Plymouth Acclaim & Dodge Spirit Automotive Repair Manual

by Robert Maddox and John H Haynes

Member of the Guild of Motoring Writers

Models covered:

All Plymouth Acclaim/Dodge Spirit Models
1989 through 1995

(10E9 - 30060)

(1779)

ABCDE
FGHIJ
KLMN

2

Haynes Publishing Group
Sparkford Nr Yeovil
Somerset BA22 7JJ England

Haynes North America, Inc
861 Lawrence Drive
Newbury Park
California 91320 USA

Acknowledgements

We are grateful to the Chrysler Corporation for assistance with technical information and certain illustrations. Technical writers who contributed to this project include Larry Warren and Mike Stubblefield.

A book in the Haynes Automotive Repair Manual Series

Printed in the U.S.A.

ISBN 1 56392 141 3

Library of Congress Catalog Card Number 95-75699

While every attempt is made to ensure that the information in this manual is correct, no liability can be accepted by the authors or publishers for loss, damage or injury caused by any errors in, or omissions from, the information given.

Contents

Haynes author, mechanic, and photographer with 1991 Plymouth Acclaim

About this manual

Its purpose

The purpose of this manual is to help you get the best value from your vehicle. It can do so in several ways. It can help you decide what work must be done, even if you choose to have it done by a dealer service department or a repair shop; it provides information and procedures for routine maintenance and servicing; and it offers diagnostic and repair procedures to follow when trouble occurs.

We hope you use the manual to tackle the work yourself. For many simpler jobs, doing it yourself may be quicker than arranging an appointment to get the vehicle into a shop and making the trips to leave it and pick it up. More importantly, a lot of money can be saved by avoiding the expense the shop must pass on to you to cover its labor and overhead costs. An added benefit is the sense of satisfaction and accomplishment that you feel after doing the job yourself.

Using the manual

The manual is divided into Chapters. Each Chapter is divided into numbered Sections, which are headed in bold type between horizontal lines. Each Section consists of consecutively numbered paragraphs.

At the beginning of each numbered Section you will be referred to any illustrations which apply to the procedures in that Section. The reference numbers used in illustration captions pinpoint the pertinent Section and the Step within that Section. That is, illustration 3.2 means the illustration refers to Section 3 and Step (or paragraph) 2 within that Section.

Procedures, once described in the text, are not normally repeated. When it's necessary to refer to another Chapter, the reference will be given as Chapter and Section number. Cross references given without use of the word "Chapter" apply to Sections and/or paragraphs in the same Chapter. For example, "see Section 8" means in the same Chapter.

References to the left or right side of the vehicle assume you are sitting in the driver's seat, facing forward.

Even though we have prepared this manual with extreme care, neither the publisher nor the author can accept responsibility for any errors in, or omissions from, the information given.

NOTE

A **Note** provides information necessary to properly complete a procedure or information which will make the procedure easier to understand.

CAUTION

A **Caution** provides a special procedure or special steps which must be taken while completing the procedure where the Caution is found. Not heeding a Caution can result in damage to the assembly being worked on.

WARNING

A **Warning** provides a special procedure or special steps which must be taken while completing the procedure where the Warning is found. Not heeding a Warning can result in personal injury.

Introduction to the Plymouth Acclaim and Dodge Spirit

These models are available in four-door sedan body styles.

Transversely mounted V6 and inline four-cylinder engines, equipped with electronic fuel injection are used. Some four-cylinder engines are turbocharged.

The engine drives the front wheels through either a five-speed manual or a three- or four-speed automatic transaxle via independent driveaxles.

The fully-independent front suspension consists of coil spring/strut units, control arms and a stabilizer bar. The rear suspension uses shock absorbers, coil springs, a solid axle with integral trailing arms and a track bar (Panhard rod).

The power-assisted rack-and-pinion steering unit is mounted behind the engine.

Front brakes are discs; the rears are either drum or optional disc-type. Power assist is standard. Four wheel disc brake-equipped models have an Anti-lock Braking System (ABS).

Vehicle identification numbers

The Vehicle Identification Number (VIN) is stamped into a metal plate fastened to the dashboard on the driver's side - it's visible through the windshield

Vehicle identification numbers

Modifications are a continuing and unpublicized process in vehicle manufacturing. Since spare parts manuals and lists are compiled on a numerical basis, the individual vehicle numbers are essential to correctly identify the component required.

Vehicle Identification Number (VIN)

The Vehicle Identification Number (VIN), which appears on the Vehicle Certificate of Title and Registration, is also embossed on a gray plate located on the upper left (driver's side) corner of the dashboard, near the windshield (see illustration). The VIN tells you when and where a vehicle was manufactured, its country of origin, make, type, passenger safety system, line, series, body style, engine and assembly plant.

Body Code Plate

The body code plate, which is located on the left (driver's side) front side shield, wheel housing or the upper radiator support (see illustration), provides more specific information about the vehicle - type of engine, transaxle, paint, etc. - to which it's attached.

Engine Identification Number (EIN)

On four-cylinder engines, the Engine Identification Number (EIN) is located on the rear face of the engine block, directly under the left (driver's side) end of the cylinder head (2.2L engines or on the right front side of the engine block (2.5L engines). On V6 engines, the EIN is on the block, directly below the cylinder head, on the front (radiator) side.

Engine Serial Number

Besides the EIN, four-cylinder engines also have a serial number, which is helpful when ordering parts. On 2.2L engines, the serial number is on the left (driver's side) rear face of the engine block, directly below the EIN; on 2.5L engines, it's located on the right (passenger's side) of the block, next to the exhaust manifold stud.

Transaxle Identification Number (TIN)

The Transaxle Identification Number (TIN) is stamped on a boss located on top of the transaxle housing (see illustration).

Transaxle Serial Number

Besides the TIN, the transaxle also has a serial number which you'll need to reference when buying transaxle parts. On manual transaxles, the serial number is embossed on a metal tag attached to the front side of the transaxle; on automatic transaxles, the serial number is located on a pad just above the oil pan at the rear of the transaxle.

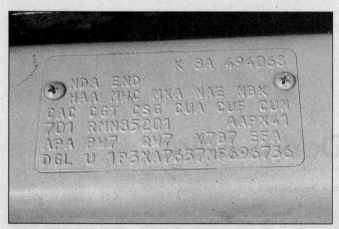

The Body Code Plate is located on the driver's side of the front shield, the wheel housing or the upper radiator support (shown) - it provides information about the type of engine, transaxle, paint, etc. of the model to which it's attached

The Transaxle Identification Number (TIN) is stamped into a flat spot on top of the transaxle housing

Buying parts

Replacement parts are available from many sources, which generally fall into one of two categories - authorized dealer parts departments and independent retail auto parts stores. Our advice concerning these parts is as follows:

Retail auto parts stores: Good auto parts stores will stock frequently needed components which wear out relatively fast, such as clutch components, exhaust systems, brake parts, tune-up parts, etc. These stores often supply new or reconditioned parts on an exchange basis, which can save a considerable amount of money. Discount auto parts stores are often very good places to buy materials and parts needed for general vehicle maintenance such as oil, grease, filters, spark plugs, belts, touch-up paint, bulbs, etc. They also usually sell tools and general accessories, have convenient hours, charge lower prices and can often be found not far from home.

Authorized dealer parts department: This is the best source for parts which are unique to the vehicle and not generally available elsewhere (such as major engine parts, transmission parts, trim pieces, etc.).

Warranty information: If the vehicle is still covered under warranty, be sure that any replacement parts purchased - regardless of the source - do not invalidate the warranty!

To be sure of obtaining the correct parts, have engine and chassis numbers available and, if possible, take the old parts along for positive identification.

Maintenance techniques, tools and working facilities

Maintenance techniques

There are a number of techniques involved in maintenance and repair that will be referred to throughout this manual. Application of these techniques will enable the home mechanic to be more efficient, better organized and capable of performing the various tasks properly, which will ensure that the repair job is thorough and complete.

Fasteners

Fasteners are nuts, bolts, studs and screws used to hold two or more parts together. There are a few things to keep in mind when working with fasteners. Almost all of them use a locking device of some type, either a lockwasher, locknut, locking tab or thread adhesive. All threaded fasteners should be clean and straight, with undamaged threads and undamaged corners on the hex head where the wrench fits. Develop the habit of replacing all damaged nuts and bolts with new ones. Special locknuts with nylon or fiber inserts can only be used once. If they are removed, they lose their locking ability and must be replaced with new ones.

Rusted nuts and bolts should be treated with a penetrating fluid to ease removal and prevent breakage. Some mechanics use turpentine in a spout-type oil can, which works quite well. After applying the rust penetrant, let it work for a few minutes before trying to loosen the nut or bolt. Badly rusted fasteners may have to be chiseled or sawed off or removed with a special nut breaker, available at tool stores.

If a bolt or stud breaks off in an assembly, it can be drilled and removed with a special tool commonly available for this purpose. Most automotive machine shops can perform this task, as well as other repair procedures, such as the repair of threaded holes that have been stripped out.

Flat washers and lockwashers, when removed from an assembly, should always be replaced exactly as removed. Replace any damaged washers with new ones. Never use a lockwasher on any soft metal surface (such as aluminum), thin sheet metal or plastic.

Fastener sizes

For a number of reasons, automobile manufacturers are making wider and wider use of metric fasteners. Therefore, it is important to be able to tell the difference between standard (sometimes called U.S. or SAE) and metric hardware, since they cannot be interchanged.

All bolts, whether standard or metric, are sized according to diameter, thread pitch and length. For example, a standard 1/2 - 13 x 1 bolt is 1/2 inch in diameter, has 13 threads per inch and is 1 inch long. An M12 - 1.75 x 25 metric bolt is 12 mm in diameter, has a thread pitch of 1.75 mm (the distance between threads) and is 25 mm long. The two bolts are nearly identical, and easily confused, but they are not interchangeable.

In addition to the differences in diameter, thread pitch and length, metric and standard bolts can also be distinguished by examining the bolt heads. To begin with, the distance across the flats on a standard bolt head is measured in inches, while the same dimension on a metric bolt is sized in millimeters (the same is true for nuts). As a result, a standard wrench should not be used on a metric bolt and a metric wrench should not be used on a standard bolt. Also, most standard bolts have slashes radiating out from the center of the head to denote the grade or strength of the bolt, which is an indication of the amount of torque that can be applied to it. The greater the number of slashes, the greater the strength of the bolt. Grades 0 through 5 are commonly used on automobiles. Metric bolts have a property class (grade) number, rather than a slash, molded into their heads to indicate bolt strength. In this case, the higher the number, the stronger the bolt. Property class numbers 8.8, 9.8 and 10.9 are commonly used on automobiles.

Strength markings can also be used to distinguish standard hex nuts from metric hex nuts. Many standard nuts have dots stamped into one side, while metric nuts are marked with a number. The greater the number of dots, or the higher the number, the greater the strength of the nut.

Metric studs are also marked on their ends according to property class (grade). Larger studs are numbered (the same as metric bolts), while smaller studs carry a geometric code to denote grade.

It should be noted that many fasteners, especially Grades 0 through 2, have no distinguishing marks on them. When such is the case, the only way to determine whether it is standard or metric is to measure the thread pitch or compare it to a known fastener of the same size.

Standard fasteners are often referred to as SAE, as opposed to metric. However, it should be noted that SAE technically refers to a non-metric fine thread fastener only. Coarse thread non-metric fasteners are referred to as USS sizes.

Grade 1 or 2   Grade 5   Grade 8

Bolt strength marking (standard/SAE/USS; bottom - metric)

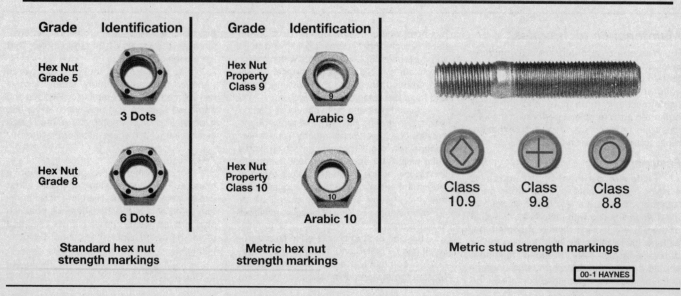

Grade	Identification	Grade	Identification
Hex Nut Grade 5	3 Dots	Hex Nut Property Class 9	Arabic 9
Hex Nut Grade 8	6 Dots	Hex Nut Property Class 10	Arabic 10

Class 10.9   Class 9.8   Class 8.8

Standard hex nut strength markings   **Metric hex nut strength markings**   **Metric stud strength markings**

Since fasteners of the same size (both standard and metric) may have different strength ratings, be sure to reinstall any bolts, studs or nuts removed from your vehicle in their original locations. Also, when replacing a fastener with a new one, make sure that the new one has a strength rating equal to or greater than the original.

Tightening sequences and procedures

Most threaded fasteners should be tightened to a specific torque value (torque is the twisting force applied to a threaded component such as a nut or bolt). Overtightening the fastener can weaken it and cause it to break, while undertightening can cause it to eventually come loose. Bolts, screws and studs, depending on the material they are made of and their thread diameters, have specific torque values, many of which are noted in the Specifications at the beginning of each Chapter. Be sure to follow the torque recommendations closely. For fasteners not assigned a specific torque, a general torque value chart is presented here as a guide. These torque values are for dry (unlubricated) fasteners threaded into steel or cast iron (not aluminum). As was previously mentioned, the size and grade of a fastener determine the amount of torque that can safely be applied to it. The figures listed here are approximate for Grade 2 and Grade 3 fasteners. Higher grades can tolerate higher torque values.

Fasteners laid out in a pattern, such as cylinder head bolts, oil pan bolts, differential cover bolts, etc., must be loosened or tightened in sequence to avoid warping the component. This sequence will normally be shown in the appropriate Chapter. If a specific pattern is not given, the following procedures can be used to prevent warping.

Metric thread sizes	Ft-lbs	Nm
M-6	6 to 9	9 to 12
M-8	14 to 21	19 to 28
M-10	28 to 40	38 to 54
M-12	50 to 71	68 to 96
M-14	80 to 140	109 to 154

Pipe thread sizes		
1/8	5 to 8	7 to 10
1/4	12 to 18	17 to 24
3/8	22 to 33	30 to 44
1/2	25 to 35	34 to 47

U.S. thread sizes		
1/4 - 20	6 to 9	9 to 12
5/16 - 18	12 to 18	17 to 24
5/16 - 24	14 to 20	19 to 27
3/8 - 16	22 to 32	30 to 43
3/8 - 24	27 to 38	37 to 51
7/16 - 14	40 to 55	55 to 74
7/16 - 20	40 to 60	55 to 81
1/2 - 13	55 to 80	75 to 108

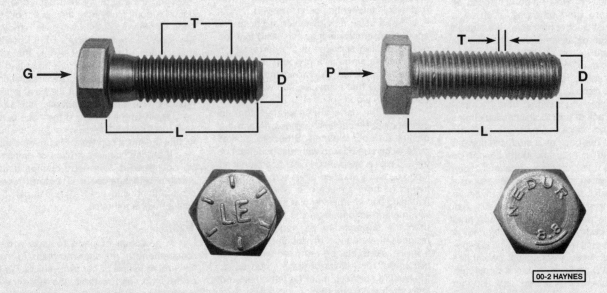

00-2 HAYNES

Standard (SAE and USS) bolt dimensions/grade marks

G   Grade marks (bolt strength)
L   Length (in inches)
T   Thread pitch (number of threads per inch)
D   Nominal diameter (in inches)

Metric bolt dimensions/grade marks

P   Property class (bolt strength)
L   Length (in millimeters)
T   Thread pitch (distance between threads in millimeters)
D   Diameter

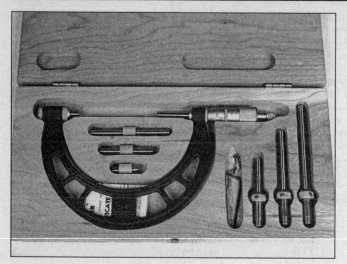

Micrometer set

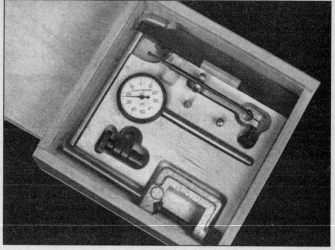

Dial indicator set

Initially, the bolts or nuts should be assembled finger-tight only. Next, they should be tightened one full turn each, in a criss-cross or diagonal pattern. After each one has been tightened one full turn, return to the first one and tighten them all one-half turn, following the same pattern. Finally, tighten each of them one-quarter turn at a time until each fastener has been tightened to the proper torque. To loosen and remove the fasteners, the procedure would be reversed.

Component disassembly

Component disassembly should be done with care and purpose to help ensure that the parts go back together properly. Always keep track of the sequence in which parts are removed. Make note of special characteristics or marks on parts that can be installed more than one way, such as a grooved thrust washer on a shaft. It is a good idea to lay the disassembled parts out on a clean surface in the order that they were removed. It may also be helpful to make sketches or take instant photos of components before removal.

When removing fasteners from a component, keep track of their locations. Sometimes threading a bolt back in a part, or putting the washers and nut back on a stud, can prevent mix-ups later. If nuts and bolts cannot be returned to their original locations, they should be kept in a compartmented box or a series of small boxes. A cupcake or muffin tin is ideal for this purpose, since each cavity can hold the bolts and nuts from a particular area (i.e. oil pan bolts, valve cover bolts, engine mount bolts, etc.). A pan of this type is especially helpful when working on assemblies with very small parts, such as the carburetor, alternator, valve train or interior dash and trim pieces. The cavities can be marked with paint or tape to identify the contents.

Whenever wiring looms, harnesses or connectors are separated, it is a good idea to identify the two halves with numbered pieces of masking tape so they can be easily reconnected.

Gasket sealing surfaces

Throughout any vehicle, gaskets are used to seal the mating surfaces between two parts and keep lubricants, fluids, vacuum or pressure contained in an assembly.

Many times these gaskets are coated with a liquid or paste-type gasket sealing compound before assembly. Age, heat and pressure can sometimes cause the two parts to stick together so tightly that they are very difficult to separate. Often, the assembly can be loosened by striking it with a soft-face hammer near the mating surfaces. A regular hammer can be used if a block of wood is placed between the hammer and the part. Do not hammer on cast parts or parts that could be easily damaged. With any particularly stubborn part, always recheck to make sure that every fastener has been removed.

Avoid using a screwdriver or bar to pry apart an assembly, as they can easily mar the gasket sealing surfaces of the parts, which must remain smooth. If prying is absolutely necessary, use an old broom handle, but keep in mind that extra clean up will be necessary if the wood splinters.

After the parts are separated, the old gasket must be carefully scraped off and the gasket surfaces cleaned. Stubborn gasket material can be soaked with rust penetrant or treated with a special chemical to soften it so it can be easily scraped off. A scraper can be fashioned from a piece of copper tubing by flattening and sharpening one end. Copper is recommended because it is usually softer than the surfaces to be scraped, which reduces the chance of gouging the part. Some gaskets can be removed with a wire brush, but regardless of the method used, the mating surfaces must be left clean and smooth. If for some reason the gasket surface is gouged, then a gasket sealer thick enough to fill scratches will have to be used during reassembly of the components. For most applications, a non-drying (or semi-drying) gasket sealer should be used.

Hose removal tips

Warning: *If the vehicle is equipped with air conditioning, do not disconnect any of the A/C hoses without first having the system depressurized by a dealer service department or a service station.*

Hose removal precautions closely parallel gasket removal precautions. Avoid scratching or gouging the surface that the hose mates against or the connection may leak. This is especially true for radiator hoses. Because of various chemical reactions, the rubber in hoses can bond itself to the metal spigot that the hose fits over. To remove a hose, first loosen the hose clamps that secure it to the spigot. Then, with slip-joint pliers, grab the hose at the clamp and rotate it around the spigot. Work it back and forth until it is completely free, then pull it off. Silicone or other lubricants will ease removal if they can be applied between the hose and the outside of the spigot. Apply the same lubricant to the inside of the hose and the outside of the spigot to simplify installation.

As a last resort (and if the hose is to be replaced with a new one anyway), the rubber can be slit with a knife and the hose peeled from the spigot. If this must be done, be careful that the metal connection is not damaged.

If a hose clamp is broken or damaged, do not reuse it. Wire-type clamps usually weaken with age, so it is a good idea to replace them with screw-type clamps whenever a hose is removed.

Tools

A selection of good tools is a basic requirement for anyone who plans to maintain and repair his or her own vehicle. For the owner who has few tools, the initial investment might seem high, but when compared to the spiraling costs of professional auto maintenance and repair, it is a wise one.

To help the owner decide which tools are needed to perform the tasks detailed in this manual, the following tool lists are offered: *Maintenance and minor repair,*

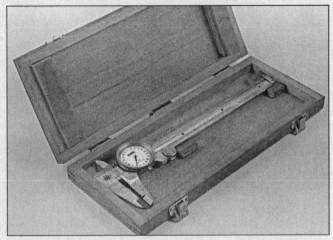

Dial caliper

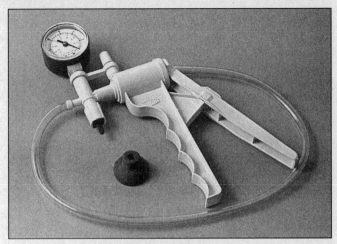

Hand-operated vacuum pump

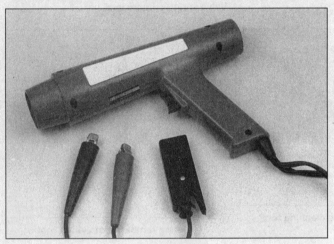

Timing light

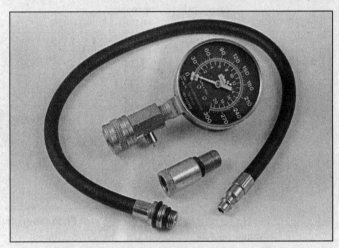

Compression gauge with spark plug hole adapter

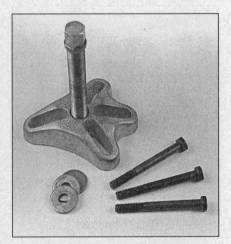

Damper/steering wheel puller

General purpose puller

Hydraulic lifter removal tool

Repair/overhaul and *Special.*

The newcomer to practical mechanics should start off with the *maintenance and minor repair* tool kit, which is adequate for the simpler jobs performed on a vehicle. Then, as confidence and experience grow, the owner can tackle more difficult tasks, buying additional tools as they are needed.

Eventually the basic kit will be expanded into the *repair and overhaul* tool set. Over a period of time, the experienced do-it-yourselfer will assemble a tool set complete enough for most repair and overhaul procedures and will add tools from the special category when it is felt that the expense is justified by the frequency of use.

Maintenance and minor repair tool kit

The tools in this list should be considered the minimum required for performance of routine maintenance, servicing and minor repair work. We recommend the purchase of combination wrenches (box-end and open-

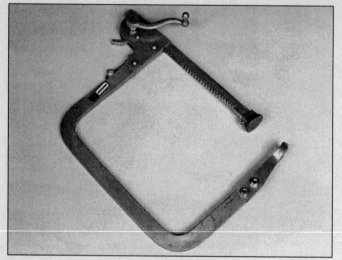

Valve spring compressor

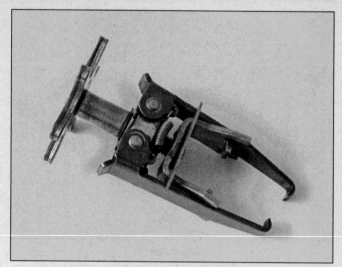

Valve spring compressor

Ridge reamer

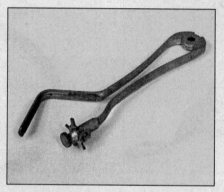

Piston ring groove cleaning tool

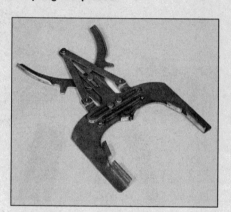

Ring removal/installation tool

end combined in one wrench). While more expensive than open end wrenches, they offer the advantages of both types of wrench.

> Combination wrench set (1/4-inch to 1 inch or 6 mm to 19 mm)
> Adjustable wrench, 8 inch
> Spark plug wrench with rubber insert
> Spark plug gap adjusting tool
> Feeler gauge set
> Brake bleeder wrench
> Standard screwdriver (5/16-inch x 6 inch)
> Phillips screwdriver (No. 2 x 6 inch)
> Combination pliers - 6 inch
> Hacksaw and assortment of blades
> Tire pressure gauge
> Grease gun
> Oil can
> Fine emery cloth
> Wire brush
> Battery post and cable cleaning tool
> Oil filter wrench
> Funnel (medium size)
> Safety goggles
> Jackstands (2)
> Drain pan

Note: If basic tune-ups are going to be part of routine maintenance, it will be necessary to purchase a good quality stroboscopic timing light and combination tachometer/dwell meter. Although they are included in the list of special tools, it is mentioned here because they are absolutely necessary for tuning most vehicles properly.

Repair and overhaul tool set

These tools are essential for anyone who plans to perform major repairs and are in addition to those in the maintenance and minor repair tool kit. Included is a comprehensive set of sockets which, though expensive, are invaluable because of their versatility, especially when various extensions and drives are available. We recommend the 1/2-inch drive over the 3/8-inch drive. Although the larger drive is bulky and more expensive, it has the capacity of accepting a very wide range of large sockets. Ideally, however, the mechanic should have a 3/8-inch drive set and a 1/2-inch drive set.

> Socket set(s)
> Reversible ratchet
> Extension - 10 inch
> Universal joint
> Torque wrench (same size drive as sockets)
> Ball peen hammer - 8 ounce
> Soft-face hammer (plastic/rubber)

Ring compressor

> Standard screwdriver (1/4-inch x 6 inch)
> Standard screwdriver (stubby - 5/16-inch)
> Phillips screwdriver (No. 3 x 8 inch)
> Phillips screwdriver (stubby - No. 2)
> Pliers - vise grip
> Pliers - lineman's
> Pliers - needle nose
> Pliers - snap-ring (internal and external)
> Cold chisel - 1/2-inch

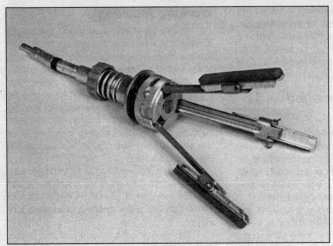

Cylinder hone

Brake hold-down spring tool

Scribe
Scraper (made from flattened copper
    tubing)
Centerpunch
Pin punches (1/16, 1/8, 3/16-inch)
Steel rule/straightedge - 12 inch
Allen wrench set (1/8 to 3/8-inch or
    4 mm to 10 mm)
A selection of files

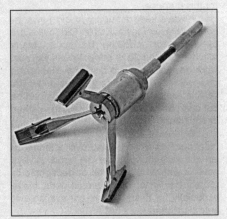

Brake cylinder hone

Wire brush (large)
Jackstands (second set)
Jack (scissor or hydraulic type)

Note: *Another tool which is often useful is an electric drill with a chuck capacity of 3/8-inch and a set of good quality drill bits.*

Special tools

The tools in this list include those which are not used regularly, are expensive to buy, or which need to be used in accordance with their manufacturer's instructions. Unless these tools will be used frequently, it is not very economical to purchase many of them. A consideration would be to split the cost and use between yourself and a friend or friends. In addition, most of these tools can be obtained from a tool rental shop on a temporary basis.

This list primarily contains only those tools and instruments widely available to the public, and not those special tools produced by the vehicle manufacturer for distribution to dealer service departments. Occasionally, references to the manufacturer's special tools are included in the text of this manual. Generally, an alternative method of doing the job without the special tool is offered. How-ever, sometimes there is no alternative to their use. Where this is the case, and the tool cannot be purchased or borrowed, the work should be turned over to the dealer service department or an automotive repair shop.

Valve spring compressor
Piston ring groove cleaning tool
Piston ring compressor
Piston ring installation tool
Cylinder compression gauge
Cylinder ridge reamer
Cylinder surfacing hone
Cylinder bore gauge
Micrometers and/or dial calipers
Hydraulic lifter removal tool
Balljoint separator
Universal-type puller
Impact screwdriver
Dial indicator set
Stroboscopic timing light (inductive
    pick-up)
Hand operated vacuum/pressure pump
Tachometer/dwell meter
Universal electrical multimeter
Cable hoist
Brake spring removal and installation
    tools
Floor jack

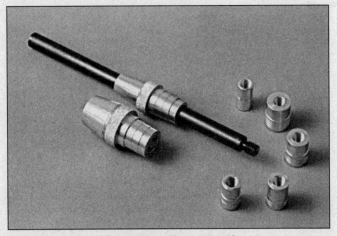

Clutch plate alignment tool

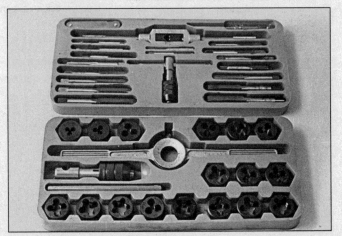

Tap and die set

Buying tools

For the do-it-yourselfer who is just starting to get involved in vehicle maintenance and repair, there are a number of options available when purchasing tools. If maintenance and minor repair is the extent of the work to be done, the purchase of individual tools is satisfactory. If, on the other hand, extensive work is planned, it would be a good idea to purchase a modest tool set from one of the large retail chain stores. A set can usually be bought at a substantial savings over the individual tool prices, and they often come with a tool box. As additional tools are needed, add-on sets, individual tools and a larger tool box can be purchased to expand the tool selection. Building a tool set gradually allows the cost of the tools to be spread over a longer period of time and gives the mechanic the freedom to choose only those tools that will actually be used.

Tool stores will often be the only source of some of the special tools that are needed, but regardless of where tools are bought, try to avoid cheap ones, especially when buying screwdrivers and sockets, because they won't last very long. The expense involved in replacing cheap tools will eventually be greater than the initial cost of quality tools.

Care and maintenance of tools

Good tools are expensive, so it makes sense to treat them with respect. Keep them clean and in usable condition and store them properly when not in use. Always wipe off any dirt, grease or metal chips before putting them away. Never leave tools lying around in the work area. Upon completion of a job, always check closely under the hood for tools that may have been left there so they won't get lost during a test drive.

Some tools, such as screwdrivers, pliers, wrenches and sockets, can be hung on a panel mounted on the garage or workshop wall, while others should be kept in a tool box or tray. Measuring instruments, gauges, meters, etc. must be carefully stored where they cannot be damaged by weather or impact from other tools.

When tools are used with care and stored properly, they will last a very long time. Even with the best of care, though, tools will wear out if used frequently. When a tool is damaged or worn out, replace it. Subsequent jobs will be safer and more enjoyable if you do.

How to repair damaged threads

Sometimes, the internal threads of a nut or bolt hole can become stripped, usually from overtightening. Stripping threads is an all-too-common occurrence, especially when working with aluminum parts, because aluminum is so soft that it easily strips out.

Usually, external or internal threads are only partially stripped. After they've been cleaned up with a tap or die, they'll still work. Sometimes, however, threads are badly damaged. When this happens, you've got three choices:

1) *Drill and tap the hole to the next suitable oversize and install a larger diameter bolt, screw or stud.*

2) *Drill and tap the hole to accept a threaded plug, then drill and tap the plug to the original screw size. You can also buy a plug already threaded to the original size. Then you simply drill a hole to the specified size, then run the threaded plug into the hole with a bolt and jam nut. Once the plug is fully seated, remove the jam nut and bolt.*

3) *The third method uses a patented thread repair kit like Heli-Coil or Slimsert. These easy-to-use kits are designed to repair damaged threads in straight-through holes and blind holes. Both are available as kits which can handle a variety of sizes and thread patterns. Drill the hole, then tap it with the special included tap. Install the Heli-Coil and the hole is back to its original diameter and thread pitch.*

Regardless of which method you use, be sure to proceed calmly and carefully. A little impatience or carelessness during one of these relatively simple procedures can ruin your whole day's work and cost you a bundle if you wreck an expensive part.

Working facilities

Not to be overlooked when discussing tools is the workshop. If anything more than routine maintenance is to be carried out, some sort of suitable work area is essential.

It is understood, and appreciated, that many home mechanics do not have a good workshop or garage available, and end up removing an engine or doing major repairs outside. It is recommended, however, that the overhaul or repair be completed under the cover of a roof.

A clean, flat workbench or table of comfortable working height is an absolute necessity. The workbench should be equipped with a vise that has a jaw opening of at least four inches.

As mentioned previously, some clean, dry storage space is also required for tools, as well as the lubricants, fluids, cleaning solvents, etc. which soon become necessary.

Sometimes waste oil and fluids, drained from the engine or cooling system during normal maintenance or repairs, present a disposal problem. To avoid pouring them on the ground or into a sewage system, pour the used fluids into large containers, seal them with caps and take them to an authorized disposal site or recycling center. Plastic jugs, such as old antifreeze containers, are ideal for this purpose.

Always keep a supply of old newspapers and clean rags available. Old towels are excellent for mopping up spills. Many mechanics use rolls of paper towels for most work because they are readily available and disposable. To help keep the area under the vehicle clean, a large cardboard box can be cut open and flattened to protect the garage or shop floor.

Whenever working over a painted surface, such as when leaning over a fender to service something under the hood, always cover it with an old blanket or bedspread to protect the finish. Vinyl covered pads, made especially for this purpose, are available at auto parts stores.

Booster battery (jump) starting

Observe these precautions when using a booster battery to start a vehicle:

a) *Before connecting the booster battery, make sure the ignition switch is in the Off position.*
b) *Turn off the lights, heater and other electrical loads.*
c) *Your eyes should be shielded. Safety goggles are a good idea.*
d) *Make sure the booster battery is the same voltage as the dead one in the vehicle.*
e) *The two vehicles MUST NOT TOUCH each other!*
f) *Make sure the transaxle is in Neutral (manual) or Park (automatic).*
g) *If the booster battery is not a maintenance-free type, remove the vent caps and lay a cloth over the vent holes.*

Connect the red jumper cable to the positive (+) terminals of each battery **(see illustration)**.

Connect one end of the black jumper cable to the negative (-) terminal of the booster battery. The other end of this cable should be connected to a good ground on the vehicle to be started, such as a bolt or bracket on the body.

Start the engine using the booster battery, then, with the engine running at idle speed, disconnect the jumper cables in the reverse order of connection.

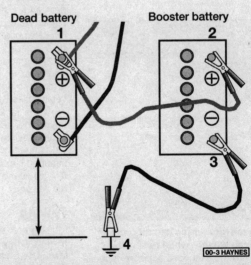

Make the booster battery cable connections in the numerical order shown (note that the negative cable of the booster battery is NOT attached to the negative terminal of the dead battery)

Jacking and towing

Jacking

Warning: *The jack supplied with the vehicle should only be used for changing a tire or placing jackstands under the frame. Never work under the vehicle or start the engine while this jack is being used as the only means of support.*

1   The vehicle should be on level ground. Place the shift lever in Park (automatic transaxle) or Reverse (manual). Block the wheel diagonally opposite the wheel being changed. Set the parking brake.

2   Peel back the floor mat in the rear cargo area. Remove the cover from the spare tire well and remove the spare tire, scissors-type jack and lug nut wrench from the spare tire well.

There's jack locator pin like this (arrow) near each wheel - when raising the vehicle with the standard scissors-type jack, make sure the jack head is securely engaged with the pin nearest he wheel you're raising

3   Insert a screwdriver or the tapered end of the lug nut wrench between the wheel and the wheel cover, then twist the handle and lever the screwdriver or lug wrench against the wheel and pry off the wheel cover. Loosen - but don't remove - the wheel lug nuts about one-half turn.

4   On the bottom of each rocker panel, you'll find a small jack locator pin near each wheel **(see illustration)**. Place the jack under the pin nearest the tire you're changing, then turn the handle clockwise until the jack head is engaged with the pin. **Warning:** *DON'T RAISE THE VEHICLE UNTIL THE JACK IS PROPERLY ENGAGED.*

5   Turn the jack handle clockwise until the tire clears the ground. Raise the vehicle just enough for the tire to clear the ground. The higher the vehicle, the less the stability.

6   Remove the lug nuts and pull the wheel off. Replace it with the spare.

7   Replace the lug nuts with the beveled edges facing in. Tighten them snugly. Don't attempt to tighten them completely until the vehicle is lowered or it could slip off the jack. Turn the jack handle counterclockwise to lower the vehicle. Remove the jack and tighten the lug nuts in a criss-cross pattern.

8   Install the cover and be sure it's snapped into place all the way around.

9   Stow the tire, jack and wrench. Unblock the wheels.

Towing

Safety is a major consideration when towing. Obey all applicable state and local laws. Use a safety chain system at all times. Remember that power steering and power brakes will not work with the engine off.

Always use equipment specifically designed for towing. Attach it to the main structural members of the vehicle, not the bumpers or brackets.

Towing vehicles with an automatic transaxle

If the transaxle is working, your vehicle can be towed - from the front only - with all four wheels on the ground, for a distance of up to 15 miles. Keep the speed below 25 mph. **Caution:** *Never tow a vehicle with an automatic transaxle from the rear with the front wheels on the ground.*

Always check the transmission fluid level before towing (see Chapter 1). If the level is below the HOT line on the dipstick, add fluid or use a towing dolly. Release the parking brake, put the transaxle in Neutral and place the ignition key in the Off - not the Lock or Accessory - position.

If the transaxle is inoperative, or the vehicle must be towed more than 15 miles, tow the vehicle with the front wheels raised or on a dolly.

Towing vehicles with a manual transaxle

Vehicles with a manual transaxle can be towed any distance at any legal highway speed. Place the shift lever in Neutral. Place the ignition switch in the Off - not in the Lock or Accessory - position. Release the parking brake.

If the transaxle isn't operative, tow the vehicle with the front wheels off the ground.

Towing a vehicle without an ignition key

If the vehicle must be towed with the ignition in the Lock position, raise the front (drive) wheels off the ground. If they can't be raised, place them on a dolly.

Automotive chemicals and lubricants

A number of automotive chemicals and lubricants are available for use during vehicle maintenance and repair. They include a wide variety of products ranging from cleaning solvents and degreasers to lubricants and protective sprays for rubber, plastic and vinyl.

Cleaners

Carburetor cleaner and choke cleaner is a strong solvent for gum, varnish and carbon. Most carburetor cleaners leave a dry-type lubricant film which will not harden or gum up. Because of this film it is not recommended for use on electrical components.

Brake system cleaner is used to remove grease and brake fluid from the brake system, where clean surfaces are absolutely necessary. It leaves no residue and often eliminates brake squeal caused by contaminants.

Electrical cleaner removes oxidation, corrosion and carbon deposits from electrical contacts, restoring full current flow. It can also be used to clean spark plugs, carburetor jets, voltage regulators and other parts where an oil-free surface is desired.

Demoisturants remove water and moisture from electrical components such as alternators, voltage regulators, electrical connectors and fuse blocks. They are non-conductive, non-corrosive and non-flammable.

Degreasers are heavy-duty solvents used to remove grease from the outside of the engine and from chassis components. They can be sprayed or brushed on and, depending on the type, are rinsed off either with water or solvent.

Lubricants

Motor oil is the lubricant formulated for use in engines. It normally contains a wide variety of additives to prevent corrosion and reduce foaming and wear. Motor oil comes in various weights (viscosity ratings) from 0 to 50. The recommended weight of the oil depends on the season, temperature and the demands on the engine. Light oil is used in cold climates and under light load conditions. Heavy oil is used in hot climates and where high loads are encountered. Multi-viscosity oils are designed to have characteristics of both light and heavy oils and are available in a number of weights from 5W-20 to 20W-50.

Gear oil is designed to be used in differentials, manual transmissions and other areas where high-temperature lubrication is required.

Chassis and wheel bearing grease is a heavy grease used where increased loads and friction are encountered, such as for wheel bearings, balljoints, tie-rod ends and universal joints.

High-temperature wheel bearing grease is designed to withstand the extreme temperatures encountered by wheel bearings in disc brake equipped vehicles. It usually contains molybdenum disulfide (moly), which is a dry-type lubricant.

White grease is a heavy grease for metal-to-metal applications where water is a problem. White grease stays soft under both low and high temperatures (usually from -100 to +190-degrees F), and will not wash off or dilute in the presence of water.

Assembly lube is a special extreme pressure lubricant, usually containing moly, used to lubricate high-load parts (such as main and rod bearings and cam lobes) for initial start-up of a new engine. The assembly lube lubricates the parts without being squeezed out or washed away until the engine oiling system begins to function.

Silicone lubricants are used to protect rubber, plastic, vinyl and nylon parts.

Graphite lubricants are used where oils cannot be used due to contamination problems, such as in locks. The dry graphite will lubricate metal parts while remaining uncontaminated by dirt, water, oil or acids. It is electrically conductive and will not foul electrical contacts in locks such as the ignition switch.

Moly penetrants loosen and lubricate frozen, rusted and corroded fasteners and prevent future rusting or freezing.

Heat-sink grease is a special electrically non-conductive grease that is used for mounting electronic ignition modules where it is essential that heat is transferred away from the module.

Sealants

RTV sealant is one of the most widely used gasket compounds. Made from silicone, RTV is air curing, it seals, bonds, waterproofs, fills surface irregularities, remains flexible, doesn't shrink, is relatively easy to remove, and is used as a supplementary sealer with almost all low and medium temperature gaskets.

Anaerobic sealant is much like RTV in that it can be used either to seal gaskets or to form gaskets by itself. It remains flexible, is solvent resistant and fills surface imperfections. The difference between an anaerobic sealant and an RTV-type sealant is in the curing. RTV cures when exposed to air, while an anaerobic sealant cures only in the absence of air. This means that an anaerobic sealant cures only after the assembly of parts, sealing them together.

Thread and pipe sealant is used for sealing hydraulic and pneumatic fittings and vacuum lines. It is usually made from a Teflon compound, and comes in a spray, a paint-on liquid and as a wrap-around tape.

Chemicals

Anti-seize compound prevents seizing, galling, cold welding, rust and corrosion in fasteners. High-temperature anti-seize, usually made with copper and graphite lubricants, is used for exhaust system and exhaust manifold bolts.

Anaerobic locking compounds are used to keep fasteners from vibrating or working loose and cure only after installation, in the absence of air. Medium strength locking compound is used for small nuts, bolts and screws that may be removed later. High-strength locking compound is for large nuts, bolts and studs which aren't removed on a regular basis.

Oil additives range from viscosity index improvers to chemical treatments that claim to reduce internal engine friction. It should be noted that most oil manufacturers caution against using additives with their oils.

Gas additives perform several functions, depending on their chemical makeup. They usually contain solvents that help dissolve gum and varnish that build up on carburetor, fuel injection and intake parts. They also serve to break down carbon deposits that form on the inside surfaces of the combustion chambers. Some additives contain upper cylinder lubricants for valves and piston rings, and others contain chemicals to remove condensation from the gas tank.

Miscellaneous

Brake fluid is specially formulated hydraulic fluid that can withstand the heat and pressure encountered in brake systems. Care must be taken so this fluid does not come in contact with painted surfaces or plastics. An opened container should always be resealed to prevent contamination by water or dirt.

Weatherstrip adhesive is used to bond weatherstripping around doors, windows and trunk lids. It is sometimes used to attach trim pieces.

Undercoating is a petroleum-based, tar-like substance that is designed to protect metal surfaces on the underside of the vehicle from corrosion. It also acts as a sound-deadening agent by insulating the bottom of the vehicle.

Waxes and polishes are used to help protect painted and plated surfaces from the weather. Different types of paint may require the use of different types of wax and polish. Some polishes utilize a chemical or abrasive cleaner to help remove the top layer of oxidized (dull) paint on older vehicles. In recent years many non-wax polishes that contain a wide variety of chemicals such as polymers and silicones have been introduced. These non-wax polishes are usually easier to apply and last longer than conventional waxes and polishes.

Conversion factors

Length (distance)

Inches (in)	X	25.4	= Millimetres (mm)	X 0.0394	= Inches (in)
Feet (ft)	X	0.305	= Metres (m)	X 3.281	= Feet (ft)
Miles	X	1.609	= Kilometres (km)	X 0.621	= Miles

Volume (capacity)

Cubic inches (cu in; in^3)	X	16.387	= Cubic centimetres (cc; cm^3)	X 0.061	= Cubic inches (cu in; in^3)
Imperial pints (Imp pt)	X	0.568	= Litres (l)	X 1.76	= Imperial pints (Imp pt)
Imperial quarts (Imp qt)	X	1.137	= Litres (l)	X 0.88	= Imperial quarts (Imp qt)
Imperial quarts (Imp qt)	X	1.201	= US quarts (US qt)	X 0.833	= Imperial quarts (Imp qt)
US quarts (US qt)	X	0.946	= Litres (l)	X 1.057	= US quarts (US qt)
Imperial gallons (Imp gal)	X	4.546	= Litres (l)	X 0.22	= Imperial gallons (Imp gal)
Imperial gallons (Imp gal)	X	1.201	= US gallons (US gal)	X 0.833	= Imperial gallons (Imp gal)
US gallons (US gal)	X	3.785	= Litres (l)	X 0.264	= US gallons (US gal)

Mass (weight)

Ounces (oz)	X	28.35	= Grams (g)	X 0.035	= Ounces (oz)
Pounds (lb)	X	0.454	= Kilograms (kg)	X 2.205	= Pounds (lb)

Force

Ounces-force (ozf; oz)	X	0.278	= Newtons (N)	X 3.6	= Ounces-force (ozf; oz)
Pounds-force (lbf; lb)	X	4.448	= Newtons (N)	X 0.225	= Pounds-force (lbf; lb)
Newtons (N)	X	0.1	= Kilograms-force (kgf; kg)	X 9.81	= Newtons (N)

Pressure

Pounds-force per square inch (psi; lbf/in^2; lb/in^2)	X	0.070	= Kilograms-force per square centimetre (kgf/cm^2; kg/cm^2)	X 14.223	= Pounds-force per square inch (psi; lbf/in^2; lb/in^2)
Pounds-force per square inch (psi; lbf/in^2; lb/in^2)	X	0.068	= Atmospheres (atm)	X 14.696	= Pounds-force per square inch (psi; lbf/in^2; lb/in^2)
Pounds-force per square inch (psi; lbf/in^2; lb/in^2)	X	0.069	= Bars	X 14.5	= Pounds-force per square inch (psi; lbf/in^2; lb/in^2)
Pounds-force per square inch (psi; lbf/in^2; lb/in^2)	X	6.895	= Kilopascals (kPa)	X 0.145	= Pounds-force per square inch (psi; lbf/in^2; lb/in^2)
Kilopascals (kPa)	X	0.01	= Kilograms-force per square centimetre (kgf/cm^2; kg/cm^2)	X 98.1	= Kilopascals (kPa)

Torque (moment of force)

Pounds-force inches (lbf in; lb in)	X	1.152	= Kilograms-force centimetre (kgf cm; kg cm)	X 0.868	= Pounds-force inches (lbf in; lb in)
Pounds-force inches (lbf in; lb in)	X	0.113	= Newton metres (Nm)	X 8.85	= Pounds-force inches (lbf in; lb in)
Pounds-force inches (lbf in; lb in)	X	0.083	= Pounds-force feet (lbf ft; lb ft)	X 12	= Pounds-force inches (lbf in; lb in)
Pounds-force feet (lbf ft; lb ft)	X	0.138	= Kilograms-force metres (kgf m; kg m)	X 7.233	= Pounds-force feet (lbf ft; lb ft)
Pounds-force feet (lbf ft; lb ft)	X	1.356	= Newton metres (Nm)	X 0.738	= Pounds-force feet (lbf ft; lb ft)
Newton metres (Nm)	X	0.102	= Kilograms-force metres (kgf m; kg m)	X 9.804	= Newton metres (Nm)

Vacuum

Inches mercury (in. Hg)	X	3.377	= Kilopascals (kPa)	X 0.2961	= Inches mercury
Inches mercury (in. Hg)	X	25.4	= Millimeters mercury (mm Hg)	X 0.0394	= Inches mercury

Power

Horsepower (hp)	X	745.7	= Watts (W)	X 0.0013	= Horsepower (hp)

Velocity (speed)

Miles per hour (miles/hr; mph)	X	1.609	= Kilometres per hour (km/hr; kph)	X 0.621	= Miles per hour (miles/hr; mph)

Fuel consumption*

Miles per gallon, Imperial (mpg)	X	0.354	= Kilometres per litre (km/l)	X 2.825	= Miles per gallon, Imperial (mpg)
Miles per gallon, US (mpg)	X	0.425	= Kilometres per litre (km/l)	X 2.352	= Miles per gallon, US (mpg)

Temperature

Degrees Fahrenheit = (°C x 1.8) + 32   Degrees Celsius (Degrees Centigrade; °C) = (°F - 32) x 0.56

*It is common practice to convert from miles per gallon (mpg) to litres/100 kilometres (l/100km), where mpg (Imperial) x l/100 km = 282 and mpg (US) x l/100 km = 235

Safety first!

Regardless of how enthusiastic you may be about getting on with the job at hand, take the time to ensure that your safety is not jeopardized. A moment's lack of attention can result in an accident, as can failure to observe certain simple safety precautions. The possibility of an accident will always exist, and the following points should not be considered a comprehensive list of all dangers. Rather, they are intended to make you aware of the risks and to encourage a safety conscious approach to all work you carry out on your vehicle.

Essential DOs and DON'Ts

DON'T rely on a jack when working under the vehicle. Always use approved jackstands to support the weight of the vehicle and place them under the recommended lift or support points.

DON'T attempt to loosen extremely tight fasteners (i.e. wheel lug nuts) while the vehicle is on a jack - it may fall.

DON'T start the engine without first making sure that the transmission is in Neutral (or Park where applicable) and the parking brake is set.

DON'T remove the radiator cap from a hot cooling system - let it cool or cover it with a cloth and release the pressure gradually.

DON'T attempt to drain the engine oil until you are sure it has cooled to the point that it will not burn you.

DON'T touch any part of the engine or exhaust system until it has cooled sufficiently to avoid burns.

DON'T siphon toxic liquids such as gasoline, antifreeze and brake fluid by mouth, or allow them to remain on your skin.

DON'T inhale brake lining dust - it is potentially hazardous (see *Asbestos* below).

DON'T allow spilled oil or grease to remain on the floor - wipe it up before someone slips on it.

DON'T use loose fitting wrenches or other tools which may slip and cause injury.

DON'T push on wrenches when loosening or tightening nuts or bolts. Always try to pull the wrench toward you. If the situation calls for pushing the wrench away, push with an open hand to avoid scraped knuckles if the wrench should slip.

DON'T attempt to lift a heavy component alone - get someone to help you.

DON'T rush or take unsafe shortcuts to finish a job.

DON'T allow children or animals in or around the vehicle while you are working on it.

DO wear eye protection when using power tools such as a drill, sander, bench grinder, etc. and when working under a vehicle.

DO keep loose clothing and long hair well out of the way of moving parts.

DO make sure that any hoist used has a safe working load rating adequate for the job.

DO get someone to check on you periodically when working alone on a vehicle.

DO carry out work in a logical sequence and make sure that everything is correctly assembled and tightened.

DO keep chemicals and fluids tightly capped and out of the reach of children and pets.

DO remember that your vehicle's safety affects that of yourself and others. If in doubt on any point, get professional advice.

Asbestos

Certain friction, insulating, sealing, and other products - such as brake linings, brake bands, clutch linings, torque converters, gaskets, etc. - may contain asbestos. Extreme care must be taken to avoid inhalation of dust from such products, since it is hazardous to health. If in doubt, assume that they do contain asbestos.

Fire

Remember at all times that gasoline is highly flammable. Never smoke or have any kind of open flame around when working on a vehicle. But the risk does not end there. A spark caused by an electrical short circuit, by two metal surfaces contacting each other, or even by static electricity built up in your body under certain conditions, can ignite gasoline vapors, which in a confined space are highly explosive. Do not, under any circumstances, use gasoline for cleaning parts. Use an approved safety solvent.

Always disconnect the battery ground (-) cable at the battery before working on any part of the fuel system or electrical system. Never risk spilling fuel on a hot engine or exhaust component. It is strongly recommended that a fire extinguisher suitable for use on fuel and electrical fires be kept handy in the garage or workshop at all times. Never try to extinguish a fuel or electrical fire with water.

Fumes

Certain fumes are highly toxic and can quickly cause unconsciousness and even death if inhaled to any extent. Gasoline vapor falls into this category, as do the vapors from some cleaning solvents. Any draining or pouring of such volatile fluids should be done in a well ventilated area.

When using cleaning fluids and solvents, read the instructions on the container carefully. Never use materials from unmarked containers.

Never run the engine in an enclosed space, such as a garage. Exhaust fumes contain carbon monoxide, which is extremely poisonous. If you need to run the engine, always do so in the open air, or at least have the rear of the vehicle outside the work area.

If you are fortunate enough to have the use of an inspection pit, never drain or pour gasoline and never run the engine while the vehicle is over the pit. The fumes, being heavier than air, will concentrate in the pit with possibly lethal results.

The battery

Never create a spark or allow a bare light bulb near a battery. They normally give off a certain amount of hydrogen gas, which is highly explosive.

Always disconnect the battery ground (-) cable at the battery before working on the fuel or electrical systems.

If possible, loosen the filler caps or cover when charging the battery from an external source (this does not apply to sealed or maintenance-free batteries). Do not charge at an excessive rate or the battery may burst.

Take care when adding water to a non maintenance-free battery and when carrying a battery. The electrolyte, even when diluted, is very corrosive and should not be allowed to contact clothing or skin.

Always wear eye protection when cleaning the battery to prevent the caustic deposits from entering your eyes.

Household current

When using an electric power tool, inspection light, etc., which operates on household current, always make sure that the tool is correctly connected to its plug and that, where necessary, it is properly grounded. Do not use such items in damp conditions and, again, do not create a spark or apply excessive heat in the vicinity of fuel or fuel vapor.

Secondary ignition system voltage

A severe electric shock can result from touching certain parts of the ignition system (such as the spark plug wires) when the engine is running or being cranked, particularly if components are damp or the insulation is defective. In the case of an electronic ignition system, the secondary system voltage is much higher and could prove fatal.

Troubleshooting

Contents

This section provides an easy reference guide to the more common problems which may occur during the operation of your vehicle. These problems and their possible causes are grouped under headings denoting various components or systems, such as Engine, Cooling system, etc. They also refer you to the chapter and/or section which deals with the problem.

Remember that successful troubleshooting is not a mysterious black art practiced only by professional mechanics. It is simply the result of the right knowledge combined with an intelligent, systematic approach to the problem. Always work by a process of elimination, starting with the simplest solution and working through to the most complex - and never overlook the obvious. Anyone can run the gas tank dry or leave the lights on overnight, so don't assume that you are exempt from such oversights.

Finally, always establish a clear idea of why a problem has occurred and take steps to ensure that it doesn't happen again. If the electrical system fails because of a poor connection, check the other connections in the system to make sure that they don't fail as well. If a particular fuse continues to blow, find out why - don't just replace one fuse after another. Remember, failure of a small component can often be indicative of potential failure or incorrect functioning of a more important component or system.

Engine

1 Engine will not rotate when attempting to start

1 Battery terminal connections loose or corroded (Chapter 1).
2 Battery discharged or faulty (Chapter 1).
3 Automatic transaxle not completely engaged in Park (Chapter 7) or clutch not completely depressed (Chapter 8).
4 Broken, loose or disconnected wiring in the starting circuit (Chapters 5 and 12).
5 Starter motor pinion jammed in flywheel ring gear (Chapter 5).
6 Starter solenoid faulty (Chapter 5).
7 Starter motor faulty (Chapter 5).
8 Ignition switch faulty (Chapter 12).
9 Starter pinion or flywheel teeth worn or broken (Chapter 5).

2 Engine rotates but will not start

1 Fuel tank empty.
2 Battery discharged (engine rotates slowly) (Chapter 5).
3 Battery terminal connections loose or corroded (Chapter 1).
4 Leaking fuel injector(s), fuel pump, pressure regulator, etc. (Chapter 4).
5 Fuel not reaching fuel injection system (Chapter 4).
6 Ignition components damp or damaged (Chapter 5).
7 Worn, faulty or incorrectly gapped spark plugs (Chapter 1).
8 Broken, loose or disconnected wiring in the starting circuit (Chapter 5).
9 Loose distributor is changing ignition timing (Chapter 1).
10 Broken, loose or disconnected wires at the ignition coil or faulty coil (Chapter 5).

3 Engine hard to start when cold

1 Battery discharged or low (Chapter 1).
2 Malfunctioning fuel system (Chapter 4).
3 Injector(s) leaking (Chapter 4).
4 Distributor rotor carbon tracked (Chapter 5).

4 Engine hard to start when hot

1 Air filter clogged (Chapter 1).
2 Fuel not reaching the fuel injection system (Chapter 4).
3 Corroded battery connections, especially ground (Chapter 1).

5 Starter motor noisy or excessively rough in engagement

1 Pinion or flywheel gear teeth worn or broken (Chapter 5).
2 Starter motor mounting bolts loose or missing (Chapter 5).

6 Engine starts but stops immediately

1 Loose or faulty electrical connections at distributor, coil or alternator (Chapter 5).
2 Insufficient fuel reaching the fuel injector(s) (Chapters 1 and 4).
3 Vacuum leak at the gasket between the intake manifold/plenum and throttle body (Chapters 1 and 4).

7 Oil puddle under engine

1 Oil pan gasket and/or oil pan drain bolt washer leaking (Chapter 2).
2 Oil pressure sending unit leaking (Chapter 2).
3 Valve covers leaking (Chapter 2).
4 Engine oil seals leaking (Chapter 2).
5 Oil pump housing leaking (Chapter 2).
6 Turbocharger oil return line leaking (Chapter 4).

8 Engine lopes while idling or idles erratically

1 Vacuum leakage (Chapters 2 and 4).
2 Leaking EGR valve (Chapter 6).
3 Air filter clogged (Chapter 1).
4 Fuel pump not delivering sufficient fuel to the fuel injection system (Chapter 4).
5 Leaking head gasket (Chapter 2).
6 Timing belt and/or pulleys worn (Chapter 2).
7 Camshaft lobes worn (Chapter 2).

9 Engine misses at idle speed

1 Spark plugs worn or not gapped properly (Chapter 1).
2 Faulty spark plug wires (Chapter 1).
3 Vacuum leaks (Chapter 1).
4 Incorrect ignition timing (Chapter 1).
5 Uneven or low compression (Chapter 2).

10 Engine misses throughout driving speed range

1 Fuel filter clogged and/or impurities in the fuel system (Chapter 1).
2 Low fuel output at the injector(s) (Chapter 4).
3 Faulty or incorrectly gapped spark plugs (Chapter 1).
4 Incorrect ignition timing (Chapter 5).
5 Cracked distributor cap, disconnected distributor wires or damaged distributor components (Chapters 1 and 5).
6 Leaking spark plug wires (Chapters 1 or 5).
7 Faulty emission system components (Chapter 6).
8 Low or uneven cylinder compression pressures (Chapter 2).
9 Weak or faulty ignition system (Chapter 5).
10 Vacuum leak in fuel injection system, intake manifold, air control valve or vacuum hoses (Chapter 4).

11 Engine stumbles on acceleration

1 Spark plugs fouled (Chapter 1).
2 Spark plug wire(s) faulty
3 Fuel injection system needs adjustment or repair (Chapter 4).
4 Fuel filter clogged (Chapters 1 and 4).
5 Incorrect ignition timing (Chapter 1).
6 Intake manifold air leak (Chapters 2 and 4).

12 Engine surges while holding accelerator steady

1 Intake air leak (Chapter 4).

2   Fuel pump faulty (Chapter 4).
3   Loose fuel injector wire harness connectors (Chapter 4).
4   Defective ECU (Chapter 6).

13 Engine stalls

1   Fuel filter clogged and/or water and impurities in the fuel system (Chapters 1 and 4).
2   Distributor components damp or damaged (Chapter 5).
3   Faulty emissions system components (Chapter 6).
4   Faulty or incorrectly gapped spark plugs (Chapter 1).
5   Faulty spark plug wires (Chapter 1).
6   Vacuum leak in the fuel injection system, intake manifold or vacuum hoses (Chapters 2 and 4).
7   Idle speed too low (Chapter 4).

14 Engine lacks power

1   Incorrect ignition timing (Chapter 5).
2   Excessive play in distributor shaft (Chapter 5).
3   Worn rotor, distributor cap or wires (Chapters 1 and 5).
4   Faulty or incorrectly gapped spark plugs (Chapter 1).
5   Fuel injection system out of adjustment or excessively worn (Chapter 4).
6   Faulty coil (Chapter 5).
7   Brakes binding (Chapter 9).
8   Automatic transaxle fluid level incorrect (Chapter 1).
9   Clutch slipping (Chapter 8).
10   Fuel filter clogged and/or impurities in the fuel system (Chapters 1 and 4).
11   Emission control system not functioning properly (Chapter 6).
12   Low or uneven cylinder compression pressures (Chapter 2).
13   Turbocharger inoperative (Chapter 4).

15 Engine backfires

1   Emission control system not functioning properly (Chapter 6).
2   Ignition timing incorrect (Chapter 1).
3   Faulty secondary ignition system (cracked spark plug insulator, faulty plug wires, distributor cap and/or rotor) (Chapters 1 and 5).
4   Fuel injection system in need of adjustment or worn excessively (Chapter 4).
5   Vacuum leak at fuel injector(s), intake manifold, air control valve or vacuum hoses (Chapters 2 and 4).

16 Pinging or knocking engine sounds during acceleration or uphill

1   Incorrect grade of fuel.
2   Ignition timing incorrect (Chapter 1).
3   Fuel injection system in need of adjustment (Chapter 4).
4   Improper or damaged spark plugs or wires (Chapter 1).
5   Worn or damaged distributor components (Chapter 5).
6   Faulty emission system (Chapter 6).
7   Vacuum leak (Chapters 2 and 4).

17 Engine runs with oil pressure light on

1   Low oil level (Chapter 1).
2   Idle rpm below specification (Chapter 1).
3   Short in wiring circuit (Chapter 12).
4   Faulty oil pressure sender (Chapter 2).
5   Worn engine bearings and/or oil pump (Chapter 2).
6   Turbocharger oil supply line leaking (Chapter 4).

18 Engine diesels (continues to run) after switching off

1   Excessive engine operating temperature (Chapter 3).
2   Idle speed too high (Chapter 1).

Engine electrical system

19 Battery will not hold a charge

1   Alternator drivebelt defective or not adjusted properly (Chapter 1).
2   Battery electrolyte level low (Chapter 1).
3   Battery terminals loose or corroded (Chapter 1).
4   Alternator not charging properly (Chapter 5).
5   Loose, broken or faulty wiring in the charging circuit (Chapter 5).
6   Short in vehicle wiring (Chapter 12).
7   Internally defective battery (Chapters 1 and 5).

20 Alternator light fails to go out

1   Faulty alternator or charging circuit (Chapter 5).
2   Alternator drivebelt defective or out of adjustment (Chapter 1).
3   Alternator voltage regulator inoperative (Chapter 5).

21 Alternator light fails to come on when key is turned on

1   Warning light bulb defective (Chapter 12).
2   Fault in the printed circuit, dash wiring or bulb holder (Chapter 12).

Fuel system

22 Excessive fuel consumption

1   Dirty or clogged air filter element (Chapter 1).
2   Incorrectly set ignition timing (Chapter 1).
3   Emissions system not functioning properly (Chapter 6).
4   Fuel injection internal parts excessively worn or damaged (Chapter 4).
5   Low tire pressure or incorrect tire size (Chapter 1).

23 Fuel leakage and/or fuel odor

1   Leaking fuel feed or return line (Chapters 1 and 4).
2   Tank overfilled.
3   Evaporative canister filter clogged (Chapters 1 and 6).
4   Fuel injector internal parts excessively worn (Chapter 4).

Cooling system

24 Overheating

1   Insufficient coolant in system (Chapter 1).
2   Water pump drivebelt defective or out of adjustment (Chapter 1).
3   Radiator core blocked or grille restricted (Chapter 3).
4   Thermostat faulty (Chapter 3).
5   Electric coolant fan blades broken or cracked (Chapter 3).
6   Radiator cap not maintaining proper pressure (Chapter 3).
7   Ignition timing incorrect (Chapter 5).

25 Overcooling

1   Faulty thermostat (Chapter 3).
2   Inaccurate temperature gauge sending unit (Chapter 3).

26 External coolant leakage

1 Deteriorated/damaged hoses; loose clamps (Chapters 1 and 3).
2 Water pump seal defective (Chapter 3).
3 Leakage from radiator core or coolant reservoir bottle (Chapter 3).
4 Engine drain or water jacket core plugs leaking (Chapter 2).
5 Turbocharger coolant supply or return line leaking (Chapter 4).

27 Internal coolant leakage

1 Leaking cylinder head gasket (Chapter 2).
2 Cracked cylinder bore or cylinder head (Chapter 2).

28 Coolant loss

1 Too much coolant in system (Chapter 1).
2 Coolant boiling away because of overheating (Chapter 3).
3 Internal or external leakage (Chapter 3).
4 Faulty radiator cap (Chapter 3).
5 Turbocharger coolant supply or return line leaking (Chapter 4).

29 Poor coolant circulation

1 Inoperative water pump (Chapter 3).
2 Restriction in cooling system (Chapters 1 and 3).
3 Water pump drivebelt defective/out of adjustment (Chapter 1).
4 Thermostat sticking (Chapter 3).
5 Restriction in turbocharger coolant supply or return line (Chapter 4).

Clutch

30 Clutch pedal travels to floor - no pressure or very little resistance

Clutch cable broken (Chapter 8).

31 Unable to select gears

1 Faulty transaxle (Chapter 7).
2 Faulty clutch disc (Chapter 8).
3 Fork and bearing not assembled properly (Chapter 8).
4 Faulty pressure plate (Chapter 8).
5 Pressure plate-to-flywheel bolts loose (Chapter 8).

32 Clutch slips (engine speed increases with no increase in vehicle speed)

1 Clutch plate worn (Chapter 8).
2 Clutch plate is oil soaked by leaking rear main seal (Chapter 8).
3 Clutch plate not seated. It may take 30 or 40 normal starts for a new one to seat.
4 Warped pressure plate or flywheel (Chapter 8).
5 Weak diaphragm spring (Chapter 8).
6 Clutch plate overheated. Allow to cool.

33 Grabbing (chattering) as clutch is engaged

1 Oil on clutch plate lining, burned or glazed facings (Chapter 8).
2 Worn or loose engine or transaxle mounts (Chapters 2 and 7).
3 Worn splines on clutch plate hub (Chapter 8).
4 Warped pressure plate or flywheel (Chapter 8).
5 Burned or smeared resin on flywheel or pressure plate (Chapter 8).

34 Transaxle rattling (clicking)

1 Release fork loose (Chapter 8).
2 Clutch plate damper spring failure (Chapter 8).

35 Noise in clutch area

1 Fork shaft improperly installed (Chapter 8).
2 Faulty bearing (Chapter 8).

36 Clutch pedal stays on floor

1 Broken release bearing or fork (Chapter 8).
2 Clutch cable broken (Chapter 8)

37 High pedal effort

1 Pressure plate faulty (Chapter 8).
2 Damaged or binding clutch cable (Chapter 8).

Manual transaxle

38 Knocking noise at low speeds

1 Worn driveaxle constant velocity (CV) joints (Chapter 8).

2 Worn side gear shaft counterbore in differential case (Chapter 7A).*

39 Noise most pronounced when turning

Differential gear noise (Chapter 7A).*

40 Clunk on acceleration or deceleration

1 Loose engine or transaxle mounts (Chapters 2 and 7A).
2 Worn differential pinion shaft in case.*
3 Worn side gear shaft counterbore in differential case (Chapter 7A).*
4 Worn or damaged driveaxle inboard CV joints (Chapter 8).

41 Clicking noise in turns

Worn or damaged outboard CV joint (Chapter 8).

42 Vibration

1 Rough wheel bearing (Chapters 1 and 10).
2 Damaged driveaxle (Chapter 8).
3 Out-of-round tires (Chapter 1).
4 Tire out of balance (Chapters 1 and 10).
5 Worn CV joint (Chapter 8).

43 Noisy in neutral with engine running

1 Damaged input gear bearing (Chapter 7A).*
2 Damaged clutch release bearing (Chapter 8).

44 Noisy in one particular gear

1 Damaged or worn constant-mesh gears (Chapter 7A).*
2 Damaged or worn synchronizers (Chapter 7A).*
3 Bent reverse fork (Chapter 7A).*
4 Damaged fourth speed gear or output gear (Chapter 7A).*
5 Worn or damaged reverse idler gear or idler bushing (Chapter 7A).*

45 Noisy in all gears

1 Insufficient lubricant (Chapter 7A).
2 Damaged or worn bearings (Chapter 7A).*
3 Worn or damaged input gear shaft and/or output gear shaft (Chapter 7A).*

46 Slips out of gear

1 Worn or improperly adjusted linkage (Chapter 7A).
2 Transaxle loose on engine (Chapter 7A).
3 Shift linkage does not work freely, binds (Chapter 7A).
4 Input gear bearing retainer broken or loose (Chapter 7A).*
5 Dirt between clutch cover and engine housing (Chapter 7A).
6 Worn shift fork (Chapter 7A).*

47 Leaks lubricant

1 Side gear shaft seals worn (Chapter 8).
2 Excessive amount of lubricant in transaxle (Chapters 1 and 7A).
3 Loose or broken input gear shaft bearing retainer (Chapter 7A).*
4 Input gear bearing retainer O-ring and/or lip seal damaged (Chapter 7A).*

48 Locked in second gear

Lock pin or interlock pin missing (Chapter 7A).*

Although the corrective action necessary to remedy the symptoms described is beyond the scope of the home mechanic, the above information should be helpful in isolating the cause of the condition so that the owner can communicate clearly with a professional mechanic.

Automatic transaxle

Note: *Due to the complexity of the automatic transaxle, it is difficult for the home mechanic to properly diagnose and service this component. For problems other than the following, the vehicle should be taken to a dealer or transmission shop.*

49 Fluid leakage

1 Automatic transmission fluid is a deep red color. Fluid leaks should not be confused with engine oil, which can easily be blown onto the transaxle by air flow.
2 To pinpoint a leak, first remove all built-up dirt and grime from the transaxle housing with degreasing agents and/or steam cleaning. Then drive the vehicle at low speeds so air flow will not blow the leak far from its source. Raise the vehicle and determine where the leak is coming from. Common areas of leakage are:
a) *Pan (Chapters 1 and 7)*
b) *Dipstick tube (Chapters 1 and 7)*
c) *Transaxle oil lines (Chapter 7)*
d) *Speed sensor (Chapter 7)*

50 Transaxle fluid brown or has a burned smell

Transaxle fluid burned (Chapter 1).

51 General shift mechanism problems

1 Chapter 7, Part B, deals with checking and adjusting the shift linkage on automatic transaxles. Common problems which may be attributed to poorly adjusted linkage are:
a) *Engine starting in gears other than Park or Neutral.*
b) *Indicator on shifter pointing to a gear other than the one actually being used.*
c) *Vehicle moves when in Park.*
2 Refer to Chapter 7B for the shift linkage adjustment procedure.

52 Transaxle will not downshift with accelerator pedal pressed to the floor

Throttle Valve (TV) cable out of adjustment (Chapter 7B).

53 Engine will start in gears other than Park or Neutral

Neutral start switch malfunctioning (Chapter 7B).

54 Transaxle slips, shifts roughly, is noisy or has no drive in forward or reverse gears

There are many probable causes for the above problems, but the home mechanic should be concerned with only one possibility - fluid level. Before taking the vehicle to a repair shop, check the level and condition of the fluid as described in Chapter 1. Correct the fluid level as necessary or change the fluid and filter if needed. If the problem persists, have a professional diagnose the cause.

Driveaxles

55 Clicking noise in turns

Worn or damaged outboard CV joint (Chapter 8).

56 Shudder or vibration during acceleration

1 Excessive toe-in (Chapter 10).

2 Worn or damaged inboard or outboard CV joints (Chapter 8).
3 Sticking inboard CV joint assembly (Chapter 8).

57 Vibration at highway speeds

1 Out-of-balance front wheels and/or tires (Chapters 1 and 10).
2 Out-of-round front tires (Chapters 1 and 10).
3 Worn CV joint(s) (Chapter 8).

Brakes

Note: *Before assuming that a brake problem exists, make sure that:*
a) *The tires are in good condition and properly inflated (Chapter 1).*
b) *The front end alignment is correct (Chapter 10).*
c) *The vehicle is not loaded with weight in an unequal manner.*

58 Vehicle pulls to one side during braking

1 Incorrect tire pressures (Chapter 1).
2 Front end out of line (have the front end aligned).
3 Front or rear tires not matched to one another.
4 Restricted brake lines or hoses (Chapter 9).
5 Malfunctioning caliper or drum brake assembly (Chapter 9).
6 Loose suspension parts (Chapter 10).
7 Loose calipers (Chapter 9).
8 Excessive wear of brake shoe or pad material or disc/drum on one side.

59 Noise (high-pitched squeal when the brakes are applied)

1 Front disc brake pads worn out. The noise comes from the wear sensor rubbing against the disc (does not apply to all vehicles). Replace pads with new ones immediately (Chapter 9).
2 incorrectly installed new pads (many require an anti-squeal compound on the backing plates).

60 Brake roughness or chatter (pedal pulsates)

1 Excessive lateral runout (Chapter 9).
2 Uneven pad wear (Chapter 9).
3 Defective rotor (Chapter 9).

61 Excessive brake pedal effort required to stop vehicle

1 Malfunctioning power brake booster (Chapter 9).
2 Partial system failure (Chapter 9).
3 Excessively worn pads or shoes (Chapter 9).
4 Piston in caliper or wheel cylinder stuck or sluggish (Chapter 9).
5 Brake pads or shoes contaminated with oil or grease (Chapter 9).
6 New pads or shoes installed and not yet seated. It will take a while
for the new material to seat against the rotor or drum.

62 Excessive brake pedal travel

1 Partial brake system failure (Chapter 9).
2 Insufficient fluid in master cylinder (Chapters 1 and 9).
3 Air trapped in system (Chapters 1 and 9).

63 Dragging brakes

1 Incorrect adjustment of brake light switch (Chapter 9).
2 Master cylinder pistons not returning correctly (Chapter 9).
3 Restricted brake lines or hoses (Chapters 1 and 9).
4 Incorrect parking brake adjustment (Chapter 9).

64 Grabbing or uneven braking action

1 Malfunction of proportioning valve (Chapter 9).
2 Malfunction of power brake booster unit (Chapter 9).
3 Binding brake pedal mechanism (Chapter 9).

65 Brake pedal feels spongy when depressed

1 Air in hydraulic lines (Chapter 9).
2 Master cylinder mounting bolts loose (Chapter 9).
3 Master cylinder defective (Chapter 9).

66 Brake pedal travels to the floor with little resistance

1 Little or no fluid in the master cylinder reservoir caused by leaking caliper piston(s) (Chapter 9).
2 Loose, damaged or disconnected brake lines (Chapter 9).

67 Parking brake does not hold

Parking brake linkage improperly adjusted (Chapters 1 and 9).

Suspension and steering systems

Note: *Before attempting to diagnose the suspension and steering systems, perform the following preliminary checks:*

a) *Tires for wrong pressure and uneven wear.*
b) *Steering universal joints from the column to the steering gear for loose connectors or wear.*
c) *Front and rear suspension and the steering gear assembly for loose or damaged parts.*
d) *Out-of-round or out-of-balance tires, bent rims and loose and/or rough wheel bearings.*

68 Vehicle pulls to one side

1 Mismatched or uneven tires (Chapter 10).
2 Broken or sagging springs (Chapter 10).
3 Wheel alignment (Chapter 10).
4 Front brake dragging (Chapter 9).

69 Abnormal or excessive tire wear

1 Wheel alignment (Chapter 10).
2 Sagging or broken springs (Chapter 10).
3 Tire out of balance (Chapter 10).
4 Worn strut damper (Chapter 10).
5 Overloaded vehicle.
6 Tires not rotated regularly.

70 Wheel makes a thumping noise

1 Blister or bump on tire (Chapter 10).
2 Improper strut damper action (Chapter 10).

71 Shimmy, shake or vibration

1 Tire or wheel out-of-balance or out-of-round (Chapter 10).
2 Loose or worn wheel bearings (Chapters 1, 8 and 10).
3 Worn tie-rod ends (Chapter 10).
4 Worn lower balljoints (Chapters 1 and 10).
5 Excessive wheel runout (Chapter 10).
6 Blister or bump on tire (Chapter 10).

72 Hard steering

1 Lack of lubrication at balljoints, tie-rod ends and steering gear assembly (Chapter 10).
2 Front wheel alignment (Chapter 10).
3 Low tire pressure(s) (Chapters 1 and 10).

73 Poor returnability of steering to center

1 Lack of lubrication at balljoints and tie-rod ends (Chapter 10).
2 Binding in balljoints (Chapter 10).
3 Binding in steering column (Chapter 10).
4 Lack of lubricant in steering gear assembly (Chapter 10).
5 Front wheel alignment (Chapter 10).

74 Abnormal noise at the front end

1 Lack of lubrication at balljoints and tie-rod ends (Chapters 1 and 10).
2 Damaged strut mounting (Chapter 10).
3 Worn control arm bushings or tie-rod ends (Chapter 10).
4 Loose stabilizer bar (Chapter 10).
5 Loose wheel nuts (Chapters 1 and 10).
6 Loose suspension bolts (Chapter 10).

75 Wander or poor steering stability

1 Mismatched or uneven tires (Chapter 10).
2 Lack of lubrication at balljoints and tie-rod ends (Chapters 1 and 10).
3 Worn strut assemblies (Chapter 10).
4 Loose stabilizer bar (Chapter 10).
5 Broken or sagging springs (Chapter 10).
6 Wheel alignment (Chapter 10).

76 Erratic steering when braking

1 Wheel bearings worn (Chapter 10).
2 Broken or sagging springs (Chapter 10).
3 Leaking wheel cylinder or caliper (Chapter 10).
4 Warped rotors or drums (Chapter 10).

77 Excessive pitching and/or rolling around corners or during braking

1 Loose stabilizer bar (Chapter 10).
2 Worn strut dampers or mountings (Chapter 10).
3 Broken or sagging springs (Chapter 10).
4 Overloaded vehicle.

78 Suspension bottoms

1 Overloaded vehicle.
2 Worn strut dampers (Chapter 10).
3 Incorrect, broken or sagging springs (Chapter 10).

79 Cupped tires

1   Front wheel or rear wheel alignment (Chapter 10).
2   Worn strut dampers (Chapter 10).
3   Wheel bearings worn (Chapter 10).
4   Excessive tire or wheel runout (Chapter 10).
5   Worn balljoints (Chapter 10).

80 Excessive tire wear on outside edge

1   Inflation pressures incorrect (Chapter 1).
2   Excessive speed in turns.
3   Front end alignment incorrect (excessive toe-in). Have professionally aligned.
4   Suspension arm bent or twisted (Chapter 10).

81 Excessive tire wear on inside edge

1   Inflation pressures incorrect (Chapter 1).
2   Front end alignment incorrect (toe-out). Have professionally aligned.
3   Loose or damaged steering components (Chapter 10).

82 Tire tread worn in one place

1   Tires out of balance.
2   Damaged or buckled wheel. Inspect and replace if necessary.
3   Defective tire (Chapter 1).

83 Excessive play or looseness in steering system

1   Wheel bearing(s) worn (Chapter 10).
2   Tie-rod end loose (Chapter 10).
3   Steering gear loose (Chapter 10).
4   Worn or loose steering intermediate shaft (Chapter 10).

84 Rattling or clicking noise in steering gear

1   Insufficient or improper lubricant in steering gear assembly (Chapter 10).
2   Steering gear attachment loose (Chapter 10).

Chapter 1
Tune-up and routine maintenance

Contents

Specifications

Recommended lubricants and fluids

Note: *Listed here are manufacturer recommendations at the time this manual was written. Manufacturers occasionally upgrade their fluid and lubricant specifications, so check with your local auto parts store for current recommendations.*

Engine oil
  Type .... API SG or SG/CD multigrade and fuel efficient oil
  Viscosity .... See accompanying chart

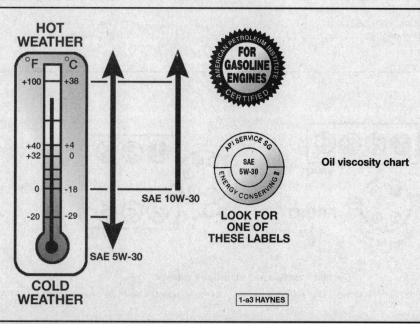

Oil viscosity chart

Recommended lubricants and fluids

Manual transaxle lubricant...	SAE 5W30 engine oil
Automatic transaxle fluid	Mopar ATF Plus 3 Type 7176 automatic transmission fluid or equivalent
Power steering fluid	Mopar 4-253 power steering fluid or equivalent
Brake fluid..	DOT 3 brake fluid
Engine coolant..	50/50 mixture of ethylene glycol-based antifreeze and water
Transaxle shift linkage grease	NLGI no. 2 chassis grease
Clutch linkage grease	NLGI no. 2 chassis grease
Parking brake mechanism grease	White lithium-based grease NLGI no. 2
Chassis lubrication grease	NLGI no. 2 EP grease
Rear wheel bearing grease	NLGI no. 2 EP high-temperature wheel bearing grease
Steering gear lubricant	API GL-4 SAE 90W gear oil
Hood, door and trunk/liftgate hinge lubricant	Engine oil
Door hinge and check spring grease................................	NLGI no. 2 multi-purpose grease
Key lock cylinder lubricant...	Graphite spray
Hood latch assembly lubricant	NLGI no. 2 multi-purpose grease
Door latch lubricant	NLGI no. 2 multi-purpose grease

Capacities*

Engine oil (including filter) - all models	4.5 qts
Automatic transaxle	
Drain and refill	4.0 qts
From dry (including torque converter).............................	8.9 qts
Manual transaxle	2.3 qts
Cooling system	9.0 qts

* All capacities approximate. Add as necessary to bring to appropriate level.

Brakes

Disc brake pad wear limit (including metal shoe)	5/16 inch
Drum brake shoe wear limit...	1/8 inch

Ignition system

Spark plug type	
Four-cylinder engines...	Champion RN12YC or equivalent
Six-cylinder engine...	Champion RN11YC4 or equivalent
Spark plug gap	
Four-cylinder engines...	0.035 inch
Six-cylinder engine...	0.044 inch
Spark plug wire resistance	
Minimum..	3000 ohms per foot
Maximum...	7200 ohms per foot
Ignition timing	See the *Vehicle Emissions Control Information* label in the engine compartment
Firing order	
Four-cylinder engines...	1-3-4-2
Six-cylinder engine...	1-2-3-4-5-6

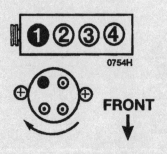

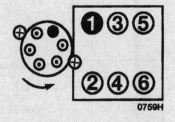

Cylinder location and distributor rotation

Distributor cap terminal routing for 3.0L V6

The blackened terminal shown on the distributor cap indicates the Number One spark plug wire position

Drivebelt deflection

Alternator
  New .... 1/8 inch
  Used .... 1/4 inch
Power steering pump
  New .... 1/4 inch
  Used .... 7/16 inch
Water pump
  New .... 1/8 inch
  Used .... 1/4 inch
Air conditioning compressor
  New .... 5/16 inch
  Used .... /16 inch
Automatic transaxle band adjustment
Kickdown (front) .... Tighten to 72 in-lbs, then back off 2-1/2 turns
Low-Reverse... Tighten to 41 in-lbs, then back off 3-1/2 turns

Torque specifications   **Ft-lbs** (unless otherwise indicated)

Throttle body mounting bolt/nut
  Turbo 40
  Non-turbo .... 175 in-lbs
Spark plugs.. 26
Wheel lug nuts 95
Automatic transaxle
  Pan bolts .... 170 in-lbs
  Filter-to-valve body screws .... 40 in-lbs

Engine compartment components - V6 model

1	*Windshield washer fluid reservoir*	*6*	*Radiator cap*	*10*	*Coolant reservoir*
2	*Power steering fluid dipstick*	*7*	*Automatic transaxle fluid dipstick*	*11*	*Distributor cap*
3	*Air filter housing*	*8*	*Engine oil dipstick*	*12*	*Upper radiator hose*
4	*Brake fluid reservoir*	*9*	*Engine oil filler cap*	*13*	*Serpentine drivebelt*
5	*Battery*				

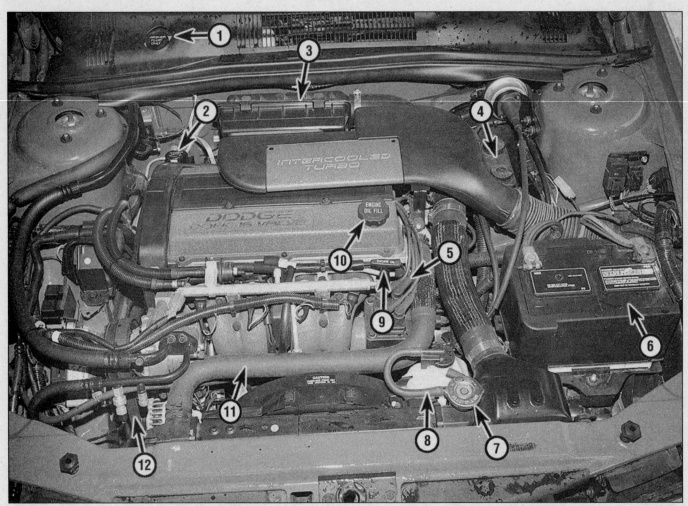

Engine compartment components - DOHC turbo model

1	Windshield washer fluid reservoir	5	Ignition coil	9	Engine oil dipstick
2	Power steering fluid reservoir	6	Battery	10	Engine oil filler cap
3	Air filter housing	7	Radiator cap	11	Upper radiator hose
4	Brake fluid reservoir	8	Coolant reservoir	12	Serpentine drivebelt

Engine compartment underside components - (V6 model shown, others similar)

1   Engine oil drain plug
2   Engine oil filter
3   Automatic transaxle fluid pan
4   Brake hose
5   Brake caliper
6   Driveaxle boot
7   Exhaust pipe
8   Front suspension strut

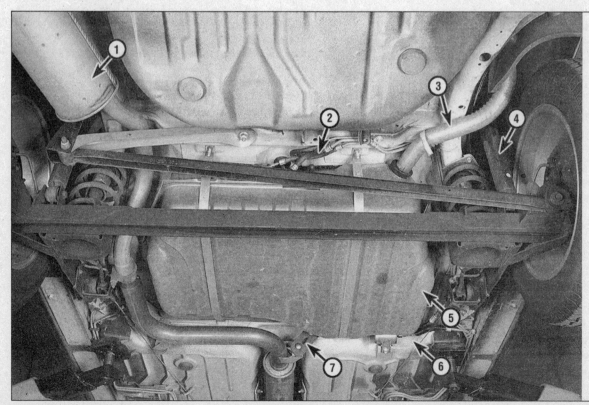

Typical rear underside components

1   Muffler
2   Fuel lines
3   Fuel filler hose
4   Shock absorber
5   Fuel tank
6   Parking brake cable
7   Exhaust system hanger

1 Dodge Spirit/Plymouth Acclaim Maintenance schedule

The following maintenance intervals are based on the assumption that the vehicle owner will be doing the maintenance or service work, as opposed to having a dealer service department do the work. Although the time/mileage intervals are loosely based on factory recommendations, most have been shortened to ensure, for example, that such items as lubricants and fluids are checked/changed at intervals that promote maximum engine/driveline service life. Also, subject to the preference of the individual owner interested in keeping his or her vehicle in peak condition at all times, and with the vehicle's ultimate resale in mind, many of the maintenance procedures may be performed more often than recommended in the following schedule. We encourage such owner initiative.

When the vehicle is new it should be serviced initially by a factory authorized dealer service department to protect the factory warranty. In many cases the initial maintenance check is done at no cost to the owner (check with your dealer service department for more information).

Every 250 miles or weekly, whichever comes first

Check the engine oil level; add oil as necessary (see Section 4)
Check the engine coolant level; add coolant as necessary (see Section 4)
Check the windshield washer fluid level (see Section 4)
Check the battery electrolyte level (see Section 4)
Check the brake fluid level (see Section 4)
Check the tires and tire pressures (see Section 5)
Check the automatic transaxle fluid level (see Section 6)
Check the power steering fluid level (see Section 7)
Check the wiper blade condition (see Section 8)
Check the operation of all lights
Check the horn operation

Every 3000 miles or 3 months, whichever comes first

Change the engine oil and filter (all models) (see Section 9)*

Every 7500 miles or 6 months, whichever comes first

Check the fuel system hoses, lines and connections for leaks and damage (see Section 24)
Check the brake hoses and lines for leaks and damage (see Section 29)
Check the suspension balljoint and steering linkage boots for damage and lubricant leaks (see Section 27)*
Check the driveaxle boots for damage and lubricant leaks (see Section 36)*
Check the manual transaxle lubricant level (see Section 12)

Every 15,000 miles or 12 months, whichever comes first

Check and clean the battery (see Section 10)

Check the drivebelts (see Section 17)
Check the fuel injection throttle body mounting nut torque (see Section 22)
Check the cooling system hoses and connections for leaks and damage (see Section 25)

Every 22,500 miles or 18 months, whichever comes first

Check the EGR system components for proper operation (see Section 20)
Check the condition of all vacuum hoses and connections (see Section 21)
Check the condition of the primary ignition wires and spark plug wires (see Section 16)
Check the distributor cap and rotor (see Section 16)
Check the exhaust pipes and hangers (see Section 26)
Check for freeplay in the steering linkage and balljoints (see Section 27)
Check the fuel evaporative emission system hoses and connections (see Section 37)
Rotate the tires (see Section 11)
Replace the fuel filter (see Section 13)
Check the brakes (see Section 29)*

Every 30,000 miles or 24 months, whichever comes first

Check and service the rear wheel bearings (see Section 28)*
Replace the air filter element (see Section 18)*
Check the PCV valve (see Section 19)
Replace the spark plugs (see Section 15)
Check the parking brake operation (see Section 29)
Lubricate the front suspension and steering balljoints (see Section 27)*
Drain and replace the engine coolant (see Section 30)
Change the manual transaxle lubricant (see Section 33)*
Change the automatic transaxle fluid and filter (see Section 34)*
Adjust the automatic transaxle bands (see Section 35)*
Check the airbag system (see Section 32)

Every 50,000 miles or 60 months, whichever comes first

Replace the PCV valve (see Section 19)
Replace the spark plug wires, distributor cap and rotor (see Section 16)
Replace the oxygen sensor (Chapter 6)

* This item is affected by "severe" operating conditions as described below. If the vehicle in question is operated under "severe" conditions, perform all maintenance procedures marked with an asterisk (*) at the following intervals:

Every 1,000 miles

Change the engine oil and filter (turbo models only)

Every 2,000 miles

Change the engine oil and filter (non-turbo models only)
Check the driveaxle, suspension and steering boots

Every 9,000 miles

Check the brakes
Service the rear wheel bearings

Every 15,000 miles

Replace the air filter element
Lubricate the tie-rod ends
Change the automatic transaxle fluid and filter
Adjust the automatic transaxle bands
Change the manual transaxle lubricant and clean the pan magnet

Consider the conditions "severe" if most driving is done . . .
In dusty areas
Towing a trailer
Idling for extended periods and/or low-speed operation
When outside temperatures remain below freezing and most trips are less than four miles
In heavy city traffic where outside temperatures regularly reach 90-degrees F or higher

1

2   Introduction

This Chapter is designed to help the home mechanic maintain the Dodge Spirit/Plymouth Acclaim with the goals of maximum performance, economy, safety and reliability in mind.

Included is a master maintenance schedule, followed by procedures dealing specifically with each item on the schedule. Visual checks, adjustments, component replacement and other helpful items are included. Refer to the accompanying illustrations of the engine compartment and the underside of the vehicle for the locations of various components.

Adhering to the mileage/time maintenance schedule and following the step-by-step procedures, which is simply a preventive maintenance program, will result in maximum reliability and vehicle service life. Keep in mind that it's a comprehensive program - maintaining some items but not others at the specified intervals will not produce the same results.

As you service the vehicle, you'll discover that many of the procedures can - and should - be grouped together because of the nature of the particular procedure you're performing or because of the close proximity of two otherwise unrelated components to one another.

For example, if the vehicle is raised, you should inspect the exhaust, suspension, steering and fuel systems while you're under the vehicle. When you're rotating the tires, it makes good sense to check the brakes, since the wheels are already removed. Finally, let's suppose you have to borrow or rent a torque wrench. Even if you only need it to tighten the spark plugs, you might as well check the torque of as many critical fasteners as time allows.

The first step in this maintenance program is to prepare yourself before the actual work begins. Read through all the procedures you're planning to do, then gather up all the parts and tools needed. If it looks like you might run into problems during a particular job, seek advice from a mechanic or an experienced do-it-yourselfer.

3   Tune-up general information

The term "tune-up" is used in this manual to represent a combination of individual operations rather than one specific procedure.

If, from the time the vehicle is new, the routine maintenance schedule is followed closely and frequent checks are made of fluid levels and high wear items, as suggested throughout this manual, the engine will be kept in relatively good running condition and the need for additional work will be minimized.

More likely than not, however, there will be times when the engine is running poorly due to lack of regular maintenance. This is even more likely if a used vehicle, which hasn't received regular and frequent maintenance checks, is purchased. In such cases, an engine tune-up will be needed outside of the regular routine maintenance intervals.

The first step in any tune-up or diagnostic procedure to help correct a poor running engine is a cylinder compression check. A compression check (see Chapter 2, Part C) will help determine the condition of internal engine components and should be used as a guide for tune-up and repair procedures. For instance, if a compression check indicates serious internal engine wear, a conventional tune-up will not improve the performance of the engine and would be a waste of time and money. Because of its importance, the compression check should be done by someone with the right equipment and the knowledge to use it properly.

The following procedures are those most often needed to bring a generally poor running engine back into a proper state of tune:

Minor tune-up

Check all engine related fluids (see Section 4)
Clean, inspect and test the battery (see Section 10)
Replace the spark plugs (see Section 15)
Inspect the distributor cap and rotor (see Section 16)
Inspect the spark plug and coil wires (see Section 16)
Check and adjust the drivebelts (see Section 17)
Check the air filter (see Section 18)
Check the PCV valve (see Section 19)
Check all underhood hoses (see Section 21)
Check the cooling system (see Section 25)
Check and adjust the ignition timing (see Section 31)

Major tune-up

All items listed under Minor tune-up plus . . .
Replace the air filter (see Section 18)
Replace the distributor cap and rotor (see Section 16)
Replace the spark plug wires (see Section 16)
Check the EGR system (see Section 20)
Check the fuel system (see Section 24)
Check the ignition system (see Chapter 5)
Check the charging system (see Chapter 5)

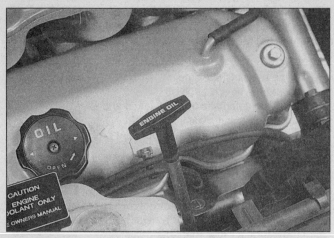

4.4a The engine oil dipstick is located on the front (radiator side) of the engine

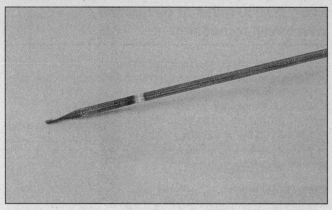

4.4b The oil level should be between the ADD and FULL marks on the dipstick - if it isn't, add enough oil to bring the level up to or near the FULL mark (it takes one quart to raise the level from the ADD to the FULL mark)

4   Fluid level checks

Note: *The following are fluid level checks to be done on a 250 mile or weekly basis. Additional fluid level checks can be found in specific maintenance procedures which follow. Regardless of the intervals, develop the habit of checking under the vehicle periodically for evidence of fluid leaks.*

1   Fluids are an essential part of the lubrication, cooling, brake and window washer systems. Because the fluids gradually become depleted and/or contaminated during normal operation of the vehicle, they must be replenished periodically. See Recommended lubricants and fluids at the beginning of this Chapter before adding fluid to any of the following components. **Note:** The vehicle must be on level ground when fluid levels are checked.

Engine oil

Refer to illustrations 4.4a, 4.4b and 4.5

2   The engine oil level is checked with a dipstick which is located on the front (radiator) side of the engine block. The dipstick extends through a tube and into the oil pan at the bottom of the engine.
3   The oil level should be checked before the vehicle has been driven, or about 15 minutes after the engine has been shut off. If the oil is checked immediately after driving the vehicle, some of the oil will remain in the upper engine components, resulting in an inaccurate reading on the dipstick.
4   Pull the dipstick out of the tube **(see illustration)** and wipe all the oil off the end with a clean rag or paper towel. Insert the clean dipstick all the way back into the tube, then pull it out again. Note the oil level at the end of the dipstick. Add oil as necessary to keep the level at the Full mark **(see illustration)**.
5   Oil is added to the engine after removing a twist-off cap located on the camshaft cover **(see illustration)**. The cap will be marked "Engine oil" or something similar. A funnel

4.5 Turn the oil filler cap counterclockwise to remove it

may help reduce spills as the oil is poured in.
6   Don't allow the level to drop below the Add mark or engine damage may occur. On the other hand, don't overfill the engine by adding too much oil - it may result in oil fouled spark plugs, oil leaks or seal failures.
7   Checking the oil level is an important preventive maintenance step. A consistently low oil level indicates oil leakage through damaged seals, defective gaskets or past worn rings or valve guides. If the oil looks milky in color or has water droplets in it, the block may be cracked. The engine should be checked immediately. The condition of the oil should also be checked. Each time you check the oil level, slide your thumb and index finger up the dipstick before wiping off the oil. If you see small dirt or metal particles clinging to the dipstick, the oil should be changed (see Section 9).

Engine coolant

Refer to illustrations 4.8 and 4.12
Warning: *Do not allow antifreeze to come in contact with your skin or painted surfaces of the vehicle. Flush contaminated areas immediately with plenty of water. Don't store new coolant or leave old coolant lying around*

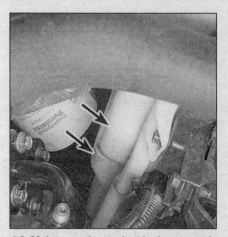

4.8 Make sure the coolant in the reservoir is between the MIN and MAX marks - if it's below the MIN mark, add more coolant mixture or water

where it's accessible to children or pets - they're attracted by its sweet smell. Ingestion of even a small amount of coolant can be fatal! Wipe up garage floor and drip pan spills immediately. Keep antifreeze containers covered and repair cooling system leaks as soon as they're noticed.

8   All vehicles covered by this manual are equipped with a pressurized coolant recovery system, which makes coolant level checks very easy. A coolant reservoir attached to the inner fender panel or the radiator itself is connected by a hose to the radiator filler neck **(see illustration)**. As the engine warms up, some coolant escapes through a valve in the radiator cap and travels through the hose into the reservoir. As the engine cools, the coolant is automatically drawn back into the cooling system to maintain the correct level.
9   The coolant level should be checked when the engine is at normal operating temperature. Simply note the fluid level in the reservoir - it should be at or near the Max mark.
10   The coolant level can also be checked by removing the radiator cap. **Warning:** *Don't*

4.12 Flip up the cap to add more coolant to the reservoir

4.15 The windshield washer reservoir is mounted in the cavity between the windshield and the engine compartment

remove the cap to check the coolant level when the engine is warm! Wait until the engine has cooled, then wrap a thick cloth around the cap and turn it to the first stop. If any steam escapes from the cap, allow the engine to cool further, then remove the cap and check the level in the radiator.

11   If only a small amount of coolant is required to bring the system up to the proper level, regular water can be used. However, to maintain the proper antifreeze/water mixture in the system, both should be mixed together to replenish a low level. High-quality antifreeze/coolant should be mixed with water in the proportion specified on the antifreeze container.

12   Coolant should be added to the reservoir after removing the cap **(see illustration)**.

13   As the coolant level is checked, note the condition of the coolant as well. It should be relatively clear. If it's brown or rust colored, the system should be drained, flushed and refilled (see Section 30).

14   If the coolant level drops consistently, there may be a leak in the system. Check the radiator, hoses, filler cap, drain plugs and water pump (see Section 25). If no leaks are noted, have the radiator filler cap pressure tested by a service station.

Windshield washer fluid

Refer to illustration 4.15

15   The fluid for the windshield washer system is stored in a plastic reservoir. The level inside each reservoir should be maintained about one inch below the filler cap. The reservoir is accessible after opening the hood **(see illustration)**.

16   In milder climates, plain water can be used in the reservoir, but it should be kept no more than two-thirds full to allow for expansion if the water freezes. In colder climates, use windshield washer system antifreeze, available at any auto parts store, to lower the freezing point of the fluid. Mix the antifreeze with water in accordance with the manufacturer's directions on the container. **Caution:** *Don't use cooling system antifreeze - it'll damage the vehicle's paint. To help prevent icing in cold weather, warm the windshield with the defroster before using the washer.*

Battery electrolyte

Refer to illustration 4.19

Warning: *Certain precautions must be followed when checking or servicing a battery. Hydrogen gas, which is highly flammable, is*

produced in the cells, so keep lighted tobacco, open flames, bare light bulbs and sparks away from the battery. The electrolyte inside the battery is dilute sulfuric acid, which can burn skin and cause serious injury if splashed in your eyes (wear safety glasses). It'll also ruin clothes and painted surfaces. Remove all metal jewelry which could contact the positive battery terminal and a grounded metal source, causing a direct short.

17   Vehicles equipped with a maintenance-free battery require no maintenance - the battery case is sealed and has no removable caps for adding water.

18   If a maintenance-type battery is installed, the caps on top of the battery should be removed periodically to check for a low electrolyte level. This check is more critical during warm summer months.

19   Remove each of the caps and add distilled water to bring the level in each cell to the split ring in the filler opening **(see illustration)**.

20   At the same time the battery water level is checked, the overall condition of the battery and related components should be noted. (see Section 10) for complete battery check and maintenance procedures.

Brake fluid

Refer to illustration 4.22

21   The brake master cylinder is located on the driver's side of the engine compartment firewall.

22   Before removing the cap(s) to check the fluid, use a rag to clean all dirt off the top of the reservoir. If any foreign matter enters the master cylinder when the caps are removed, blockage in the brake system lines can occur. Also, make sure all painted surfaces around the master cylinder are covered, since brake fluid will ruin paint. The level should be maintained at the bottom of the rings in the neck of the reservoir (there are actually two separate reservoirs, so be sure to check both of them) **(see illustration)**.

23   If additional fluid is necessary to bring the level up, carefully pour new, clean brake fluid into the master cylinder. Be careful not

4.19 Remove the cell caps to check the water level in the battery - if the level is low, add distilled water only

4.22 The brake fluid level should be kept at or near the bottom of the rings inside the reservoir filler neck

5.2 Use a tire tread depth indicator to monitor tire wear - they are available at auto parts stores and service stations and cost very little

to spill the fluid on painted surfaces. Be sure the specified fluid is used; mixing different types of brake fluid can cause damage to the system. See *Recommended lubricants and fluids* at the beginning of this Chapter or your owner's manual.

24   At this time the fluid and the master cylinder can be inspected for contamination. Normally the brake hydraulic system won't need periodic draining and refilling, but if rust deposits, dirt particles or water droplets are seen in the fluid, the system should be dismantled, cleaned and refilled with fresh fluid.

25   Reinstall the master cylinder caps.

26   The brake fluid in the master cylinder will drop slightly as the brake shoes or pads at each wheel wear down during normal operation. If the master cylinder requires repeated replenishing to keep the level up, it's an indication of leaks in the brake system which should be corrected immediately. Check all brake lines and connections, along with the wheel cylinders and booster (see Chapter 9 for more information).

27   If you discover one or both reservoirs empty or nearly empty, the brake system should be bled (see Chapter 9).

5   Tire and tire pressure checks

Refer to illustrations 5.2, 5.3, 5.4a, 5.4b and 5.8

1   Periodic inspection of the tires may spare you the inconvenience of being stranded with a flat tire. It can also provide you with vital information regarding possible problems in the steering and suspension systems before major damage occurs.

2   The original tires on this vehicle are equipped with 1/2-inch wide bands that will appear when tread depth reaches 1/16-inch, but they don't appear until the tires are worn out. Tread wear can be monitored with a simple, inexpensive device known as a tread depth indicator **(see illustration)**.

3   Note any abnormal tread wear **(see illustration)**. Tread pattern irregularities such as cupping, flat spots and more wear on one side than the other are indications of front end alignment and/or balance problems. If any of these conditions are noted, take the vehicle to a tire shop or service station to correct the problem.

4   Look closely for cuts, punctures and embedded nails or tacks. Sometimes a tire will hold air pressure for a short time or leak down very slowly after a nail has embedded itself in the tread. If a slow leak persists, check the valve stem core to make sure it's tight **(see illustration)**. Examine the tread for an object that may have embedded itself in the tire or for a "plug" that may have begun to leak (radial tire punctures are repaired with a plug that's installed in a puncture). If a puncture is suspected, it can be easily verified by spraying a solution of soapy water onto the puncture area **(see illustration)**. The soapy solution will bubble if there's a leak. Unless the puncture is unusually large, a tire shop or service station can usually repair the tire.

5   Carefully inspect the inner sidewall of each tire for evidence of brake fluid leakage. If you see any, inspect the brakes immediately.

INCORRECT TOE-IN OR EXTREME CAMBER

UNDERINFLATION

CUPPING

Cupping may be caused by:
- Underinflation and/or mechanical irregularities such as out-of-balance condition of wheel and/or tire, and bent or damaged wheel.
- Loose or worn steering tie-rod or steering idler arm.
- Loose, damaged or worn front suspension parts.

OVERINFLATION

FEATHERING DUE TO MISALIGNMENT

5.3 This chart will help you determine the condition of the tires, the probable cause(s) of abnormal wear and the corrective action necessary

5.4a If a tire loses air on a steady basis, check the valve core first to make sure it's snug (special inexpensive wrenches are commonly available at auto parts stores)

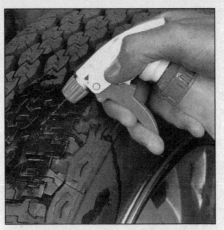

5.4b If the valve core is tight, raise the corner of the vehicle with the low tire and spray a soapy water solution onto the tread as the tire is turned slowly - leaks will cause small bubbles to appear

5.8 To extend the life of the tires, check the air pressure at least once a week with an accurate gauge (don't forget the spare)

1

6   Correct air pressure adds miles to the lifespan of the tires, improves mileage and enhances overall ride quality. Tire pressure cannot be accurately estimated by looking at a tire, especially if it's a radial. A tire pressure gauge is essential. Keep an accurate gauge in the vehicle. The pressure gauges attached to the nozzles of air hoses at gas stations are often inaccurate.

7   Always check tire pressure when the tires are cold. Cold, in this case, means the vehicle has not been driven over a mile in the three hours preceding a tire pressure check. A pressure rise of four to eight pounds is not uncommon once the tires are warm.

8   Unscrew the valve cap protruding from the wheel or hubcap and push the gauge firmly onto the valve stem **(see illustration)**. Note the reading on the gauge and compare the figure to the recommended tire pressure shown on the placard on the driver's side door pillar. Be sure to reinstall the valve cap to keep dirt and moisture out of the valve stem mechanism. Check all four tires and, if necessary, add enough air to bring them up

to the recommended pressure.

9   Don't forget to keep the spare tire inflated to the specified pressure (refer to your owner's manual or the tire sidewall). Note that the pressure recommended for the compact spare is higher than for the tires on the vehicle.

6   Automatic transaxle fluid level check

Refer to illustrations 6.3 and 6.4

1   The fluid inside the transaxle should be at normal operating temperature to get an accurate reading on the dipstick. This is done by driving the vehicle for several miles, making frequent starts and stops to allow the transaxle to shift through all gears.

2   Park the vehicle on a level surface, place the gear selector lever in Park and leave the engine running.

3   Remove the transaxle dipstick **(see**

illustration) and wipe all the fluid from the end with a clean rag.

4   Push the dipstick back into the transaxle until the cap seats completely. Remove the dipstick again and note the fluid on the end. The level should be in the area marked Hot (between the two upper holes in the dipstick) **(see illustration)**. If the fluid isn't hot (temperature about 100-degrees F), the level should be in the area marked Warm (between the two lower holes).

5   If the fluid level is at or below the Add mark on the dipstick, add enough fluid to raise the level to within the marks indicated for the appropriate temperature. Fluid should be added directly into the dipstick hole, using a funnel to prevent spills.

6   Do not overfill the transaxle. Never allow the fluid level to go above the upper hole on the dipstick - it could cause internal transaxle damage. The best way to prevent overfilling is to add fluid a little at a time, driving the vehicle and checking the level between additions.

7   Use only the transaxle fluid specified by the manufacturer. This information can be

6.3 The automatic transaxle fluid is checked by removing the dipstick on the transaxle case - don't confuse it with the engine oil dipstick

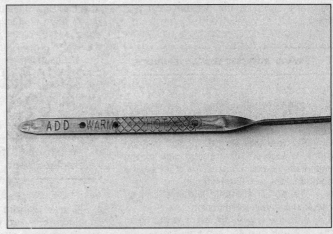

6.4 Check the fluid with the transaxle at normal operating temperature - the level should be kept in the HOT range (between the two upper holes)

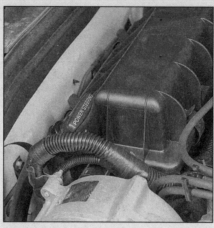

7.2a The power steering fluid reservoir is located at the front of the engine, near the passenger's side of the firewall

7.2b On V6 models, the power steering reservoir dipstick is located at the front of the engine near the firewall

7.5a The power steering fluid dipstick on four-cylinder models is marked on both sides for checking the fluid cold (shown) or hot

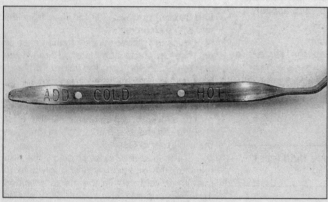

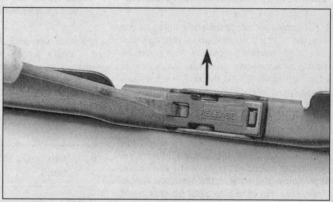

7.5b The V6 power steering dipstick is marked so the fluid can be checked hot or cold - keep the level between the two holes

8.4 Use a screwdriver to press the release lever, then slide the wire assembly off the arm in the direction shown

found in the *Recommended lubricants and fluids* Section at the beginning of this Chapter.

8   The condition of the fluid should also be checked along with the level. If it's a dark reddish-brown color, or if it smells burned, it should be changed. If you're in doubt about the condition of the fluid, purchase some new fluid and compare the two for color and smell.

7   Power steering fluid level check

Refer to illustrations 7.2a, 7.2b, 7.5a and 7.5b

1   Unlike manual steering, the power steering system relies on fluid which may, over a period of time, require replenishing.

2   The reservoir for the power steering pump is located on the rear side of the engine on the passenger's side of the engine compartment **(see illustrations)**.

3   The power steering fluid level can be checked with the engine cold.

4   With the engine off, use a rag to clean the reservoir cap and the area around the cap. This will help prevent foreign material from falling into the reservoir when the cap is removed.

5   Turn and pull out the reservoir cap, which has a dipstick attached to it. Remove the fluid at the bottom of the dipstick with a clean rag. Reinstall the cap to get a fluid level reading. Remove the cap again and note the fluid level. It should be at the Full Cold mark on the dipstick **(see illustrations)**. If the engine is warm, the level can be checked on the other side of the dipstick.

6   If additional fluid is required, pour the specified type directly into the reservoir using a funnel to prevent spills.

7   If the reservoir requires frequent fluid additions, all power steering hoses, hose connections, the power steering pump and the steering box should be carefully checked for leaks.

8   Wiper blade inspection and replacement

Refer to illustrations 8.4 and 8.5

1   The windshield wiper blade elements should be checked periodically for cracks and deterioration.

2   To gain access to the wiper blades, turn on the ignition switch and cycle the wipers to a position on the windshield where the work

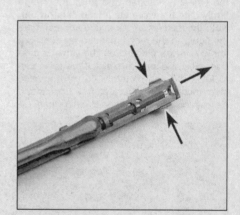

8.5 Squeeze the tabs in, then slide the element out of the wiper assembly

can be performed, then turn off the ignition.

3   Lift the wiper blade assembly away from the glass.

4   Press the release button and slide the wiper off the pin **(see illustration)**.

5   Use needle-nose pliers to squeeze the tabs, then slide the element out of the frame **(see illustration)**.

6   Slide the new element into the frame until it locks.

7   Installation is the reverse of removal.

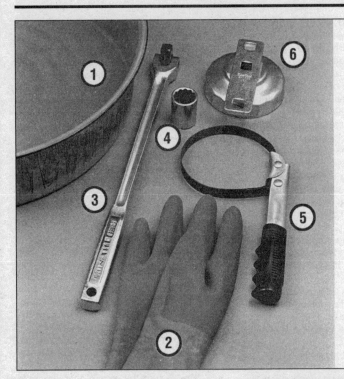

9.3 These tools are required when changing the engine oil and filter

1   **Drain pan** - *It should be fairly shallow in depth, but wide in order to prevent spills*

2   **Rubber gloves** - *When removing the drain plug and filter, it is inevitable that you will get oil on your hands (the gloves will prevent burns)*

3   **Breaker bar** - *Sometimes the oil drain plug is pretty tight and a long breaker bar is needed to loosen it*

4   **Socket** – *To be used with the breaker bar or a ratchet (must be the correct size to fit the drain plug)*

5   **Filter wrench** - *This is a metal band-type wrench, which requires clearance around the filter to be effective*

6   **Filter wrench** - *This type fits on the bottom of the filter and can be turned with a ratchet or breaker bar (different size wrenches are available for different types of filters)*

1

9   Engine oil and filter change

Refer to illustrations 9.3, 9.9, 9.14 and 9.19

1   Frequent oil changes are the most important preventive maintenance procedures that can be done by the home mechanic. When engine oil ages, it gets diluted and contaminated, which ultimately leads to premature engine wear.

2   Although some sources recommend oil filter changes every other oil change, a new filter should be installed every time the oil is changed.

3   Gather together all necessary tools and materials before beginning this procedure **(see illustration)**. **Note:** *To avoid rounding off the corners of the drain plug, use a six-point socket.*

4   In addition, you should have plenty of clean rags and newspapers handy to mop up any spills. Access to the underside of the vehicle is greatly improved if it can be lifted on a hoist, driven onto ramps or supported by jackstands. **Warning:** *Don't work under a vehicle that is supported only by a jack!*

5   If this is your first oil change on the vehicle, crawl underneath it and familiarize yourself with the locations of the oil drain plug and the oil filter. Since the engine and exhaust components will be warm during the actual work, it's a good idea to figure out any potential problems beforehand.

6   Allow the engine to warm up to normal operating temperature. If oil or tools are needed, use the warm-up time to gather everything necessary for the job. The correct type of oil to buy for your application can be found in the *Recommended lubricants and fluids* section at the beginning of this Chapter.

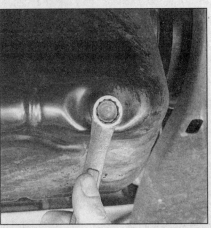

9.9 To avoid rounding off the corners, use the correct size box-end wrench or a six-point socket to remove the engine oil drain plug

7   With the engine oil warm (warm oil will drain better and more built-up sludge will be removed with it), raise the vehicle and support it securely on jackstands. They should be placed under the portions of the body designated as hoisting and jacking points (see *Jacking and towing* at the front of this manual).

8   Move all necessary tools, rags and newspapers under the vehicle. Place the drain pan under the drain plug. Keep in mind that the oil will initially flow from the engine with some force, so position the pan accordingly.

9   Being careful not to touch any of the hot exhaust components, use the breaker bar and socket to remove the drain plug near the bottom of the oil pan **(see illustration)**.

9.14 The oil filter is usually on very tight and normally will require a special wrench for removal - DO NOT use the wrench to tighten the filter!

Depending on how hot the oil is, you may want to wear gloves while unscrewing the plug the final few turns.

10   Allow the oil to drain into the pan. It may be necessary to move the pan further under the engine as the oil flow reduces to a trickle.

11   After all the oil has drained, clean the plug thoroughly with a rag. Small metal particles may cling to it and would immediately contaminate the new oil.

12   Clean the area around the oil pan opening and reinstall the plug. Tighten it securely.

13   Move the drain pan into position under the oil filter.

14   Now use the filter wrench to loosen the oil filter **(see illustration)**. Chain or metal band-type filter wrenches may distort the filter canister, but don't worry about it - the fil-

9.19 Lubricate the oil filter gasket with clean engine oil before installing the filter on the engine

ter will be discarded anyway.

15　Sometimes the oil filter is on so tight it cannot be loosened, or it's positioned in an area inaccessible with a conventional filter wrench. Other type of tools, which fit over the end of the filter and turned with a ratchet/breaker bar, are available and may be better suited for removing the filter. If the filter is extremely tight, position the filter wrench near the threaded end of the filter, close to the engine.

16　Completely unscrew the old filter. Be careful, it's full of oil. Empty the old oil inside the filter into the drain pan.

17　Compare the old filter with the new one to make sure they're identical.

18　Use a clean rag to remove all oil, dirt and sludge from the area where the oil filter mounts on the engine. Check the old filter to make sure the rubber gasket isn't stuck to the engine mounting surface.

19　Apply a light coat of oil to the rubber gasket on the new oil filter **(see illustration)**.

20　Attach the new filter to the engine following the tightening directions printed on the filter canister or packing box. Most filter manufacturers recommend against using a filter wrench due to the possibility of over-tightening and damaging the canister.

21　Remove all tools and materials from under the vehicle, being careful not to spill the oil in the drain pan. Lower the vehicle off the jackstands.

22　Move to the engine compartment and locate the oil filler cap on the engine.

23　If the filler opening is obstructed, use a funnel when adding oil.

24　Pour the specified amount of new oil into the engine. Wait a few minutes to allow the oil to drain to the pan, then check the level on the dipstick (see Section 4 if necessary). If the oil level is at or above the Add mark, start the engine and allow the new oil to circulate.

25　Run the engine for only about a minute, then shut it off. Immediately look under the vehicle and check for leaks at the oil pan drain plug and around the oil filter. If either one is leaking, tighten with a bit more force.

26　With the new oil circulated and the filter now completely full, recheck the level on the dipstick. If necessary, add enough oil to bring the level to the Full mark on the dipstick.

27　During the first few trips after an oil change, make it a point to check for leaks and keep a close watch on the oil level.

28　The old oil drained from the engine cannot be reused in its present state and should be disposed of. Oil reclamation centers, auto repair shops and gas stations will normally accept the oil. After the oil has cooled, it should be drained into containers (plastic bottles with screw-on tops are preferred) for transport to a disposal site.

10　Battery check, maintenance and charging

Refer to illustrations 10.1, 10.5, 10.6a, 10.6b, 10.7a and 10.7b

1　A routine preventive maintenance program for the battery in your vehicle is the only way to ensure quick and reliable starts. But before performing any battery maintenance, make sure that you have the proper equipment necessary to work safely around the battery **(see illustration)**.

2　There are also several precautions that should be taken whenever battery maintenance is performed. Before servicing the battery, always turn the engine and all accessories off and disconnect the cable from the negative terminal of the battery.

3　The battery produces hydrogen gas, which is both flammable and explosive. Never create a spark, smoke or light a match around the battery. Always charge the battery in a ventilated area.

4　Electrolyte contains poisonous and corrosive sulfuric acid. Do not allow it to get in your eyes, on your skin on your clothes.

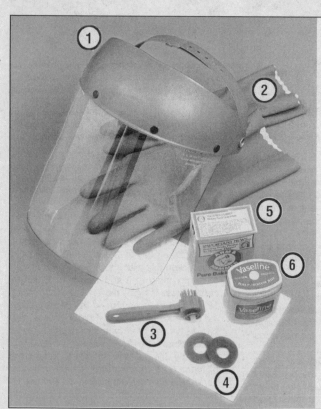

10.1 Tools and materials required for battery maintenance

1　*Face shield/safety goggles -when removing corrosion with a brush, the acidic particles can easily fly up into your eyes*

2　*Rubber gloves - Another safety item to consider when servicing the battery; remember that's acid inside the battery!*

3　*Battery terminal/cable cleaner - This wire brush cleaning tool will remove all traces of corrosion from the battery and cable*

4　*Treated felt washers - Placing one of these on each terminal, directly under the cable end, will help prevent corrosion (be sure to get the correct type for side terminal batteries)*

5　*Baking soda - A solution of baking soda and water can be used to neutralize corrosion*

6　*Petroleum jelly - A layer of this on the battery terminal bolts will help prevent corrosion*

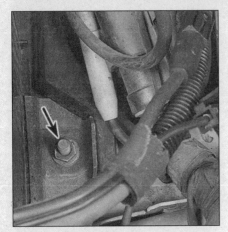

10.5 On these models the battery is secured by a clamp at the base - make sure the nut is tight (arrow)

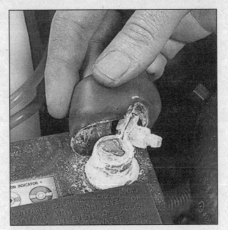

10.6a Battery terminal corrosion usually appears as light, fluffy powder

10.6b Removing the cable from a battery post with a wrench - sometimes a special battery pliers is required for this procedure if corrosion has caused deterioration of the nut hex (always remove the ground cable first and hook it up last)

Never ingest it. Wear protective safety glasses when working near the battery. Keep children away from the battery.

5   Note the external condition of the battery. If the positive terminal and cable clamp on your vehicle's battery is equipped with a rubber protector, make sure that it's not torn or damaged. It should completely cover the terminal. Look for any corroded or loose connections, cracks in the case or cover or loose hold-down clamps **(see illustration)**. Also check the entire length of each cable for cracks and frayed conductors.

6   If corrosion, which looks like white, fluffy deposits **(see illustration)** is evident, particularly around the terminals, the battery should be removed for cleaning. Loosen the cable clamp nuts with a wrench, being careful to remove the negative cable first, and slide them off the terminals **(see illustration)**. Then disconnect the hold-down clamp nuts, remove the clamp and lift the battery from the engine compartment.

7   Clean the cable clamps thoroughly with a battery brush or a terminal cleaner and a solution of warm water and baking soda **(see**

illustration). Wash the terminals and the top of the battery case with the same solution but make sure that the solution doesn't get into the battery. When cleaning the cables, terminals and battery top, wear safety goggles and rubber gloves to prevent any solution from coming in contact with your eyes or hands. Wear old clothes too - even diluted, sulfuric acid splashed onto clothes will burn holes in them. If the terminals have been extensively corroded, clean them up with a terminal cleaner **(see illustration)**. Thoroughly wash all cleaned areas with plain water.

8   Before reinstalling the battery in the engine compartment, inspect the plastic battery carrier. If it's dirty or covered with corrosion, remove it and clean it in the same solution of warm water and baking soda. Inspect the metal brackets which support the carrier to make sure that they are not covered with corrosion. If they are, wash them off. If corrosion is extensive, sand the brackets down to bare metal and spray them with a zinc-based primer (available in spray cans at auto paint and body supply stores).

9   Reinstall the battery carrier and the battery back into the engine compartment. Make

sure that no parts or wires are laying on the carrier during installation of the battery.

10   Install a pair of specially treated felt washers around the terminals (available at auto parts stores), then coat the terminals and the cable clamps with petroleum jelly or grease to prevent further corrosion. Install the cable clamps and tighten the nuts, being careful to install the negative cable last.

11   Install the hold-down clamp and nuts. Tighten the nuts only enough to hold the battery firmly in place. Overtightening these nuts can crack the battery case.

Charging

12   Remove all of the cell caps (if equipped) and cover the holes with a clean cloth to prevent spattering electrolyte. Disconnect the negative battery cable and hook the battery charger leads to the battery posts (positive to positive, negative to negative), then plug in the charger. Make sure it is set at 12 volts if it

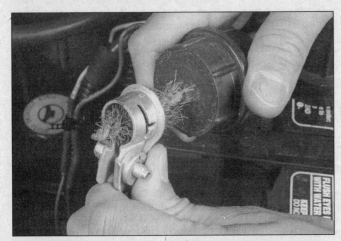

10.7a When cleaning the cable clamps, all corrosion must be removed (the inside clamp is tapered to match the taper on the post, so don't remove too much material)

10.7b Regardless of the type of tool used on the battery posts, a clean, shiny surface should be the result

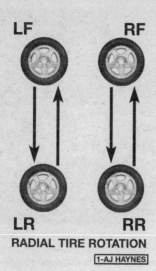

RADIAL TIRE ROTATION

1-AJ HAYNES

11.2 The recommended tire rotation pattern for these models

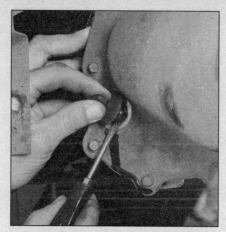

12.3 Use a screwdriver to pry the rubber fill plug out of the transaxle

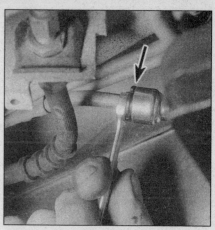

13.4a Use a small wrench to push on the black plastic ring (arrow) and release the quick-disconnect fitting - detach the hose from the fuel line first . . .

has a selector switch.

13   If you're using a charger with a rate higher than two amps, check the battery regularly during charging to make sure it doesn't overheat. If you're using a trickle charger, you can safely let the battery charge overnight after you've checked it regularly for the first couple of hours.

14   If the battery has removable cell caps, measure the specific gravity with a hydrometer every hour during the last few hours of the charging cycle. Hydrometers are available inexpensively from auto parts stores - follow the instructions that come with the hydrometer. Consider the battery charged when there's no change in the specific gravity reading for two hours and the electrolyte in the cells is gassing (bubbling) freely. The specific gravity reading from each cell should be very close to the others. If not, the battery probably has a bad cell(s).

15   Some batteries with sealed tops have built-in hydrometers on the top that indicate the state of charge by the color displayed in the hydrometer window. Normally, a bright-colored hydrometer indicates a full charge and a dark hydrometer indicates the battery still needs charging. Check the battery manufacturer's instructions to be sure you know what the colors mean.

16   If the battery has a sealed top and no built-in hydrometer, you can hook up a digital voltmeter across the battery terminals to check the charge. A fully charged battery should read 12.6 volts or higher.

17   Further information on the battery and jump starting can be found in Chapter 5 and at the front of this manual.

11   Tire rotation

Refer to illustration 11.2

1   The tires should be rotated at the speci-

fied intervals and whenever uneven wear is noticed. Since the vehicle will be raised and the tires removed anyway, this is a good time to check the brakes (see Section 29) and/or repack the rear wheel bearings (see Section 28). Read over the appropriate Section if other work will be done at the same time.

2   The rotation pattern depends on whether or not the spare is included in the rotation **(see illustration)**.

3   See the information in *Jacking and towing* at the front of this manual for the proper procedures to follow when raising the vehicle and changing a tire; however, if the brakes are to be checked, don't apply the parking brake as stated. Make sure the tires are blocked to prevent the vehicle from rolling.

4   Preferably, the entire vehicle should be raised at the same time. This can be done on a hoist or by jacking up each corner of the vehicle and lowering it onto jackstands. Always use four jackstands and make sure the vehicle is safely supported.

5   After the tire rotation, check and adjust the tire pressures as necessary and be sure to check wheel lug nut tightness.

12   Manual transaxle lubricant level check

Refer to illustration 12.3

1   Manual transaxles don't have a dipstick. The lubricant level is checked by removing a rubber plug from the side of the transaxle case. Check the lubricant level with the engine cold.

2   Locate the plug and use a rag to clean it and the surrounding area. It may be necessary to remove the left inner fenderwell cover for access to the plug.

3   Pry the plug out with a small screwdriver **(see illustration)**. If lubricant immediately starts leaking out, insert the plug back into the transaxle - the lubricant level is all right If lubricant doesn't leak out, completely remove the plug and use a finger to feel the lubricant level. The lubricant level should be even with

the bottom of the plug hole.

4   If the transaxle requires additional lubricant, use a funnel with a rubber tube or a syringe to pour or squeeze the recommended lubricant into the plug hole to restore the level. **Caution:** *Use only the specified transaxle lubricant - see* Recommended lubricants and fluids *at the beginning of this Chapter.*

5   Push the plug securely back into the transaxle. Drive the vehicle and check for leaks around the plug.

13   Fuel filter replacement

Refer to illustrations 13.4a, 13.4b and 13.6
Warning: *Gasoline is extremely flammable, so take extra precautions when you work on any part of the fuel system. Don't smoke or allow open flames or bare light bulbs near the work area, and don't work in a garage where a natural gas-type appliance (such as a water heater or clothes dryer) with a pilot light is present. If you spill any fuel on your skin, rinse it off immediately with soap and water. When you perform any kind of work on the fuel system, wear safety glasses and have a Class B type fire extinguisher on hand.*

1   Depressurize the fuel system (see Chapter 4).

2   The fuel filter is a disposable canister type and is located in the fuel line under the right rear of the vehicle, adjacent to the fuel tank.

3   Raise the rear of the vehicle and support it securely on jackstands.

4   Detach the hoses by using a small wrench to push the black plastic rings on the quick-disconnect fittings **(see illustrations)**.

5   Wrap a cloth around the fuel filter to catch the residual fuel (which may still be under slight pressure) and disconnect the hoses. It's a good idea to tie rags around your wrists to keep fuel from running down your arms.

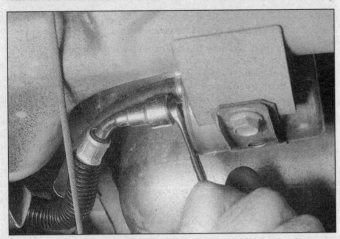

13.4b ... followed by the hose at the filter

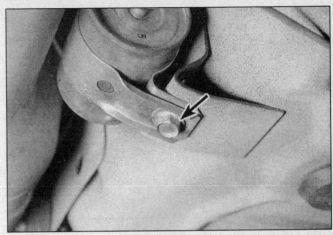

13.6 Remove this bolt (arrow) to detach the filter

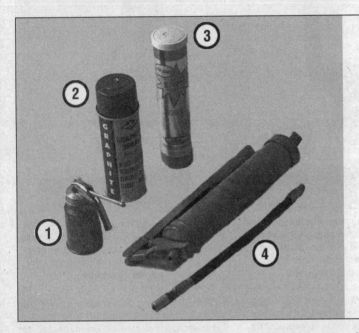

14.1 Material required for chassis and body lubrication

1   **Engine oil -** *Light engine oil in a can like this can be used for door and hood hinges*
2   **Graphite spray -** *Used to lubricate lock cylinders*
3   **Grease -** *Grease, in a variety of types and weights, is available for use in a grease gun. Check the Specifications for your requirements.*
4   **Grease gun -** *A common grease gun, shown here with a detachable hose and nozzle, is needed for chassis lubrication. After use, clean it thoroughly!*

6   Remove the bracket mounting bolt and detach the filter from the vehicle; hold your finger over the outlet to keep the residual fuel from running out **(see illustration)**.
7   Place the new filter in position, install the mounting bolt and tighten it securely. If the hoses are damaged or deteriorated, install new ones along with the new filter.
8   Insert the quick disconnect fittings into the filter until they lock in place.
9   Start the engine and check carefully for leaks at the hose connections.

14   Chassis lubrication

Refer to illustrations 14.1 and 14.6

1   A grease gun and a cartridge filled with the proper grease (see *Recommended lubricants and fluids*), graphite spray and an oil can filled with engine oil will be required to lubricate the chassis components **(see illustration)**. Occasionally, on later model vehicles, plugs will be installed rather than grease

fittings. If so, grease fittings will have to be purchased and installed.
2   Look under the vehicle and see if grease fittings or plugs are installed. If there are plugs, remove them with a wrench and buy grease fittings which will thread into the component. A dealer parts department or auto parts store will be able to supply the correct fittings. Straight and angled fittings are available.
3   For easier access under the vehicle, raise it with a jack and place jackstands under the portions of the body designated as hoisting and jacking points front and rear (see *Jacking and towing* at the front of this manual). Make sure it's securely supported by the stands.
4   Before beginning, force a little grease out of the nozzle to remove any dirt from the end of the gun. Wipe the nozzle clean with a rag.
5   With the grease gun and plenty of clean rags, crawl under the vehicle and begin lubricating the components.
6   Wipe the suspension balljoint grease fit-

ting clean and push the nozzle firmly over it **(see illustration)**. Operate the lever on the grease gun to force grease into the component. The balljoints should be lubricated until the rubber seal is firm to the touch. Don't

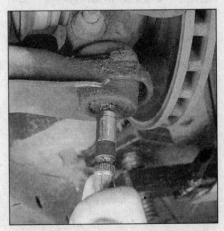

14.6 Pump the grease into the balljoint fitting until the rubber seal is firm

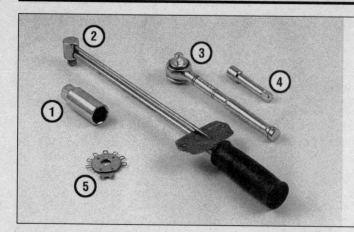

15.2 Tools required for changing spark plugs

1   **Spark plug socket** - This will have special padding inside to protect the spark plug's porcelain insulator
2   **Torque wrench** - Although not mandatory, using this tool is the best way to ensure the plugs are tightened properly
3   **Ratchet** - Standard hand tool to fit the spark plug socket
4   **Extension** - Depending on model and accessories, you may need special extensions and universal joints to reach one or more of the plugs
5   **Spark plug gap gauge** - This gauge for checking the gap comes in a variety of styles. Make sure the gap for your engine is included.

pump too much grease into the fitting as it could rupture the seal. For all other suspension and steering components, continue pumping grease into the fitting until it oozes out of the joint between the two components. If grease escapes around the grease gun nozzle, the fitting is clogged or the nozzle is not completely seated on the fitting. Re-secure the gun nozzle to the fitting and try again. If necessary, replace the fitting with a new one.

7   Wipe the excess grease from the components and the grease fitting. Repeat the procedure for the remaining fittings.

8   Lubricate the sliding contact and pivot points of the manual transaxle shift linkage with the specified grease. While you're under the vehicle, clean and lubricate the parking brake cable along with the cable guides and levers. This can be done by smearing some of the chassis grease onto the cable and related parts with your fingers. Lubricate the clutch adjuster and cable, as well as the cable positioner, with a thin film of multi-purpose grease.

9   Lower the vehicle to the ground.

10   Open the hood and smear a little chassis grease on the hood latch mechanism. Have an assistant pull the hood release lever from inside the vehicle as you lubricate the cable at the latch.

11   Lubricate all the hinges (door, hood, etc.) with the recommended lubricant to keep them in proper working order.

12   The key lock cylinders can be lubricated with spray-on graphite or silicone lubricant which is available at auto parts stores.

13   Lubricate the door weather-stripping with silicone spray. This will reduce chafing and retard wear.

15   Spark plug replacement

Refer to illustrations 15.2, 15.5a, 15.5b, 15.7, 15.9a, 15.9b and 15.11

1   The spark plugs are located on the front side of the engine, facing the radiator. **Warning:** *Before beginning work, disconnect the negative battery cable to prevent the electric cooling fan from coming on.*

2   In most cases the tools necessary for

15.5a Spark plug manufacturers recommend using a wire type gauge when checking the gap - if the wire does not slide between the electrodes with a slight drag, adjustment is required

15.5b To change the gap, bend the side electrode only, as indicated by the arrows, and be very careful not to crack or chip the porcelain insulator surrounding the center electrode

spark plug replacement include a spark plug socket which fits onto a ratchet (this special socket will be padded inside to protect the porcelain insulators on the new plugs), various extensions and a feeler gauge to check and adjust the spark plug gap **(see illustration)**. A special plug wire removal tool is available for separating the wire boot from the spark plug, but it isn't absolutely necessary. Since these engines are equipped with an aluminum cylinder head, a torque wrench should be used for tightening the spark plugs.

3   The best approach when replacing the spark plugs is to purchase the new spark plugs beforehand, adjust them to the proper gap and then replace each plug one at a time. When buying the new spark plugs, be sure to obtain the correct plug for your specific engine. This information can be found on the Vehicle Emissions Control Information label located under the hood, in the factory owner's manual or in the Specifications at the front of this Chapter. If differences exist between the sources, purchase the spark plug type specified on the VECI label as it was printed for your specific engine.

4   Allow the engine to cool completely before attempting to remove any of the plugs. During this cooling off time, each of the new spark plugs can be inspected for defects and the gaps can be checked.

5   The gap is checked by inserting the proper thickness gauge between the electrodes at the tip of the plug **(see illustration)**. The gap between the electrodes should be as specified on the VECI label in the engine compartment. The wire should touch each of the electrodes. If the gap is incorrect, use the adjuster on the thickness gauge body to bend the curved side electrode slightly until the proper gap is obtained **(see illustration)**. Also, at this time check for cracks in the spark plug body (if any are found, the plug should not be used). If the side electrode is not exactly over the center one, use the adjuster to align the two.

6   Cover the front of the vehicle to prevent damage to the paint.

7   With the engine cool, remove the spark plug wire from one spark plug. Pull only on the boot at the end of the wire; don't pull on the wire. Use a twisting motion to free the boot and wire from the plug. A plug wire removal tool (mentioned earlier) should be used if available **(see illustration)**.

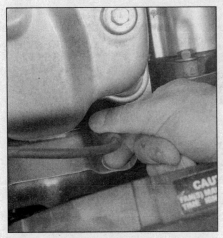

15.7 Pull on the spark plug wire boot and twist it back-and-forth while pulling it

15.9a Use a ratchet and short extension to remove the spark plugs

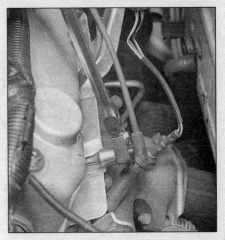

15.9b The rear bank spark plugs are accessible once the air filter assembly has been removed

1

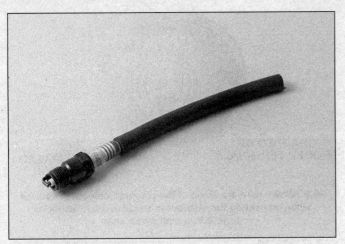

15.11 A length of 3/16-inch ID rubber hose will save time and prevent damaged threads when installing the spark plugs

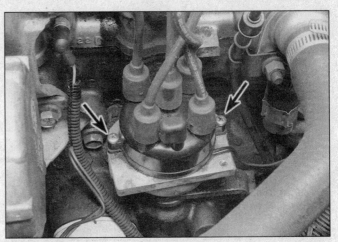

16.7a After removing the splash shield, loosen the two screws (arrows) and lift the distributor cap off (four-cylinder models)

8   If compressed air is available, use it to blow any dirt or foreign material away from the spark plug area. A common bicycle pump will also work. The idea here is to eliminate the possibility of material falling into the cylinder through the plug hole as the spark plug is removed.

9   Now place the spark plug socket over the plug and remove it from the engine by turning it in a counterclockwise direction (see illustrations).

10   Compare the spark plug with those shown in the accompanying color photos to get an indication of the overall running condition of the engine.

11   Thread one of the new plugs into the hole, tightening it as much as possible by hand. **Caution:** Be extremely careful - these engines have aluminum cylinder heads, which means the spark plug hole threads can be stripped easily. It may be a good idea to slip a short length of rubber hose over the end of the plug to use as a tool to thread it into place. The hose will grip the plug well enough to turn it, but will start to slip on the plug if the plug begins to cross-thread in the

hole - this will prevent damaged threads and the accompanying costs involved in repairing them (see illustration).

12   Attach the plug wire to the new spark plug, again using a twisting motion on the boot until it's seated on the spark plug.

13   Repeat the above procedure for the remaining spark plugs, replacing them one at a time to prevent mixing up the spark plug wires.

16   Spark plug wire, distributor cap and rotor check and replacement

Refer to illustrations 16.7a, 16.7b, 16.9 and 16.10

1   The spark plug wires should be checked at the recommended intervals or whenever new spark plugs are installed.

2   The wires should be inspected one at a time to prevent mixing up the order which is essential for proper engine operation.

3   Disconnect the plug wire from the spark plug. A removal tool can be used for this, or

you can grab the rubber boot, twist slightly and then pull the wire free. Don't pull on the wire itself, only on the rubber boot.

4   Check inside the boot for corrosion, which will look like a white, crusty powder (don't mistake the white dielectric grease used on some plug wire boots for corrosion).

5   Now push the wire and boot back onto the end of the spark plug. It should be a tight fit on the plug end. If not, remove the wire and use a pair of pliers to carefully crimp the metal connector inside the wire boot until the fit is snug.

6   Now, using a cloth, clean each wire along its entire length. Remove all built-up dirt and grease. As this is done, inspect for burned areas, cracks and any other form of damage. Bend the wires in several places to ensure that the conductive material inside hasn't hardened. Repeat the procedure for the remaining wires (don't forget the distributor cap-to-coil wire).

7   Remove the distributor cap splash shield and check the wires at the cap, making sure they aren't loose and that the wires and boots aren't cracked or damaged. **Note:**

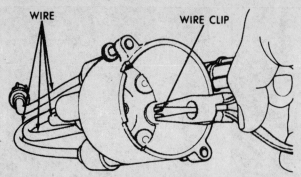

16.7b When replacing the spark plug wires, use a pair of pliers to compress the wire retaining clips inside the distributor cap before pulling the wires out

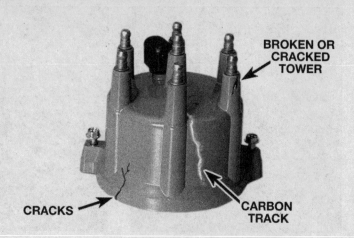

16.9 Shown here are some of the common defects to look for when inspecting the distributor cap (if in doubt about its condition, install a new one)

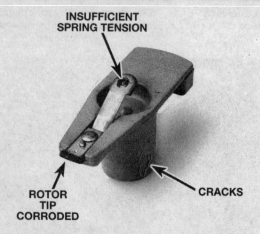

16.10 The ignition rotor should be checked for wear and corrosion as indicated here (if in doubt about its condition, buy a new one)

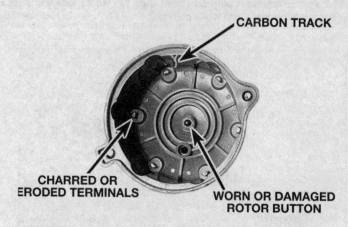

Don't attempt to pull the wires off the cap - they're retained on the inside by wire clips. The manufacturer doesn't recommend removing the wires from the cap for inspection because this could damage the integrity of the boot seal. If the wires appear to be damaged, replace them with new ones. Remove the distributor cap, release the wire clips with a pair of pliers and remove the wires **(see illustrations)**. *Insert the new wires into the cap while squeezing the boots to release any trapped air as you push them into place. Continue pushing until you feel the wire clips snap into position.*

8   A visual check of the spark plug wires can also be made. In a darkened garage (make sure there is ventilation), start the engine and look at each plug wire. Be careful not to come into contact with any moving engine parts. If there's a crack in the insulation, you'll see arcing or a small spark at the damaged area.

9   Remove the distributor cap with the wires attached and check the cap for cracks, carbon tracks and other damage. Examine the terminals inside the cap for corrosion (slight corrosion can be removed with a pocket knife) **(see illustration)**.

10   Check the rotor (now visible on the end of the distributor shaft) for cracks and a secure fit on the shaft. Make sure the terminals aren't burned, corroded or pitted excessively. A small fine file can be used to restore the rotor terminals **(see illustration)**.

11   If new spark plug wires are needed, purchase a complete pre-cut set for your particular engine. The terminals and rubber boots should already be installed on the wires. Replace the wires one at a time to avoid mixing up the firing order and make sure the terminals are securely seated in the distributor cap and on the spark plugs.

17   Drivebelt check, adjustment and replacement

Refer to illustrations 17.3, 17.4, 17.5, 17.10a and 17.10b

Warning: *The electric cooling fan on some models can activate at any time, even when the ignition switch is in the Off position. Disconnect the negative battery cable when working in the vicinity of the fan.*

1   The drivebelts, or V-belts as they are sometimes called, at the front of the engine, play an important role in the overall operation of the vehicle and its components. Due to their function and material makeup, the belts are prone to failure after a period of time and should be inspected and adjusted periodically to prevent major damage.

2   The number of belts used on a particular engine depends on the accessories installed. Drivebelts are used to turn the alternator, power steering pump, water pump and air conditioning compressor. Depending on the pulley arrangement, a single belt may be used for more than one of these components. Some later models use a serpentine drivebelt in place of multiple V-belts. A serpentine belt requires no adjustment, as this is taken care of by a tensioner.

3   With the engine off, open the hood and locate the various belts at the front of the engine. Using your fingers (and a flashlight if necessary), examine the belts. Check for cracks and separation of the plies. Look for contamination by grease or oil and glazed areas, which give the belt a shiny appearance. Both sides of each belt should be inspected, which means you'll have to twist them to check the underside **(see illustration)**.

4   The tightness of each belt is checked by pushing on it at a distance halfway between

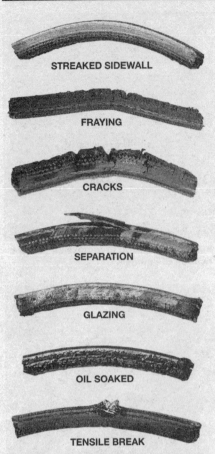

STREAKED SIDEWALL

FRAYING

CRACKS

SEPARATION

GLAZING

OIL SOAKED

TENSILE BREAK

17.3 Here are some of the more common problems associated with drivebelts (check the belts very carefully to prevent an untimely breakdown)

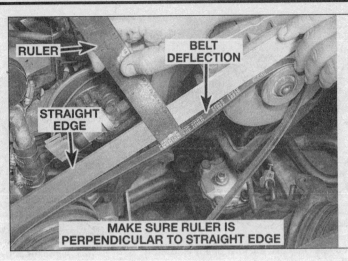

RULER

STRAIGHT EDGE

BELT DEFLECTION

17.4 Measuring drivebelt deflection with a straightedge and ruler

MAKE SURE RULER IS PERPENDICULAR TO STRAIGHT EDGE

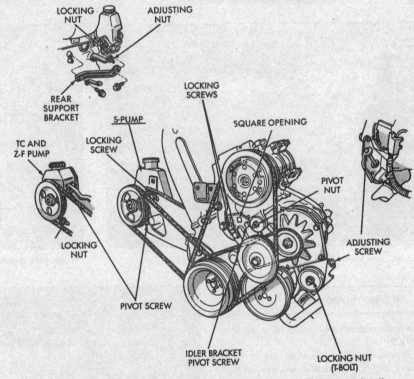

LOCKING NUT

ADJUSTING NUT

REAR SUPPORT BRACKET

LOCKING SCREWS

S-PUMP

SQUARE OPENING

TC AND Z-F PUMP

LOCKING SCREW

PIVOT NUT

LOCKING NUT

ADJUSTING SCREW

PIVOT SCREW

IDLER BRACKET PIVOT SCREW

LOCKING NUT (T-BOLT)

17.5 Typical non-turbo, four-cylinder engine drivebelt adjustment details

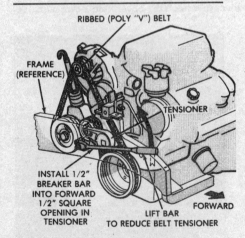

RIBBED (POLY "V") BELT

FRAME (REFERENCE)

TENSIONER

INSTALL 1/2" BREAKER BAR INTO FORWARD 1/2" SQUARE OPENING IN TENSIONER

LIFT BAR TO REDUCE BELT TENSIONER

FORWARD

17.10a Rotate the serpentine belt tensioner counterclockwise on 1990 and earlier models

the pulleys **(see illustration)**. Apply about 10 pounds of force with your thumb and see how much the belt moves down (deflects). Refer to this Chapter's Specifications for the amount of deflection allowed in each belt.

5   If adjustment is necessary, it's done by moving the belt-driven accessory on the

bracket **(see illustration)**.

6   For each component, there's a locking screw and a pivot screw or nut. Both must be loosened slightly to move the component.

7   After the two bolts have been loosened, move the component away from the engine (to tighten the belt) or toward the engine (to loosen the belt). Many accessories are equipped with a square hole designed to accept a 3/8-inch or 1/2-inch square drive breaker bar. The bar can be used to lever the component and tension the drivebelt. Hold the accessory in position and check the belt tension. If it's correct, tighten the two bolts until snug, then recheck the tension. If it's all right, tighten the two bolts completely.

8   To adjust the alternator drivebelt, loosen

the pivot nut and the locking screw or T-bolt locknut, then turn the adjusting bolt to tension the belt.

9   It may be necessary to use some sort of prybar to move a component while the belt is adjusted. If this must be done, be very careful not to damage the component being moved, or the part being pried against.

10   When replacing a serpentine belt, use a 1/2-inch drive breaker bar to rotate the tensioner counterclockwise (1990 and earlier models) or clockwise (1991-on) as required to release the belt tension **(see illustrations)**. Make sure the new belt is routed correctly (refer to the label in the engine compartment).

11   Run the engine for about 15 minutes, then recheck the belt tension.

1

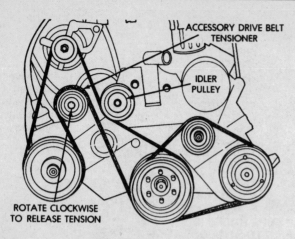

17.10b On 1991 and later models, the idler pulley is rotated clockwise to relieve belt tension

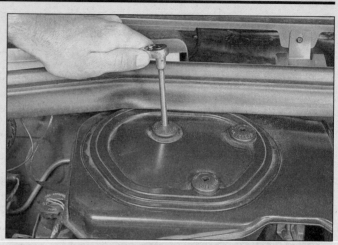

18.3 A socket and extension are required to remove air cleaner cover on EFI models

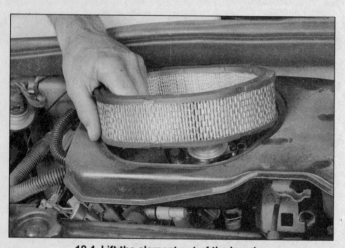

18.4 Lift the element out of the housing

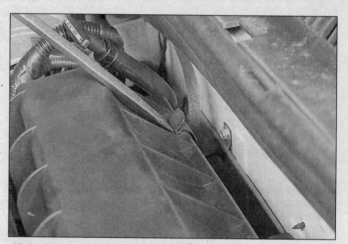

18.8a Use a screwdriver to detach the cover hold-down clips . . .

18 Air filter replacement

Refer to illustrations 18.3, 18.4, 18.8a, 18.8b and 18.9

1   At the specified intervals, the air filter element and (if equipped) crankcase ventilation filter should be replaced.

2   The air filter element is located in a housing on top of or adjacent to the engine.

Models with Throttle Body Injection (TBI)

3   Remove the screws and lift off the cover (see illustrations).

4   Lift the element out (see illustration).

5   Be careful not to drop anything down into the throttle body or air cleaner assembly. Clean the inside of the housing with a rag.

6   Pull the crankcase ventilation filter (if equipped) out of the housing. Wash the crankcase filter in solvent and oil it lightly before reinstalling.

7   Place the new filter element in position and install the cover. Be sure to tighten any hose clamps which were loosened or removed.

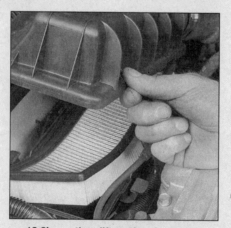

18.8b . . . then lift up the air cleaner housing cover for access to the filter element

Models with Multi-Point Injection (MPI)

8   Release the hold-down clips or bails, separate the cover from the air cleaner body or housing and lift the element out (see illustrations).

18.9 Pull the crankcase filter out of the housing

9   Pull the crankcase ventilation filter (if equipped) out of the housing (see illustration). Wash the crankcase filter in solvent and oil it lightly before reinstalling.

10   Place the new filter into the air cleaner and install the cover.

19.2a Pull the PCV valve out of the fitting

19.2b On V6 models, pull off the hose and use a wrench to unscrew the PCV valve from the manifold

1

19   Positive Crankcase Ventilation (PCV) valve check and replacement

Refer to illustrations 19.2a and 19.2b

1   The PCV valve is located in the rubber hoses connected to the rocker arm cover.

2   With the engine idling at normal operating temperature, pull the valve (with the hose attached) from the rubber fitting **(see illustration)**. On V6 models, detach the hose, unscrew the valve, then reconnect the hose **(see illustration)**.

3   Place your finger over the valve opening. If there's no vacuum at the valve, check for a plugged hose, manifold port or valve. Replace any plugged or deteriorated hoses.

4   Turn off the engine and shake the PCV valve, listening for a rattle. If the valve doesn't rattle, replace it with a new one.

5   To replace the valve, pull it from the end of the hose, noting its installed position and direction.

6   When purchasing a replacement PCV valve, make sure it's for your particular vehicle and engine size. Compare the old valve with the new one to make sure they're the same.

7   Push the valve into the end of the hose until it's seated.

8   Inspect the rubber fitting for damage and replace it with a new one if necessary.

9   Push the PCV valve and hose securely into position.

20   Exhaust Gas Recirculation (EGR) system check

Refer to illustration 20.2

1   The EGR valve is located on the intake manifold, adjacent to the throttle body.

2   Check the EGR valve hose and pipe for damage and leaks **(see illustration)**.

3   With the engine idling at normal operating temperature, watch the stem under the valve for movement and increase the engine speed to approximately 2500 rpm.

4   The stem should move up and down as the engine speed changes, indicating that the EGR system is operating properly.

5   See Chapter 6 for more information on the EGR system.

21   Underhood hose check and replacement

Warning: *Replacement of air conditioning hoses must be left to a dealer service department or air conditioning shop equipped to depressurize the system safely. Never remove air conditioning components or hoses until the system has been depressurized.*

General

1   High temperatures under the hood can cause the deterioration of the rubber and plastic hoses used for engine, accessory and emission systems operation. Periodic inspection should be made for cracks, loose clamps, material hardening and leaks.

2   Information specific to the cooling system hoses can be found in Section 25.

3   Some, but not all, hoses use clamps to secure the hoses to fittings. Where clamps are used, check to be sure they haven't lost their tension, allowing the hose to leak. Where clamps are not used, make sure the

hose hasn't expanded and/or hardened where it slips over the fitting, allowing it to leak.

Vacuum hoses

4   It's quite common for vacuum hoses, especially those in the emissions system, to be color coded or identified by colored stripes molded into the hose. Various systems require hoses with different wall thicknesses, collapse resistance and temperature resistance. When replacing hoses, make sure the new ones are made of the same material.

5   Often the only effective way to check a hose is to remove it completely from the vehicle. Where more than one hose is removed, be sure to label the hoses and their attaching points to insure proper reattachment.

6   When checking vacuum hoses, be sure to include any plastic T-fittings in the check. Check the fittings for cracks and the hose where it fits over the fitting for enlargement, which could cause leakage.

7   A small piece of vacuum hose (1/4-inch inside diameter) can be used as a stethoscope to detect vacuum leaks. Hold one end of the hose to your ear and probe around vacuum hoses and fittings, listening for the "hissing" sound characteristic of a vacuum leak. **Warning:** *When probing with the vacuum hose stethoscope, be careful not to allow your body or the hose to come into contact with moving engine components such as the drivebelt, cooling fan, etc.*

Fuel hose

Warning: *Gasoline is extremely flammable, so take extra precautions when you work on any part of the fuel system. Don't smoke or allow open flames or bare light bulbs near the work area, and don't work in a garage where a natural gas-type appliance (such as a water heater or clothes dryer) with a pilot light is present. If you spill any fuel on your skin, rinse it off immediately with soap and water. When you perform any kind of work on the fuel system, wear safety glasses and have a Class B type fire extinguisher on hand. Before working on any part of the fuel system, relieve the fuel system pressure (see Chapter 4).*

20.2 Inspect the rubber hose on the EGR valve (arrow) for hardening and cracks

22.4 Throttle body bolt locations (arrows) - upper arrows point to rear bolts, which are not visible

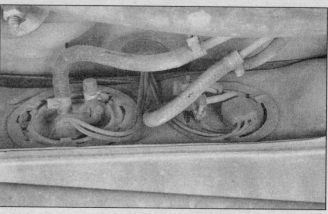

24.6 Check the fuel tank hoses for damage and deterioration

8   Check all rubber fuel hoses for damage and deterioration. Check especially for cracks in areas where the hose bends and just before clamping points, such as where a hose attaches to the fuel injection unit.

9   High quality fuel line, specifically designed for fuel injection systems, should be used for fuel line replacement. **Warning:** *Never use vacuum line, clear plastic tubing or water hose for fuel lines.*

10   Spring-type clamps are commonly used on fuel lines. These clamps often lose their tension over a period of time, and can be "sprung" during the removal process. Therefore it is recommended that all spring-type clamps be replaced with screw clamps whenever a hose is replaced.

Metal lines

11   Sections of metal line are often used for fuel line between the fuel pump and fuel injection unit. Check carefully to be sure the line has not been bent and crimped and that cracks have not started in the line.

12   If a section of metal fuel line must be replaced, only seamless steel tubing should be used, since copper and aluminum tubing do not have the strength necessary to withstand normal engine operating vibration.

13   Check the metal brake lines where they enter the master cylinder and brake proportioning unit (if used) for cracks in the lines or loose fittings. Any sign of brake fluid leakage calls for an immediate thorough inspection of the brake system.

22 Throttle body mounting bolt torque check

Refer to illustration 22.4

1   The fuel injection throttle body is attached to the intake manifold by bolts. The bolts can sometimes work loose during normal engine operation and cause a vacuum leak.

2   To properly tighten the mounting bolts or nuts, a torque wrench is necessary. If you do not own one, they can usually be rented on a daily basis.

3   Remove the air cleaner assembly.

4   Locate the mounting bolts at the base of the throttle body **(see illustration)**. Decide what special tools or adapters will be necessary, if any, to tighten the bolts with a socket and the torque wrench.

5   Tighten the bolts to the torque listed in this Chapter's Specifications. Do not overtighten the bolts, as the threads may strip.

6   If you suspect a vacuum leak exists at the bottom of the throttle body, obtain a short length of rubber hose. Start the engine and place one end of the hose next to your ear as you probe around the base of the throttle body with the other end. You should hear a hissing sound if a leak exists.

7   If, after the bolts are properly tightened, a vacuum leak still exists, the throttle body must be removed and a new gasket installed. See Chapter 4 for more information.

8   After tightening the bolts, reinstall the air cleaner housing.

23 Heated inlet air system check

1   TBI-equipped models are equipped with a heated inlet air cleaner which draws air to the fuel injection throttle body from different locations, depending on engine temperature.

2   This is a simple visual check; however, the outside air duct must be removed.

3   Locate the vacuum air control valve in the air cleaner assembly. It's located inside the air cleaner duct fitting, where you removed the outside air duct from. Make sure the flexible heat duct under the air cleaner is securely attached and undamaged.

4   The check should be done when the engine and outside air are cold (less than 65-degrees F). Start the engine and look through the duct fitting at the valve (which should move up to the "heat on" position). With the valve up, air cannot enter through the end of the duct fitting, but instead enters the air cleaner through the heat duct attached to the exhaust manifold.

5   As the engine warms up to operating temperature, the valve should move down to the "heat off" position to allow air through the duct fitting. Depending on outside air temper-

ature, this may take 10 to 15 minutes. To speed up the check you can reconnect the outside air duct, drive the vehicle and then check to see if the valve has moved down.

6   If the air cleaner isn't operating properly, see Chapter 6 for more information.

24 Fuel system check

Refer to illustration 24.6

Warning: *Gasoline is extremely flammable, so take extra precautions when you work on any part of the fuel system. Don't smoke or allow open flames or bare light bulbs near the work area, and don't work in a garage where a natural gas-type appliance (such as a water heater or clothes dryer) with a pilot light is present. If you spill any fuel on your skin, rinse it off immediately with soap and water. When you perform any kind of work on the fuel system, wear safety glasses and have a Class B type fire extinguisher on hand.*

1   These models are equipped with fuel injection and the fuel system is under pressure even when the engine is off. Consequently, the fuel system must be depressurized (see Chapter 4) whenever it is worked on. Even after depressurization, if any fuel lines are disconnected for servicing, be prepared to catch some fuel as it spurts out. Plug all disconnected fuel lines immediately to prevent the tank from emptying itself.

2   The fuel system is most easily checked with the vehicle raised on a hoist where the components on the underside are readily visible and accessible.

3   If the smell of gasoline is noticed while driving, or after the vehicle has been parked in the sun, the fuel system should be thoroughly inspected immediately.

4   Remove the gas tank cap and check for damage, corrosion and a proper sealing imprint on the gasket. Replace the cap with a new one if necessary.

5   Inspect the gas tank and filler neck for punctures, cracks and other damage. The connection between the filler neck and the tank is especially critical. Sometimes a rubber filler neck will leak due to loose clamps or deterio-

Check for a chafed area that could fail prematurely.

Check for a soft area indicating the hose has deteriorated inside.

Overtightening the clamp on a hardened hose will damage the hose and cause a leak.

Check each hose for swelling and oil-soaked ends. Cracks and breaks can be located by squeezing the hose.

25.4 Hoses, like drivebelts, have a habit of failing at the worst possible time - to prevent the inconvenience of a blown radiator or heater hose, inspect them carefully as shown here

rated rubber; problems a home mechanic can usually rectify. **Warning:** Do not, under any circumstances, try to repair a fuel tank yourself (except to replace rubber components). A welding torch or any open flame can easily cause the fuel vapors to explode if the proper precautions are not taken.

6   Carefully check all rubber hoses and metal lines leading away from the fuel tank. Check for loose connections, deteriorated hoses, crimped lines and damage of any kind **(see illustration)**. Follow the lines up to the front of the vehicle, carefully inspecting them all the way. Repair or replace damaged sections as necessary (see Chapter 4).

25   Cooling system check

Refer to illustration 25.4
Warning: *The electric cooling fan on these*

models can activate at any time, even when the ignition switch is in the Off position. Disconnect the fan motor or the negative battery cable when working in the vicinity of the fan.

1   Many major engine failures can be attributed to a faulty cooling system. If the vehicle is equipped with an automatic transaxle, the cooling system is also used to cool the transaxle fluid.

2   The cooling system should be checked with the engine cold. Do this before the vehicle is driven for the day or after it has been shut off for three or four hours.

3   Remove the radiator cap and thoroughly clean the cap (inside and out) with water. Also clean the filler neck on the radiator. All traces of corrosion should be removed.

4   Carefully check the upper and lower radiator hoses along with the smaller diameter heater hoses. Inspect the entire length of each hose, replacing any that are cracked, swollen or deteriorated. Cracks may become more apparent when a hose is squeezed **(see illustration)**.

5   Also check that all hose connections are tight. A leak in the cooling system will usually show up as white or rust-colored deposits on the areas adjoining the leak.

6   Use compressed air or a soft brush to remove bugs, leaves, and other debris from the front of the radiator or air conditioning condenser. Be careful not to damage the delicate cooling fins, or cut yourself on them.

7   Finally, have the cap and system pressure tested. If you do not have a pressure tester, most gas stations and repair shops will do this for a minimal charge.

26   Exhaust system check

1   With the engine cold (at least three hours after the vehicle has been driven), check the complete exhaust system from its starting point at the engine to the end of the tailpipe. This should be done on a hoist where unrestricted access is available.

2   Check the pipes and connections for signs of leakage and/or corrosion indicating a potential failure. Make sure that all brackets

27.3 This leaking fluid indicates a blown seal, which means the shock absorbers must be replaced

and hangers are in good condition and tight.

3   At the same time, inspect the underside of the body for holes, corrosion and open seams which may allow exhaust gases to enter the passenger compartment. Seal all body openings with silicone sealant or body putty.

4   Rattles and other noises can often be traced to the exhaust system, especially the mounts and hangers. Try to move the pipes, muffler and catalytic converter. If the components can come into contact with the body, secure the exhaust system with new mounts.

5   This is also an ideal time to check the running condition of the engine by inspecting the very end of the tailpipe. The exhaust deposits here are an indication of engine state-of-tune. If the pipe is black and sooty or coated with white deposits, the engine may be in need of a tune-up (including a thorough fuel injection system inspection and adjustment).

27   Steering and suspension check

Refer to illustrations 27.3 and 27.4

1   Whenever the front of the vehicle is raised for service it is a good idea to visually check the suspension and steering components for wear and damage.

2   Indications of wear and damage include excessive play in the steering wheel before the front wheels react, excessive lean around corners, body movement over rough roads or binding at some point as the steering wheel is turned.

3   Before the vehicle is raised for inspection, test the shock absorbers by pushing down to rock the vehicle at each corner. If it does not come back to a level position within one or two bounces, the shocks are worn and should be replaced. As this is done, check for squeaks and unusual noises from the suspension components. Check the shock absorbers for fluid leakage **(see illustration)**. Information on shock absorbers and suspension components can be found in Chapter 10.

4   Check the balljoints for wear by grasping the grease fittings securely and attempting to move them **(see illustration)**. If the

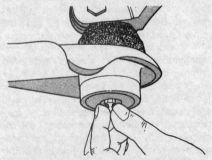

27.4 With the vehicle weight resting on the suspension, try to move the balljoint grease fittings with your fingers - if the fittings can be moved easily, the balljoints are worn and must be replaced

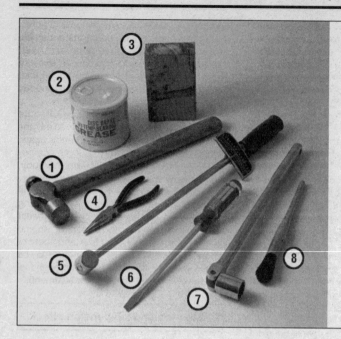

28.1 Tools and materials needed for front wheel bearing maintenance

1   *Hammer* - *A common hammer will do just fine*
2   *Grease* - *High temperature grease that is formulated specially for front wheel bearings should be used*
3   *Wood block* - *If you have a scrap piece of 2x4, it can be used to drive the new seal into the hub*
4   *Needle-nose pliers* - *Used to straighten and remove the cotter pin in the spindle*
5   *Torque wrench* - *This is very important in this procedure; if the bearing is too tight, the wheel won't turn freely - if it's too loose, the wheel will "wobble" on the spindle. Either way, it could mean extensive damage*
6   *Screwdriver* - *Used to remove the seal from the hub (a long screwdriver would be preferred)*
7   *Socket/breaker bar* - *Needed to loosen the nut on the spindle if it's extremely tight*
8   *Brush* - *Together with some clean solvent, this will be used to remove old grease from the hub and spindle*

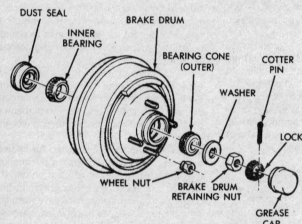

28.7 An exploded view of the rear brake drum/hub and bearing components (bearing assembly on rear disc brake models similar)

28.8 Pull the brake drum/hub out slightly to dislodge the outer wheel bearing, then remove the washer and bearing

grease fittings move easily, the balljoints are worn and must be replaced with new ones.

5   Now raise the front end of the vehicle and support it securely with jackstands placed under the jacking and hoisting points (see *Jacking and towing* at the front of this manual). Because of the work to be done, the vehicle must be stable and safely supported.

6   Check the front wheel hub nuts for correct tightness and make sure they're properly crimped in place.

7   Crawl under the vehicle and check for loose bolts, broken or disconnected parts and deteriorated rubber bushings on all suspension and steering components. Look for grease or fluid leaking from around the steering gear boots. Check the power steering hoses and connections for leaks. Check the steering joints for wear.

8   Have an assistant turn the steering wheel from side-to-side and check the steering components for free movement, chafing and binding. If the wheels don't respond the

movement of the steering wheel, try to determine where the slack is located.

28   Rear wheel bearing check, repack and adjustment

Refer to illustrations 28.1, 28.7, 28.8, 28.14 and 28.26

1   In most cases the rear wheel bearings won't need servicing until the brake shoes are changed. However, the bearings should be checked whenever the rear of the vehicle is raised for any reason. Several items, including a torque wrench and special grease, are required for this procedure **(see illustration)**.

2   With the vehicle securely supported on jackstands, spin each wheel and check for noise, rolling resistance and freeplay.

3   Grasp the top of each tire with one hand and the bottom with the other. Move the

wheel in-and-out on the spindle. If there's any noticeable movement, the bearings should be checked and then repacked with grease or replaced if necessary.

4   Remove the wheel. On rear-disc brake-equipped models, remove the caliper (see Chapter 9).

5   Pry the grease cap out of the hub with a screwdriver or hammer and chisel.

6   Straighten the bent ends of the cotter pin, then pull the cotter pin out of the lock. Discard the cotter pin and use a new one during reassembly.

7   Remove the lock and the hub nut from the end of the spindle **(see illustration)**.

8   Pull the brake drum/hub assembly out slightly, then push it back into its original position. This should force the outer bearing and washer off the spindle enough so they can be removed **(see illustration)**.

9   Pull the brake drum/hub assembly off the spindle. If it does not come off easily, back off the adjuster as described in the

28.14 Work the grease into each bearing from the large diameter side until it's forced out of the small diameter side

28.26 Tap the grease cap into place with a large punch and a hammer (work around the outer edge)

29.5 There's an inspection hole like this in each caliper - by looking through the hole you can determine the thickness of the remaining friction material on both the inner and outer pads (arrow)

1

drum brake shoe replacement procedure in Chapter 9.

10   Use a screwdriver to pry the dust seal out of the rear of the hub. As this is done, note how the seal is installed.

11   Remove the inner wheel bearing from the hub.

12   Use solvent to remove all traces of old grease from the bearings, hub and spindle. A small brush may prove helpful; however, make sure no bristles from the brush embed themselves inside the bearing rollers. Allow the parts to air dry.

13   Carefully inspect the bearings for cracks, heat discoloration, worn rollers, etc. check the bearing races inside the hub for wear and damage. If the bearing races are defective, the hubs should be taken to a machine shop with the facilities to remove the old races and press new ones in. Note that the bearings and races come as matched sets - old bearings should never be installed on new races and vice-versa.

14   Use high-temperature wheel bearing grease to pack the bearings. Work the grease completely into the bearings, forcing it between the rollers, cone and cage from the back side **(see illustration)**.

15   Apply a thin coat of grease to the spindle at the outer bearing seat, inner bearing seat, shoulder and seal seat.

16   Put a small quantity of grease on the inner side of each bearing race inside the hub. Using your finger, form a dam at these points to provide extra grease availability and to keep thinned grease from flowing out of the bearing.

17   Place the grease-packed inner bearing into the rear of the hub and put a little more grease on the outer side of the bearing.

18   Place a new dust seal over the inner bearing and tap the seal evenly into place with a hammer and block of wood until it's flush with the hub.

19   Carefully place the drum/hub assembly on the spindle and push the grease-packed outer bearing into position.

20   Install the washer and nut. Tighten the

nut only slightly (no more than 12 ft-lbs of torque).

21   Spin the drum/hub in a forward direction to seat the bearings and remove any grease or burrs which could cause excessive bearing play later.

22   Verify that the tightness of the nut is still approximately 12 ft-lbs.

23   Loosen the nut until it's just loose, no more.

24   Using your hand (not a wrench of any kind), tighten the nut until it's snug. Install the lock and a new cotter pin through the hole in the spindle and lock. If the lock slots don't line up, take it off and rotate it to another position.

25   Bend the ends of the cotter pin until they're flat against the nut. Cut off any extra length which could interfere with the grease cap.

26   Install the grease cap, tapping it into place with a hammer **(see illustration)**.

27   Install the wheel and tighten the lug nuts.

28   Grasp the top and bottom of the tire and check the bearings in the manner described earlier in this Section.

29   Lower the vehicle.

29   Brake system check

Refer to illustrations 29.5, 29.14, and 29.16

1   The brakes should be inspected every time the wheels are removed or whenever a defect is suspected. Indications of a potential brake system problem include the vehicle pulling to one side when the brake pedal is depressed, noises coming from the brakes when they are applied, excessive brake pedal travel, pulsating pedal and leakage of fluid, usually seen on the inside of the tire or wheel.

Disc brakes

2   Disc brakes can be visually checked without removing any parts except the wheels.

3   Raise the vehicle and place it securely

on jackstands. Remove the wheels (see *Jacking and towing* at the front of this manual if necessary).

4   Now visible is the disc brake caliper which contains the pads. There is an outer brake pad and an inner pad. Both should be checked for wear.

5   Note the pad thickness by looking at each end of the caliper and through the inspection hole in the caliper body **(see illustration)**. If the combined thickness of the pad lining and metal shoe is 5/16-inch or less, the pads should be replaced.

6   Since it'll be difficult, if not impossible, to measure the exact thickness of the pad, if you're in doubt as to the pad quality, remove them for further inspection or replacement. See Chapter 9 for disc·brake pad replacement.

7   Before installing the wheels, check for leakage around the brake hose connections leading to the caliper and for damaged brake hoses (cracks, leaks, chafed areas, etc.). Replace the hoses or fittings as necessary (see Chapter 9).

8   Also check the disc for score marks, wear and burned spots. If these conditions exist, the hub/disc assembly should be removed for servicing (see Chapter 9).

Drum brakes (rear)

9   Raise the vehicle and support it securely on jackstands. Block the front tires to prevent the vehicle from rolling; however, don't apply the parking brake or it will lock the drums in place.

10   Remove the wheels, referring to *Jacking and towing* at the front of this manual if necessary.

11   Mark the hub so it can be reinstalled in the same position. Use a scribe, chalk, etc. on the drum, hub and backing plate.

12   Remove the brake drum as described in Section 28.

13   With the drum removed, carefully clean off any accumulations of dirt and dust using

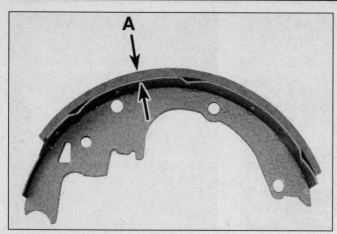

29.14 If the lining is bonded to the brake shoe, measure the lining thickness from the outer surface to the metal shoe, as shown here; if the lining is riveted to the shoe, measure the lining outer surface to the rivet head

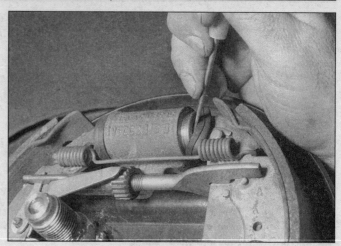

29.16 Use a small screwdriver to carefully pry the boot away from the cylinder and check for fluid leakage

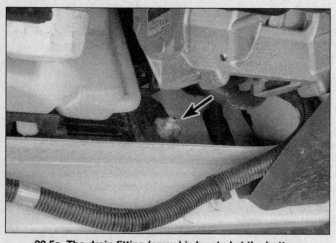

30.5a The drain fitting (arrow) is located at the bottom of the radiator

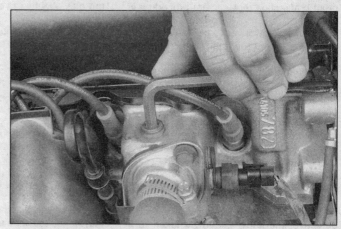

30.5b To allow the system to drain on four-cylinder engines, remove the vacuum switch or bleeder plug (shown here) on top of the thermostat housing

brake system cleaner. **Warning:** *Don't blow the dust out with compressed air and don't inhale any of it (it may contain asbestos, which is harmful to your health).*

14   Note the thickness of the lining material on both front and rear brake shoes. If the material has worn away to within 1/8-inch of the recessed rivets or metal backing, the shoes should be replaced **(see illustration).** The shoes should also be replaced if they're cracked, glazed (shiny areas), or covered with brake fluid.

15   Make sure all the brake assembly springs are connected and in good condition.

16   Check the brake components for signs of fluid leakage. Carefully pry back the rubber cups on the wheel cylinder located at the top of the brake shoes **(see illustration).** Any leakage here is an indication that the wheel cylinders should be overhauled immediately (see Chapter 9). Also, check all hoses and connections for signs of leakage.

17   Wipe the inside of the drum with a clean rag and denatured alcohol or brake cleaner. Again, be careful not to breathe the dangerous asbestos dust.

18   Check the inside of the drum for cracks, score marks, deep scratches and "hard spots" which will appear as small discolored areas. If imperfections cannot be removed with fine emery cloth, the drum must be taken to an automotive machine shop for resurfacing.

19   Repeat the procedure for the remaining wheel. If the inspection reveals that all parts are in good condition, reinstall the brake drums. Install the wheels and lower the vehicle to the ground.

30   Cooling system servicing (draining, flushing and refilling)

Refer to illustrations 30.5a and 30.5b
Warning: *Do not allow engine coolant (antifreeze) to come in contact with your skin or painted surfaces of the vehicle. Rinse off spills immediately with plenty of water. Antifreeze is highly toxic if ingested. Never leave antifreeze lying around in an open container or in puddles on the floor; children and pets are attracted by it's sweet smell and may*

drink it. Check with local authorities about disposing of used antifreeze. Many communities have collection centers which will see that antifreeze is disposed of safely.

1   Periodically, the cooling system should be drained, flushed and refilled to replenish the antifreeze mixture and prevent formation of rust and corrosion, which can impair the performance of the cooling system and cause engine damage. When the cooling system is serviced, all hoses and the radiator cap should be checked and replaced, if necessary.

Draining

2   At the same time the cooling system is serviced, all hoses and the radiator cap should be inspected and replaced if faulty (see Section 25).

3   With the engine cold, remove the radiator cap and set the heater control to Heat (Max).

4   Move a large container under the radiator to catch the coolant mixture as it's drained.

5   Open the drain fitting at the bottom of the radiator **(see illustration).** Remove the

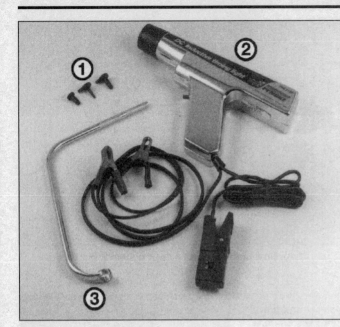

31.2 Tools needed to check and adjust the ignition timing

1   *Vacuum plugs - Vacuum hoses will, in most cases, have to be disconnected and plugged. Molded plugs in various shapes and sizes are available for this.*
2   *Inductive pick-up timing light - Flashes a bright concentrated beam of light when the number one spark plug fires. Connect the leads according to the instructions supplied with the light.*
3   *Distributor wrench - On some models, the hold-down bolt for the distributor is difficult to reach and turn with conventional wrenches or sockets. A special wrench like this must be used.*

1

vacuum switch or bleeder plug from the top of the thermostat housing on the engine on four-cylinder engines **(see illustration)**.
6   On V6 engines, remove the drain plugs located on each side of the block.
7   Disconnect the coolant reservoir hose, remove the reservoir and flush it with clean water.
8   Place a hose (a common garden hose is fine) in the radiator filler neck at the top of the radiator and flush the system until the water runs clear at all drain points.

Flushing

9   In severe cases of contamination or clogging of the radiator, remove it (see Chapter 3) and reverse flush it. This involves inserting the hose in the bottom radiator outlet to allow the clean water to run against the normal flow, draining through the top. A radiator repair shop should be consulted if further cleaning or repair is necessary.
10   Where the coolant is regularly drained and the system refilled with the correct antifreeze mixture there should be no need to employ chemical cleaners or descalers.

Refilling

11   Install the coolant reservoir, reconnect the hoses and close the drain fitting. On V6 models install the block drain plugs.
12   Add coolant to the radiator. On four-cylinder engines, add coolant until it reaches the bottom of the threaded bleeder plug hole in the thermostat housing. Reinstall the plug or vacuum switch in the hole and tighten it securely. Continue adding coolant to the radiator until it reaches the radiator cap seat.
13   Add coolant to the reservoir until the level is between the Min and Max marks.
14   Run the engine until normal operating temperature is reached and, with the engine idling, add coolant up the correct level.
15   Always refill the system with a mixture of antifreeze and water in the proportion called

for on the antifreeze container or in you owner's manual. Chapter 3 also contains information on antifreeze mixtures.
16   Keep a close watch on the coolant level and the various cooling system hoses during the first few miles of driving. Tighten the hose clamps and add more coolant mixture as necessary.

31   Ignition timing check and adjustment

Refer to illustrations 31.2, 31.5a, 31.5b and 31.10

1   All vehicles are equipped with a *Vehicle Emissions Control Information* label inside the engine compartment. The label contains important ignition timing specifications and the proper timing procedure for your specific vehicle. If the information on the emissions label is different from the information included in this Section, follow the procedure on the label.
2   At the specified intervals, or when the distributor has been removed, the ignition

timing must be checked and adjusted if necessary. Tools required for this procedure include an inductive pick-up timing light, a tachometer and a distributor wrench **(see illustration)**.
3   Before you check the timing, make sure the engine is at normal operating temperature.
4   Connect a timing light in accordance with the manufacturer's instructions. Usually, the light must be connected to the battery and the number one spark plug is some fashion. The number one spark plug wire or terminal should be marked at the distributor; trace it back to the spark plug and attach the timing light lead near the plug. **Caution:** *If an inductive pick-up timing light isn't available, don't puncture the spark plug wire to attach the timing light pick-up lead. Instead, use an adapter between the spark plug and plug wire. If the insulation on the plug wire is damaged, the secondary voltage will jump to ground at the damaged point and the engine will misfire.*
5   Locate the timing marks at the window in the transaxle bellhousing or front of the engine **(see illustrations)**.

31.5a The bellhousing window (on four-cylinder engines) allows you to view the flywheel/driveplate notch (arrow) - mark this notch and the mark along the side of the window that corresponds to the number of degrees specified on the Vehicle Emissions Control label in the engine compartment

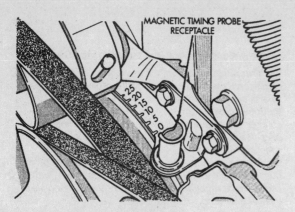

31.5b On V6 engines, the timing marks are attached to the front of the engine and the crankshaft pulley has a groove in it for reference

31.10 Unplug the coolant sensor connector (arrow)

6   Locate the notched groove across the flywheel/driveplate. It may be necessary to have an assistant temporarily turn the ignition on and off in short bursts without starting the engine in order to bring the groove into a position where it can easily be cleaned and marked. **Warning:** *Stay clear of all moving engine components when the engine is turned over in this manner.*

7   Use white chalk or paint to mark the groove in the flywheel **(see illustration 31.5a)**. Also, mark the number corresponding to the number of degrees specified on the *Vehicle Emissions Control Information* label in the engine compartment.

8   Connect a tachometer to the engine, setting the selector to the correct cylinder position.

9   Make sure the wiring for the timing light is clear of all moving engine components, then start the engine.

10   Disconnect the coolant temperature sensor connector (located on the thermostat housing) **(see illustration)**.

11   Aim the timing light at the marks, again being careful not to come into contact with moving parts. The marks you made should appear stationary. If the marks are in alignment, the timing is correct. If the marks are not aligned, turn off the engine.

12   Loosen the hold-down bolt at the base of the distributor. Loosen the bolt only slightly, just enough to turn the distributor (see Chapter 5).

13   Now restart the engine and turn the distributor very slowly until the timing marks are aligned.

14   Shut off the engine and tighten the distributor bolt, being careful not to move the distributor.

15   Start the engine and recheck the timing to make sure the marks are still in alignment. Reconnect the coolant temperature sensor.

32   Airbag system check

1   At the specified intervals, the airbag sys-

tem should be checked.

2   Turn the ignition switch On and make sure the airbag warning light goes on, then after ten seconds goes out. If the light does-n't go on or goes on and stays lit for more than ten seconds, take the vehicle to a dealer and have the system checked.

3   Refer to Chapter 12 for more information on the airbag system.

33   Manual transaxle lubricant change

1   Raise the front of the vehicle and support it securely on jackstands. Apply the parking brake.

2   If the transaxle is equipped with a drain plug, remove plug and drain fluid into a suitable container.

3   If not equipped with a drain plug, draw the fluid out through the fill plug opening with a suction syringe.

4   Replace the drain plug, if equipped, and tighten securely.

5   Fill the transaxle with the recommended lubricant (see *Recommended lubricants and fluids* at the beginning of this Chapter) until the level is at the bottom edge of the filler plug. Drive the vehicle and check the cover for leaks.

34   Automatic transaxle fluid and filter change

Refer to illustrations 34.3, 34.4 and 34.8

1   The automatic transaxle fluid and filter should be changed, the magnet cleaned and the bands adjusted at the recommended intervals.

2   Raise the front of the vehicle and support it securely on jackstands. Apply the parking brake.

3   Position a container under the transaxle fluid pan. Loosen the pan bolts. Completely remove the bolts along the rear of the pan.

34.3 Use a soft-face hammer to break he gasket seal at the corner of the pan so the fluid will drain out

Tap the corner of the pan **(see illustration)** to break the seal and allow the fluid to drain into the container (the remaining bolts will prevent the pan from separating from the transaxle). Remove the remaining bolts and detach the pan.

4   Remove the filter screws and detach the filter (a special Torx bit may be required for the screws) **(see illustration)**.

5   Refer to Section 35 and adjust the bands before proceeding with the fluid change.

6   Install the new gasket and filter. Tighten the filter screws securely.

7   Carefully remove all traces of old sealant from the pan and transaxle body (don't nick or gouge the sealing surfaces). Clean the magnet in the pan with a clean, lint-free cloth.

8   Apply a 1/8-inch bead of RTV sealant to the pan sealing surface and position it on the transaxle **(see illustration)**. Install the bolts and tighten them to the torque listed in this Chapter's Specifications following a criss-cross pattern. Work up to the final torque in three or four steps.

9   Lower the vehicle and add three quarts of the specified fluid (see *Recommended*

34.4 A Torx-head tool may be required for removing the filter screws

34.8 Apply a 1/8-inch diameter bead of RTV sealant and install the pan before the sealant dries

1

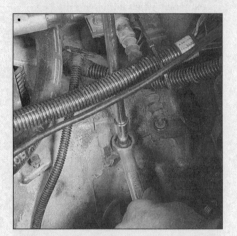

35.7 Hold the screw so it won't turn and tighten the locknut with a box-end wrench

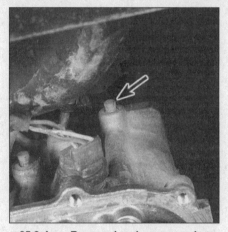

35.9 Low-Reverse band pressure plug location (arrow)

35.10 Insert feeler gauges between the Low-Reverse band ends to measure wear - if the gap is less than 0.080-inch, a new band is needed

lubricants and fluids at the beginning of this Chapter) to the transaxle. Start the engine and allow it to idle for at least two minutes, then move the shift lever through each of the gear positions, ending in Park or Neutral. Check for fluid leakage around the pan.

10   Add more fluid until the level is between the Add and Full marks. Add fluid a little at a time until it is (be careful not to overfill it).

11   Make sure the dipstick is seated completely or dirt could get into the transaxle.

35   Automatic transaxle band adjustment (three-speed models only)

Refer to illustrations 35.7, 35.9, 35.10, 35.11a, 35.11b, 35.12a, 35.12b and 35.15

1   The transaxle bands should be adjusted when specified in the maintenance schedule or at the time of a fluid and filter change (see Section 34).

Kickdown band

2   The kickdown band adjustment screw is located at the top left side of the transaxle case.

3   On some models the accelerator cable may interfere with band adjustment. If so, mark its position and then remove the accelerator cable adjustment bolt. Move the cable away from the band adjustment screw.

4   Loosen the locknut approximately five turns and make sure the adjusting screw turns freely.

5   Tighten the adjusting screw to the torque listed in this Chapter's Specifications.

6   Back the adjusting screw off the specified number of turns (see the Specifications section at the beginning of this Chapter).

7   Hold the screw in position and tighten the locknut securely **(see illustration)**.

Low-Reverse band

8   To gain access to the Low-Reverse band, the transaxle pan must be removed (see Section 34).

9   To determine if the band is worn excessively, remove the Low-Reverse pressure plug from the transaxle case **(see illustration)** and apply 30 psi of air pressure to the port.

10   Measure the gap between the band ends **(see illustration)**. It should be 0.080-inch minimum. If it's less than that, the band should be replaced with a new one.

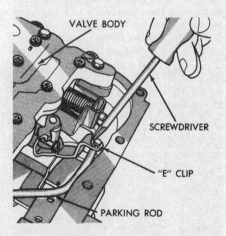

35.11a Use a screwdriver to pry off the parking rod E-clip . . .

11   To proceed with adjustment, pry off the parking rod E-clip and remove the rod **(see illustrations)**.

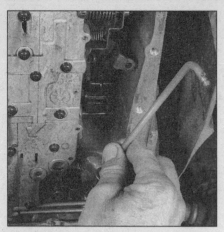

35.11b . . . then lower the rod from the transaxle

35.12a Loosen the locknut five turns

35.12b it may be necessary to use a universal joint between the socket and extension when tightening the Low-Reverse band adjusting screw

12   Loosen the locknut approximately five turns **(see illustration)**. Use an inch-pound torque wrench to tighten the adjusting screw to the torque listed in this Chapter's Specifications **(see illustration)**.

13   Back the screw off the specified number of turns (see the Specifications section at the beginning of this Chapter).

14   Hold the adjusting screw in position and tighten the locknut securely.

15   Push the shift pawl in the transaxle case to the rear and reinstall the parking rod **(see illustration)**.

16   Install the pan and refill the transaxle (see Section 34).

36   Driveaxle boot check

Refer to illustration 36.3

1   If the driveaxle boots are damaged or deteriorated, serious and costly damage can occur to the CV joints the boots are designed to protect. The boots should be inspected very carefully at the recommended intervals.

2   Raise the front of the vehicle and support it securely on jackstands (see *Jacking*

and towing at the front of this manual if necessary).

3   Crawl under the vehicle and check the four driveaxle boots (two on each driveaxle) very carefully for cracks, tears, holes, deteriorated rubber and loose or missing clamps **(see illustration)**. If the boots are dirty, wipe them clean before beginning the inspection.

4   If damage or deterioration is evident, replace the boots with new ones and check the CV joints for damage (see Chapter 8).

37   Evaporative emissions control system check

1   The function of the evaporative emissions control system is to draw fuel vapors from the gas tank and fuel system, store them in a charcoal canister and route them to the intake manifold during normal engine operation.

2   The most common symptom of a fault in the evaporative emissions system is a strong fuel odor in the engine compartment. If a fuel odor is detected, inspect the charcoal canister, located in the engine compartment on the

passenger's side, behind the headlight. Check the canister and all hoses for damage and deterioration.

3   The evaporative emissions control system is explained in more detail in Chapter 6.

38   Seat belt check

1   Check the seat belts, buckles, latch plates and guide loops for obvious damage and signs of wear.

2   See if the seat belt reminder light comes on when the key is turned to the Run or Start positions. A chime should also sound.

3   The seat belts are designed to lock up during a sudden stop or impact, yet allow free movement during normal driving. Make sure the retractors return the belt against your chest while driving and rewind the belt fully when the buckle is unlatched.

4   If any of the above checks reveal problems with the seat belt system, replace parts as necessary.

35.15 Push the shift pawl back with your finger before inserting the parking rod

36.3 Push on the boot to check for damage and look for signs of grease (arrow) indicating a leak

Chapter 2 Part A
Four-cylinder engines

Contents

Specifications

General

Firing order	1-3-4-2
Cylinder numbers (drivebelt end-to-transaxle end)	1-2-3-4
Bore and stroke	
2.2L	3.44 X 3.62 inches
2.5L	3.44 X 4.09 inches
Displacement	
2.2L	135 cubic inches
2.5L	153 cubic inches

Camshaft

SOHC engine	
Endplay	0.005 to 0.013 inch
Runout	0.0004 inch
Journal diameter	
Standard	1.375 to 1.376 inch
Oversize	1.395 to 1.396 inch
DOHC engine	
Endplay	0.001 to 0.008 inch
Journal diameter	1.886 to 1.887 inch
Lobe wear (maximum) (all engines)	0.010 inch
Belt tension (DOHC engine)	
New belt	110 lbs
Used belt	70 lbs

FRONT

Cylinder location chart

*The blackened terminal shown on the
distributor cap indicates the Number
One spark plug wire position*

Cylinder head

Cylinder head warpage limit (all engines) .... 0.004 inch
Intake/exhaust manifolds
    Warpage limit
        SOHC engine .... 0.008 in per foot of manifold length
        DOHC engine .... 0.006 in per foot of manifold length

Oil pump

Outer rotor-to-housing clearance
    Standard .... 0.010 inch
    Service limit .... 0.014 inch
Outer rotor thickness
    Standard .... 0.944 to 0.945 inch
    Service limit .... 0.9435 inch
Inner rotor-to-outer rotor tip clearance
    Standard .... 0.004 inch
    Service limit .... 0.008 inch
Inner and outer rotor-to-housing clearance
    Standard .... 0.001 to 0.003 inch
    Service limit .... 0.0035 inch
Pump cover flatness
    Standard .... 0.002 inch maximum
    Service limit .... 0.003 inch
Relief spring free length .... 1.95 inch

Torque specifications   **Ft-lbs** (unless otherwise indicated)

Camshaft
    SOHC engines
        Bearing cap bolts .... 215 in-lbs
        Sprocket bolt 65
    DOHC engines
        Thrust plate retaining nut .... 55 to 72 in-lbs
        Sprocket bolt 47
Crankshaft
    SOHC engines
        Front oil seal housing bolts .... 105 in-lbs
        Pulley Torx head bolts .... 250 in-lbs
    Sprocket bolt
        1987 through 1989 50
        1990 on 85
    DOHC engines
        Sprocket bolt 80
        Pulley bolts .... 280 in-lbs
Cylinder head bolts (engine cold) - SOHC and DOHC engines
    First step 45
    Second step 65
    Third step 65
    Fourth step 1/4-turn
Driveplate-to-crankshaft bolts 50
Exhaust manifold bolts (DOHC engines) .... 210 in-lbs
Flywheel-to-crankshaft bolts 60
Intake/exhaust manifold nuts/bolts (SOHC engines) 16
Intake manifold bolts (DOHC engines) .... 200 in-lbs
Intermediate shaft
    SOHC engines
        Oil seal housing bolts .... 105 in-lbs
        Sprocket bolt 65
    DOHC engines
        Sprocket bolt 53
Oil pan drain plug 20
Oil pan-to-engine block fasteners
    SOHC engines
        M8 16
        M6 .... 105 in-lbs
    DOHC engines
        M8 21
        M6 18
Oil pick-up tube-to-oil pump housing bolt 16

Torque specifications

	Ft-lbs (unless otherwise indicated)
Oil pump cover bolts	105 in-lbs
Oil pump mounting bolts	21
Rear main oil seal housing bolts	105 in-lbs
Rocker arm assemblies (DOHC engine)	
Initial	105 in-lbs
Final	17
Timing belt	
SOHC engines	
Tensioner bolt	45
DOHC engines	
Tensioner bolt	40
Idler pulley bolt	40
Valve cover bolts/nuts (all engines)	105 in-lbs
Water pump hub bolt	21

1   General information

This Part of Chapter 2 is devoted to in-vehicle repair procedures for the four-cylinder engines. All information concerning engine removal and installation and engine block and cylinder head overhaul can be found in Part C of this Chapter. The following repair procedures are based on the assumption that the engine is installed in the vehicle. If the engine has been removed from the vehicle and mounted on a stand, many of the steps outlined in this Part of Chapter 2 will not apply.

The Specifications included in this Part of Chapter 2 apply only to the procedures contained in this Part. Part C of Chapter 2 contains the Specifications necessary for cylinder head and engine block rebuilding.

2   Repair operations possible with the engine in the vehicle

Many major repair operations can be accomplished without removing the engine from the vehicle.

Clean the engine compartment and the exterior of the engine with some type of degreaser before any work is done. It will make the job easier and help keep dirt out of the internal areas of the engine. Depending on the components involved, it may be helpful to remove the hood to improve access to the engine as repairs are performed (refer to Chapter 11 if necessary). Cover the fenders to prevent damage to the paint. Special pads are available, but an old bedspread or blanket will also work.

If vacuum, exhaust, oil or coolant leaks develop, indicating a need for gasket or seal replacement, the repairs can generally be made with the engine in the vehicle. The intake and exhaust manifold gaskets, oil pan gasket, crankshaft oil seals and cylinder head gasket are all accessible with the engine in place.

Exterior engine components, such as the intake and exhaust manifolds, the oil pan (and the oil pump), the water pump, the starter motor, the alternator, the distributor and the fuel system components can be removed for repair with the engine in place.

Since the cylinder head can be removed without pulling the engine, camshaft and valve component servicing can also be accomplished with the engine in the vehicle. Replacement of the timing belt and sprockets is also possible with the engine in the vehicle.

In extreme cases caused by a lack of necessary equipment, repair or replacement of piston rings, pistons, connecting rods and rod bearings is possible with the engine in the vehicle. However, this practice is not recommended because of the cleaning and preparation work that must be done to the components involved.

3   Top Dead Center (TDC) for number one piston - locating

Refer to illustrations 3.6a, 3.6b, 3.6c, 3.6d, 3.8a and 3.8b

Note: *The following procedure is based on the assumption that the spark plug wires and distributor are correctly installed. If you are trying to locate TDC to install the distributor correctly, piston position must be determined by feeling for compression at the number one spark plug hole, then aligning the ignition timing marks as described in step 8.*

1   Top Dead Center (TDC) is the highest point in the cylinder that each piston reaches as it travels up-and-down when the crankshaft turns. Each piston reaches TDC on the compression stroke and again on the exhaust stroke, but TDC generally refers to piston position on the compression stroke.

2   Positioning the piston(s) at TDC is an essential part of many procedures such as camshaft and timing belt/sprocket removal and distributor removal.

3   Before beginning this procedure, be sure to place the transmission in Neutral and apply the parking brake or block the rear wheels. Also, disable the ignition system by disconnecting the electrical connector(s) from the distributor or, on models equipped with a Direct Ignition System (DIS), by disconnecting the electrical connectors at the ignition module (see Chapter 5). Remove the spark plugs (see Chapter 1).

4   In order to bring any piston to TDC, the crankshaft must be turned using one of the methods outlined below. When looking at the front of the engine, normal crankshaft rotation is clockwise.

a) *The preferred method is to turn the crankshaft with a socket and ratchet attached to the bolt threaded into the front of the crankshaft.*

b) *A remote starter switch, which may save some time, can also be used. Follow the instructions included with the switch. Once the piston is close to TDC, use a socket and ratchet as described in the previous paragraph.*

c) *If an assistant is available to turn the ignition switch to the Start position in short bursts, you can get the piston close to TDC without a remote starter switch. Make sure your assistant is out of the vehicle, away from the ignition switch, then use a socket and ratchet as described in Paragraph a) to complete the procedure.*

5   If the vehicle is powered by a 2.2L DOHC engine with Direct Ignition System (DIS), you won't be able to perform the following procedure entirely (those steps concerning the crankshaft pulley still apply; those steps concerning the position of the distributor rotor don't apply - 2.2L DOHC engines don't have a distributor). Instead, you'll have to remove the spark plug for the number one cylinder and place your finger over the spark plug hole to verify compression. When the piston in the number one cylinder comes up to TDC on the compression stroke, the valves will be closed, so you'll be able to feel the pressure at the spark plug hole; if the piston is coming up on the exhaust stroke, the exhaust valve will be open, so you won't feel pressure at the plug hole.

6   On all other engines, note the position of the terminal for the number one spark plug wire on the distributor cap. If the terminal isn't marked, follow the plug wire from the number one cylinder spark plug to the cap. Use a felt-tip pen or chalk to make a mark on the distributor body directly under the termi-

3.6a On four-cylinder engines, use a felt-tip marker or chalk to mark the distributor housing directly beneath the number one spark plug wire terminal (arrow)

3.6b Use a felt-tip marker or chalk to mark the distributor housing directly beneath the rotor on V6 engines, but note that . . .

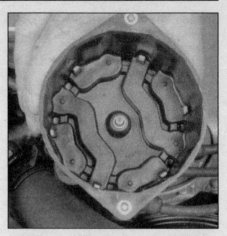

3.6c . . . the terminals inside the V6 distributor cap are offset from their respective spark plug wire terminals on top of the cap, so it's easy to become confused by the rotor's position relative to the apparent spark plug wire terminal when the number one piston is at TDC

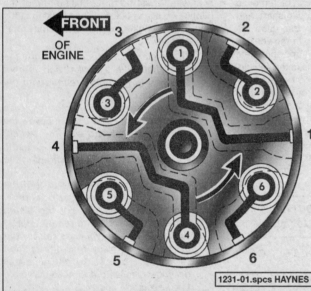

3.6d To avoid confusion, refer to this terminal guide for the V6 distributor cap whenever you're trying to locate TDC for the number one piston (or doing any procedure that involves alignment of the rotor with the correct terminal) - this view is from the top of the cap

nal **(see illustrations)**. **Note:** *This procedure differs slightly on V6 engines, because they use a distributor cap with offset terminals - the terminals inside the distributor cap are offset from their respective spark plug terminals on the top of the cap* **(see illustrations)**.

7   Detach the cap from the distributor and set it aside (see Chapter 1 if necessary).

8   On four-cylinder engines, locate the round window in the bellhousing. You'll see the timing increments on the edge of the window. Turn the crankshaft (see Paragraph 3 above) until the TDC mark (zero) on the edge of the bellhousing is aligned with the groove in the flywheel **(see illustration)**. On V6 engines, turn the crankshaft until the notch in the crankshaft pulley is aligned with the "0" mark on the timing cover **(see illustration)**.

9   Look at the distributor rotor - it should be pointing directly at the mark you made on the distributor body. If the rotor is pointing at the mark, go to Step 12. If it isn't, go to Step 10.

10   If the rotor is 180-degrees off, the number one piston is at TDC on the exhaust stroke.

11   To get the piston to TDC on the compression stroke, turn the crankshaft one complete turn (360-degrees) clockwise. The rotor should now be pointing at the mark on the distributor. When the rotor is pointing at the number one spark plug wire terminal in the distributor cap and the ignition timing marks are aligned, the number one piston is at TDC on the compression stroke.

12   After the number one piston has been positioned at TDC on the compression stroke, TDC for any of the remaining pistons can be located by turning the crankshaft and following the firing order. Mark the remaining spark plug wire terminal locations on the distributor body just like you did for the number one terminal, then number the marks to correspond with the cylinder numbers. As you turn the

3.8a When you're bringing the number one piston to TDC on four-cylinder engines, look at the timing mark on the edge of the flywheel/driveplate through the opening in the bellhousing, and align the mark with the 0-degree mark on the bellhousing - you may have to remove a plug from the bellhousing to see the flywheel

3.8b To bring the number one piston to TDC on V6 engines, watch the timing notch on the edge of the crankshaft pulley and align it with the 0-degree mark on the timing cover (arrow)

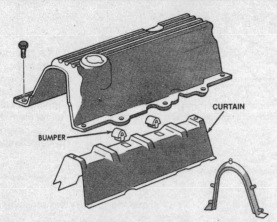

4.4a An exploded view of a typical valve cover assembly (eight-valve engines)

4.4b Remove the valve cover bolts (arrows) (eight-valve engines)

crankshaft, the rotor will also turn. When it's pointing directly at one of the marks on the distributor, the piston for that particular cylinder is at TDC on the compression stroke. On models with a Distributorless Ignition System, rotate the engine 180-degrees in the normal direction of rotation to find TDC for the next cylinder in the firing order.

4   Valve cover - removal and installation

SOHC engines

Removal

Refer to illustrations 4.4a, 4.4b, 4.5 and 4.6

1   Detach the cable from the negative battery terminal.
2   Detach the accelerator cable from the cable bracket.
3   Wipe off the valve cover thoroughly to prevent debris from falling onto the exposed cylinder head or camshaft/valve train assembly.
4   Remove the upper half of the timing cover (see Section 6). Remove the valve

cover bolts **(see illustrations)**.
5   Carefully lift off the valve cover and gasket. If the gasket is stuck to the cylinder head, use a putty knife or flat-bladed screwdriver to remove it **(see illustration)**. Set the cover aside.
6   If the vehicle is fuel-injected or turbocharged, you'll note a "curtain" under the valve cover. If you're simply replacing a leaking valve cover gasket, you don't need to remove the curtain. If you want to adjust the valves or service the camshaft assembly or cylinder head, remove the curtain **(see illustration)**. Don't lose the two small rubber "bumpers" which act as cushions between the curtain and the valve cover.

Installation

Refer to illustrations 4.9a and 4.9b

7   Make sure the gasket mating surfaces of the cylinder head and the valve cover are clean.
8   If the engine is equipped with a curtain (and it has been removed), install it now, manifold side first, with the cutouts over the cam towers and contacting the cylinder head floor, then press the opposite (distributor) side into position below the gasket mating

4.5 Carefully pry the valve cover off the cylinder head - be careful not to bend the rails, which could cause oil leaks later on (eight-valve engines)

surface. Be sure to install the rubber bumpers on top of the curtain.
9   Install new gaskets on the valve cover. Install the molded rubber seals to the ends of the cover by pushing the tabs through the slots in the cover **(see illustration)**. Apply a

4.6 Lift the curtain off the cylinder head (eight-valve engine)

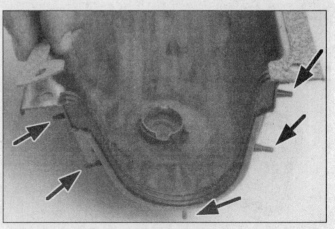

4.9a Use a small pair of pliers to pull the tabs (arrows) through the housing, insuring the seal is flush against the valve cover - also, make sure the gasket slightly overlaps the rubber seal at the corners (eight-valve engines)

4.9b Apply a small amount of RTV sealant to the corners of the cylinder head to prevent oil leaks (eight-valve engines)

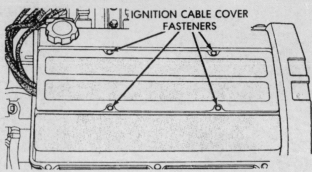

4.13 Remove these four fasteners (arrows) and remove the ignition cable cover from the valve covers (16-valve engines)

1/8-inch wide bead of RTV sealant to the cylinder head rail **(see illustration)**, then install the cover and bolts and tighten them to the torque listed in this Chapter's Specifications.

10   Turbo versions of the newer 2.2L engine also use a molded one-piece rubber gasket, but the gasket is attached differently. A continuous slot molded into the valve cover retains the gasket. Install the gasket by pressing the gasket rail section into the slot. Install the cover and bolts and tighten the bolts to the torque listed in this Chapter's Specifications.

11   The remainder of installation is the reverse of removal.

DOHC engines

Refer to illustrations 4.13 and 4.16

12   Remove the fresh air duct (see Chapter 4).

13   Remove the ignition cable cover **(see illustration)**.

14   Remove the six bolts from each valve cover and remove the valve covers.

15   Before installing the valve covers, clean the mating surfaces of the cylinder head and valve covers. **Caution:** *Make sure no oil or solvents contact the timing belt as they can*

deteriorate the rubber and cause the teeth to skip.

16   Install the valve covers and gaskets **(see illustration)** on the head and tighten the bolts to the torque listed in this Chapter's Specifications.

17   Install the ignition cable cover and tighten the fasteners securely.

18   Install the fresh air duct (see Chapter 4).

5   Intake/exhaust manifold - removal and installation

Warning: *Gasoline is extremely flammable, so take extra precautions when you work on any part of the fuel system. Don't smoke or allow open flames or bare light bulbs near the work area, and don't work in a garage where a natural gas-type appliance (such as a water heater or clothes dryer) with a pilot light is present. If you spill any fuel on your skin, rinse it off immediately with soap and water. When you perform any kind of work on the fuel system, wear safety glasses and have a Class B type fire extinguisher on hand.*

SOHC engines (except turbos)
Removal
Refer to illustrations 5.15 and 5.18
Note: *On these models the throttle body assembly and intake manifold must be removed as a unit before the exhaust manifolds can be removed.*

1   Relieve the fuel system pressure (see Chapter 4).

2   Detach the cable from the negative battery terminal.

3   Drain the cooling system (see Chapter 1).

4   Remove the air cleaner (see Chapter 4).

5   Clearly label, then detach all vacuum lines, electrical wiring and fuel lines.

6   Detach the accelerator cable from the throttle linkage (see Chapter 4).

7   Loosen the power steering pump (if equipped) and remove the drivebelt (see Chapter 1).

8   Detach the power brake vacuum hose from the intake manifold.

9   If you're working on a Canadian model with a 2.2L engine, you may have to remove the coupling hose from the air injection tube.

10   Remove the water hoses from the coolant crossover lines.

11   Raise the front of the vehicle and support it securely on jackstands. Detach the exhaust pipe from the exhaust manifold (see Chapter 4).

12   Remove the power steering pump (if equipped) and set it aside (see Chapter 10).

13   Remove the intake manifold support bracket and detach the EGR tube from the exhaust manifold.

14   If you're working on a Canadian model with a 2.2L engine, you may have to remove the air injection tube assembly.

15   Remove the intake manifold fasteners **(see illustration)**.

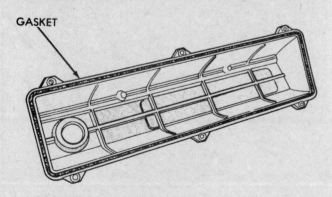

4.16 A valve cover with the gasket correctly positioned (16-valve engines)

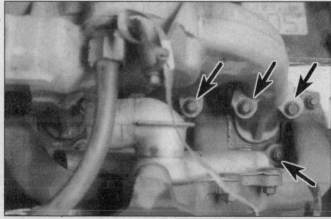

5.15 Intake manifold fasteners (2.2L TBI engine)

5.18 Exhaust manifold fasteners (2.2L TBI engine)

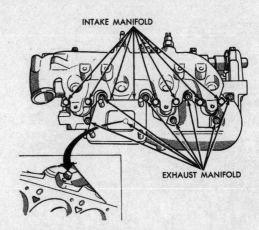

5.36 Intake/exhaust manifold fasteners on the turbo engine

16   Lower the vehicle.

17   Remove the throttle body and the intake manifold as a single assembly. Detach the throttle body and gasket from the intake manifold (see Chapter 4) after the unit is on the bench.

18   Remove the exhaust manifold nuts **(see illustration)** and detach the exhaust manifold. Discard the old gaskets and clean all gasket mating surfaces.

19   Clean the manifolds with solvent and dry them with compressed air.

20   Check the mating surfaces of the manifolds for flatness with a precision straightedge and feeler gauges. Refer to this Chapter's Specifications for the warpage limit.

21   Inspect the manifolds for cracks and distortion.

22   If the manifolds are cracked or warped, replace them or see if they can be resurfaced/repaired at an automotive machine shop.

Installation

23   If you're replacing either manifold, transfer the studs from the old manifold to the new one.

24   When working on a SOHC engine:

a)   *Apply a thin coat of gasket sealant to the manifold sides of the new gaskets and place them in position on the manifolds.*

b)   *Place the exhaust manifold in position on the cylinder head and install the nuts. Starting at the center, tighten the nuts in a criss-cross pattern until the torque listed in this Chapter's Specifications is reached.*

c)   *Position the intake manifold on the head.*

d)   *Raise the vehicle and support it securely on jackstands.*

e)   *Working under the vehicle, install the intake manifold bolts finger tight. Starting at the center and working out in both directions, tighten the bolts in a criss-cross pattern until the torque listed in this Chapter's Specifications is reached.*

25   The remainder of the installation procedure is the reverse of removal.

Turbo SOHC engines

Removal

Refer to illustration 5.36

26   Disconnect the negative cable from the battery.

27   Drain the cooling system (see Chapter 1).

28   Raise the front of the vehicle and support it securely on jackstands.

29   Remove the front engine mount through bolt and rotate the engine away from the cowl.

30   Working under the vehicle, remove the turbocharger (see Chapter 4).

31   Lower the vehicle.

32   Working in the engine compartment, remove the air cleaner assembly along with the throttle body, hose and air cleaner box and bracket (see Chapter 4).

33   Disconnect the throttle linkage and throttle body electrical connector and vacuum hoses.

34   Position the fuel rail out of the way (complete with injectors, wiring harness and fuel line) by removing the hose retainer bracket screw, the four bracket screws from the intake manifold and the two retaining clips (see Chapter 4).

35   Disconnect the upper radiator hose from the thermostat housing.

36   Remove the bolts and nuts securing the intake and exhaust manifolds **(see illustration)**.

37   Remove the manifolds as an assembly.

38   Place the manifolds on a clean working surface. Discard the old gaskets and clean both surfaces (manifolds and cylinder head).

39   Check the gasket mating surfaces of the manifolds for flatness with a precision straightedge and feeler gauges. Refer to this Chapter's Specifications for the warpage limit.

40   Inspect the manifolds for cracks, corrosion and damage. If they're warped or cracked, an automotive machine shop may be able to resurface/repair them.

Installation

41   Install a new gasket. **Note:** *Don't use*

sealant on the manifold gasket.

42   Place the exhaust manifold in position. Apply anti-seize compound to the threads and install the mounting nuts. Working from the center out in both directions, tighten the nuts in 1/4-turn increments to the torque listed in this Chapter's Specifications.

43   Place the intake manifold in position and install the bolts and washers. Working from the center out in both directions, tighten the bolts in 1/4-turn increments until all bolts are at the torque listed in this Chapter's Specifications.

44   Place the turbocharger in position on the exhaust manifold (see Chapter 4). Apply anti-seize compound to the threads and install the retaining nuts. Tighten the nuts to the torque listed in this Chapter's Specifications. Tighten the connector tube clamps securely.

45   Install the coolant return tube in the water box connector, tighten the tube nut and install the tube support bracket on the cylinder head.

46   Connect the turbocharger oil feed line.

47   Install the air cleaner assembly and reconnect the throttle linkage, wires and vacuum hoses.

48   Install the fuel rail (see Chapter 4).

49   Reconnect the exhaust pipe.

50   Connect the upper radiator hose to the thermostat housing.

51   Fill the cooling system (see Chapter 1).

52   Connect the negative battery cable.

DOHC engine

Intake manifold

Removal

Refer to illustrations 5.63 and 5.66

53   Relieve the fuel system pressure (see Chapter 4).

54   Detach the cable from the negative terminal of the battery.

55   Drain the cooling system (see Chapter 1).

56   Remove the fresh air duct from the air filter housing and the inlet hose from the intercooler (see Chapter 4).

Chapter 2 Part A Four-cylinder engines

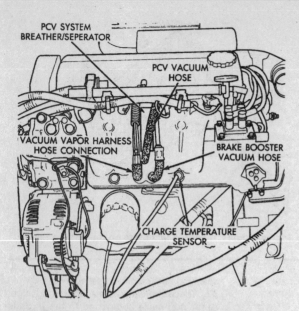

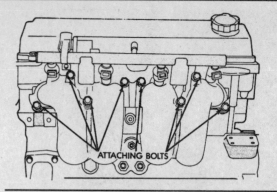

5.66 Intake manifold mounting bolts (turbo DOHC engine

5.63 Detach the vacuum hoses for the brake booster, the vacuum vapor harness hose, the fuel pressure regulator harness, the PCV vacuum hose and breather/separator box from the intake manifold and unplug the electrical connector for the charge temperature sensor (turbo DOHC engine)

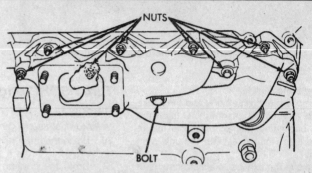

5.82 The mounting bolts and nuts for the exhaust manifold (turbo DOHC engine)

57   Detach the radiator hose from the thermostat housing (see Chapter 3).
58   Remove the DIS ignition coils from the intake manifold (see Chapter 5).
59   Detach the accelerator and cruise control cables from the engine (see Chapter 4).
60   Disconnect the intercooler-to-throttle body outlet hose (see Chapter 4).
61   Disconnect the vacuum hoses from the throttle body and remove the vacuum harness (see Chapter 4).
62   Unplug the electrical connectors from the Automatic Idle Speed (AIS) motor (see Chapter 6) and the Throttle Position Sensor (TPS) (see Chapter 4).
63   Detach the vacuum hoses for the brake booster, the vacuum vapor harness and the fuel pressure regulator harness **(see illustration)**. Remove the PCV breather/separator box (see Chapter 6).
64   Unplug the charge temperature sensor **(see illustration 5.63)**. Unplug the electrical connector for the fuel injector harness.
65   Disconnect the fuel supply and return hose fittings (see Chapter 4).
66   Remove the eight intake manifold bolts **(see illustration)** and remove the intake manifold. Note that each bolt has a washer - don't lose these washers.
67   Discard the gasket and clean all gasket surfaces of the manifold (see Steps 38, 39 and 40).

Installation

68   Install a new intake manifold gasket and intake manifold onto the cylinder head and tighten the fasteners to the torque listed in this Chapter's Specifications.

69   Install the PCV breather/separator box and the vacuum harness assembly. Connect the brake booster, vacuum vapor harness and vacuum hose to the fuel pressure regulator.
70   Inspect the quick-connect fittings for damage and, if necessary, replace them (see Chapter 4). Lubricate the fuel tube with clean 30w engine oil, connect the fuel supply and return hoses to the chassis fuel lines. Check each connection by pulling on the connector to verify that it's locked together.
71   Reconnect the fuel injector, charge temperature sensor, Automatic Idle Speed (AIS) and Throttle Position Sensor (TPS) electrical connectors.
72   Reconnect the vacuum hoses to the throttle body (see Chapter 4).
73   Install the hose between the intercooler and the throttle body and tighten the hose clamps securely.
74   Reattach the accelerator and speed control cables (see Chapter 4).
75   Install the DIS ignition coil pack (see Chapter 5).
76   Install the upper radiator hose and tighten the hose clamps securely.
77   Fill the cooling system (see Chapter 1).
78   Attach the fresh air duct to the air filter housing.
79   Attach the inlet hose to the intercooler and tighten the hose clamp securely.
80   Connect the cable to the negative battery cable.

Exhaust manifold

Refer to illustration 5.82

81   Remove the turbocharger assembly (see

Chapter 4).
82   Remove all nine exhaust manifold mounting bolts and nuts and remove the manifold **(see illustration)**.
83   Discard the old gasket and clean the mating surfaces of the manifold and cylinder head.
84   Test the manifold and cylinder head gasket surfaces for flatness with a precision straightedge and a feeler gauge. These surfaces must be flat within the allowable deviation listed in this Chapter's Specifications.
85   Inspect the manifold for cracks or distortion. Replace if necessary.
86   Install a new manifold gasket. Do NOT apply any type of sealant.
87   Install the exhaust manifold and - starting at the center and working your way out in both directions - tighten the mounting bolts and nuts to the torque listed in this Chapter's Specifications.
88   Install the turbocharger assembly (see Chapter 4).

---

6   Timing belt and sprockets - removal, inspection and installation

SOHC engines

Timing belt removal

Refer to illustrations 6.3, 6.4, 6.5, 6.6a, 6.6b, 6.6c, 6.7, 6.8a, 6.8b and 6.8c

1   Detach the cable from the negative battery terminal.
2   Remove all accessory drivebelts (see

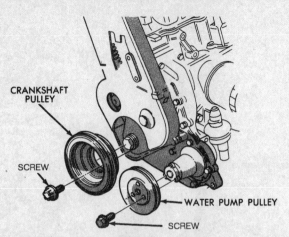

6.3 Details of the crankshaft and water pump pulleys (SOHC engines)

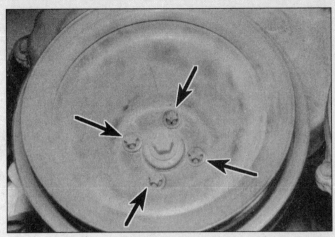

6.4 Remove the four Torx head bolts (arrows) from the crankshaft pulley (SOHC engines)

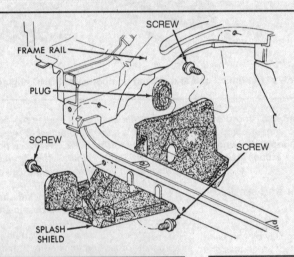

6.5 Raise the vehicle and detach the right inner splash shield to remove the crankshaft pulley (SOHC engines)

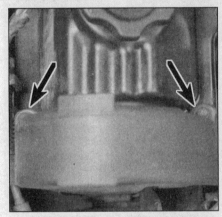

6.6a Remove the two bolts (arrows) that secure the upper timing cover to the valve cover (SOHC engines)

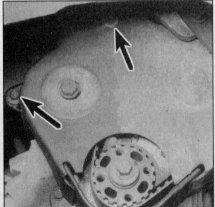

6.6b Remove the bolts (arrows) from the lower timing cover (the third bolt is located behind the water pump) (SOHC engines)

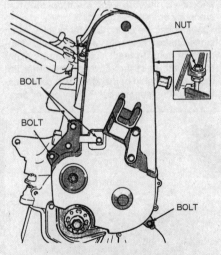

6.6c Remove the fasteners and detach the two timing cover halves (SOHC engines)

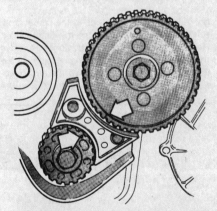

6.7 If you have correctly positioned the number one piston at TDC, the marks on the crankshaft and intermediate shaft sprockets will be aligned (SOHC engines)

Chapter 1).

3   Remove the bolts and detach the water pump pulley (see illustration).

4   Remove the crankshaft pulley bolts (see illustration).

5   Raise the vehicle, support it securely on jackstands and remove the right inner splash shield (see illustration). Remove the crankshaft pulley.

6   Remove the screws and nuts holding the timing belt cover to the cylinder head and block (see illustrations). Remove both halves of the timing belt cover.

7   Position the number one piston at Top Dead Center on the compression stroke (see Section 3). The marks on the crankshaft and intermediate shaft sprocket will be aligned (see illustration) and the arrows on the camshaft sprocket will line up with the bearing cap parting line (see illustration 6.19).

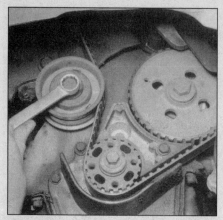

6.8a Loosen the tensioner locking bolt and remove the tensioner (SOHC engines)

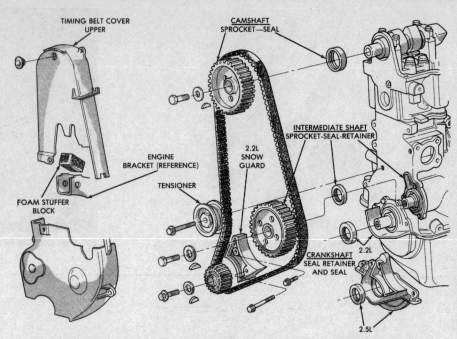

6.8c An exploded view of the timing belt and related components (SOHC engines)

Labels in illustration: TIMING BELT COVER UPPER; CAMSHAFT SPROCKET—SEAL; INTERMEDIATE SHAFT SPROCKET-SEAL-RETAINER; 2.2L SNOW GUARD; ENGINE BRACKET (REFERENCE); TENSIONER; FOAM STUFFER BLOCK; 2.2L; CRANKSHAFT SEAL RETAINER AND SEAL; 2.5L

6.8b Remove the air conditioning compressor, then unscrew the bolts (arrows) and lift off the compressor bracket from the engine (SOHC engines)

8   Use a wrench to loosen the center bolt, releasing the tension from the timing belt. Remove the belt **(see illustrations)**. Remove the tensioner. **Note:** *If the engine is equipped with air conditioning, remove the air conditioning compressor (see Chapter 3) and the*

bracket **(see illustration)**. Also, in order to remove the belt from the engine compartment, it is necessary to support the engine with a block of wood and a floor jack and remove the engine mount.

Timing belt, tensioner and sprocket inspection

Refer to illustration 6.10

9   Rotate the tensioner pulley by hand and move it side-to-side to detect roughness and excessive play. Replace it if it doesn't turn smoothly or if play is noted.

10   Inspect the timing belt for cracks, wear, signs of stretching, ply separation and damaged or missing teeth. Look for contamination by oil, gasoline, coolant and other liquids, which could damage the belt **(see illustration)**. Replace the belt if it's worn or damaged. **Note:** *Unless the engine has very low mileage, it's common practice to replace the timing belt with a new one every time it's removed. Don't reinstall the original belt unless it's in like-new condition. Never reinstall a belt in questionable condition.*

11   Visually inspect the sprockets for wear and damage. If any of the sprockets are damaged or worn, replace them.

12   Inspect the area directly below each sprocket for leaking engine oil. If there is oil below a sprocket, the seal behind that sprocket is leaking and must be replaced (see Sections 7, 8 and 9).

Sprocket removal and installation

Refer to illustrations 6.13, 6.14, 6.16 and 6.19

13   Remove the intermediate shaft sprocket bolt while holding the sprocket with a pin

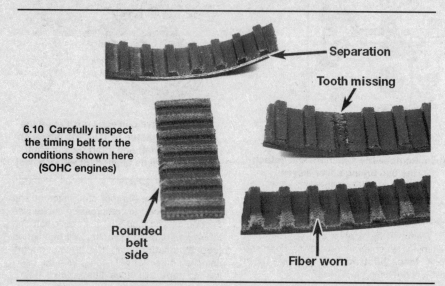

6.10 Carefully inspect the timing belt for the conditions shown here (SOHC engines)

Separation

Tooth missing

Rounded belt side

Fiber worn

6.13 A pin spanner (or homemade substitute like this one shown here) will hold the intermediate shaft sprocket while the bolt is loosened (SOHC engines)

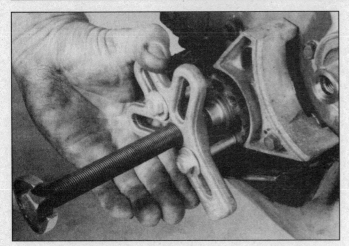

6.14 Use a puller to get the crankshaft sprocket off (SOHC engines)

6.16 Use a straightedge to make the marks (dimples) line up with the centers of the sprocket bolt holes (SOHC engines)

2A

6.19 The small hole must be at the top (arrow) and the triangles on the camshaft sprocket must be aligned with the bearing cap parting line (arrows) (SOHC engines)

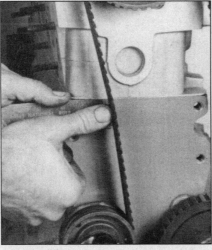

6.23 Use a ruler to measure the timing belt deflection (SOHC engines)

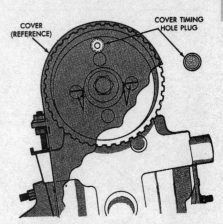

6.25 To check the camshaft timing when the timing belt cover is installed, bring the number one piston to TDC on the compression stroke and verify the small hole in the camshaft sprocket is aligned with the hole in the cover - DO NOT rotate the engine unless the marks are correctly aligned (SOHC engines)

spanner or a homemade substitute **(see illustration)**. Pull the sprocket off the shaft.

14   Remove the bolt and use a puller to remove the crankshaft sprocket **(see illustration)**.

15   Hold the camshaft sprocket as described in Step 13 and remove the bolt, then detach the sprocket from the cam.

16   Make sure the Woodruff keys are in place, then install the crankshaft and intermediate shaft sprockets. Turn the shafts until the marks are aligned **(see illustration)**.

17   Install the crankshaft sprocket bolt, lock the crankshaft to keep it from rotating and tighten the bolt to the torque listed in this Chapter's Specifications.

18   Install the intermediate shaft sprocket bolt and tighten it to the torque listed in this Chapter's Specifications. Double-check to make sure the marks are aligned as shown in **illustration 6.16**.

19   Install the camshaft sprocket and bolt. Tighten the bolt to the torque listed in this Chapter's Specifications. The triangles on the sprocket hub must align with the camshaft bearing cap parting line **(see illustration)**.

Timing belt installation

Refer to illustrations 6.23 and 6.25

20   When installing the timing belt, the marks on the sprockets MUST BE ALIGNED as described in Steps 16 and 19.

21   Install the timing belt without turning any of the sprockets.

22   Install the tensioner pulley with the bolt finger tight.

23   With the help of an assistant, apply tension to the timing belt and temporarily tighten the tensioner bolt. Measure the deflection of the belt half-way between the camshaft sprocket and tensioner pulley. Adjust the tensioner until belt deflection is approximately 5/16-inch **(see illustration)**.

24   Turn the crankshaft two complete revolutions in a clockwise direction (viewed from the front). This will align the belt on the pulleys. Recheck the belt deflection and tighten the tensioner pulley. **Note:** *When tightening the tensioner, use two wrenches. One wrench must keep the larger bolt in a stationary position (adjusted position) while the other*

wrench tightens the smaller bolt (locking bolt).

25   Recheck the camshaft timing mark with the timing belt cover installed and the number one piston at TDC on the compression stroke. The small hole in the camshaft sprocket must be centered in the timing belt cover hole **(see illustration)**.

26   The remainder of installation is the reverse of removal.

DOHC engines

Timing belt removal

Refer to illustrations 6.29, 6.35 and 6.37

27   Detach the cable from the negative battery terminal.

28   Remove the PCV tube (see Chapter 6).

29   Remove the upper timing belt cover

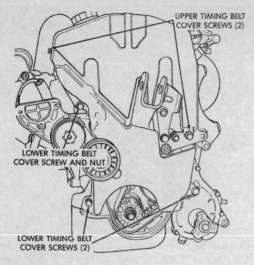

6.29 Timing belt cover screws (DOHC engine)

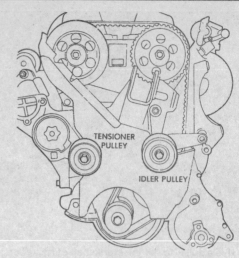

6.35 Idler pulley and tensioner for the accessory drivebelt (DOHC engine)

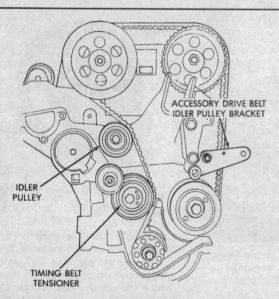

6.37 Bracket for the accessory drivebelt idler pulley, idler pulley and timing belt tensioner (DOHC engine)

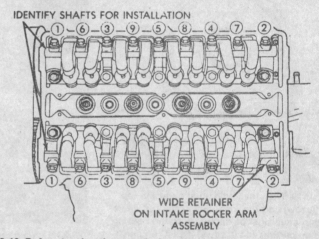

6.42 Before turning the camshaft or crankshaft sprockets, always loosen the rocker arm assemblies about three turns to allow all the open valves to close so they won't be damaged by hitting a piston - the circled numbers indicate the correct sequence for loosening the retaining bolts for the rocker arm assembly (DOHC engine)

screws **(see illustration)** and remove the cover.

30   Remove all accessory drivebelts (see Chapter 1).

31   Loosen - but don't remove - the lug nuts for the right (passenger's side) front wheel. Raise the front of the vehicle and place it securely on jackstands. Remove the right front wheel.

32   Remove the inner splash shield **(see illustration 6.5)**.

33   Bring the number one piston to TDC (see Section 3).

34   Remove the retaining bolts from the water pump pulley and the crankshaft pulley **(see illustration 6.3)** and remove both pulleys. **Note:** *Even though the valve timing mark for the engine is on the flywheel, it's a good idea to have a more convenient timing mark for installing the timing belt. So check the*

mark on the flywheel one more time (it may have moved when you loosened the bolt(s) for the crankshaft pulley), then scribe or paint an alignment mark on the crankshaft sprocket and the block.

35   Remove the idler and tensioner pulleys for the accessory drivebelt **(see illustration)**.

36   Support the engine with a hoist, or a floor jack and a block, and remove the right (passenger's side) engine mount **(see illustration 16.4b)**.

37   Remove the bracket for the accessory drivebelt idler pulley **(see illustration)**.

38   Loosen the timing belt tensioner and remove the drivebelt and the idler pulley. **Caution:** *Do NOT turn the crankshaft or the camshafts while the drivebelt is removed; if you move them while the belt is off, they'll have to be re-timed prior to installation of the drivebelt.*

Timing belt, tensioner, idler pulley and sprocket inspection

39   Refer to Steps 9 through 12 above for these procedures. **Note:** *Inspect the "idler pulley" the same way you inspect the tensioner.*

Sprocket removal and installation

40   Refer to Steps 13 through 19 above for these procedures. **Note:** *It's not necessary to time the intermediate shaft sprocket on this engine because the intermediate shaft doesn't drive the distributor.*

Timing belt installation

Refer to illustrations 6.42, 6.43, 6.44 and 6.50

41   If you haven't already done so, remove the ignition cable cover and the valve cover (see Section 4).

42   Loosen the rocker arm assemblies **(see**

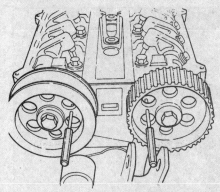

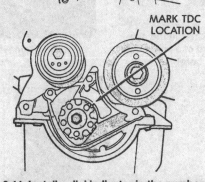

LOCATE TOP DEAD CENTER
FOR NUMBER 1 CYLINDER

6.43 Align and pin both camshaft sprockets with pin punches or 3/32-inch drill bits (DOHC engine)

MARK TDC
LOCATION

6.44 Install a dial indicator in the number one spark plug hole, rotate the crankshaft until the number one piston is at Top Dead Center on the compression stroke and verify that the TDC marks you made on the crankshaft sprocket and the block are still aligned (DOHC engine)

illustration) about three turns.

43 Align and pin both camshaft sprockets with pin punches or 3/32-inch drill bits **(see illustration)**. **Note:** *Don't worry about the intermediate shaft sprocket - it doesn't have to be timed.*

44 Remove the spark plug from the number one spark plug hole and install a dial indicator in its place **(see illustration)**.

45 Rotate the crankshaft until the number one piston is at Top Dead Center on the compression stroke. Verify that the mark on the flywheel is still aligned with the stationary pointer on the bellhousing and the mark you made on the crankshaft sprocket is aligned with the mark you made on the block (If you didn't make a mark before, it would be a good idea to make one now, across the crank sprocket and the block).

46 Install the timing belt and the idler pulley as follows:

a) With the marks on the flywheel and the bellhousing and the marks on the crankshaft pulley and the block lined up, and the camshaft sprockets pinned into place, install the belt in a counterclockwise direction, starting with the crankshaft sprocket, then the intermediate shaft sprocket, then the intake cam sprocket, then the exhaust cam sprocket. There must be no slack in the

belt so far; if you leave any slack in the belt up to this point, the camshafts will be out of time with the crankshaft within one revolution.

b) Install the idler pulley exactly as shown (with the teeth on the belt facing away from the pulley), push the belt over the flange on the tensioner, rotate the tensioner clockwise to remove all slack from the belt and tighten the tensioner bolt to the torque listed in this Chapter's Specifications.

47 Remove the dial indicator from the cylin-

der head and remove the pins or drill bits from the camshaft sprockets.

48 Ideally, the tension of the drivebelt should be adjusted with a belt tension gauge placed between the camshaft sprockets and the indicated tension should be the same as the figure listed in this Chapter's Specifications. However, if you remove all slack on the run between the exhaust camshaft sprocket and the crankshaft sprocket, the belt tension should be okay.

49 To verify that you've installed the belt correctly, rotate the crankshaft *clockwise* through two full revolutions and verify that all the marks still line up. If they don't, go back to Step 45 and repeat this procedure. **Caution:** *Do NOT rotate the crankshaft backwards - counterclockwise - or attempt to rotate the crank by turning the camshaft or intermediate shaft sprockets.*

50 Make sure the camshaft lobes still point away from the rocker arm lash adjusters, i.e. the valves are still closed, for the number one piston, then tighten the rocker arm shafts, in the sequence shown **(see illustration)**, to the initial, then the final, torque listed in this Chapter's Specifications.

51 The remainder of installation is the reverse of removal.

7   Camshaft oil seal - replacement

Refer to illustrations 7.2 and 7.5

Note: *The following procedure applies to the camshaft oil seals on all engines.*

1   Remove the timing belt and camshaft sprocket (see Section 6).

2   Wrap the tip of a small screwdriver with tape and use it to carefully pry out the seal. Don't nick or scratch the camshaft journal or the new seal will leak **(see illustration)**.

3   Thoroughly clean and inspect the seal bore and the seal journal on the camshaft. Both must be clean and smooth. Use emery cloth or 400-grit sandpaper to remove small burrs.

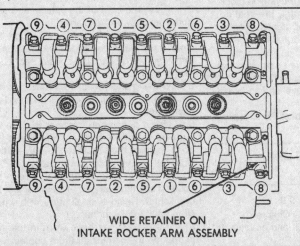

6.50 Make sure the camshaft lobes still point away from the rocker arm lash adjuster, i.e. the valves are still closed, for the number one piston, then tighten the rocker arm assemblies in the sequence indicated by the circled numbers

WIDE RETAINER ON
INTAKE ROCKER ARM ASSEMBLY

7.2 Wrap tape around the end of a small screwdriver and pry the seal out of the housing (SOHC engine shown, DOHC engine similar)

2A

7.5 If you don't have a socket large enough to drive in the new seal, tap around the outer edge with the large end of a punch (but be careful not to cock the seal in the bore)

8.3 Remove the bolts and detach the seal housing

4   If a groove has been worn into the journal on the camshaft (from contact with the seal lip), installing a new seal probably won't stop the leak.

Such wear normally indicates the camshaft or the bearing surfaces in the caps are worn. It's probably time to overhaul the cylinder head (see Chapter 2, Part C) or replace the head or camshaft.

5   Coat the lip of the new seal with clean engine oil or moly-base grease and carefully tap the seal into place with a large socket or piece of pipe and a hammer. If you don't have a socket as large in diameter as the seal, tap around the outer edge of the seal with the large end of a punch **(see illustration)**.

6   Install the camshaft sprocket and timing belt (see Section 6).

7   Start the engine and check for oil leaks.

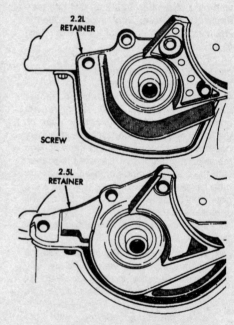

8.7 Using a soft-face hammer, carefully tap the new seal into the housing - be careful not to cock the seal in the bore

8   Intermediate shaft oil seal - replacement

Refer to illustrations 8.3 and 8.7

Note: *The following procedure applies to the intermediate (accessory) shaft oil seal on all engines.*

1   Drain the engine oil (see Chapter 1).

2   Remove the timing belt and intermediate shaft sprocket (see Section 6).

3   Remove the oil seal housing **(see illustration)**.

4   Pry the old seal out of the housing with a screwdriver (wrap the tip of the screwdriver with tape). Make sure you don't scratch the seal bore.

5   Thoroughly clean and inspect the seal bore and the seal journal on the intermediate shaft. Both must be clean and smooth. Remove small burrs with emery cloth or 400-grit sandpaper.

6   If a groove has been worn in the seal journal (from contact with the seal lip), installing a new seal probably won't stop the leak. Such wear normally indicates the intermediate shaft or shaft bearing surfaces in the

engine block are worn. It's probably time to overhaul the engine (see Chapter 2, Part C).

7   Using a soft-face hammer, carefully tap the new seal into the housing **(see illustration)**.

8   Coat the lip of the seal with clean engine oil or moly-base grease and install the housing and seal on the front of the engine block. Make sure you don't damage the seal lip. Install the housing bolts and tighten them to the torque listed in this Chapter's Specifications.

9   Install the intermediate shaft sprocket and the timing belt (see Section 6).

10   Check the engine oil level and add oil, if necessary (see Chapter 1).

11   Start the engine and check for oil leaks.

9   Crankshaft front oil seal - replacement

Refer to illustrations 9.5 and 9.9

1   Drain the engine oil (see Chapter 1).

2   Remove the timing belt and crankshaft sprocket (see Section 6).

9.5 Remove the bolts and detach the housing/seal assembly

3   Raise the front of the vehicle and support it securely on jackstands.

4   Remove the oil pan (see Section 12).

Note: *It is possible to remove the seal without removing the oil pan, if a special seal puller tool is used.*

5   Working underneath the vehicle, remove the bolts and detach the oil seal housing **(see illustration)**.

6   Use a punch and hammer to drive the old seal out of the housing. Make sure you don't damage the seal bore. To prevent this, wrap the tip of the punch with tape.

7   Thoroughly clean the seal bore in the housing and the seal journal on the end of the crankshaft. Remove small burrs with emery cloth or 400-grit sandpaper.

8   If a groove has been worn in the seal journal on the crankshaft (from contact with

9.9 Tap the new crankshaft oil seal into the housing with a soft-face hammer

10.3 The camshaft bearing caps are numbered from 1 to 5 (arrow) so they don't get mixed up - if the caps aren't numbered, mark them (they must be reinstalled in their original locations)

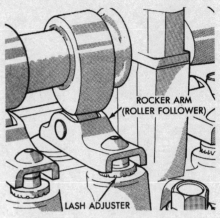

10.5 Mark the rocker arms and lash adjusters before removing them

2A

the seal lip), installing a new seal probably won't stop the leak. Such wear normally indicates the crankshaft and/or the main bearings are excessively worn. It's probably time to overhaul the engine (see Chapter 2, Part C).

9   Apply a thin coat of RTV sealant to the surface of the seal bore, lay the housing on a clean, flat work surface, position the new seal in the bore and tap it into place with a soft face hammer **(see illustration)**. Make sure the seal lip faces the proper direction (towards the engine).

10   Lubricate the seal lip with multi-purpose grease and apply a 1 mm wide bead of anaerobic gasket sealant to the engine block mating surface of the seal housing. Position the housing on the engine. Install the retaining bolts and tighten them to the torque listed in this Chapter's Specifications.

11   Reinstall the crankshaft sprocket, timing belt and related components.

12   Install the oil pan (see Section 12).

13   Check the engine oil level and add oil, if necessary (see Chapter 1).

14   Start the engine, let it warm up and check for leaks.

---

10   Camshaft and hydraulic lash adjusters/rocker arms - removal, inspection and installation

SOHC engines

Removal

Refer to illustrations 10.3, 10.5, 10.6 and 10.8

1   Remove the valve cover (see Section 4).

2   Remove the timing belt cover, timing belt and camshaft sprocket (see Section 6). **Note:** *If you want to save time by not removing and installing the timing belt, you can unfasten the camshaft sprocket and suspend it out of the way - with the belt still attached - on a piece of wire. Be sure the wire maintains tension on the belt so it won't disengage any of the sprockets.*

3   The camshaft rides on five bearings. Each bearing cap is held by two fasteners. On some engines, the bearing caps are numbered from 1 to 5, beginning at the drivebelt end of the engine **(see illustration)**. **Note:** *All*

numbers face either the spark plug or manifold side of the engine. This is to ensure you install the caps facing the correct direction.

4   On some engines, the bearing caps aren't numbered. If this is the case, you must mark them before removal. Be sure to put the marks on the same ends of all the caps to prevent incorrect orientation of the caps during installation.

5   Also mark the rocker arms **(see illustration)** to ensure they're installed in the same position during reassembly.

6   Remove the bolts from all the bearing caps **(see illustration)** except cap numbers 2 and 4. Next, loosen each of the four fasteners on 2 and 4 a little at a time to relieve valve spring tension evenly until the caps are loose. If any of the caps stick, gently tap them with a soft-face hammer. **Caution:** *Failure to follow this procedure exactly as described could tilt the camshaft in the housing, which could damage the housing or bend the camshaft.*

7   Lift out the camshaft, wipe it off with a clean shop towel and set it aside.

8   Lift out each rocker arm and lash adjuster **(see illustration)**, wipe them off and set them aside in labeled plastic bags or an egg carton.

10.6 Remove the bolts (arrows) from the camshaft bearing caps

10.8 The lash adjusters should slide out easily if they aren't coated with varnish

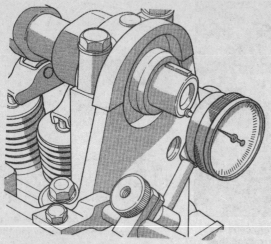

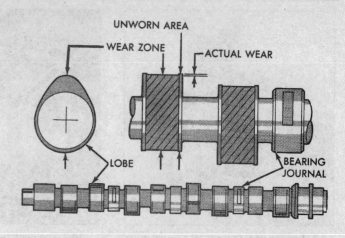

10.9 To check camshaft endplay, set up a dial indicator like this with the gauge plunger touching the nose of the camshaft (SOHC engine shown, procedure for DOHC engines similar)

10.12 Measure the height of the camshaft lobes at the wear zone and unworn area, then subtract the wear zone measurement from the unworn area measurement to get the actual wear - compare the wear to the limit listed in this Chapter's Specifications

Inspection

Refer to illustrations 10.9 and 10.12

9   To check camshaft endplay:

a) *Install the camshaft and secure it with caps 1 and 5.*

b) *Mount a dial indicator on the head (see illustration).*

c) *Using a large screwdriver as a lever at the opposite end, move the camshaft forward-and-backward and note the dial indicator reading.*

d) *Compare the reading with the endplay listed in this Chapter's Specifications.*

e) *If the indicated reading is higher, either the camshaft or the head is worn. Replace parts as necessary.*

10   To check camshaft runout:

a) *Support the camshaft with a pair of V-blocks and attach a dial indicator with the stem resting against the center bearing journal on the camshaft.*

b) *Rotate the camshaft and note the indicated runout.*

c) *Compare the results to the camshaft runout listed in this Chapter's Specifications.*

d) *If the indicated runout exceeds the specified runout, replace the camshaft.*

11   Check the camshaft bearing journals and caps for scoring and signs of wear. If they are worn, replace the cylinder head with a new or rebuilt unit. Measure the journals on the camshaft with a micrometer, comparing your readings with this Chapter's Specifications. If the diameter of any of the journals is out of specification, replace the camshaft. **Note:** *When servicing the camshaft or cylinder head, it is necessary to be certain that oversized camshafts are used only with oversized journals. Cylinder heads with oversized journals can be identified by green paint on the tops of the camshaft bearing caps and OS/J stamped to the rear of the oil gallery plug on the air pump end of the cylinder*

head. Camshafts with oversized journals are identified by green paint on the barrel of the shaft and OS/J stamped on the end of the shaft.

12   Check the cam lobes for wear:

a) *Check the toe and ramp areas of each cam lobe for score marks and uneven wear. Also check for flaking and pitting.*

b) *If there's wear on the toe or the ramp, replace the camshaft, but first try to find the cause of the wear. Check the lash adjusters, look for abrasive substances in the oil and inspect the oil pump and oil passages for blockage. Lobe wear is usually caused by inadequate lubrication or dirty oil.*

c) *Using a micrometer, calculate the lobe wear (see illustration). If the lobe wear is greater than listed in this Chapter's Specifications, replace the camshaft.*

13   Inspect the rocker arms and hydraulic lash adjusters for wear, galling and pitting of the contact surfaces.

14   If any of the conditions described above are noted, the cylinder head is probably getting insufficient lubrication or dirty oil, so make sure you track down the cause of this problem (low oil level, low oil pump capacity, clogged oil passage, etc.) before installing a new head, camshaft or followers.

Installation

Refer to illustrations 10.17, 10.20 and 10.21

15   Thoroughly clean the camshaft, the bearing surfaces in the head and caps, the rocker arms and hydraulic lash adjusters. Remove all sludge and dirt. Wipe off all components with a clean, lint-free cloth.

16   Lubricate the lash adjuster and the contact surfaces on the top of the rocker arms with assembly lube or moly-base grease. Install the lash adjusters and rocker arms, making sure you put them in their original locations.

17   Lubricate the camshaft bearing surfaces

10.17 Install the camshaft with the lobes pointing away from the number one cylinder intake and exhaust valves

in the head and the bearing journals and lobes on the camshaft with assembly lube or moly-base grease. Carefully lower the camshaft into position with the lobes for the number one cylinder pointing away from the cam followers or rocker arms **(see illustration). Caution:** *Failure to adequately lubricate the camshaft and related components can cause serious damage to bearing and friction surfaces during the first few seconds after engine start-up, when the oil pressure is low or nonexistent.*

18   Apply a thin coat of assembly lube or moly-base grease to the bearing surfaces of the camshaft bearing caps and install the caps in their original locations.

19   Install the bolts for bearing caps 2 and 4. Gradually tighten all four fasteners - 1/4-turn at a time - until the camshaft is drawn down and seated in the bearing saddles. Don't tighten the fasteners completely at this time.

20   Apply anaerobic-type sealant to the contact surfaces of bearing caps 1 and 5 **(see illustration).**

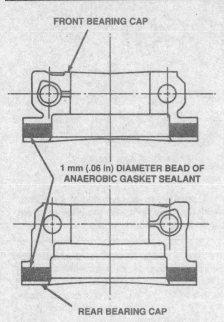

FRONT BEARING CAP

1 mm (.06 in) DIAMETER BEAD OF
ANAEROBIC GASKET SEALANT

REAR BEARING CAP

10.20 Apply anaerobic-type gasket sealant to the dark areas only on the front and rear camshaft bearing caps

10.21 Apply RTV sealant to the outer circumference of the camshaft rear plug before installing the number 5 cap

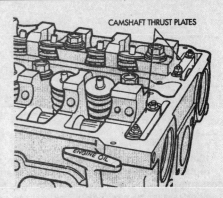

CAMSHAFT THRUST PLATES

ENGINE OIL

10.32 Camshaft thrust plate(s) - note that the intake cam uses a wider thrust than the exhaust cam; because of their different thicknesses, the thrust plates can't be interchanged (DOHC engine)

2A

21   Install bearing caps 3 and 5 **(see illustration)** and tighten the fasteners the same way you did for caps 2 and 4.

22   Install a new oil seal on the front of the camshaft, then install bearing cap 1. Don't tighten the fasteners completely at this time.

23   Remove any excess sealant from the two end bearing caps.

24   Working in a criss-cross pattern, tighten the fasteners for bearing caps 2 and 4 to the torque listed in this Chapter's Specifications. Then torque the fasteners for bearing caps 3 and 5 the same way. Finally, tighten the fasteners for bearing cap 1.

25   Install the camshaft sprocket, timing belt, timing belt cover and related components (see Section 6). If you suspended the camshaft sprocket out of the way and didn't disturb the timing belt or sprockets, the valve timing should still be correct. Rotate the camshaft as necessary to reattach the sprocket to the camshaft. If the valve timing was disturbed, align the sprockets and install the belt as described in Section 6.

26   Remove the spark plugs and rotate the crankshaft by hand to make sure the valve timing is correct. After two revolutions, the timing marks on the sprockets should still be aligned. If they're not, re-index the timing belt to the sprockets (see Section 6). **Note:** *If you feel resistance while rotating the crankshaft, stop immediately and check the valve timing* (see Section 6).

DOHC engine

Removal

Refer to illustrations 10.32, 10.34 and 10.35
Note: *The following procedure applies to either camshaft.*

27   Remove the valve cover (see Section 4).

28   Remove the timing belt cover, the timing belt and the camshaft sprocket(s) (see Section 6).

29   Remove the cylinder head (see Section 11).

30   If you're removing both camshafts, scribe or paint identifying marks on the rocker arm shafts to prevent them from being accidentally switched during installation.

31   Remove the retaining bolts, in the proper sequence, from the rocker arm assembly(ies) **(see illustration 6.42)**. Before you remove either rocker arm assembly, secure the hydraulic lash adjusters with tape or rubber bands to prevent them from falling out of the rocker arms when you lift up the rocker arm assembly. Remove the rocker arm assembly(ies).

32   Remove the thrust plate(s) from the rear of the camshaft(s) **(see illustration)**. **Note:** *If you're removing both camshafts, note that the intake cam uses a wider thrust plate than the exhaust cam; because of their different thicknesses, the thrust plates can't be interchanged.*

33   Note the direction in which each cam lobe points before removing either cam. This is how the cam lobes look when the number one piston is at TDC. Make a mental note of this image so you'll reinstall the cam(s) correctly. It's not a bad idea to make a sketch.

34   Using a screwdriver placed between the cylinder head casting and a cam lobe, lever the cam(s) out of the cylinder head far enough to push out the seal(s) **(see illustration)**.

35   Remove the camshaft(s) from the cylinder head **(see illustration)**. Make sure you don't scratch the bearing surfaces on the cam(s) or in the head.

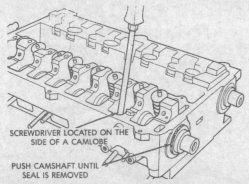

SCREWDRIVER LOCATED ON THE SIDE OF A CAMLOBE

PUSH CAMSHAFT UNTIL SEAL IS REMOVED

10.34 Using a screwdriver placed between the cylinder head casting and a cam lobe, lever the cam(s) out of the cylinder head far enough to push out the seal(s)

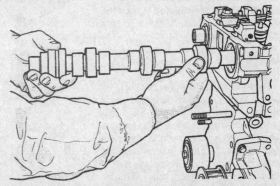

10.35 Make sure you don't scratch the bearing surfaces on the cam(s) or in the head when removing the camshaft(s) from the cylinder head

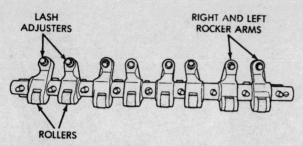

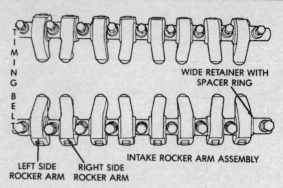

10.37 If you have to disassemble a rocker arm assembly to replace a worn or damaged rocker or shaft, make sure you reassemble it with the rocker arms arranged like this, with the flat sides of each pair of rockers adjacent to each other - if you reassemble a rocker assembly incorrectly, the rockers will go on the shaft, but the lash adjusters won't line up with the valve stems

10.42 If you removed both rocker arm assemblies at the same time, make sure you install the assembly with the wide retainer and spacer ring on the intake side of the head

Inspection

Refer to illustration 10.37

36   There are a few differences in the rocker arm assemblies on SOHC and DOHC engines: The rocker arm assembly on SOHC engines is below the camshaft; on the DOHC engine, the rocker arm assemblies are above the cam. Because of this arrangement, and because there are twice as many camshafts, rocker arms, hydraulic lash adjusters and valves on the DOHC design (as well as a pair of rocker arm shafts), the lash adjusters on the DOHC engine are smaller than those used on a SOHC head and are housed in the rocker arms themselves instead of the cylinder head. But the procedures for inspecting the camshaft(s), hydraulic lash adjusters and rocker arms used on DOHC engines are the same as those used for SOHC engines. Refer to Steps 9 through 14.

37   If you have to disassemble a rocker arm shaft to replace worn or damaged rocker arms, refer to the accompanying illustration to assure correct reassembly **(see illustration)**.

Installation

Refer to illustration 10.42

38   Lubricate the camshaft journals with clean engine oil and carefully install the camshaft into the head. **Caution:** *If you have removed both cams, make sure you don't switch them - they're not interchangeable; the intake cam has a wider thrust plate groove.*

39   Install the thrust plate(s) and tighten the retaining nuts to the torque listed in this Chapter's Specifications.

40   Install a new camshaft oil seal(s) flush with the cylinder head surface (see Section 7).

41   If you disassembled either rocker arm assembly to replace worn or damaged rockers or shafts, make sure the rocker assembly is correctly assembled **(see illustration 10.37)** and the lash adjusters are at least partially filled with oil. To verify that an adjuster has enough oil inside, try to compress it with your thumb and index finger. If there's little or no plunger travel, the adjuster has plenty of oil in it; if it compresses easily, the adjuster needs more oil. Immerse the adjuster in fresh oil, compress it and release it - when you

release the plunger, it will suck oil into the adjuster.

42   Install the rocker arm assembly(ies). If you removed both rocker arm assemblies, note that the intake rocker arm assembly has a wide retainer with a spacer ring **(see illus-** tration). Tighten the rocker arm assembly retaining bolts in the sequence shown in illustration 6.50, to the initial, then the final, torque listed in this Chapter's Specifications.

43   The remainder of installation is the reverse of removal.

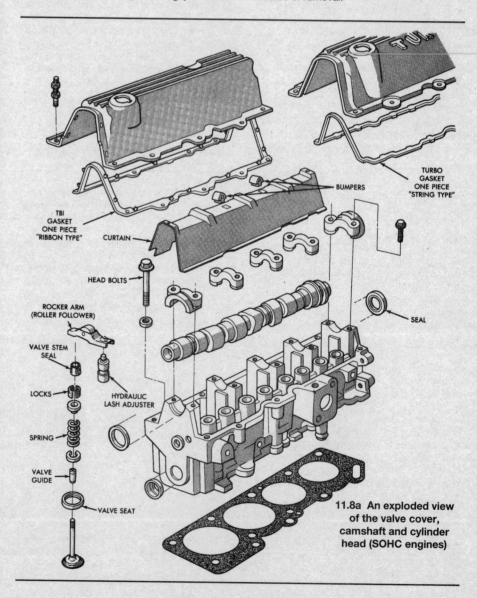

11.8a An exploded view of the valve cover, camshaft and cylinder head (SOHC engines)

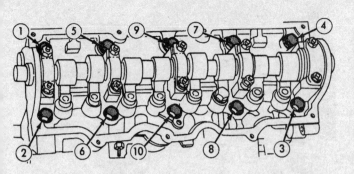

11.8b Loosen the head bolts 1/4-turn at a time, in the sequence shown, until they can be removed by hand (SOHC engines)

11.9 If the cylinder head is difficult to remove, pry only on the protrusions located on the side of the cylinder head, as this will not damage the cylinder head surface (SOHC engines)

2A

11 Cylinder head - removal and installation

Caution: *Allow the engine to cool completely before beginning this procedure.*

SOHC engines

Removal

Refer to illustrations 11.8a, 11.8b and 11.9

1 Position the number one piston at Top Dead Center (see Section 3).
2 Disconnect the negative cable from the battery.
3 Drain the cooling system and remove the spark plugs (see Chapter 1).
4 Remove the intake/exhaust manifold (see Section 5). **Note:** *If you're only replacing the cylinder head gasket, it isn't necessary to remove the manifolds. If you leave the manifold attached, you may need an assistant to help lift the head off the engine.*
5 Remove the distributor (see Chapter 5), including the cap and wires.
6 Remove the timing belt (see Section 6).
7 Remove the valve cover (see Section 4).
8 Loosen the head bolts in 1/4-turn increments until they can be removed by hand. Follow the recommended sequence to avoid warping the head **(see illustrations).**
9 Lift the head off the engine. If resistance is felt, don't pry between the head and block gasket mating surfaces - damage to the mating surfaces will result. Instead, pry against the casting protrusions on the sides of the cylinder head **(see illustration).** Set the head on blocks of wood to prevent damage to the gasket sealing surfaces.
10 Cylinder head disassembly and inspection procedures are covered in detail in Chapter 2, Part C. It's a good idea to have the head checked for warpage, even if you're just replacing the gasket.

Installation

Refer to illustrations 11.12, 11.14, 11.15a, 11.15b and 11.16

11 The mating surfaces of the cylinder head and block must be perfectly clean when the head is installed.

11.12 Use a gasket scraper to remove the old head gasket (SOHC engines)

12 Use a gasket scraper to remove all traces of carbon and old gasket material **(see illustration),** then clean the mating surfaces with lacquer thinner or acetone. If there's oil on the mating surfaces when the head is installed, the gasket may not seal correctly and leaks may develop. When working on the block, stuff the cylinders with clean shop rags to keep out debris. Use a vacuum cleaner to remove material that falls into the cylinders. Since the head is made of aluminum, aggressive scraping can cause damage. Be extra careful not to nick or gouge the mating surfaces with the scraper.

11.14 Use a die to remove sealant and corrosion from the head bolts prior to installation (SOHC engines)

13 Check the block and head mating surfaces for nicks, deep scratches and other damage. If damage is slight, it can be removed with a file; if it's excessive, machining may be the only alternative.
14 Use a tap of the correct size to chase the threads in the head bolt holes. Mount each head bolt in a vise and run a die down the threads to remove corrosion and restore the threads **(see illustration).** Dirt, corrosion, sealant and damaged threads will affect torque readings.
15 Place a new gasket on the block **(see**

11.15a When you put the new head gasket in position on the engine block, be sure it's right side up and facing the right direction; the holes in the gasket must match the passages in the block for coolant and oil to circulate properly (SOHC engine shown, but same principles apply to DOHC engine as well)

THESE GASKETS ARE NOT INTERCHANGEABLE

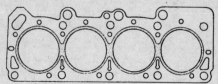

2.2/2.5L NATURAL ASPIRATED AND 2.2L TURBO I ENGINES

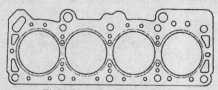

2.2L TURBO 2 & 4 AND 2.5L TURBO I ENGINES

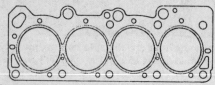

TURBO III ENGINES ONLY

11.15b Note the differences among these three head gaskets - make sure you've got the right gasket for the engine you're servicing

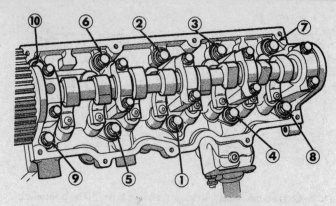

11.16 Cylinder head bolt tightening sequence (SOHC engines)

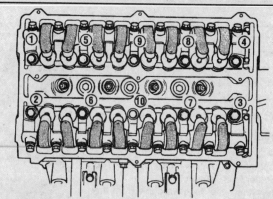

11.25 Cylinder head bolt loosening sequence (DOHC engine)

illustrations) and set the cylinder head in position.

16   Install the bolts. They must be tightened in four steps, following a specific sequence (see illustration), to the torque listed in this Chapter's Specifications.

17   Reinstall the timing belt (see Section 6).

18   Reinstall the remaining parts in the reverse order of removal.

19   Be sure to refill the cooling system and check all fluid levels.

20   Rotate the crankshaft clockwise slowly by hand through two complete revolutions. Recheck the camshaft timing marks (see Section 6).

21   Start the engine and check the ignition timing (see Chapter 1).

22   Run the engine until normal operating temperature is reached. Check for leaks and proper operation.

DOHC engine

Removal

Refer to illustration 11.25

23   Refer to Steps 1 through 4, 5 and 7 above.

24   Remove the compressor mounting bracket (see Chapter 3).

25   To avoid warping the cylinder head, loosen the head bolts in the recommended sequence, in 1/4-turn increments (see illustration).

26   Lift the head off the engine and set it on blocks of wood to prevent damage to the

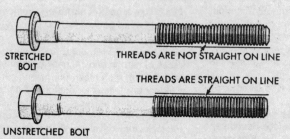

STRETCHED BOLT   THREADS ARE NOT STRAIGHT ON LINE

THREADS ARE STRAIGHT ON LINE

UNSTRETCHED BOLT

11.30 If the threads of a cylinder head bolt are "necked" down, replace the bolt

gasket sealing surfaces. If the head is stuck, pry against the casting protrusions on the sides of the cylinder head. **Caution:** *DON'T pry between the gasket mating surfaces of the head and the block, or you might damage them.*

27   Cylinder head disassembly and inspection procedures are covered in detail in Chapter 2, Part C. It's a good idea to have the head checked for warpage, even if you're just replacing the gasket.

Installation

Refer to illustrations 11.30 and 11.32

28   Refer to Steps 11 through 13 above.

29   Place a new gasket on the block. Note that the gasket used on the DOHC engine is different from those used on other four-cylinder engines (see illustration 11.15b). Make sure you've got the right one before you lay the cylinder on the block.

30   The bolts used on the DOHC engine are

also different than those used on other four-cylinder engines; you can distinguish them from the bolts used on other cylinder heads by their 11mm heads. These bolts are also tightened using a different procedure, so examine them carefully before you install them: Replace any bolts with "necked" down threads. To determine whether the threads of a head bolt are necked down, hold a metal straightedge or ruler against the threads (see illustration). If some of the threads don't contact the straight edge, replace the bolt.

31   Once you've determined that the bolts are in satisfactory condition, clean and lubricate the threads of each bolt (see Step 14 above).

32   Install the cylinder head bolts and tighten them in the sequence shown (see illustration), using the four-step method listed in this Chapter's Specifications.

33   The remainder of installation is the reverse of removal.

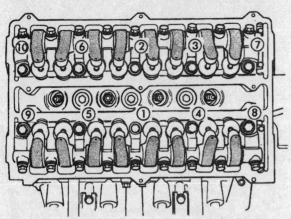

11.32 Cylinder head bolt tightening sequence (DOHC engine)

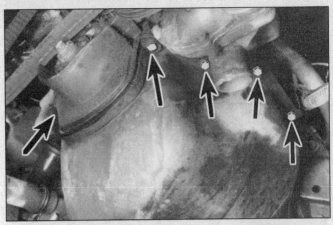

12.4 Remove the bolts (arrows) from the oil pan

2A

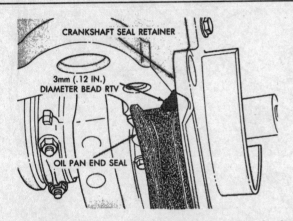

12.8a Install the new oil pan end seals and hold them in place with a bead of RTV sealant as shown here

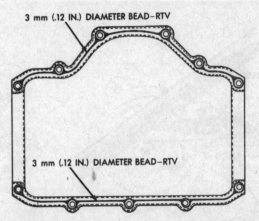

12.8b Apply a continuous 1/8-inch wide bead of RTV sealant to the oil pan, then install the pan

12 Oil pan - removal and installation

Refer to illustrations 12.4, 12.8a and 12.8b
Note: *The following procedure is based on the assumption that the engine is in the vehicle.*

1   Warm up the engine, then drain the oil and replace the oil filter (see Chapter 1).
2   Detach the cable from the negative battery terminal.
3   Raise the vehicle and support it securely on jackstands.
4   Remove the bolts securing the oil pan to the engine block **(see illustration).**
5   Tap on the pan with a soft-face hammer to break the gasket seal, then detach the oil pan from the engine. Don't pry between the block and oil pan mating surfaces.
6   Using a gasket scraper, remove all traces of old gasket and/or sealant from the engine block and oil pan. Remove the seals from each end of the engine block or oil pan. Clean the mating surfaces with lacquer thinner or acetone. Make sure the threaded bolt holes in the block are clean.
7   Clean the oil pan with solvent and dry it thoroughly. Check the gasket flanges for distortion, particularly around the bolt holes. If necessary, place the pan on a block of wood

and use a hammer to flatten and restore the gasket surfaces.
8   Install new seals in the retainers at the front and rear of the engine block **(see illustration).** Apply a 1/8-inch wide bead of RTV sealant to the oil pan gasket surfaces. Continue the bead across the end seals. Make sure the sealant is applied to the inside of the bolt holes **(see illustration).**
9   Carefully place the oil pan in position.
10   Install the bolts and tighten them in 1/4-turn increments to the torque listed in this Chapter's Specifications. Start with the bolts closest to the center of the pan and work out in a spiral pattern. Don't overtighten them or leakage may occur. **Note:** *Some 2.2L engines have bolts with different diameters, which require different torque values.*
11   Add oil, run the engine and check for oil leaks.

13 Oil pump - removal, inspection and installation

Removal

Refer to illustrations 13.2a, 13.2b and 13.2c
1   Remove the oil pan (see Section 12).

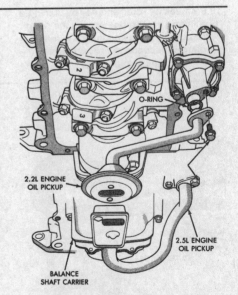

13.2a Engine oil pump mounting and brace bolt locations (arrows)

2   Remove the oil pump mounting bolts. If equipped, also remove the brace bolt **(see illustrations).**
3   Remove the oil pump assembly.

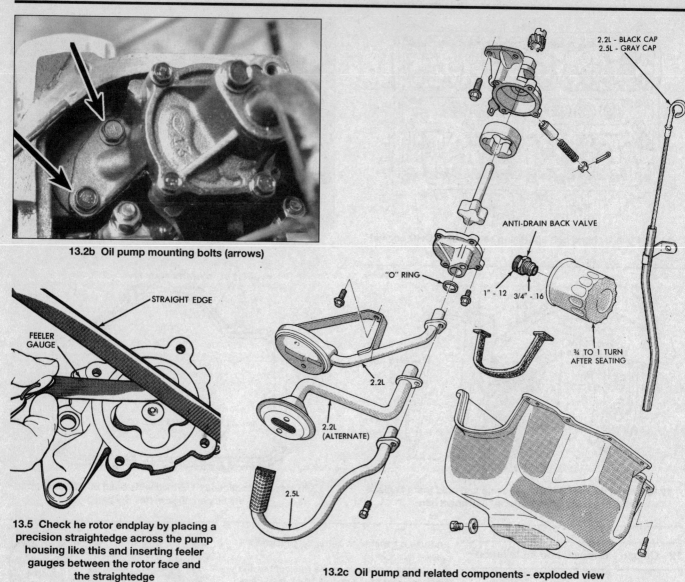

13.2b Oil pump mounting bolts (arrows)

2.2L - BLACK CAP
2.5L - GRAY CAP

ANTI-DRAIN BACK VALVE

"O" RING

1" - 12   3/4" - 16

¾ TO 1 TURN
AFTER SEATING

2.2L

2.2L
(ALTERNATE)

2.5L

STRAIGHT EDGE

FEELER
GAUGE

13.5 Check he rotor endplay by placing a
precision straightedge across the pump
housing like this and inserting feeler
gauges between the rotor face and
the straightedge

13.2c Oil pump and related components - exploded view

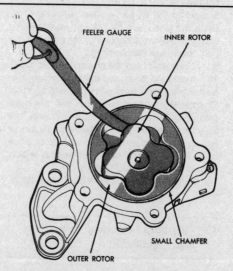

MICROMETER

OUTER ROTOR

LARGE CHAMFER

13.6 Measure the thickness of the oil
pump outer rotor with a micrometer

FEELER GAUGE   INNER ROTOR

OUTER ROTOR

SMALL CHAMFER

13.7 Check the inner rotor-to-outer rotor
tip clearance with feeler gauge

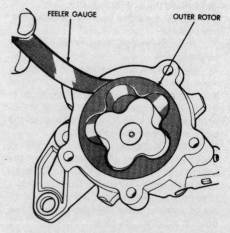

FEELER GAUGE

OUTER ROTOR

13.8 Check the outer rotor-to-pump body
clearance with feeler gauges

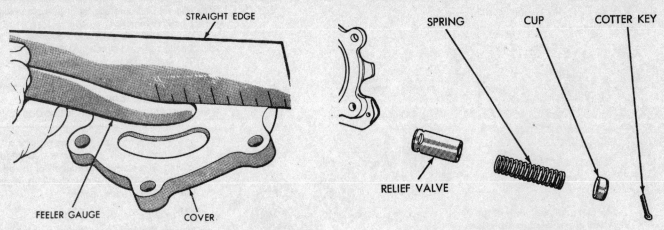

13.9 Check the oil pump cover for warpage with a straightedge and feeler gauge

13.10 An exploded view of the oil pressure relief valve components

Inspection

Refer to illustrations 13.5, 13.6, 13.7, 13.8, 13.9 and 13.10

4   Remove the bolts and lift off the oil pump cover.

5   Check the rotor endplay with feeler gauges and a straightedge **(see illustration)**.

6   Remove the outer rotor and measure its thickness **(see illustration)**.

7   Check the clearance between the inner and outer rotor tips with feeler gauges **(see illustration)**.

8   Measure the outer rotor-to-pump body clearance **(see illustration)**.

9   Check the oil pump cover for warpage with feeler gauges and a straightedge **(see illustration)**.

10   Remove the cotter pin and cup, then extract the spring and oil pump relief valve from the pump housing **(see illustration)**. Measure the free length of the oil pressure relief valve spring.

11   Compare the measurements to the oil pump Specifications at the beginning of this Chapter. If any of them are outside the limits, replace the pump.

12   Install the rotor with the large chamfered edge facing toward the pump body. Install the oil pressure relief valve and spring assembly. Install the pump cover and tighten the bolts to the torque listed in this Chapter's Specifications.

Installation

Refer to illustration 13.15

13   Apply a thin coat of RTV sealant to the mating surface of the pump and place the pump in position. Rotate it back-and-forth a little to ensure there's positive contact between the pump and the engine block.

14   Coat the threads of the mounting bolts with sealant and, while holding the pump securely in place, install the bolts. Tighten them to the torque listed in this Chapter's Specifications.

15   Install a new O-ring in the oil pump pick-up opening **(see illustration)**.

16   Carefully work the pick-up tube into the pump, install the retaining bolt and tighten it to the torque listed in this Chapter's Specifications.

17   Install the brace bolt and tighten it securely.

18   Install the oil pan (see Section 12).

14   Flywheel/driveplate - removal and installation

Removal

Refer to illustrations 14.3 and 14.4

1   Raise the vehicle and support it securely on jackstands, then refer to Chapter 7 and remove the transaxle. If it's leaking, now would be a very good time to replace the front pump seal/O-ring (automatic transaxle only).

2   Remove the pressure plate and clutch disc (see Chapter 8) (manual transaxle equipped vehicles). Now is a good time to check/replace the clutch components and pilot bearing.

3   Make alignment marks on the flywheel/driveplate and crankshaft **(see illustration)** to ensure correct alignment during reinstallation.

13.15 Before attaching the oil pick-up tube assembly, lubricate the new O-ring and install it in the oil pump

14.3 It isn't necessary to mark the crankshaft and flywheel if the bolts are arranged in a staggered pattern - note the two bolts (arrows) are spaced much farther apart than the others

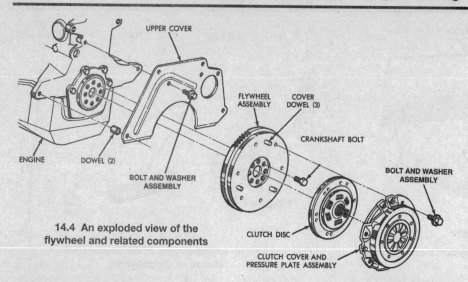

14.4 An exploded view of the flywheel and related components

15.4 Carefully pry the seal from the retainer

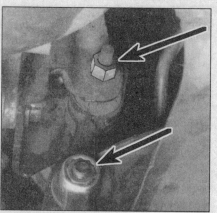

16.4a Remove the bolts and nuts that hold the rear strut onto the crossmember and the engine

4   Remove the bolts that secure the fly-wheel/driveplate to the crankshaft (see illus-tration). If the crankshaft turns, wedge a screwdriver through the starter opening to jam the flywheel.

5   Remove the flywheel/driveplate from the crankshaft. Since the flywheel is fairly heavy, be sure to support it while removing the last bolt.

6   Clean the flywheel to remove grease and oil. Inspect the surface for cracks, rivet grooves, burned areas and score marks. Light scoring can be removed with emery cloth. Check for cracked and broken ring gear teeth. Lay the flywheel on a flat surface and use a straightedge to check for warpage.

7   Clean and inspect the mating surfaces of the flywheel/driveplate and the crankshaft. If the crankshaft rear seal is leaking, replace it before reinstalling the flywheel/driveplate.

Installation

8   Position the flywheel/driveplate against the crankshaft. Be sure to align the marks made during removal. Note: *Some engines have an alignment dowel or staggered bolt holes to ensure correct installation. Before installing the bolts, apply thread locking com-pound to the threads.*

9   Wedge a screwdriver through the starter motor opening to keep the flywheel/drive-plate from turning as you tighten the bolts to the torque listed in this Chapter's Specifica-tions.

10   The remainder of installation is the reverse of the removal procedure.

15   Rear main oil seal - replacement

Refer to illustration 15.4

1   Remove the transaxle (see Chapter 7).

2   If the vehicle has a manual transaxle, remove the clutch and flywheel (see Chap-ter 8 and Section 14 of this Chapter).

3   If the vehicle has an automatic trans-axle, remove the driveplate (see Section 14).

4   Pry the oil seal from the retainer with a screwdriver (see illustration). Be careful not to nick or scratch the crankshaft or the seal retainer bore. Thoroughly clean the seal bore in the seal housing with a shop towel. Remove all traces of oil and dirt.

5   Lubricate the lips of the new seal with engine oil or multi-purpose grease. Install the seal over the end of the crankshaft (make sure the lips of the seal point toward the

engine) and carefully tap it into place with a plastic hammer.

6   Install the driveplate or flywheel (see Section 14) and clutch (see Chapter 8).

7   Install the transaxle (see Chapter 7).

16   Engine mounts - check, replacement and adjustment

1   Engine mounts seldom require atten-tion, but broken or deteriorated mounts should be replaced immediately or the added strain placed on the driveline components may cause damage or wear.

Check

Refer to illustrations 16.4a, 16.4b, 16.4c, 16.4d and 16.4e

2   During the check, the engine must be raised slightly to remove the weight from the mounts.

3   Raise the vehicle and support it securely on jackstands, then position a jack under the engine oil pan. Place a large block of wood between the jack head and the oil pan, then carefully raise the engine just enough to take the weight off the mounts. Warning: *DO NOT place any part of your body under the engine when it's supported only by a jack!*

4   Check the mount insulators (see illus-trations) to see if the rubber is cracked, hardened or separated from the metal plates. Sometimes the rubber will split right down the center.

5   Check for relative movement between the mount plates and the engine or frame (use a large screwdriver or prybar to attempt to move the mounts). If movement is noted, lower the engine and tighten the mount fas-teners.

6   Rubber preservative should be applied to the insulators to slow deterioration.

Replacement

7   Disconnect the negative battery cable from the battery, then raise the vehicle and support it securely on jackstands (if not already done).

8   Remove the fasteners and detach the insulator from the frame bracket.

9   Raise the engine slightly with a jack or hoist. Remove the insulator-to-engine bolts and detach the insulator.

10   Installation is the reverse of removal. Use thread locking compound on the mount bolts and be sure to tighten them securely.

Adjustment

Refer to illustration 16.15

11   The right and left engine mounts are adjustable to allow drivetrain movement in relation to driveaxle assembly length (see Chapter 8).

12   Always adjust the mounts when:

a) *You service the driveaxles.*

b) *The vehicle sustains front end structural damage.*

c) *You replace an mount.*

13   Remove the load on the engine mounts by carefully supporting the engine and transaxle assembly with a floor jack.
14   Loosen the right insulator vertical fasteners and the front engine mount bracket-to-front crossmember bolts and nuts.
15   The left engine mount insulator is sleeved over the shaft and long support bolt **(see illustration)** to provide lateral movement adjustment.
16   Pry the engine right or left as required to achieve the proper driveaxle length (see Chapter 8).
17   Tighten the right engine mount insulator vertical bolts securely, tighten the front engine mount bolts and nuts securely and center the left engine mount insulator.
18   Recheck the driveaxle length.

17 Valve spring, retainer and seals - replacement

Refer to illustrations 17.9, 17.15 and 17.17
Note: *Broken valve springs and defective valve stem seals can be replaced without removing the cylinder heads. Two special tools and a compressed air source are nor-*

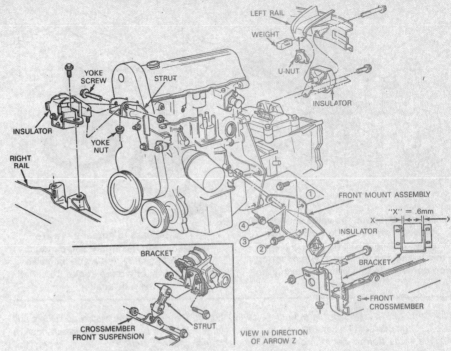

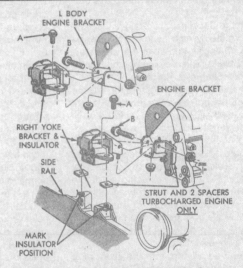

16.4b An exploded view of typical engine mounts

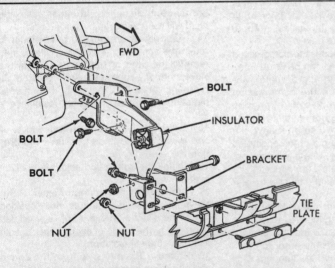

16.4c An exploded view of a typical front engine mount

16.4d An exploded view of a typical right engine mount

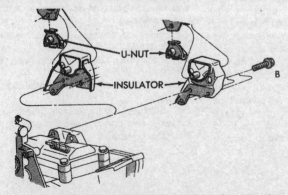

16.4e An exploded view of a typical left engine mount

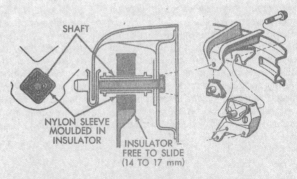

16.15 Cutaway view of the left insulator sleeve assembly

2A

17.9 Using this tool, the valve springs can be depressed and the rocker arms removed without removing the camshaft - this is also the preferred type of spring compressor to use when removing the valve keepers

17.15 Be sure to note if there are differences in the intake and exhaust valve stem seals - use a special valve stem seal tool or a deep socket to install the new seal(s)

17.17 Apply a small dab of grease to each keeper before installation to hold it in place on the valve stem until the spring compressor is released

mally required to perform this operation, so read through this Section carefully and rent or buy the tools before beginning the job. If compressed air isn't available, a length of nylon rope can be used to keep the valves from falling into the cylinder during this procedure.

1   Refer to Section 4 and remove the valve cover from the cylinder head. If you're working on a V6 engine and all of the valve stem seals are being replaced, remove both valve covers (see Chapter 2, Part B).

2   Remove the spark plug from the cylinder which has the defective component. If all of the valve stem seals are being replaced, all of the spark plugs should be removed.

3   Turn the crankshaft until the piston in the affected cylinder is at top dead center on the compression stroke (refer to Section 3 for instructions). If you're replacing all of the valve stem seals, begin with cylinder number one and work on the valves for one cylinder at a time. Move from cylinder-to-cylinder following the firing order sequence (see this Chapter's Specifications).

4   Thread an adapter into the spark plug hole and connect an air hose from a compressed air source to it. Most auto parts stores can supply the air hose adapter. **Note:** *Many cylinder compression gauges utilize a screw-in fitting that may work with your air hose quick-disconnect fitting.*

5   Remove the rocker arm (see Section 10) for the valve with the defective part. If all of the valve stem seals are being replaced, all of the rocker arms should be removed.

6   Apply compressed air to the cylinder. **Warning:** *The piston may be forced down by compressed air, causing the crankshaft to turn suddenly. If the wrench used when posi-*

tioning the number one piston at TDC is still attached to the bolt in the crankshaft nose, it could cause damage or injury when the crankshaft moves.

7   The valves should be held in place by the air pressure. If the valve faces or seats are in poor condition, leaks may prevent air pressure from retaining the valves - refer to the alternative procedure below.

8   If you don't have access to compressed air, an alternative method can be used. Position the piston at a point approximately 45-degrees before TDC on the compression stroke, then feed a long piece of nylon rope through the spark plug hole until it fills the combustion chamber. Be sure to leave the end of the rope hanging out of the engine so it can be removed easily. Use a large ratchet and socket to rotate the crankshaft in the normal direction of rotation until slight resistance is felt.

9   Stuff shop rags into the cylinder head holes around the valve spring area to prevent parts and tools from falling into the engine, then use a valve spring compressor to compress the spring. Remove the keepers with small needle-nose pliers or a magnet **(see illustration).**

10   Remove the spring retainer, shield and valve spring, then remove the umbrella type guide seal. **Note:** *If air pressure fails to hold the valve in the closed position during this operation, the valve face or seat is probably damaged. If so, the cylinder head will have to be removed for additional repair operations.*

11   Wrap a rubber band or tape around the top of the valve stem so the valve won't fall into the combustion chamber, then release the air pressure. **Note:** *If a rope was used instead of air pressure, turn the crankshaft*

slightly in the direction opposite normal rotation.

12   Inspect the valve stem for damage. Rotate the valve in the guide and check the end for eccentric movement, which would indicate that the valve is bent.

13   Move the valve up-and-down in the guide and make sure it doesn't bind. If the valve stem binds, either the valve is bent or the guide is damaged. In either case, the head will have to be removed for repair.

14   Reapply air pressure to the cylinder to retain the valve in the closed position, then remove the tape or rubber band from the valve stem. If a rope was used instead of air pressure, rotate the crankshaft in the normal direction of rotation until slight resistance is felt.

15   Lubricate the valve stem with engine oil and install a new guide seal **(see illustration).**

16   Install the spring and shield in position over the valve.

17   Install the valve spring retainer. Compress the valve spring and carefully position the keepers in the groove. Apply a small dab of grease to the inside of each keeper to hold it in place **(see illustration).**

18   Remove the pressure from the spring tool and make sure the keepers are seated.

19   Disconnect the air hose and remove the adapter from the spark plug hole. If a rope was used in place of air pressure, pull it out of the cylinder.

20   Refer to Section 10 and install the rocker arm(s).

21   Install the spark plug(s) and hook up the wire(s).

22   Refer to Section 4 and install the valve cover(s).

23   Start and run the engine, then check for oil leaks and unusual sounds coming from the valve cover area.

Chapter 2 Part B
3.0L V6 engine

Contents

Specifications

General

Displacement	181 cubic inches
Compression ratio	8.85:1
Firing order	1-2-3-4-5-6
Cylinder numbers (drivebelt end-to-transaxle end)	
Rear (firewall side)	1-3-5
Front (radiator side)	2-4-6

Camshaft and related components

Camshaft runout limit	0.004 inch
Lobe height	1.624 inch
Lobe wear limit	0.02 inch

Oil pump

Case-to-outer rotor clearance	0.004 to 0.007 inch
Rotor end clearance	0.0015 to 0.0035 inch
Case-to-inner rotor clearance	0.0010 to 0.0028 inch

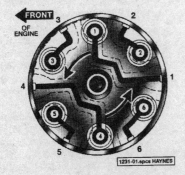

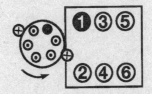

The blackened terminal shown on the distributor cap indicates the Number One spark plug wire position

Cylinder location and distributor rotation

Torque specifications

	Ft-lbs (unless otherwise indicated)
Rocker arm shaft bolts	180 in-lbs
Intake manifold nuts/bolts	174 in-lbs
Distributor drive adapter bolts	130 in-lbs
Engine mounts (see illustration 21.1)	
A	125
B	00
C	75
D	50
E	40
F	16
G	16
Exhaust manifold nuts	175 in-lbs
Exhaust manifold heat shield bolts	130 in-lbs
Exhaust pipe-to-manifold bolts	21
Exhaust crossover pipe bolts	51
Crankshaft pulley-to-crankshaft bolt	112
Camshaft sprocket bolt	70
Timing belt cover (see Section 10)	
A (M6 X 20)	115 in-lbs
B (M6 X 55)	115 in-lbs
C (M6 X 25)	115 in-lbs
D (M6 X 10)	115 in-lbs
Timing belt tensioner locking bolt	21
Cylinder head bolts	70
Flywheel/driveplate mounting bolts*	72 to 80
Oil pan mounting bolts	50 in-lbs
Oil pump assembly mounting bolts	130 in-lbs
Oil pump relief plug	36
Oil pick-up tube-to-pump bolts	191 in-lbs
Oil pump cover bolts	104 in-lbs
Valve cover bolts	88 in-lbs

*Apply a thread locking compound to the threads prior to installation

1   General information

This Part of Chapter 2 is devoted to in-vehicle repair procedures for the 3.0L V6 engine. All information concerning engine removal and installation and engine block and cylinder head overhaul can be found in Part C of this Chapter.

The following repair procedures are based on the assumption that the engine is installed in the vehicle. If the engine has been removed from the vehicle and mounted on a stand, many of the steps outlined in this Part of Chapter 2 will not apply.

The Specifications included in this Part of Chapter 2 apply only to the procedures contained in this Part. Part C of Chapter 2 contains the Specifications necessary for cylinder head and engine block rebuilding.

The 60-degree V6 has a cast iron block and aluminum heads with a camshaft in each head. The block has thin-walled sections for light weight. A "cradle frame" main bearing casting - the main bearing caps are cast as a unit, with a bridge, or truss, connecting them - supports the cast ductile iron crankshaft.

Both camshafts are driven off the crankshaft by a cog belt. A spring loaded tensioner, adjusted by an eccentric type locknut, maintains belt tension. Each camshaft actuates two valves per cylinder through hydraulic lash adjusters and shaft-mounted forged aluminum rocker arms.

Each cast aluminum three-ring piston has two compression rings and a three-piece oil control ring. The piston pins are pressed into forged steel connecting rods. The flat-topped pistons produce a 8.85:1 compression ratio.

The distributor, which is mounted on the drivebelt end of the front cylinder head, is driven by a helical gear on the camshaft. The water pump, which is bolted to the timing belt end of the block, is driven off the crankshaft by a drivebelt and pulley. The gear type oil pump is mounted in the oil pump case and attached to the timing belt cover. It is driven by the crankshaft.

From the oil pump, oil travels through the filter to the main oil gallery, from which it is routed either directly to the main bearings, crankshaft, connecting rod bearings and pistons and cylinder walls or to the cylinder heads.

2   Repair operations possible with the engine in the vehicle

Many major repair operations can be accomplished without removing the engine from the vehicle.

Clean the engine compartment and the exterior of the engine with some type of degreaser before any work is done. It will make the job easier and help keep dirt out of the internal areas of the engine.

Depending on the components involved, it may be helpful to remove the hood to improve access to the engine as repairs are performed (refer to Chapter 11 if necessary). Cover the fenders to prevent damage to the paint. Special pads are available, but an old bedspread or blanket will also work.

If vacuum, exhaust, oil or coolant leaks develop, indicating a need for gasket or seal replacement, the repairs can generally be made with the engine in the vehicle. The intake and exhaust manifold gaskets, oil pan gasket, camshaft and crankshaft oil seals and cylinder head gaskets are all accessible with the engine in place.

Exterior engine components, such as the intake and exhaust manifolds, the oil pan (and the oil pump), the water pump, the starter motor, the alternator, the distributor and the fuel system components can be removed for repair with the engine in place.

Since the cylinder heads can be removed without pulling the engine, camshaft and valve component servicing can also be accomplished with the engine in the vehicle. Replacement of the timing belt and sprockets is also possible with the engine in the vehicle.

In extreme cases caused by a lack of necessary equipment, repair or replacement of piston rings, pistons, connecting rods and rod bearings is possible with the engine in the vehicle. However, this practice is not recommended because of the cleaning and preparation work that must be done to the components involved.

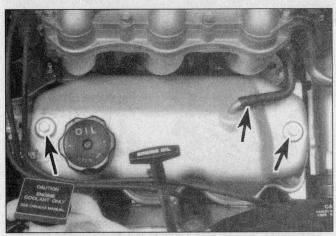

4.3 To remove the front (radiator side) valve cover, the breather hose and the spark plug wires, then remove the two cover retaining bolts and washers

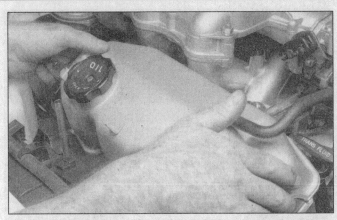

4.7 Try to break the valve cover loose with your hands - if it's stuck to the head, try to jar it loose with a block of wood and a hammer or slip a flexible putty knife between the head and cover to break the gasket seal; don't pry at the cover-to-head joint or you may damage the sealing surfaces (which will cause an oil leak)

3 Top Dead Center (TDC) for number one piston - locating

Note: *The following procedure is based on the assumption that the spark plug wires and distributor are correctly installed. If you are trying to locate TDC to install the distributor correctly, piston position must be determined by feeling for compression at the number one spark plug hole as the crankshaft is slowly turned clockwise, then aligning the ignition timing marks as described in Step 8.3.*

1   Top Dead Center (TDC) is the highest point in the cylinder that each piston reaches as it travels up-and-down when the crankshaft turns. Each piston reaches TDC on the compression stroke and again on the exhaust stroke, but TDC generally refers to piston position on the compression stroke.

2   Positioning the piston(s) at TDC is an essential part of many procedures such as camshaft and timing belt/sprocket removal and distributor removal.

3   Before beginning this procedure, be sure to place the transmission in Neutral and apply the parking brake or block the rear wheels. Also, disable the ignition system by detaching the coil wire from the terminal marked 'C' on the distributor cap and grounding it on the block with a jumper wire. Remove the spark plugs (see Chapter 1).

4   In order to bring any piston to TDC, the crankshaft must be turned using one of the methods outlined below. When looking at the drivebelt end of the engine, normal crankshaft rotation is clockwise.

  a) *The preferred method is to turn the crankshaft with a socket and ratchet attached to the bolt threaded into the front of the crankshaft.*

  b) *A remote starter switch, which may save some time, can also be used. Follow the instructions included with the switch. Once the piston is close to TDC, use a socket and ratchet as described in the previous paragraph.*

  c) *If an assistant is available to turn the ignition switch to the Start position in short bursts, you can get the piston close to TDC without a remote starter switch. Make sure your assistant is out of the vehicle, away from the ignition switch, then use a socket and ratchet as described in Paragraph a) to complete the procedure.*

5   Note the position of the terminal for the number one spark plug wire on the distributor cap. If the terminal isn't marked, follow the plug wire from the number one cylinder spark plug to the cap.

6   Use a felt-tip pen or chalk to make a mark on the distributor body directly under the terminal.

7   Detach the cap from the distributor and set it aside (see Chapter 1 if necessary).

8   Turn the crankshaft (see Step 3 above) until the "0" notch in the crankshaft pulley is aligned with the timing indicator (located at the front of the engine).

9   Look at the distributor rotor - it should be pointing directly at the mark you made on the distributor body. If it is, go to Step 12.

10   If the rotor is 180-degrees off, the number one piston is at TDC on the exhaust stroke - proceed to the next Step.

11   To get the piston to TDC on the compression stroke, turn the crankshaft one complete turn (360-degrees) clockwise. The rotor should now be pointing at the mark on the distributor. When the rotor is pointing at the number one spark plug wire terminal inside the distributor cap and the ignition timing marks are aligned, the number one piston is at TDC on the compression stroke.

12   After the number one piston has been positioned at TDC on the compression stroke, TDC for any of the remaining pistons can be located by turning the crankshaft and following the firing order.

13   Mark the remaining spark plug wire terminal locations on the distributor body just like you did for the number one terminal, then number the marks to correspond with the cylinder numbers. As you turn the crankshaft, the rotor will also turn. When it's pointing directly at one of the marks on the distributor, the piston for that particular cylinder is at TDC on the compression stroke.

4 Valve covers - removal and installation

1   Relieve the fuel system pressure (see Chapter 4).

2   Disconnect the negative cable from the battery.

Removal

Front (radiator side) cover

Refer to illustrations 4.3 and 4.7

3   Detach the breather hose by sliding back the hose clamp (if equipped) and pulling the hose off the fitting on the valve cover **(see illustration)**.

4   Remove the spark plug wires from the spark plugs. Mark them clearly with pieces of masking tape to prevent confusion during installation.

5   Remove the wires and hoses attached to the valve cover.

6   Remove the valve cover bolts and washers.

7   Detach the valve cover **(see illustration)**. **Caution:** *If the cover is stuck to the head, bump one end with a block of wood and a hammer to jar it loose. If that doesn't work, try to slip a flexible putty knife between the head and cover to break the gasket seal. Don't pry at the cover-to-head joint or damage to the sealing surfaces may occur (leading to oil leaks in the future).*

Rear (firewall side) cover

Refer to illustration 4.12

8   Detach the breather hose from the cover.

9   Tag and detach the spark plug wires.

10   Loosen the front alternator mounting

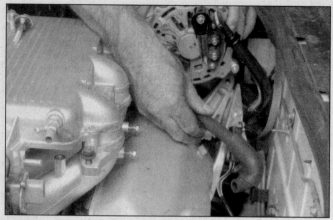

4.12 The rear valve cover is a little trickier to remove because of its close proximity to the intake plenum, the alternator and the firewall - but if you swing the alternator up like this, you can work the cover off without removing the plenum/intake assembly

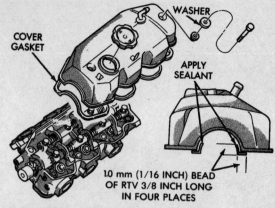

4.15 It isn't necessary to use RTV gasket sealant on the inside of the gasket if the gasket is a tight fit and doesn't budge once it's installed inside the valve cover - but it IS necessary to apply RTV to the edge (arrows) on the outside of the gasket where it mates with the camshaft seal

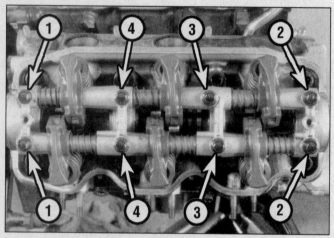

5.2 Loosen the bolts for the rocker arm shafts a little at a time in the sequence shown

5.4a Before you lift the rocker assembly off the head, make sure you tape the hydraulic lash adjusters into their respective bores in the tips of the rocker arms, or they'll fall out when you remove the rockers

bolt and nut, remove the rear bolt and nut and pivot the alternator up and forward to clear the valve cover (see Chapter 5).

11   Remove the valve cover bolts and washers.

12   Lift off the valve cover (see illustration). Read the Caution in Step 7.

Installation

Refer to illustration 4.15

13   The mating surfaces of each cylinder head and valve cover must be perfectly clean when the covers are installed. Use a gasket scraper to remove all traces of sealant and old gasket material, then clean the mating surfaces with lacquer thinner or acetone. If there's sealant or oil on the mating surfaces when the cover is installed, oil leaks may develop.

14   If necessary, clean the mounting screw threads with a die to remove any corrosion and restore damaged threads. Make sure the threaded holes in the head are clean - run a tap into them to remove corrosion and restore damaged threads.

15   The gaskets should be mated to the covers before the covers are installed. Apply a bead of RTV sealant to the cover in the areas indicated (see illustration), then position the gasket inside the cover and allow the sealant to set up so the gasket adheres to the cover. If the sealant isn't allowed to set, the gasket may fall out of the cover as it's installed on the engine.

16   Carefully position the cover on the head and install the bolts.

17   Tighten the bolts in three or four steps to the torque listed in this Chapter's Specifications.

18   The remaining installation steps are the reverse of removal.

19   Start the engine and check carefully for oil leaks as the engine warms up.

5   Rocker arm components - removal and installation

Refer to illustrations 5.2, 5.4a, 5.4b, 5.4c, 5.5a, 5.5b and 5.5c

1   Position the engine at TDC compression for the number 1 cylinder (see Section 3).

Remove the valve cover (see Section 4).

2   Loosen the rocker arm shaft bolts (see illustration) in two or three stages, working your way from the ends toward the middle of the shafts. **Caution:** *Some of the valves will be open when you loosen the rocker arm shaft bolts and the rocker arm shafts will be under a certain amount of valve spring pressure. Therefore, the bolts must be loosened gradually. Loosening a bolt all at once near a rocker arm under spring pressure could bend or break the rocker arm shaft.*

3   Prior to removal, scribe or paint identifying marks on the rockers to ensure they will be installed in their original locations. Wrap the ends of the rockers arms with tape to prevent the hydraulic lash adjusters from falling out when the rockers are removed.

4   Remove the bolts and lift off the rocker arm shaft assemblies (see illustration). Lay them down on a nearby workbench in the same relationship to each other that they're in when installed (see illustration). They must be reinstalled on the same cylinder head. Note the location of the stamped bearing cap number and the position of the

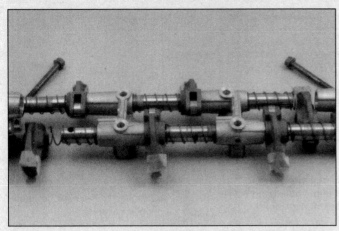

5.4b The rocker assembly is spring-loaded, so it pops apart when you remove it from the cylinder head; so, it's a good idea to set the assembly on a clean surface with all the parts in order

5.4c A numeral ("1," "2," etc..) should be stamped on each bearing cap, listing its position on the head (center arrow) (if the number's missing, mark one with a scribe or punch) - also note the flat space (left and right arrows); when you reassemble the rocker assembly, position the flats as shown

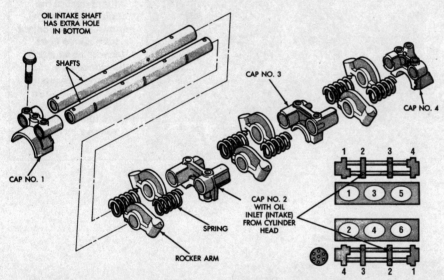

5.5a An exploded view of the rocker arm assembly - note that bearing cap #2 on each head *must* be in the proper position to ensure that the rocker assembly gets oil from the galley in each head directly below the #2 cap

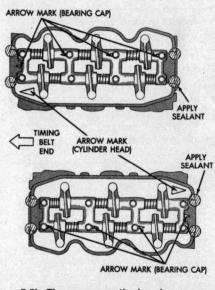

5.5b The arrows on the bearing caps should point in the same direction as the arrows on the cylinder heads

notches **(see illustration)**.

5   Installation is the reverse of the removal procedure **(see illustration)**. Note: *Be sure the arrows stamped into the cylinder head and the bearing caps **(see illustration)** are pointing in the same direction. Tighten the rocker arm shaft bolts, in several steps, to the torque listed in this Chapter's Specifications. Work from the ends of the shafts toward the middle - the reverse of the order in which you loosened the rocker arm shaft bolts in Step 2* **(see illustration)**.

6   Hydraulic lash adjusters - check, removal and installation

Check

Refer to illustration 6.1

1   Check the hydraulic lash adjusters for

5.5c Using an inch-pound torque wrench, tighten the rocker arm assembly bolt pairs in the exact opposite order in which you loosened them

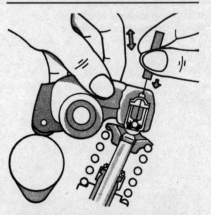

6.1 When performing the freeplay test, make sure the adjuster that's being tested has the corresponding camshaft lobe pointing away from the rocker arm (closed valve)

freeplay by inserting a small wire through the air bleed hole in the rocker arm while lightly pushing the check ball down **(see illustration)**.
2   While lightly holding the check ball down, move the rocker arm up and down to check for freeplay. There should be a small amount of movement. If there is no freeplay, replace the adjuster with a new unit.

Removal and installation

Refer to illustration 6.4

3   Remove the valve cover(s) (see Section 4) and the rocker arm shaft components (see Section 5).
4   Pull the hydraulic lash adjuster(s) out of the rocker arm(s) **(see illustration)**. Note: *Be sure to label each rocker arm and adjuster and place them in a partitioned box or something suitable to keep them from getting mixed with each other.*
5   Installation is the reverse of removal.

7   Intake manifold - removal and installation

Removal

Refer to illustrations 7.10 and 7.11

1   Relieve the fuel system pressure (see Chapter 4).
2   Disconnect the cable from the negative terminal of the battery.

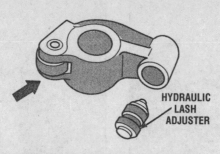

6.4 The hydraulic lash adjusters are precision units installed in the machined openings in the rocker arm assembly

HYDRAULIC LASH ADJUSTER

7.10 Location of the MAP sensor bracket bolts (arrows)

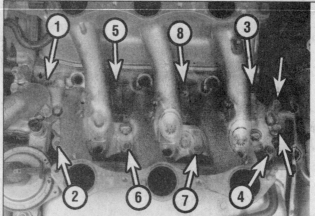

7.11 To remove the intake manifold, detach the PCV valve hose (right next to the coolant tube flange), remove the two coolant tube flange bolts (arrows at far right) then loosen the eight nuts in the sequence shown, in 1/4-turn increments, until they're loose enough to remove by hand

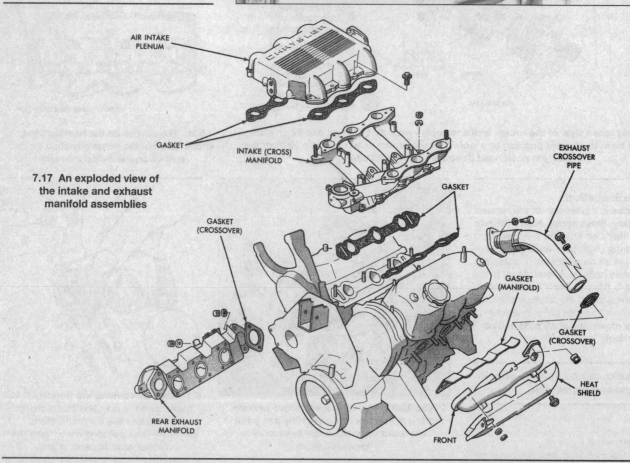

AIR INTAKE PLENUM

GASKET

INTAKE (CROSS) MANIFOLD

GASKET

GASKET (CROSSOVER)

7.17 An exploded view of the intake and exhaust manifold assemblies

GASKET

EXHAUST CROSSOVER PIPE

GASKET (MANIFOLD)

GASKET (CROSSOVER)

HEAT SHIELD

REAR EXHAUST MANIFOLD

FRONT

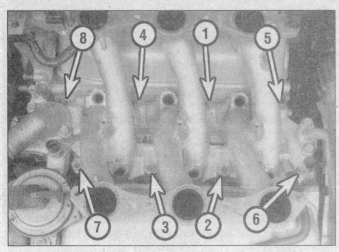

7.20 Nut tightening sequence for the intake manifold

8.5 If you're removing the front exhaust manifold, remove the bolts from the front flange of the crossover pipe (left arrow); if you're removing the rear manifold, remove the bolts from the rear flange (right arrow); If you're removing both manifolds, remove all the bolts (only the upper flange bolts are visible in this photo)

3   Drain the cooling system (don't forget to drain the cylinder block) (see Chapter 1).
4   Remove the air cleaner assembly (see Chapter 4).
5   Disconnect the coil high tension spark plug lead and the three spark plug leads to the rear cylinder (see Chapter 1) - they're in the way of the bolt at the right rear corner of the plenum.
6   Remove the coil assembly (see Chapter 5).
7   Disconnect the accelerator cable and the TV cable from the throttle body (see Chapter 4).
8   Remove the air intake plenum and the throttle body as a single assembly (see Chapter 4). It's unnecessary to separate the two parts.
9   Remove the fuel injectors (see Chapter 4).
10   Remove the MAP sensor bracket bolts (see illustration).
11   Detach the PCV valve hose (see illustration).
12   Remove the coolant tube flange bolts.
13   Loosen the manifold retaining nuts in 1/4-turn increments until they can be removed by hand. Loosen the outer nuts first, then the inner nuts. Remove the washers.
14   The manifold will probably be stuck to the cylinder heads and force may be required to break the gasket seal. **Caution:** *Don't pry between the manifold and the heads or damage to the gasket sealing surfaces may occur, leading to vacuum leaks.*

Installation
Refer to illustrations 7.17 and 7.20
Note: *The mating surfaces of the cylinder heads and manifold must be perfectly clean when the manifold is installed. Gasket removal solvents in aerosol cans are available at most auto parts stores and may be helpful when removing old gasket material that's stuck to the heads and manifold (since they're made of aluminum, aggressive scraping can cause damage). Be sure to follow the directions printed on the container.*
15   Use a gasket scraper to remove all

traces of sealant and old gasket material, then clean the mating surfaces with lacquer thinner or acetone. If there's old sealant or oil on the mating surfaces when the manifold is installed, oil or vacuum leaks may develop. Use a vacuum cleaner to remove any material that falls into the intake ports in the heads.
16   Use a tap of the correct size to chase the threads in the bolt holes, then use compressed air (if available) to remove the debris from the holes. **Warning:** *Wear safety glasses or a face shield to protect your eyes when using compressed air!*
17   Position the gaskets on the cylinder heads (see illustration). No sealant is required, but make sure the beaded sealant side is facing up.
18   If you're installing a new intake manifold, remove the coolant temperature sending unit (single-wire connector) and coolant temperature sensor (two-wire connector) from the old manifold and install them in the new unit. Be sure to coat the threads with Teflon tape or thread sealant. Also remove the PCV valve, check it (see Chapter 1) and install it in the new manifold (see Chapter 1).
19   Make sure all intake port openings, coolant passage holes and bolt holes are aligned correctly, then carefully set the manifold in place. Be careful not to disturb the gaskets.

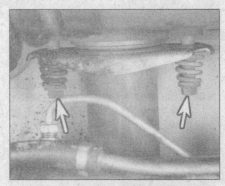

8.6 If you're removing the rear exhaust manifold, remove the exhaust pipe flange bolts

20   Install the washers and nuts and tighten them in the recommended sequence **(see illustration)** to the torque listed in this Chapter's Specifications. Work up to the final torque in two steps.
21   Coat the coolant tube flange gasket with sealant, place it on the flange, place the flange in position, install the flange bolts and tighten them securely.
22   Install the MAP sensor bracket bolts and tighten them securely.
23   The remainder of installation is the reverse of removal. Start the engine and check carefully for oil and coolant leaks at the intake manifold joints.

8   Exhaust manifolds - removal and installation

Refer to illustrations 8.5, 8.6, 8.8, 8.9a, 8.9b, 8.9c, 8.12a and 8.12b
Warning: *Let the engine cool completely before this procedure is performed.*

Removal
1   Disconnect the negative cable from the battery. Raise the vehicle and support it securely on jackstands.
2   Spray penetrating oil on the exhaust manifold fasteners and allow it to soak in.
3   If you're removing the front exhaust manifold, remove the coolant reservoir (see Chapter 3) and the dipstick tube (follow the tube down the front of the block and you'll find a single bracket bolt securing the tube to the block).
4   If you're removing the rear exhaust manifold, remove the air cleaner assembly and the intake ducting (see Chapter 4).
5   Remove the bolts and nuts that attach the flange(s) of the crossover pipe to the front and/or rear exhaust manifold(s) **(see illustration)**.
6   If you're removing the rear exhaust manifold, disconnect the exhaust pipe flange bolts **(see illustration)**.

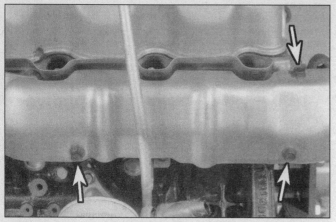

8.8 If you're removing the front exhaust manifold, remove the dipstick tube (see next illustration) and the heat shield bolts (arrows)

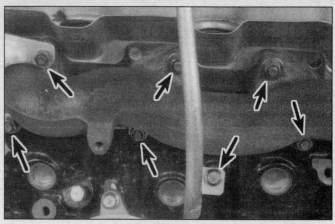

8.9a Front exhaust manifold bolts and dipstick tube bracket bolt (arrows)

8.9b Rear exhaust manifold lower bolts (arrows) . . .

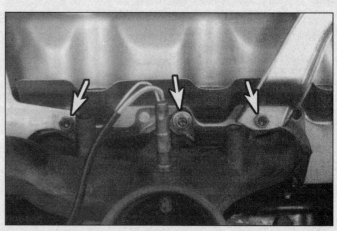

8.9c . . . and upper bolts (arrows)

7   If you're removing the rear exhaust manifold, disconnect the EGR tube (see Chapter 6).

8   If you're removing the front exhaust manifold, remove the three heat shield bolts **(see illustration)** and remove the shield.

9   Remove the exhaust manifold(s) and gasket(s) **(see illustrations)**.

10   Carefully inspect the manifold(s) and fasteners for cracks and damage.

11   Use a scraper to remove all traces of old gasket material and carbon deposits from the manifold and cylinder head mating surfaces. If the gasket was leaking, have the manifold checked for warpage at an automotive machine shop and resurfaced if necessary.

Installation

12   Position the new gasket(s) over the cylinder head studs. **Note:** *Install the gasket with the numbers 1-3-5 on the top onto the rear bank (cylinder head) and install the gasket with the numbers 2-4-6 onto the front bank (cylinder head)* **(see illustrations)**.

13   Install the manifold and thread the

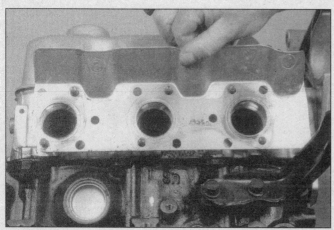

8.12a Install a new steel exhaust manifold gasket onto the manifold studs (rear gasket shown, front gasket similar)

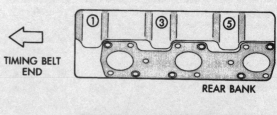

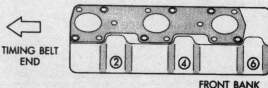

8.12b Be sure to install the correct exhaust manifold gasket onto the corresponding cylinder head

9.4a To remove the two-piece pulley from the vibration damper, remove these bolts (arrow); then remove the large center bolt and use a puller to remove the damper

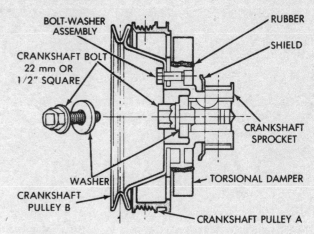

9.4b This cross-section view shows the relationship between the two pulley halves and the vibration damper - note the keyway (half-moon piece) which locks the damper onto the nose of the crankshaft

mounting nuts into place.

14   Working from the center out, tighten the nuts to the torque listed in this Chapter's Specifications in three or four equal steps.

15   Reinstall the remaining parts in the reverse order of removal. Use new gaskets when connecting the exhaust crossover pipe to the exhaust manifold(s).

16   Run the engine and check for exhaust leaks.

9   Crankshaft pulley/vibration damper - removal and installation

Removal

Refer to illustrations 9.4a, 9.4b, 9.5a and 9.5b

1   Disconnect the negative cable from the battery.

2   Loosen the lug nuts of the right front wheel, raise the front of the vehicle and support it securely on jackstands. Remove the wheel. Remove the right inner splash shield **(see illustration 6.5 in Chapter 2, Part A)**.

3   Remove the accessory drivebelts (see Chapter 1).

4   Remove the bolts **(see illustration)** attaching the pulley to the vibration damper and remove the pulley. **Note:** *The crankshaft pulley is actually a two-piece design* **(see illustration)**.

5   Wrap a cloth around the vibration damper to protect the belt surface and attach a chain wrench to the pulley. Hold the crankshaft from turning and use a socket wrench to loosen the damper bolt. If you don't have a chain wrench, make a crank holding tool with a piece of angle iron and a couple of bolts of the correct diameter and thread pitch, drill a couple of holes in the angle iron the same distance apart as any two holes in the crank pulley, insert the bolts through the angle iron and thread them into the pulley holes **(see illustration)**. Or, remove

9.5a If you don't have a chain wrench, you can fabricate a crankshaft holding tool with a piece of angle iron and a couple of bolts of the same thread pitch and diameter as the holes in the crankshaft pulley . . .

the flywheel/driveplate cover **(see illustration)** and lock the crank by jamming a screwdriver between the ring gear teeth and the bellhousing.

6   Remove the vibration damper. If it's stuck, install a vibration damper/steering wheel puller onto the damper and pull it off the nose of the crankshaft.

Installation

7   Lightly lubricate the seal contact surface with engine oil and position it on the nose of the crankshaft. Align the keyway in the pulley with the key in the crankshaft and push the pulley into place by hand. If necessary, tap lightly on the damper using a block of wood and a hammer.

8   Prevent the crankshaft from turning as described in Step 5, then install the bolt and tighten it to the torque listed in this Chapter's Specifications.

9   Reinstall the remaining parts in the reverse order of removal.

9.5b . . . or remove the flywheel/driveplate cover and immobilize the crank by jamming a large screwdriver between the ring gear and the bellhousing

10   Timing belt - removal, installation and adjustment

Removal

Refer to illustrations 10.5, 10.6a, 10.6b, 10.6c, 10.6d, 10.7, 10.8, 10.10, 10.11, 10.12a, 10.12b, 10.13a, 10.13b, 10.13c, 10.14, 10.16

1   Disconnect the cable from the negative terminal of the battery.

2   Loosen the lug nuts on the right front wheel, raise the front of the vehicle and support it securely on jackstands. Remove the right front wheel. Remove the right inner splash shield **(see illustration 6.5 in Chapter 2, Part A)**.

3   Position the number one piston at TDC on the compression stroke (see Section 3).

4   Remove the drivebelt for the air conditioning compressor and the serpentine belt for the alternator and power steering pump (see Chapter 1).

10.5 Remove the bolts (arrows) and remove the tensioner pulley assembly for the serpentine belt

10.6a Remove these bolts (arrows) and remove the tensioner pulley assembly for the air conditioning compressor drivebelt

10.6b Remove this compressor bracket bolt (arrow), push the compressor and bracket assembly aside and support it with a piece of wire

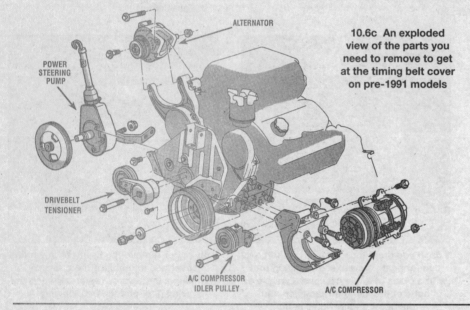

10.6c An exploded view of the parts you need to remove to get at the timing belt cover on pre-1991 models

5   Remove the tensioner pulley assembly for the serpentine belt (see illustration).
6   Remove the tensioner pulley assembly for the compressor drivebelt (see illustration) and the compressor mounting bracket (see illustrations).
7   Remove the bolts from the power steering pump mounting bracket and set the pump and bracket aside (see illustration).
8   Remove the crankshaft pulley and vibration damper (see Section 9). Remove the crankshaft sprocket flange (see illustration). **Note:** *Don't allow the crankshaft to rotate during removal of the pulley. If the crankshaft moves, the number one piston won't be at TDC.*
9   Position a floor jack and a block of wood under the engine oil pan for support.
10   Scribe or mark the relationship of the engine support assembly to the engine bracket, then remove the right engine mount

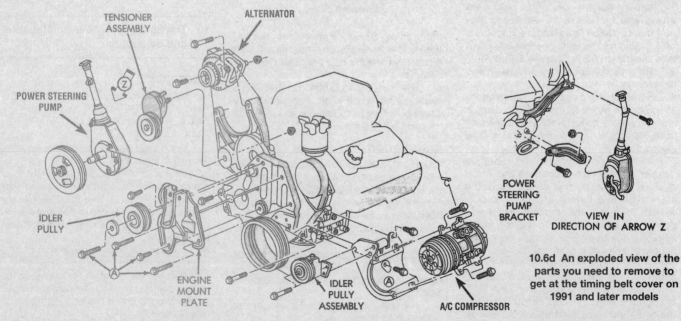

10.6d An exploded view of the parts you need to remove to get at the timing belt cover on 1991 and later models

VIEW IN DIRECTION OF ARROW Z

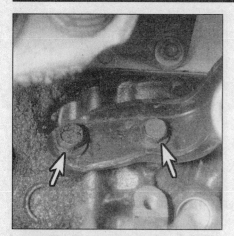

10.7 Remove these two bolts from the power steering pump bracket, swing the pump and bracket assembly aside and support it with a piece of wire

10.8 After you've removed the crankshaft pulley and vibration damper, remove this crankshaft sprocket flange

10.10 To remove the right engine mount, remove the bolts from the engine mount bracket and the vehicle body (arrows)

10.11 Remove these three bolts (arrows) and remove the engine mount bracket

(see illustration).

11   Remove the engine mount bracket **(see illustration).**

12   Remove the timing belt covers **(see**

10.12a You need to remove a total of ten bolts (arrows) to remove the three timing belt covers (not all the bolts are visible in this photo)

2B

illustrations). Note the various type and sizes of bolts by recording a diagram or making specific notes while the timing belt cover is being removed. The bolts must be reinstalled in their original locations.

13   Confirm that the number one piston is still at TDC on the compression stroke by verifying that the timing marks on all three timing belt sprockets are aligned with their respective stationary alignment marks **(see illustrations).**

14   Relieve tension on the timing belt by

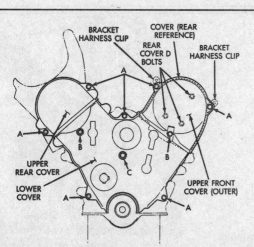

10.12b There are four different lengths of timing belt cover bolts - in this illustration, the bolts are designated as A, B, C, and D, according to their size

10.13a To confirm that the number one piston is still at TDC on the compression stroke, verify that the timing mark on the rear timing belt sprocket . . .

10.13b ... the front timing belt sprocket ...

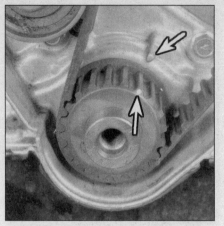

10.13c ... and the crankshaft sprocket are aligned with their respective stationary alignment marks (some models, such as the one shown, don't have a mark on the crankshaft sprocket, so you'll have to make your own)

10.14 To relieve tension on the timing belt, loosen this nut (arrow) on the timing belt tensioner pulley

loosening the nut on the timing belt tensioner pulley **(see illustration)**.

15 Check to see that the timing belt is marked with an arrow as to which side faces out. If there isn't a mark, paint one on (only if the same belt will be reinstalled). Slide the timing belt off the sprockets. Check the condition of the tensioner.

16 Inspect the timing belt **(see illustration)**. Look at the backside (the side without the teeth): If it's cracked or peeling, or it's hard, glossy and inflexible, and leaves no indent when pressed with your fingernail, replace the belt. Now look at the drive side: If any teeth are missing, cracked or excessively worn, replace the belt.

Installation

Refer to illustrations 10.17a and 10.17b

17 Prepare to install the timing belt by prying the tensioner away from the spring to the end of the adjustment slot **(see illustration)**, then temporarily tightening the locking bolt. Make sure the tensioner spring is positioned properly **(see illustration)**.

18 Install the belt on the crankshaft sprocket first, and simultaneously keep the belt tight on the tension side.

19 Install the belt on the front (radiator side) camshaft sprocket and then onto the water pump pulley and finally the rear camshaft sprocket and timing belt tensioner. Be careful not to nudge the camshaft sprocket(s) or crankshaft gear off the timing marks. Install the timing belt with the directional arrow pointing away from the engine.

20 Align the factory-made white lines on the timing belt with the punch mark on each of the camshaft sprockets and the crankshaft sprocket. Make sure all three sets of timing marks are properly aligned **(see illustrations 10.13a, 10.13b and 10.13c)**. Note: *Be sure to install the crankshaft sprocket flange onto the crankshaft gear (see illustration 10.8)*.

Adjustment

Refer to illustrations 10.23 and 10.25

21 Loosen the tensioner nut and let the tensioner assembly spring toward the belt - the

spring tension will automatically apply the proper amount of tension to the belt.

22 Slowly turn the crankshaft clockwise two full revolutions, returning the number one piston to TDC on the compression stroke. **Caution:** *If excessive resistance is felt while turning the crankshaft, it's an indication that the pistons are coming into contact with the*

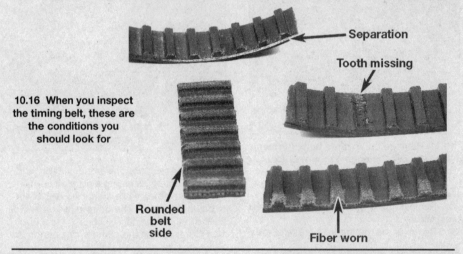

10.16 When you inspect the timing belt, these are the conditions you should look for

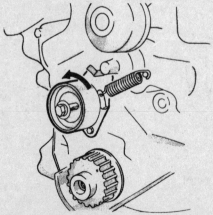

10.17a Before installing the timing belt, rotate the tensioner away from the spring (counterclockwise) to the end of the adjustment slot ...

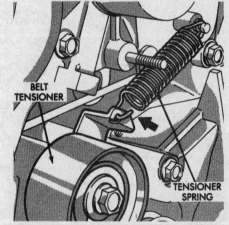

10.17b ... then temporarily tighten the locking bolt with the spring positioned as shown

valves. Go back over the procedure to correct the situation before proceeding.

23 Make sure all the timing marks are still aligned properly **(see illustration)**. Tighten the tensioner bolt to the torque listed in this Chapter's Specifications while keeping the tensioner steady with your hand.

24 Check the deflection of the timing belt by observing the force the tensioner pulley applies to the timing belt. If the belt seems loose, replace the tensioner spring.

25 Install the various components removed during disassembly, referring to the appropriate sections as necessary **(see illustration)**.

11 Crankshaft front oil seal - replacement

Refer to illustrations 11.3, 11.4, 11.7, 11.8a and 11.8b

1 Disconnect the negative cable from the battery.

2 Remove the drivebelts (see Chapter 1), crankshaft pulley and timing belt (see Sections 9 and 10).

3 You should be able to slide the crankshaft sprocket **(see illustration)** off by hand. If the sprocket is stuck, wedge two screwdrivers behind it and carefully pry the sprocket off the crankshaft. Some sprockets are more difficult to remove because corrosion fuses them onto the nose of the crankshaft. If the pulley on your engine is really difficult to pry off, don't damage the oil pump with the screwdrivers. Instead, try the following solution.

4 If the sprocket won't come loose, drill and tap two holes into the face of the sprocket and use a bolt-type puller to slip it off the crankshaft **(see illustration)**. **Caution:** *Do not reuse a drilled sprocket - replace it.*

5 Turn the bolt of the puller until the pulley comes off. Remove the timing belt plate.

6 Carefully pry the oil seal out with a screwdriver or seal removal tool. Don't scratch or nick the crankshaft in the process!

2B

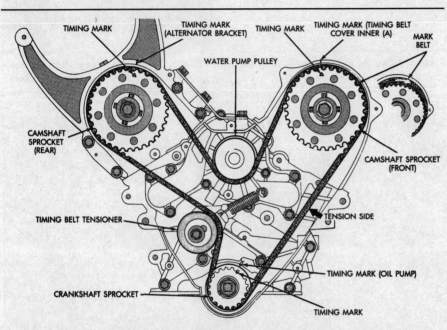

10.23 After turning the crankshaft two full revolutions and returning the number one piston to TDC, the timing belt and marks should look like this - if they don't, loosen the tensioner pulley, remove the belt, realign the marks and reinstall the belt

11.3 If you're lucky, you'll be able to pull the crankshaft sprocket off by hand

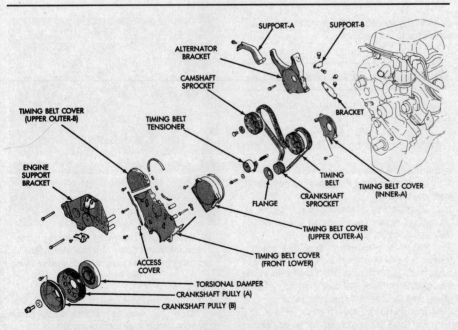

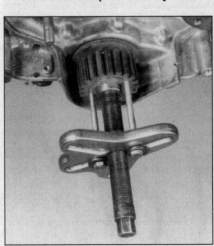

10.25 An exploded view of the timing belt assembly and related components

11.4 If the crankshaft sprocket is stuck on the nose of the crank and you can't pry it off with a pair of screwdrivers, here's the last-resort solution: drill and tap two holes and remove the sprocket with a bolt-type puller

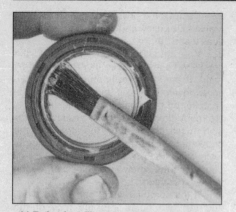

11.7 Apply a film of grease to the lips of the new seal before installing it - if you apply a small amount of grease to the outer edge, it will be easier to push into the bore

11.8a Fabricate a seal installation tool from a piece of pipe and a large washer . . .

11.8b . . . and push the seal into the bore - the pipe must bear against the outer edge of the seal as the bolt is tightened

12.3 Fabricate a sprocket holding tool from a piece of angle iron and a couple of bolts to lock the camshaft sprocket in place while you loosen the retaining bolt

12.4a If you're replacing the seal on the front camshaft, remove the inner timing cover bolts (arrows) and remove the cover

7   Before installation, apply a coat of multi-purpose grease to the inside of the seal (see illustration).

8   Fabricate a seal installation tool with a short length of pipe of equal or slightly smaller outside diameter than the seal itself. File the end of the pipe that will bear down on the seal until it's free of sharp edges. You'll also need a large washer, slightly larger in diameter than the pipe, on which the bolt head can seat (see illustration). Install the oil seal by pressing it into position with the seal installation tool (see illustration). When you see and feel the seal stop moving, don't turn the bolt any more or you'll damage the seal.

9   Slide the timing belt plate onto the nose of the crankshaft.

10   Make sure the Woodruff key is in place in the crankshaft.

11   Apply a thin coat of assembly lube to the inside of the timing belt sprocket and slide it onto the crankshaft.

12   Installation of the remaining components is the reverse of removal. Be sure to refer to Section 10 for the timing belt installation and adjustment procedure. Tighten all

bolts to the torque values listed in this Chapter's Specifications.

12   Camshaft oil seal - replacement

Refer to illustrations 12.3, 12.4a, 12.4b, 12.5a, 12.5b, 12.6, 12.7a and 12.7b

Note: *The 3.0L engine is equipped with two camshaft oil seals on the front (timing belt side) as well as two camshaft oil plugs on the rear (transaxle side) of the engine.*

1   Disconnect the negative battery cable from the battery.

2   Remove the drivebelts (see Chapter 1), crankshaft pulley (see Section 9) and timing belt (see Section 10).

3   Fabricate a camshaft sprocket holding tool from a piece of angle iron and a couple of large bolts that will fit through the holes in the sprocket, then lock the camshaft sprocket in place and loosen the sprocket retaining bolt (see illustration). Once the bolt is out, the sprocket can be removed by hand. **Note:** *Don't mix up the camshaft sprockets. If you're removing both sprockets, mark each one with*

12.4b If you're removing the seal on the rear camshaft, remove the alternator bracket bolts (arrows) and then remove the bracket

an "F" (front, radiator side) or an "R" (rear, firewall side). They must be installed on the same cam from which they were removed.

4   If you're replacing the seal for the front camshaft, remove the inner timing belt cover

12.5a To remove the distributor drive adapter, remove the distributor hold-down nut (upper arrow), remove the distributor (see Chapter 5) and remove the three adapter retaining bolts (arrows)

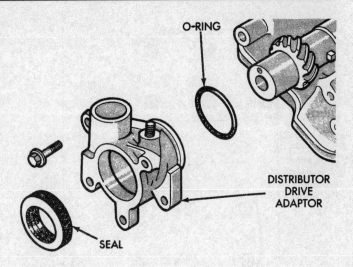

12.5b An exploded view of the distributor drive adapter assembly

12.6 To extract a camshaft seal, drill a couple of small holes in the old seal, thread a pair of sheetmetal screws into the holes and lever the seal out with a screwdriver and a claw hammer

12.7a You can press a new seal into place with a large socket and a bolt of the proper size and thread pitch

12.7b As a last resort, you can also drive a cam seal into place with a hammer and a large socket, but make sure you don't damage the sprocket positioning pin on the end of the camshaft

(see illustration). If you're removing the seal for the rear camshaft, remove the alternator bracket (see illustration).

5   If you're replacing the seal on the front camshaft, it's a good idea to replace the O-ring between the distributor drive adapter and the cylinder head. Remove the distributor (see Chapter 5) and the adapter (see illustrations). Note: *If you remove the adapter, skip the following Steps describing on-vehicle seal replacement. Instead, pry out the old seal, install a new seal with the adapter on the bench, reattach the adapter, tighten the bolts securely and install the distributor.*

6   Drill a couple of small holes in the old seal, thread a pair of sheetmetal screws into the holes, then carefully remove the old oil seal with a screwdriver and a claw hammer (see illustration). Don't nick or scratch the camshaft in the process.

7   There are several ways to install the new seal. If you've already fabricated the

crankshaft seal installation described in Step eight in Section 11, use that. It will also work on camshaft seals. If you haven't, use a very large socket (see illustration) with an inside diameter big enough to clear the nose of the camshaft. If you have the socket, but not the bolt, you can even drive the seal into place - if you're careful - (see illustration), but we don't recommend this third method, because of the danger of damaging the sprocket positioning pin (unless you can pull it out) in the nose of the cam.

8   If you replaced the front cam seal, reattach the inner timing belt cover.

9   When you install the sprocket, make sure the R or F mark faces out! The side of the pulley with the deep recess must face the engine, which means the shallow recess must face out.

10   Using your sprocket holding tool, tighten the bolt to the torque listed in this Chapter's Specifications.

11   Installation of the remaining components is the reverse of removal.

13   Valve spring, retainer and seals - replacement

This procedure is essentially the same as for the 2.2/2.5 liter four-cylinder engines. Refer to Part A, Section 17 and follow the procedure outlined there.

14   Cylinder head(s) - removal and installation

Note: *Allow the engine to cool completely before beginning this procedure.*

Removal

1   Position the engine at TDC on the compression stroke for the number 1 cylinder (see Section 3). Drain the engine coolant (see Chapter 1).

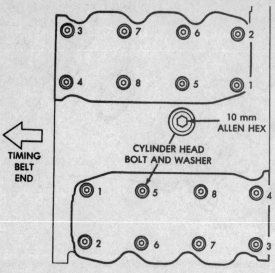

14.12 Cylinder head bolt REMOVAL sequence

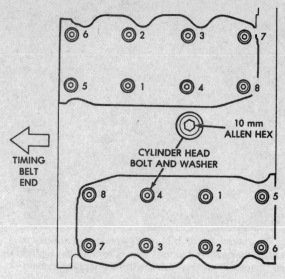

14.23 Cylinder head bolt TIGHTENING sequence

2   Remove the timing belt cover, timing belt and the camshaft sprockets see Sections 10 and 12).

3   Remove the intake manifold (see Section 7).

4   Remove the rocker arm components (see Section 5) and hydraulic lash adjusters (see Section 6).

5   Remove the exhaust manifold(s) as described in Section 8. **Note:** *If desired, each manifold may remain attached to the cylinder head until after the head is removed from the engine. However, the manifold must still be disconnected from the exhaust system and/or crossover pipe.*

Front (radiator side) cylinder head

6   Remove the distributor (crank angle sensor) (see Chapter 5).

7   Remove the air conditioning compressor from the bracket without disconnecting any hoses (see Chapter 3) and set it aside. It may be helpful to secure the compressor to the vehicle with rope or wire to make sure it doesn't hang by its hoses.

8   Remove the air conditioning compressor bracket (see Chapter 3).

Rear (firewall side) cylinder head

9   Detach the heater hoses and brackets from the transaxle end of the head.

10   Remove the air cleaner housing from the engine compartment (see Chapter 4).

11   Remove the alternator (see Chapter 5) and bracket **(see illustration 12.4b)** from the cylinder head.

Both sides

Refer to illustration 14.12

12   Loosen the cylinder head bolts with a 10 mm hex drive tool in 1/4-turn increments until they can be removed by hand. Be sure to follow the proper numerical sequence **(see illustration)**.

13   Head bolts must be reinstalled in their original locations. To keep them from getting mixed up, store them in cardboard holders marked to indicate the bolt pattern. Mark the holders F (front) and R (rear) and indicate the timing belt end of the engine.

14   Lift the head off the block. If resistance is felt, dislodge the head by striking it with a wood block and hammer. If prying is required, pry only on a casting protrusion - be very careful not to damage the head or block!

15   If necessary, remove the camshaft(s) as described in Section 15.

Installation

Refer to illustration 14.23

16   Remove all traces of old gasket material from the cylinder heads and the engine block. The mating surfaces of the cylinder heads and block must be perfectly clean when the heads are installed.

17   Use a gasket scraper to remove all traces of carbon and old gasket material, then clean the mating surfaces with lacquer thinner or acetone. If there's oil on the mating surfaces when the heads are installed, the gaskets may not seal correctly and leaks may develop. Use a vacuum cleaner to remove any debris that falls into the cylinders.

18   Check the block and head mating surfaces for nicks, deep scratches and other damage. If damage is slight, it can be removed with a file - if it's excessive, machining may be the only alternative.

19   Use a tap of the correct size to chase the threads in the head bolt holes. Mount each bolt in a vise and run a die down the threads to remove corrosion and restore the threads. Dirt, corrosion, sealant and damaged threads will affect torque readings. Ensure that the threaded holes in the block are clean and dry.

20   Position the new gaskets over the dowel pins on the block.

21   Carefully position the heads on the block without disturbing the gaskets.

22   Lightly oil the threads and install the bolts in their original locations. Tighten them finger tight.

23   Follow the recommended sequence and tighten the bolts in three steps to the torque listed in this Chapter's Specifications **(see illustration)**.

24   The remaining installation steps are the reverse of removal.

25   Add coolant and change the engine oil and filter (see Chapter 1), then start the engine and check carefully for oil and coolant leaks.

15   Camshaft(s) - removal and installation

Removal

Refer to illustration 15.4

1   Position the engine at TDC on the compression stroke for the number 1 cylinder (see Section 3).

2   If you're removing the front (radiator side) cylinder head, remove the bolts and gently pry off the distributor drive adapter **(see illustration 12.5a)**.

3   Remove the rocker arm assembly (see Section 5).

4   Carefully pry the camshaft plugs from the rear section (transaxle end) of the cylinder head **(see illustration)**. Don't scratch or nick the camshaft in the process!

5   Carefully lift the camshaft from the cylinder head. Inspect the camshaft as described in Section 16.

Installation

6   Lubricate the camshaft bearing journals and lobes with moly-base grease or engine assembly lube, then install it carefully in the head. Don't scratch the bearing surfaces with

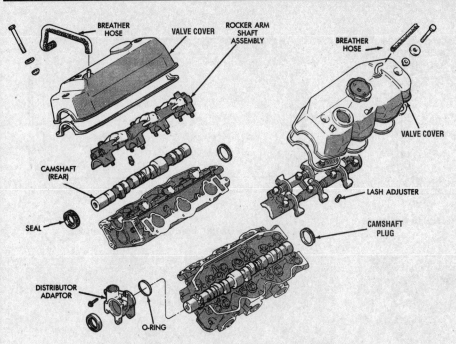

15.4 An exploded view of the cylinder head assembly

16.2 You'll need a dial indicator and a set of V-blocks to measure the camshaft runout

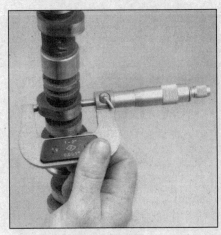

16.3 Use a micrometer to measure cam lobe height

the cam lobes!

7   Install the distributor drive adapter retaining bolts and tighten it to the torque listed in this Chapter's Specifications.

8   Check to make sure the mark on the crankshaft sprocket is still aligned with its mark on the oil pump. Slide the camshaft sprockets onto the camshafts and align the marks on the sprockets with their corresponding marks on the cylinder heads.

9   The remaining steps are the reverse of the removal procedure.

16   Camshaft and bearing surfaces - inspection

Refer to illustrations 16.2 and 16.3

1   Visually check the camshaft bearing surfaces for pitting, score marks, galling and abnormal wear. If the bearing surfaces are damaged, the head will have to be replaced.

2   Check camshaft runout by placing the camshaft between two V-blocks and set up a dial indicator on the center journal (see illustration). Zero the dial indicator. Turn the camshaft slowly and note the total indicator reading. Record your readings and compare them with the specified runout in this Chapter. If the measured runout exceeds the runout listed in this Chapter's Specifications, replace the camshaft.

3   Check the camshaft lobe height by measuring each lobe with a micrometer (see illustration). Compare the measurement to the cam lobe height listed in this Chapter's Specifications. Then subtract the measured cam lobe height from the specified height to compute wear on the cam lobes. Compare it to the specified wear limit. If it's greater than

the specified wear limit, replace the camshaft.

4   Inspect the contact and sliding surfaces of each hydraulic lash adjuster for scoring or damage (see Section 6). Replace any defective parts.

5   Check the rocker arms and shafts for abnormal wear, pits, galling, score marks and rough spots. Don't attempt to restore rocker arms by grinding the pad surfaces. Replace any defective parts.

17   Oil pan - removal and installation

Removal

Refer to illustration 17.11

1   Disconnect the negative cable from the battery.

2   Raise the vehicle and support it securely on jackstands.

3   Remove the under-vehicle splash pan.

4   Drain the engine oil and install a new oil filter (see Chapter 1).

5   Unbolt the exhaust pipe from the rear manifold (see Section 8).

6   Support the engine/transaxle securely with a hoist from above or a jack under the bellhousing. Protect the bellhousing by placing a wood block on the jack pad. **Warning:** *Be absolutely certain the engine/transaxle is securely supported! DO NOT place any part of your body under the engine/transaxle - it could crush you if the jack or hoist fails!*

7   Unbolt the engine mounts (see Section 21). Raise the engine/transaxle assembly to provide clearance for oil pan removal.

8   Remove the oil pan bolts.

9   Detach the oil pan. Don't pry between

the pan and block or damage to the sealing surfaces may result and oil leaks could develop. If the pan is stuck, dislodge it with a hammer and a block of wood.

10   Use a gasket scraper to remove all traces of old gasket material and sealant from the block and pan. Clean the mating surfaces with lacquer thinner or acetone.

11   Unbolt the oil pick-up tube and screen assembly (see illustration).

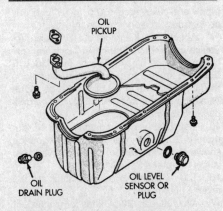

17.11 An exploded view of the oil pan and oil pick-up assemblies

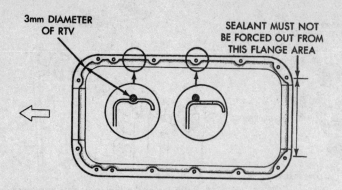

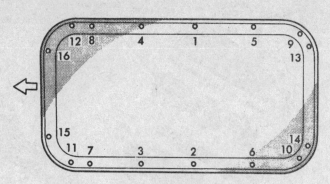

17.14 The bead of RTV sealant shouldn't interfere with the holes for the oil pan bolts

17.15 Oil pan bolt tightening sequence

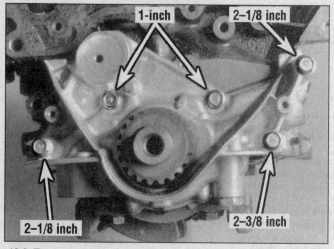

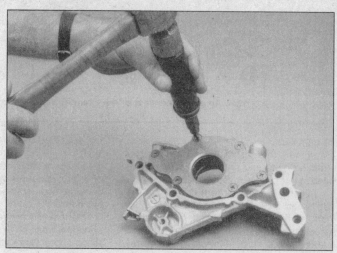

18.3 To remove the oil pump assembly from the engine, remove these bolts (arrows) - note the correct locations for the different length bolts for reassembly

18.7 The Phillips screws retaining the pump cover are screwed on tightly at the factory - you'll probably need to use an impact driver to break them loose (otherwise, you'll strip out the heads)

Installation

Refer to illustrations 17.14 and 17.15

12   Replace the gasket on the flange of the oil pick-up tube and reinstall the tube. Tighten the pick-up tube bolts to the torque listed in this Chapter's Specifications.

13   Ensure that the threaded holes in the block are clean (use a tap to remove any sealant or corrosion from the threads).

14   Apply a small amount of RTV sealant (or equivalent) to the oil pump-to-block and rear seal retainer-to-block junctions **(see illustration)** and apply a thin continuous bead along the circumference of the oil pan flange. **Note:** *Allow the sealant to "set-up" (slightly harden) before installing the gasket.*

15   Install the oil pan and tighten the bolts in three or four steps following the sequence shown **(see illustration)** to the torque listed in this Chapter's Specifications.

16   The remaining installation steps are the reverse of removal.

17   Allow at least 30 minutes for the sealant to dry. Fill the crankcase with oil (see Chapter 1), start the engine and check for oil pressure and leaks.

18   Oil pump - removal, inspection and installation

Removal

Refer to illustration 18.3

1   Remove the timing belt and the crankshaft sprocket (see Sections 10 and 11). Remove the oil pan and pick-up assemblies (see Section 17).

2   Unbolt the power steering pump (see Chapter 10) without disconnecting the hoses. Remove the power steering pump bracket **(see illustration 10.7)**.

3   Remove the oil pump-to-engine block bolts from the front of the engine **(see illustration)**.

4   Use a block of wood and a hammer to break the oil pump loose.

5   Pull out on the oil pump to remove it from the engine block.

6   Use a scraper to remove old gasket material and sealant from the oil pump and engine block mating surfaces. Clean the mating surfaces with lacquer thinner or acetone.

Inspection

Refer to illustrations 18.7, 18.9, 18.10a, 18.10b, 18.10c, 18.10d, 18.10e and 18.10f

7   Remove the screws holding the rear cover to the oil pump **(see illustration)**.

8   Clean all components with solvent, then inspect them for wear and damage.

9   Remove the oil pressure relief valve plug, washer, spring and valve (plunger) **(see illustration)**. Check the oil pressure relief valve sliding surface and valve spring. If either the spring or the valve is damaged, they must be replaced as a set.

10   Check the following clearances with a feeler gauge **(see illustrations)** and compare the measurements to the clearances listed in this Chapter's Specifications:

Case-to-outer rotor
Rotor end clearance
Case-to-inner rotor

   If any of the clearances are excessive, replace the entire oil pump assembly.

11   Pack the cavities of the oil pump with petroleum jelly to prime it. Assemble the oil pump and tighten the screws to the torque

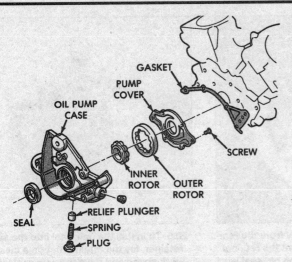

18.9 An exploded view of the oil pump assembly

18.10a Use a feeler gauge to determine the clearance between the outer rotor and the case

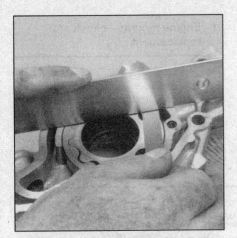

18.10b Use a straightedge and a feeler gauge to determine the rotor end clearance (the clearance between the rotor face and the pump cover)

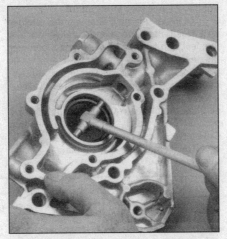

18.10c Determining the third measurement, the clearance between the inner rotor and the case, is trickier; first, measure the inside diameter of the inner rotor bore in the case with a bore gauge . . .

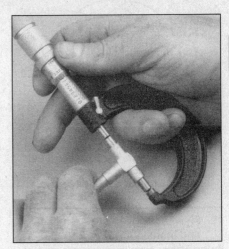

18.10d . . . measure the bore gauge with a micrometer . . .

listed in this Chapter's Specifications. Install the oil pressure relief valve, spring and washer, then tighten the oil pressure relief valve plug to the torque listed in this Chapter's Specifications.

Installation

12   Apply a thin film of RTV sealant to the new oil pump gasket.

13   Installation is the reverse of the removal procedure. Align the flats on the crankshaft with the flats in the inner rotor of the oil pump. Tighten all fasteners to the torque values listed in this Chapter's Specifications.

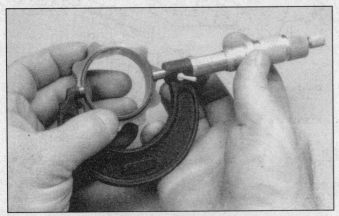

18.10e . . . measure the diameter of the inner rotor with a micrometer . . .

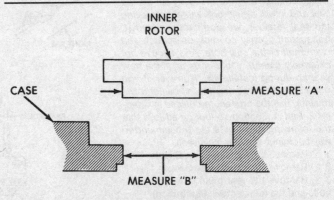

18.10f . . . and subtract the two (I.D. of the rotor bore in the case minus the O.D. of the inner rotor)

2B

20.3 To remove the rear main oil seal retainer, remove these five bolts

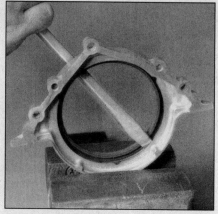

20.4 To remove the old seal from the rear main oil seal retainer, mount the retainer in bench vise and pry out the old seal with a screwdriver

20.5 To install the new seal into the seal retainer, lay the retainer flat on a clean work space and drive the new seal into place with a block of wood and a hammer

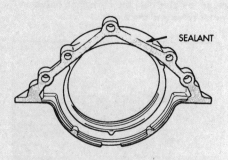

20.6 Before installing the rear main oil seal retainer onto the block, coat the mating surfaces of the retainer with silicone rubber adhesive sealant

19 Flywheel/driveplate - removal and installation

This procedure is essentially the same for all engines. Refer to Part A and follow the procedure outlined there, but use the bolt torque listed in this Chapter's Specifications.

20 Rear main oil seal - replacement

Refer to illustrations 20.3, 20.4, 20.5 and 20.6
Note: *Although it's possible to pry out the old seal and install a new one without removing the seal retainer, we don't recommend it, because it's easy to nick or scratch the crankshaft or the seal bore. And if you're not extremely careful, you can damage the new seal lip during installation. However, if you don't feel like removing the oil pan and the retainer, use the procedure outlined in Chapter 2, Part A, Section 15 (but be advised that the following method is the recommended way to change the rear main seal).*
1   Remove the transaxle (see Chapter 7).
2   Remove the oil pan (See Section 17).
3   Remove the rear main oil seal retainer bolts and the retainer **(see illustration)**.
4   Put the retainer in a bench vise and pry

out the old seal **(see illustration)**.
5   To install the new seal, lay the retainer on a clean, flat surface and carefully drive in the seal with a block of wood and a hammer **(see illustration)**.
6   Coat the mating surface of the with silicone rubber adhesive sealant **(see illustration)**, apply a light coating of clean oil to the seal lip, install the retainer and tighten the retainer bolts to the torque listed in this Chapter's Specifications.
7   The remainder of installation is the reverse of removal.

21 Engine mounts - check and replacement

Refer to illustration 21.1
This procedure is essentially the same for all engines. See Part A of this Chapter and follow the procedure outlined there, but use the torque values listed in this Chapter's Specifications. Use the accompanying exploded view for reference **(see illustration)**.

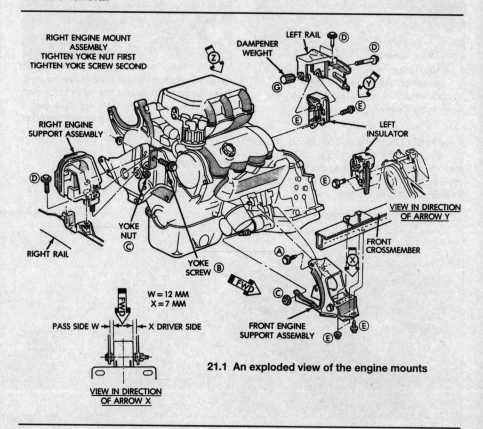

21.1 An exploded view of the engine mounts

Chapter 2 Part C
General engine overhaul procedures

Contents

2C

Specifications

Four-cylinder engines

General
Displacement	
2.2L	135 cubic inches
2.5L	153 cubic inches
Cylinder compression pressure	130 to 150 psi at 250 rpm
Oil pressure (at 3000 rpm)	25 to 80 psi

Engine block
Cylinder taper limit	0.005 inch
Cylinder out-of-round limit	0.002 inch

Pistons and rings
Piston diameter	
2.2L engine	3.443 to 3.445 inches
2.5L engine	
1989 and 1990	3.442 to 3.445 inches
1991 and 1992	3.443 to 3.444 inches
2.5L Turbo engine	3.443 to 3.444 inches
2.2L turbo engine	
1991	3.443 to 3.444 inches
1992	3.441 to 3.444 inches
Piston-to-bore clearance	0.001 to 0.003 inch

Four-cylinder engines (continued)

Pistons and rings

Piston ring side clearance
  Non-turbo
    Top compression ring
      Standard.. 0.0015 to 0.0031 inch
      Service limit .... 0.004 inch
  Second compression ring
    Standard.. 0.0015 to 0.0037 inch
    Service limit .... 0.004 inch
    Oil ring .... 0.008 inch
  Turbo
    Top compression ring
      Standard .... 0.0016 to 0.0030 inch
      Service limit .... Not available
    Second compression ring
      SOHC engines
        Standard .... 0.0016 to 0.0035 inch
        Service limit .... Not available
      DOHC engine
        Standard .... 0.0016 to 0.0030 inch
        Service limit .... Not available
  Oil ring
    SOHC engines.. 0.008 inch
    DOHC engine
      1991 .... 0.000 to 0.004 inch
      1992 .... 0.0007 to 0.002 inch
Piston ring end gap
  Non-turbo
    Top compression ring .... 0.010 to 0.020 inch
    Second compression ring .... 0.011 to 0.021 inch
    Oil ring
      Standard .... 0.015 to 0.055 inch
      Service limit .... 0.074 inch
  Turbo
    Top compression ring
      SOHC engines .... 0.010 to 0.020 inch
      DOHC engine .... 0.014 to 0.020 inch
    Second compression ring
      SOHC engines .... 0.009 to 0.019 inch
      DOHC engine .... 0.014 to 0.020 inch
    Oil ring (all engines)
      Standard .... 0.015 to 0.055 inch
      Service limit .... 0.074 inch

Crankshaft and connecting rods

Endplay
  Standard.. 0.002 to 0.007 inch
  Service limit .... 0.014 inch
Main bearing journal
  Diameter.. 2.362 to 2.363 inches
  Taper limit... 0.0003 inch
  Out-of-round limit.. 0.0003 inch
Connecting rod journal
  Diameter.. 1.968 to 1.969 inches
  Out-of-round/taper limits .... 0.0003 inch
Main bearing oil clearance
  Standard.. 0.0004 to 0.0028 inch
  Service limit .... 0.004 inch
Connecting rod bearing oil clearance
  Standard.. 0.0008 to 0.0034 inch
  Service limit .... 0.004 inch
Connecting rod endplay (side clearance) .... 0.005 to 0.013 inch

Camshaft

Endplay
  Standard.. 0.005 to 0.013 inch
  Service limit .... 0.020 inch

Cylinder head and valves

Head warpage limit...	0.004 inch
Valve seat angle..	45-degrees
Valve face angle..	45-degrees
Valve margin width	
SOHC engines	
Intake	
Standard...	1/16 inch
Service limit..	1/32 inch
Exhaust	
Standard...	1/16 inch
Service limit..	3/64 inch
DOHC engine	
Intake	
Standard...	3/64 inch
Service limit..	Not available
Exhaust	
Standard...	3/64 inch
Service limit..	Not available
Valve stem diameter	
Intake	0.3124 inch
Exhaust...	0.3103 inch
Valve stem-to-guide clearance	
SOHC engines	
Intake	0.0009 to 0.0026 inch
Exhaust..	0.003 to 0.0047 inch
DOHC engine	
Intake	0.001 to 0.0023 inch
Exhaust..	0.002 to 0.0031 inch
Valve spring free length	
Non-turbo engines	2.39 inches
Turbo engines	
SOHC engines	2.28 inches
DOHC engine	2.094 inches
Valve spring installed height	1.65 inches

Torque specifications*

	Ft-lbs (unless otherwise indicated)
Main bearing cap bolts	30 plus 1/4-turn
Connecting rod bearing cap nuts	40 plus 1/4-turn
Counterbalance assembly	
Double-ended stud and gear cover bolts	105 in-lbs
Crankshaft sprocket bolts	130 in-lbs
Tensioner bolts...	105 in-lbs
Guide bolts...	105 in-lbs
Balance shaft gear bolt	21

* **Note:** *Refer to Part A for additional torque specifications.*

V6 engine

General

Displacement..	181 cubic inches
Cylinder compression pressure...	178 at 250 rpm

Engine block

Cylinder diameter	3.586 to 3.587 inches

Pistons and rings

Piston diameter..	3.585 to 3.586 inches
Piston ring side clearance	
Top compression ring	
Standard	0.0020 to 0.0035 inch
Service limit...	0.004 inch
Second compression ring	
Standard	0.0008 to 0.0020 inch
Service limit...	0.0039 inch

2C

V6 engine (continued)

Pistons and rings (continued)

Piston ring end gap

  Top compression ring

    Standard .... 0.012 to 0.018 inch

    Service limit .... 0.032 inch

  Second compression ring

    Standard .... 0.010 to 0.016 inch

    Service limit .... 0.032 inch

  Oil ring

    Standard .... 0.012 to 0.035 inch

    Service limit .... 0.040 inch

Crankshaft and connecting rods

Endplay (standard) .... 0.002 to 0.010 inch

Main bearing journal

  Diameter .... 2.361 to 2.362 inches

  Taper limit .... 0.0002 inch

  Out-of-round limit .... 0.001 inch

Connecting rod journal

  Diameter .... 1.968 to 1.969 inches

  Taper limit .... 0.0002 in

  Out-of-round limit .... 0.001 inch

Main bearing oil clearance .... 0.0006 to 0.0020 inch

Connecting rod bearing oil clearance .... 0.0006 to 0.0020 inch

Connecting rod endplay (side clearance)

  Standard .... 0.004 to 0.010 inch

  Service limit .... 0.016 inch

Cylinder head and valves

Head warpage limit .... 0.002 inch

Valve seat angle 45-degrees

Valve face angle 45-degrees

Valve margin width

  Intake

    Standard .... 0.047 inch

    Service limit .... 0.027 inch

  Exhaust

    Standard .... 0.079 inch

    Service limit .... 0.059 inch

Valve stem-to-guide clearance

  Intake

    Standard .... 0.001 to 0.002 inch

    Service limit .... 0.004 inch .

  Exhaust

    Standard .... 0.0020 to 0.0030 inch

    Service limit .... 0.006 inch

Valve spring free length

  Standard .... 1.960 inches

  Service limit .... 1.921 inches

Valve spring installed height

  Standard .... 1.590 inches

  Service limit .... Not available

Valve stem diameter

  Intake .... 0.313 to 0.314 inch

  Exhaust .... 0.312 to 0.313 inch

Torque specifications*

                                     Ft-lbs (unless otherwise indicated)

Main bearing cap bolts 60

Connecting rod bearing cap nuts 34

* **Note:** *Refer to Part B for additional torque specifications.*

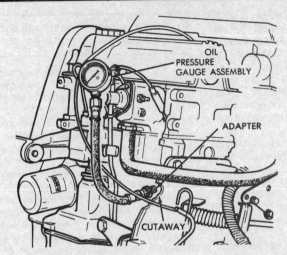

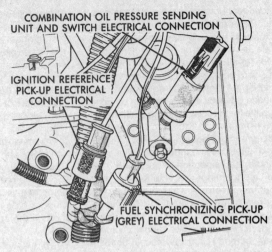

2.4a Remove the oil high pressure sending unit (switch) and install a pressure gauge in its place (four-cylinder engine shown)

2.4b Location of the oil pressure sending unit on the turbo SOHC engine

1 General information

Included in this portion of Chapter 2 are the general overhaul procedures for the cylinder head(s) and internal engine components.

The information ranges from advice concerning preparation for an overhaul and the purchase of replacement parts to detailed, step-by-step procedures covering removal and installation of internal engine components and the inspection of parts.

The following Sections have been written based on the assumption the engine has been removed from the vehicle. For information concerning in-vehicle engine repair, as well as removal and installation of the external components necessary for the overhaul, see Part A (four-cylinder engines) or B (V6 engine) of this Chapter.

The Specifications included in this Part are only those necessary for the inspection and overhaul procedures which follow. Refer to Parts A and B for additional Specifications.

2 Engine overhaul - general information

Refer to illustrations 2.4a, 2.4b and 2.4c

It's not always easy to determine when, or if, an engine should be completely overhauled, as a number of factors must be considered.

High mileage isn't necessarily an indication an overhaul is needed, while low mileage doesn't preclude the need for an overhaul. Frequency of servicing is probably the most important consideration. An engine that's had regular and frequent oil and filter changes, as well as other required maintenance, will most likely give many thousands of miles of reliable service. Conversely, a neglected engine may require an overhaul very early in its life.

Excessive oil consumption is an indication that piston rings, valve seals and/or valve

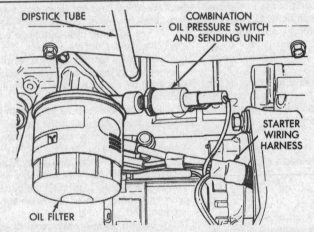

2.4c Location of the oil pressure sending unit on the V6 engine

guides are in need of attention. Make sure oil leaks aren't responsible before deciding the rings and/or guides are bad. Perform a cylinder compression check to determine the extent of the work required (see Section 3).

Remove the oil pressure sending unit and check the oil pressure with a gauge installed in its place **(see illustrations)**. Compare the results to this Chapter's Specifications. As a general rule, engines should have ten psi oil pressure for every 1,000 rpm. If the pressure is extremely low, the bearings and/or oil pump are probably worn out.

Loss of power, rough running, knocking or metallic engine noises, excessive valve train noise and high fuel consumption rates may also point to the need for an overhaul, especially if they're all present at the same time. If a complete tune-up doesn't remedy the situation, major mechanical work is the only solution.

An engine overhaul involves restoring the internal parts to the specifications of a new engine. During an overhaul, the piston rings are replaced and the cylinder walls are reconditioned (rebored and/or honed). If a rebore is done by an automotive machine shop, new oversize pistons will also be

installed. The main bearings, connecting rod bearings and camshaft bearings are generally replaced with new ones and, if necessary, the crankshaft may be reground to restore the journals. Generally, the valves are serviced as well, since they're usually in less-than-perfect condition at this point. While the engine is being overhauled, other components, such as the starter and alternator, can be rebuilt as well. The end result should be a like new engine that will give many trouble free miles. **Note:** *Critical cooling system components such as the hoses, drivebelts, thermostat and water pump MUST be replaced with new parts when an engine is overhauled. The radiator should be checked carefully to ensure it isn't clogged or leaking (see Chapter 3). Also, we don't recommend overhauling the oil pump - always install a new one when an engine is rebuilt.*

Before beginning the engine overhaul, read through the entire procedure to familiarize yourself with the scope and requirements of the job.

Overhauling an engine isn't particularly difficult, if you follow all of the instructions carefully, have the necessary tools and equipment and pay close attention to all specifications; however, it can be time consuming. Plan on the vehicle being tied up for a minimum of two weeks, especially if parts must be taken to an automotive machine shop for repair or reconditioning. Check on availability of parts and make sure any necessary special tools and equipment are obtained in advance. Most work can be done with typical hand tools, although a number of precision measuring tools are required for inspecting parts to determine if they must be replaced. Often an automotive machine shop will handle the inspection of parts and offer advice concerning reconditioning and replacement. **Note:** *Always wait until the engine has been completely disassembled and all components, especially the engine block, have been inspected before deciding what service and repair operations must be performed by an automotive machine shop. Since the block's condition will be the major factor to consider when determining whether to overhaul the original engine or buy a rebuilt one, never purchase parts or have machine work done on other components until the block has been thoroughly inspected.* As a general rule, time is the primary cost of an overhaul, so it doesn't pay to install worn or substandard parts.

As a final note, to ensure maximum life and minimum trouble from a rebuilt engine, everything must be assembled with care in a spotlessly clean environment.

3   Cylinder compression check

Refer to illustration 3.6

1   A compression check will tell you what mechanical condition the upper end (pistons, rings, valves, head gaskets) of the engine is in. Specifically, it can tell you if the compression is down due to leakage caused by worn piston rings, defective valves and seats or a blown head gasket. **Note:** *The engine must be at normal operating temperature and the battery must be fully charged for this check.*

2   Begin by cleaning the area around the spark plugs before you remove them. Compressed air should be used, if available, otherwise a small brush or even a bicycle tire pump will work. The idea is to prevent dirt from getting into the cylinders as the compression check is being done.

3   Remove all of the spark plugs from the engine (see Chapter 1).

4   Block the throttle wide open.

5   Disable the ignition system by disconnecting the primary wires from the coil (see Chapter 5). Also, disable the fuel injection system by unplugging the electrical connector to the injector wiring harness.

6   Install the compression gauge in the number one spark plug hole **(see illustration)**.

7   Crank the engine over at least seven compression strokes and watch the gauge. The compression should build up quickly in a healthy engine. Low compression on the first

stroke, followed by gradually increasing pressure on successive strokes, indicates worn piston rings. A low compression reading on the first stroke, which doesn't build up during successive strokes, indicates leaking valves or a blown head gasket (a cracked head could also be the cause). Deposits on the undersides of the valve heads can also cause low compression. Record the highest gauge reading obtained.

8   Repeat the procedure for the remaining cylinders and compare the results to this Chapter's Specifications.

9   If the readings are below normal, add some engine oil (about three squirts from a plunger-type oil can) to each cylinder, through the spark plug hole, and repeat the test.

10   If the compression increases after the oil is added, the piston rings are definitely worn. If the compression doesn't increase significantly, the leakage is occurring at the valves or head gasket. Leakage past the valves may be caused by burned valve seats and/or faces or warped, cracked or bent valves.

11   If two adjacent cylinders have equally low compression, there's a strong possibility the head gasket between them is blown. The appearance of coolant in the combustion chambers or the crankcase would verify this condition.

12   If one cylinder is about 20-percent lower than the others, and the engine has a slightly rough idle, a worn exhaust lobe on the camshaft could be the cause.

13   If the compression is unusually high, the combustion chambers are probably coated with carbon deposits. If that's the case, the cylinder head(s) should be removed and decarbonized.

14   If compression is way down or varies greatly between cylinders, it would be a good idea to have a leak-down test performed by an automotive repair shop. This test will pinpoint exactly where the leakage is occurring and how severe it is.

3.6 A compression gauge with a threaded fitting for the spark plug hole is preferred over the type that requires hand pressure to maintain the seal

4   Engine removal - methods and precautions

If you've decided the engine must be removed for overhaul or major repair work, several preliminary steps should be taken.

Locating a suitable place to work is extremely important. Adequate work space, along with storage space for the vehicle, will be needed. If a shop or garage isn't available, at the very least a flat, level, clean work surface made of concrete or asphalt is required.

Cleaning the engine compartment and engine before beginning the removal procedure will help keep tools clean and organized.

An engine hoist or A-frame will also be necessary. Make sure the equipment is rated in excess of the combined weight of the engine and transaxle. Safety is of primary importance, considering the potential hazards involved in lifting the engine out of the vehicle.

If the engine is being removed by a novice, a helper should be available. Advice and aid from someone more experienced would also be helpful. There are many instances when one person cannot simultaneously perform all of the operations required when lifting the engine out of the vehicle.

Plan the operation ahead of time. Arrange for or obtain all of the tools and equipment you'll need prior to beginning the job. Some of the equipment necessary to perform engine removal and installation safely and with relative ease are (in addition to an engine hoist) a heavy duty floor jack, complete sets of wrenches and sockets as described in the front of this manual, wooden blocks and plenty of rags and cleaning solvent for mopping up spilled oil, coolant and gasoline. If the hoist must be rented, be sure to arrange for it in advance and perform all of the operations possible without it beforehand. This will save you money and time.

Plan for the vehicle to be out of use for quite a while. A machine shop will be required to perform some of the work which the do-it-yourselfer can't accomplish without special equipment. These shops often have a busy schedule, so it would be a good idea to consult them before removing the engine in order to accurately estimate the amount of time required to rebuild or repair components that may need work.

Always be extremely careful when removing and installing the engine. Serious injury can result from careless actions. Plan ahead, take your time and a job of this nature, although major, can be accomplished successfully.

5   Engine - removal and installation

Refer to illustrations 5.5, 5.18 and 5.26
Warning: *Gasoline is extremely flammable, so take extra precautions when disconnecting any part of the fuel system. Don't smoke or*

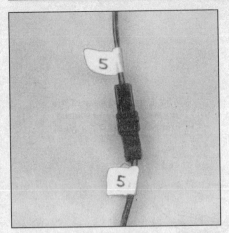

5.5. Label each wire before unplugging the connector

5.18 Use a box-end wrench to remove the torque converter bolts

allow open flames or bare light bulbs in or near the work area and don't work in a garage where a natural gas appliance (such as a clothes dryer or water heater) is installed. If you spill gasoline on your skin, rinse it off immediately. Have a fire extinguisher rated for gasoline fires handy and know how to use it! Also, the air conditioning system is under high pressure - have a dealer service department or service station discharge the system before disconnecting any of the hoses or fittings.

Note: Read through the following steps carefully and familiarize yourself with the procedure before beginning work.

Removal

1   If the vehicle is equipped with air conditioning, have the air conditioning system discharged by a dealer service department or service station. (This isn't necessary on most 2.2L and 2.5L models - the air conditioning compressor can be unbolted and repositioned without disconnecting the hoses.)

2   Refer to Chapter 4 and relieve the fuel system pressure, then disconnect the negative cable from the battery.

3   Cover the fenders and cowl and remove the hood (see Chapter 11). Special pads are available to protect the fenders, but an old bedspread or blanket will also work.

4   Remove the air cleaner assembly (see Chapter 4).

5   Label the vacuum lines, emissions system hoses, wiring connectors, ground straps and fuel lines to ensure correct reinstallation, then detach them. Pieces of masking tape with numbers or letters written on them work well **(see illustration)**. If there's any possibility of confusion, make a sketch of the engine compartment and clearly label the lines, hoses and wires.

6   Raise the vehicle and support it securely on jackstands. Drain the cooling system (see Chapter 1).

7   Label and detach all coolant hoses from the engine.

8   Remove the coolant reservoir, cooling fan, shroud and radiator (see Chapter 3).

9   Remove the drivebelt(s) and idler, if

equipped (see Chapter 1).

10   Disconnect the fuel lines running from the engine to the chassis (see Chapter 4). Plug or cap all open fittings/lines.

11   Disconnect the accelerator linkage (and TV linkage/cruise control cable, if equipped) from the engine (see Chapters 4 and 7).

12   Unbolt the power steering pump and set it aside (see Chapter 10). Leave the lines/hoses attached and make sure the pump is kept in an upright position in the engine compartment.

13   Unbolt the air conditioning compressor (see Chapter 3) and set it aside. Do not disconnect the hoses.

14   Drain the engine oil and remove the filter (see Chapter 1).

15   Remove the starter and the alternator (see Chapter 5).

16   Check for clearance and remove the brake master cylinder, if necessary, to allow clearance for the transaxle (see Chapter 9).

17   Disconnect the exhaust system from the engine (see Chapter 4). If the engine is equipped with a turbocharger, be sure to disconnect any lines or hoses that will hinder the removal of the engine.

18   Mark the relationship of the torque converter to the driveplate, then remove the torque converter bolts **(see illustration)**. The bolts are much easier to access at this time

before the engine and transaxle are removed. Do not remove any of the transaxle-to-engine mounting bolts yet.

19   Support the transaxle with a jack. Position a block of wood on the jack head to prevent damage to the transaxle. Or lay a piece of wood lengthwise above the transaxle and support it with short section of chain.

20   Attach an engine sling or a length of chain to the lifting brackets on the engine.

21   Roll the hoist into position and connect the sling to it. Take up the slack in the sling or chain, but don't lift the engine. **Warning:** *DO NOT place any part of your body under the engine when it's supported only by a hoist or other lifting device.*

22   Remove the right engine mount. Refer to the appropriate chapter (Chapter 2A or 2B) for complete illustrations of the engine mounts.

23   Remove the front engine mount.

24   Remove the rear engine mount.

25   Recheck to be sure nothing is still connecting the engine to the vehicle (or transaxle, where applicable). Disconnect anything still remaining.

26   Raise the engine (or engine/transaxle assembly) slightly to disengage the mounts. Slowly raise the engine out of the vehicle **(see illustration)**. Check carefully to make sure nothing is hanging up as the hoist is raised.

27   Once the engine/transaxle assembly is out of the vehicle, lower it to the ground and support it on wood blocks. Remove the transaxle-to-engine block bolts and carefully separate the engine from the transaxle. If you're working on a vehicle with an automatic transaxle, be sure the torque converter stays with the transaxle (clamp a pair of vise-grips to the housing to keep the converter from sliding out). If you're working on a vehicle with a manual transaxle, the input shaft must be completely disengaged from the clutch.

28   Remove the clutch and flywheel or driveplate and mount the engine on an engine stand.

Installation

29   Check the engine and transaxle mounts. If they're worn or damaged, replace them.

30   If you're working on a manual transaxle equipped vehicle, install the clutch and pres-

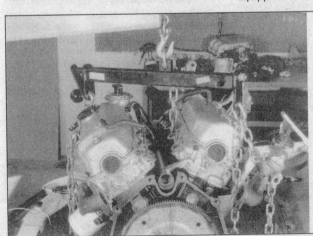

5.26 Lift the engine off the mounts and guide it carefully around any obstacles as an assistant raises the hoist until it clears the front of the vehicle

2C

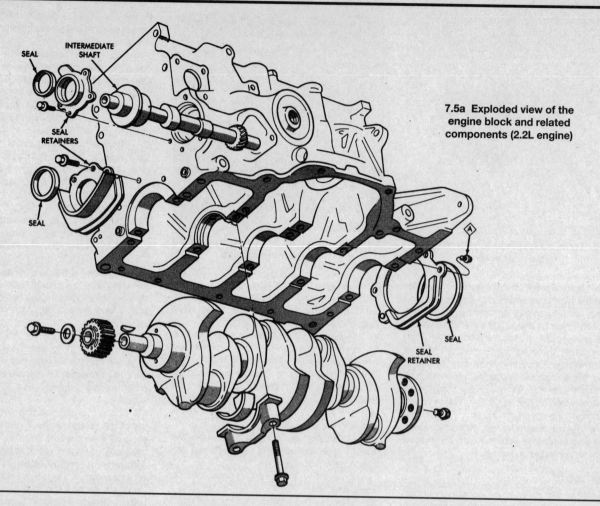

7.5a Exploded view of the engine block and related components (2.2L engine)

sure plate (see Chapter 7). Now is a good time to install a new clutch. Apply a dab of high-temperature grease to the input shaft.
Caution: *DO NOT use the transaxle-to-engine bolts to force the transaxle and engine together. If you're working on an automatic transaxle equipped vehicle, take great care when installing the torque converter, following the procedure outlined in Chapter 7.*
31   Carefully lower the engine/transaxle into the engine compartment - make sure the mounts line up. Reinstall the remaining components in the reverse order of removal. Double-check to make sure everything is hooked up right.
32   Add coolant, oil, power steering and transmission fluid as needed. If the brake master cylinder was removed, bleed the brakes (see Chapter 9). Recheck the fluid level and test the brakes.
33   Run the engine and check for leaks and proper operation of all accessories, then install the hood and test drive the vehicle.
34   If the air conditioning system was discharged, have it evacuated, recharged and leak tested by the shop that discharged it.

---

6   Engine rebuilding alternatives

The home mechanic is faced with a number of options when performing an engine overhaul. The decision to replace the engine block, piston/connecting rod assemblies and crankshaft depends on a number of factors, with the number one consideration being the condition of the block. Other considerations are cost, access to machine shop facilities, parts availability, time required to complete the project and the extent of prior mechanical experience.
Some of the rebuilding alternatives include:

Individual parts - If the inspection procedures reveal the engine block and most engine components are in reusable condition, purchasing individual parts may be the most economical alternative. The block, crankshaft and piston/connecting rod assemblies should all be inspected carefully. Even if the block shows little wear, the cylinder bores should be surface honed.

Short block - A short block consists of an engine block with a crankshaft and piston/connecting rod assemblies already installed. All new bearings are incorporated and all clearances will be correct. The existing camshaft, valve train components, cylinder head(s) and external parts can be bolted to the short block with little or no machine shop work necessary.

Long block - A long block consists of a short block plus an oil pump, oil pan, cylinder head(s), valve cover(s), camshaft and valve train components, timing sprockets and chain and timing chain cover. All components are installed with new bearings, seals and gaskets incorporated throughout. The installation of manifolds and external parts is all that's necessary.
Give careful thought to which alternative is best for you and discuss the situation with local automotive machine shops, auto parts dealers and experienced rebuilders before ordering or purchasing replacement parts.

---

7   Engine overhaul - disassembly sequence

Refer to illustrations 7.5a, 7.5b and 7.5c
1   It's much easier to disassemble and work on the engine if it's mounted on a portable engine stand. A stand can often be rented quite cheaply from an equipment rental yard. Before it's mounted on a stand, the flywheel/driveplate should be removed from the engine.
2   If a stand isn't available, it's possible to disassemble the engine with it blocked up on the floor. Be extra careful not to tip or drop the engine when working without a stand.

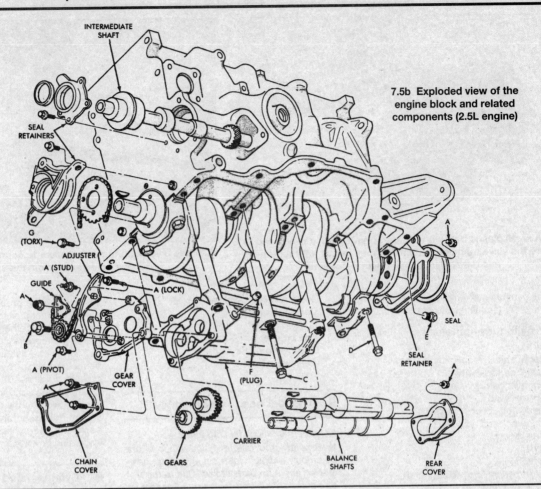

7.5b Exploded view of the engine block and related components (2.5L engine)

INTERMEDIATE SHAFT

SEAL RETAINERS

G (TORX)

ADJUSTER

A (STUD)

GUIDE

A (LOCK)

A (PIVOT)

GEAR COVER

CHAIN COVER

GEARS

CARRIER

F (PLUG)

SEAL

SEAL RETAINER

BALANCE SHAFTS

REAR COVER

2C

3   If you're going to obtain a rebuilt engine, all external components must come off first, to be transferred to the replacement engine, just as they will if you're doing a complete engine overhaul yourself. These include:

Alternator and brackets
Emissions control components
Ignition coil/module assembly, spark plug wires and spark plugs
Thermostat and housing cover
Water pump
EFI components
Intake/exhaust manifolds
Oil filter
Engine mounts
Clutch and flywheel/driveplate

Note: *When removing the external components from the engine, pay close attention to details that may be helpful or important during installation. Note the installed position of gaskets, seals, spacers, pins, brackets, washers, bolts and other small items.*

4   If you're obtaining a short block, which consists of the engine block, crankshaft, pistons and connecting rods all assembled, then the cylinder head(s), oil pan and oil pump will have to be removed as well. See Engine rebuilding alternatives for additional information regarding the different possibilities to be considered.

5   If you're planning a complete overhaul, the engine must be disassembled and the

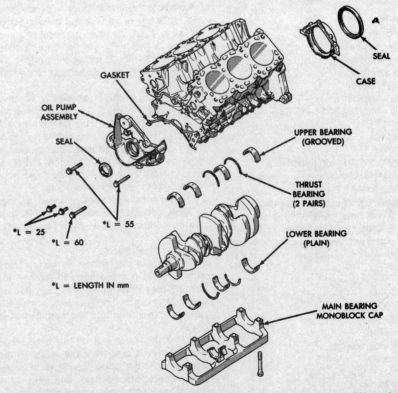

GASKET

OIL PUMP ASSEMBLY

SEAL

SEAL

CASE

UPPER BEARING (GROOVED)

THRUST BEARING (2 PAIRS)

LOWER BEARING (PLAIN)

MAIN BEARING MONOBLOCK CAP

*L = 25
*L = 60
*L = 55
*L = LENGTH IN mm

7.5c Exploded view of the engine block and related components (V6 engine)

8.2 A small plastic bag, with an appropriate label, can be used to store the valve train components so they can be kept together and reinstalled in their original locations

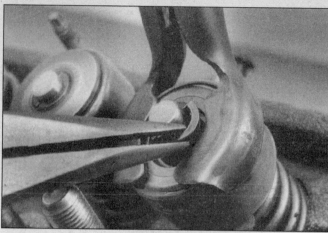

8.3 Use a valve spring compressor to compress the spring, then remove the keepers from the valve stem

internal components removed in the following general order **(see illustrations):**

Four-cylinder engines

Valve cover
Intake/exhaust manifolds
Rocker arm assembly
Hydraulic lash adjusters
Cylinder head
Timing belt cover
Timing belt and sprockets
Camshaft
Oil pan
Oil pump
Piston/connecting rod assemblies
Crankshaft and main bearings

V6 engine

Valve covers
Exhaust manifolds
Rocker arm assemblies and camshafts
Intake manifold
Cylinder heads
Timing chain/belt cover
Timing chain/belt and sprockets
Camshaft
Oil pan
Oil pump
Piston/connecting rod assemblies
Rear main oil seal housing
Crankshaft and main bearings

6   Before beginning the disassembly and overhaul procedures, make sure the following items are available. Also, refer to *Engine overhaul - reassembly sequence* for a list of tools and materials needed for engine reassembly.

Common hand tools
Small cardboard boxes or plastic bags for storing parts
Gasket scraper
Ridge reamer
Vibration damper puller
Micrometers
Telescoping gauges
Dial indicator set
Valve spring compressor
Cylinder surfacing hone

Piston ring groove cleaning tool
Electric drill motor
Tap and die set
Wire brushes
Oil gallery brushes
Cleaning solvent

8   Cylinder head - disassembly

Refer to illustrations 8.2, 8.3 and 8.4
Note: *New and rebuilt cylinder heads are commonly available for most engines at dealerships and auto parts stores. Due to the fact that some specialized tools are necessary for the disassembly and inspection procedures, and replacement parts aren't always readily available, it may be more practical and economical for the home mechanic to purchase replacement head(s) rather than taking the time to disassemble, inspect and recondition the original(s).*

1   Cylinder head disassembly involves removal of the intake and exhaust valves and related components. The camshafts and housings must be removed before beginning the cylinder head disassembly procedure (see Part A or B of this Chapter). Label the parts or store them separately so they can be reinstalled in their original locations.
2   Before the valves are removed, arrange to label and store them, along with their related components, so they can be kept separate and reinstalled in their original locations **(see illustration).**
3   Compress the springs on the first valve with a spring compressor and remove the keepers **(see illustration).** Carefully release the valve spring compressor and remove the retainer, the spring and the spring seat (if used).
4   Pull the valve out of the head, then remove the oil seal from the guide. If the valve binds in the guide (won't pull through), push it back into the head and deburr the area around the keeper groove with a fine file or whetstone **(see illustration).**

5   Repeat the procedure for the remaining valves. Remember to keep all the parts for each valve together so they can be reinstalled in the same locations.
6   Once the valves and related components have been removed and stored in an organized manner, the head should be thoroughly cleaned and inspected. If a complete engine overhaul is being done, finish the engine disassembly procedures before beginning the cylinder head cleaning and inspection process.

9   Cylinder head - cleaning

1   Thorough cleaning of the cylinder head(s) and related valve train components, followed by a detailed inspection, will enable you to decide how much valve service work must be done during the engine overhaul. **Note:** *If the engine was severely overheated, the cylinder head is probably warped.*
2   Scrape all traces of old gasket material and sealant off the head gasket, intake mani-

8.4 If the valve won't pull through the guide, deburr the edge of the stem end and the area around the top of the keeper groove with a file or whetstone

10.2 Check the cylinder head gasket surface for warpage by trying to slip a feeler gauge under the straightedge (see this Chapter's Specifications for the maximum warpage allowed and use a feeler gauge of that thickness)

10.4 A dial indicator can be used to determine the valve stem-to-guide clearance (move the valve as indicated by the arrows)

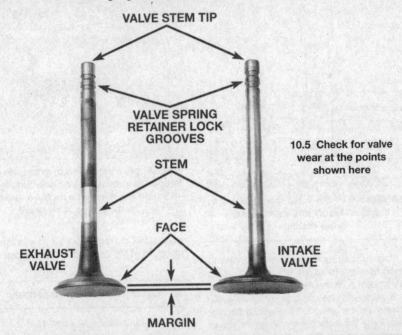

VALVE STEM TIP

VALVE SPRING RETAINER LOCK GROOVES

STEM

FACE

EXHAUST VALVE

INTAKE VALVE

MARGIN

10.5 Check for valve wear at the points shown here

10 Cylinder head - inspection

Refer to illustrations 10.2, 10.4, 10.5, 10.6, 10.7 and 10.8

Note: *Be sure to perform all of the following inspection procedures before concluding machine shop work is required. Make a list of the items that need attention.*

Cylinder head

1   Inspect the head very carefully for cracks, evidence of coolant leakage and other damage. If cracks are found, check with an automotive machine shop concerning repair. If repair isn't possible, a new cylinder head should be obtained.

2   Using a straightedge and feeler gauge, check the head gasket mating surface for warpage **(see illustration)**. If the warpage exceeds the limit in this Chapter's Specifications, it can be resurfaced at an automotive machine shop. **Note:** *If the V6 engine heads are resurfaced, the intake manifold flanges will also require machining.*

3   Examine the valve seats in each of the combustion chambers. If they're pitted, cracked or burned, the head will require valve service that's beyond the scope of the home mechanic.

4   Check the valve stem-to-guide clearance by measuring the lateral movement of the valve stem with a dial indicator attached securely to the head **(see illustration)**. The valve must be in the guide and approximately 1/16-inch off the seat. The total valve stem movement indicated by the gauge needle must be divided by two to obtain the actual clearance. After this is done, if there's still some doubt regarding the condition of the valve guides, they should be checked by an automotive machine shop (the cost should be minimal).

Valves

5   Carefully inspect each valve face for uneven wear, deformation, cracks, pits and burned areas. Check the valve stem for scuff-

fold and exhaust manifold mating surfaces. Be very careful not to gouge the cylinder head. Special gasket removal solvents that soften gaskets and make removal much easier are available at auto parts stores.

3   Remove all built up scale from the coolant passages.

4   Run a stiff wire brush through the various holes to remove deposits that may have formed in them.

5   Run an appropriate size tap into each of the threaded holes to remove corrosion and thread sealant that may be present. If compressed air is available, use it to clear the holes of debris produced by this operation. **Warning:** *Wear eye protection when using compressed air!*

6   Clean the rocker arm bolt threads with a wire brush.

7   Clean the cylinder head with solvent and dry it thoroughly. Compressed air will speed the drying process and ensure that all holes

and recessed areas are clean. **Note:** *Decarbonizing chemicals are available and may prove very useful when cleaning cylinder heads and valve train components. They're very caustic and should be used with caution. Be sure to follow the instructions on the container.*

8   Clean the rocker arm parts with solvent and dry them thoroughly (don't mix them up during the cleaning process). Compressed air will speed the drying process and can be used to clean out the oil passages.

9   Clean all the valve springs, spring seats, keepers and retainers with solvent and dry them thoroughly. Do the components from one valve at a time to avoid mixing up the parts.

10   Scrape off any heavy deposits that may have formed on the valves, then use a motorized wire brush to remove deposits from the valve heads and stems. Again, make sure the valves don't get mixed up.

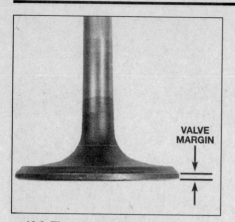

10.6 The margin width on each valve must be as specified (if no margin exists, the valve cannot be reused)

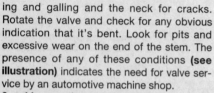

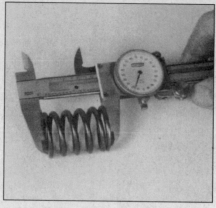

10.7 Measure the free length of each valve spring with a dial or vernier caliper

10.8 Check each valve spring for squareness

ing and galling and the neck for cracks. Rotate the valve and check for any obvious indication that it's bent. Look for pits and excessive wear on the end of the stem. The presence of any of these conditions **(see illustration)** indicates the need for valve service by an automotive machine shop.

6   Measure the margin width on each valve **(see illustration)**. Any valve with a margin narrower than specified in this Chapter will have to be replaced with a new one.

Valve components

7   Check each valve spring for wear (on the ends) and pits. Measure the free length and compare it to this Chapter's Specifications **(see illustration)**. Any springs that are shorter than specified have sagged and shouldn't be reused. The tension of all springs should be checked with a special fixture before deciding they're suitable for use in a rebuilt engine (take the springs to an automotive machine shop for this check).

8   Stand each spring on a flat surface and check it for squareness **(see illustration)**. If any of the springs are distorted or sagged, replace all of them with new parts.

9   Check the spring retainers and keepers for obvious wear and cracks. Any questionable parts should be replaced with new ones, as extensive damage will occur if they fail during engine operation.

10   If the inspection process indicates the valve components are in generally poor condition and worn beyond the limits specified, which is usually the case in an engine that's being overhauled, reassemble the valves in the cylinder head and refer to Section 11 for valve servicing recommendations.

11 Valves - servicing

1   Because of the complex nature of the job and the special tools and equipment needed, servicing of the valves, the valve seats and the valve guides, commonly known as a valve job, should be done by a professional.

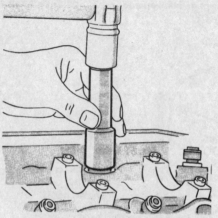

12.4 Make sure the valve stem seals are installed evenly and carefully to avoid damage

2   The home mechanic can remove and disassemble the head, do the initial cleaning and inspection, then reassemble and deliver it to a dealer service department or an automotive machine shop for the actual service work. Doing the inspection will enable you to see what condition the head and valvetrain components are in and will ensure that you know what work and new parts are required when dealing with an automotive machine shop.

3   The dealer service department, or automotive machine shop, will remove the valves and springs, recondition or replace the valves and valve seats, recondition the valve guides, check and replace the valve springs, rotators, spring retainers and keepers (as necessary), replace the valve seals with new ones, reassemble the valve components and make sure the installed spring height is correct. The cylinder head gasket surface will also be resurfaced if it's warped.

4   After the valve job has been performed by a professional, the head will be in like new condition. When the head is returned, be sure to clean it again before installation on the engine to remove any metal particles and abrasive grit that may still be present from the valve service or head resurfacing opera-

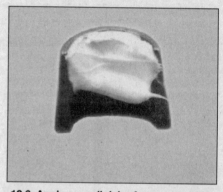

12.6 Apply a small dab of grease to each keeper as shown here before installation - it'll hold them in place on the valve stem as the spring is released

tions. Use compressed air, if available, to blow out all the oil holes and passages.

12 Cylinder head - reassembly

Refer to illustrations 12.4 and 12.6

1   Regardless of whether or not the head was sent to an automotive repair shop for valve servicing, make sure it's clean before beginning reassembly.

2   If the head was sent out for valve servicing, the valves and related components will already be in place. Begin the reassembly procedure with Step 8.

3   Install the spring seats or valve rotators (if equipped) before the valve seals.

4   Install new seals on each of the valve guides. Using a hammer and a deep socket or seal installation tool, gently tap each seal into place until it's completely seated on the guide **(see illustration)**. Don't twist or cock the seals during installation or they won't seal properly on the valve stems.

5   Beginning at one end of the head, lubricate and install the first valve. Apply moly-base grease or clean engine oil to the valve stem.

6   Position the valve springs (and shims, if used) over the valves. Compress the springs

13.1 A ridge reamer is required to remove the ridge from the top of each cylinder - do this before removing the pistons!

13.3 Check the connecting rod side clearance with a feeler gauge as shown

with a valve spring compressor and carefully install the keepers in the groove, then slowly release the compressor and make sure the keepers seat properly. Apply a small dab of grease to each keeper to hold it in place if necessary **(see illustration)**.

7   Repeat the procedure for the remaining valves. Be sure to return the components to their original locations - don't mix them up!

8   Check the installed valve spring height with a ruler graduated in 1/32-inch increments or a dial caliper. If the head was sent out for service work, the installed height should be correct (but don't automatically assume it is). The measurement is taken from the top of each spring seat to the bottom of the retainer. If the height is greater than specified in this Chapter, shims can be added under the springs to correct it. **Caution:** *Do not, under any circumstances, shim the springs to the point where the installed height is less than specified.*

9   Apply moly-base grease to the rocker arm faces and the shaft, then install the rocker arm assembly on the cylinder head.

10   Refer to Part A or B and install the camshafts, hydraulic lash adjusters and rocker arm assemblies onto the head.

13   Pistons and connecting rods - removal

Refer to illustrations 13.1, 13.3 and 13.6

Note: *Prior to removing the piston/connecting rod assemblies, remove the cylinder head(s), the oil pan and the oil pump by referring to the appropriate Sections in Parts A or B of Chapter 2.*

1   Use your fingernail to feel if a ridge has formed at the upper limit of ring travel (about 1/4-inch down from the top of each cylinder). If carbon deposits or cylinder wear have produced ridges, they must be completely removed with a special tool **(see illustration)**. Follow the manufacturer's instructions provided with the tool. Failure to remove the ridges before attempting to remove the pis-

ton/connecting rod assemblies may result in piston breakage.

2   After the cylinder ridges have been removed, turn the engine upside-down so the crankshaft is facing up.

3   Before the connecting rods are removed, check the endplay with feeler gauges. Slide them between the first connecting rod and the crankshaft throw until the play is removed **(see illustration)**. The endplay is equal to the thickness of the feeler gauge(s). If the endplay exceeds the service limit, new connecting rods will be required. If new rods (or a new crankshaft) are installed, the endplay may fall under the minimum specified in this Chapter (if it does, the rods will have to be machined to restore it - consult an automotive machine shop for advice if necessary). Repeat the procedure for the remaining connecting rods.

4   Check the connecting rods and caps for identification marks. If they aren't plainly marked, use a small center-punch to make the appropriate number of indentations on each rod and cap (1, 2, 3, etc., depending on the engine type and cylinder they're associated with).

5   Loosen each of the connecting rod cap nuts 1/2-turn at a time until they can be removed by hand. Remove the number one connecting rod cap and bearing insert. Don't drop the bearing insert out of the cap.

6   Slip a short length of plastic or rubber hose over each connecting rod cap bolt to protect the crankshaft journal and cylinder wall as the piston is removed **(see illustration)**.

7   Remove the bearing insert and push the connecting rod/piston assembly out through the top of the engine. Use a wooden or plastic hammer handle to push on the upper bearing surface in the connecting rod. If resistance is felt, double-check to make sure all of the ridge was removed from the cylinder.

8   Repeat the procedure for the remaining cylinders.

9   After removal, reassemble the connecting rod caps and bearing inserts in their respective connecting rods and install the

13.6 To prevent damage to the crankshaft journals and cylinder walls, slip sections of rubber or plastic hose over the rod bolts before removing the pistons

cap nuts finger tight. Leaving the old bearing inserts in place until reassembly will help prevent the connecting rod bearing surfaces from being accidentally nicked or gouged.

10   Don't separate the pistons from the connecting rods (see Section 19 for additional information).

14   Counterbalance shafts (four-cylinder engines) - removal, installation and chain tensioning

Note: *The counterbalance shafts can be removed only after the engine has been removed from the vehicle. It's assumed the flywheel or driveplate, timing belt, oil pan and oil pump (see Chapter 2, Part A) and piston/connecting rod assemblies have already been removed.*

Removal

Refer to illustrations 14.2, 14.3, 14.4 and 14.5

1   The balance shafts are installed in a carrier that is mounted to the lower block **(see illustration 7.5b)**. The shafts are intercon-

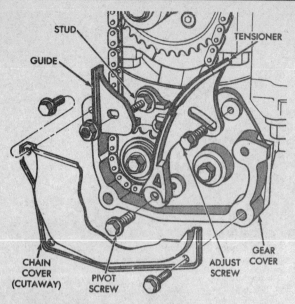

14.2 An exploded view of the chain cover, guide and tensioner

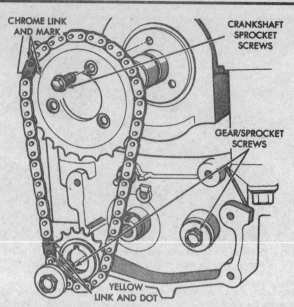

14.3 Note the location of the timing marks and the colored links before removing the assembly

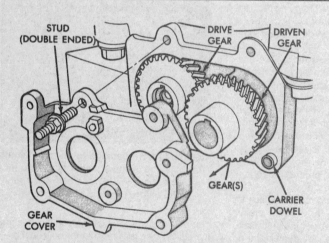

14.4 When you remove the gear cover, note the differently sized hubs on each balance shaft

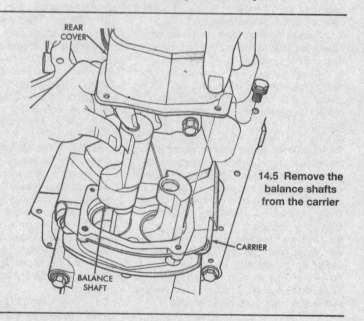

14.5 Remove the balance shafts from the carrier

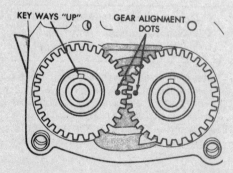

14.8 Note the position of the keyways and the alignment marks on the gears

nected through two gears rotating them in opposite directions. These gears are driven by a chain from the crankshaft and they are geared to rotate twice the crankshaft speed. This motion will counterbalance certain reciprocating masses within the engine.

2   Remove the chain cover, guide and tensioner from the engine block **(see illustration)**.

3   Remove the balance shaft gear and chain sprocket retaining bolts (Torx) that retain the crankshaft sprocket **(see illustration)**. Remove the chain and sprocket assembly.

4   Remove the special stud (double-ended) from the gear cover and remove the cover and balance shaft gears **(see illustration)**.

5   Remove the rear cover from the carrier and remove the balance shafts **(see illustration)**.

6   Remove the six bolts that retain the carrier to the crankcase.

Installation

Refer to illustrations 14.8 and 14.11

7   Install the balance shafts into the carrier.

8   Turn the balance shafts until both shaft keyways face up **(see illustration)**. Install the short hub drive gear on the sprocket driven shaft and the long hub gear on the gear driven shaft.

9   Install the gear cover and tighten the double-ended stud to the torque listed in this Chapter's Specifications.

10   Install the crankshaft sprocket and tighten the bolts (Torx) to the torque listed in this Chapter's Specifications.

11   Turn the crankshaft until number one is at Top Dead Center (TDC) (see Chapter 2A).

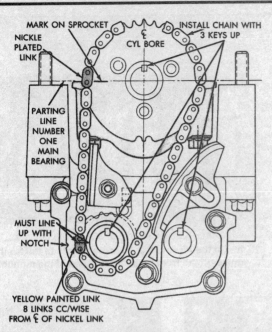

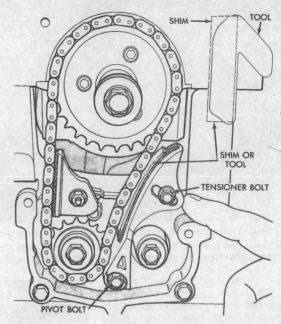

14.11 The mark on the crankshaft sprocket, the colored chain links and the mark on the counterbalance sprocket must be aligned for correct timing

14.16 Apply tension to the chain directly behind he adjustment bolt on the tensioner

The timing marks on the chain sprocket should line up with the parting line on the left side of number one main bearing cap **(see illustration)**.

12   Place the chain over the crankshaft sprocket so that the nickel plated link of the chain is over the timing mark on the crankshaft sprocket.

13   Install the balance shaft sprocket into the chain so that the timing mark on the sprocket (yellow dot) mates with the yellow painted link on the chain.

14   With the balance shaft keyways pointing up, slide the balance shaft sprocket onto the end of the balance shaft. **Note:** *The timing mark on the sprocket, the painted link and the arrow on the side of the gear cover should line up if the balance shafts are correctly timed.*

15   Install the balance shaft bolts and tighten the bolts to the torque listed in this Chapter's Specifications. **Note:** *Place a block of wood between the crankcase and the counterbalance crankshaft to prevent any gear rotation while tightening the bolts.*

Chain tensioning

Refer to illustration 14.16

16   Install the chain tensioner loosely. Place a shim (0.039 X 2.75 inch) between the tensioner and the chain **(see illustration)** or a special tool, if available. Push the tensioner up against the chain. Apply firm pressure directly behind the adjustment slot to take up all the slack.

17   With the load applied, tighten the top tensioner bolt first then the bottom pivot bolt. Tighten the bolts to the torque listed in this Chapter's Specifications. Remove the shim tool.

18   Place the chain guide onto the double

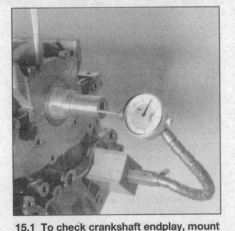

15.1 To check crankshaft endplay, mount a dial indicator on the front of the block and, using a screwdriver, pry the crankshaft back and forth

ended stud making sure the tab on the guide fits into the slot on the gear cover. Tighten the bolt to the torque listed in this Chapter's Specifications.

19   Install the carrier covers and tighten the bolts to the torque listed in this Chapter's Specifications.

15   Crankshaft - removal

Refer to illustrations 15.1, 15.3, 15.4a and 15.4b

Note: *The crankshaft can be removed only after the engine has been removed from the vehicle. It's assumed the flywheel or drive-plate, crankshaft balancer/vibration damper, timing chain or belt, oil pan, oil pump, counterbalance shafts (if equipped) and*

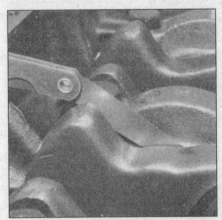

15.3 To check crankshaft endplay with a feeler gauge, place the gauge between the thrust main bearing and the crank

piston/connecting rod assemblies have already been removed. The rear main oil seal housing must be unbolted and separated from the block before proceeding with crankshaft removal.

1   Before the crankshaft is removed, check the endplay. Mount a dial indicator with the stem in line with the crankshaft, touching one of the crank throws **(see illustration)**.

2   Push the crankshaft all the way to the rear and zero the dial indicator. Next, pry the crankshaft to the front as far as possible and check the reading on the dial indicator. The distance it moves is the endplay. If it's greater than the value listed in this Chapter's Specifications, check the crankshaft thrust surfaces for wear. If no wear is evident, new main bearings should correct the endplay.

3   If a dial indicator isn't available, feeler gauges can be used. Gently pry or push the

15.4a Use a center punch or number stamping dies to mark the main bearing caps to ensure installation in their original locations on the block (make the punch marks near one of the bolt heads)

15.4b On the V6 engines, an arrow points to the front of the engine on the front main bearing cap of the monoblock

crankshaft all the way to the front of the engine. Slip feeler gauges between the crankshaft and the front face of the thrust main bearing to determine the clearance **(see illustration)**.

4   Check the main bearing caps to see if they're marked to indicate their locations. They should be numbered consecutively from the front of the engine to the rear. If they aren't, mark them with number stamping dies or a center-punch **(see illustrations)**. Main bearing caps generally have a cast-in arrow, which points to the front of the engine **(see illustration)**. Loosen the main bearing cap bolts 1/4-turn at a time each, until they can be removed by hand. **Note:** *If any stud bolts are used and make sure they're returned to their original locations when the crankshaft is reinstalled.*

5   Gently tap the caps with a soft-face hammer, then separate them from the engine block. If necessary, use the bolts as levers to remove the caps. Try not to drop the bearing inserts if they come out with the caps.

6   Carefully lift the crankshaft out of the engine. It may be a good idea to have an assistant available, since the crankshaft is quite heavy. With the bearing inserts in place in the engine block and main bearing caps, return the caps to their respective locations on the engine block and tighten the bolts finger tight.

16   Engine block - cleaning

Refer to illustrations 16.4a, 16.4b, 16.8 and 16.10

1   Remove the main bearing caps and separate the bearing inserts from the caps and the engine block. Tag the bearings, indicating which cylinder they were removed from and whether they were in the cap or the block, then set them aside.

2   Using a gasket scraper, remove all traces of gasket material from the engine block. Be very careful not to nick or gouge

16.4a A hammer and a large punch can be used to knock the core plugs sideways in their bores

16.4b Pull the core plugs from the block with pliers

the gasket sealing surfaces.

3   Remove all of the covers and threaded oil gallery plugs from the block. The plugs are usually very tight - they may have to be drilled out and the holes retapped. Use new plugs when the engine is reassembled.

4   Remove the core plugs from the engine block. To do this, knock one side of the plug into the block with a hammer and a punch, then grasp them with large pliers and pull them out **(see illustrations)**.

5   If the engine is extremely dirty, it should be taken to an automotive machine shop to be steam cleaned or hot tanked.

6   After the block is returned, clean all oil holes and oil galleries one more time. Brushes specifically designed for this purpose are available at most auto parts stores. Flush the passages with warm water until the water runs clear, dry the block thoroughly and wipe all machined surfaces with a light, rust preventive oil. If you have access to compressed air, use it to speed the drying process and blow out all the oil holes and galleries. **Warning:** *Wear eye protection when using compressed air!*

7   If the block isn't extremely dirty or sludged up, you can do an adequate cleaning job with hot soapy water and a stiff brush. Take plenty of time and do a thorough job. Regardless of the cleaning method used, be sure to clean all oil holes and galleries very thoroughly, dry the block completely and coat all machined surfaces with light oil.

8   The threaded holes in the block must be clean to ensure accurate torque readings during reassembly. Run the proper size tap into each of the holes to remove rust, corrosion, thread sealant or sludge and restore damaged threads **(see illustration)**. If possible, use compressed air to clear the holes of debris produced by this operation. Now is a good time to clean the threads on the head bolts and the main bearing cap bolts as well.

9   Reinstall the main bearing caps and tighten the bolts finger tight.

10   After coating the sealing surfaces of the new core plugs with Permeate no. 2 sealant, install them in the engine block **(see illustration)**. Make sure they're driven in straight and seated properly or leakage could result. Special tools are available for this purpose, but a large socket, with an outside diameter that

16.8 All bolt holes in the block - particularly the main bearing cap and head bolt holes - should be cleaned and restored with a tap (be sure to remove debris from the holes after this is done)

16.10 A large socket on an extension can be used to drive the new core plugs into the bores

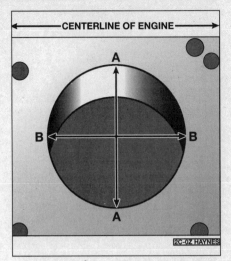

17.4a Measure the diameter of each cylinder at a right angle to the engine centerline (A), and parallel to engine centerline (B) - out-of-round is the difference between A and B; taper is the difference between A and B at the top of the cylinder and A and B at the bottom of the cylinder

will just slip into the core plug, a 1/2-inch drive extension and a hammer will work just as well.

11   Apply non-hardening sealant (such as Permeate no. 2 or Teflon pipe sealant) to the new oil gallery plugs and thread them into the holes in the block. Make sure they're tightened securely.

12   If the engine isn't going to be reassembled right away, cover it with a large plastic trash bag to keep it clean.

17   Engine block - inspection

Refer to illustrations 17.4a, 17.4b and 17.4c

1   Before the block is inspected, it should be cleaned as described in Section 16.

2   Visually check the block for cracks, rust and corrosion. Look for stripped threads in the threaded holes. It's also a good idea to have the block checked for hidden cracks by an automotive machine shop that has the

special equipment to do this type of work. If defects are found, have the block repaired, if possible, or replaced.

3   Check the cylinder bores for scuffing and scoring.

4   Measure the diameter of each cylinder at the top (just under the ridge area), center and bottom of the cylinder bore, parallel to the crankshaft axis **(see illustrations)**. **Note:** *These measurements should not be made with the bare block mounted on an engine stand - the cylinders will be distorted and the measurements will be inaccurate.*

5   Next, measure each cylinder's diameter at the same three locations across the crankshaft axis. Compare the results to this Chapter's Specifications.

6   If the required precision measuring tools aren't available, the piston-to-cylinder clearances can be obtained, though not quite as accurately, using feeler gauge stock. Feeler gauge stock comes in 12-inch lengths and various thicknesses and is generally available at auto parts stores.

7   To check the clearance, select a feeler

gauge and slip it into the cylinder along with the matching piston. The piston must be positioned exactly as it normally would be. The feeler gauge must be between the piston and cylinder on one of the thrust faces (90-degrees to the piston pin bore).

8   The piston should slip through the cylinder (with the feeler gauge in place) with moderate pressure.

9   If it falls through or slides through easily, the clearance is excessive and a new piston will be required. If the piston binds at the lower end of the cylinder and is loose toward the top, the cylinder is tapered. If tight spots are encountered as the piston/feeler gauge is rotated in the cylinder, the cylinder is out-of-round.

10   Repeat the procedure for the remaining

17.4b The ability to "feel" when the telescoping gauge is at the correct point will be developed over time, so work slowly and repeat the check until you're satisfied the bore measurement is accurate

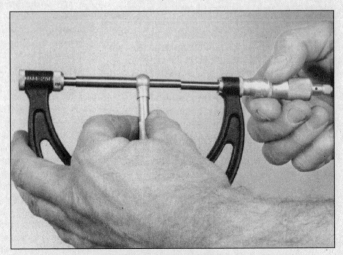

17.4c The gauge is then measured with a micrometer to determine the bore size

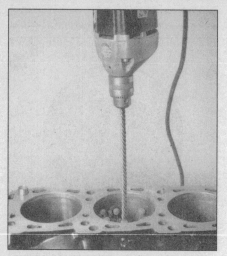

18.3a A "bottle brush" hone will produce better results if you've never honed cylinders before

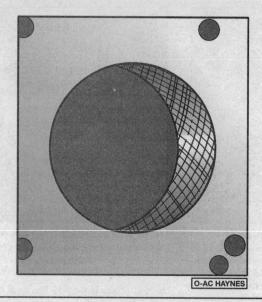

18.3b The cylinder hone should leave a smooth, crosshatch pattern with the lines intersecting at approximately a 60-degree angle

O-AC HAYNES

pistons and cylinders.

11   If the cylinder walls are badly scuffed or scored, or if they're out-of- round or tapered beyond the limits given in this Chapter's Specifications, have the engine block rebored and honed at an automotive machine shop. If a rebore is done, oversize pistons and rings will be required.

12   If the cylinders are in reasonably good condition and not worn to the outside of the limits, and if the piston-to-cylinder clearances can be maintained properly, they don't have to be rebored. Honing is all that's necessary (see Section 18).

18   Cylinder honing

Refer to illustrations 18.3a and 18.3b

1   Prior to engine reassembly, the cylinder bores must be honed so the new piston rings will seat correctly and provide the best possible combustion chamber seal. **Note:** *If you don't have the tools or don't want to tackle the honing operation, most automotive machine shops will do it for a reasonable fee.*

2   Before honing the cylinders, install the main bearing caps and tighten the bolts to the torque listed in this Chapter's Specifications.

3   Two types of cylinder hones are commonly available - the flex hone or "bottle brush" type and the more traditional surfacing hone with spring-loaded stones. Both will do the job, but for the less experienced mechanic the "bottle brush" hone will probably be easier to use. You'll also need some honing oil (kerosene will work if honing oil isn't available), rags and an electric drill motor. Proceed as follows:

   a)   *Mount the hone in the drill motor, compress the stones and slip it into the first cylinder* **(see illustration)**. *Be sure to wear safety goggles or a face shield!*

   b)   *Lubricate the cylinder with plenty of*

honing oil, turn on the drill and move the hone up-and-down in the cylinder at a pace that will produce a fine crosshatch pattern on the cylinder walls. Ideally, the crosshatch lines should intersect at approximately a 60-degree angle **(see illustration)**. *Be sure to use plenty of lubricant and don't take off any more material than is absolutely necessary to produce the desired finish.* **Note:** *Piston ring manufacturers may specify a smaller crosshatch angle than the traditional 60-degrees - read and follow any instructions included with the new rings.*

   c)   *Don't withdraw the hone from the cylinder while it's running. Instead, shut off the drill and continue moving the hone up-and-down in the cylinder until it comes to a complete stop, then compress the stones and withdraw the hone. If you're using a "bottle brush" type hone, stop the drill motor, then turn the chuck in the normal direction of rotation while withdrawing the hone from the cylinder.*

   d)   *Wipe the oil out of the cylinder and repeat the procedure for the remaining cylinders.*

4   After the honing job is complete, chamfer the top edges of the cylinder bores with a small file so the rings won't catch when the pistons are installed. Be very careful not to nick the cylinder walls with the end of the file.

5   The entire engine block must be washed again very thoroughly with warm, soapy water to remove all traces of the abrasive grit produced during the honing operation. **Note:** *The bores can be considered clean when a lint-free white cloth - dampened with clean engine oil - used to wipe them out doesn't pick up any more honing residue, which will show up as gray areas on the cloth.* Be sure to run a brush through all oil holes and galleries and flush them with running water.

6   After rinsing, dry the block and apply a

coat of light rust preventive oil to all machined surfaces. Wrap the block in a plastic trash bag to keep it clean and set it aside until reassembly.

19   Pistons and connecting rods - inspection

Refer to illustrations 19.4a, 19.4b, 19.10 and 19.11

1   Before the inspection process can be carried out, the piston/connecting rod assemblies must be cleaned and the original piston rings removed from the pistons. **Note:** *Always use new piston rings when the engine is reassembled.*

2   Using a piston ring installation tool, carefully remove the rings from the pistons. Be careful not to nick or gouge the pistons in the process.

3   Scrape all traces of carbon from the top of the piston. A hand held wire brush or a piece of fine emery cloth can be used once the majority of the deposits have been scraped away. Do not, under any circumstances, use a wire brush mounted in a drill motor to remove deposits from the pistons. The piston material is soft and may be eroded away by the wire brush.

4   Use a piston ring groove cleaning tool to remove carbon deposits from the ring grooves. If a tool isn't available, a piece broken off the old ring will do the job. Be very careful to remove only the carbon deposits - don't remove any metal and do not nick or scratch the sides of the ring grooves **(see illustrations)**.

5   Once the deposits have been removed, clean the piston/rod assemblies with solvent and dry them with compressed air (if available). **Warning:** *Wear eye protection. Make sure the oil return holes in the back sides of the ring grooves are clear.*

6   If the pistons and cylinder walls aren't

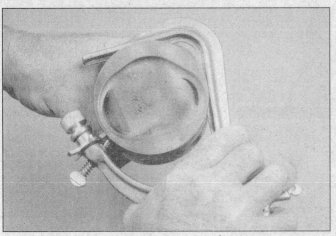

19.4a The piston ring grooves can be cleaned with a special tool, as shown here . . .

19.4b . . . or a section of a broken ring

19.10 Check the ring side clearance with a feeler gauge at several points around the groove

19.11 Measure the piston diameter at a 90-degree angle to the piston pin and in line with it

2C

damaged or worn excessively, and if the engine block isn't rebored, new pistons won't be necessary. Normal piston wear appears as even vertical wear on the piston thrust surfaces and slight looseness of the top ring in its groove. New piston rings, however, should always be used when an engine is rebuilt.

7   Carefully inspect each piston for cracks around the skirt, at the pin bosses and at the ring lands.

8   Look for scoring and scuffing on the thrust faces of the skirt, holes in the piston crown and burned areas at the edge of the crown. If the skirt is scored or scuffed, the engine may have been suffering from overheating and/or abnormal combustion, which caused excessively high operating temperatures. The cooling and lubrication systems should be checked thoroughly. A hole in the piston crown is an indication that abnormal combustion (pre-ignition) was occurring. Burned areas at the edge of the piston crown are usually evidence of spark knock (detonation). If any of the above problems exist, the causes must be corrected or the damage will occur again. The causes may include intake air leaks, incorrect fuel/air mixture, low

octane fuel, ignition timing and EGR system malfunctions.

9   Corrosion of the piston, in the form of small pits, indicates coolant is leaking into the combustion chamber and/or the crankcase. Again, the cause must be corrected or the problem may persist in the rebuilt engine.

10   Measure the piston ring side clearance by laying a new piston ring in each ring groove and slipping a feeler gauge in beside it **(see illustration)**. Check the clearance at three or four locations around each groove. Be sure to use the correct ring for each groove - they are different. If the side clearance is greater than specified in this Chapter, new pistons will have to be used.

11   Check the piston-to-bore clearance by measuring the bore (see Section 17) and the piston diameter. Make sure the pistons and bores are correctly matched. Measure the piston across the skirt, at a 90-degree angle to the piston pin **(see illustration)**. The measurement must be taken at a specific point, depending on the engine type, to be accurate.

 a) *The piston diameter on 2.2L four-cylin-*

der engines is measured in line with the piston pin centerline, 1.14 inches (28.9 mm) below the top of the piston. On 2.5L engines, piston diameter is measured slightly below centerline with the piston pin.

 b) *V6 engine pistons are measured 0.080 inches (2.0 mm) above the bottom of the piston skirt.*

12   Subtract the piston diameter from the bore diameter to obtain the clearance. If it's greater than specified, the block will have to be rebored and new pistons and rings installed.

13   Check the piston-to-rod clearance by twisting the piston and rod in opposite directions. Any noticeable play indicates excessive wear, which must be corrected. The piston/connecting rod assemblies should be taken to an automotive machine shop to have the pistons and rods resized and new pins installed.

14   If the pistons must be removed from the connecting rods for any reason, they should be taken to an automotive machine shop. While they are there have the connecting rods checked for bend and twist, since auto-

20.1 The oil holes should be chamfered so sharp edges don't gouge or scratch the new bearings

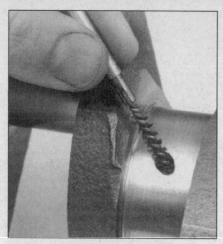

20.2 Use a wire or stiff plastic bristle brush to clean the oil passages in the crankshaft

20.4 Rubbing a penny lengthwise on each journal will reveal its condition - if copper rubs off and is embedded in the crankshaft, the journals should be reground

motive machine shops have special equipment for this purpose. **Note:** *Unless new pistons and/or connecting rods must be installed, do not disassemble the pistons and connecting rods.*

15   Check the connecting rods for cracks and other damage. Temporarily remove the rod caps, lift out the old bearing inserts, wipe the rod and cap bearing surfaces clean and inspect them for nicks, gouges and scratches. After checking the rods, replace the old bearings, slip the caps into place and tighten the nuts finger tight. **Note:** *If the engine is being rebuilt because of a connecting rod knock, be sure to install new rods.*

20   Crankshaft - inspection

Refer to illustrations 20.1, 20.2, 20.4, 20.6 and 20.8

1   Remove all burrs from the crankshaft oil holes with a stone, file or scraper **(see illustration)**.

2   Clean the crankshaft with solvent and dry it with compressed air (if available). **Warning:** *Wear eye protection when using compressed air. Be sure to clean the oil holes with a stiff brush* **(see illustration)** *and flush them with solvent.*

3   Check the main and connecting rod bearing journals for uneven wear, scoring, pits and cracks.

4   Rub a penny across each journal several times **(see illustration)**. If a journal picks up copper from the penny, it's too rough and must be reground.

5   Check the rest of the crankshaft for cracks and other damage. It should be magnafluxed to reveal hidden cracks - an automotive machine shop will handle the procedure.

6   Using a micrometer, measure the diameter of the main and connecting rod journals and compare the results to this Chapter's Specifications **(see illustration)**. By measuring the diameter at a number of points around each journal's circumference, you'll

be able to determine whether or not the journal is out-of-round. Take the measurement at each end of the journal, near the crank throws, to determine if the journal is tapered.

7   If the crankshaft journals are damaged, tapered, out-of-round or worn beyond the limits given in the Specifications, have the crankshaft reground by an automotive machine shop. Be sure to use the correct size bearing inserts if the crankshaft is reconditioned.

8   Check the oil seal journals at each end of the crankshaft for wear and damage. If the seal has worn a groove in the journal, or if it's nicked or scratched **(see illustration)**, the new seal may leak when the engine is reassembled. In some cases, an automotive machine shop may be able to repair the journal by pressing on a thin sleeve. If repair isn't feasible, a new or different crankshaft should be installed.

9   Refer to Section 21 and examine the main and rod bearing inserts.

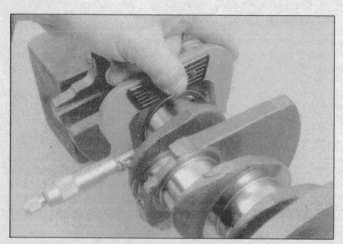

20.6 Measure the diameter of each crankshaft journal at several points to detect taper and out-of-round conditions

20.8 If the seals have worn grooves in the crankshaft journals, or if the seal contact surfaces are nicked or scratched, the new seals will leak

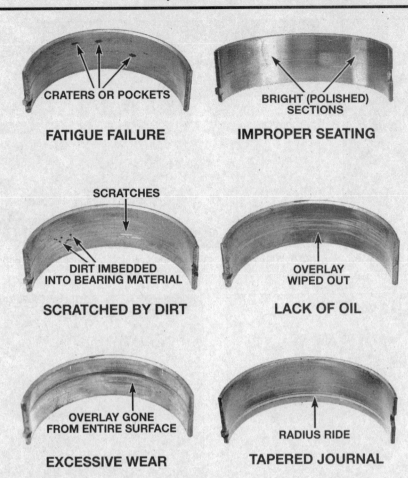

FATIGUE FAILURE — CRATERS OR POCKETS

IMPROPER SEATING — BRIGHT (POLISHED) SECTIONS

SCRATCHED BY DIRT — SCRATCHES / DIRT IMBEDDED INTO BEARING MATERIAL

LACK OF OIL — OVERLAY WIPED OUT

EXCESSIVE WEAR — OVERLAY GONE FROM ENTIRE SURFACE

TAPERED JOURNAL — RADIUS RIDE

21.1 Typical bearing failures

21 Main and connecting rod bearings - inspection

Refer to illustration 21.1

1   Even though the main and connecting rod bearings should be replaced with new ones during the engine overhaul, the old bearings should be retained for close examination, as they may reveal valuable information about the condition of the engine **(see illustration)**.

2   Bearing failure occurs because of lack of lubrication, the presence of dirt or other foreign particles, overloading the engine and corrosion. Regardless of the cause of bearing failure, it must be corrected before the engine is reassembled to prevent it from happening again.

3   When examining the bearings, remove them from the engine block, the main bearing caps, the connecting rods and the rod caps and lay them out on a clean surface in the same general position as their location in the engine. This will enable you to match any bearing problems with the corresponding crankshaft journal.

4   Dirt and other foreign particles get into the engine in a variety of ways. It may be left in the engine during assembly, or it may pass through filters or the PCV system. It may get into the oil, and from there into the bearings. Metal chips from machining operations and normal engine wear are often present. Abrasives are sometimes left in engine components after reconditioning, especially when parts aren't thoroughly cleaned using the proper cleaning methods. Whatever the source, these foreign objects often end up embedded in the soft bearing material and are easily recognized. Large particles won't embed in the bearing and will score or gouge the bearing and journal. The best prevention for this cause of bearing failure is to clean all parts thoroughly and keep everything spotlessly clean during engine assembly. Frequent and regular engine oil and filter changes are also recommended.

5   Lack of lubrication (or lubrication breakdown) has a number of interrelated causes. Excessive heat (which thins the oil), overloading (which squeezes the oil from the bearing face) and oil leakage or throw off (from excessive bearing clearances, worn oil pump or high engine speeds) all contribute to lubrication breakdown. Blocked oil passages, which usually are the result of misaligned oil holes in a bearing shell, will also oil starve a bearing and destroy it. When lack of lubrication is the cause of bearing failure, the bearing material is wiped or extruded from the steel backing of the bearing. Temperatures may increase to the point where the steel backing turns blue from overheating.

6   Driving habits can have a definite effect on bearing life. Full throttle, low speed operation (lugging the engine) puts very high loads on bearings, which tends to squeeze out the oil film. These loads cause the bearings to flex, which produces fine cracks in the bearing face (fatigue failure). Eventually the bearing material will loosen in pieces and tear away from the steel backing. Short trip driving leads to corrosion of bearings because insufficient engine heat is produced to drive off the condensed water and corrosive gases. These products collect in the engine oil, forming acid and sludge. As the oil is carried to the engine bearings, the acid attacks and corrodes the bearing material.

7   Incorrect bearing installation during engine assembly will lead to bearing failure as well. Tight fitting bearings leave insufficient oil clearance and will result in oil starvation. Dirt or foreign particles trapped behind a bearing insert result in high spots on the bearing which lead to failure.

22 Engine overhaul - reassembly sequence

1   Before beginning engine reassembly, make sure you have all the necessary new parts, gaskets and seals as well as the following items on hand:

Common hand tools
Torque wrench (1/2-inch drive)
Piston ring installation tool
Piston ring compressor
Vibration damper installation tool
Short lengths of rubber or plastic hose to fit over connecting rod bolts
Plastigage
Feeler gauges
Fine-tooth file
New engine oil
Engine assembly lube or moly-base grease
Gasket sealant
Thread locking compound

2   In order to save time and avoid problems, engine reassembly must be done in the following general order:

Four-cylinder engines

Crankshaft and main bearings
Rear main oil seal housing
Piston/connecting rod assemblies
Balance shafts (if equipped)
Oil pump
Timing belt and sprockets
Timing belt cover
Oil pan
Cylinder head, camshaft, pushrods and rocker arms
Intake/exhaust manifolds
Valve cover
Engine rear plate (if equipped)
Flywheel/driveplate

2C

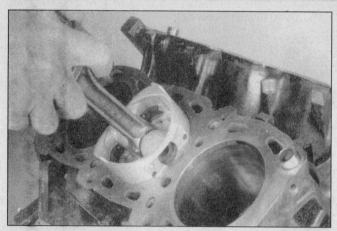

23.3 When checking piston ring and gap, the ring must be square in the cylinder bore (this is done by pushing the ring down with the top of a piston as shown)

23.4 With the ring square in the cylinder, measure the end gap with a feeler gauge

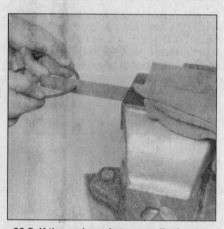

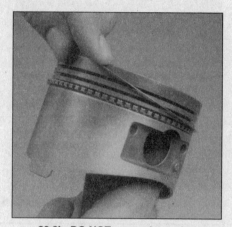

23.5 If the end gap is too small, clamp a file in a vise and file the ring ends (from the outside in only) to enlarge the gap slightly

23.9a Installing the spacer/expander in the oil control ring groove

23.9b DO NOT use a piston ring installation tool when installing the oil ring side rails

V6 engine

Crankshaft and main bearings
Rear main oil seal housing
Piston/connecting rod assemblies
Oil pump
Oil pan
Timing belt cover
Timing belt and sprockets
Cylinder heads and camshafts
Intake and exhaust manifolds
Valve covers
Flywheel/driveplate

23 Piston rings - installation

Refer to illustrations 23.3, 23.4, 23.5, 23.9a, 23.9b and 23.12

1   Before installing the new piston rings, the ring end gaps must be checked. It's assumed the piston ring side clearance has been checked and verified correct (see Section 19).

2   Lay out the piston/connecting rod assemblies and the new ring sets so the ring sets will be matched with the same piston

and cylinder during the end gap measurement and engine assembly.

3   Insert the top (number one) ring into the first cylinder and square it up with the cylinder walls by pushing it in with the top of the piston **(see illustration)**. The ring should be near the bottom of the cylinder, at the lower limit of ring travel.

4   To measure the end gap, slip feeler gauges between the ends of the ring until a gauge equal to the gap width is found **(see illustration)**. The feeler gauge should slide between the ring ends with a slight amount of drag. Compare the measurement to this Chapter's Specifications. If the gap is larger or smaller than specified, double-check to make sure you have the correct rings before proceeding.

5   If the gap is too small, it must be enlarged or the ring ends may come in contact with each other during engine operation, which can cause serious engine damage. The end gap can be increased by filing the ring ends very carefully with a fine file. Mount the file in a vise equipped with soft jaws, slip the ring over the file with the ends contacting the file teeth and slowly move the ring to remove material from the ends. When performing this

operation, file only from the outside in **(see illustration)**.

6   Excess end gap isn't critical unless it's greater than 0.040-inch. Again, double-check to make sure you have the correct rings for the engine.

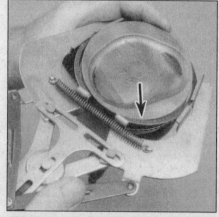

23.12 Installing the compression rings with a ring expander - the mark (arrow) must face up

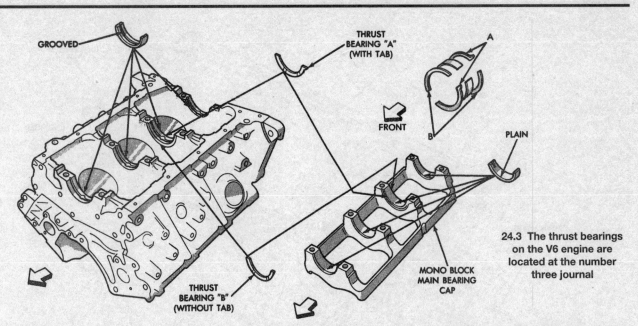

24.3 The thrust bearings on the V6 engine are located at the number three journal

7   Repeat the procedure for each ring that will be installed in the first cylinder and for each ring in the remaining cylinders. Remember to keep rings, pistons and cylinders matched up.

8   Once the ring end gaps have been checked/corrected, the rings can be installed on the pistons.

9   The oil control ring (lowest one on the piston) is usually installed first. It's composed of three separate components. Slip the spacer/expander into the groove **(see illustration)**. If an anti-rotation tang is used, make sure it's inserted into the drilled hole in the ring groove. Next, install the lower side rail. Don't use a piston ring installation tool on the oil ring side rails, as they may be damaged. Instead, place one end of the side rail into the groove between the spacer/expander and the ring land, hold it firmly in place and slide a finger around the piston while pushing the rail into the groove **(see illustration)**. Next, install the upper side rail in the same manner.

10   After the three oil ring components have been installed, check to make sure both the upper and lower side rails can be turned smoothly in the ring groove.

11   The number two (middle) ring is installed next. It's usually stamped with a mark, which must face up, toward the top of the piston. **Note:** *Always follow the instructions printed on the ring package or box - different manufacturers may require different approaches. Don't mix up the top and middle rings, as they have different cross sections.*

12   Use a piston ring installation tool and make sure the identification mark is facing the top of the piston, then slip the ring into the middle groove on the piston **(see illustration)**. Don't expand the ring any more than necessary to slide it over the piston.

13   Install the number one (top) ring in the same manner. Make sure the mark is facing up. Be careful not to confuse the number one and number two rings.

14   Repeat the procedure for the remaining pistons and rings.

24   Crankshaft - installation and main bearing oil clearance check

Refer to illustrations 24.3, 24.11, 24.13 and 24.15

1   Crankshaft installation is the first step in engine reassembly. It's assumed at this point that the engine block and crankshaft have been cleaned, inspected and repaired or reconditioned.

2   Position the engine with the bottom facing up.

3   Remove the main bearing cap bolts and lift out the caps. Lay them out in the proper order to ensure correct installation **(see illustration)**.

4   If they're still in place, remove the original bearing inserts from the block and the main bearing caps. Wipe the bearing surfaces of the block and caps with a clean, lint-free cloth. They must be kept spotlessly clean.

Main bearing oil clearance check

Note: *Don't touch the faces of the new bearing inserts with your fingers. Oil and acids from your skin can etch the bearings.*

5   Clean the back sides of the new main bearing inserts and lay one in each main bearing saddle in the block. If one of the bearing inserts from
each set has a large groove in it, make sure the grooved insert is installed in the block. Lay the other bearing from each set in the corresponding main bearing cap. Make sure the tab on the bearing insert fits into the recess in the block or cap. **Caution:** *The oil holes in the block must line up with the oil holes in the bearing inserts. Do not hammer*

the bearing into place and don't nick or gouge the bearing faces. No lubrication should be used at this time.

6   The thrust bearing must be installed in the number three (center) cap and saddle.

7   Clean the faces of the bearings in the block and the crankshaft main bearing journals with a clean, lint-free cloth.

8   Check or clean the oil holes in the crankshaft, as any dirt here can go only one way - straight through the new bearings.

9   Once you're certain the crankshaft is clean, carefully lay it in position in the main bearings.

10   Before the crankshaft can be permanently installed, the main bearing oil clearance must be checked.

11   Cut several pieces of the appropriate size Plastigage (they should be slightly shorter than the width of the main bearings) and place one piece on each crankshaft main bearing journal, parallel with the journal axis **(see illustration)**.

24.11 Lay the Plastigage strips (arrow) on the main bearing journals, parallel to the crankshaft centerline

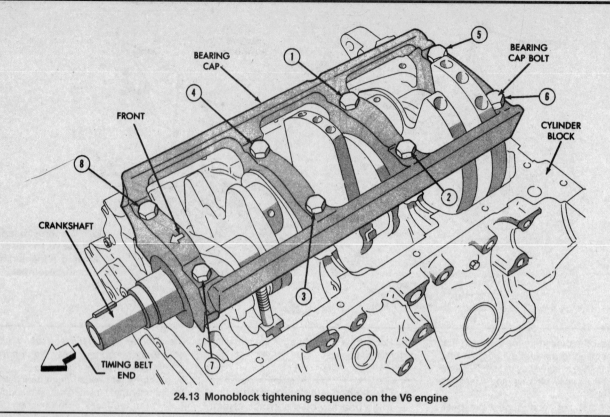

24.13 Monoblock tightening sequence on the V6 engine

12   Clean the faces of the bearings in the caps and install the caps in their original locations (don't mix them up) with the arrows pointing toward the front of the engine. Don't disturb the Plastigage.

13   Starting with the center main and working out toward the ends, tighten the main bearing cap bolts, in three steps, to the torque figure listed in this Chapter's Specifications. Don't rotate the crankshaft at any time during this operation. **Note:** *On 3.0L engines, tighten the mono-block bolts in the correct sequence* **(see illustration).**

14   Remove the bolts and carefully lift off the main bearing caps. Keep them in order. Don't disturb the Plastigage or rotate the crankshaft. If any of the main bearing caps are difficult to remove, tap them gently from side-to-side with a soft-face hammer to loosen them.

15   Compare the width of the crushed Plastigage on each journal to the scale printed on the Plastigage envelope to obtain the main bearing oil clearance **(see illustration).** Check the Specifications to make sure it's correct.

16   If the clearance is not as specified, the bearing inserts may be the wrong size (which means different ones will be required). Before deciding different inserts are needed, make sure no dirt or oil was between the bearing inserts and the caps or block when the clearance was measured. If the Plastigage was wider at one end than the other, the journal may be tapered (see Section 20).

17   Carefully scrape all traces of the Plastigage material off the main bearing journals

and/or the bearing faces. Use your fingernail or the edge of a credit card - don't nick or scratch the bearing faces.

Final crankshaft installation

18   Carefully lift the crankshaft out of the engine.

19   Clean the bearing faces in the block, then apply a thin, uniform layer of moly-base grease or engine assembly lube to each of the bearing surfaces. Be sure to coat the thrust faces as well as the journal face of the thrust bearing.

20   Make sure the crankshaft journals are clean, then lay the crankshaft back in place in the block.

21   Clean the faces of the bearings in the caps, then apply lubricant to them.

22   Install the caps in their original locations with the arrows pointing toward the front of the engine.

23   Install the bolts.

24   Tighten all except the thrust bearing cap bolts to the specified torque (work from the center out and approach the final torque in three steps).

25   Tighten the thrust bearing cap bolts to 10-to-12 ft-lbs.

26   Tap the ends of the crankshaft forward and backward with a lead or brass hammer to line up the main bearing and crankshaft thrust surfaces.

27   Retighten all main bearing cap bolts to the torque listed in this Chapter's Specifications, starting with the center main and working out toward the ends.

28   Rotate the crankshaft a number of times by hand to check for any obvious binding.

29   The final step is to check the crankshaft endplay with feeler gauges or a dial indicator as described in Section 15. The endplay should be correct if the crankshaft thrust faces aren't worn or damaged and new bearings have been installed.

30   Refer to Section 25 and install the new rear main oil seal.

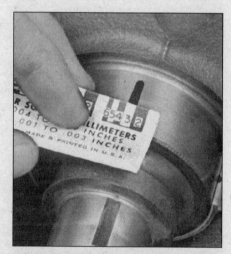

24.15 **Compare the width of the crushed Plastigage to the scale on the envelope to determine the main bearing oil clearance (always take the measurement at the widest point of the Plastigage); be sure to use the correct scale - standard and metric ones are included**

25.1 To remove the old rear main oil seal from the housing, support the housing on a pair of wood blocks and drive out the seal with a punch or screwdriver and hammer - make sure you don't damage the seal bore

25.2 To install the new seal in he housing, simply lay the housing on a clean, flat workbench lay a block of wood on the seal and carefully tap it into place with a hammer

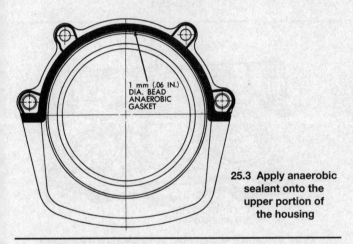

1 mm (.06 IN.) DIA. BEAD ANAEROBIC GASKET

25.3 Apply anaerobic sealant onto the upper portion of the housing

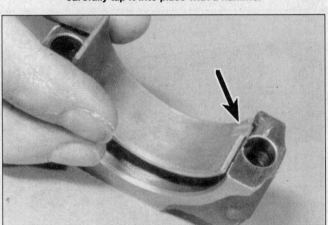

26.4 The tab on the bearing (arrow) must fit into the cap recess so the bearing will seat properly

2C

25 Rear main oil seal - installation

Refer to illustrations 25.1, 25.2 and 25.3
Note: *The crankshaft must be installed and the main bearing caps bolted in place before the new seal and housing assembly can be bolted to the block.*

1   Remove the old seal from the housing with a hammer and punch by driving it out from the back side **(see illustration)**. Be sure to note how far it's recessed into the housing bore before removing it; the new seal will have to be recessed an equal amount. Be very careful not to scratch or otherwise damage the bore in the housing or oil leaks could develop.

2   Make sure the housing is clean, then apply a thin coat of engine oil to the outer edge of the new seal. The seal must be pressed squarely into the housing bore, so hammering it into place isn't recommended. If you don't have access to a press, sandwich the housing and seal between two smooth pieces of wood and press the seal into place with the jaws of a large vise. If you don't have a vise big enough, lay the housing on a work-

bench and drive the seal into place with a block of wood and hammer **(see illustration)**. The pieces of wood must be thick enough to distribute the force evenly around the entire circumference of the seal. Work slowly and make sure the seal enters the bore squarely.

3   Apply anaerobic sealant on the upper portion of the retainer **(see illustration)** before installing the housing. Lubricate the seal lips with clean engine oil or multi-purpose grease before you slip the seal/housing over the crankshaft and bolt it to the block.

4   Tighten the housing bolts a little at a time until they're all snug.

26 Pistons and connecting rods - installation and rod bearing oil clearance check

Refer to illustrations 26.4, 26.5, 26.9a, 26.9b, 26.9c, 26.11, 26.13 and 26.17

1   Before installing the piston/connecting rod assemblies, the cylinder walls must be perfectly clean, the top edge of each cylinder

must be chamfered, and the crankshaft must be in place.

2   Remove the cap from the end of the number one connecting rod (check the marks made during removal). Remove the original bearing inserts and wipe the bearing surfaces of the connecting rod and cap with a clean, lint-free cloth. They must be kept spotlessly clean.

Connecting rod bearing oil clearance check

Note: *Don't touch the faces of the new bearing inserts with your fingers. Oil and acids from your skin can etch the bearings.*

3   Clean the back side of the new upper bearing insert, then lay it in place in the connecting rod. Make sure the tab on the bearing fits into the recess in the rod. Don't hammer the bearing insert into place and be very careful not to nick or gouge the bearing face. Don't lubricate the bearing at this time.

4   Clean the back side of the other bearing insert and install it in the rod cap. Again, make sure the tab on the bearing fits into the recess in the cap **(see illustration)**, and don't

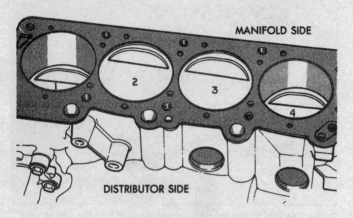

26.5 Position the ring gaps as shown here before installing the piston/connecting rod assemblies in the engine

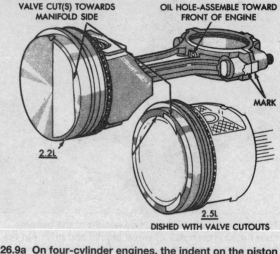

26.9a On four-cylinder engines, the indent on the piston and the oil hole in the rod must face the front of the engine (timing belt end) and the valve cut(s) must face the manifold side of the engine

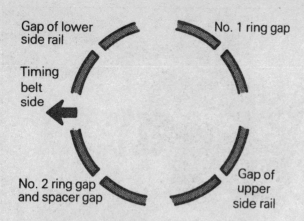

26.9b Piston orientation after installation for four-cylinder engines

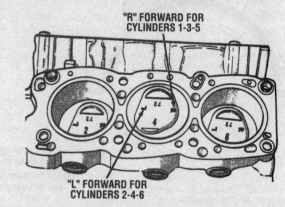

26.9c Piston orientation after installation for V6 engines

apply any lubricant. It's critically important that the mating surfaces of the bearing and connecting rod are perfectly clean and oil free when they're assembled.

5   Position the piston ring gaps at 120-degree intervals around the piston (see illustration).

6   Slip a section of plastic or rubber hose over each connecting rod cap bolt.

7   Lubricate the piston and rings with clean engine oil and attach a piston ring compressor to the piston. Leave the skirt protruding about 1/4-inch to guide the piston into the cylinder. The rings must be compressed until they're flush with the piston.

8   Rotate the crankshaft until the number one connecting rod journal is at BDC (bottom dead center) and apply a coat of engine oil to the cylinder walls.

9   With the mark or notch on top of the piston (see illustrations) facing the front of the engine, gently insert the piston/connecting rod assembly into the number one cylinder bore and rest the bottom edge of the ring compressor on the engine block. If you're working on a four-cylinder engine, make sure

the oil hole in the lower end of the connecting rod is facing the front (timing belt) side of the engine.

10   Tap the top edge of the ring compressor to make sure it's contacting the block around its entire circumference.

11   Gently tap on the top of the piston with the end of a wooden or plastic hammer handle (see illustration) while guiding the end of the connecting rod into place on the crankshaft journal. The piston rings may try to pop out of the ring compressor just before entering the cylinder bore, so keep some pressure on the ring compressor. Work slowly, and if any resistance is felt as the piston enters the cylinder, stop immediately. Find out what's hanging up and fix it before proceeding. Do not, for any reason, force the piston into the cylinder - you might break a ring and/or the piston.

12   Once the piston/connecting rod assembly is installed, the connecting rod bearing oil clearance must be checked before the rod cap is permanently bolted into place.

13   Cut a piece of the appropriate size Plastigage slightly shorter than the width of the

connecting rod bearing and lay it in place on the number one connecting rod journal, parallel with the journal axis (see illustration).

14   Clean the connecting rod cap bearing face, remove the protective hoses from the connecting rod bolts and install the rod cap. Make sure the mating mark on the cap is on the same side as the mark on the connecting rod.

15   Install the nuts and tighten them to the torque listed in this Chapter's Specifications. Work up to it in three steps. Note: Use a thin-wall socket to avoid erroneous torque readings that can result if the socket is wedged between the rod cap and nut. If the socket tends to wedge itself between the nut and the cap, lift up on it slightly until it no longer contacts the cap. Do not rotate the crankshaft at any time during this operation.

16   Remove the nuts and detach the rod cap, being very careful not to disturb the Plastigage.

17   Compare the width of the crushed Plastigage to the scale printed on the Plastigage envelope to obtain the oil clearance (see illustration). Compare it to this Chapter's

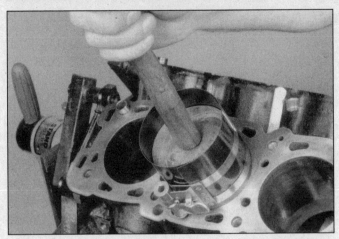

26.11 Gently drive the piston into the cylinder bore with the end of a wooden or plastic hammer handle

26.13 Lay the Plastigage strips on each rod bearing journal, parallel to the crankshaft centerline

Specifications to make sure the clearance is correct.

18   If the clearance is not as specified, the bearing inserts may be the wrong size (which means different ones will be required). Before deciding different inserts are needed, make sure no dirt or oil was between the bearing inserts and the connecting rod or cap when the clearance was measured. Also, recheck the journal diameter. If the Plastigage was wider at one end than the other, the journal may be tapered (refer to Section 20).

Final connecting rod installation

19   Carefully scrape all traces of the Plastigage material off the rod journal and/or bearing face. Be very careful not to scratch the bearing - use your fingernail or the edge of a credit card.

20   Make sure the bearing faces are perfectly clean, then apply a uniform layer of clean moly-base grease or engine assembly lube to both of them. You'll have to push the piston into the cylinder to expose the face of the bearing insert in the connecting rod - be sure to slip the protective hoses over the rod bolts first.

21   Slide the connecting rod back into place on the journal, remove the protective hoses from the rod cap bolts, install the rod cap and tighten the nuts to the torque listed in this Chapter's Specifications. Again, work up to the torque in three steps.

22   Repeat the entire procedure for the remaining pistons/connecting rods.

23   The important points to remember are:

a) Keep the back sides of the bearing inserts and the insides of the connecting rods and caps perfectly clean when assembling them.

b) Make sure you have the correct piston/rod assembly for each cylinder.

c) The arrow or mark on the piston must face the front (timing chain end) of the engine.

d) Lubricate the cylinder walls with clean oil.

e) Lubricate the bearing faces when installing the rod caps after the oil clearance has been checked.

24   After all the piston/connecting rod assemblies have been properly installed, rotate the crankshaft a number of times by hand to check for any obvious binding.

25   As a final step, the connecting rod end-play must be checked. Refer to Section 13 for this procedure.

26   Compare the measured endplay to this Chapter's Specifications to make sure it's correct. If it was correct before disassembly and the original crankshaft and rods were reinstalled, it should still be right. If new rods or a new crankshaft were installed, the endplay may be inadequate. If so, the rods will have to be removed and taken to an automotive machine shop for resizing.

27   Initial start-up and break-in after overhaul

Warning: *Have a fire extinguisher handy when starting the engine for the first time.*

1   Once the engine has been installed in the vehicle, double-check the engine oil and coolant levels.

2   With the spark plugs out of the engine and the ignition system disabled (see Section 3), crank the engine until oil pressure registers on the gauge or the light goes out.

3   Install the spark plugs, hook up the plug wires and restore the ignition system functions (see Section 3).

4   Start the engine. It may take a few moments for the fuel system to build up pressure, but the engine should start without a great deal of effort. **Note:** *If backfiring occurs through the throttle body, recheck the valve timing and ignition timing.*

5   After the engine starts, it should be allowed to warm up to normal operating temperature. While the engine is warming up, make a thorough check for fuel, oil and coolant leaks.

26.17 Measuring the width of the crushed Plastigage to determine the rod bearing oil clearance (be sure to use the correct scale - standard and metric ones are included)

6   Shut the engine off and recheck the engine oil and coolant levels.

7   Drive the vehicle to an area with minimum traffic, accelerate at full throttle from 30 to 50 mph, then allow the vehicle to slow to 30 mph with the throttle closed. Repeat the procedure 10 or 12 times. This will load the piston rings and cause them to seat properly against the cylinder walls. Check again for oil and coolant leaks.

8   Drive the vehicle gently for the first 500 miles (no sustained high speeds) and keep a constant check on the oil level. It isn't unusual for an engine to use oil during the break-in period.

9   At approximately 500 to 600 miles, change the oil and filter.

10   For the next few hundred miles, drive the vehicle normally. Don't pamper it or abuse it.

11   After 2000 miles, change the oil and filter again and consider the engine broken in.

Notes

Chapter 3
Cooling, heating and air conditioning systems

Contents

Specifications

General

Radiator cap pressure rating	14 to 17 psi
Thermostat rating (opening temperature)	195-degrees F
Cooling system capacity	See Chapter 1
Refrigerant capacity	32 ounces

Torque specifications

	Ft-lbs (unless otherwise indicated)
Thermostat cover-to-engine bolts/nuts	
Four-cylinder engines	21
V6 engine	113 in-lbs
Water pump	
Four-cylinder engines	
Pulley bolts	21
Cover-to-housing bolts	105 in-lbs
Housing-to-block bolts	
Upper three bolts	21
Lower bolt	40 in-lbs
V6 engine	20

1 General information

Engine cooling system

All vehicles covered by this manual employ a pressurized engine cooling system with thermostatically controlled coolant circulation. An impeller-type water pump mounted on the front of the block pumps coolant through the engine. The coolant flows around the combustion chambers and toward the rear of the engine. Cast-in coolant passages direct coolant near the intake ports, exhaust ports, and spark plug areas.

A wax pellet-type thermostat is located in a housing near the front of the engine. During warm-up, the closed thermostat prevents coolant from circulating through the radiator. As the engine nears normal operating temperature, the thermostat opens and allows hot coolant to travel through the radiator, where it's cooled before returning to the engine.

The cooling system is sealed by a pressure-type radiator cap, which raises the boiling point of the coolant and increases the cooling efficiency of the radiator. If the system pressure exceeds the cap pressure relief value, the excess pressure in the system forces the spring-loaded valve inside the cap off its seat and allows the coolant to escape through the overflow tube into a coolant reservoir. When the system cools the excess coolant is automatically drawn from the reservoir back into the radiator.

The coolant reservoir serves as both the point at which fresh coolant is added to the cooling system to maintain the proper fluid level and as a holding tank for overheated coolant. This type of cooling system is known as a closed design because coolant that escapes past the pressure cap is saved and reused.

Heating system

The heating system consists of a blower fan and heater core located in the heater box,

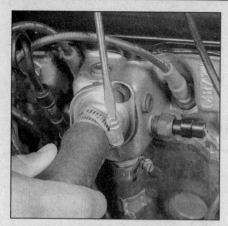

3.8 Remove the hose from the thermostat cover (SOHC engines)

3.10 Detach the thermostat cover from the engine . . .

3.11 . . . then lift the thermostat out of the cover (SOHC engine shown)

the hoses connecting the heater core to the engine cooling system and the heater/air conditioning control head on the dashboard. Hot engine coolant is circulated through the heater core. When the heater mode is activated, a flap door opens to expose the heater box to the passenger compartment. A fan switch on the control head activates the blower motor, which forces air through the core, heating the air.

Air conditioning system

The air conditioning system consists of a condenser mounted in front of the radiator, an evaporator mounted adjacent to the heater core, a compressor mounted on the engine, a filter/drier or receiver/drier (accumulator) which contains a high pressure relief valve and the plumbing connecting all of the above components.

A blower fan forces the warmer air of the passenger compartment through the evaporator core, transferring the heat from the air to the refrigerant (sort of a "radiator in reverse"). The liquid refrigerant boils off into low pressure vapor, taking the heat with it when it leaves the evaporator.

---

2   Antifreeze - general information

Warning: *Do not allow antifreeze to come in contact with your skin or painted surfaces of the vehicle. Rinse off spills immediately with plenty of water. Antifreeze is highly toxic if ingested. Never leave antifreeze lying around in an open container or in puddles on the floor; children and pets are attracted by it's sweet smell and may drink it. Antifreeze is also flammable, so don't store or use it near open flames. Check with local authorities about disposing of used antifreeze. Many communities have collection centers which will see that antifreeze is disposed of safely. Never dump anti-freeze on the ground or pour it into drains.*
Note: *Non-toxic antifreeze is available at most auto parts stores, but even these types should be disposed of properly.*

The cooling system should be filled with a water/ethylene glycol based antifreeze solution, which will prevent freezing down to at least 20-degrees F, or lower if local climate requires it. It also provides protection against corrosion and increases the coolant boiling point.

The cooling system should be drained, flushed and refilled at the specified intervals (see Chapter 1). Old or contaminated antifreeze solutions are likely to cause damage and encourage the formation of rust and scale in the system. Use distilled water with the antifreeze.

Before adding antifreeze, check all hose connections, because antifreeze tends to leak through very minute openings. Engines don't normally consume coolant, so if the level goes down, find the cause and correct it.

The exact mixture of antifreeze-to-water which you should use depends on the relative weather conditions. The mixture should contain at least 50-percent antifreeze, but should never contain more than 70-percent antifreeze. Consult the mixture ratio chart on the antifreeze container before adding coolant. Hydrometers are available at most auto parts stores to test the coolant. Use antifreeze which meets the vehicle manufacturer's specifications.

---

3   Thermostat - check and replacement

Warning: *Do not remove the radiator cap, drain the coolant or replace the thermostat until the engine has cooled completely.*

Check

1   Before assuming the thermostat is to blame for a cooling system problem, check the coolant level, drivebelt tension (see Chapter 1) and temperature gauge operation.
2   If the engine seems to be taking a long time to warm up (based on heater output or temperature gauge operation), the thermostat is probably stuck open. Replace the thermostat with a new one.

3   If the engine runs hot, use your hand to check the temperature of the upper radiator hose. If the hose isn't hot, but the engine is, the thermostat is probably stuck closed, preventing the coolant inside the engine from escaping to the radiator. Replace the thermostat. **Caution:** *Don't drive the vehicle without a thermostat. The computer may stay in open loop and emissions and fuel economy will suffer.*
4   If the upper radiator hose is hot, it means that the coolant is flowing and the thermostat is open. Consult the *Troubleshooting* section at the front of this manual for cooling system diagnosis.

Replacement
SOHC Four-cylinder engines
Refer to illustrations 3.8, 3.10, 3.11, 3.12 and 3.13
5   Disconnect the negative battery cable from the battery.
6   Drain the cooling system (see Chapter 1). If the coolant is relatively new or in good condition, save it and reuse it.
7   Follow the upper radiator hose to the engine to locate the thermostat housing.
8   Loosen the hose clamp, then detach the hose from the fitting **(see illustration)**. If it's stuck, grasp it near the end with a pair of adjustable pliers and twist it to break the seal, then pull it off. If the hose is old or deteriorated, cut it off and install a new one.
9   If the outer surface of the large fitting that mates with the hose is deteriorated (corroded, pitted, etc.) it may be damaged further by hose removal. If it is, the thermostat housing cover will have to be replaced.
10   Remove the fasteners and detach the housing cover **(see illustration)**. If the cover is stuck, tap it with a soft-face hammer to jar it loose. Be prepared for some coolant to spill as the gasket seal is broken.
11   Note how it's installed (which end is facing up), then remove the thermostat **(see illustration)**.
12   Remove all traces of old gasket material and sealant from the housing and cover with a gasket scraper **(see illustration)**.

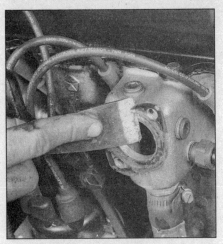

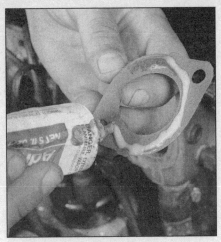

3.12 Carefully scrape all of the old gasket off (SOHC engine shown)

3.13 Be sure to apply sealant to both sides of the gasket before installing it (SOHC engine shown)

13   Apply a thin, uniform layer of RTV sealant to both sides of the new gasket and position it on the housing (see illustration). Install the new thermostat in the housing. Make sure the correct end faces up (the spring end should be directed into the engine).

14   Install the cover and fasteners. Tighten the fasteners to the torque listed in this Chapter's Specifications.

15   Reattach the hose to the fitting and tighten the hose clamp securely.

16   Refill the cooling system (see Chapter 1).

17   Start the engine and allow it to reach normal operating temperature, then check for leaks and proper thermostat operation (as described in Steps 2 through 4).

Other engines

Refer to illustrations 3.18a and 3.18b

18   The procedure for replacing the thermostat on a DOHC four-cylinder engine or a V6 engine (see illustrations) is essentially the same as the above procedure for SOHC fours. Refer to Steps 5 through 17.

---

4   Coolant reservoir - removal and installation

Refer to illustration 4.1

1   Detach the overflow hose at the reservoir (see illustration). Plug the hose to prevent leakage.

2   Remove the reservoir retaining bolt and lift the reservoir out of the engine compartment.

3   Installation is the reverse of removal.

---

5   Engine cooling fan - check and replacement

Warning: *To avoid possible injury or damage, DO NOT operate the engine with a damaged fan. Do not attempt to repair fan blades - replace a damaged fan with a new one.*

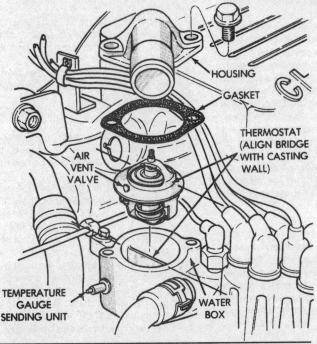

3.18a An exploded view of the thermostat assembly on a V6 engine

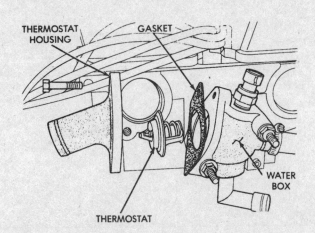

3.18b An exploded view of the thermostat on a DOHC engine

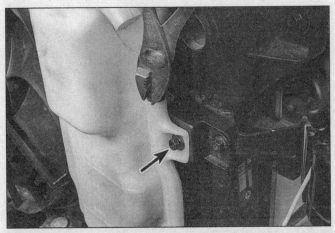

4.1 Detach the coolant overflow hose from the reservoir, then remove the retaining bolt (arrow) and lift the reservoir out of the engine compartment

3

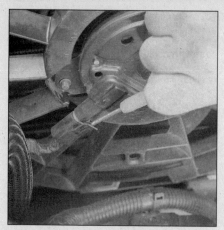

5.1 To unplug the electrical connector from the fan motor, pry loose the locking tang with a small screwdriver

5.5a To remove the fan shroud assembly, remove the left (driver's side) retaining bolt . . .

5.5b . . . pry off the U-clip . . .

Check

Refer to illustration 5.1

1   If the engine is overheating and the cooling fan is not coming on, unplug the electrical connector at the motor **(see illustration)** and use jumper wires to connect the fan

5.5c . . . remove the right (passenger's side) retaining bolt . . .

directly to the battery. If the fan still doesn't work, replace the motor.

2   If the motor is OK, but the cooling fan still doesn't come on when the engine gets hot, the fault lies in the coolant temperature sensor in the thermostat housing, the engine control computer or the wiring which connects the components. Unplug the electrical connector from the sensor. If the fan operates, the sensor is defective. If the fan still doesn't come on, use a voltmeter or test light to check the fan circuit (wiring diagrams are included at the end of Chapter 12). Carefully check all wiring and connections. If no obvious problems are found, further diagnosis should be done by a dealer service department or repair shop.

Replacement

Warning: *On airbag-equipped models, always disconnect the negative battery cable and wait at least two minutes before working in the vicinity of the impact sensors, steering column or center console to avoid the accidental deployment of the airbag, which could cause personal injury.*

Fan

Refer to illustrations 5.5a through 5.5h, 5.6a and 5.6b

3   Disconnect the negative battery cable, then unplug the electrical connector from the fan if you haven't already done so **(see illustration 4.1)**

4   Disconnect the reservoir hose from the radiator filler neck and remove the reservoir (see Section 4).

5   Remove the fan shroud mounting bolts, detach the clips at the top and bottom of the shroud with a small screwdriver, detach the wire harness clips from the shroud, then carefully lift it out of the engine compartment **(see illustrations)**.

6   To detach the fan blade from the motor, remove the clip from the motor shaft with a small screwdriver **(see illustration)**. If the fan blade is stuck on the shaft, apply a little penetrant to the end of the shaft and fan bushing, let it sit for awhile and try again. If the fan is still stuck, gently tap the tip of the shaft with a small hammer or rubber mallet. To detach the motor from the shroud, remove the retaining nuts or Torx screws **(see illustration)** and slide the motor out of the shroud.

7   Installation is the reverse of removal.

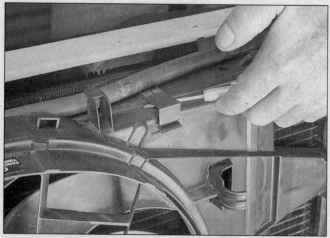

5.5d . . . pry off the upper retaining clip that attaches the shroud to the radiator . . .

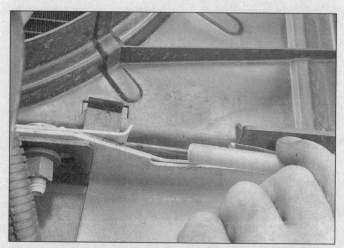

5.5e . . . pry off the lower retaining clip that secures the shroud to the lower crossmember . . .

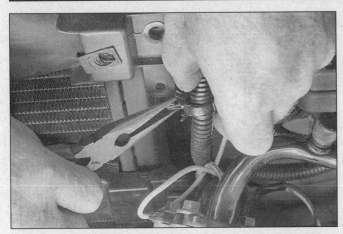

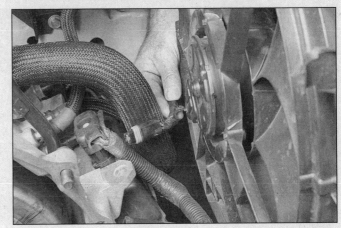

5.5f . . . detach this wire harness clip from the fan shroud by pinching together its tangs (they protrude through the front side of the shroud) with a pair of pliers . . .

5.5g . . . detach the fan motor wire harness clip from the shroud the same way . . .

5.5h . . . and lift the fan shroud assembly off the lower crossmember, away from the radiator out of the engine compartment

13 Plug in the electrical connector.
14 Fill the cooling system (see Chapter 1).
15 Start the engine and check for leaks.

6 Radiator - removal and installation

Warning 1: *Wait until the engine is completely cool before beginning this procedure.*
Warning 2: *On airbag-equipped models, always disconnect the negative battery cable and wait at least two minutes before working in the vicinity of the impact sensors, steering column or center console to avoid the accidental deployment of the airbag, which could cause personal injury.*

Removal

Refer to illustrations 6.4a, 6.4b, 6.7a, 6.7b, 6.7c and 6.7d
1 Disconnect the negative battery cable.
2 Drain the cooling system (see Chapter 1). If the coolant is relatively new and in

Coolant temperature sensor

Refer to illustration 5.9
8 Drain the coolant (see Chapter 1).
9 Unplug the electrical connector from the sensor **(see illustration)**.

10 Unscrew the sensor from the thermostat housing.
11 Wrap the threads of the new sensor with Teflon tape to prevent leaks.
12 Install the sensor and tighten it securely.

5.6a To remove the fan from the motor, pry off this spring clip with a small screwdriver (if the fan is stuck on the motor shaft, try loosening it up with a little penetrant; if that doesn't work, tap the end of the shaft with a small hammer)

5.6b To remove the fan motor from the shroud, remove these three Torx screws (arrows) (some earlier models use retaining nuts instead)

5.9 To remove the coolant temperature sensor, unplug the electrical connector and unscrew the sensor – be sure to wrap the threads of the new sensor with Teflon tape or thread sealant (V6 engine shown, see Section 3 for illustrations of a typical four-cylinder sensor)

6.4a Disconnect the upper coolant hose from the radiator . . .

6.4b . . . detach the lower hose (bottom arrow) and (if the vehicle is equipped with an automatic transaxle) the transmission cooler lines (two upper arrows)

6.7a To remove the radiator, remove the upper left (driver's side) mounting bolt (arrow) . . .

6.7b . . . remove the upper right (passenger's side) mounting bolt (arrow) . . .

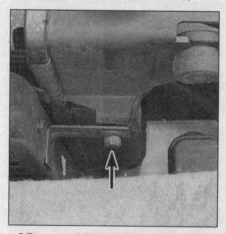

6.7c . . . and, if the vehicle is equipped with air conditioning, remove the upper left (driver's side) condenser retaining bolt (arrow) . . .

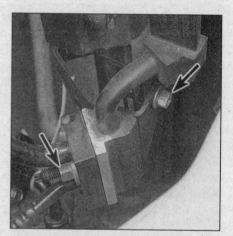

6.7d . . . remove the upper right (passenger's side) condenser retaining bolt (upper arrow) and carefully lift the radiator out of the engine compartment – if you're removing the condenser itself, you'll need to disconnect the refrigerant lines by removing the single nut at the connection (lower arrow)

good condition, save it and reuse it.

3   Disconnect the overflow hose from the radiator filler neck and remove the reservoir (see Section 4).

4   Loosen the hose clamps, then detach the upper and lower coolant hoses from the radiator (see illustrations). If they're stuck, grasp each hose near the end with a pair of adjustable pliers and twist it to break the seal, then pull it off - be careful not to distort the radiator fittings! If the hoses are old or deteriorated, cut them off and install new ones.

5   If the vehicle is equipped with an automatic transmission, disconnect and plug the cooler lines (see illustration 6.4b).

6   Unplug the electrical connector from the coolant temperature sensor (see Section 5).

7   Remove the radiator mounting bolts (see illustrations). If the vehicle is equipped with air conditioning, remove the condenser retaining bolts (see illustrations).

8   Carefully lift out the radiator. Don't spill coolant on the vehicle or scratch the paint.

9   Check the radiator for leaks and damage. If it needs repair, have a radiator shop or dealer service department perform the work,

as special techniques are required.

10   Remove bugs and dirt from the radiator with compressed air and a soft brush (don't bend the cooling fins).

Installation

11   Inspect the radiator mounts for deterioration and make sure there's no dirt or gravel in them when the radiator is installed.

12   Installation is the reverse of the removal procedure. Make sure the radiator is properly seated on the lower mounting insulators before fastening the top brackets.

13   After installation, fill the cooling system with the proper mixture of antifreeze and water. See Chapter 1 if necessary.

14   Start the engine and check for leaks. Allow the engine to reach normal operating temperature, indicated by the upper radiator hose becoming hot. Recheck the coolant level and add more if required.

15   If you're working on an automatic transmission equipped vehicle, check and add fluid as needed.

7   Water pump - check

1   A failure in the water pump can cause serious engine damage due to overheating.

2   There are three ways to check the operation of the water pump while it's installed on the engine. If the pump is defective, it should be replaced with a new or rebuilt unit.

3   With the engine running at normal operating temperature, squeeze the upper radiator hose. If the water pump is working properly, a pressure surge should be felt as the hose is released. Warning: *Keep your hands away from the fan blades!*

4   Water pumps are equipped with weep or vent holes. If a failure occurs in the pump seal, coolant will leak from the hole. In most cases you'll need a flashlight to find the hole on the water pump from underneath to check for leaks.

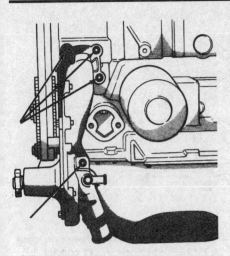

8.8 Water pump mounting bolt locations (four-cylinder engines)

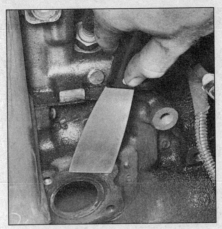

8.10 Scrape the old sealant material off the engine block and the water pump housing (four-cylinder engines)

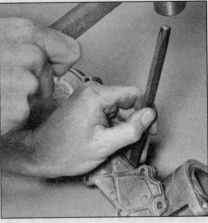

8.11a You may have to use a hammer and chisel to separate the water pump from the housing, but be extremely careful – don't damage the mating surface of the housing (four-cylinder engines)

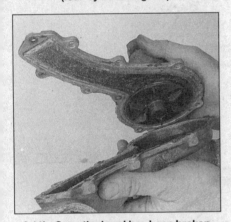

8.11b Once the bond has been broken, separate the pump form the housing (four-cylinder engines)

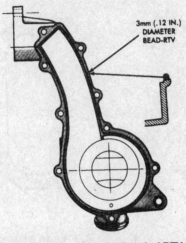

8.14 Apply a continuous bead of RTV-type sealant between the bolt holes and the inner edge of the housing (four-cylinder engines)

3mm (.12 IN.) DIAMETER BEAD-RTV

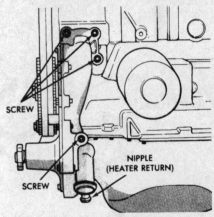

SCREW

NIPPLE (HEATER RETURN)

SCREW

8.15 On DOHC engines, install the coolant deflector into the block before installing the pump, and install the spacer between the pump and the block at the lower mounting bolt

5   If the water pump shaft bearings fail there may be a howling sound at the front of the engine while it's running. Shaft wear can be felt if the water pump pulley is rocked up-and-down. Don't mistake drivebelt slippage, which causes a squealing sound, for water pump bearing failure.

8   Water pump - replacement

Warning: *Wait until the engine is completely cool before beginning this procedure.*

1   Disconnect the negative battery cable from the battery.
2   Drain the cooling system (see Chapter 1). If the coolant is relatively new or in good condition, save and reuse it.

Four-cylinder models

Refer to illustrations 8.8, 8.10, 8.11a, 8.11b, 8.14 and 8.15

3   Remove the cooling fan and shroud (see Section 5).
4   Remove the drivebelts (see Chapter 1) and the pulley at the end of the water pump shaft.

5   On air-conditioned models, unbolt the compressor (see Section 15). **Warning:** *Simply set the compressor aside - don't disconnect the lines.*
6   Remove the alternator (see Chapter 5).
7   Loosen the clamps and detach the hoses from the water pump. If they're stuck, grasp each hose near the end with a pair of adjustable pliers and twist it to break the seal, then pull it off. If the hoses are deteriorated, cut them off and install new ones.
8   Remove the bolts **(see illustration)** and detach the water pump and housing from the engine. Note the locations of the various lengths and different types of bolts as they're removed to ensure correct installation. On DOHC engines, there's also a spacer between the pump and the block at the lower bolt.
9   Clean the bolt threads and the threaded holes in the engine to remove corrosion and sealant.
10   Remove all traces of old gasket material

from the engine and pump housing with a gasket scraper **(see illustration)**.
11   Separate the water pump from the housing **(see illustrations)**.
12   If you're installing a new pump, compare the new pump to the old pump to make sure they're identical.
13   Clean the mating surfaces of the housing. Remove all old sealant material. Remove the old O-ring from the housing groove.
14   Apply a bead of RTV sealant to the mating surface of the housing **(see illustration)**. Install a new O-ring in the housing groove.
15   Attach the new pump to the housing and tighten the bolts to the torque listed in this Chapter's Specifications. On DOHC engines, install the coolant deflector **(see illustration)** into the block before installing the pump on the engine, and install the spacer between the pump and the block before torquing the lower bolt.
16   Install the pump/housing assembly on the engine (make sure a new gasket is used)

3

8.20 To remove the water pump assembly on a V6 engine, remove these mounting bolts (arrows), then pull the pump assembly off the coolant inlet pipe connected to the pump housing (the pipe's a snug fit but it's only sealed by an O-ring)

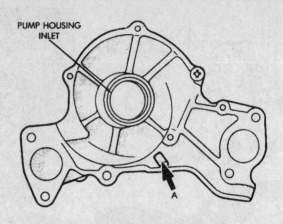

8.21 Before you install the old pump, make sure there's no trace of coolant leakage from the weep hole (A) (V6 engine)

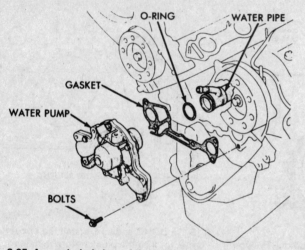

8.25 An exploded view of the water pump assembly (V6 engine)

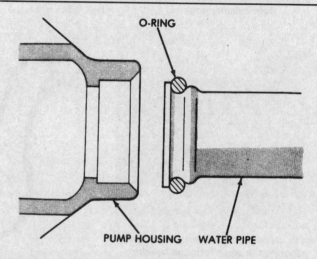

8.26 When installing the water pump onto the block, press on the pump body until the coolant inlet pipe seats properly into the housing (V6 engine)

and tighten the bolts to the torque listed in this Chapter's Specifications.

17   Reinstall all parts removed for access to the pump.

18   Refill the cooling system and check the drivebelt tension (see Chapter 1). Run the engine and check for leaks.

V6 models

Refer to illustrations 8.20, 8.21, 8.25 and 8.26

19   Remove the timing belt (see Chapter 2, Part B).

20   Remove the water pump mounting bolts **(see illustration)**. Pull on the pump assembly to detach it from the coolant inlet pipe connected to the pump housing (the pipe fits snugly but it's only sealed by an O-ring). Remove the pump assembly and the old gasket.

21   Even if you're planning to reinstall the same pump, now is a good time to inspect it. Look for cracks in the pump cover or housing. Note whether there is any trace of coolant leakage out the weep hole **(see illus-**

tration). Turn the pump pulley. Does the impeller make a rubbing sound inside the pump body? Does the bearing feel loose or rough when you turn it? If the pump exhibits any of these conditions, replace it.

22   If you're replacing the water pump, you can buy a complete water pump assembly from a dealer, or just the cover assembly (pulley, shaft, bearing, seal, impeller and front cover, with no housing) from some auto parts stores. However, no torque specification is available for the cover-to-housing bolts at the time of publication.

23   Scrape all old gasket material off the block and, if you're reinstalling the old pump, clean out the bore in the housing into which the coolant pipe is inserted.

24   Install a new O-ring on the coolant inlet pipe and wet the O-ring with a little water - DON'T use oil or grease - to facilitate installation of the pump.

25   Place the new gasket in position on the water pump and install the pump **(see illustration)**.

26   Press on the pump assembly until the coolant inlet pipe seats properly into the housing **(see illustration)**.

27   Install the pump-to-mounting bolts and tighten them to the torque listed in this Chapter's Specifications.

28   Install the timing belt and the timing belt cover (see Chapter 2, Part B).

29   The remainder of installation is the reverse of removal.

9   Heater or heater/air conditioner control assembly - removal and installation

Refer to illustrations 9.3 and 9.4
Warning: *On airbag-equipped models, always disconnect the negative battery cable and wait at least two minutes before working in the vicinity of the impact sensors, steering column or center console to avoid the accidental deployment of the airbag, which could cause personal injury.*

9.3 To detach the heater or heater/air conditioning control assembly from the dash, remove these two screws (arrows) . . .

9.4 . . . then unplug the electrical connector, disconnect the cables and detach the vacuum hoses (it's a good idea to label the vacuum hoses to prevent switched connections during reassembly)

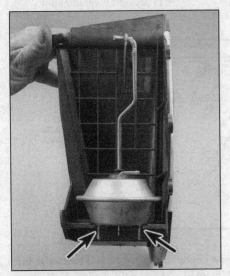

10.5 To separate the blower housing from the heater/air conditioner assembly, remove all eight mounting screws (arrows) from the housing (housing removed from vehicle for sake of clarity)

3

10.4 The actuator is the diaphragm-like device with the vertical arm connected to the air door lever arm – to remove it, remove the two sheet metal nuts from the studs on the bottom and detach the rod from the door lever arm (blower housing and actuator removed from the vehicle for clarity in this illustration)

1   Disconnect the negative battery cable.
2   Remove the center bezel (see Chapter 11).
3   Remove the two control mounting screws **(see illustration)**.
4   Slide the control assembly back, detach the cables, wires and vacuum hoses **(see illustration)**, then remove the control unit.
5   Installation is the reverse of removal.

10   Heater and air conditioner blower motor - removal and installation

Refer to illustrations 10.4, 10.5, 10.6 and 10.7
Warning: *On airbag-equipped models,*

always disconnect the negative battery cable and wait at least two minutes before working in the vicinity of the impact sensors, steering column or center console to avoid the accidental deployment of the airbag, which could cause personal injury.

1   Disconnect the battery negative cable.
2   Remove the glove box (see Chapter 11).
3   Detach the panel underneath the right end of the dash. It has four fasteners, all of them facing up - two screws in front (side toward the passenger seat) and two sheet metal nuts on the backside (toward the firewall).
4   On air-conditioned models, detach the two vacuum lines from the air door actuator **(see illustration)**, remove the two sheet metal nuts from the studs that secure the actuator to the blower housing, reach up to the top of the actuator rod, disconnect the rod from the door lever arm and remove the actuator. **Note:** *You have to remove the actuator to get at the blower housing mounting screw behind it.*
5   Remove all eight mounting screws from the blower housing **(see illustration)** and

10.6 To detach the fan from the motor, remove this retaining clamp from the fan hub and slide the fan off the shaft

remove the housing.
6   Remove the retaining clamp from the fan hub **(see illustration)** and slide the fan off the motor shaft.

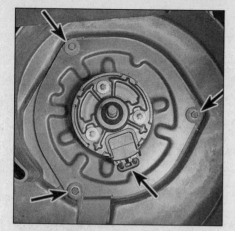

10.7 Unplug or, on some models, unsolder, the blower motor electrical connector, remove the three motor mounting screws (arrows) and pull out the motor

11.24 After draining the cooling system, disconnect these heater hoses at the firewall and plug the heater core tubes to avoid spilling coolant inside the vehicle

11.25a Unplug the electrical connector, remove the sealing plate bolt (arrow), disconnect the refrigerant lines from the expansion valve at the firewall and seal them to prevent contamination

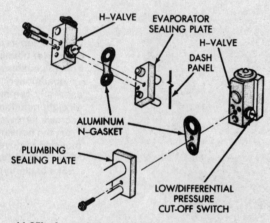

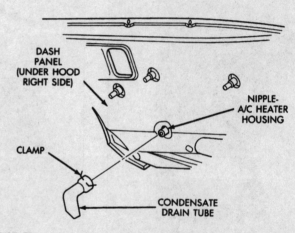

11.25b An exploded view of two typical expansion valve assemblies

11.27 The air conditioner condensate drain tube is located in the engine compartment, on the firewall (typical drain shown)

7   Unplug or, on some models, unsolder, the blower motor electrical connector (see illustration).

8   Remove the three blower motor mounting screws and remove the motor.

9   Install the fan on the new blower motor and secure it to the shaft with the retaining clamp.

10   Installation is the reverse of removal.

11   Heater/air conditioner assembly - removal and installation

Refer to illustrations 11.24, 11.25a, 11.25b and 11.27

Warning 1: *The air conditioning system is under high pressure. Do not loosen any hose fittings or remove any components until after the system has been discharged by a dealer service department or service station. Always wear eye protection when disconnecting air conditioning system fittings.*

Warning 2: *On airbag-equipped models, always disconnect the negative battery cable and wait at least two minutes before working in the vicinity of the impact sensors, steering column or center console to avoid the accidental deployment of the airbag, which could cause personal injury.*

1   Remove the blower motor (see Section 10).

2   Remove the relay panel above the glove compartment opening.

3   Through the glove compartment opening, disconnect the air conditioning vacuum line connector and the radio noise capacitor connectors.

4   Remove the trim cover from the left windshield pillar.

5   Remove the trim cover from the left lower side cowl.

6   Remove the attaching screws from the hood release handle mechanism.

7   Remove the trim covers from the steering column.

8   Disconnect the connecting rod from the

parking brake release mechanism (you can reach it through the fuse panel opening).

9   Remove the left lower silencer from the instrument panel.

10   Remove the left lower reinforcement from the instrument panel.

11   Remove the center bezel from the dash (see Chapter 11).

12   Remove the forward floor console (see Chapter 11).

13   Remove the radio (see Chapter 12).

14   Remove the heater or heater/air conditioner control assembly (see Section 9).

15   Remove the cigarette lighter.

16   Remove the message center-trip computer, if equipped.

17   Disconnect the side window demister tubes from the top of the heater/air conditioner unit.

18   Remove the upper attaching bolts from the steering column and allow the steering wheel to rest on the driver's seat.

19   Remove the cover from the upper defroster outlet in the dash.

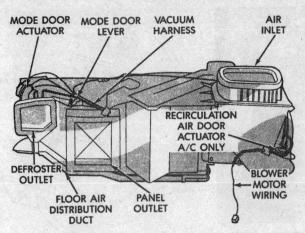

12.1 Typical heater/air conditioner assembly

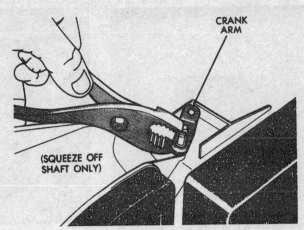

12.3 To remove the crank arm, squeeze the blend air door crank off the shaft with a pair of pliers

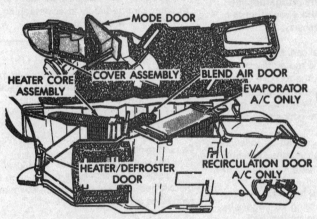

12.5 Typical heater/air conditioner assembly with the cover removed

at the air inlet plenum and the eleven screws that point down into the housing. Lift the cover from the heater/air conditioner assembly (see illustration).

6   You can now remove the heater core (or the air conditioner evaporator unit).

7   Installation is the reverse of removal.

13   Air conditioning system - check and maintenance

Warning: *The air conditioning system is under high pressure. Do not loosen any hose fittings or remove any components until after the system has been discharged by a dealer service department or service station. Always wear eye protection when disconnecting air conditioning system fittings.*

Check

Refer to illustration 13.7

1   The following maintenance checks should be performed on a regular basis to ensure the air conditioner continues to operate at peak efficiency.

a) *Check the compressor drivebelt. If it's worn or deteriorated, replace it (see Chapter 1).*
b) *Check the drivebelt tension and, if necessary, adjust it (see Chapter 1).*
c) *Check the system hoses. Look for cracks, bubbles, hard spots and deterioration. Inspect the hoses and all fittings for oil bubbles and seepage. If there's any evidence of wear, damage or leaks, replace the hose(s).*
d) *Inspect the condenser fins for leaves, bugs and other debris. Use a "fin comb" or compressed air to clean the condenser.*
e) *Make sure the system has the correct refrigerant charge.*

2   It's a good idea to operate the system for about 10 minutes at least once a month, particularly during the winter. Long term non-use can cause hardening, and subsequent

20   Remove the upper attaching screws for the dash (just below the windshield opening).

21   Loosen - but don't remove - the lower left attaching screw from the dash.

22   Remove the lower right attaching screw from the dash.

23   Carefully pull out the right end of the dash and allow it to rest on the passenger's seat.

24   From the engine compartment, drain the cooling system and disconnect the heater hoses **(see illustration)** from the heater core pipes. Plug the pipes to avoid spilling coolant inside the vehicle.

25   Unplug the electrical connector and disconnect the refrigerant lines from the expansion valve at the firewall on the right side of the vehicle **(see illustrations)**. Seal the refrigerant lines to prevent contamination.

26   Remove the expansion valve from the evaporator plate. Seal the valve to avoid contamination.

27   Remove the condensation drain tube **(see illustration)**.

28   Remove the silencer for the heater/air conditioner unit from the dash panel and remove the heater/air conditioner assembly from the vehicle.

29   Installation is the reverse of removal. Be sure to refill the cooling system (see Chap-

ter 1) and recharge the air conditioning system (see Section 13).

12   Heater core - removal and installation

Refer to illustrations 12.1, 12.3 and 12.5

Warning: *On airbag-equipped models, always disconnect the negative battery cable and wait at least two minutes before working in the vicinity of the impact sensors, steering column or center console to avoid the accidental deployment of the airbag, which could cause personal injury.*

1   Remove the heater/air conditioner assembly (see Section 11) and place it on a work bench **(see illustration)**.

2   Locate and remove one retaining nut from the blend-air door pivot shaft.

3   To remove the top cover from the air conditioner/heater housing, remove the crank arm **(see illustration)**.

4   Disconnect the vacuum lines from the defroster and panel model vacuum actuators and position them out of the way.

5   Remove the three heater/air conditioner cover screws that point up at the defroster outlet chamber, the two screws that point up

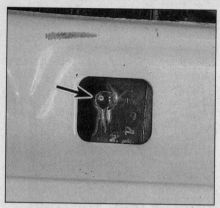

13.7 The sight glass on top of the filter-drier enables you to view the condition of the refrigerant while the system is operating – if the refrigerant looks foamy, the charge is low

14.1 The filter-drier is located near the right corner of the engine compartment, just behind the upper crossmember – to remove it, detach the refrigerant line fittings and remove the three mounting bolts (arrows)

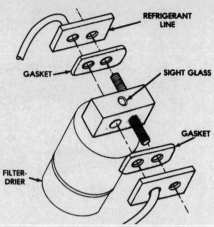

14.4 An exploded view of the filter-drier assembly – if you're planning to reinstall the same unit, be sure to plug the openings immediately after detaching the refrigerant lines

failure, of the seals.

3   Because of the complexity of the air conditioning system and the special equipment necessary to service it, in-depth troubleshooting and repairs are not included in this manual (refer to the *Haynes Automotive Heating and Air Conditioning Repair Manual*). However, simple checks and component replacement procedures are provided in this Chapter.

4   The most common cause of poor cooling is simply a low system refrigerant charge. If a noticeable drop in cool air output occurs, the following quick check will help you determine if the refrigerant level is low.

5   Warm the engine up to normal operating temperature.

6   Place the air conditioning temperature selector at the coldest setting and put the blower at the highest setting. Open the doors (to make sure the air conditioning system doesn't cycle off as soon as it cools the passenger compartment).

7   With the compressor engaged - the clutch will make an audible click and the center of the clutch will rotate - inspect the sight glass **(see illustration)**. If the refrigerant looks foamy, it's low. Charge the system as described later in this Section.

8   If there's no sight glass, feel the inlet and outlet pipes at the compressor. One side should be cold and one hot. If there's no perceptible difference between the two pipes, there's something wrong with the compressor or the system. It might be a low charge - it might be something else. Take the vehicle to a dealer service department or an automotive air conditioning shop.

Adding refrigerant

9   Buy an automotive charging kit at an auto parts store. A charging kit includes a 14-ounce can of refrigerant, a tap valve and a short section of hose that can be attached between the tap valve and the system low side service valve. Because one can of refrigerant may not be sufficient to bring the system charge up to the proper level, it's a good

idea to buy an additional can. Make sure that one of the cans contains red refrigerant dye. If the system is leaking, the red dye will leak out with the refrigerant and help you pinpoint the location of the leak. **Warning:** *Never add more than two cans of refrigerant to the system.*

10   Hook up the charging kit by following the manufacturer's instructions. **Warning:** *DO NOT hook the charging kit hose to the system high side!*

11   Start the engine and turn on the air conditioner. Keep the charging kit hose away from the fan and other moving parts.

12   Place a thermometer in the dashboard vent nearest the evaporator and add refrigerant until the indicated temperature is around 40 to 45-degrees F.

14   Air conditioning filter-drier - removal and installation

Refer to illustrations 14.1 and 14.4
Warning: *The air conditioning system is under high pressure. DO NOT disassemble any part of the system (hose, compressor, line fittings, etc.) until after the system has been depressurized by a dealer service department or service station.*
Caution: *Replacement filter-drier/receiver-drier units are so effective at absorbing moisture that they can quickly saturate upon exposure to the atmosphere. When installing a new unit, have all tools and supplies ready for quick reassembly to avoid having the system open any longer than necessary.*

1   The filter-drier, or receiver-drier, acts as a reservoir for the system refrigerant. It's located on the right side of the engine compartment, just behind the upper crossmember **(see illustration)**.

2   Have the system discharged (see the Warning at the beginning of this Section).

3   Disconnect the cable from the negative

terminal of the battery.

4   Disconnect the refrigerant lines from the filter-drier **(see illustration)**. Use a back-up wrench to prevent twisting the tubing.

5   Plug the open fittings to prevent entry of dirt and moisture.

6   Loosen the mounting bracket bolts and lift out the filter-drier.

7   Installation is the reverse of removal.

8   Take the vehicle back to the shop that discharged it. Have the system evacuated, recharged and leak tested.

15   Air conditioning compressor - removal and installation

Refer to illustration 15.5, 15.6a and 15.6b
Warning: *The air conditioning system is under high pressure. DO NOT disassemble any part of the system (hoses, compressor, line fittings, etc.) until after the system has been depressurized by a dealer service department or service station.*
Note: *The filter-drier/receiver-drier (see Section 14) should be replaced whenever the compressor is replaced.*

1   Have the system discharged (see Warning above).

2   Disconnect the negative cable from the battery.

3   Unplug the electrical connector from the compressor clutch. On some models, the connector is on the compressor clutch; on others, it's at the end of a short lead.

4   Remove the drivebelt (see Chapter 1).

5   Disconnect the refrigerant lines from the compressor **(see illustration)**. Plug the open fittings to prevent entry of dirt and moisture.

6   Unbolt the compressor from the mounting bracket **(see illustrations)** and lift it out of the vehicle.

7   If a new compressor is being installed, pour out the oil from the old compressor into

15.5 To remove a compressor, unplug the connector at the end of the short electrical lead from the clutch (connector not visible in this illustration), remove the two pairs of bolts which attach the refrigerant lines (arrows), detach the lines and remove the four bolts (arrows) which attach the compressor to the mounting bracket (fixed-displacement V6 unit shown, others similar)

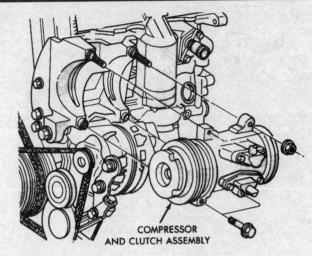

15.6a An exploded view of a typical air conditioning compressor installation (four-cylinder engines)

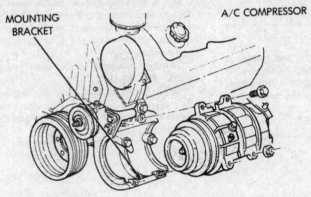

15.6b Another typical air conditioning compressor installation (this one's a late-model variable-displacement unit on a V6 engine

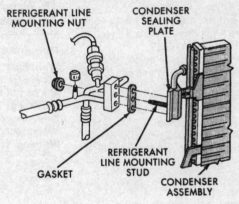

16.5 An exploded view of the refrigerant line connection at the condenser (see illustration 6.7d for the assembled unit)

3

a graduated container and add that amount of new refrigerant oil to the new compressor. Also follow any directions included with the new compressor.

8   The clutch may have to be transferred from the original to the new compressor.

9   Installation is the reverse of removal. Replace all O-rings with new ones specifically made for air conditioning system use and lubricate them with refrigerant oil.

10   Have the system evacuated, recharged and leak tested by the shop that discharged it.

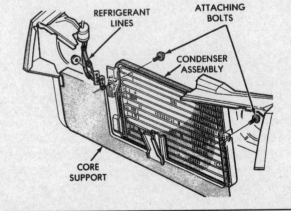

16.6 Condenser mounting details

16   Air conditioning condenser - removal and installation

Refer to illustrations 16.5 and 16.6

Warning 1: *The air conditioning system is under high pressure. DO NOT disassemble any part of the system (hoses, compressor, line fittings, etc.) until after the system has been depressurized by a dealer service department or service station.*

Warning 2: *On airbag-equipped models, always disconnect the negative battery cable*

and wait at least two minutes before working in the vicinity of the impact sensors, steering column or center console to avoid the accidental deployment of the airbag, which could cause personal injury.

Note: *The filter-drier/receiver-drier should be replaced whenever the condenser is replaced (see Section 14).*

1   Have the system discharged (see Warning above).

2   Remove the battery (see Chapter 5).

3   Drain the cooling system (see Chapter 1).

4   Remove the radiator (see Section 6).

5   Disconnect the refrigerant lines from the condenser **(see illustration)**.

6   Lift the condenser out of the vehicle and plug the lines to keep dirt and moisture out **(see illustration)**.

7   Inspect the rubber insulator pads (on the

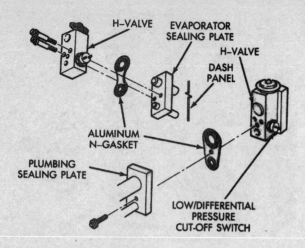

17.2a An exploded view of the expansion valve assembly

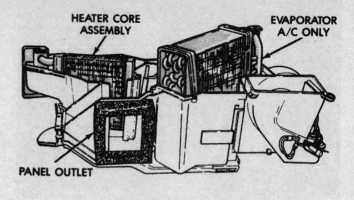

17.2b Lift the evaporator straight up out of the heater and air conditioner assembly

lower crossmember) on which the condenser sits. Replace them if they're dried or cracked.

8   If the original condenser will be reinstalled, store it with the line fittings on top to prevent oil from draining out.

9   If a new condenser is being installed, pour one ounce of refrigerant oil into it prior to installation.

10   Reinstall the components in the reverse order of removal. Be sure the rubber pads are in place under the condenser.

11   Have the system evacuated, recharged and leak tested by the shop that discharged it.

17   Air conditioning evaporator - removal and installation

Refer to illustrations 17.2a and 17.2b

Warning 1: *The air conditioning system is under high pressure. DO NOT disassemble any part of the system (hoses, compressor, line fittings, etc.) until after the system has been depressurized by a dealer service department or service station.*

Warning 2: *On airbag-equipped models,* always disconnect the negative battery cable and wait at least two minutes before working in the vicinity of the impact sensors, steering column or center console to avoid the accidental deployment of the airbag, which could cause personal injury.

1   Remove the heater and air conditioning unit assembly (see Section 11).

2   Remove the expansion valve sealing plate seal and the seal screw from under the plate **(see illustration)** and lift the evaporator **(see illustration)** out of the housing.

3   Installation is the reverse of removal.

Chapter 4
Fuel and exhaust systems

Contents

4

Specifications

Fuel pressure

Note: *Fuel pressure tests performed with the vacuum hose connected to the fuel pressure regulator*

Four-cylinder models	
Turbo	55 psi
Non-turbo	
1989 and 1990	14.5 psi
1991 on	39 psi
V6 models	48 psi

Torque specifications

	Ft-lbs (unless otherwise indicated)
Air intake plenum mounting bolts (3.0L engine)	115 in-lbs
Fuel pressure regulator mounting screws (single-point EFI)	40 in-lbs
Fuel injector cap mounting screws	35 to 45 in-lbs
Throttle Position Sensor (TPS) mounting screws	
Single-point systems	20 in-lbs
Multi-point systems	17 in-lbs
Automatic Idle Speed (AIS) mounting screws	
Single-point systems	20 in-lbs
Multi-point systems	17 in-lbs
Fuel rail mounting bolts	16
Air cleaner housing support bracket bolt	40
Exhaust pipe-to-manifold bolt/nut	21

Torque specifications (continued)

	Ft-lbs (unless otherwise indicated)
Throttle body-to-intake manifold bolts	
2.5L engine	175 in-lbs
3.0L engine	175 in-lbs
Turbo	175 to 225 in-lbs
Turbocharger-to-exhaust manifold nuts	40
Turbocharger fuel rail bolts	20
Turbocharger support bracket bolts	
To engine block	40
To turbocharger	20

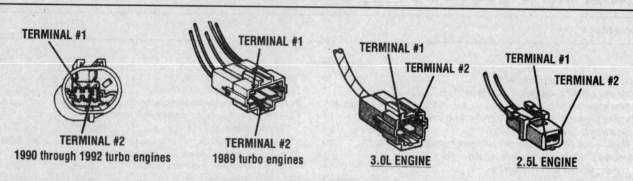

2.4 If an injector is not accessible, ground the number 1 terminal on the injector side of the harness connector and apply battery voltage to the number 2 terminal to actuate the injector and release the pressurized fuel

1   General information

Fuel system

The fuel system consists of the fuel tank, an electric fuel pump, an air cleaner, a fuel injection system and the hoses and lines which connect these components.

Two different fuel injection systems are used. A single-point (one injector) Electronic Fuel Injection (EFI) system is used on normally aspirated four-cylinder models. A multi-point (one injector per cylinder) EFI system is used on turbo and V6 models.

Exhaust system

The exhaust system consists of the exhaust manifold, exhaust pipes, catalytic converter and muffler. For information regarding the removal and installation of the exhaust manifold, refer to Chapter 2, Part A. For information regarding exhaust system and catalytic converter servicing, see Section 30. For further information regarding the catalytic converter, refer to Chapter 6.

2   Fuel pressure relief procedure

Refer to illustrations 2.4, 2.5a and 2.5b

Warning: *Gasoline is extremely flammable, so take extra precautions when you work on any part of the fuel system. Don't smoke or allow open flames or bare light bulbs near the work area, and don't work in a garage where a natural gas-type appliance (such as a water heater or clothes dryer) with a pilot light is present. If you spill any fuel on your skin, rinse*

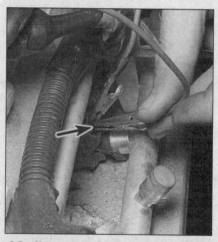

2.5a If one of the injectors is accessible, unplug the most convenient injector connector and bleed the fuel pressure in short bursts by grounding one of the terminals and touching the other terminal (arrow) with the jumper wire clip (multi-point system shown)

2.5b Relieving he fuel pressure on a single-point system

it off immediately with soap and water. When you perform any kind of work on the fuel system, wear safety glasses and have a Class B type fire extinguisher on hand.

1   The fuel system operates under pressure and may be under residual pressure even when the engine is off. Consequently, any time the fuel system is worked on (such as when the fuel filter is replaced), the system must be depressurized to avoid the spraying of fuel when a component is disconnected.

2   Loosen the fuel tank cap to release any pressure in the tank.

3   Unplug the electrical connector from the fuel injector. If you're working on a multi-point system disconnect the electrical connector from the injector that is the most easily accessible. If access to the injector(s) is difficult, unplug the injector harness connector from the engine or main harness.

4   If the injector is accessible, ground one of the terminals with a jumper wire. If it was necessary to disconnect the main injector harness due to inadequate access to the injector(s), ground the injector terminal number 1 (on the engine side of the harness) using a jumper wire **(see illustration)**.

5   Connect a jumper wire between the other terminal (number 2 on the injector har-

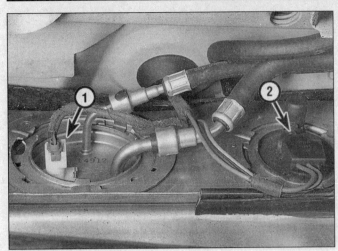

3.4 The electrical connectors for the fuel pump (1) and fuel gauge sending unit (2) are easily accessible at the fuel tank

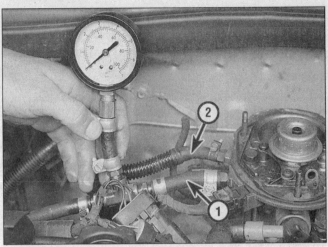

3.8a Be sure the fuel gauge is connected to the inlet line (1) and not the return line (2) (single-point system)

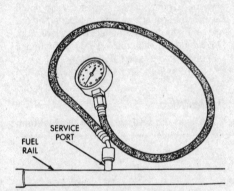

3.8b The fuel rail on multi-point systems has a service port that can be used to attach the fuel pressure gauge

3.10 Attach the fuel pressure gauge between the fuel tank and the fuel filter

ness) and the positive (+) post of the battery, which will open the injector and depressurize the fuel system (see illustrations). Caution: *Do not energize the injectors for more than five seconds to avoid damage to the fuel injector. It's recommended that the pressure be bled in several spurts of one to two seconds to make sure the injector isn't damaged. The fuel pressure can be heard escaping into the throttle body or intake port. When the sound is no longer heard, the system is depressurized.*

3 Fuel pump/fuel pressure - check

Warning: *Gasoline is extremely flammable, so take extra precautions when you work on any part of the fuel system. Don't smoke or allow open flames or bare light bulbs near the work area, and don't work in a garage where a natural gas-type appliance (such as a water heater or clothes dryer) with a pilot light is present. If you spill any fuel on your skin, rinse it off immediately with soap and water. When you perform any kind of work on the fuel sys-*

tem, wear safety glasses and have a Class B type fire extinguisher on hand.

Voltage check

Refer to illustration 3.4

1   Remove the fuel tank cap and place your ear close to the filler neck. Have an assistant turn the ignition key to On while you listen for the sound of the in-tank pump. It should make a whirring sound. If you don't hear the pump, check the fuses. If the fuses are okay, make the following quick checks.

2   Relieve the fuel system pressure (see Section 2).

3   Raise the rear of the vehicle and place it securely on jackstands.

4   Lower the fuel tank slightly (see Section 5) and locate the wire harness (see illustration) to the fuel pump. Unplug the fuel pump electrical connector.

5   Using a test light, verify that there's voltage to the pump for two seconds after the key is turned to the On position, and also when the key is turned to the Start position.

a) *If there is voltage, replace the pump (see Section 4).*

b) *If there is no voltage to the pump, refer to the wiring diagrams at the end of the manual. Trace the wires for a open or short circuit condition.*

6   If the pump still doesn't work, have the vehicle checked by a dealer service department or other repair shop, as further testing requires special equipment.

Fuel pressure check

Refer to illustrations 3.8a, 3.8b, 3.10 and 3.12

7   Relieve the fuel pressure (see Section 2).

8   On single-point fuel injection systems (TBI), disconnect the 5/16-inch fuel line from the throttle body and connect a fuel pressure gauge between the fuel inlet hose and the throttle body (see illustration). On multipoint fuel injection systems, remove the fitting on the fuel rail (see illustration) and install the pressure gauge. **Note:** *Late models are equipped with a quick disconnect coupler installed in the fuel line near the fuel filter.*

9   Start the engine and record the fuel pressure, comparing your findings with the values listed in this Chapter's Specifications.

10   If the fuel pressure is BELOW specifications, install the fuel pressure gauge between the fuel filter and the fuel tank (see illustration).

11   If the fuel pressure increases, the fuel filter or line (between the filter and throttle body or fuel rail) is plugged or restricted. If the fuel pressure is still low, pinch the return line with a pair of pliers (wrap a rag around the hose first to prevent damage). If the pressure now goes up, replace the fuel pressure regulator. If no change in the fuel pressure is observed, check for a plugged fuel pump sock filter (screen) or a defective fuel pump.

12   If the fuel pressure is ABOVE specifications, disconnect the primary wires from the ignition coil, remove the return hose from the throttle body or fuel rail and connect a short

4

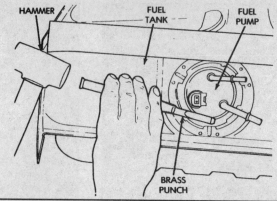

4.2 Use a hammer and a brass punch to turn the lock ring in a counterclockwise direction

3.12 Disconnect the return line and attach a length of fuel hose, directing the free end of the hose into a container - if the fuel pressure is within specifications when an assistant cranks the engine (with the ignition system disabled), check for a plugged return line

section of hose to it. Direct the end of the hose into a suitable container and have an assistant crank the engine **(see illustration)**.
13   If the pressure is now correct, the problem is a restricted return line.
14   If fuel pressure is still incorrect, suspect the fuel pressure regulator.

---

4   Fuel pump - removal and installation

Refer to illustration 4.2
Warning: *Gasoline is extremely flammable, so take extra precautions when you work on any part of the fuel system. Don't smoke or allow open flames or bare light bulbs near the work area, and don't work in a garage where a natural gas-type appliance (such as a water heater or clothes dryer) with a pilot light is present. If you spill any fuel on your skin, rinse it off immediately with soap and water. When you perform any kind of work on the fuel sys-*

tem, wear safety glasses and have a Class B type fire extinguisher on hand.

Removal

1   Remove the fuel tank (see Section 5).
2   Use a hammer and a BRASS punch (a steel punch may cause a spark, which could be extremely dangerous when working on the fuel tank!) to remove the fuel pump lock ring. Drive it in a counterclockwise direction until it can be removed **(see illustration)**.
3   Lift the fuel pump and O-ring out of the fuel tank.

Installation

4   Clean the sealing area of the fuel tank

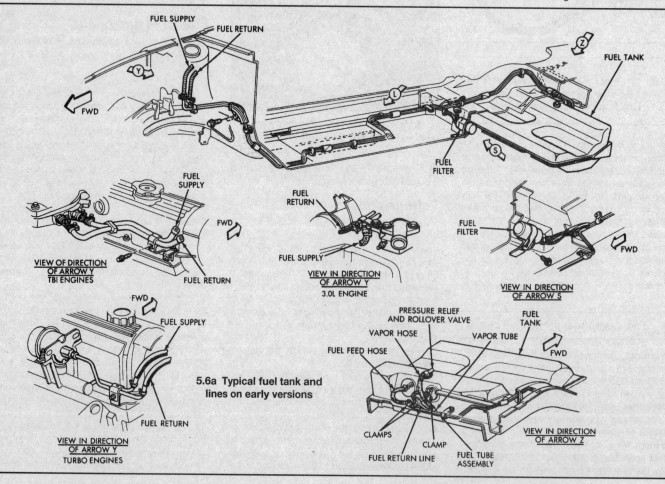

5.6a Typical fuel tank and lines on early versions

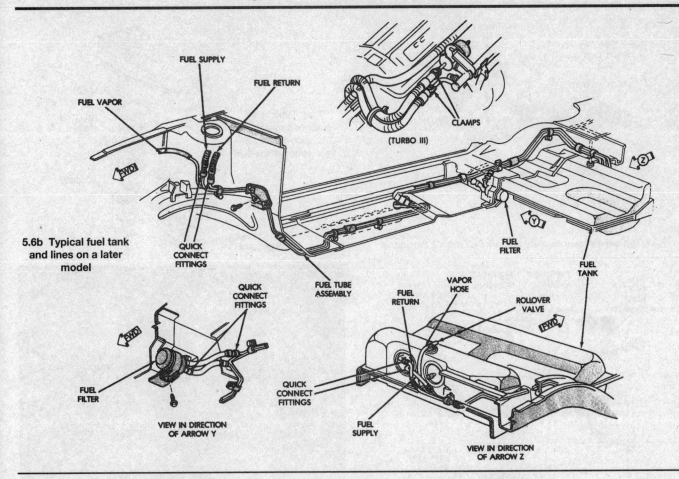

5.6b Typical fuel tank and lines on a later model

(TURBO III)

FUEL VAPOR

FUEL SUPPLY

FUEL RETURN

CLAMPS

QUICK CONNECT FITTINGS

FUEL TUBE ASSEMBLY

FUEL FILTER

FUEL TANK

QUICK CONNECT FITTINGS

FUEL FILTER

VIEW IN DIRECTION OF ARROW Y

FUEL RETURN

VAPOR HOSE

ROLLOVER VALVE

QUICK CONNECT FITTINGS

FUEL SUPPLY

VIEW IN DIRECTION OF ARROW Z

4

and install a new O-ring. Prior to installation, inspect the fuel inlet sock filter on the fuel pump suction tube for damage and contamination. Replace it with a new one if necessary.

5   Place the fuel pump in position in the tank, install the locking ring and use a hammer and a BRASS punch to lock the pump in place.

6   Install the fuel tank.

5   Fuel tank - removal and installation

Refer to illustrations 5.6a, 5.6b and 5.9

Warning: *Gasoline is extremely flammable, so take extra precautions when you work on any part of the fuel system. Don't smoke or* allow open flames or bare light bulbs near the work area, and don't work in a garage where a natural gas-type appliance (such as a water heater or clothes dryer) with a pilot light is present. If you spill any fuel on your skin, rinse it off immediately with soap and water. When you perform any kind of work on the fuel system, wear safety glasses and have a Class B type fire extinguisher on hand. **Note:** *The following procedure is much easier if the tank is empty. Some tanks have a drain plug - if it doesn't, use a siphoning kit (available at most auto parts stores) and siphon the fuel into an approved fuel container. Don't start the siphoning action by mouth!*

1   Remove the filler cap to relieve the tank pressure.

2   Relieve the fuel system pressure (see Section 2).

3   Detach the cable from the negative terminal of the battery.

4   If the tank has a drain plug, remove it and allow the fuel to drain into an approved gasoline container.

5   Raise the vehicle and place it securely on jackstands.

6   Disconnect the fuel lines and the fuel filler tube **(see illustrations)**.

Note: *The fuel lines are different diameters, so reattachment is simplified. If you have any doubts, however, clearly label the lines and the fittings. Be sure to plug the hoses to prevent leakage and contamination of the fuel system.*

7   If the tank doesn't have a drain plug, siphon the fuel from the tank at the fuel feed - not the return - line. **Warning:** *Never start the siphoning action by mouth! Use a siphoning kit, which can be purchased at most auto parts stores.*

8   Support the tank with a floor jack. Position a piece of wood between the jack head and the tank to protect the tank.

9   Disconnect both fuel tank retaining straps and pivot them down until they're hanging out of the way **(see illustration)**.

10   Lower the tank enough to disconnect the electrical connectors from the fuel gauge and fuel pump.

11   Remove the tank from the vehicle.

12   Installation is the reverse of removal.

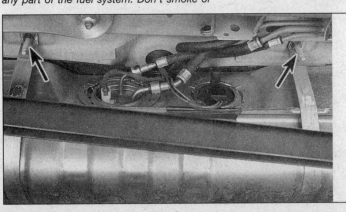

5.9 Remove the nuts and carefully slide the retaining straps over the studs

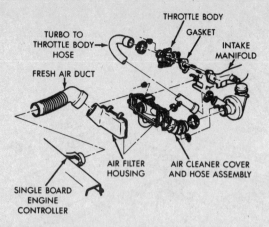

7.3a Typical air cleaner assembly - 2.5L Turbo 1 models

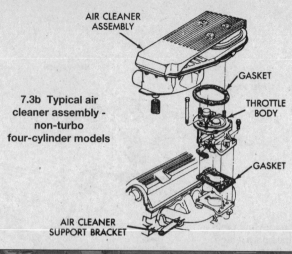

7.3b Typical air cleaner assembly - non-turbo four-cylinder models

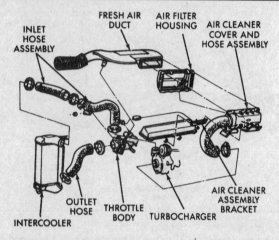

7.3c Air cleaner assembly - 2.2L Turbo III models

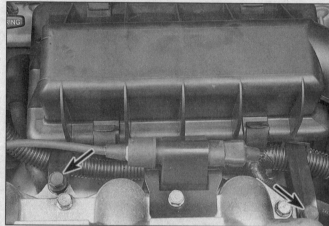

7.4 Mounting bolts (arrows) for the air cleaner assembly on V6 models

6 Fuel tank cleaning and repair - general information

1   All repairs to the fuel tank or filler neck should be carried out by a professional who has experience in this critical and potentially dangerous work. Even after cleaning and flushing of the fuel system, explosive fumes can remain and ignite during repair of the tank.

2   If the fuel tank is removed from the vehicle, it shouldn't be placed in an area where sparks or open flames could ignite the fumes coming out of the tank. Be especially careful inside garages where a natural gas-type appliance is located, because the pilot light could cause an explosion.

7 Air cleaner housing - removal and installation

Refer to illustrations 7.3a, 7.3b, 7.3c and 7.4

1   Detach the cable from the negative battery terminal.

2   Remove the air filter element (see Chapter 1).

3   Clearly label, then detach all remaining vacuum lines, tubes and hoses from the lower half of the air cleaner assembly **(see illustrations)**.

4   Remove the fasteners from the air cleaner mounting brackets and detach the air cleaner **(see illustration)**.

5   Installation is the reverse of removal.

8 Accelerator cable - replacement

Non-turbo models

Refer to illustrations 8.1, 8.2a, 8.2b, 8.2c and 8.2d

1   Working inside the vehicle, remove the

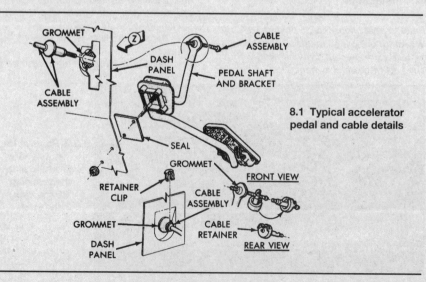

8.1 Typical accelerator pedal and cable details

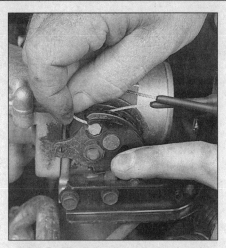

8.2a Use a small pair of needle-nose pliers to remove the retaining clip from the throttle lever

8.2b On V8 engines, rotate the throttle valve and remove the cable end from the slot

8.2c Squeeze the grommet with a pair of pliers to allow the tabs to clear the bracket

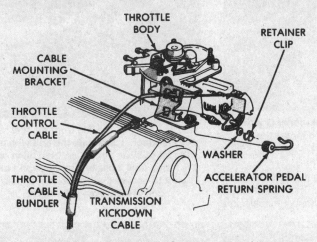

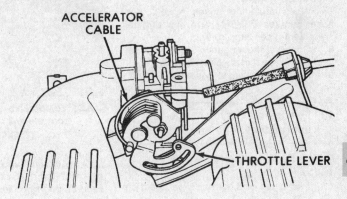

8.2d Throttle and transmission kickdown cable details (non-turbo four-cylinder model)

8.7 Rotate the throttle shaft until the cable is out of the guide groove in the bellcrank, then slide the cable end out of the bellcrank

4

retainer or plug and detach the cable end from the accelerator pedal shaft **(see illustration)**. Remove the retainer clip from the cable assembly housing at the grommet and pull the cable through the firewall.

2   Working in the engine compartment, remove the retainer clip and separate the cable from the pin or stud on the throttle lever **(see illustration)**, then detach the cable from the mounting bracket **(see illustration)**. Compress the cable-to-bracket fitting with a pair of pliers **(see illustration)**, then pull the cable through the bracket. **Note:** *If the vehicle is equipped with cruise control, mark the position of the retaining clip on the throttle lever with paint before disconnecting it* **(see illustration)**.

3   Remove the cable from the engine compartment.

4   Installation is the reverse of removal.

Turbo models

Refer to illustration 8.7

5   Working inside the vehicle, disconnect the throttle cable from the pedal shaft, then disconnect the cable from the firewall **(see illustration 8.1)**.

6   Working in the engine compartment, pull the cable housing end fitting out of the dash panel grommet, making sure the grommet remains in place.

7   Remove the throttle retainer and disconnect the throttle cable and cruise control cable (if equipped) from the throttle body **(see illustration)**. Use a pair of pliers to compress the end fitting tabs so the cable can be separated from the mounting bracket.

8   To install the cable, insert the housing into the throttle valve on the throttle body. Insert the cable through the firewall grommet and connect it to the throttle pedal.

9   Fuel lines and fittings - replacement

Refer to illustrations 9.5a, 9.5b and 9.5c
Warning: *Gasoline is extremely flammable, so take extra precautions when you work on*

any part of the fuel system. Don't smoke or allow open flames or bare light bulbs near the work area, and don't work in a garage where a natural gas-type appliance (such as a water heater or clothes dryer) with a pilot light is present. If you spill any fuel on your skin, rinse it off immediately with soap and water. When you perform any kind of work on the fuel system, wear safety glasses and have a Class B type fire extinguisher on hand. **Note:** *Since the EFI system is under considerable pressure, always replace all clamps released or removed with new ones of the correct type.*

1   Remove the air cleaner assembly.

2   Relieve the fuel system pressure (see Section 2).

3   Disconnect the negative cable from the battery.

4   On standard connections, loosen the hose clamps, wrap a cloth around each end of the hose to catch the residual fuel and twist and pull to remove the hose.

5   On quick-connect fittings, push the plastic ring on the end of the fitting IN then

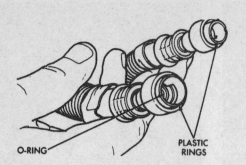

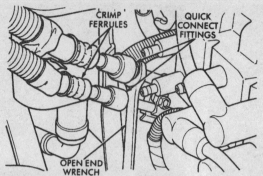

9.5a Typical quick-connect fittings have an inner plastic lockring (fitting for V6 engine shown, others similar)

detach the fitting from the component **(see illustrations)**.

6   When reconnecting quick-connect fittings, the ends of the fuel lines must be lubricated with a light coat of 30-weight engine oil. After the connection has been made, tug on the lines to ensure the connection has been made properly.

7   When replacing hoses, always use hoses marked EFI/EFM and new original equipment-type clamps only.

8   Connect the negative battery cable, start the engine and check for leaks.

9   Install the air cleaner assembly.

10 Fuel injection system - general information

Refer to illustrations 10.1a, 10.1b, 10.2a, 10.2b and 10.2c

   Two types of Electronic Fuel Injection

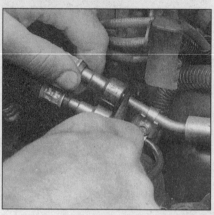

9.5b To detach a quick-connect fitting from the fuel rail, depress the plastic ring . . .

(EFI) systems are used on these models; single-point and multi-point. Single-point EFI is used on non-turbo four-cylinder models and

9.5c . . . and pull the line from the fuel rail - to reattach it, lubricate the end with a little bit of clean engine oil, then push on the fitting until it clicks into place and tug on it to ensure that the connection is locked into place (V6 engine)

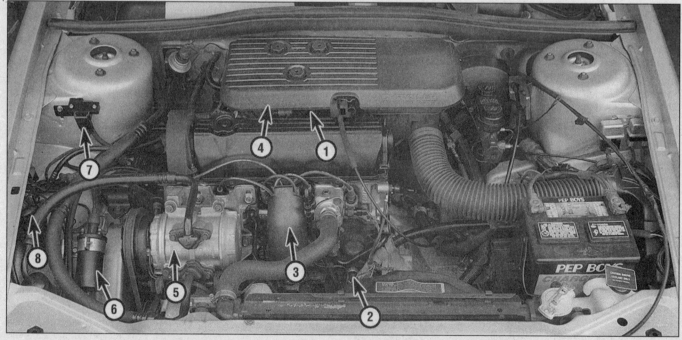

10.1a Underhood view of a typical single-point, fuel-injected (TBI) engine

1	Throttle body (not visible)	4	Air cleaner housing	7	MAP sensor
2	Oil pressure sending unit	5	Air conditioning compressor	8	Charcoal canister
3	Distributor	6	Ignition coil		

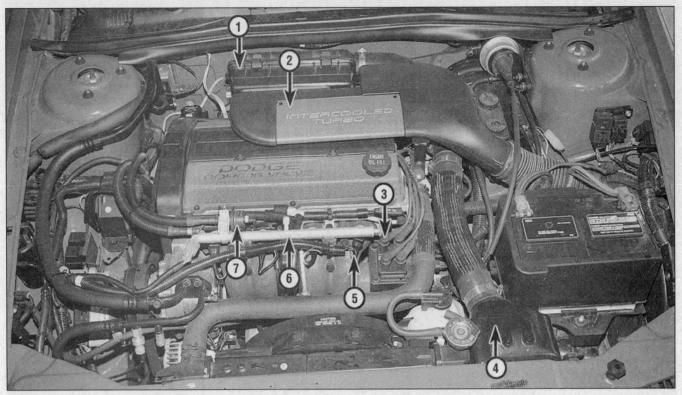

10.1b Underhood view of a typical multi-point, fuel-injected (MPI) Turbo III engine

1	Air cleaner housing	3	DISC unit	5	Fuel injector	7	Fuel pressure regulator
2	Air intake ducts	4	Intercooler	6	Fuel rail		

multi-point on turbo and V6 models **(see illustrations)**.

Both types are similar in operation. Each is an electronically controlled system which combines electronic fuel injection and elec-tronic spark advance. The main sub-systems include the air induction, fuel delivery, fuel control, emission control, control module and data sensors. On 1989 models, the control module is called the Single Module Engine Controller (SMEC). On 1990 and later models it's called the Single Board Engine Controller (SBEC) **(see illustrations)**. Each system differs slightly in the position and type of components installed.

4

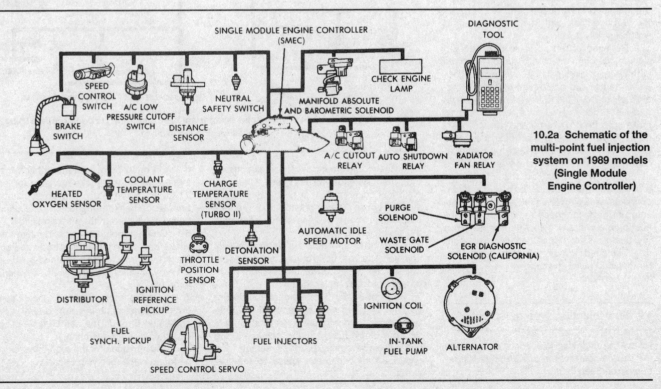

10.2a Schematic of the multi-point fuel injection system on 1989 models (Single Module Engine Controller)

Air induction system

The air induction system includes the air cleaner, throttle body, Throttle Position Sensor (TPS), Automatic Idle Speed (AIS) motor and turbocharger (if equipped).

Fuel delivery system

The fuel delivery system provides fuel from the fuel tank into the fuel control system. It also returns any excess fuel back into the fuel tank. The system includes an in-tank electric fuel pump, fuel filter, check valves and return line. Power is supplied to the fuel pump through the power module via the Automatic Shutdown (ASD) relay. The ASD relay also controls the ignition coil, the fuel injectors and parts of the power module.

Fuel control system

The remaining components of the fuel control system are the fuel pressure regulator, fuel injectors and fuel rail (multi-point) or TBI unit (single-point).

Emission control system

The emission system is directly linked to the SMEC/SBEC. The fuel injection system and the emission system are closely linked in function and design. For additional information, refer to Chapter 6.

Fuel injectors

On both the single and multi-point EFI, the conventional carburetor is replaced by a throttle body and injector (single-point) or throttle body, fuel rail and injectors (multi-point). On single-point EFI, the fuel is mixed with air in the throttle body and sprayed into the intake manifold, which directs it to the intake ports and cylinders. On multi-port EFI, the fuel is sprayed directly into the ports by the fuel injectors, with the intake manifold supplying only the air.

Because of the complexity of the EFI system, the home mechanic can do very little in the way of diagnosis because of the special expertise and equipment required. However, checking of the EFI system components and electrical and vacuum connections to make sure they're secure and not obviously damaged is one thing the home mechanic can do which can often detect a potential or current problem. Since the power module is completely dependent on the information provided by the many sensors and vacuum connections, a simple visual check and tightening of loose connections can save diagnostic time and a possibly unnecessary trip to a dealer service department or repair shop.

Damaged or faulty EFI components can be replaced using the procedures in the following Sections.

11 Fuel injection system - check

Note: *The following procedure is based on the assumption that the fuel pressure is adequate (see Section 3).*

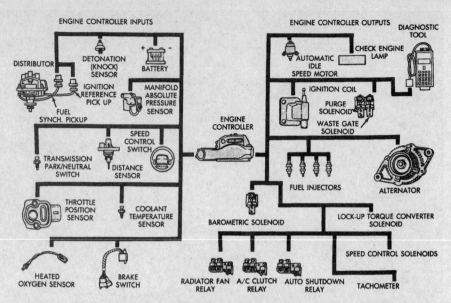

10.2b Schematic of the multi-point system on 1990 and later Turbo I model (Single Board Engine Controller)

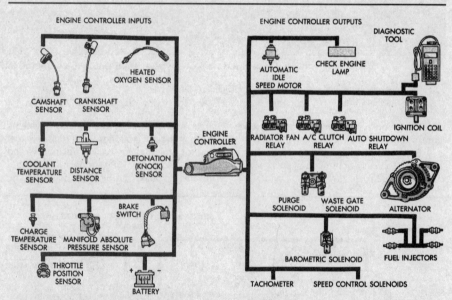

10.2c Schematic of the multi-point system on 1991 and later Turbo III models (Single Board Engine Controller)

1   Check the ground wire connections on the intake manifold for tightness. Check all electrical connectors that are related to the system. Loose connectors and poor grounds can cause many problems that resemble more serious malfunctions.
2   Check to see that the battery is fully charged, as the control unit and sensors depend on an accurate supply voltage in order to properly meter the fuel.
3   Check the air filter element - a dirty or partially blocked filter will severely impede performance and economy (see Chapter 1).
4   If a blown fuse is found, replace it and see if it blows again. If it does, search for a grounded wire in the harness to the fuel pump.
5   On multi-point systems, check the air intake duct to the intake manifold for leaks, which will result in an excessively lean mixture. Also check the condition of all vacuum hoses connected to the intake manifold.
6   On multi-point systems, remove the air intake duct from the throttle body and check for dirt, carbon or other residue build-up. If it's dirty, clean it with carburetor cleaner and a toothbrush.
7   With the engine running, place a screwdriver against each injector, one at a time, and listen through the handle for a clicking sound, indicating operation.
8   The remainder of the system checks can be found in the following Sections.

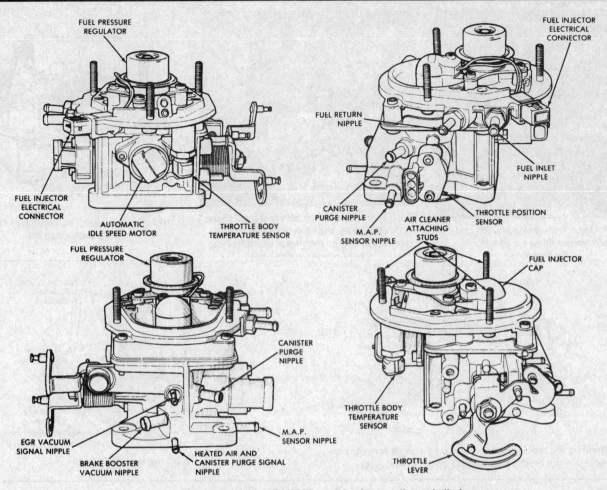

FUEL PRESSURE REGULATOR

FUEL INJECTOR ELECTRICAL CONNECTOR

FUEL INJECTOR ELECTRICAL CONNECTOR

AUTOMATIC IDLE SPEED MOTOR

THROTTLE BODY TEMPERATURE SENSOR

FUEL RETURN NIPPLE

FUEL INLET NIPPLE

CANISTER PURGE NIPPLE

M.A.P. SENSOR NIPPLE

AIR CLEANER ATTACHING STUDS

THROTTLE POSITION SENSOR

FUEL PRESSURE REGULATOR

FUEL INJECTOR CAP

CANISTER PURGE NIPPLE

EGR VACUUM SIGNAL NIPPLE

BRAKE BOOSTER VACUUM NIPPLE

HEATED AIR AND CANISTER PURGE SIGNAL NIPPLE

M.A.P. SENSOR NIPPLE

THROTTLE BODY TEMPERATURE SENSOR

THROTTLE LEVER

12.4 Throttle body details (1989 models shown, others similar)

12 Throttle body (single-point EFI) - removal and installation

Warning: *Gasoline is extremely flammable, so take extra precautions when you work on any part of the fuel system. Don't smoke or allow open flames or bare light bulbs near the work area, and don't work in a garage where a natural gas-type appliance (such as a water heater or clothes dryer) with a pilot light is present. If you spill any fuel on your skin, rinse it off immediately with soap and water. When you perform any kind of work on the fuel system, wear safety glasses and have a Class B type fire extinguisher on hand.*

Removal

Refer to illustrations 12.4 and 12.8

1   Remove the air cleaner assembly (see Section 7).
2   Relieve the fuel system pressure (see Section 2).
3   Disconnect the negative cable from the battery.
4   Mark and disconnect the vacuum hoses and electrical connectors **(see illustration)**.
5   Disconnect the throttle linkage and (if equipped) the cruise control and transaxle

kickdown cable.
6   Remove the throttle return spring.
7   Place rags or newspapers under the fuel hoses to catch the residual fuel. Loosen the clamps, wrap a cloth around each fuel hose and pull them off. Remove the copper washers from the hoses, noting their locations.
8   Remove the mounting bolts or nuts **(see illustration)** and lift the throttle body off the manifold. Remove all traces of old gasket material from the mating surfaces of the throttle body and intake manifold.

Installation

9   Inspect the mating surfaces of the throttle body and the manifold for nicks, burrs and debris that could cause air leaks.
10   Using a new gasket, place the throttle body in position and install the mounting bolts or nuts. Tighten the bolts or nuts to the torque listed in this Chapter's Specifications, following a criss-cross pattern. Work up to the final torque in three or four steps.
11   Check all of the vacuum hoses and electrical connectors for damage, replacing them with new parts if necessary, then connect them.
12   Connect the throttle linkage and (if equipped) cruise control and kickdown cable.

12.8 Remove the two long bolts (center and right arrows) and the two short bolts (arrow) from the throttle body (the rear short bolt is hidden from view)

13   Connect the throttle return spring.
14   Using new clamps, install the fuel hoses.
15   Check the operation of the throttle linkage.
16   Install the air cleaner assembly.
17   Connect the negative battery cable.
18   Start the engine and check for fuel leaks.

4

13.5 Use a Torx driver (no. 25) and remove the three screws from the regulator

13.7 If the regulator is still fastened to the throttle body after the bolts have been removed, wiggle the regulator to free-up the hardened rubber seal

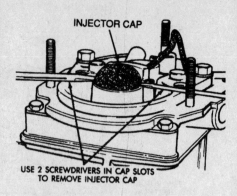

14.7 Use two small screwdrivers to pry the injector cap off

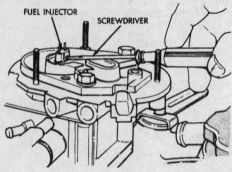

14.8 Remove the fuel injector by inserting a small screwdriver into the slot on the injector and gently prying it up

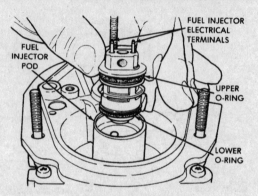

14.9 Fuel injector details

13 Fuel pressure regulator (single-point EFI) - check, removal and installation

Warning: *Gasoline is extremely flammable, so take extra precautions when you work on any part of the fuel system. Don't smoke or allow open flames or bare light bulbs near the work area, and don't work in a garage where a natural gas-type appliance (such as a water heater or clothes dryer) with a pilot light is present. If you spill any fuel on your skin, rinse it off immediately with soap and water. When you perform any kind of work on the fuel system, wear safety glasses and have a Class B type fire extinguisher on hand.*

Check

1   Follow the fuel pressure checking procedure in Section 3 for diagnosis of the fuel pressure regulator.

Removal

Refer to illustrations 13.5 and 13.7

2   Remove the air cleaner assembly (see Section 7).
3   Relieve the fuel system pressure (see Section 2).
4   Disconnect the negative cable from the battery.

5   Remove the three screws (this will require a no. 25 Torx driver) from the regulator **(see illustration)**.
6   Wrap a cloth around the fuel inlet chamber to catch any residual fuel.
7   Withdraw the pressure regulator from the throttle body **(see illustration)**.
8   Carefully remove the O-ring from the pressure regulator, followed by the gasket.

Installation

9   Place a new gasket in position on the pressure regulator and carefully install a new O-ring.
10   Place the pressure regulator in position on the throttle body, press it into position and install the three mounting screws. Tighten the screws to the torque listed in this Chapter's Specifications.
11   Connect the negative battery cable. Check carefully for any fuel leaks.
12   Install the air cleaner assembly (see Section 7).

14 Fuel injector (single-point EFI) - check, removal and installation

Warning: *Gasoline is extremely flammable, so take extra precautions when you work on any part of the fuel system. Don't smoke or allow open flames or bare light bulbs near the*

work area, and don't work in a garage where a natural gas-type appliance (such as a water heater or clothes dryer) with a pilot light is present. If you spill any fuel on your skin, rinse it off immediately with soap and water. When you perform any kind of work on the fuel system, wear safety glasses and have a Class B type fire extinguisher on hand.

Check

1   With the engine running, or cranking, listen to the sound from the injector with an automotive stethoscope and verify that the injector sounds as if it's operating normally. If you don't have a stethoscope, touch the area of the throttle body immediately above the fuel injector with your finger and try to determine whether the injector feels like it's operating smoothly. It should sound/feel smooth and uniform and its sound/feel should rise and fall with engine rpm. If the injector isn't operating, or sounds/feels erratic, check the injector electrical connector. If the connectors are snug, check for voltage to the injector using a special injector harness test light (available at most auto parts stores). If there's voltage to the injector and it isn't operating, or if it's operating erratically, replace it.

Removal

Refer to illustrations 14.7, 14.8 and 14.9

2   Remove the air cleaner assembly (see

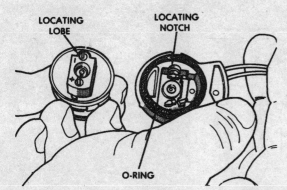

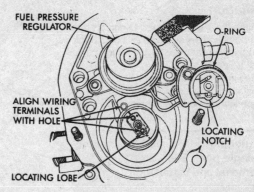

14.12a Alignment details of the cap and injector (early models)

14.12b Alignment details of the cap and injector (later models)

Section 7).

3   Relieve the fuel system pressure (See Section 2).

4   Disconnect the negative cable from the battery.

5   On some early model TBI units, it may be necessary to remove the fuel pressure regulator (see Section 13) to access the fuel injector.

6   Remove the Torx screw that holds the injector cap.

7   Use two small screwdrivers and carefully pry the cap off the injector using the appropriate slots **(see illustration)**.

8   Place a small screwdriver into the hole in the injector and gently pry the injector from the throttle body unit **(see illustration)**.

9   Peel the upper and lower O-rings off the fuel injector **(see illustration)**. If the lower O-ring isn't on the injector, be sure to retrieve it from the throttle body.

Installation

Refer to illustrations 14.12a, 14.12b and 14.13

10   Install new O-rings on the injector and a new O-ring on the injector cap. **Note:** *New injectors come equipped with a new upper O-ring. Coat the O-rings with a light film of engine oil to help injector installation.*

11   Insert the injector into the throttle body.

12   Place the injector cap onto the injector. The injector and cap are keyed and must be aligned properly **(see illustrations)**.

13   Rotate the cap and injector to line up the attachment hole **(see illustration)**. Tighten the screws to the torque listed in this Chapter's Specifications.

14   Connect the negative battery cable, start the engine and check for leaks.

15   Turn off the engine and install the air cleaner assembly.

15   Throttle Position Sensor (TPS) (single-point EFI) - check, removal and installation

Warning: *Gasoline is extremely flammable, so take extra precautions when you work on*

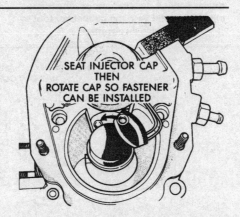

14.13 Rotate the cap so the screw aligns with the slot in the cap

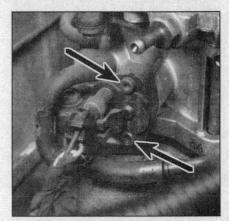

15.5 Use a Torx driver (no. 25) and remove the two bolts (arrows)

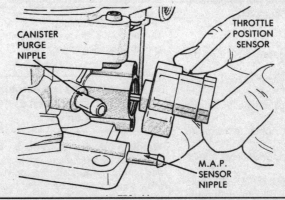

15.6 Don't strike the TPS with a hammer or a hard object to loosen it from the throttle body

any part of the fuel system. Don't smoke or allow open flames or bare light bulbs near the work area, and don't work in a garage where a natural gas-type appliance (such as a water heater or clothes dryer) with a pilot light is present. If you spill any fuel on your skin, rinse it off immediately with soap and water. When you perform any kind of work on the fuel system, wear safety glasses and have a Class B type fire extinguisher on hand.*

Check

1   The Throttle Position Sensor (TPS) is monitored by the SMEC or SBEC (computer) located in the engine compartment. If the TPS malfunctions, a trouble code is stored in the logic module's memory. To get the com-

puter to display any stored trouble codes, refer to the appropriate Section in Chapter 6. If a Code 24 is displayed, first check the circuit and, if necessary, replace the TPS.

Removal

Refer to illustrations 15.5 and 15.6

2   Disconnect the negative cable from the battery.

3   Remove the air cleaner (see Section 7).

4   Unplug the electrical connector from the TPS.

5   Remove the two TPS-to-throttle body screws (a no. 25 Torx driver will be required) **(see illustration)**.

6   Separate the TPS from the throttle shaft **(see illustration)** and remove the O-ring.

4

Installation

7   Place the TPS with a new O-ring on the throttle body and install the retaining screws. Tighten the screws to the torque listed in this Chapter's Specifications.
8   Plug in the electrical connector.
9   Install the air cleaner.
10 Connect the negative battery cable.

16 Automatic Idle Speed (AIS) motor (single-point EFI) - check, removal and installation

Warning: *Gasoline is extremely flammable, so take extra precautions when you work on any part of the fuel system. Don't smoke or allow open flames or bare light bulbs near the work area, and don't work in a garage where a natural gas-type appliance (such as a water heater or clothes dryer) with a pilot light is present. If you spill any fuel on your skin, rinse it off immediately with soap and water. When you perform any kind of work on the fuel system, wear safety glasses and have a Class B type fire extinguisher on hand.*

Check

1   The Automatic Idle Speed (AIS) motor is monitored by the SMEC or the SBEC (computer). If the AIS motor malfunctions, a trouble code is stored in the computer's memory. To get the computer to display any stored trouble codes, refer to the appropriate Section in Chapter 6. If a Code 25 is displayed, check the AIS motor circuit for problems. If necessary, replace the AIS motor.

Removal

2   Disconnect the negative cable from the battery.
3   Remove the air cleaner assembly (see Section 7).
4   Unplug the electrical connector on the AIS motor.
5   Remove the throttle body temperature sensor (see Section 17).
6   Remove the two retaining screws (no. 25 Torx) from the AIS motor.
7   Pull the AIS from the throttle body. Make sure the O-ring doesn't fall into the throttle body opening.

Installation

Refer to illustration 16.8

8   Prior to installation, make sure the 6 is in the retracted position. If the pintle protrudes more than 1-inch (25 mm), the AIS motor must be taken to a dealer service department to be retracted **(see illustration)**.
9   Install a new O-ring and insert the AIS motor into the housing, making sure the O-ring isn't dislodged.
10 Install the two retaining screws. Tighten the screws to the torque listed in this Chapter's Specifications.
11 Plug in the electrical connector.
12 Install the throttle body temperature

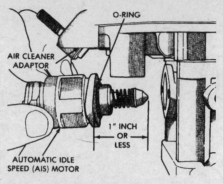

16.8 Measure the length of the pintle - if it protrudes more than 1-inch, take it to a dealer service department or other repair shop equipped with the necessary tool to have it retracted

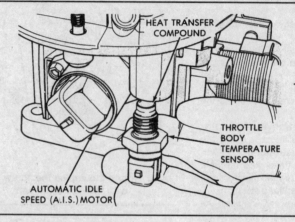

sensor (see Section 17).
13 Install the air cleaner assembly and connect the negative battery cable.

17 Throttle body temperature sensor (single-point EFI) - check and replacement

Warning: *Gasoline is extremely flammable, so take extra precautions when you work on any part of the fuel system. Don't smoke or allow open flames or bare light bulbs near the work area, and don't work in a garage where a natural gas-type appliance (such as a water heater or clothes dryer) with a pilot light is present. If you spill any fuel on your skin, rinse it off immediately with soap and water. When you perform any kind of work on the fuel system, wear safety glasses and have a Class B type fire extinguisher on hand.*

Check

1   The throttle body temperature sensor is monitored by the engine controller (computer). If the sensor malfunctions, a trouble code is stored in the computer's memory. To get the computer to display any stored trouble codes, refer to the appropriate section in Chapter 6. If a Code 23 is displayed, replace the sensor.

17.4 Remove the two bolts (arrows) that retain the cable bracket to the throttle body

17.6 Carefully unscrew the sensor from the throttle body

Removal

Refer to illustrations 17.4 and 17.6

2   Disconnect the negative cable from the battery.
3   Remove the air cleaner assembly (see Section 7).
4   Disconnect the throttle cable from the throttle body, remove the two cable bracket screws and lay the bracket aside **(see illustration)**.
5   Unplug the electrical connector from the sensor.
6   Remove the sensor by unscrewing it **(see illustration)**.

Installation

7   Apply a thin coat of heat transfer compound (provided with the new sensor) to the tip of the sensor.
8   Screw the sensor into the throttle body and tighten it securely.
9   Plug in the electrical connector.
10 Connect the throttle cable.
11 Install the air cleaner and connect the negative battery cable.

18 Throttle body (multi-point EFI) - removal and installation

Warning: *Gasoline is extremely flammable,*

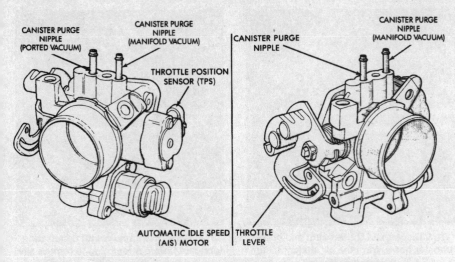

18.5a Throttle body external details (2.5L Turbo I shown, 2.2L Turbo III similar)

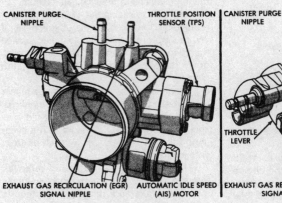
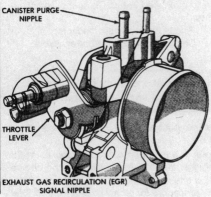

18.5b Throttle body external details (V6 engine)

so take extra precautions when you work on any part of the fuel system. Don't smoke or allow open flames or bare light bulbs near the work area, and don't work in a garage where a natural gas-type appliance (such as a water heater or clothes dryer) with a pilot light is present. If you spill any fuel on your skin, rinse it off immediately with soap and water. When you perform any kind of work on the fuel system, wear safety glasses and have a Class B type fire extinguisher on hand.

Removal

Refer to illustrations 18.5a, 18.5b and 18.7

1   Disconnect the negative cable from the battery.
2   Remove the clamp and air cleaner hose from the throttle body (see Section 7). Remove the air cleaner assembly.
3   Remove the return spring, disconnect the accelerator cable (see Section 8) and remove the cruise control and automatic transaxle kickdown cable (if equipped).
4   Detach the throttle cable from the bracket.
5   Unplug any electrical connectors from

the throttle body **(see illustrations)**.
6   Mark and disconnect any vacuum hoses from the throttle body.
7   Remove the bolts/nuts and detach the throttle body from the intake manifold **(see illustration)**.

18.7 Remove the nuts (arrows) and separate the throttle body from the air intake plenum

Installation

8   Place the throttle body in position and install the mounting bolts. Tighten them in a criss-cross pattern to the torque listed in this Chapter's Specifications.
9   Connect the vacuum hoses.
10   Plug in the electrical connectors.
11   Install the bracket and connect the throttle cable, return spring and (if equipped) cruise control and automatic transaxle kick-down cable.
12   Install the air cleaner hose and adapter. Tighten the clamps securely.
13   Connect the negative battery cable.

19   Throttle Position Sensor (TPS) (multi-point EFI) - check, removal and installation

Check

1   The Throttle Position Sensor (TPS) is monitored by the SMEC or the SBEC (computer). If the TPS malfunctions, a trouble code is stored in the computer's memory. To get the vehicle to display any stored trouble codes, refer to the appropriate section in Chapter 6. If a Code 24 is displayed, check the TPS.

Removal

Refer to illustration 19.5

2   Disconnect the negative cable from the battery.
3   Unplug the electrical connector from the TPS.
4   Remove the TPS-to-throttle body screws.
5   Withdraw the TPS from the throttle shaft **(see illustration)**.

Installation

6   Install the TPS on the throttle body. Tighten the screws to the torque listed in this Chapter's Specifications.
7   Plug in the three-way connector and connect the negative battery cable.

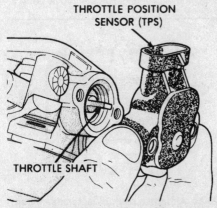

19.5 Remove the throttle position sensor from the throttle body

4

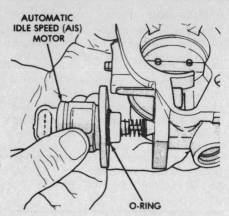

20.5 Carefully remove the AIS motor from the throttle body

20   Automatic Idle Speed (AIS) motor (multi-point EFI) - check, removal and installation

Check

1   The Automatic Idle Speed (AIS) motor is monitored by the SMEC or the SBEC (computer). If the AIS motor malfunctions, a trouble code is stored in the computer's memory. To get the computer to display any stored trouble codes, refer to the appropriate Section in Chapter 6. If a Code 25 is displayed, check the AIS system.

Removal

Refer to illustration 20.5

2   Disconnect the negative cable from the battery.
3   Unplug the four-way electrical connector from the AIS.
4   Remove the two AIS motor-to-throttle body screws.
5   Remove the AIS motor from the throttle body. Make sure the O-ring remains on the motor **(see illustration)**.

Installation

6   Carefully position the AIS motor (using new O-rings - new motors should be already equipped with O-rings) on the throttle body.

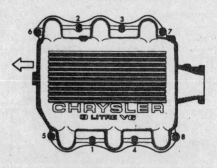

21.6a Air intake plenum fasteners - when installing the plenum, tighten the bolts in the order shown (V6 engine)

21.1 Disconnect the vacuum and brake booster hoses from the air intake plenum (V6 engine shown)

7   Install the screws and tighten them to the torque listed in this Chapter's Specifications.
8   Plug in the four-way connector.
9   Connect the negative battery cable.

21   Air intake plenum (V6 engine) - removal and installation

Refer to illustrations 21.1, 21.2, 21.6a and 21.6b
Note: *The following procedure applies to V6 engines; the 2.5L four-cylinder turbo engine has a one-piece plenum and intake manifold. The procedure for removing and installing the turbo plenum/intake manifold is in Chapter 2, Part A.*

1   Disconnect the vacuum and brake booster hoses from the air intake plenum **(see illustration)**.
2   Remove the mounting bolts from the EGR tube flange **(see illustration)**, unplug any electrical connectors from the throttle body or plenum and detach the vacuum harness connectors from the air intake plenum.
3   Detach the ignition coil from the air intake plenum (see Chapter 5).
4   Disconnect any vacuum lines located at

21.6b Be sure to note the position of the coil bolt before removing it from the plenum

21.2 Spray the threads with penetrating lubricant before attempting to remove the flange nuts

the opposite end of the air intake plenum.
5   If you're replacing the air intake plenum, remove the throttle body (see Section 18); if you're simply removing the plenum to service the lower intake manifold, the heads, etc., don't remove the throttle body from the plenum.
6   Remove the air intake plenum fasteners **(see illustrations)** from the intake manifold, remove the plenum and discard the old gaskets. Cover the intake manifold with a clean shop towel to prevent dirt and debris from entering the engine.
7   Installation is the reverse of removal. Remove the shop towel from the lower intake manifold. Make sure the gasket surface is spotless. Place the new gaskets on the lower intake manifold (the beaded sealant faces up). Put the air intake plenum in place, install the mounting fasteners and tighten them to the torque listed in this Chapter's Specifications following the correct sequence **(see illustration 21.6a)**.

22   Fuel rail assembly (multi-point EFI) - removal and installation

Warning: *Gasoline is extremely flammable, so take extra precautions when you work on any part of the fuel system. Don't smoke or allow open flames or bare light bulbs near the work area, and don't work in a garage where a natural gas-type appliance (such as a water heater or clothes dryer) with a pilot light is present. If you spill any fuel on your skin, rinse it off immediately with soap and water. When you perform any kind of work on the fuel system, wear safety glasses and have a Class B type fire extinguisher on hand.*

1   Relieve the fuel system pressure (see Section 2).
2   Disconnect the negative cable from the battery.
3   Remove the air cleaner assembly (see Section 7).

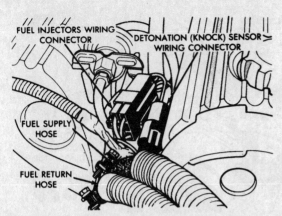

22.5a Disconnect any electrical connectors relating to the fuel injectors and fuel rail assembly (multi-point system)

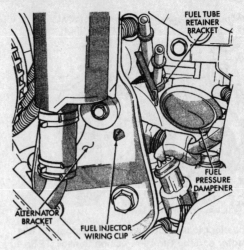

22.5b The fuel injector harness is clipped into the alternator bracket - to release it, pinch the tabs together and push it through the hole (Turbo III models)

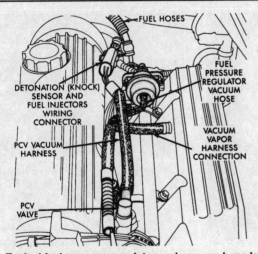

22.6 Typical fuel pressure regulator and vacuum hose layout on multi-point fuel injector systems

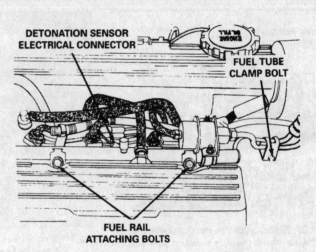

22.8a Remove the fuel rail attaching bolts (Turbo I model)

Turbo engines

Removal

Refer to illustrations 22.5a, 22.5b, 22.6, 22.8a and 22.8b

4   Remove the quick-disconnect fittings from the chassis fuel lines, or the hose clamps and hoses from the fuel rail assembly.

5   Disconnect any electrical connectors (fuel injector, detonation knock sensor, etc.) from the injector wiring harness (**see illustrations**).

6   Disconnect the vacuum hose from the fuel pressure regulator (**see illustration**) and loosen the regulator/return line nut using two wrenches. Detach the hose from the regulator.

7   Remove the PCV vacuum harness and vacuum vapor harness from the intake manifold if equipped (**see illustration 22.6**).

8   Remove the fuel rail mounting bolts (**see illustrations**).

9   Grasp the fuel rail and injector assembly and pull the injectors straight out of their ports. Working carefully, to avoid damaging the injector O-rings, remove the rail assembly from the vehicle. The fuel injectors must not

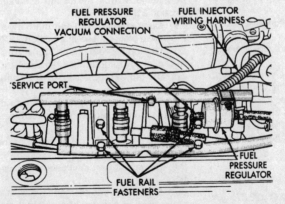

22.8b Fuel rail assembly on a Turbo III model

be removed until the fuel rail is detached from the vehicle.

10   Support the fuel rail and disconnect the remaining fuel hoses.

Installation

11   Prior to installation, make sure the injectors are securely seated in the fuel rail with the lock rings in place.

12   Inspect the injector holes to make sure

they're clean.

13   Lubricate the injector O-rings with clean engine oil.

14   Insert the injector assemblies carefully into their ports and install the bolts and ground straps. Tighten the bolts evenly in a criss-cross pattern so the injectors are drawn evenly into place. Once the injectors are seated, tighten the bolts to the torque listed in this Chapter's Specifications.

4

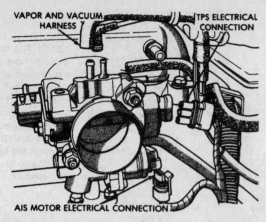

22.22 Unplug the electrical connectors for the Automatic Idle Speed (AIS) motor and the Throttle Position Sensor (TPS)

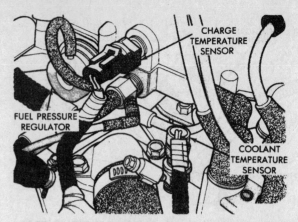

22.26 Unplug the electrical connectors from the charge temperature sensor and the coolant temperature sensor

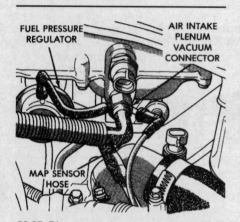

22.27 Disconnect the vacuum hoses from the air intake plenum vacuum connector

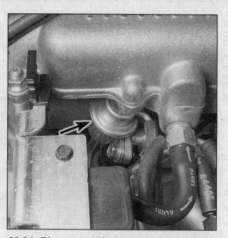

22.31 Disconnect the vacuum hoses from the fuel rail and the fuel pressure regulator (arrow)

22.32 Pinch the two plastic tangs while simultaneously lifting the injector to remove it from the connector

15   Connect the injector electrical connectors to the injectors and secure the harness with the clips.
16   Install the fuel rail-to-valve cover bracket bolt.
17   Connect the fuel pressure regulator vacuum hose.
18   Reconnect the fuel supply hose. Clamp on the rail and tighten the clamp securely.
19   Check to make sure the ground straps, hoses, wiring electrical and connectors are securely installed in their original locations.
20   Connect the negative battery cable.

V6 engine

Removal

Refer to illustrations 22.22, 22.26, 22.27, 22.31, 22.32, 22.34a and 22.34b

21   Detach the accelerator cable (see Section 8) and transaxle kickdown cable (see Chapter 7).
22   Unplug the electrical connectors for the Automatic Idle Speed (AIS) motor and the Throttle Position Sensor (TPS) **(see illustration)**.
23   Disconnect the vacuum hose connections from the throttle body **(see illustration 22.22)**.

24   Disconnect the vacuum and brake booster hoses from the air intake plenum (see Section 21).
25   Disconnect the EGR tube flange from the intake plenum **(see illustration 21.2)**.
26   Unplug the electrical connectors from the charge temperature sensor and the coolant temperature sensor **(see illustration)**.
27   Detach the vacuum hoses from the air intake plenum vacuum connector **(see illustration)**.
28   Disconnect the fuel hoses from the fuel rail.
29   Remove the air intake plenum (see Section 21).
30   Cover the intake manifold with clean shop rags to prevent dirt and debris from entering the engine.
31   Disconnect the vacuum hoses from the fuel rail and the fuel pressure regulator **(see illustration)**.
32   Unplug the electrical connectors for the fuel injectors **(see illustration)**.
33   Remove the fuel pressure regulator.
34   Remove the fuel rail mounting bolts and lift the fuel rail assembly from the intake manifold **(see illustrations)**.

Installation

35   Make sure the injector holes are clean and all plugs have been removed.
36   Lube the injector O-rings with a drop of clean engine oil to facilitate installation.
37   Make sure all injectors are properly seated into their receiver cups with the lock

22.34a Remove the bolts (arrows) from the fuel rail assembly

22.34b When you are removing or installing the fuel rail, you can twist either fuel rail tube independently to help wiggle the injectors loose or seat them

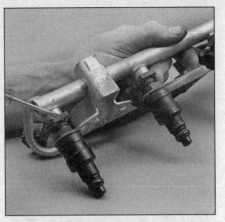

23.3a Pry the injector lock rings off with a screwdriver

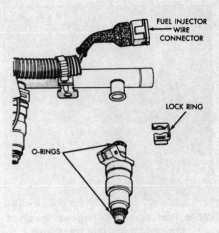

23.3b Pull the injector straight out of the fuel receiver cup

rings in place (see Section 23).

38   Put the tip of each injector into its respective port. Push the assembly into place until the injectors are seated in their ports.

39   Install the fuel rail mounting bolts and tighten them to the torque listed in this Chapter's Specifications.

40   Install the fuel pressure regulator and hose assembly. Make sure the hose clamps are snug.

41   Install the hold-down bolt for the fuel supply and return tube and the hold-down bolt for the vacuum crossover tube. Tighten both bolts securely.

42   Plug in the electrical connector for the fuel injector wiring harness.

43   Reattach the vacuum harness for the fuel pressure regulator and the fuel rail assembly.

44   Install the air intake plenum (see Section 21).

45   Connect the fuel line to the fuel rail and tighten the hose clamps securely.

46   Connect the vacuum harness to the air intake plenum.

47   Plug in the electrical connectors for the charge temperature sensor and coolant temperature sensor.

48   Reattach the EGR tube flange to the air intake plenum.

49   Reconnect the PCV and brake booster supply hoses to the intake plenum.

50   Plug in the electrical connectors for the

automatic idle speed (AIS) motor and throttle position sensor (TPS).

51   Reconnect the vacuum vapor harness to the throttle body.

52   Reattach the accelerator cable (see Section 8) and transaxle kickdown linkage (see Chapter 7).

53   Install the air cleaner assembly.

54   Connect the negative battery cable.

23 Fuel injector(s) (multi-point EFI) - check, removal and installation

Refer to illustrations 23.3a, 23.3b, 23.4a, 23.4b, 23.4c, 23.5 and 23.6

Warning: *Gasoline is extremely flammable, so take extra precautions when you work on any part of the fuel system. Don't smoke or allow open flames or bare light bulbs near the work area, and don't work in a garage where a natural gas-type appliance (such as a water heater or clothes dryer) with a pilot light is present. If you spill any fuel on your skin, rinse it off immediately with soap and water. When you perform any kind of work on the fuel system, wear safety glasses and have a Class B type fire extinguisher on hand.*

Check

1   With the engine running or cranking, listen to the sound from each injector with an automotive stethoscope and verify the injectors are all clicking the same. If you don't

have a stethoscope, place the tip of a screwdriver against the injectors and press your ear against the handle of the screwdriver. Also feel the operation of each injector with your finger. It should sound/feel smooth and uniform and its sound/feel should rise and fall with engine RPM. If an injector isn't operating, or sounds/feels erratic, check the injector connector and the wire electrical connector. If the connectors are snug, check for voltage to the injector, using a special injector harness test light (available at most auto parts stores). If there's voltage to the injector but it injector isn't operating, or it sounds/feels erratic, replace the injector.

Removal

2   Remove the fuel rail assembly (see Section 22) and place the fuel rail assembly on a clean work surface so the fuel injectors are accessible.

3   Remove the injector lock ring from the fuel rail and injector by prying it off with a small screwdriver. Pull the injector straight out of the receiver cup **(see illustrations)**.

4   Inspect the injector O-rings for damage. Replace them with new ones if necessary **(see illustrations)**.

4

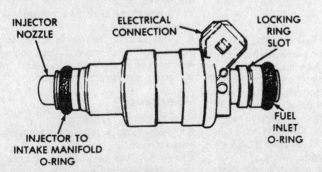

23.4a The fuel injector has two different size O-rings

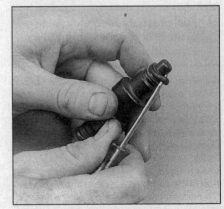

23.4b Insert a small screwdriver under the O-ring and pry it off - be careful not to damage the injector tip

23.4c Push the new O-ring over the tip of the injector and into the groove

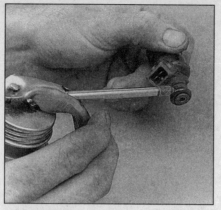

23.5 A drop of clean engine oil will allow the injector to seat easily

23.6 Push the injector straight into the receiver cup

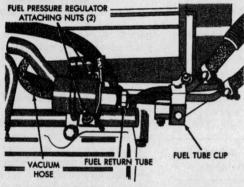

24.3a Fuel pressure regulator assembly (2.5L Turbo I)

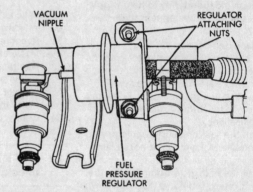

24.3b Fuel pressure regulator assembly (2.2L Turbo III)

Installation

5   Prior to installation, lubricate the O-rings with a light film of clean engine oil **(see illustration)**.

6   Push the top of the injector straight into the fuel rail receiver cup, taking care not to damage the O-ring **(see illustration)**.

7   Slide the open end of the injector clip into the top slot of the injector, onto the receiver cup ridge and into the side slots of the clip.

8   Install the fuel rail (see Section 22).

24 Fuel pressure regulator (multi-point EFI) - removal and installation

Warning: *Gasoline is extremely flammable, so take extra precautions when you work on any part of the fuel system. Don't smoke or allow open flames or bare light bulbs near the work area, and don't work in a garage where a natural gas-type appliance (such as a water heater or clothes dryer) with a pilot light is present. If you spill any fuel on your skin, rinse it off immediately with soap and water. When you perform any kind of work on the fuel system, wear safety glasses and have a Class B type fire extinguisher on hand.*

1   Relieve the system fuel pressure (see Section 2).

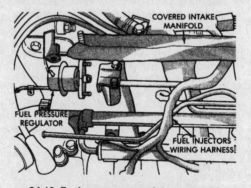

24.10 Fuel pressure regulator assembly (V6 engine)

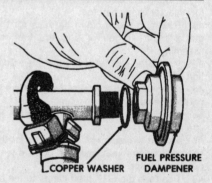

25.4 Fuel pressure damper assembly (2.5L turbo engine)

2   Disconnect the cable from the negative battery terminal.

Turbo engines

Refer to illustrations 24.3a and 24.3b

3   Disconnect the vacuum hose from the fuel pressure regulator **(see illustrations)**.

4   Loosen the fuel return hose clamp at the fuel pressure regulator and remove the hose.

5   On 2.5L Turbo I engines, use two flare nut or open end wrenches - one on the regulator and the other on the fuel return tube nut - loosen the tube nut. Failure to use a backup wrench will cause damage.

6   Remove the fuel pressure regulator attaching nuts and remove the regulator from the fuel rail.

7   Inspect the O-ring for damage. If it's damaged, replace it.

8   Installation is the reverse of removal. Be sure to lube the O-ring with clean engine oil. And be sure to use a backup wrench when tightening the fuel return tube fitting.

V6 engine

Refer to illustration 24.10

9   Refer to Section 21 and remove the air intake plenum.

10   Remove the fuel pressure regulator fasteners **(see illustration)** and the regulator.

11   Inspect the regulator O-ring. If it's damaged, replace it.

12   Installation is the reverse of removal. Be sure to lube the regulator O-ring with a light film of clean engine oil.

25   Fuel pressure damper (2.5L Turbo I models) - removal and installation

Refer to illustration 25.4

Warning: *Gasoline is extremely flammable, so take extra precautions when you work on any part of the fuel system. Don't smoke or allow open flames or bare light bulbs near the work area, and don't work in a garage where a natural gas-type appliance (such as a water heater or clothes dryer) with a pilot light is present. If you spill any fuel on your skin, rinse it off immediately with soap and water. When you perform any kind of work on the fuel system, wear safety glasses and have a Class B type fire extinguisher on hand.*

1   Relieve system fuel pressure (see Section 2).

2   Detach the cable from the negative battery terminal.

3   Disconnect the PCV system hose from the intake manifold and valve cover (see Chapter 6).

4   Place a shop towel under the fuel pressure damper to absorb fuel spillage. Using two flare nut or open end wrenches - one on the flats of the fuel rail and the other on the fuel pressure damper - remove the fuel pressure damper and copper sealing washer **(see illustration)**. Don't try to remove the damper without a backup wrench or you'll damage the fuel rail.

5   Installation is the reverse of removal. Be sure to use a new copper sealing washer and tighten the damper securely.

26   Turbocharger - general information

The turbocharger increases power by using an exhaust gas-driven turbine to pressurize the fuel/air mixture before it enters the combustion chambers. The amount of boost (intake manifold pressure) is controlled by the wastegate (exhaust bypass valve). The wastegate is operated by a spring-loaded actuator assembly which controls the maximum boost level by allowing some of the exhaust gas to bypass the turbine. The wastegate is controlled by the SBEC or SMEC.

The models covered by this manual have different options available depending on the engine and type of turbocharger. Turbo I is the most common option available with the 2.5L engine and multi-point fuel injection system. The Turbo III (2.2L engine) system uses an intercooler to reduce the temperature of the compressed intake air.

The computerized fuel injection (SBEC or SMEC) and emission control system is equipped with self diagnosis capabilities that can access certain turbocharging system components. Refer to Chapter 6 for information pertaining to trouble codes and diagnosis.

27   Turbocharger - check

1   While it is a relatively simple device, the turbocharger is also a precision component which can be severely damaged by an interrupted oil or coolant supply or loose or damaged ducts.

2   Due to the special techniques and equipment required, checking and diagnosis of suspected problems should be left to a dealer service department. The home mechanic can, however, check the connections and linkages for security, damage and other obvious problems.

3   Because each turbocharger has its own distinctive sound, a change in the noise level can be a sign of potential problems.

4   A high-pitched or whistling sound is a symptom of an inlet air or exhaust gas leak.

5   If an unusual sound comes from the vicinity of the turbine, the turbocharger can be removed and the turbine wheel inspected. **Caution:** *All checks must be made with the engine off and cool to the touch and the turbocharger stopped or personal injury could result. Operating the engine without all the turbocharger ducts and filters installed is also dangerous and can result in damage to the turbine wheel blades.*

6   With the engine turned off, reach inside the housing and turn the turbine wheel to make sure it spins freely. If it doesn't, it's possible the cooling oil has sludged or coked from overheating. Push in on the turbine wheel and check for binding. The turbine should rotate freely with no binding or rubbing on the housing. If it does the turbine bearing is worn out.

7   Check the exhaust manifold for cracks and loose connections.

8   Because the turbine wheel rotates at speeds up to 140,000 rpm, severe damage can result from the interruption of coolant or contamination of the oil supply to the turbine bearings. Check for leaks in the coolant and oil inlet lines and obstructions in the oil drain-back line, as this can cause severe oil loss through the turbocharger seals. Burned oil on the turbine housing is a sign of this. **Caution:** *Whenever a major engine bearing such as a main, connecting rod or camshaft bearing is replaced, the turbocharger should be flushed with clean oil.*

28   Turbocharger - removal and installation

Refer to illustrations 28.2, 28.4a, 28.4b, 28.5 and 28.7

Note: *The turbocharger is removed from below the vehicle. It is not necessary to remove the cylinder head from the engine to gain access to the turbocharger and related components.*

Removal

1   Disconnect the cable from the negative terminal of the battery.

2   Drain the cooling system (see Chapter 1) and remove the air cleaner housing and ducts **(see illustration)**. For Turbo III exploded view, refer to **illustration 7.3c.**

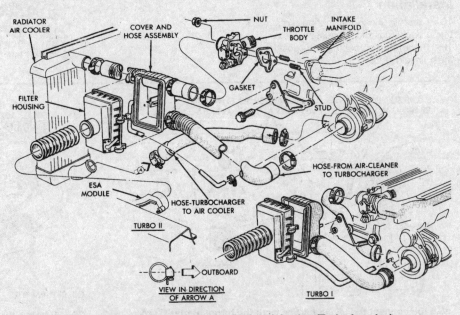

28.2 Details of the air cleaner and related ducting (Turbo I engine)

Working above the engine

3   Remove the through bolt from the front engine mount (see Chapter 2, Part A) and move the top of the engine forward (away from the firewall).
4   Remove the coolant line from the water box and the turbocharger housing (see illustrations).
5   Separate the oil feed line from the turbocharger housing (see illustration).
6   Remove the wastegate rod-to-gate retaining clip.
7   Remove the three (two upper and one lower) driver's side nuts retaining the turbocharger to the exhaust manifold (see illustration).
8   Disconnect the oxygen sensor wire (see Chapter 6) and any vacuum lines that might be in the way.

Working below the engine

9   Loosen the right front wheel lug nuts and hub nut (see Chapter 8), raise the front of the vehicle and support it securely on jackstands.
10   Remove the right front wheel.
11   Remove the right front driveaxle (see Chapter 8).
12   Remove the bracket support from the lower portion of the turbocharger (see illustration 28.4a).
13   Separate the oil drain-back tube fitting from the turbocharger housing and remove the fitting and the hose.
14   Remove the last remaining turbocharger-to-exhaust manifold nut.
15   Disconnect the exhaust pipe joint from the turbocharger housing.
16   Remove the lower coolant line and turbocharger inlet fitting.
17   Lift the turbocharger off its mounting studs and lower the assembly down and out of the vehicle.

Installation

18   Carefully clean the mating surfaces of the turbocharger and exhaust manifold.
19   Place the turbocharger in position on the manifold studs.

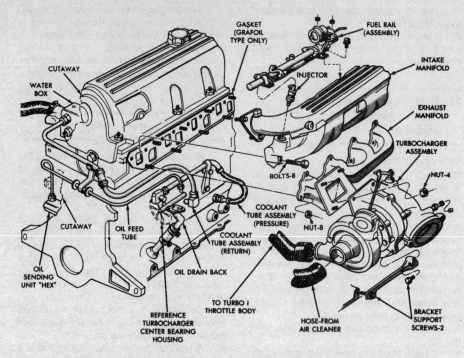

28.4a Exploded view of the turbocharger and intake and exhaust manifolds (Turbo I engine)

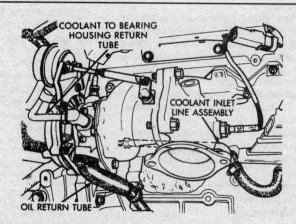

28.4b Disconnect the coolant inlet line from the turbocharger (Turbo III model shown)

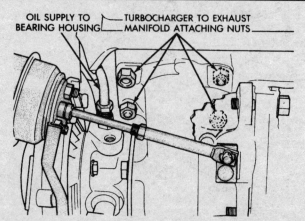

28.5 Disconnect the oil supply line from the turbocharger (Turbo III model shown)

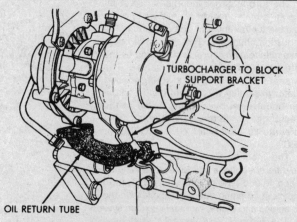

28.7 Remove the turbocharger-to-block support bracket (Turbo III model shown)

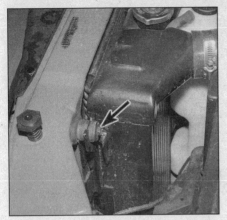

29.3 Remove the mounting bolt (arrow) from the chassis

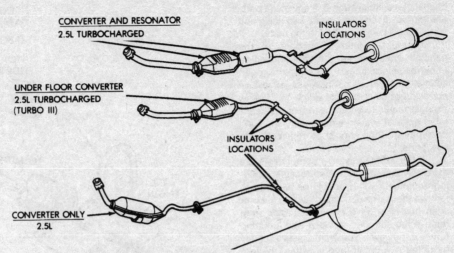

CONVERTER AND RESONATOR
2.5L TURBOCHARGED

UNDER FLOOR CONVERTER
2.5L TURBOCHARGED
(TURBO III)

CONVERTER ONLY
2.5L

INSULATORS LOCATIONS

INSULATORS LOCATIONS

30.1a Typical exhaust system components

20   Apply anti-seize compound to the studs and install the nuts. Tighten the nuts to the torque listed in this Chapter's Specifications.

21   Apply thread sealant into the lower inlet coolant line fitting and install the fitting into the turbocharger housing.

22   Install the lower coolant line.

23   Install the oil drain-back tube and fitting, along with a new gasket, to the turbocharger housing.

24   Install the turbocharger-to-block support bracket and bolts. Tighten the bolts to the torque listed in this Chapter's Specifications.

25   Reposition the exhaust pipe and tighten the bolts to the torque listed in this Chapter's Specifications.

26   Install the driveaxle (see Chapter 8) and the right front wheel.

27   Reconnect the oxygen sensor electrical connector and any vacuum lines that were disconnected.

28   Install the wastegate rod-to-gate retaining clip.

29   Attach the oil feed line to the turbocharger bearing housing. Tighten the fitting securely.

30   Apply sealant to the water box and coolant line fittings and install the lines. Tighten them securely.

31   Align the engine mount within the crossmember bracket and tighten the bolts to the torque listed in the Chapter 2A Specifications.

32   Check the coolant level and add some, if necessary (see Chapter 1).

33   Change the engine oil (see Chapter 1).

29   Intercooler - removal and installation

Refer to illustration 29.3

1   The intercooler lowers the temperature of the intake air on turbo engines.

2   Loosen the hose clamps **(see illustration 7.3c),** then disconnect the air hoses from the intercooler.

3   Remove the mounting bolts **(see illustration)** and lift the intercooler from the engine compartment.

4   Inspect the intercooler for cracks and damage to the flanges, tubes and fins. Replace it or have it repaired if necessary.

5   Installation is the reverse of removal.

30   Exhaust system servicing - general information

Refer to illustrations 30.1a, 30.1b, 30.1c and 30.4

Warning: *Inspection and repair of exhaust system components should be done only with the engine and exhaust components completely cool. Also, when working under the vehicle, make sure it's securely supported on jackstands.*

1   The exhaust system **(see illustration)** consists of the exhaust manifold(s), the catalytic converter, the muffler, the tailpipe and all connecting pipes, brackets, hangers and clamps. The exhaust system is attached to

4

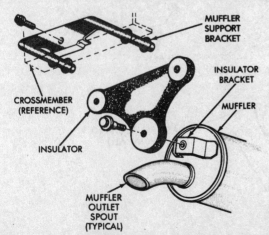

MUFFLER SUPPORT BRACKET

INSULATOR BRACKET

MUFFLER

CROSSMEMBER (REFERENCE)

INSULATOR

MUFFLER OUTLET SPOUT (TYPICAL)

30.1b Typical tailpipe and muffler support/insulator assembly

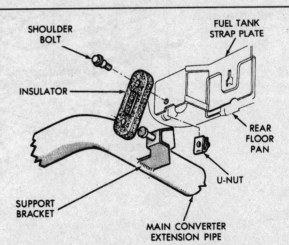

SHOULDER BOLT

INSULATOR

SUPPORT BRACKET

FUEL TANK STRAP PLATE

REAR FLOOR PAN

U-NUT

MAIN CONVERTER EXTENSION PIPE

30.1c Typical exhaust pipe hanger

the body with mounting brackets and rubber hangers **(see illustrations)**. If any of the parts are improperly installed, excessive noise and vibration will be transmitted to the body.

2   Conduct regular inspections of the exhaust system to keep it safe and quiet. Look for any damaged or bent parts, open seams, holes, loose connections, excessive corrosion or other defects which could allow exhaust fumes to enter the vehicle. Deteriorated exhaust system components shouldn't be repaired; they should be replaced with new parts.

3   If the exhaust system components are extremely corroded or rusted together, welding equipment will probably be required to remove them. The convenient way to accomplish this is to have a muffler repair shop remove the corroded sections with a cutting torch. If, however, you want to save money by doing it yourself (and you don't have a welding outfit with a cutting torch), simply cut off the old components with a hacksaw. If you have compressed air, special pneumatic cutting chisels can also be used. If you decide to tackle the job at home, be sure to wear safety goggles to protect your eyes from metal chips and work gloves to protect your hands.

4   Here are some simple guidelines to follow when repairing the exhaust system:
a) *Work from the back to front when removing exhaust system components.*
b) *Apply penetrating oil to the component*

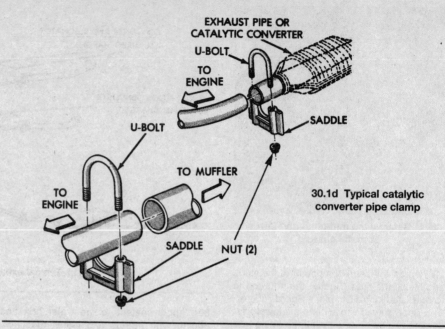

30.1d Typical catalytic converter pipe clamp

fasteners to make them easier to remove.
c) *Use new gaskets, hangers and clamps when installing exhaust system components.*
d) *Apply anti-seize compound to the threads of all exhaust system fasteners during reassembly.*

e) *Be sure to allow sufficient clearance between newly installed parts and all points on the underbody to avoid overheating the floor pan and possibly damaging the interior carpet and insulation. Pay particularly close attention to the catalytic converter and heat shields **(see illustration)**.*

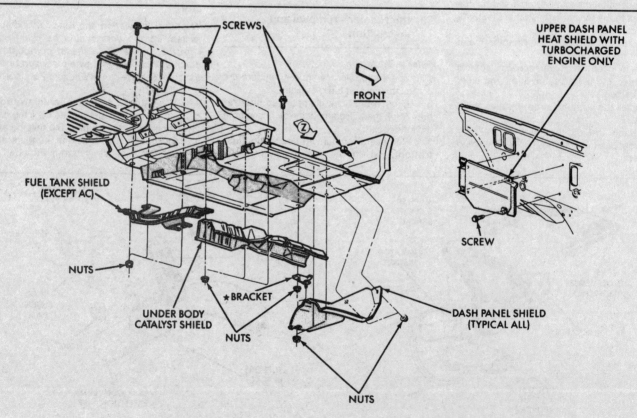

30.4 Installation details of the catalytic converter heat shields (typical)

Chapter 5
Engine electrical systems

Contents

5

Specifications

Ignition coil resistance (conventional ignition)

Diamond (epoxy) (2.5L four-cylinder engine)
Primary ... 0.97 to 1.18 ohms
Secondary ... 11.3 to 15.3 K-ohms
Diamond (epoxy) (V6 engine)
Primary ... 0.97 to 1.18 ohms
Secondary ... 11.0 to 15.3 K-ohms
Diamond (oil-filled)
Primary ... 1.34 to 1.55 ohms
Secondary ... 15 to 19 K-ohms
Essex
Primary ... 1.34 to 1.55 ohms
Secondary ... 9 to 12.2 K-ohms
Prestolite
Primary ... 1.34 to 1.55 ohms
Secondary ... 9.4 to 11.7 K-ohms
Toyodenso
Primary ... 0.95 to 1.20 ohms
Secondary ... 11.3 to 13.3 K-ohms

Ignition coil resistance (Direct Ignition System [DIS])

Diamond (2.2L Turbo III engine)
Primary ... 0.52 to 0.63 ohms
Secondary ... 11.6 to 15.8 K-ohms

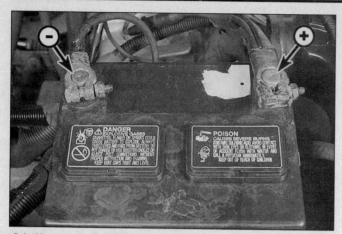

3.1 Always disconnect the cable from the negative terminal first, then disconnect the positive cable

3.2 To remove the battery, unscrew the hold-down bolt (arrow) and remove the hold-down clamp

1   General information

The engine electrical systems include all ignition, charging and starting components. Because of their engine-related functions, these components are discussed separately from chassis electrical devices such as the lights, the instruments, etc. (which are included in Chapter 12). Always observe the following precautions when working on the electrical systems:

a) Be extremely careful when servicing engine electrical components. They are easily damaged if checked, connected or handled improperly.

b) Never leave the ignition switch on for long periods of time with the engine off.

c) Don't disconnect the battery cables while the engine is running.

d) Maintain correct polarity when connecting a battery cable from another vehicle during jump starting.

e) Always disconnect the negative cable first and hook it up last or the battery may be shorted by the tool being used to loosen the cable clamps. It's also a good idea to review the safety-related information regarding the engine electrical systems located in the Safety First section near the front of this manual before beginning any operation included in this Chapter.

2   Battery - emergency jump starting

Refer to the Booster battery (jump) starting procedure at the front of this manual.

3   Battery - removal and installation

Refer to illustrations 3.1 and 3.2

1   **Warning:** Always disconnect the negative cable first and hook it up last or the battery may be shorted by the tool being used to loosen the cable clamps. Disconnect both cables from the battery terminals **(see illustration)**.

2   Remove the battery hold-down clamp **(see illustration)**.

3   Lift out the battery. Be careful - it's heavy.

4   While the battery is out, inspect the carrier (tray) for corrosion (see Chapter 1).

5   If you're replacing the battery, make sure you purchase one that's identical, with the same dimensions, amperage rating, cold cranking rating, etc.

6   Installation is the reverse of removal.

4   Battery cables - check and replacement

1   Periodically inspect the entire length of each battery cable for damage, cracked or burned insulation and corrosion. Poor battery cable connections can cause starting problems and decreased engine performance.

2   Check the cable-to-terminal connections at the ends of the cables for cracks, loose wire strands and corrosion. The presence of white, fluffy deposits under the insulation at the cable terminal connection is a sign that the cable is corroded and should be replaced. Check the terminals for distortion, missing mounting bolts and corrosion.

3   When removing the cables, always disconnect the negative cable first and hook it up last or the battery may be shorted by the tool used to loosen the cable clamps. Even if only the positive cable is being replaced, be sure to disconnect the negative cable from the battery first (see Chapter 1 for further information regarding battery cables).

4   Disconnect the old cables from the battery, then trace each of them to their opposite ends and detach them from the starter solenoid and ground terminals. Note the routing of each cable to ensure correct installation.

5   If you're replacing either or both of the old cables, take them with you when buying new cables. It's very important to replace the cables with identical parts. Cables have characteristics that make them easy to identify: Positive cables are usually red, larger in cross-section and have a larger diameter battery post clamp; ground cables are usually black, smaller in cross-section and have a slightly smaller diameter clamp for the negative post.

6   Clean the threads of the solenoid or ground connection with a wire brush to remove rust and corrosion. Apply a light coat of battery terminal corrosion inhibitor, or petroleum jelly, to the threads to prevent future corrosion.

7   Attach the cable to the solenoid or ground connection and tighten the mounting nut/bolt securely.

8   Before connecting a new cable to the battery, make sure it reaches the battery post without having to be stretched.

9   Connect the positive cable first, followed by the negative cable.

5   Ignition system - general information

The ignition system includes the ignition switch, the battery, the coil, the primary (low voltage) and secondary (high voltage) wiring circuits, the distributor (except 2.2L Turbo III models) and the spark plugs. Models with the 2.2L Turbo III DOHC engines do not have a distributor but instead are equipped with a direct (distributorless) ignition system (DIS). The three main components are the coil pack, the crankshaft timing sensor and the camshaft reference sensor. The crankshaft and camshaft sensors are both Hall Effect timing devices (for more information on the crankshaft and camshaft sensors, refer to Chapter 6).

The ignition system on early models is controlled by a computer known as the Single Module Engine Controller (SMEC). The SMEC monitors coolant temperature, engine rpm and available intake manifold vacuum to ensure a perfectly timed spark under all driving conditions. Later versions of the ignition

6.2 To use a calibrated ignition tester (available at most auto parts stores), simply disconnect a spark plug wire, attach the wire to the tester and clip the tester to a good ground - if there is enough power to fire the plug, sparks will be clearly visible between the electrode tip and the tester body as the engine is turned over

computer are referred to by Chrysler as the Single-Board Engine Controller (SBEC), but they're functionally similar to the SMEC. For more information regarding the SMEC or the SBEC, refer to Chapter 6.

6 Ignition system - check

Refer to illustrations 6.2, 6.13a, 6.13b and 6.15

Warning: *The secondary ignition system voltage is very high (over 30,000 volts). Use extreme care when performing the following checks so you don't get shocked.*

1   If the engine turns over but won't start, disconnect the spark plug wire from any spark plug and attach it to a calibrated ignition tester (available at most auto parts stores).
2   Connect the clip on the tester to a bolt or metal bracket on the engine **(see illustration)**.
3   Crank the engine and watch the end of

the tester or spark plug wire to see if bright blue, well-defined sparks occur. If you're not using a calibrated tester, have an assistant crank the engine for you. **Warning:** *Keep clear of drivebelts and other moving engine components that could injure you.*
4   If sparks occur, sufficient voltage is reaching the plug to fire it (repeat the check at the remaining plug wires to verify the wires and coils [2.2L Turbo III models] or wires, distributor cap and rotor [all others] are OK). However, the plugs themselves may be fouled, so remove them and check them as described in Chapter 1.
5   If no sparks, or intermittent sparks occur on a DIS-type system, check the coil pack (see Section 7). On a conventional ignition system, if no sparks or intermittent sparks occur, remove the distributor cap and check the cap and rotor as described in Chapter 1. If moisture is present, dry out the cap and rotor, then reinstall the cap.
6   If there's still no spark, detach the coil secondary wire from the distributor cap and hook it up to the tester (reattach the plug wire to the spark plug), then repeat the spark check. Again, if you don't have a tester, hold the end of the wire about 1/4-inch from a good ground. If sparks occur now, the distributor cap, rotor or plug wire(s) may be defective.
7   If no sparks occur, check the wire connections at the coil to make sure they're clean and tight. Check for voltage to the coil. Make any necessary repairs, then repeat the check again.
8   If there's still no spark, the coil-to-cap wire may be bad (check the resistance with an ohmmeter - it should be 7000 ohms per foot or less). If a known good wire doesn't make any difference in the test results, check

the coil (see Section 7). If it's OK, the pick-up assembly (see Section 9) or the SMEC/SBEC may be defective.
9   Connect a voltmeter to the coil positive terminal and crank the engine for five seconds. If the voltage is near zero during this test, check to see if any trouble codes are stored in the computer (see Chapter 6, Section 3).
10   If the voltage is at near battery voltage (approximately 12.4 volts) at the start of the test but drops to zero after one to two seconds of cranking, check to see if any trouble codes are stored in the computer (see Chapter 6, Section 3).
11   If the voltage remains at near battery voltage for the five seconds, turn off the ignition key, remove the 14-way (or 60-way on later models) connector from the SMEC/SBEC and check for any spread terminals.
12   Remove the coil positive terminal lead and connect a jumper wire between the battery positive terminal and the coil positive terminal.
13   On SMEC-equipped engines (1989 models), momentarily ground terminal No. 12 of the 14-way connector **(see illustration)** with a jumper wire. On SBEC-equipped engines (1990 and later models), ground terminal No. 19 of the 60-way connector **(see illustration)**.
14   If a spark is generated, replace the SMEC/SBEC.
15   If no spark is generated, connect a special jumper wire **(see illustration)** to ground the coil negative terminal.
16   If a spark is now produced, check the wiring harness for an open condition.
17   If no spark is produced, check the coil (see Section 7).

5

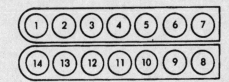

6.13a Terminal guide for SMEC 14-way electrical connector (1989 2.5L engine)

TERMINAL SIDE

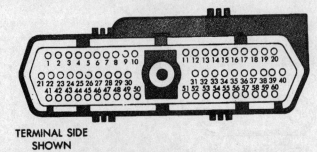

TERMINAL SIDE SHOWN

6.13b Terminal guide for SBEC 60-way electrical connector - when grounding to a terminal, be extremely careful not to touch any other terminal or you may damage the SBEC (1990 and later 2.5L engine)

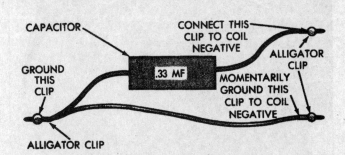

CAPACITOR
CONNECT THIS CLIP TO COIL NEGATIVE
ALLIGATOR CLIP
GROUND THIS CLIP
.33 MF
MOMENTARILY GROUND THIS CLIP TO COIL NEGATIVE
ALLIGATOR CLIP

6.15 You'll need to fabricate a special jumper wire to ground the negative terminal of the coil on a 2.5L engine

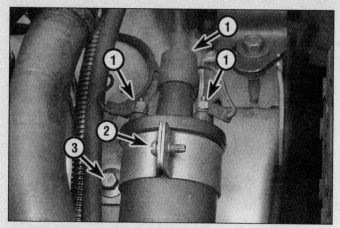

7.2a To remove the earlier type coil from the fenderwell, disconnect the primary wires and the high-tension cable (1), then remove the mounting bracket bolt - if the coil is bad, loosen the clamp pinch screw (2) and transfer the clamp/mounting bracket to the new coil

7.2b To remove the later type coil from the engine, disconnect the primary electrical connector and the high-tension cable (top and bottom arrows), then remove the mounting bolts (center arrows)

7 Ignition coil - check and replacement

Conventional coil

Refer to illustrations 7.2a, 7.2b, 7.2c, 7.2d, 7.4a, 7.4b, 7.5a and 7.5b

1   Detach the cable from the negative battery terminal.

2   Mark the wires and terminals with pieces of numbered tape, then remove the primary wires and the high-tension cable from the coil (see illustrations). Disconnect the coil mounting bracket, remove the coil/bracket assembly, clean the outer case and check it for cracks and other damage.

3   Clean the coil primary terminals and check the coil tower terminal for corrosion. Clean it with a wire brush if any corrosion is found.

4   Check the coil primary resistance by

7.2c Be sure to release the locking tab on the electrical connector for the primary wires on the later type engine-mounted coil before disconnecting it

7.2d On V6 engines, remove the mounting bolts from the intake plenum (arrow) and intake manifold (not visible)

7.4a To check the coil primary resistance on an earlier type coil, touch the leads of an ohmmeter to the positive and negative primary terminals (arrows) and compare your reading with the coil primary resistance listed in this Chapter's Specifications

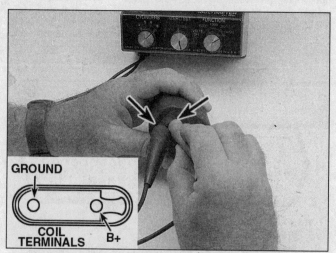

7.4b To check the coil primary resistance on a later type coil, touch the leads of an ohmmeter to the positive and negative primary terminals (arrows) and compare your reading with the coil primary resistance listed in this Chapter's Specifications

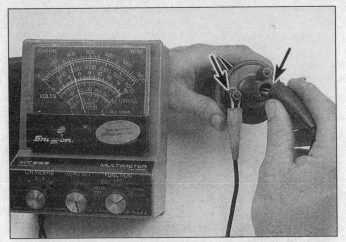

7.5a To check the coil secondary resistance on an earlier type coil, touch one lead of the ohmmeter to one of the primary terminals and the other lead to the high-tension terminals (arrows)

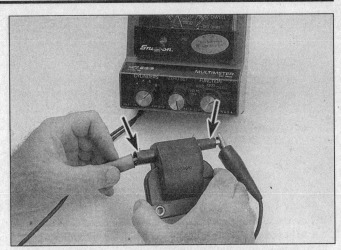

7.5b To check the coil secondary resistance on a later type coil, touch one lead of ohmmeter to one of the primary terminals and the other lead to the high-tension terminal (arrow)

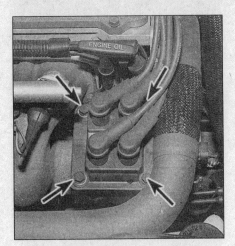

7.11 To detach the coil pack from an engine equipped with the Distributorless Ignition System (DISC), remove these four bolts (arrows)

attaching the leads of an ohmmeter to the positive and negative terminals **(see illustrations)**. Compare your readings to the primary resistance listed in this Chapter's Specifications.

5   Check the coil secondary resistance by hooking one of the ohmmeter leads to one of the primary terminals and the other ohmmeter lead to the large center (high-tension) terminal **(see illustrations)**. Compare your readings to the secondary resistance listed in this Chapter's Specifications.

6   If the measured resistances are not as specified, the coil is probably defective and should be replaced with a new one.

7   For proper ignition system operation, all coil terminals and wire leads must be kept clean and dry.

8   Install the coil and hook up the wires.

9   Attach the cable to the negative battery terminal.

Direct Ignition System (DIS) coil pack (2.2L Turbo III models)

Refer to illustrations 7.11, 7.13 and 7.14
Note: *The DIS coil pack doesn't have to be removed from the engine for testing - we've*

done so only for the sake of clarity.

10   Clearly label the four spark plug wires, then detach them from the coil pack. Measure the resistance of each cable. It should be 3 to 12 k-ohms per foot of cable. Replace any cable not within tolerance.

11   Remove the four coil pack mounting bolts **(see illustration)**.

12   Lift up the coil pack and unplug the electrical connector.

13   Measure the resistance on the primary side of each coil with a digital ohmmeter **(see illustration)**. At the coil, connect an ohmmeter between the B+ pin and the pin corresponding to the particular cylinder. Compare your readings with the resistance values listed in this Chapter's Specifications.

14   Measure the secondary resistance of the coil between the paired high tension towers of each group of cylinders **(see illustration)**. Compare your readings with the resistance values listed in this Chapter's Specifications.

15   If any coil in the coil pack fails either of the above tests, replace the coil pack.

16   Installation is the reverse of removal.

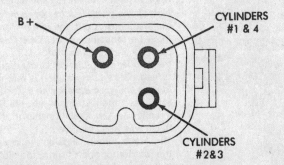

7.13 Terminal guide for measuring the primary resistance of the coil pack at the electrical connector (coil-pack-side of the connector shown) - check between the B+ terminal and each of the other terminals in the connector

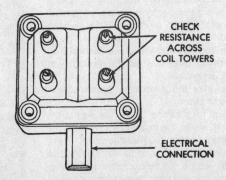

7.14 To measure the secondary resistance of each coil in the DISC coil pack, touch the test lead probes to the twin terminals of the paired high-tension towers

8.3a If you remove the distributor, trace the wire for the Hall Effect pick-up from the distributor down to this connector (arrow) and unplug it (four-cylinder engines)

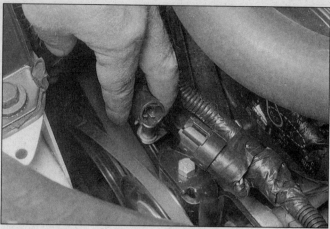

8.3b The distributor electrical connector is located near the belt tensioner on V6 engines

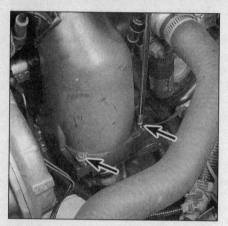

8.4 Remove these two screws (arrows) and remove the distributor splash shield

8.7a Mark the position of the rotor tip on the distributor base and mark the relationship of the base to the block (arrow)

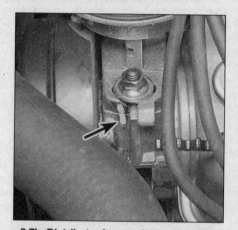

8.7b Distributor base paint mark on the V6 engine

8   Distributor - removal and installation

Removal

Refer to illustrations 8.3a, 8.3b, 8.4, 8.7a, 8.7b and 8.8

1   Disconnect the cable from the negative terminal of the battery.

2   Detach the primary lead from the coil.

3   Unplug the electrical connector for the Hall Effect pick-up on four-cylinder engines **(see illustration)** or from the photo optic sensing unit on V6 engines **(see illustration)**. Follow the wires as they exit the distributor to find the connector.

4   Remove the distributor splash shield **(see illustration)**.

5   Look for a raised "1" on the distributor cap. This marks the location for the number one cylinder spark plug wire terminal. If the cap doesn't have a mark for the number one terminal, locate the number one spark plug and trace the wire back to the terminal on the cap.

6   Remove the distributor cap (see Chapter 1) and turn the engine over until the rotor is pointing toward the number one spark plug

wire terminal (see the locating TDC procedure in Chapter 2, Part C, if necessary).

7   Make a mark on the edge of the distributor base directly below the rotor tip and in line with it. Also, mark the distributor base and the engine block to ensure that the dis-

8.8 Remove the hold-down bolt and clamp, then pull the distributor straight up

tributor will be reinstalled correctly **(see illustrations)**.

8   Remove the distributor hold-down bolt and clamp **(see illustration)**, then pull the distributor straight up and remove it. **Caution:** *DO NOT turn the crankshaft while the distributor is out of the engine, or the alignment marks will be useless.*

Installation

Refer to illustrations 8.10a and 8.10b

Note: *If the crankshaft has been moved while the distributor is out, the number one piston must be repositioned at TDC. This can be done by feeling for compression pressure at the number one plug hole as the crankshaft is turned. Once compression is felt, align the ignition timing zero mark with the pointer.*

9   Insert the distributor into the engine in exactly the same relationship to the block that it was when removed.

10   Make sure the lugs on the lower end of the distributor shaft fit into the slots in the upper end of the oil pump shaft **(see illustrations)**. If they don't, the distributor won't seat completely. Recheck the alignment marks between the distributor base and block to verify the distributor is in the same position it was before removal. Also check the rotor to

8.10a When you install the distributor, be sure to align the lugs (arrows) on the end of the distributor shaft . . .

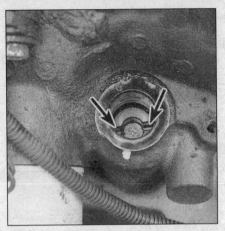

8.10b . . . with slots (arrows) in the top of the oil pump drive shaft

9.4 To replace the Hall Effect pick-up assembly on 2.5L four-cylinder engines, simply remove the rotor and lift the pick-up unit off the distributor housing (distributor removed for clarity)

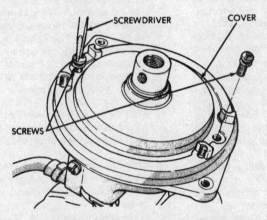

9.8 To get at the photo-optic sensing unit on a V6 distributor, remove these two screws (arrows) and the protective cover

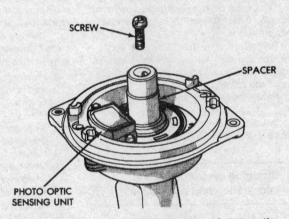

9.9 Remove the screw from the spacer and remove the spacer (V6 engine)

see if it's aligned with the mark you made on the edge of the distributor base.

11   Place the hold-down clamp in position and loosely install the bolt.

12   Install the distributor cap.

13   Plug in the Hall Effect pick-up electrical connector.

14   Reattach the spark plug wires to the plugs (if removed).

15   Connect the cable to the negative terminal of the battery.

16   Check the ignition timing (see Chapter 1) and tighten the distributor hold-down bolt securely.

9   Pick-up assembly - replacement

1   Disconnect the cable from the negative terminal of the battery.

Hall effect pick-up assembly (2.5L four-cylinder engines)

Refer to illustration 9.4

Note: *The Hall Effect pick-up assembly inside*

the distributor supplies the basic ignition timing signal to the computer. *The check for the Hall Effect pick-up assembly is part of a larger diagnostic procedure for the entire electronic spark advance system, and is beyond the scope of the home mechanic. But the replacement procedure itself is easy once you've verified that the Hall Effect unit is bad.*

2   Remove the distributor splash shield and cap and disconnect the Hall Effect electrical connector (**see illustration 8.3a**).

3   Remove the distributor cap and rotor (see Chapter 1).

4   Lift the pick-up assembly off the distributor shaft (**see illustration**).

5   Installation is the reverse of removal.

Photo-optical sensing unit (V6 engine)

Refer to illustrations 9.8, 9.9, 9.10a, 9.10b and 9.12

6   Remove the distributor (see Section 8).

7   Remove the rotor (see Chapter 1).

8   Remove the protective cover from the distributor housing (**see illustration**).

9   Remove the screw from the spacer (see

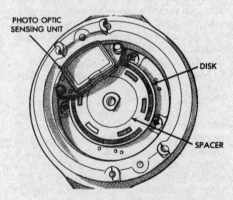

9.10a Carefully remove the upper disk spacer, the disk and the lower disk spacer (underneath the disk, not visible in this illustration)

illustration) and remove the spacer.

10   Carefully remove the upper disk spacer, the disk and the lower disk spacer (**see illustration**). **Note:** *The disk and spacers are*

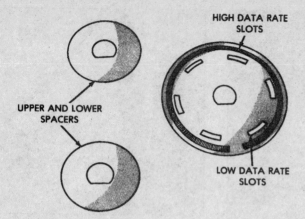

HIGH DATA RATE
SLOTS

UPPER AND LOWER
SPACERS

LOW DATA RATE
SLOTS

9.10b Note how the upper and lower disk spacers and the disk itself are keyed to prevent incorrect reassembly

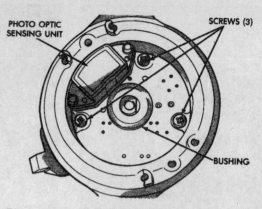

PHOTO OPTIC
SENSING UNIT

SCREWS (3)

BUSHING

9.12 Remove the bushing from the photo-optic sensing unit, remove these three screws (arrows) and remove the photo-optic sensing unit

keyed to ensure proper reassembly **(see illustration)**.

11   Check the disk for warpage, cracks or damaged slots. If any damage is evident, replace the disk.

12   Remove the bushing from the photo-optic sensing unit, remove the three screws from the sensing unit **(see illustration)** and remove the sensing unit.

13   Reassembly is the reverse of disassembly.

14   Install the distributor (see Section 8) and install the rotor and cap (see Chapter 1).

10   Charging system - general information and precautions

The charging system includes the alternator, a voltage regulator within the SMEC or SBEC (computer), a charge indicator, the battery, a fusible link and the wiring between all the components. The charging system supplies electrical power for the ignition system, the lights, the radio, etc. The alternator is driven by a drivebelt at the front of the engine.

The purpose of the voltage regulator is to limit the alternator's voltage to a preset value. This prevents power surges, circuit overloads, etc., during peak voltage output.

The fusible link is a short length of insulated wire integral with the engine compartment wiring harness. The link is four wire gauges smaller in diameter than the circuit it protects. Production fusible links and their identification flags are identified by the flag color. See Chapter 12 for additional information regarding fusible links.

The charging system doesn't ordinarily require periodic maintenance. However, the drivebelt, battery and wires and connections should be inspected at the intervals outlined in Chapter 1.

The dashboard warning light should come on when the ignition key is turned to Start, then go off immediately. If it remains on, there is a malfunction in the charging sys-

tem (see Section 11). Some vehicles are also equipped with a voltmeter. If the voltmeter indicates abnormally high or low voltage, check the charging system (see Section 11).

Be very careful when making electrical circuit connections to a vehicle equipped with an alternator and note the following:

a) When reconnecting wires to the alternator from the battery, be sure to note the polarity.

b) Before using arc welding equipment to repair any part of the vehicle, disconnect the wires from the alternator and the battery terminals.

c) Never start the engine with a battery charger connected.

d) Always disconnect both battery leads before using a battery charger.

e) The alternator is turned by an engine drivebelt which could cause serious injury if your hands, hair or clothes become entangled in it with the engine running.

f) Because the alternator is connected directly to the battery, it could arc or cause a fire if overloaded or shorted out.

g) Wrap a plastic bag over the alternator and secure it with rubber bands before steam cleaning the engine.

h) Never disconnect the battery while the engine is running.

11   Charging system - check

1   If a malfunction occurs in the charging circuit, don't automatically assume the alternator is causing the problem. First check the following items:

a) Check the drivebelt tension and condition (Chapter 1). Replace it if it's worn or deteriorated.

b) Make sure the alternator mounting and adjustment bolts are tight.

c) Inspect the alternator wiring harness and the connectors at the alternator and voltage regulator. They must be in good condition and tight.

d) Check the fusible link (if equipped) located between the starter solenoid and the alternator. If it's burned, determine the cause, repair the circuit and replace the link (the vehicle won't start and/or the accessories won't work if the fusible link blows). Sometimes a fusible link may look good, but still be bad. If in doubt, remove it and check it for continuity.

e) Start the engine and check the alternator for abnormal noises (a shrieking or squealing sound indicates a bad bearing).

f) Check the specific gravity of the battery electrolyte. If it's low, charge the battery (doesn't apply to maintenance free batteries).

g) Make sure the battery is fully charged (one bad cell in a battery can cause overcharging by the alternator).

h) Disconnect the battery cables (negative first, then positive). Inspect the battery posts and the cable clamps for corrosion. Clean them thoroughly if necessary (see Chapter 1). Reconnect the cable to the negative terminal.

i) With the key off, connect a test light between the negative battery post and the disconnected negative cable clamp.

   1) If the test light does not come on, reattach the clamp and proceed to the next Step.

   2) If the test light comes on, there is a short (drain) in the electrical system of the vehicle. The short must be repaired before the charging system can be checked.

   3) Disconnect the alternator wiring harness.

      (a) If the light goes out, the alternator is bad.

      (b) If the light stays on, pull each fuse until the light goes out (this will tell you which component is shorted).

2   Using a voltmeter, check the battery voltage with the engine off. If should be approximately 12-volts.

12.2a To disconnect the electrical connector from the alternator, remove these nuts (arrows) (Bosch alternator shown, other units similar)

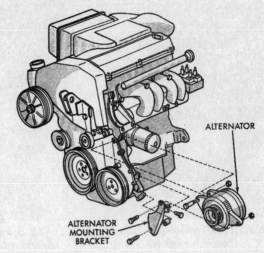

12.2b Exploded view of the alternator on a 2.2L Turbo III model

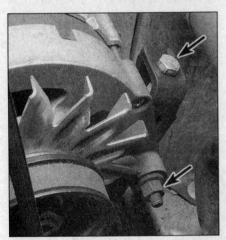

12.3a To remove the alternator drivebelt, back off the adjustment bolt (upper arrow) and loosen the upper (lower arrow) . . .

12.3b . . . and lower mounting nuts - to remove the alternator, remove the mounting bolts and nuts (mounting and adjustment system for Bosch unit shown, others similar)

13.2 On Bosch alternators, loosen the brush holder mounting screws (arrows) in small increments, moving from screw to screw, so the holder won't be warped . . .

3   Start the engine and check the battery voltage again. It should now be approximately 14 to 15-volts.
4   Turn on the headlights. The voltage should drop, and then come back up, if the charging system is working properly.
5   If the voltage reading is more than the specified charging voltage, replace the voltage regulator (see Section 14). On some models, the regulator is inside the computer and can't be replaced; on these vehicles, you'll have to replace the computer (see Chapter 6).
6   If the voltage reading is less than the specified voltage, the alternator diode(s), stator or rectifier may be bad or the voltage regulator may be malfunctioning.

12 Alternator - removal and installation

Refer to illustrations 12.2a, 12.2b, 12.3a and 12.3b
1   Detach the cable from the negative ter-

minal of the battery.
2   Detach the electrical connector(s) from the alternator (see illustrations).
3   Loosen the alternator adjustment and mounting bolts and detach the drivebelt (see illustrations).
4   Remove the adjustment and pivot bolts and separate the alternator from the engine.
5   If you're replacing the alternator, take the old one with you when purchasing a replacement unit. Make sure the new/rebuilt unit looks identical to the old alternator. Look at the terminals - they should be the same in number, size and location as the terminals on the old alternator. Finally, look at the identification numbers - they will be stamped into the housing or printed on a tag attached to the housing. Make sure the numbers are the same on both alternators.
6   Many new/rebuilt alternators DO NOT have a pulley installed, so you may have to switch the pulley from the old unit to the new/rebuilt one. When buying an alternator,

find out the shop's policy regarding pulleys some shops will perform this service free of charge.
7   Installation is the reverse of removal.
8   After the alternator is installed, adjust the drivebelt tension (see Chapter 1).
9   Check the charging voltage to verify proper operation of the alternator (see Section 11).

13 Alternator brushes - replacement

1   Disconnect the negative cable at the battery. Label the wires and detach them from the alternator terminals.

Bosch alternator

Refer to illustrations 13.2, 13.3 and 13.5
2   Loosen the brush holder mounting screws a little at a time to prevent distortion of the holder, then remove them (see illustration).

13.3 . . . and remove the brush holder assembly

13.5 Using an ohmmeter, check for continuity between each brush and the appropriate field terminal (if there's no continuity, switch one of the leads to the other field terminal or brush)

3   Remove the brush holder from the alternator (see illustration).
4   If the brushes appear to be significantly worn, or if they don't move smoothly in the brush holder, replace the brush holder assembly.
5   Before installing the brush holder assembly, check for continuity between each brush and the appropriate field terminal (see illustration).
6   Install the brush holder. Make sure the

brushes seat correctly.
7   Hold the brush holder securely in place and install the screws. Tighten them evenly, a little at a time, so the holder isn't distorted. Once the screws are snug, tighten them securely.
8   Reconnect the negative battery cable.

Chrysler 60, 65 and 78 amp alternators

Refer to illustration 13.11
9   Remove the alternator.
10   The brushes are mounted in plastic holders which locate them in the proper position.
11   Remove the brush mounting screws and insulating washers and separate the brush assemblies from the rectifier end shield (see illustration).
12   If the brushes appear to be significantly worn or are oil soaked or damaged, replace them with new ones.
13   Make sure the brushes move smoothly in the holders.
14   Insert the brush assemblies into the rectifier end shield and install the screws and washers. Tighten the screws securely. Make sure the brushes aren't grounded.
15   Install the alternator.

Chrysler 40 and 90 amp alternators

Refer to illustrations 13.16, 13.17a, 13.17b and 13.18
16   Remove the nut and detach the dust cover from the rear of the alternator (see illustration).
17   Remove the brush holder mounting

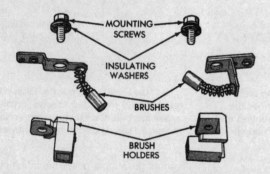

13.11 On Chrysler 60, 65, and 78-amp alternators, the brushes are held in the holders with screws - when installing the brushes, the insulating washers must be in place

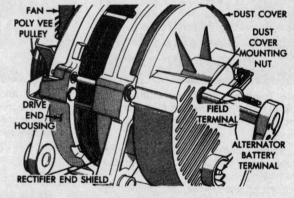

13.16 On Chrysler 40 and 90-amp alternators, remove the nut and detach the dust cover

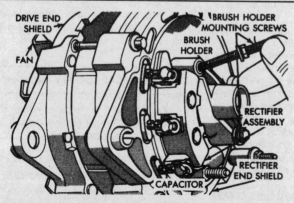

13.17a To replace the brushes on Chrysler 40 and 90-amp alternators, remove the brush holder mounting screws . . .

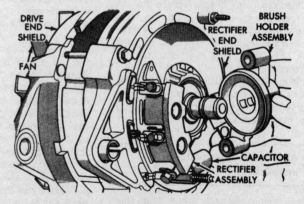

13.17b . . . and detach the brush holder

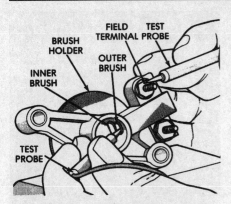

13.18 Before installing the brush holder assembly on 40 and 90-amp Chrysler alternators, use an ohmmeter to verify continuity between each brush and the appropriate field terminal (if there's no continuity, switch one of the leads to the other field terminal or brush)

13.20 To replace the brushes on Nippondenso alternators, remove the B+ terminal insulator nut, washer and insulator

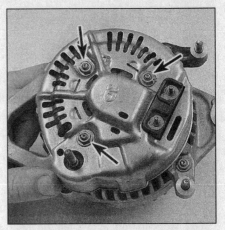

13.21 Remove the rear cover attaching nuts (arrows) and remove the rear cover (Nippodenso alternators)

screws and separate the brush holder from the end shield **(see illustrations)**.

18   Before installing the new brush holder assembly, check for continuity between each brush and the appropriate field terminal **(see illustration)**.

19   Installation is the reverse of removal. Be careful when sliding the brushes over the slip rings and don't overtighten the brush holder screws.

Nippondenso alternators

Refer to illustrations 13.20, 13.21, 13.22a, 13.22b and 13.24

20   With the alternator removed from the vehicle (see the previous Section), remove the B+ insulator nut and insulator **(see illustration)**.

21   Remove the rear cover attaching nuts and remove the rear cover **(see illustration)**.

22   Remove the brush holder attaching screws and lift the brush holder from the alternator **(see illustrations)**.

23   Before installing the new brush holder assembly, check for continuity between each brush and the appropriate field terminal **(see illustrations 13.5 and 13.18)**.

24   To install the brush holder assembly, use your finger to depress the brushes **(see illustration)**, then slide the holder over the commutator slip rings and screw it into place.

25   Installation is otherwise the reverse of removal. When installing the B+ insulator, be sure to align the guide tang with the hole in the rear cover.

14   Voltage regulator - general information

The voltage regulator is integrated into the computer - the Single Module Engine Controller (SMEC) or the Single Board Engine Controller (SBEC) - of the fuel injection system. Special diagnostic tools are needed to

13.22a Remove the brush holder attaching screws (arrows) . . .

13.22b . . . and remove the brush holder assembly (Nippondenso alternator)

check the regulator. Only a dealer service department and some repair shops have these tools. If the regulator is faulty, the computer must be replaced. Computer replacement is covered by a Federally-mandated extended warranty (see your owner's manual or consult your dealer for details). If the computer is out of warranty and you want to replace it yourself, see Chapter 6.

15   Starting system - general information and precautions

The sole function of the starting system is to turn over the engine quickly enough to allow it to start.

The starting system consists of the battery, the starter motor, the starter solenoid, the switch and the wires connecting them. The solenoid is mounted directly on the starter motor.

The solenoid/starter motor assembly is installed on the lower part of the engine, next to the transaxle bellhousing.

When the ignition key is turned to the Start position, the starter solenoid is actuated

5

13.24 Depress the brushes with your index finger as you slide the brush holder into place

through the starter control circuit. The starter solenoid then connects the battery to the starter. The battery supplies the electrical energy to the starter motor, which does the actual work of cranking the engine.

The starter on a vehicle equipped with an automatic transaxle can only be operated

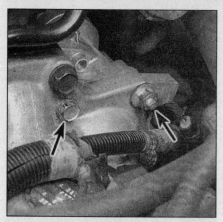

17.2 Working from above, remove the upper mounting bolt and the nut (arrows)

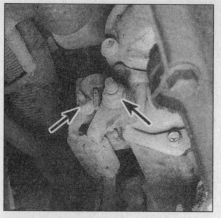

17.4 Label the wires (arrows) before disconnecting them from the starter assembly

17.5 Remove the starter motor lower mounting bolt (arrow)

when the gear selector lever is in Park or Neutral.

Always observe the following precautions when working on the starting system:

a) *Excessive cranking of the starter motor can overheat it and cause serious damage. Never operate the starter motor for more than 15 seconds at a time without pausing to allow it to cool for at least two minutes.*

b) *The starter is connected directly to the battery and could arc or cause a fire if mishandled, overloaded or shorted out.*

c) *Always detach the cable from the negative terminal of the battery before working on the starting system.*

16 Starter motor - in-vehicle check

Note: *Before diagnosing starter problems, make sure the battery is fully charged.*

1   If the starter motor doesn't turn at all when the switch is operated, make sure the shift lever is in Neutral or Park (automatic transaxle models).

2   Make sure the battery is charged and all cables, both at the battery and starter solenoid terminals, are clean and secure.

3   If the starter motor spins but the engine isn't cranking, the overrunning clutch in the starter motor is slipping and the starter motor must be replaced, or the teeth on the flywheel/driveplate are broken.

4   If, when the switch is actuated, the starter motor doesn't operate at all but the solenoid clicks, then the problem lies with either the battery, the main solenoid contacts or the starter motor itself (or the engine is seized).

5   If the solenoid plunger can't be heard when the switch is actuated, the battery is bad, the fusible link is burned (the circuit is open) or the solenoid itself is defective.

6   To check the solenoid, connect a jumper lead between the battery (+) and the ignition switch wire terminal (the small terminal) on the solenoid. If the starter motor now

operates, the solenoid is OK and the problem is in the ignition switch, neutral start switch or the wiring.

7   If the starter motor still doesn't operate, remove the starter/solenoid assembly for disassembly, testing and repair.

8   If the starter motor cranks the engine at an abnormally slow speed, first make sure the battery is fully charged and all terminal connections are tight. If the engine is partially seized, or has the wrong viscosity oil in it, it will crank slowly.

9   Run the engine until normal operating temperature is reached, then turn the engine off and disconnect the primary wires from the coil or coil pack.

10   Connect a voltmeter positive lead to the positive battery post and connect the negative lead to the negative post.

11   Crank the engine and take the voltmeter readings as soon as a steady figure is indicated. Don't allow the starter motor to turn for more than 15 seconds at a time. A reading of 9-volts or more, with the starter motor turning at normal cranking speed, is normal. If the reading is 9-volts or more but the cranking speed is slow, the motor is faulty. If the reading is less than 9-volts and the cranking speed is slow, the solenoid contacts are probably burned, the starter motor is bad, the battery is discharged or there's a bad connection.

17 Starter motor assembly - removal and installation

Refer to illustrations 17.2, 17.4 and 17.5

1   Detach the cable from the negative terminal of the battery.

2   Remove the upper mounting bolt and nut **(see illustration)**.

3   Raise the vehicle and support it securely on jackstands.

4   Clearly label, then disconnect the wires from the terminals on the starter motor and solenoid **(see illustration)**.

5   Remove the lower mounting bolt **(see illustration)** and detach the starter.

6   Installation is the reverse of removal.

18 Starter motor/solenoid/gear reduction assembly - replacement

1   Disconnect the cable from the negative terminal of the battery.

2   Remove the starter motor (see Section 17).

Bosch starter

Refer to illustrations 18.3a, 18.3b, 18.3c, 18.4 and 18.5

3   Remove the field terminal nut, disconnect the field terminal and remove the washer

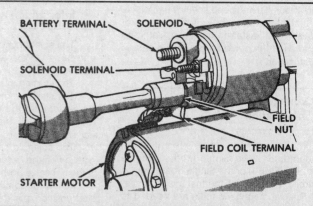

18.3a Before disconnecting the solenoid from a Bosch starter motor, remove the field terminal nut . . .

BATTERY TERMINAL
SOLENOID
SOLENOID TERMINAL
FIELD NUT
FIELD COIL TERMINAL
STARTER MOTOR

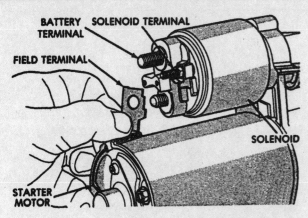

18.3b . . . disconnect the field terminal . . .

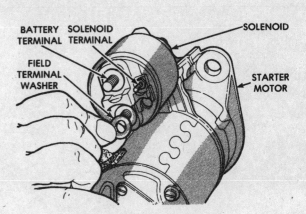

18.3c . . . and remove the washer

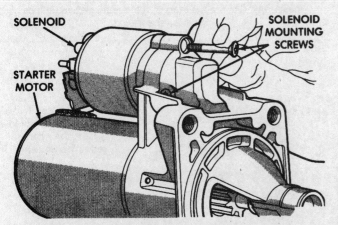

18.4 To detach the solenoid from a Bosch starter motor, remove the mounting screws (arrows)

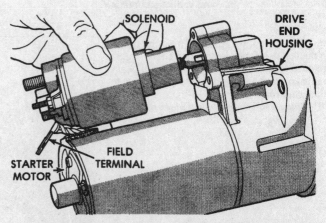

18.5 On a Bosch starter motor, work the solenoid off the shift fork and detach it from the drive end housing

5

18.7 If you're replacing the starter motor or solenoid on a Nippondenso starter motor, disconnect the field coil strap from the solenoid terminal (if you're replacing the gear reduction assembly, you can leave the solenoid and starter wired together and simply disconnect both of them as a single unit from the gear reduction housing)

18.8a To detach a Nippondenso starter motor from the gear reduction assembly, remove these two long through-bolts (arrows) . . .

(see illustrations).
4   Remove the three solenoid mounting screws (see illustration).
5   Work the solenoid off the shift fork and detach it from the drive end housing (see illustration).
6   Installation is the reverse of removal.

Nippondenso starter

Refer to illustrations 18.7, 18.8a, 18.8b, 18.9a and 18.9b

7   If you're replacing the starter motor or solenoid, disconnect the field coil strap from the solenoid terminal (see illustration); if

you're replacing the gear reduction assembly, skip this step and proceed to the next step.
8   To detach the starter motor from the gear reduction assembly, simply remove the two long through-bolts and pull off the starter (see illustrations).

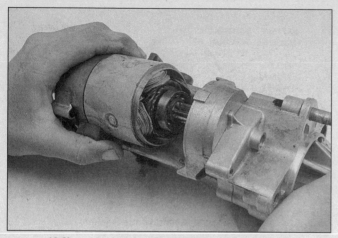

18.8b ... and separate the starter motor from the
gear reduction housing

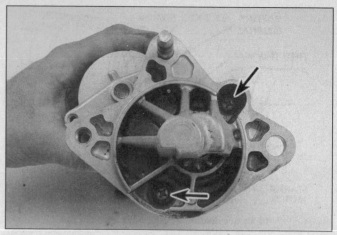

18.9a To detach a Nippondenso solenoid from the gear reduction
assembly, remove the starter, remove these two Phillips
screws (arrows) ...

9   To detach the solenoid from the gear
reduction assembly, remove the starter, then
remove the two Phillips screws from the gear
reduction assembly and pull off the solenoid
(see illustrations).
10   Installation is the reverse of removal.

18.9b ... and
separate the solenoid
from the gear
reduction housing

Chapter 6
Emissions control systems

Contents

Specifications

Torque specifications

Camshaft reference sensor retaining bolt (Turbo III)................	145 in-lbs
Crankshaft reference sensor retaining bolt (Turbo III)................	145 in-lbs
EGR valve (all engines)	
EGR valve mounting bolts................	200 in-lbs
EGR tube bolts................	200 in-lbs
EGR tube-to-valve screws	95 in-lbs

1 General information

Refer to illustrations 1.3a through 1.3g and 1.6

To prevent pollution of the atmosphere from incompletely burned and evaporating gases, and to maintain good driveability and fuel economy, a number of emission control systems are incorporated. The principal systems are:

Positive Crankcase Ventilation (PCV) system
Fuel evaporative emission control system
Heated inlet air system (thermostatically controlled air cleaner)
Exhaust Gas Recirculation (EGR) system
Air aspirator system
Oxygen sensor
Catalytic converter
SMEC or SBEC (computer) and sensors

The Sections in this Chapter include general descriptions, checking procedures within the scope of the home mechanic and component replacement procedures (when possible) for each of the systems listed above.

Before assuming an emissions control system is malfunctioning, check the fuel and ignition systems carefully. The diagnosis of some emission control devices requires specialized tools, equipment and training. If checking and servicing become too difficult or if a procedure is beyond your ability, consult a dealer service department. Remember, the most frequent cause of emissions problems is simply a loose or broken vacuum hose or wire, so always check the hose **(see illustrations)** and electrical connections first.

This doesn't mean, however, that emission control systems are particularly difficult to maintain and repair. You can quickly and easily perform many checks and do most of the regular maintenance at home with common tune-up and hand tools. **Note:** *Because of a Federally mandated extended warranty which covers the emission control system components, check with your dealer about warranty coverage before working on any emissions-related systems. Once the warranty has expired, you may wish to perform some of the component checks and/or replacement procedures in this Chapter to save money.*

Pay close attention to any special precautions outlined in this Chapter. It should be noted that the illustrations of the various systems may not exactly match the system installed on your vehicle because of changes made by the manufacturer during production or from year-to-year.

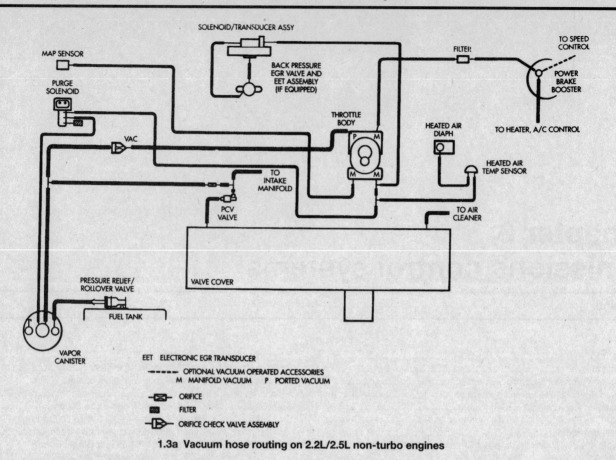

1.3a   Vacuum hose routing on 2.2L/2.5L non-turbo engines

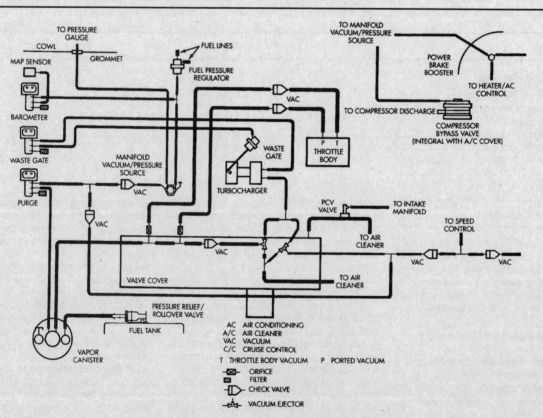

1.3b   Vacuum hose routing on 2.5L Turbo I engines

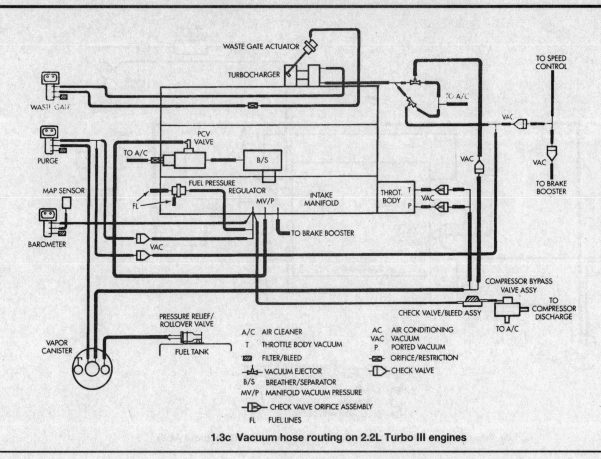

1.3c Vacuum hose routing on 2.2L Turbo III engines

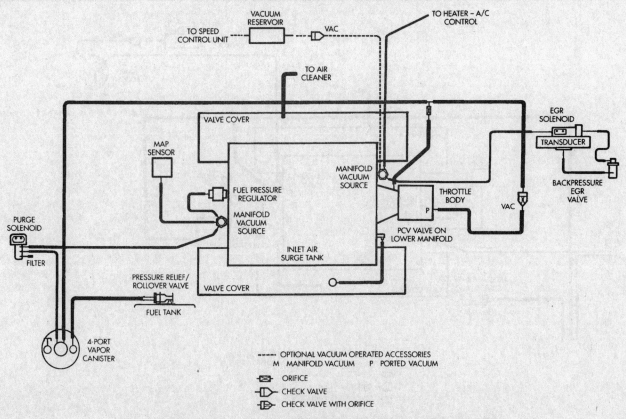

1.3d Vacuum hose routing on V6 engines (California models with ABS)

6

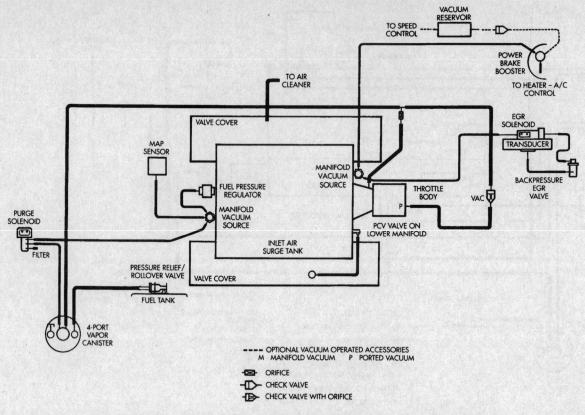

1.3e Vacuum hose routing on V6 engines (California models without ABS)

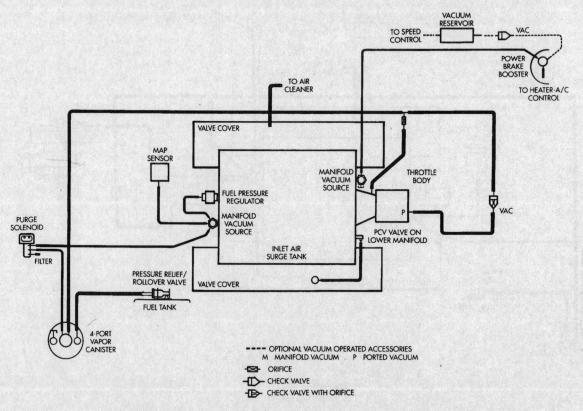

1.3f Vacuum hose routing on V6 engines (Canadian and 49 State models without ABS)

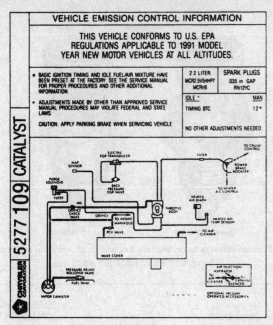

1.6 Typical Vehicle Emission Control Information (VECI) label.

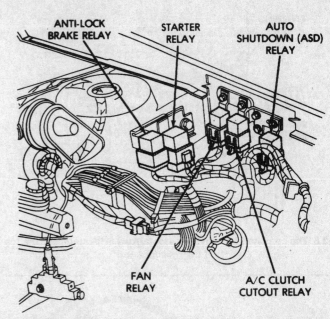

2.6 Relay location on 1 1992 Turbo I model (other models similar)

A Vehicle Emissions Control Information (VECI) label is located in the engine compartment **(see illustration)**. This label contains important emissions specifications and adjustment information. When servicing the engine or emissions systems, the VECI label in your particular vehicle should always be checked for up-to-date information.

2 Single Module Engine Controller (SMEC)/Single Board Engine Controller (SBEC) and information sensors - description

1   The electronic fuel injection (EFI) system provides the correct air-fuel ratio under all driving conditions. The 2.5L non-turbo engine is equipped with a computer-controlled, "single-point" (one injector in the throttle body) electronic fuel injection (EFI) system. The 2.5L and 2.2L turbo and V6 engines are equipped with similar "multi-point" (injector in each intake port) EFI systems.

2   The "brain" of all EFI systems is a computer known as a Single Module Engine Controller (SMEC) (1989 models) or a Single Board Engine Controller (SBEC) (1990 and later models) **(see illustrations 10.2a, 10.2b and 10.2c in Chapter 4)**. The SMEC/SBEC is located at the front corner of the engine compartment.

3   The SMEC/SBEC receives variable voltage inputs from a variety of sensors, switches and relays. All inputs are converted into digital signals which are "read" by the SMEC/SBEC, which constantly fine-tunes such variables as ignition timing, spark advance, ignition coil dwell, fuel injector pulse width and idle speed to minimize exhaust emissions and enhance driveability.

It also controls the operation of the radiator cooling fan, the alternator charging rate and such emissions-related components as the EGR solenoids and the purge solenoid for the EVAP canister. The SMEC/SBEC even updates and revises its own programming in response to changing operating conditions.

4   The SMEC/SBEC also constantly monitors many of its own input and output circuits. If a fault is found in the EFI system, the information is stored in the SMEC/SBEC memory. You really can't check or test the components of the EFI system without an expensive factory tool, the Diagnostic Readout Box DRB II or its equivalent, but you can often determine where a problem is coming from, or at least which circuit it's in. This process always begins with reading any stored fault codes to identify the general location of a problem, followed by a thorough visual inspection of the system components to ensure that everything is properly connected and/or plugged in. The most common cause of a problem in any EFI system is a loose or corroded electrical connector or a loose vacuum line. To learn how to output this information and display it on the "Check Engine" light on the dash, refer to Section 4.

Information sensors
Refer to illustration 2.6

5   Various components provide basic information to the SMEC/SBEC; they include:

Air conditioning cut-out relay (2.5L, turbo and V6 engines)
Auto shutdown relay (all engines)
Brake switch (turbo and V6 engines)
Camshaft reference sensor (2.2L Turbo III engines)
Charge temperature sensor (2.2L Turbo III engines)

Coolant temperature sensor (all engines)
Crankshaft reference sensor (2.2L Turbo III engine)
Detonation (knock) sensor (turbo engines)
Manifold Absolute Pressure (MAP) sensor (all engines)
Neutral safety switch (all engines)
Oxygen sensor (all engines)
Speed control switch (all engines)
Throttle body temperature sensor (2.5L engines)
Throttle Position Sensor (TPS) (all engines)
Transmission neutral-safety switch (turbo and 3.0L engine)
Vehicle distance sensor (2.5L and turbo engines)
Vehicle speed sensor (V6 engines)

Air conditioning cut-out relay
Refer to illustration 2.6

6   The air conditioning cut-out relay **(see illustration)** is connected in series electrically with the air conditioner damped pressure switch, the air conditioner switch and (on 2.5L engines) the radiator/condenser fan relay. The cut-out relay is energized (in its closed position) when the engine is operating. When the SMEC/SBEC senses a low idle speed, or the throttle position sensor indicates a wide open throttle condition, the cut-out relay is de-energized, its contacts open and the air conditioner clutch is prevented from engaging. The cut-out relay is located on the left inner fender panel, next to the battery and right above the SMEC/SBEC.

Auto shutdown relay (all engines)

7   If there's no ignition (distributor) signal (2.5L, 2.5L Turbo I and V6 engines), or cam or

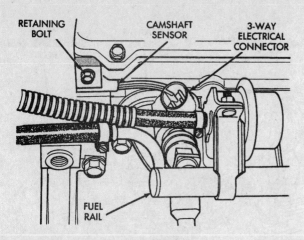

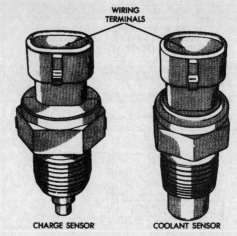

2.8 The camshaft reference sensor (arrow) is located near the top of the cylinder head

2.9 Typical charge temperature sensor (2.2L engine) and coolant temperature sensor (all engines)

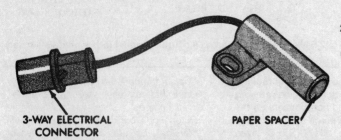

2.11 The crankshaft reference sensor used on 2.2L engine

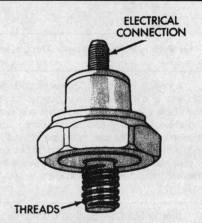

2.12 The detonation (knock) sensor used on turbo engines

crank reference sensor signal (2.2L Turbo III engine), present when the ignition key is turned to the RUN position, the auto shut-down relay interrupts power to the electric fuel pump, the fuel injectors, the ignition coil and the heated oxygen sensor. The cut-out relay is located on the left inner fender panel, next to the battery and right above the SMEC/SBEC (see illustration 2.6).

Camshaft reference sensor (2.2L Turbo III engine)

Refer to illustration 2.8

8   The camshaft reference sensor (see illustration) is mounted on top of the engine timing chain cover. The sensor reads camshaft position by sensing slots on the cam sprocket. The sensor then sends a coded signal to the SBEC, which uses this information to determine whether the fuel injectors and ignition coils are correctly synchronized.

Charge temperature sensor (Turbo III engines)

Refer to illustration 2.9

9   The charge temperature sensor (see illustration), which is mounted in the underside of the intake manifold, measures the temperature of the incoming air and sends this information to the SMEC/SBEC. This data is used by the SMEC/SBEC to modify the air/fuel mixture and the turbocharger boost level.

Coolant temperature sensor (all engines)

10   The coolant temperature sensor (see illustration 2.9), which is threaded into the thermostat housing, monitors coolant temperature and sends this information to the SMEC/SBEC. This data, along with the information from the charge temperature sensor, is used by the SMEC/SBEC to determine the correct air/fuel mixture and idle speed while the engine is warming up. The sensor is also used to turn on the radiator fan.

Crankshaft reference sensor (2.2L Turbo III engine)

Refer to illustration 2.11

11   The crank timing sensor (see illustration) is mounted on the transaxle bellhousing. This sensor sends information to the SBEC regarding engine crankshaft position. The sensor "reads" slots (sets of four per cylinder) on the torque converter driveplate.

Detonation (knock) sensor (turbo engines)

Refer to illustration 2.12

12   The detonation (knock) sensor (see illustration) generates a signal when spark knock occurs in the combustion chambers. It's mounted on the intake manifold where detonation in each cylinder can be detected. The sensor provides information used by the

SMEC/SBEC to modify spark advance and eliminate detonation.

Distributor pick-up (1991 and later 2.5L and V6 engines)

13   On 1991 and later 2.5L and V6 engines, engine speed input is supplied to the SMEC/SBEC by the distributor Hall effect pick-up (2.5L engines) or the optical system pick-up (V6 engines). The distributor uses an internal shutter and Hall effect sensor (2.5L engines) or an internal metal disc and optical sensor (V6 engines) to create a pulsing signal that is sent to the SMEC/SBEC. These electronic pulses are converted to engine rpm information.

Manifold Absolute Pressure (MAP) sensor (all engines)

Refer to illustrations 2.14a, 2.14b, 2.14c and 2.14d

14   The MAP sensor (see illustrations) is located on the firewall. It monitors intake manifold vacuum through a vacuum line to the throttle body. The MAP sensor transmits

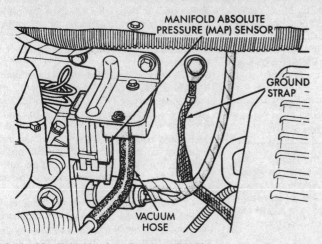

2.14a Manifold Absolute Pressure (MAP) sensor used on single point (TBI) engines

2.14b Manifold Absolute Pressure (MAP) sensor used on the V6 engine

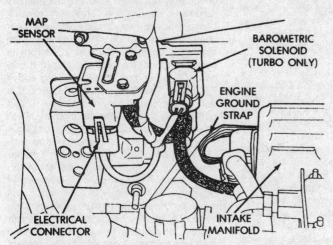

2.14c Manifold Absolute Pressure (MAP) sensor used on 2.5L Turbo I engines

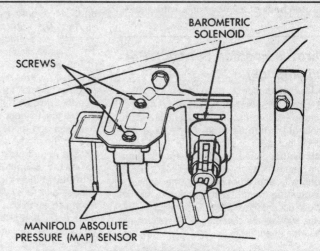

2.14d Manifold Absolute (MAP) sensor used on 2.2L Turbo III engines

6

this data, along with data on barometric pressure, in the form of a variable voltage output to the SMEC/SBEC. When combined with data from other sensors, this information helps the SMEC/SBEC determine the correct air-fuel mixture ratio.

Miscellaneous switches (all engines)

15 Various switches (such as the transmission neutral safety switch, the air conditioning switch, the speed control switch and the brake light switch) provide information to the SMEC/SBEC, which adjusts engine operation in accordance with what switch states are present at these inputs. The state of these switch inputs (high/low) is difficult to determine without the DRB II diagnostic meter.

Oxygen sensor (all engines)

Refer to illustration 2.16

16 The oxygen sensor **(see illustration)**, which is mounted in the exhaust manifold (the rear manifold on the V6 engines), produces a voltage signal when exposed to the oxygen

2.16 Typical heated oxygen sensor used on all engines

present in the exhaust gases. The sensor is electrically heated internally for faster switching when the engine is running. When there's a lot of oxygen present (lean mixture), the sensor produces a low voltage signal; when there's little oxygen present (rich mixture), it produces a signal of higher voltage. By monitoring the oxygen content and converting it to electrical voltage, the sensor acts as a lean-rich switch. The voltage signal to the SMEC/SBEC alters the pulse width of the injector(s).

Throttle body temperature sensor (2.5L engine)

17 The throttle body temperature sensor, which is mounted in the throttle body, monitors the temperature of the throttle body (fuel temperature). When transmitted to the SMEC/SBEC, this data helps determine the correct air/fuel mixture during a hot restart condition.

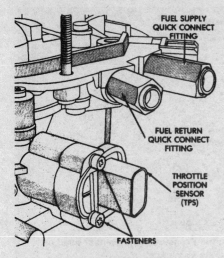

FUEL SUPPLY
QUICK CONNECT
FITTING

FUEL RETURN
QUICK CONNECT
FITTING

THROTTLE
POSITION
SENSOR
(TPS)

FASTENERS

2.18 Throttle Position Sensor (TPS) on the throttle body of a 2.5L engine with single-point EFI

Throttle Position Sensor (TPS) (all engines)

Refer to illustration 2.18

18   The TPS **(see illustration)**, which is located on the throttle body, monitors the angle of the throttle plate. The voltage produced increases or decreases in accordance with the opening angle of the throttle plate. This data, when relayed to the SMEC/SBEC, along with data from several other sensors, enables the computer to adjust the air/fuel ratio in accordance with the operating conditions, such as acceleration, deceleration, idle and wide open throttle.

Vehicle distance (speed) sensor

19   The vehicle distance (speed) sensor, which is located in the transaxle extension housing, senses vehicle motion. It generates eight pulses for every revolution of the driveaxle and transmits them as voltage signals to the SMEC/SBEC. These signals are compared by the SMEC/SBEC with a closed throttle signal from the throttle position sensor so it can distinguish between a closed throttle deceleration and a normal idle (vehi-

cle stopped) condition. Under deceleration conditions, the SMEC/SBEC controls the AIS motor to maintain the desired MAP value; under idle conditions, the SMEC/SBEC adjusts the AIS motor to maintain the desired engine speed.

---

3   Self diagnosis system - description and code access

Note 1: *Before outputting the trouble codes, thoroughly inspect ALL electrical connectors and hoses. Make sure all electrical connections are tight, clean and free of corrosion; make sure all hoses are properly connected, fit tightly and are in good condition (no cracks or tears).*

Note 2: *On the models covered by this manual, the CHECK ENGINE light, located in the instrument panel, flashes on for three seconds as a bulb test when the engine is started. The light comes on and stays on when there's a problem in the EFI.*

1   The self diagnosis information contained in the SBEC or SMEC (computer) can be accessed either by the ignition key or by using a special tool called the Diagnostic Readout Box (DRB II). This tool is attached to the diagnostic connector in the engine compartment and reads the codes and parameters on the digital display screen. The tool is expensive and most home mechanics prefer to use the alternate method. The drawback with the ignition method is that it does not access all the available codes for display. Most problems can be solved or diagnosed quite easily and if the information cannot be obtained readily, have the vehicle's self diagnosis system analyzed by a dealer service department or other properly-equipped repair shop.

2   To obtain the codes using the ignition key method, first set the parking brake and put the transaxle in Park (automatic) or Neutral (manual). Raise the engine speed to approximately 2500 rpm and slowly let the speed down to idle. Also cycle the air conditioning system (on briefly, then off). Next, if the vehicle is equipped with an automatic transmission, with your foot on the brake, select each position on the transmission (Reverse, Drive, Low etc.) and bring the

shifter back to Park. This will allow the computer to obtain any fault codes that might be linked to any of the sensors controlled by the transmission, engine speed or air conditioning system.

3   To display the codes on the dashboard (POWER LOSS or CHECK ENGINE light), turn the ignition key ON, OFF, ON, OFF and finally ON. The codes will begin to flash. The light will blink the number of the first digit then pause and blink the number of the second digit. For example: Code 23, throttle body temperature sensor circuit, would be indicated by two flashes, then a pause followed by three flashes.

4   Certain criteria must be met for a fault code to be entered into the engine controller memory. The criteria may be a specific range of engine rpm, engine temperature or input voltage to the engine controller. It is possible that a fault code for a particular monitored circuit may not be entered into the memory despite a malfunction. This may happen because one of the fault code criteria has not been met. For example; The engine must be operating between 750 and 2000 rpm in order to monitor the Map sensor circuit correctly. If the engine speed is raised above 2400 rpm, the MAP sensor output circuit shorts to ground and will not allow a fault code to be entered into the memory. Then again, the exact opposite could occur: A code is entered into the memory that suggests a malfunction within another component that is not monitored by the computer. For example; A fuel pressure problem cannot register a fault directly but instead, it will cause a rich/lean fuel mixture problem. Consequently, this will cause an oxygen sensor malfunction resulting in a stored code in the computer for the oxygen sensor. Be aware of the interrelationship of the sensors and circuits and the overall relationship of the emissions control and fuel injection systems.

5   The following table is a list of the typical trouble codes which may be encountered while diagnosing the system. Also included are simplified troubleshooting procedures. If the problem persists after these checks have been made, more detailed service procedures will have to be performed by a dealer service department or other qualified repair shop.

Trouble codes

Note: *Not all trouble codes apply to all models.*

Code 11*	No distributor reference signal detected during engine cranking. Check the circuit between the distributor and the SMEC/SBEC.
Code 12*	Problem with stand-by memory circuit. Direct battery input to controller disconnected within the last 50 ignition key-ons.
Code 13**	Indicates a problem with the MAP sensor pneumatic (vacuum) system.
Code 14**	MAP sensor voltage too low or too high.
Code 15**	A problem with the vehicle distance/speed signal. No distance/speed sensor signal detected during road load conditions.

Code 16	Loss of battery voltage.
Code 17*	Engine is cold too long. Engine coolant temperature remains below normal operating temperatures during operation (check the thermostat).
Code 21**	Problem with oxygen sensor signal circuit. Sensor voltage to computer not fluctuating.
Code 22**	Coolant sensor voltage too high or too low. Test coolant temperature sensor.
Code 23	Indicates that the throttle body temperature sensor/charge temperature sensor input is below the minimum acceptable voltage or the throttle body temperature sensor input is above the maximum acceptable voltage.
Code 24**	Throttle position sensor voltage high or low. Test the throttle position sensor.
Code 25	Automatic Idle Speed (AIS) motor circuits(s) indicate a shorted condition detected in one or more of the circuits. Check the circuits.
Code 26	Peak injector current has not been reached (non-turbo) or a problem with an injector circuit (turbo). Check the injector(s) and electrical harnesses.
Code 27	One of the injector control circuit output drivers does not respond properly to the control signal. Check the circuits.
Code 31**	Problem with the canister purge solenoid circuit.
Code 32**	An open or shorted condition detected in the EGR transducer solenoid circuit. Possible air/fuel ratio imbalance not detected during diagnosis
Code 33*	Air conditioner clutch relay circuit. An open or shorted condition detected in the air conditioning clutch relay circuit.
Code 34*	Open or shorted condition detected in the speed control vacuum or vent solenoid circuits.
Code 35*	Radiator fan relay circuit indicates an open or shorted condition.
Code 36**	Indicates a problem with the wastegate solenoid circuit (turbo models) or the air switching solenoid circuit (non-turbo models).
Code 37*	Torque converter unlock solenoid circuit. An open or shorted condition detected in the torque converter part throttle unlock solenoid circuit (automatic transaxle models only).
Code 41**	Problem with the charging system. Occurs when battery voltage from the ASD relay is below 11.75-volts.
Code 42*	Auto shutdown relay (ASD) control circuit indicates an open or shorted circuit condition.
Code 43	Problem with the spark interface/injection control circuit (1989 models) or ignition coil #1 primary circuit not achieved with maximum dwell time (1991 and later Turbo III) or ignition coil #2 primary circuit not achieved with maximum dwell time (1991 and later Turbo III).
Code 44	No FJ2 voltage present at controller. Failure in the SMEC/SBEC.
Code 45	MAP sensor reading above overboost limit detected.
Code 46**	Charging system voltage too high. Computer indicates that the battery voltage is not properly regulated. Check the SMEC or SBEC.
Code 47**	Charging system voltage too low. Battery voltage sense input below target charging voltage during engine operation and no significant change in voltage detected during active test of alternator output.
Code 51**	Oxygen sensor signal input indicates lean fuel/air ratio condition during engine operation.
Code 52**	Oxygen sensor signal input indicates rich fuel/air ratio condition during engine operation.
Code 53*	Internal SMEC/SBEC failure detected.
Code 54*	Problem with the distributor synchronization circuit.
Code 55	Completion of fault code display on CHECK ENGINE lamp. This is an "End of message" code.
Code 61**	An open or short circuit detected in the baro read solenoid circuit (Turbo III).
Code 62**	Unsuccessful attempt to update EMR mileage in the controller EEPROM.
Code 63*	Controller failure. EEPROM write denied. Check the SMEC or SBEC.

6

*CHECK ENGINE light may not illuminate in some instances. **These codes light up the CHECK ENGINE light on the instrument panel on California vehicles with special emission controls.

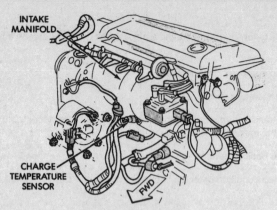

4.8 Charge temperature sensor location on the 2.2L Turbo III engine

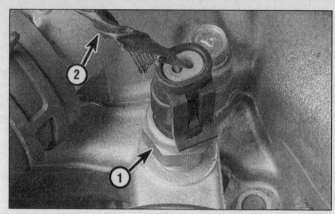

4.13a Coolant temperature sensor (V6 engine)

4   Information sensors - replacement

Camshaft reference sensor (2.2L Turbo III engine)

1   Unplug the cam reference sensor lead at the electrical connector (see illustration 2.8).
2   Loosen the cam reference sensor retaining bolt.
3   Remove the sensor from the cylinder head. The sensor might be difficult to pull out of the cover, but it will come if you persist. **Caution:** *Don't pull on the sensor wire or you will damage it.*
4   If you're reinstalling the same sensor, remove the old spacer, clean off the sensor face and install a new spacer on the face. Inspect the O-ring too. Replace it if it's damaged.
5   If you are installing a new sensor, make sure a new paper spacer is already installed on the face and the O-ring is properly positioned in its groove.
6   Apply a couple of drops of oil to the O-ring prior to installation. When you install the sensor, push it down until it contacts the cam timing gear. Hold it in this position while you tighten the retaining bolt to the torque listed in this Chapter's Specifications.
7   After you plug in the sensor lead, make sure the lead is routed away from the accessory drivebelt.

Charge temperature sensor (2.2L Turbo III engine)

Refer to illustration 4.8
8   Locate the charge temperature sensor on the air intake plenum (see illustration).
9   Unplug the electrical connector from the sensor.
10   Unscrew the sensor.
11   Coat the threads of the new sensor (or the old one, if you're reinstalling it) with teflon tape, screw it in and tighten securely.
12   Reattach the electrical connector.

Coolant temperature sensor

Refer to illustrations 4.13a, 4.13b and 4.13c
Warning: *Wait until the engine is completely*

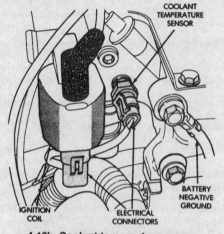

4.13b Coolant temperature sensor (2.5L Turbo I engine)

cool before replacing the coolant temperature sensor.
13   The coolant temperature sensor on most models is mounted in the thermostat housing (see illustrations).
14   Open the radiator cap to release any residual pressure. Squeeze the upper radiator hose and reinstall the cap (this will create a slight vacuum in the cooling system, which will minimize coolant loss).
15   Unplug the electrical connector from the coolant temperature sensor, unscrew the

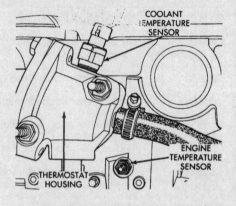

4.13c Coolant temperature sensor (2.2L Turbo III engine)

sensor and remove it.
16   Coat the threads of the new sensor (or the old one, if you're reinstalling it) with teflon tape, or a non-hardening thread sealant, screw it in, tighten securely and reattach the electrical connector.
17   Check the coolant level and add coolant if necessary.

Crankshaft reference sensor (2.2L Turbo III engine)

Refer to illustration 4.18
18   Unplug the electrical connector from the

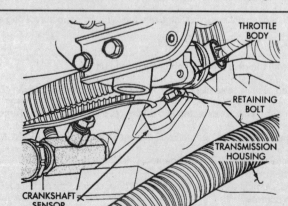

4.18 Crankshaft reference sensor (2.2L Turbo III engine)

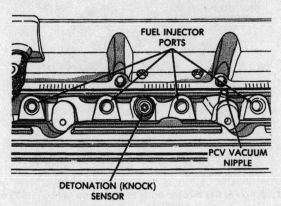

DETONATION (KNOCK) SENSOR

FUEL INJECTOR PORTS

PCV VACUUM NIPPLE

4.25a Location of the detonation (knock) sensor (Turbo I engine)

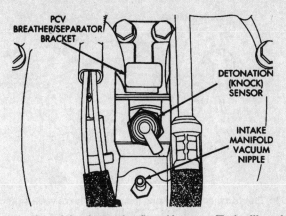

PCV BREATHER/SEPARATOR BRACKET

DETONATION (KNOCK) SENSOR

INTAKE MANIFOLD VACUUM NIPPLE

4.25b Location of the detonation (knock) sensor (Turbo III engine)

4.28 Location of the distance (speed) sensor

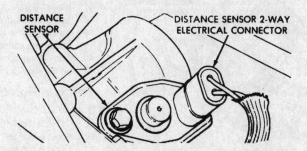

DISTANCE SENSOR

DISTANCE SENSOR 2-WAY ELECTRICAL CONNECTOR

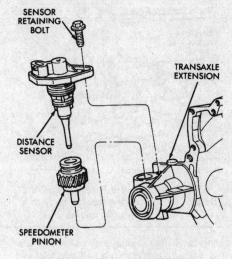

SENSOR RETAINING BOLT

TRANSAXLE EXTENSION

DISTANCE SENSOR

SPEEDOMETER PINION

4.30 Exploded view of the distance sensor and speedometer pinion

crankshaft reference sensor **(see illustration)**.

19   Loosen the crank reference sensor retaining bolt.

20   Remove the sensor from the transaxle housing.

21   If you're reinstalling the same sensor, remove the old spacer, clean off the sensor face and install a new spacer on the face.

22   If you installing a new sensor, make sure a new paper spacer is already installed on the face.

23   When you install the sensor, push it down until it contacts the driveplate. Hold it in this position while you tighten the retaining bolt to the torque listed in this Chapter's Specifications.

24   Plug in the sensor electrical connector.

Detonation (knock) sensor (turbo engines)

Refer to illustrations 4.25a and 4.25b

25   Unplug the electrical connector to the detonation (knock) sensor **(see illustrations)**.

26   Unscrew the sensor.

27   Installation is the reverse of removal.

Distance (speed) sensor

Refer to illustrations 4.28 and 4.30

28   The distance (speed) sensor is located in the transaxle extension housing **(see illustration)**.

29   Unplug the electrical connector.

30   Remove the retaining bolt and lift the sensor from the transaxle **(see illustration)**.

31   Installation is the reverse of removal.

Manifold Absolute Pressure (MAP) sensor

32   Detach the vacuum hose from the sensor **(see illustrations 2.14a through 12.14d)**.

33   Unplug the electrical connector from the sensor.

34   Remove the sensor mounting bolts and remove the sensor.

35   Installation is the reverse of removal.

Oxygen sensor

Refer to illustrations 4.36a, 4.36b and 4.36c

36   Unplug the oxygen sensor electrical connector **(see illustrations)**.

37   The sensor is threaded into the exhaust manifold. To locate it, simply trace the electri-

cal lead. On some models it may be easier to remove if you raise the front of the vehicle (support it securely on jackstands) for access to the underside of the engine compartment.

38   Unscrew the sensor. It is recommended that a special tool for heated sensors, available at most auto parts stores, be used (more

6

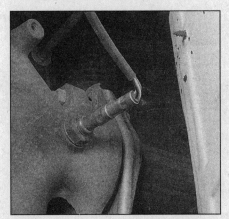

4.36a Location of the oxygen sensor on the V6 engine

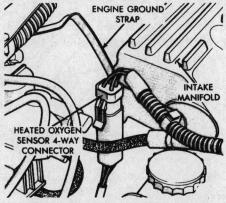

ENGINE GROUND STRAP

INTAKE MANIFOLD

HEATED OXYGEN SENSOR 4-WAY CONNECTOR

4.36b Electrical connector for the oxygen sensor on the 2.5L Turbo I engine

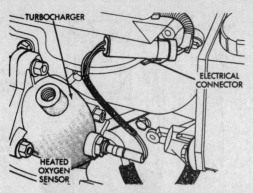

4.36c Electrical connector and location of the oxygen sensor on the 2.2L Turbo III engine

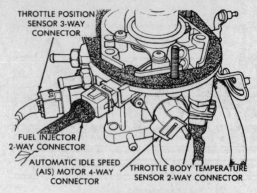

4.45 Location of the throttle body temperature sensor (1989 and 1990 2.5L engine)

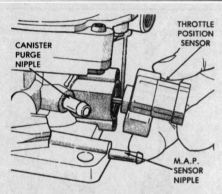

4.52a Removing the Throttle Position Sensor (TPS) from the throttle body of a 2.5L non-turbo engine

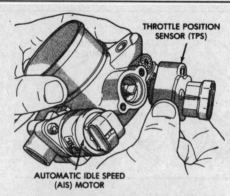

4.52b Removing the Throttle Position Sensor (TPS) from the throttle body of a turbo or V6 engine

important if, for example, you're simply removing a good sensor from a bad manifold and planning to reinstall it in another manifold).

39 Use a tap to clean the threads in the exhaust manifold.

40 If you're reinstalling the same sensor, apply a film of anti-seize compound to the threads. A new sensor should already have the anti-seize compound on the threads; if it doesn't, put some on.

41 Install the sensor, tighten it securely and plug in the electrical connector.

Throttle body temperature sensor (1989 and 1990 2.5L non-turbo engine)

Refer to illustration 4.45

42 Remove the air cleaner (see Chapter 4).

43 Disconnect the throttle cables from the throttle lever (see Chapter 4).

44 Remove the screws from the throttle cable bracket and remove the bracket.

45 Pulling down, unplug the electrical con-

nector from the sensor (see illustration).

46 Remove the sensor.

47 Apply heat transfer compound (included with sensor) to the sensor tip.

48 Install the sensor and tighten it securely.

49 The remainder of installation is the reverse of removal.

Throttle Position Sensor (TPS)

Refer to illustrations 4.52a and 4.52b

50 On 2.5L non-turbo engines, remove the air cleaner assembly (see Chapter 4).

51 Unplug the electrical connector from the TPS (three-wire connector).

52 Remove the two screws retaining the TPS to the throttle body, pull the TPS off the throttle shaft and remove it (see illustrations).

53 Installation is the reverse of removal. Make sure the flat tip of the throttle shaft seats properly into the slot in the TPS. Tighten the retaining screws securely.

5   Positive Crankcase Ventilation (PCV) system

Refer to illustrations 5.1a, 5.1b, 5.1c and 5.1d

1   The Positive Crankcase Ventilation (PCV)

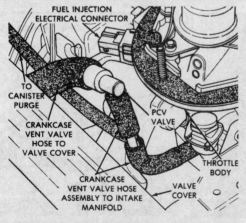

5.1a Positive Crankcase Ventilation (PCV) system on the 2.5L non-turbo engine

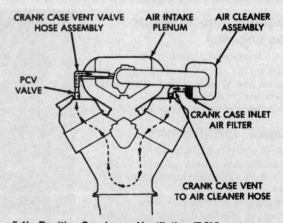

5.1b Positive Crankcase Ventilation (PCV) system on the V6 engine

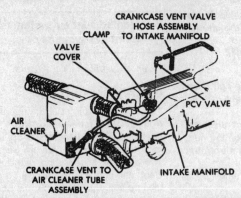

5.1c Positive Crankcase Ventilation (PCV) system on the 2.5L Turbo I engine

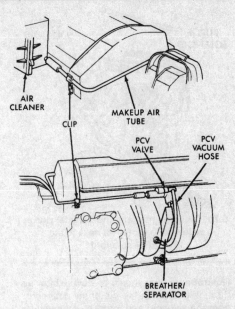

5.1d Positive Crankcase Ventilation (PCV) system on the 2.2L Turbo III engine

system **(see illustrations)** reduces hydrocarbon emissions by scavenging vapors from the crankcase. It does this by circulating fresh air from the air cleaner through the crankcase, where it mixes with blow-by gases and is then rerouted through a PCV valve to the intake manifold.

2   The main components of the PCV system are the PCV valve, a fresh air filtered inlet and the vacuum hoses connecting these two components with the engine.

3   To maintain idle quality, the PCV valve restricts the flow when the intake manifold vacuum is high. If abnormal operating conditions (such as piston ring problems) arise, the system is designed to allow excessive amounts of blow-by gases to flow back through the crankcase vent tube into the air cleaner to be consumed by normal combustion.

4   Checking and replacement of the PCV valve and filter is also covered in Chapter 1.

Check and component replacement

Refer to illustration 5.5

5   With the engine running at idle, pull the PCV valve out of the mount and place your finger over the valve inlet **(see illustration)**. A strong vacuum will be felt and a hissing noise will be heard if the valve is operating properly. Replace the valve with a new one, as described in Chapter 1, if it is not functioning as described. Do not attempt to clean the old valve.

6   Evaporative emissions control system

Refer to illustrations 6.7a, 6.7b, 6.7c, 6.7d, 6.7e and 6.8

General description

1   This system is designed to trap and store fuel that evaporates from the fuel system that would normally enter the atmosphere in the form of hydrocarbon (HC) emissions.

2   The system is very simple and consists of a charcoal-filled canister, canister purge solenoid, a combination rollover/pressure relief valve and connecting lines and hoses.

3   When the engine is off and pressure begins to build up in the fuel tank (caused by fuel evaporation), the charcoal in the canister absorbs the fuel vapor. When the engine is started (cold), the charcoal continues to absorb and store fuel vapor. As the engine warms up, the stored fuel vapors are routed to the intake manifold or air cleaner and combustion chambers where they are burned during normal engine operation.

4   The canister is purged using engine vacuum through the purge solenoid, which is controlled by the SMEC or SBEC. Single-point fuel injection systems use a bi-level canister purge system. This system uses a dual source of vacuum to remove the vapors from the canister. Multi-point fuel injection systems use a tri-level canister purge system.

The vapors are drawn in through the throttle body and air cleaner. Also, the vapors are drawn in at closed, part or wide open throttle. When the engine coolant temperature is below 70-degrees F the computer energizes the solenoid by grounding it so vacuum won't flow through it to the vacuum canister. Once the coolant temperature rises above 70-degrees F the solenoid is de-energized and vacuum then acts on the canister.

5   The relief valve, which is mounted in the fuel tank filler cap, is calibrated to open when the fuel tank vacuum or pressure reaches a certain level. This vents the fuel tank and relieves the high vacuum or pressure.

Check

6   Check the canister, hoses and lines for cracks and other damage. To check the filler cap, look for a damaged or deformed gasket as described in Chapter 1.

7   To check the purge solenoid, disconnect one of the vacuum hoses from it and attach a short length of hose to the port **(see**

6

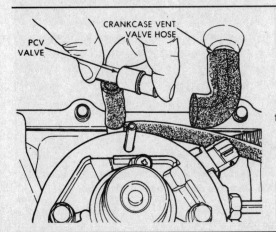

5.5 To check the PCV valve, detach it with the engine running - you should hear a hissing sound coming from the valve and you should feel a strong vacuum when you place your finger over the end of the valve

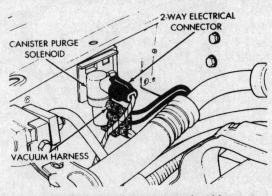

6.7a Typical canister purge solenoid

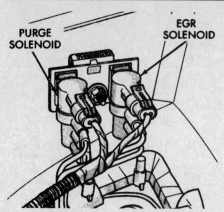

6.7b On some models, the canister purge solenoid is mounted next to the EGR solenoid

illustrations). You should be able to blow air through it. Unplug the electrical connector from the solenoid and apply battery voltage to the terminals using two jumper wires. Now when you blow into the hose, the valve should not pass air. **Caution:** *Don't leave the*

jumper wires connected to the solenoid any longer than necessary to perform this check.

Component replacement

Canister

8　The canister is located in the right front corner of the engine compartment, behind the headlight **(see illustration)**.
9　To replace the canister, disconnect the vacuum hoses, unscrew the mounting nuts and lower the canister, removing it from the engine compartment.
10　Installation is the reverse of removal.

Canister purge solenoid

11　The canister purge solenoid is located on the engine compartment firewall or the fenderwell area **(see illustrations 6.7a through 6.7c)**. On models equipped with an EGR solenoid, this solenoid is mounted together with the canister purge solenoid.
12　Disconnect the vacuum hose(s), unplug the electrical connector(s), remove the mounting bolt and detach the solenoid(s) and bracket assembly from the fender panel.
13　Installation is the reverse of removal.

7　Heated inlet air system (single-point EFI systems only)

Refer to illustrations 7.1, 7.8 and 7.10

General description

1　The heated inlet air (temperature control) system **(see illustration)** provides heated intake air during warm-up, then maintains the inlet air temperature within a 70 to 105-degrees F operating range by mixing warm and cool air. This allows leaner fuel/air mixture settings for the throttle body, which reduces emissions and improves driveability.
2　Two fresh air inlets - one warm and one cold - are used. The balance between the two is controlled by intake manifold vacuum. A vacuum diaphragm, which operates a heat duct valve in the air cleaner, is actuated by intake vacuum.
3　When the underhood temperature is cold, warm air radiating off the exhaust manifold is routed by a shroud which fits over the manifold up through a hot air inlet tube and into the air cleaner. This provides warm air for

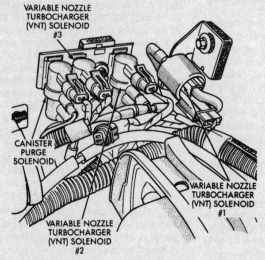

6.7c Canister purge solenoid location on turbo engines

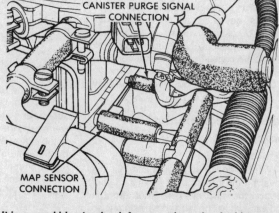

6.7d It is a good idea to check for any crimped or leaking vacuum lines by applying vacuum directly at the throttle body (single-point system shown)

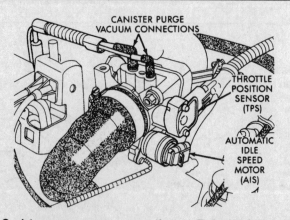

6.7e Canister purge vacuum connections on Turbo I throttle body

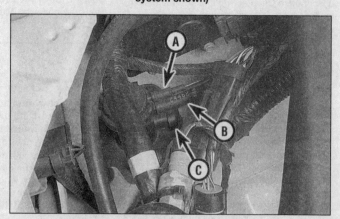

6.8 Charcoal canister hose designation

A　*Canister signal hose*　　　C　*Tank vent hose*
B　*Purge hose*

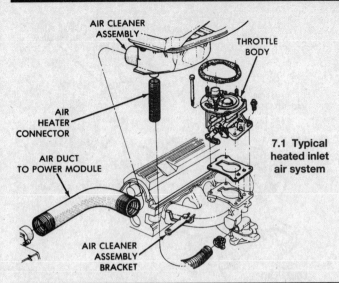

AIR CLEANER ASSEMBLY

THROTTLE BODY

AIR HEATER CONNECTOR

AIR DUCT TO POWER MODULE

AIR CLEANER ASSEMBLY BRACKET

7.1 Typical heated inlet air system

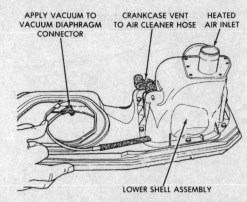

APPLY VACUUM TO VACUUM DIAPHRAGM CONNECTOR

CRANKCASE VENT TO AIR CLEANER HOSE

HEATED AIR INLET

LOWER SHELL ASSEMBLY

7.8 To check the vacuum diaphragm, unplug the vacuum source hose from the sensor and attach a hand-held vacuum pump - when vacuum is applied, the diaphragm should open the door and hold it open without leaking down - if the diaphragm fails to open the door or leaks, replace it with a new unit

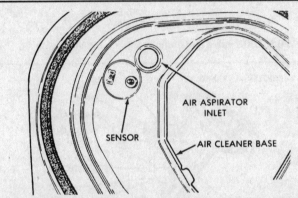

AIR ASPIRATOR INLET

SENSOR

AIR CLEANER BASE

7.10 The heated air sensor is attached to the air cleaner housing

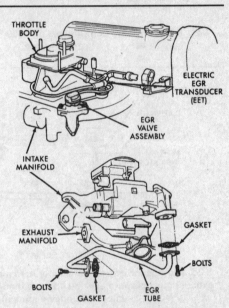

THROTTLE BODY

ELECTRIC EGR TRANSDUCER (EET)

EGR VALVE ASSEMBLY

INTAKE MANIFOLD

EXHAUST MANIFOLD

BOLTS

GASKET

GASKET

EGR TUBE

BOLTS

8.2a Typical EGR system on four-cylinder non-turbo engines

the throttle body, resulting in better driveability and faster warm-up. As the temperature inside the air cleaner rises, the heat duct valve is gradually closed by the vacuum diaphragm (which, in turn is controlled by a bi-metal temperature sensor inside the air cleaner) and the air cleaner draws air through a cold air duct instead. The result is a consistent intake air temperature.

Check

Note: *Refer to Chapter 1 for the initial system check. If the system doesn't operate as described in Chapter 1, proceed as described below.*

4   Always check the vacuum source and the integrity of all vacuum hoses between the source and the vacuum diaphragm before beginning the following test. Don't proceed until you're sure they're okay.
5   Apply the parking brake and block the wheels.
6   Detach, but do not remove, the air cleaner housing and element (see Chapter 4).
7   Turn the air cleaner housing upside down so the vacuum diaphragm door is visible. The door should be open. If it isn't, it might be binding or sticking. Make sure it's not rusted in an open or closed position by attempting to move it by hand. If it's rusted, it can usually be freed by cleaning and oiling the hinge. If it fails to work properly after ser-

vicing, replace it.
8   If the vacuum diaphragm door is okay, but the diaphragm still fails to operate correctly, check carefully for a leak in the hose leading to it. Check the vacuum source to and from the diaphragm, and the operation of the diaphragm itself **(see illustration)** with a hand vacuum pump. If no leak is found, replace the vacuum diaphragm. If the diaphragm is okay, check the heated air temperature sensor.

Component replacement

9   On some models, the vacuum diaphragm is secured with a rivet, which must be removed with a drill. Use a self-tapping screw to install the new diaphragm.
10   To replace the heated inlet air temperature sensor, disconnect the hoses from each end of the valve, then install the new sensor facing the same direction as the old one **(see illustration)**.

8   Exhaust Gas Recirculation (EGR) system

General description

Refer to illustrations 8.2a, 8.2b, 8.2c, 8.2d, 8.2e and 8.4
Note: *All California vehicles with EGR sys-*

tems have a self diagnosis system for the EGR valve and system. The diagnostic system is activated only during selected engine/driving conditions to avoid misdiagnosis. Refer to the Self diagnosis section in this Chapter (see Section 3) for a detailed explanation. **Note:** *1992 and later turbo models do not use an EGR valve.*
1   This system recirculates a portion of the exhaust gases into the intake manifold to reduce the combustion temperatures and decrease the amount of oxides of nitrogen (NOx) produced.
2   The main component in the system is the EGR valve **(see illustrations)**. It uses a backpressure transducer and an EGR solenoid. The backpressure transducer **(see illustration)** measures the amount of exhaust gas backpressure on the exhaust side of the EGR valve and varies the strength of the vacuum signal applied to the EGR valve. The

6

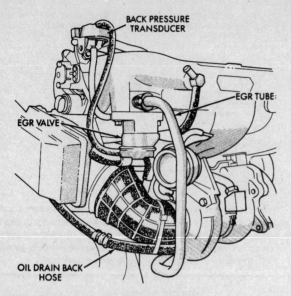

8.2b **EGR valve and components on 1989 through 1991 2.5L Turbo I engines**

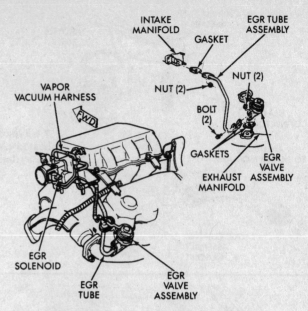

8.2c **EGR valve and components on the V6 engine**

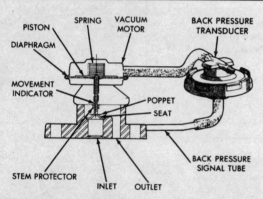

8.2d **The Backpressure Transducer measures the amount of exhaust gas pressure exerted on the exhaust side of the EGR valve (2.5L engine shown)**

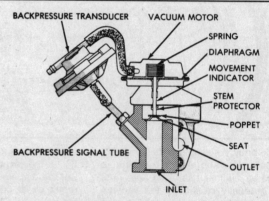

8.2e **EGR valve and Backpressure Transducer (non-California V6 engine)**

transducer uses this signal to provide the correct amount of recirculated exhaust gas under various conditions.

3   These systems do not allow EGR at idle. Single-point fuel injection systems allow EGR at all temperatures. Multi-point fuel injection systems do not allow EGR if the coolant temperature is below 40-degrees F at engine start-up. At higher engine temperatures (170-degrees F) the coolant valve opens, allowing vacuum to be applied to the EGR valve so the exhaust gas can recirculate.

4   The EGR valve and transducer (some models are equipped with an electric vacuum solenoid mounted directly above the transducer) are controlled by the EGR solenoid (operated by the SBEC or SMEC) which controls the vacuum flow to the EGR valve body in accordance with engine temperature and driving conditions. The solenoid may be mounted on the right side of the engine compartment or on the Electric EGR Transducer (EET) **(see illustration)**. Symptoms of problems associated with the EGR system are rough idling or stalling when at idle, rough engine performance during light throttle application and stalling during deceleration.

Check

5   Check all hoses for cracks, kinks, broken sections and proper connection. Inspect all system connections for damage, cracks and leaks.

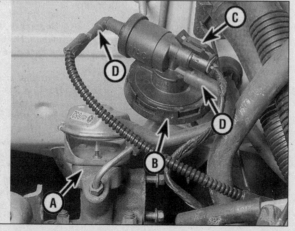

8.4 **The Electric Transducer (EET) is mounted near the EGR valve (V6 California model engine shown)**

A   *EGR valve*
B   *Electric EGR Transducer (EET)*
C   *EET electrical connector*
D   *Vacuum connections*

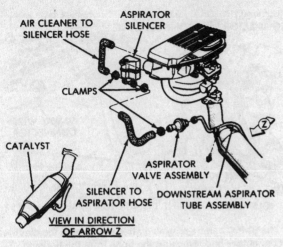

9.1 Typical air aspirator system

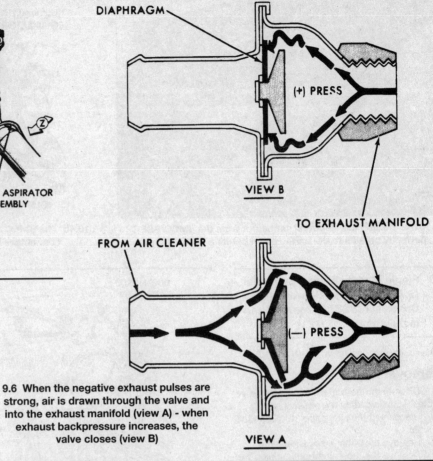

9.6 When the negative exhaust pulses are strong, air is drawn through the valve and into the exhaust manifold (view A) - when exhaust backpressure increases, the valve closes (view B)

6   To check the EGR valve operation, bring the engine up to operating temperature with the transaxle in Neutral (tires blocked to prevent movement).

7   Disconnect the hose from the transducer **(see illustration 8.2a through 8.2e)** and connect a vacuum pump. Start the engine, raise the engine speed to approximately 2000 rpm, hold it there and apply ten inches of vacuum with the pump. The EGR valve stem should move and stay open for at least 30 seconds if the control system is working properly.

8   If the stem moves but won't stay open, the EGR valve/backpressure transducer assembly is faulty and must be replaced with a new one.

9   If the EGR valve stem doesn't move except when vacuum from the pump is applied, remove the throttle body (see Chapter 4) and clean the EGR ports in the throttle bore and body with solvent.

10   If the engine exhibits rough idle, dies when returned to idle or the idle is both rough and slow, the EGR valve is leaking in the closed position. Inspect the EGR tube for leaks at the connection to the manifold. Loosen the tube connection and then tighten it securely. Remove the EGR valve and transducer assembly and inspect the poppet to make sure it's seated. If it isn't, replace the EGR valve transducer assembly with a new one; don't attempt to clean the EGR valve.

Component replacement

11   To remove the EGR valve and backpressure transducer, disconnect the vacuum hose from the backpressure transducer assembly, then pull the assembly out of the mounting clip.

12   Remove the bolts or unscrew the tube nut and disconnect the crossover tube from the EGR valve.

13   Remove the mounting bolts and detach the EGR valve and backpressure transducer

assembly from the engine. Clean off all old gasket material from the mating surfaces of the valve and manifold, and be sure to use a new gasket when installing the valve.

14   The EGR solenoid is located on the engine compartment firewall **(see illustration 6.7b).**

9   Air aspirator system

General description

Refer to illustration 9.1

1   The air aspirator system **(see illustration)** uses exhaust pulsations to draw fresh air from the air cleaner into the exhaust system. This reduces carbon monoxide (CO) and, to a lesser degree, hydrocarbon (HC) emissions.

2   The system is composed of a valve, hoses and tubes between the air cleaner assembly and the exhaust system.

3   The aspirator valve works most efficiently at idle and slightly off idle, where the negative exhaust pulses are strongest. The valve remains closed at higher engine speeds.

Check

Refer to illustration 9.6

4   Aspirator valve failure results in exces-

sive exhaust system noise from under the hood and hardening of the rubber hose from the valve to the air cleaner.

5   If exhaust noise is excessive, check the aspirator tube-to-exhaust manifold joint and the valve and air cleaner hose connections for leaks. If the manifold joint is leaking, retighten the tube fitting. If the hose connections are leaking, install new hose clamps (if the hose hasn't hardened). If the hose has hardened, replace it with a new one as well.

6   To determine if the valve has failed, disconnect the hose from the inlet. With the engine idling (transmission in Neutral), hold a strip of paper in front of the inlet - the paper should be sucked against the opening of the valve if it's working properly. If a steady stream of exhaust gas is escaping from the inlet (which will blow the paper away from the valve), the valve is defective and should be replaced with a new one **(see illustration)**. **Warning:** *Don't use your hand to feel for the exhaust pulses - the exhaust gas can be very hot!*

Component replacement

7   The valve can be replaced by removing the hose clamp, detaching the hose and unscrewing it from the tube.

8   The aspirator tube can be replaced by removing the valve, unscrewing the fitting at the manifold and removing the bracket bolt.

6

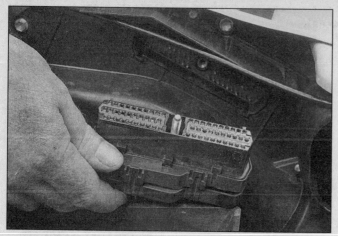

10.4a Detach the electrical connector from the SMEC/SBEC perfectly parallel to the unit to avoid bending any of the pins

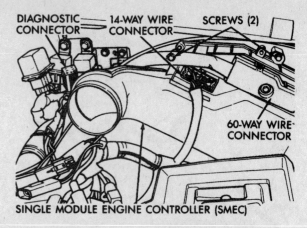

SINGLE MODULE ENGINE CONTROLLER (SMEC)

10.4b The SMEC can be removed after unplugging the electrical connectors and removing the bolts from the housing

10 Single Module Engine Controller (SMEC) or Single Board Engine Controller (SBEC) - removal and installation

Refer to illustrations 10.4a, 10.4b and 10.4c

Removal

1   Disconnect the battery cables (negative cable first, followed by the positive cable).
2   Disconnect the air cleaner duct from the module.
3   Remove the battery (see Chapter 5).
4   Remove the mounting bolts, unplug the connectors **(see illustrations)** and remove the SMEC or SBEC from the engine compartment **(see illustration)**.

Installation

5   Hold the module in position, install the bolts and plug in the connectors.
6   Connect the air cleaner duct.
7   Install the battery and connect the battery cables (positive first, then negative).

11 Catalytic converter

Note: *Because of a Federally mandated extended warranty which covers emissions-related components such as the catalytic converter, check with a dealer service department before replacing the converter at your own expense.*

General description

1   The catalytic converter is an emission control device added to the exhaust system to reduce pollutants in the exhaust gas stream. There are two types of converters.

10.4c The SBEC is located directly behind the battery tray

The conventional oxidation catalyst reduces the levels of hydrocarbon (HC) and carbon monoxide (CO). The three-way catalyst lowers the levels of oxides of nitrogen (NOx) as well as hydrocarbons (HC) and carbon monoxide (CO).

Check

2   The test equipment for a catalytic converter is expensive and highly sophisticated. If you suspect the converter is malfunctioning, take the vehicle to a dealer service department or authorized emissions inspection facility for diagnosis and repair.
3   Whenever the vehicle is raised for servicing of underbody components, check the converter for leaks, corrosion, dents and other damage. Check the welds/flange bolts that attach the front and rear ends of the converter to the exhaust system. If damage is discovered, the converter should be replaced.
4   Although catalytic converters don't

break too often, they can become plugged. The easiest way to check for a restricted converter is to use a vacuum gauge to diagnose the effect of a blocked exhaust on intake vacuum.

a) *Open the throttle until the engine speed is about 2000 rpm.*
b) *Release the throttle quickly.*
c) *If there's no restriction, the gauge will quickly drop to not more than 2 in-Hg or more above its normal reading.*
d) *If the gauge doesn't show 5 in-Hg or more above its normal reading, or seems to momentarily hover around its highest reading for a moment before it returns, the exhaust system, or the converter, is plugged (or an exhaust pipe is bent or dented, or the core inside the muffler has shifted).*

Component replacement

5   Refer to the exhaust system servicing procedures in Chapter 4.

Chapter 7 Part A
Manual transaxle

Contents

Specifications

Lubricant type and capacity .... See Chapter 1

Torque specifications
Shift linkage lock pin .... 108 in-lbs
Shift cable adjusting screws .... 70 in-lbs
Speedometer drive pinion bolt .... 60 in-lbs
Transaxle-to-engine block bolts .... 70 ft-lbs

1 General information

The vehicles covered by this manual are equipped with either a five-speed manual transaxle or a three-speed or four-speed automatic transaxle. Information on the manual transaxle is included in this Part of Chapter 7. Service procedures for the automatic transaxle are contained in Chapter 7, Part B.

The manual transaxle is a compact, two-piece, lightweight aluminum alloy housing containing both the transmission and differential assemblies.

Because of the complexity, unavailability of replacement parts and special tools required, internal repair of the manual transaxle by the home mechanic is not recommended. The bulk of information in this Chapter is devoted to removal and installation procedures.

2 Shift cables - check and adjustment

Warning: *On airbag-equipped models, always disconnect the negative battery cable and wait at least two minutes before working in the vicinity of the impact sensors, steering*

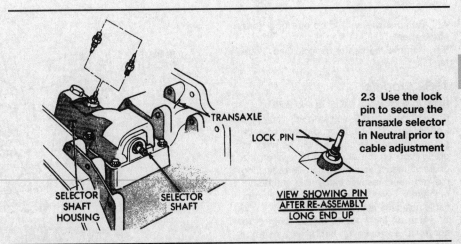

2.3 Use the lock pin to secure the transaxle selector in Neutral prior to cable adjustment

column or center console to avoid the accidental deployment of the airbag, which could cause personal injury.

All models
Refer to illustrations 2.3 and 2.4

1   In the event of hard shifting, disconnect both cables at the transaxle and then operate the shifter from the driver's seat. If the shift lever moves smoothly through all positions with the cables disconnected, then the cable assembly itself should be adjusted as described below.
2   Raise the hood and place a pad or blanket over the left fender to protect it.
3   Remove the lock pin from the transaxle selector shaft housing. Reverse the lock pin so the longer end is down, reinstall it in the hole and move the selector shaft in. When the lock pin aligns with the hole in the selector shaft, thread it into place so the shaft is locked in Neutral **(see illustration)**.

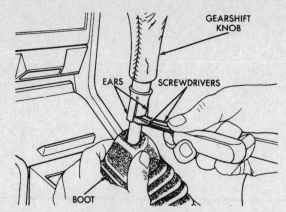

2.4 Use two screwdrivers to detach the gearshift knob on 1990 and later models

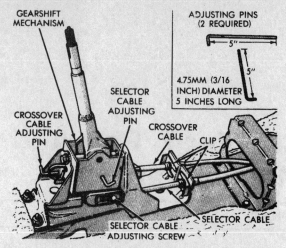

2.6 Fabricate the cable adjusting pins, loosen the adjusting screws and install the pins as shown here

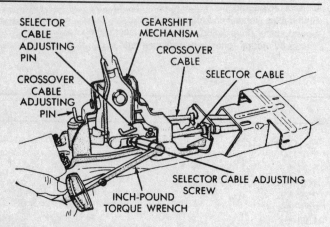

2.7a Adjust the selector cable by tightening the adjusting screw

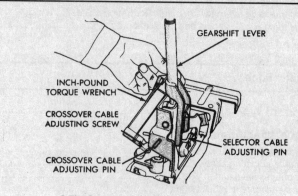

2.7b Crossover cable adjustment details

4   Remove the shift knob and boot **(see illustration)**.
5   Remove the center console (see Chapter 11).

1989 models

Refer to illustrations 2.6, 2.7a and 2.7b

6   Fabricate two 5-inch long adjusting pins from 5/16-inch wire. Bend one end of each pin at right angles so they will be easy to grasp. Loosen the adjusting screws on the gearshift mechanism and insert one adjusting pin into the crossover cable hole of the shift mechanism and the other into the selector cable hole **(see illustration)**.
7   Use an inch-pound torque wrench to tighten the crossover cable and selector cable adjusting screws to the torque listed in this Chapter's Specifications **(see illustrations)**. Remove the adjusting pins.

1990 and later models

Refer to illustration 2.8

8   Loosen the crossover cable adjusting screw and then tighten it to the torque listed in this Chapter's Specifications **(see illustration)**. Make sure the crossover bellcrank doesn't move as the adjusting screw is tightened.

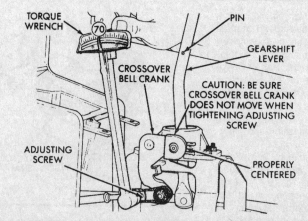

2.8 On 1990 and later models, loosen, then tighten the adjusting screw - make sure the crossover bellcrank remains stationary

All models

9   Install the console, boot and shift knob.
10   Remove the lock pin, reverse it so the longer end is upright, screw it into place and then tighten it to the torque listed in this Chapter's Specifications.
11   Check the shifter operation in First and Reverse and make sure the reverse lockout mechanism works properly.

3   Speedometer drive pinion - removal and installation

Refer to illustration 3.2

1   The speedometer drive pinion is located in the transaxle differential extension housing. The drive pinion must be removed for certain operations, such as to allow right side

driveaxle removal and installation. The manufacturer recommends that the oil seal be replaced before reinstalling the pinion.

2   Remove the retaining bolt and carefully work the speedometer drive assembly up and out of the transaxle extension housing **(see illustration)**.

3   Inspect the pinion for signs that lubricant has leaked past the adapter or into the cable.

4   If there is leakage, pry off the retainer, detach the adapter from the pinion gear and replace the O-ring.

5   Connect the adapter to the pinion, making sure the retainer is secure.

6   Make sure the mating surfaces of the adapter and extension housing are clean because any debris could cause misalignment of the gear.

7   Insert the assembly into the transaxle, install the bolt and tighten it securely.

4   Oil seal replacement

1   Oil leaks frequently occur due to wear of the driveaxle oil seals and/or the speedometer pinion drive gear O-ring. Replacement of the seals is relatively easy, since the repairs can usually be performed without removing the transaxle from the vehicle.

2   The driveaxle oil seals are located at the sides of the transaxle, where the driveaxles are attached. If leakage at the seal is suspected, raise the vehicle and support it securely on jackstands. If the seal is leaking, lubricant will be found on the sides of the transaxle.

3   Refer to Chapter 8 and remove the driveaxle(s).

4   Using a screwdriver or prybar, carefully pry the oil seal out of the transaxle bore.

5   If the oil seal can't be removed with a

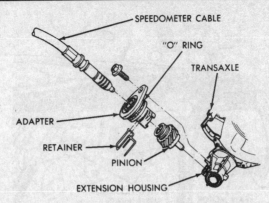

3.2 Speedometer drive pinion installation details - models equipped with a mechanical speedometer use a cable (shown); those equipped with electronic speedometers use a wire harness instead of a cable

screwdriver or prybar, a special oil seal removal tool (available at auto parts stores) will be required.

6   Using a large section of pipe or a large deep socket as a drift, install the new oil seal. Drive it into the bore squarely and make sure it's completely seated. Apply multi-purpose grease to the seal lip before installing the driveaxle.

7   Install the driveaxle(s). Be careful not to damage the lip of the new seal.

8   The speedometer cable and extension housing is located on the transaxle housing. Look for lubricant around the cable housing to determine if the O-ring is leaking.

9   Remove the speedometer drive pinion and replace the O-ring (see Section 3).

5   Transaxle mount - check and replacement

1   Insert a large screwdriver or prybar between the mount and the transaxle bracket and pry back and forth.

2   The transaxle bracket should not move

away from the mount. If it does, replace the mount.

3   To replace the mount, support the transaxle with a jack, remove the nut and through bolt and the bracket-to-transaxle bolts, then detach the mount. It may be necessary to raise or lower the transaxle slightly to provide enough clearance to remove the mount.

4   Installation is the reverse of removal.

6   Manual transaxle - removal and installation

Refer to illustrations 6.4, 6.16 and 6.19

Removal

1   Disconnect the negative cable from the battery.

2   Raise the vehicle and support it securely on jackstands.

3   Drain the transaxle lubricant (see Chapter 1).

4   Disconnect the shift and clutch linkage from the transaxle **(see illustration)**.

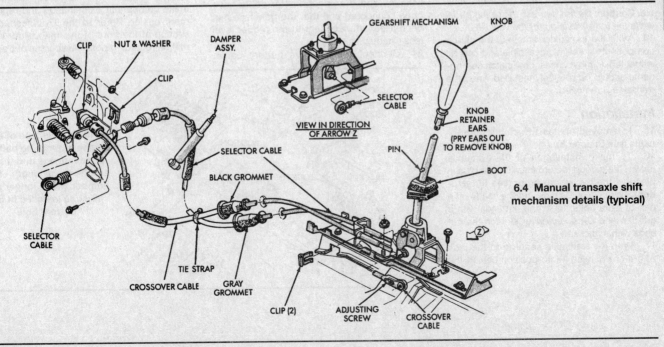

6.4 Manual transaxle shift mechanism details (typical)

7A

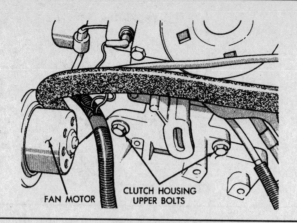

6.16 Transaxle installation will be easier if you replace these two bolts temporarily with guide pins made from a pair of extra bolts

FAN MOTOR   CLUTCH HOUSING UPPER BOLTS

5   Detach the speedometer cable (mechanical speedometer) and wire harness connectors from the transaxle.
6   Remove the exhaust system components as necessary for clearance.
7   Support the engine. This can be done from above with an engine hoist or special fixture or by placing a jack (with a block of wood as an insulator) under the engine oil pan. The engine must remain supported at all times while the transaxle is out of the vehicle!
8   Remove any chassis or suspension components that will interfere with transaxle removal (see Chapter 10).
9   Disconnect the driveaxles from the transaxle (see Chapter 8).
10   Support the transaxle with a jack, then remove the bolts securing the transaxle to the engine.
11   Remove the transaxle mount nuts and bolts.
12   Make a final check that all wires and hoses have been disconnected from the transaxle, then carefully pull the transaxle and jack away from the engine.
13   Once the input shaft is clear, lower the transaxle and remove it from under the vehicle. **Caution:** *Do not depress the clutch pedal while the transaxle is out of the vehicle.*
14   With the transaxle removed, the clutch components are now accessible and can be inspected. In most cases, new clutch components should be routinely installed when the transaxle is removed.

Installation

15   If removed, install the clutch components (see Chapter 8).
16   To make installation of the transaxle easier, it's a good idea to install guide pins in place of the two upper bolts **(see illustration)**. To make guide pins, cut the heads off a pair of extra bolts, taper the cut ends with a grinder, and cut screwdriver slots in the cut ends with a hacksaw.
17   With the transaxle secured to the jack with a chain, raise it into position behind the

engine, then carefully slide it forward, engaging the input shaft with the clutch plate hub splines. Do not use excessive force to install the transaxle - if the input shaft does not slide into place, readjust the angle of the transaxle so it is level and/or turn the input shaft so the splines engage properly with the clutch plate hub.
18   Install the transaxle-to-engine bolts. Tighten the bolts securely.
19   Install the transaxle mount nuts or bolts. **Caution:** *On later models, be sure to install the longer bolt in position number 2* **(see illustration)**. *If it is installed in position number 3 it may damage the selector shaft housing.*
20   Install the chassis and suspension components which were removed. Tighten all nuts and bolts securely.
21   Remove the jacks supporting the transaxle and engine.
22   Install the various items removed previously, referring to Chapter 8 for installation of the driveaxles and Chapter 4 for information regarding the exhaust system components.
23   Make a final check that all wires, hoses, linkages and the speedometer cable have been connected and that the transaxle has been filled with lubricant to the proper level (see Chapter 1).
24   Connect the negative battery cable.

Road test the vehicle for proper operation and check for leaks.

7   Manual transaxle overhaul - general information

Overhauling a manual transaxle is a difficult job for the do-it-yourselfer. It involves the disassembly and reassembly of many small parts. Numerous clearances must be precisely measured and, if necessary, changed with select-fit spacers and snap-rings. As a result, if transaxle problems arise, it can be removed and installed by a competent do-it-yourselfer, but overhaul should be left to a transmission repair shop. Rebuilt transaxles may be available - check with your dealer parts department and auto parts stores. At any rate, the time and money involved in an overhaul is almost sure to exceed the cost of a rebuilt unit.

Nevertheless, it's not impossible for an inexperienced mechanic to rebuild a transaxle if the special tools are available and the job is done in a deliberate step-by-step manner so nothing is overlooked.

The tools necessary for an overhaul include internal and external snap-ring pliers, a bearing puller, a slide hammer, a set of pin punches, a dial indicator and possibly a hydraulic press. In addition, a large, sturdy workbench and a vise or transaxle stand will be required.

During disassembly of the transaxle, make careful notes of how each piece comes off, where it fits in relation to other pieces and what holds it in place. Before taking the transaxle apart for repair, it will help if you have some idea what area of the transaxle is malfunctioning.

Certain problems can be closely tied to specific areas in the transaxle, which can make component examination and replacement easier. Refer to the *Troubleshooting* section at the front of this manual for information regarding possible sources of trouble.

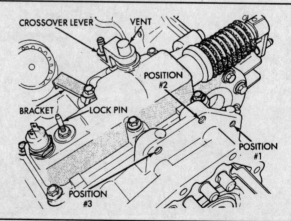

CROSSOVER LEVER   VENT

POSITION #2

BRACKET   LOCK PIN

POSITION #1

POSITION #3

6.19 On this type of left engine mount, the bolts in positions one and three are the same length - bolt number two is longer and must be installed in the correct hole

Chapter 7 Part B
Automatic transaxle

Contents

Specifications

Fluid type and capacity .... See Chapter 1

Torque specifications
Ft-lbs (unless otherwise noted)

Neutral start and back-up light switch	25
Shift cable adjustment bolt	105 in-lbs
Throttle pressure cable adjustment bracket lock bolt/screw	108 in-lbs
Transaxle case-to-engine bolts	70
Torque converter-to-driveplate bolts	55
Transaxle mount through-bolts	40
Transaxle mount attaching bolts	40

1 General information

All vehicles covered in this manual come equipped with either a five-speed manual transaxle or a three-speed or four-speed automatic transaxle. All information on the automatic transaxle is included in this Part of Chapter 7. Information on the manual transaxle can be found in Part A of this Chapter.

Due to the complexity of the automatic transaxle and the need for special equipment and expertise to perform most service operations, this Chapter contains only general diagnosis, seal replacement, adjustments and removal and installation procedures.

If the transaxle requires major repair work, it should be left to a dealer service department or an automotive or transmission repair shop. You can, however, remove and install the transaxle yourself and save the expense, even if the repair work is done by a transmission shop.

2 Diagnosis - general

Note: *Automatic transaxle malfunctions may be caused by four general conditions: Poor engine performance, improper adjustments, hydraulic malfunctions or mechanical malfunctions. Diagnosis of these problems should always begin with a check of the easily repaired items: Fluid level and condition (see Chapter 1), shift linkage adjustment and throttle linkage adjustment. Next, perform a road test to determine if the problem has been corrected or if more diagnosis is necessary. If the problem persists after the preliminary tests and corrections are completed, additional diagnosis should be done by a dealer service department or transmission repair shop. Refer to the Troubleshooting section at the front of this manual for transaxle problem diagnosis.*

Preliminary checks

1 Drive the vehicle to warm the transaxle to normal operating temperature.

2 Check the fluid level as described in Chapter 1:

a) *If the fluid level is unusually low, add enough fluid to bring the level within the designated area on the dipstick, then check for external leaks.*

b) *If the fluid level is abnormally high, drain off the excess, then check the drained fluid for contamination by coolant. The presence of engine coolant in the automatic transmission fluid indicates that a failure has occurred in the internal radiator walls that separate the coolant from the transmission fluid (see Chapter 3).*

c) *If the fluid is foaming, drain it and refill the transaxle, then check for coolant in the fluid or a high fluid level.*

3 Check the engine idle speed. **Note:** *If the engine is malfunctioning, don't proceed with the preliminary checks until it has been repaired and runs normally.*

4 Check the throttle pressure cable or rod

7B

for freedom of movement. Adjust it if necessary (see Section 4). **Note:** *The throttle pressure cable may function properly when the engine is shut off and cold, but it may malfunction once the engine is hot. Check it cold and at normal engine operating temperature.*

5   Inspect the shift cable (see Section 3). Make sure it's properly adjusted and operates smoothly.

Fluid leak diagnosis

6   Most fluid leaks are easy to locate visually. Repair usually consists of replacing a seal or gasket. If a leak is difficult to find, the following procedure may help.

7   Identify the fluid. Make sure it's transmission fluid and not engine oil or brake fluid (automatic transmission fluid is a deep red color).

8   Try to pinpoint the source of the leak. Drive the vehicle several miles, then park it over a large sheet of cardboard. After a minute or two, you should be able to locate the leak by determining the source of the fluid dripping onto the cardboard.

9   Make a careful visual inspection of the suspected component and the area immediately around it. Pay particular attention to gasket mating surfaces. A mirror is often helpful for finding leaks in areas that are hard to see.

10   If the leak still can't be found, clean the suspected area thoroughly with a degreaser or solvent, then dry it.

11   Drive the vehicle for several miles at normal operating temperature and varying speeds. After driving the vehicle, visually inspect the suspected component again.

12   Once the leak has been located, the cause must be determined before it can be properly repaired. If a gasket is replaced but the sealing flange is bent, the new gasket won't stop the leak. The bent flange must be straightened.

13   Before attempting to repair a leak, check to make sure the following conditions are corrected or they may cause another leak. **Note:** *Some of the following conditions can't be fixed without highly specialized tools and expertise. Such problems must be referred to a transmission shop or a dealer service department.*

Gasket leaks

14   Check the pan periodically. Make sure the bolts are all in place (none missing) and tight, the gasket is in good condition and the pan is flat (dents in the pan may indicate damage to the valve body inside).

15   If the pan gasket is leaking, the fluid level or the fluid pressure may be too high, the vent may be plugged, the pan bolts may be too tight, the pan sealing flange may be warped, the sealing surface of the transaxle housing may be damaged, the gasket may be damaged or the transaxle casting may be cracked or porous. If sealant is used in place of a gasket, it may be the wrong sealant.

Seal leaks

16   If a transaxle seal is leaking, the fluid

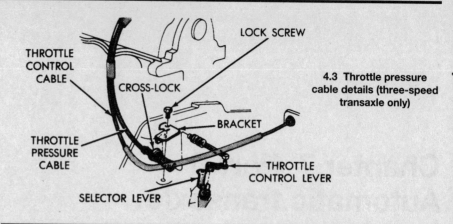

4.3 Throttle pressure cable details (three-speed transaxle only)

level or pressure may be too high, the vent may be plugged (these models are vented through the hollow dipstick), the seal bore may be damaged, the seal itself may be damaged or improperly installed, the surface of the shaft protruding through the seal may be damaged or a loose bearing may be causing excessive shaft movement.

17   Make sure the dipstick tube seal is in good condition and the tube is properly seated. Periodically check the area around the speedometer gear or sensor for leakage. If transmission fluid is evident, check the O-ring for damage. Also inspect the side gear shaft oil seals for leakage.

Case leaks

18   If the case itself appears to be leaking, the casting is porous and will have to be repaired or replaced.

19   Make sure the oil cooler hose fittings are tight and in good condition.

Fluid comes out the filler opening

20   If this condition occurs, the transaxle is overfilled, there is coolant in the fluid, the dipstick is incorrect, the vent is plugged or the drain back holes are plugged.

3   Shift cable - check and adjustment

Check

1   Check the operation of the transaxle in each shift lever position (try to start the engine in each position - the starter should operate in the Park and Neutral positions only).

Adjustment

2   Place the shift lever in Park.

3   Working in the engine compartment, loosen the shift cable clamp bolt on the transaxle bracket.

4   Pull the shift lever all the way to the front detent (Park position) by hand.

5   Keep pressure on the shift lever and tighten the cable clamp bolt.

6   Check the shift lever in the Neutral and Drive positions to make sure it's within the

confines of the lever stops. The engine should start only when the lever is in the Park or Neutral position.

4   Throttle pressure cable or rod - adjustment

Refer to illustration 4.3

1   The throttle pressure cable (four-cylinder models) or rod (V6 models) controls a valve in the transaxle which governs shift quality and speed. If shifting is harsh or erratic, the throttle pressure cable or rod should be adjusted.

2   The adjustment must be made with the engine at normal operating temperature.

Cable adjustment

3   Loosen the cable mounting bracket lock screw and position the bracket so the alignment tabs are in contact with the transaxle casting **(see illustration)**. Tighten the lock screw to the torque listed in this Chapter's Specifications.

4   Release the cross-lock on the cable assembly by pulling up on it. To ensure proper adjustment, the cable must be free to slide all the way toward the engine, against the stop, after the cross-lock is released.

5   Move the transaxle throttle control lever clockwise as far as possible (against the internal stop) and press the cross-lock down into the locked position.

6   Check the cable action. Move the transaxle throttle cable all the way forward, release it slowly and make sure it returns completely.

Rod adjustment

7   Loosen the adjustment swivel lock screw and make sure the swivel slides freely along the flat end of the throttle rod. If it doesn't, disassemble the linkage and clean or repair it as necessary.

8   Move the transaxle throttle lever toward the engine, hold it firmly against its stop, and tighten the lock screw to the torque listed in this Chapter's Specifications.

9   It's a good idea to lubricate the linkage at this point (see Chapter 1).

5.1 There are two switches at the lower front of the transaxle on four-speed modes (three-speeds have just one) - the switch on the right is the Neutral start and back-up light switch; the switch on the left is for the PRNDL indicator; the connector above the switches is for the output speed sensor

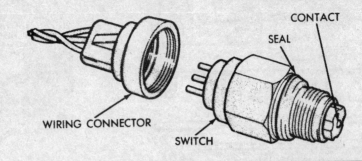

5.6 Neutral start and back-up light switch details

5 Neutral start and back-up light switch - check and replacement

Refer to illustrations 5.1 and 5.6

1   The Neutral start and back-up light switch is located at the lower front edge of the transaxle **(see illustration)**. The switch controls the back-up lights and the center terminal of the switch grounds the starter solenoid circuit when the transaxle is in Park or Neutral, allowing the engine to start.

2   Prior to checking the switch, make sure the shift cable is properly adjusted (see Section 3).

3   Unplug the connector and use an ohmmeter to check for continuity between the center terminal and the case. Continuity should exist only when the transaxle is in Park or Neutral.

4   Check for continuity between the two outer terminals. Continuity should exist only when the transaxle is in Reverse. No continuity should exist between either outer terminal and the case.

5   If the switch fails any of the tests, replace it with a new one.

6   Position a drain pan under the switch to catch the fluid released when the switch is removed. Unscrew the switch from the transaxle, using a box-end wrench to avoid damage to the switch housing **(see illustration)**.

7   Move the shift lever from Park to Neutral and check to see if the switch operating fingers are centered in the opening.

8   Wrap the threads of the new switch with Teflon tape, install it in the case and tighten it to the torque listed in this Chapter's Specifications. Plug in the connector and repeat the checks on the new switch.

9   Check the fluid level and add fluid as required (see Chapter 1).

6 Automatic transaxle - removal and installation

Removal

Refer to illustrations 6.7, 6.19, 6.20, 6.21, 6.22a and 6.22b

1   Disconnect the negative cable from the battery.

2   Raise the vehicle and support it securely on jackstands. Remove the front wheels.

3   Drain the transaxle fluid (see Chapter 1).

4   On V6 models, drain the cooling system and remove the coolant return extension (See Chapter 3).

5   Remove the torque converter cover and the left splash shield.

6   Remove the driveaxles from the transaxle (see Chapter 8).

7   Mark the torque converter and driveplate so they can be reinstalled in the same position **(see illustration)**.

8   Remove the torque converter-to-driveplate bolts. Turn the crankshaft to bring each bolt into view. The crankshaft bolt can be reached through an access cover in the passenger side splash shield.

9   Remove the starter motor (see Chapter 5).

10   Disconnect the speedometer cable (mechanical speedometer) or electrical connector (electronic speedometer) (see Chapter 7A).

11   Unplug the electrical connector from the Neutral start/back-up light switch. On four-speed transaxles, disconnect the PRNDL switch connector, output speed sensor connector, and input speed sensor connector as well **(see illustration 5.1)**. On models equipped with a lockup torque converter, disconnect the converter electrical connector near the dipstick.

12   On models so equipped, disconnect the vacuum hose(s).

13   Remove any exhaust components that will interfere with transaxle removal (see Chapter 4).

14   On three-speed transaxles, disconnect the throttle pressure cable or rod.

15   Disconnect the shift cable.

16   Support the engine with a hoist from above or a jack from below (position a block of wood between the jack and oil pan to spread the load).

17   Support the transaxle with a jack - preferably a special jack made for this purpose. Safety chains will help steady the transaxle on the jack.

18   Remove any chassis or suspension components that will interfere with transaxle removal.

7B

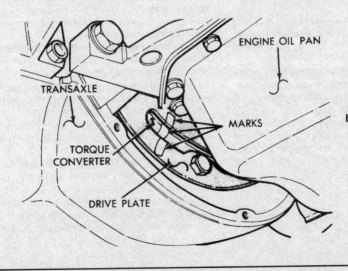

6.7 Mark across the torque converter and driveplate so they can be reassembled in the same way

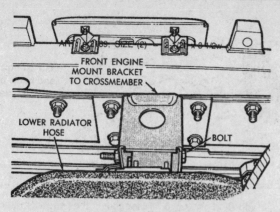

6.19 Remove the mounting bracket

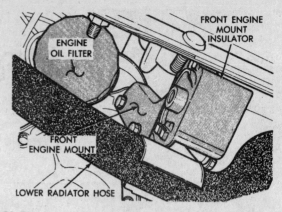

6.20 Remove the front mounting insulator through-bolt and unbolt the insulator from the transaxle

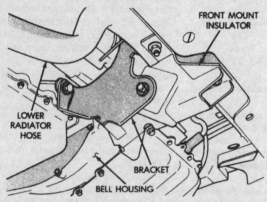

6.21 On four-speed models, remove this front engine mount

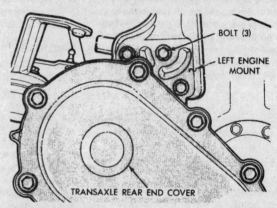

6.22a Remove the left engine mount attaching bolts . . .

Three-speed models

19   Remove the engine mount bracket from the front crossmember (see illustration).
20   Remove the front mounting insulator through-bolt and unbolt the insulator from the torque converter housing (see illustration).

Four-speed models

21   Remove the front engine mount insulator and its bracket (see illustration).

All models

22   Remove the left engine mount attaching bolts and through-bolt (see illustrations).
23   Remove the bolts securing the transaxle to the engine.
24   Lower the transaxle slightly and disconnect and plug the transaxle cooler lines.
25   Move the transaxle back to disengage it from the engine block dowel pins and make sure the torque converter is detached from the driveplate. Attach a small C-clamp to the transaxle case to prevent the torque converter from falling out during removal. Lower the transaxle from the vehicle.

Installation

26   Prior to installation, make sure the torque converter hub is securely engaged in the pump.
27   With the transaxle secured to the jack, raise it into position. Be sure to keep it level so the torque converter doesn't slide out. Connect the fluid cooler lines.
28   Turn the torque converter to line up the bolts with the holes in the driveplate. The marks on the torque converter and driveplate must line up.
29   Move the transaxle forward carefully until the dowel pins and transaxle housing are engaged.
30   Install the transaxle housing-to-engine bolts. Tighten them securely.
31   Install the torque converter-to-driveplate bolts. Tighten the bolts to the torque listed in this Chapter's Specifications.
32   Install the engine mounts and any suspension and chassis components that were removed. Tighten the bolts and nuts to the torque listed in this Chapter's Specifications.
33   Remove the jacks supporting the transaxle and engine.
34   Install the starter motor (see Chapter 5).
35   Connect the vacuum hose(s) (if equipped).
36   Connect the shift linkage (and throttle pressure linkage on three-speed models).
37   Attach the electrical connectors to the Neutral start/back-up light switch.
38   Install the torque converter cover and left splash shield.
39   Connect the driveaxles (see Chapter 8).
40   Connect the speedometer cable (mechanical speedometer).
41   Adjust the shift cable (see Section 3).
42   Install any exhaust system components that were removed or disconnected.
43   Lower the vehicle.
44   Fill the transaxle (see Chapter 1), run the vehicle and check for fluid leaks.

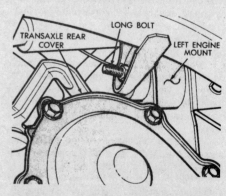

6.22b . . . and this long through-bolt

Chapter 8
Clutch and driveaxles

Contents

Specifications

Clutch disc lining thickness (minimum) 1/32-inch

Driveaxle dimensions
1989
Non-turbo models
A.C.I. — **Inch**
- Right ... 18-13/16 to 19-7/64
- Left ... 7-13/16 to 8-5/16

S.S.G.
- Right ... 18.0 to 18-1/2
- Left ... 7-13/64 to 7-29/32

S.S.G. 82-98
- Right ... 18-29/32 to 19-13/64
- Left ... 8-1/2 to 8-13/16

Turbo models
S.S.G.
Automatic
- Right ... 18.0 to 18-1/2
- Left ... 7-13/64 to 7-29/32
- Manual (right and left) ... 7-13/32 to 7-45/64

S.S.G. 82-98
Automatic
- Right ... 18-29/32 to 19-13/64
- Left ... 8-1/2 to 8-13/16
- Manual (right and left) ... 8-1/2 to 8-13/16

Driveaxle dimensions (continued)

1990
Non-turbo models
  A.C.I.
    Right.. 18-13/16 to 19-7/64
    Left... 7-13/16 to 8-5/16
  S.S.G.
    Right.. 18.0 to 18-1/2
    Left... 7-13/64 to 7-29/32
  S.S.G. 82-98
    Right.. 18-29/32 to 19-13/64
    Left... 8-1/2 to 8-13/16
Turbo models
  S.S.G.
    Automatic
      Right .... 18.0 to 18-1/2
      Left.. 7-13/64 to 7-29/32
    Manual (right and left)... 7-13/32 to 7-45/64
  S.S.G. 82-98
    Automatic
      Right .... 18-29/32 to 19-13/64
      Left.. 8-1/2 to 8-13/16
    Manual (right and left)... 8-1/2 to 8-13/16
1991 on
Non-turbo models
  Automatic
    Right.. 17.0 to 17-1/2
    Left... 6-29/32 to 7-19/64
  Manual
    Right.. 17.0 to 17-1/2
    Left... 6-1/2 to 6-292/32
Turbo models
  Automatic
    Right.. 17 to 17-1/2
    Left... 6-29/32 to 7-19/64
Manual
  2.5L Turbo (right and left) .... 6-1/2 to 6-29/32
  2.2L Turbo III (right and left) .... 7-19/32 to 8.0

Torque specifications

	Ft-lbs
Pressure plate-to-flywheel bolts	21
Bearing bracket bolts for intermediate shaft	21
Driveaxle nut	180

1   General information

The information in this Chapter deals with the components from the rear of the engine to the front (drive) wheels (except for the transaxle, which is covered in the previous Chapter). In this Chapter, the components are grouped into two categories: Clutch and driveaxles. Separate Sections within this Chapter offer general information, checks and repair procedures for components in each of the two groups. **Warning:** *Since nearly all the procedures included in this Chapter involve working under the vehicle, make sure it's securely supported on sturdy jackstands or on a hoist where it can be easily raised and lowered.*

2   Clutch - description and check

1   All vehicles with a manual transaxle have a single dry plate, diaphragm spring-type clutch. The clutch disc has a splined hub which allows it to slide along the splines of the transaxle input shaft or mainshaft. The clutch disc is held in place against the flywheel by the pressure plate springs. During disengagement (when shifting gears for example), the clutch pedal is depressed, which operates a cable, actuating the release lever so the release bearing or plate pushes on the pressure plate springs, disengaging the clutch.
2   The release mechanism incorporates a self-adjusting device which compensates for clutch disc wear (see illustration 3.2). A spring in the clutch pedal arm maintains tension on the cable and the adjuster pivot grabs the positioner adjuster when the pedal is depressed and the clutch is released. Consequently, the slack is always taken up in the cable, making adjustment unnecessary.
3   When pressure is applied to the pedal to release the clutch, the cable pulls against the end of the release lever, which turns a shaft connected to the clutch release fork. As the fork pivots, the release bearing pushes against the fingers of the diaphragm springs in the pressure plate assembly, which in turn disengages the clutch plate.
4   Terminology can be a problem when discussing the clutch components because common names are in some cases different

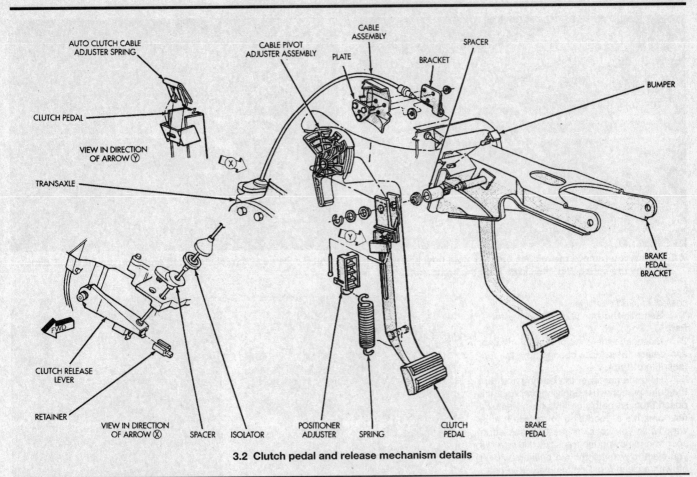

AUTO CLUTCH CABLE ADJUSTER SPRING

CLUTCH PEDAL

VIEW IN DIRECTION OF ARROW Ⓨ

TRANSAXLE

CLUTCH RELEASE LEVER

RETAINER

VIEW IN DIRECTION OF ARROW Ⓧ

FWD

SPACER

ISOLATOR

CABLE PIVOT ADJUSTER ASSEMBLY

PLATE

CABLE ASSEMBLY

SPACER

BRACKET

BUMPER

BRAKE PEDAL BRACKET

POSITIONER ADJUSTER

SPRING

CLUTCH PEDAL

BRAKE PEDAL

3.2 Clutch pedal and release mechanism details

from those used by the manufacturer. For example, the clutch disc is also called the clutch plate or driven plate, the clutch release bearing is sometimes called a throwout bearing and the release fork is sometimes called the release lever.

5   Other than to replace components with obvious damage, some preliminary checks should be performed to diagnose clutch problems.

a) *The first check should be of the clutch cable adjustment (if applicable). If there's too much slack in the cable, the clutch won't release completely, making gear engagement difficult or impossible.*

b) *To check clutch "spin-down time," run the engine at normal idle speed with the transaxle in Neutral (clutch pedal up - engaged). Disengage the clutch (pedal down), wait several seconds and shift the transaxle into Reverse. No grinding noise should be heard. A grinding noise would most likely indicate a problem in the pressure plate or the clutch disc.*

c) *To check for complete clutch release, run the engine (with the parking brake applied to prevent vehicle movement) and hold the clutch pedal approximately 1/2-inch from the floor. Shift the transaxle between First and Reverse gear several times. If the shift is rough, component failure is indicated, or as*

stated above, the cable is out of adjustment.

d) *Visually inspect the pivot bushing at the top of the clutch pedal to make sure there's no binding or excessive play.*

e) *A clutch pedal that's difficult to operate is most likely caused by a faulty clutch cable. Check the cable where it enters the housing for frayed wires, rust and other signs of corrosion. If it looks good, lubricate the cable with penetrating oil. If pedal operation improves, the cable is worn out and should be replaced.*

3   Clutch cable - removal and installation

Refer to illustration 3.2

1   Raise the front of the vehicle and support it securely on jackstands. Apply the parking brake and block the rear wheels so the vehicle can't roll off the stands.

2   On 1989 and 1990 models, remove the clip and disengage the cable housing from the retainer bracket on the strut tower **(see illustration)**.

3   Remove the clutch cable retainer and disengage the cable end from the clutch release lever on the transmission **(see illustration 3.2)**.

4   Pull the lower end of the cable out of the

grommet in the transmission mount.

5   Working inside the vehicle, disengage the cable end from the clutch pedal.

6   Pull the cable through the firewall to remove it. On 1991 and later models, pass the cable through the hoop on the strut tower.

7   When installing the new cable, hook the ends to the pedal and transmission lever first, then pull on the housing and engage the cable in the retainer bracket. On 1989 and 1990 models, don't forget to install the clip.

8   Operate the pedal several times to allow the self-adjuster mechanism to take up slack in the cable.

4   Clutch release bearing and release fork - removal and installation

Refer to illustrations 4.2, 4.4a, 4.4b and 4.4c
Warning: *Dust produced by clutch wear and deposited on clutch components may contain asbestos, which is a health hazard. DO NOT blow it out with compressed air or inhale any of it. DO NOT use gasoline or petroleum-based solvents to clean off the dust. Brake system cleaner should be used to flush the dust into a drain pan. After the clutch components are wiped clean with rags, dispose of the contaminated rags and cleaner in a*

8

4.2 Before you remove the release bearing, note how it's retained by the spring clip, then slide it off the input shaft

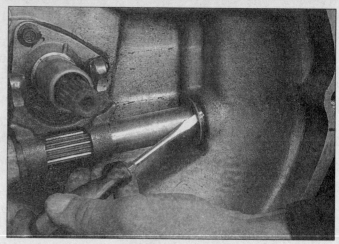

4.4a To Remove the release shaft and fork, pry off this E-clip . . .

sealed, marked container.

1   Remove the transaxle (see Chapter 7, Part A).

2   Disengage the ends of the wire retainer and detach the release bearing from the fork **(see illustration)**.

3   Hold the center of the bearing and turn the outer portion while applying pressure. If it doesn't turn smoothly or if it's noisy, install a new one. It's a good idea to replace it anyway, when you consider the time and effort spent on removing the transaxle. However, if you elect to reinstall the old bearing, wipe it off with a clean rag. Don't immerse the bearing in solvent - it's sealed for life and would be ruined by the solvent.

4   Check the release fork ends for excessive wear. If the fork must be replaced, remove the E-clip from the clutch release shaft, slide the shaft out of the clutch housing and remove the fork **(see illustrations)**.

5   If the shaft bushings are worn, replace them.

6   Lubricate the release shaft bushings with high-temperature grease, slide the shaft part way into the housing and hold the fork in position. Continue to slide the shaft into place, through the fork, until it seats in the inner bushing.

7   Install the E-clip in the shaft groove. Make sure it's seated correctly.

8   Lubricate the release fork ends with a small amount of high-temperature grease (don't overdo it). Lubricate the release bearing bore with the same grease.

9   Install the release bearing on the fork. Make sure the wire retainer is properly engaged.

10   Install the transaxle.

5   Clutch components - removal, inspection and installation

Warning: *Dust produced by clutch wear and deposited on clutch components may contain asbestos, which is a health hazard. DO*

4.4b . . . slide the shaft out far enough to pull off the housing . . .

NOT blow it out with compressed air or inhale any of it. DO NOT use gasoline or petroleum-based solvents to clean off the dust. Brake system cleaner should be used to flush the dust into a drain pan. After the clutch components are wiped clean with rags, dispose of the contaminated rags and cleaner in a sealed, marked container.

Removal

Refer to illustration 5.6

1   Access to the clutch components is normally accomplished by removing the transaxle, leaving the engine in the vehicle. Of course, if the engine is being removed for major overhaul, then check the clutch for wear and replace worn components as necessary. However, the relatively low cost of the clutch components, compared to the time and trouble spent gaining access to them, warrants their replacement anytime the engine or transaxle is removed (unless they're new or in near perfect condition). The following procedures are based on the assumption the engine will stay in place.

2   Referring to Chapter 7, Part A, remove the transaxle from the vehicle. Support the

4.4c . . . slide off the fork and remove the shaft

engine while the transaxle is out. Preferably, an engine hoist should be used to support it from above. However, if a jack is used underneath the engine, make sure a piece of wood is positioned between the jack and oil pan to spread the load. **Caution:** *The pick-up for the oil pump is very close to the bottom of the oil pan. If the pan is bent or distorted in any way, engine oil starvation could occur.*

3   The clutch release fork and release bearing can remain attached to the transaxle housing (see Section 4 for the procedures to follow when checking and replacing the release bearing and related components).

4   To support the clutch disc during removal, install a clutch alignment tool through the clutch disc hub.

5   Carefully inspect the flywheel and pressure plate for indexing marks. The marks are usually an X, an O or a white letter. If they can't be found, scribe marks yourself so the pressure plate and flywheel will be in the same alignment during installation.

6   Loosen the pressure plate-to-flywheel bolts a little at a time, following a criss-cross pattern, until all spring pressure is relieved. Hold the pressure plate in place and remove

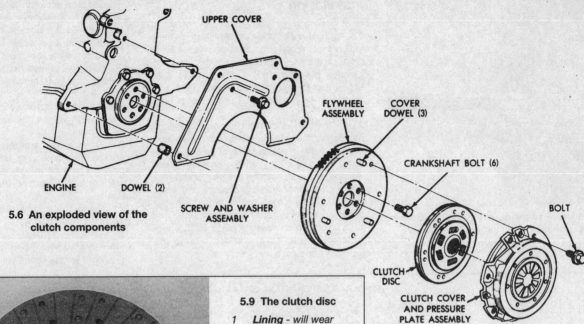

5.6 An exploded view of the clutch components

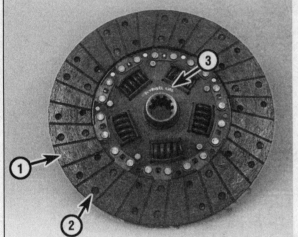

5.9 The clutch disc

1 **Lining** - will wear down in use
2 **Rivets** - secure the lining and will damage the pressure plate or flywheel surface if allowed to contact it
3 **Marks** - "flywheel side" or something similar

the bolts, then detach the pressure plate and clutch disc **(see illustration)**.

Inspection

Refer to illustrations 5.9 and 5.11

7 Ordinarily, when a problem occurs in the clutch, it can be attributed to wear of the clutch disc. However, all components should be inspected at this time. **Note:** *If the clutch components are contaminated with oil, there will be shiny, black, glazed spots on the*

clutch disc lining, which will cause the clutch to slip. Replacing clutch components won't completely solve the problem - be sure to check the crankshaft rear oil seal and the transaxle input shaft/mainshaft seal for leaks. If it looks like a seal is leaking, be sure to install a new one to avoid the same problem with a new clutch.

8 Inspect the flywheel for cracks, heat checking, grooves and other obvious defects. If the imperfections are slight, a

machine shop can machine the surface flat and smooth, which is highly recommended regardless of the surface appearance. Refer to Chapter 2, Part A, for the flywheel removal and installation procedure.

9 Inspect the lining on the clutch disc. There should be at least 1/32-inch of lining above the rivet heads. Check for loose rivets, distortion, cracks, broken springs and other obvious damage **(see illustration)**. As mentioned above, ordinarily the clutch disc is routinely replaced, so if in doubt about its condition, replace it with a new one.

10 The release bearing should also be replaced along with the clutch disc (see Section 4).

11 Check the machined surfaces and the diaphragm spring fingers of the pressure plate **(see illustration)**. If the surface is scored or otherwise damaged, replace the pressure plate. Also check for obvious damage, distortion, cracks, etc. Light glazing can be removed with emery cloth. If the pressure plate must be replaced, new and factory-rebuilt units are available.

8

 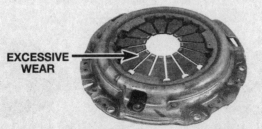 

NORMAL FINGER WEAR | EXCESSIVE FINGER WEAR | BROKEN OR BENT FINGERS

5.11 Replace the pressure plate if excessive wear or damage is noted

5.13 Use an alignment tool to center the clutch disc, then tighten the pressure plate bolts

Installation

Refer to illustration 5.13

12 Before installation, clean the flywheel and pressure plate machined surfaces with lacquer thinner, acetone or brake system cleaner. It's important to keep these surfaces, and the clutch disc lining, clean and free of oil or grease. Handle the parts only with clean hands.

13 Position the clutch disc and pressure plate against the flywheel with the clutch held in place with an alignment tool **(see illustration)**. Make sure it's installed properly (most replacement clutch plates will be marked "flywheel side" or something similar - if it's not marked, install the clutch disc with the damper springs toward the transaxle).

14 Tighten the pressure plate-to-flywheel bolts only finger tight, working around the pressure plate.

15 Center the clutch disc by ensuring the alignment tool extends through the splined hub and into the pocket in the crankshaft. Wiggle the tool up, down or side-to-side as needed to center the disc. Tighten the pressure plate-to-flywheel bolts a little at a time, working in a criss-cross pattern to prevent cover distortion. After all the bolts are snug, tighten them to the torque listed in this Chapter's Specifications. Remove the alignment tool.

16 Using high-temperature grease, lubricate the release bearing (see Section 4). Also apply a light coat of grease on the release lever contact areas and the transaxle input shaft.

17 Install the clutch release bearing as described in Section 4.

18 Install the transaxle and all components removed previously. Tighten all fasteners to the proper torque specifications.

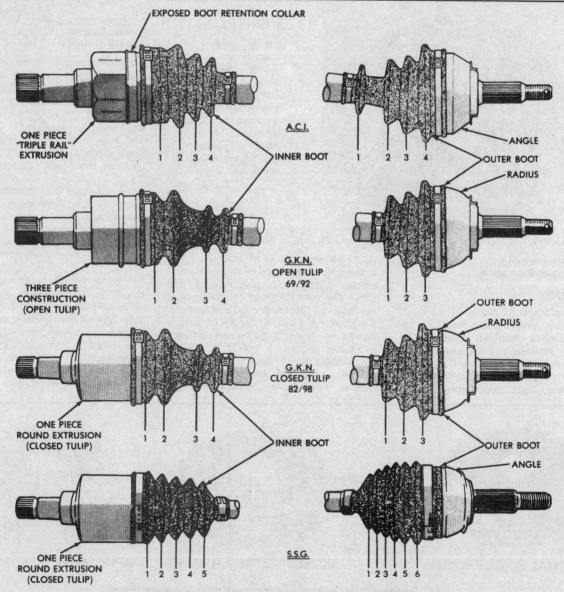

6.4a Use this chart to identify the driveaxles (early models) . . .

6   Driveaxles - general information and inspection

General information

Refer to illustrations 6.4a and 6.4b

Power from the engine passes through the clutch and transaxle to the front wheels via two driveaxles. Non-turbo models have unequal length driveaxles; most turbo models use equal-length driveaxles. On most turbo models, the inner end of the right driveaxle is connected to an intermediate shaft; the point at which the two are connected is supported by a bearing and bracket. The inner end of the intermediate shaft is connected to the differential side gear via a Cardan-type joint.

Each driveaxle assembly consists of three parts: A "tripod" type inner CV joint, an "Rzeppa" type outer CV joint and an axle-shaft which connects the two. Outer CV joint housings on both equal and unequal length driveaxles have a splined stub axle which engages with the front hub and is retained by a large nut. Inner CV joint housings have a short, splined stub axle which engages with the differential side gear (the CV joint housing for the right driveaxle on equal length systems engages with the intermediate shaft). The inner splined end of the CV joint housing is held in place by a spring inside the CV joint housing which pushes the housing toward the transaxle, keeping the stub axle fully seated in the differential side gears.

As the driveaxles move through their range of travel, ball bearings inside the CV joint housings allow them to operate at various lengths and angles. These bearings must be lubricated with special grease and protected by rubber boots. You should periodically inspect these boots for tears and/or grease leaking out. Torn boots allow dirt and moisture to enter the CV joints; if not fixed, a simple tear accelerates bearing wear and eventually causes premature failure.

The vehicles covered by this manual can be equipped with driveaxles manufactured by ACI, GKN, SSG or Saginaw **(see illustrations)**. If, after referring to the illustration, you're still unable to determine the manufacturer, take the driveaxle assembly with you when buying boots or CV joint parts. Don't try to substitute one brand of driveaxle for another or swap parts from one brand to another.

Inspection

Periodically, inspect the boots for leaks, damage and deterioration (see Chapter 1). Replace damaged CV joint boots immediately or the CV joints may be damaged. You must remove the driveaxle (see Section 7) to replace the boots. Some auto parts stores carry a convenient alternative: "Split-type" replacement boots can be installed without removing the driveaxle from the vehicle. This design is handy for emergency repairs when you're traveling, but it's not a substitute for one-piece boots. When a boot is torn, you

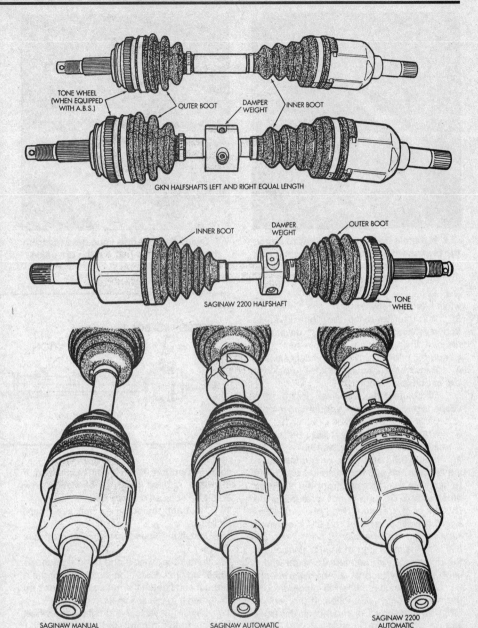

6.4b . . . this chart identifies driveaxles used on later models

must remove the driveaxle and disassemble, clean and inspect the CV joint to make sure no moisture and dirt - which greatly accelerate bearing wear - have already caused damage.

The most common symptom of worn or damaged CV joints, besides lubricant leaks, is a clicking noise in turns, a clunk when accelerating from a coasting condition or vibration at highway speeds.

To check for wear in the CV joints and driveaxle shafts, grasp each axle (one at a time) and rotate it in both directions while holding the CV joint housings. Watch for movement, indicating worn splines or sloppy CV joints. Also, check the driveaxle shafts for cracks and distortion.

7   Driveaxles - removal and installation

Removal

Refer to illustrations 7.2, 7.7 and 7.8

1   Remove the wheel cover (or hub cover). Remove the front hub nut cotter pin, nut lock and wave washer, if equipped. With the weight of the vehicle on the wheels, loosen the hub nut.

2   Loosen the wheel lug nuts, raise the front of the vehicle and support it securely on jackstands (apply the parking brake and block the rear wheels). Remove the lug nuts, the front wheel, the hub nut and the big

7.2 If there's no assistant handy to apply the brakes while you unscrew the hub nut, use a large screwdriver or pry bar to immobilize the hub

7.7 Swing the steering knuckle away from the transaxle and pull out the driveaxle

7.8 Pry the inner end of the CV joint out of the differential side gears with a large screwdriver or pry bar

washer **(see illustration)**.

3   If you're removing the right driveaxle from a vehicle with unequal length driveaxles, remove the speedometer drive gear (see Chapter 7) prior to removing the right axle.

4   Remove the steering knuckle-to-balljoint clamp bolt (see Chapter 10).

5   Disconnect the stabilizer bar from the suspension arm to allow enough movement to separate the balljoint (see Chapter 10).

6   Pry the lower balljoint stud out of the steering knuckle (see Chapter 10).

7   Grasp the outer CV joint and the steering knuckle and pull the steering knuckle out to separate the driveaxle from the hub **(see illustration)**. Be careful not to damage the CV joint boot. **Caution:** *Don't pry on or damage the wear sleeve on the CV joint when separating it from the hub.*

8   Pry the inner end of the CV joint out of the differential (or intermediate shaft) with a large screwdriver or pry bar **(see illustration)**.

9   The driveaxles, when in place, secure the hub bearing assemblies. If the vehicle must be supported or moved on the front wheels while the driveaxles are out, install bolts through the hubs and thread nuts onto them to keep the bearings from loosening.

Installation

10   Prior to installation, clean the wear sleeve on the driveaxle outer CV joint and the seal in the hub. Lubricate the entire circumference of the seal lip and fill the seal cavity with grease. Apply a 1/4-inch bead of grease to the wear sleeve seal contact area as well.

11   Apply a small amount of multi-purpose grease to the splines at each end of the driveaxle. Place the driveaxle in position and carefully insert the inner end of the shaft into the transaxle.

12   Push the steering knuckle out and insert the outer splined shaft of the CV joint into the hub.

13   Insert the balljoint stud into the steering knuckle, install the clamp bolt and tighten it to the torque listed in the Chapter 10 Specifi-

cations. **Caution:** *This is a self-locking bolt. If it's worn, replace it with an equivalent new bolt. Don't use an ordinary bolt.*

14   Reattach the stabilizer bar (see Chapter 10).

15   Install the speedometer drive gear (see Chapter 7).

16   Install the wheels and hand tighten the wheel lug nuts. Install the spacer washer and hub nut and tighten the nut securely (don't try to tighten it to the specified torque yet).

17   Lower the vehicle and tighten the wheel lug nuts to the torque listed in the Chapter 1 Specifications.

18   Tighten the driveaxle hub nut to the torque listed in this Chapter's Specifications, then install the wave washer, nut lock and a new cotter pin.

Driveaxle position check

Refer to illustration 7.21

19   All models have engine mounts with slotted holes that allow for side-to-side positioning of the engine. If the vertical bolts on the right or left upper engine mounts have been loosened for any reason, or if the vehicle has been damaged structurally at the front end, driveaxle length must be checked/corrected. A driveaxle that's shorter than required will result in objectionable noise, while a driveaxle that's longer than necessary may result in damage.

20   The vehicle must be completely assembled, the front wheels must be properly

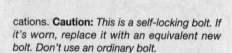

7.21 Measure the distance between arrows to verify that the driveaxle is the correct length when installed

aligned and pointing straight ahead and the weight of the vehicle must be on all four wheels.

21   Using a tape measure, check the distance from the inner edge on the outside of the boot to the inner edge of inside the boot on both driveaxles. Take the measurement at the lower edge of the driveaxles (six o'clock position) **(see illustration)**. Compare the measurement with the length listed in this Chapter's Specifications. Note that the required dimension varies with transaxle type and driveaxle manufacturer **(see illustrations 6.4a and 6.4b** to identify the driveaxle type).

22   If the dimensions aren't as specified, the mount bolts can be loosened and the engine repositioned to obtain the specified driveaxle lengths. If the engine can't be moved enough within the range of the slotted engine mounts, check for damaged or distorted support brackets and side rails.

23   If the engine is moved, see Chapter 7 and adjust the shift linkage.

8   Intermediate shaft (turbo models only) - removal and installation

Removal

Refer to illustration 8.3

1   Remove the right driveaxle (see Section 7).

2   Remove the speedometer drive gear

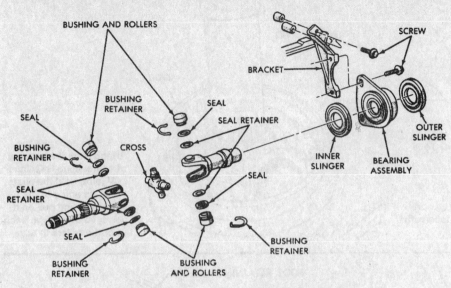

BUSHING AND ROLLERS

BRACKET · SCREW

SEAL · SEAL RETAINER · OUTER SLINGER

BUSHING RETAINER · SEAL

SEAL · CROSS · INNER SLINGER · BEARING ASSEMBLY

BUSHING RETAINER

SEAL RETAINER · SEAL

SEAL · BUSHING RETAINER

BUSHING RETAINER · BUSHING AND ROLLERS · BUSHING RETAINER

8.3 Exploded view of the intermediate shaft assembly

from the transaxle extension housing (see Chapter 7).

3   Remove the bearing bracket mounting bolts **(see illustration)**.

4   Place a drain pan underneath the right side of the transaxle to catch any lubricant that leaks out during removal of the intermediate shaft. Grasp the intermediate shaft securely with both hands and pull it out of the transaxle.

Installation

5   Place the intermediate shaft and bearing assembly in position and carefully insert the splined stub axle into the transaxle.

6   Place the bearing bracket in position, install the bracket mounting bolts and tighten them to the torque listed in this Chapter's Specifications.

7   Lubricate the splines inside the pilot

bore of the intermediate shaft with a liberal amount of multi-purpose grease.

8   Install the right driveaxle (see Section 7).

9   Check and, if necessary, add the recommended type of transaxle lubricant to bring it up to the proper level (see Chapter 1).

9   Constant velocity (CV) joints - disassembly, inspection and reassembly

1   Loosen the hub nut and the wheel lug nuts, then raise the vehicle and support it securely on jackstands.

2   Remove the driveaxles (see Section 7) and identify which types of CV joints are installed (see Section 6).

3   Place one of the driveaxles in a vise, using wood blocks to protect it from the vise jaws. If the CV joint has been operating properly with no noise or vibration, replace the boot as described in Section 10. If the CV joint is badly worn or has run for some time with no lubricant due to a damaged boot, it should be disassembled and inspected.

Inner CV joint

Refer to illustrations 9.4 through 9.8, 9.10, 9.11a, 9.11b, 9.12, 9.18, 9.19, 9.24 and 9.27

4   Remove the clamps and slide the boot back to gain access to the tripod **(see illustration)**. Depending on the type of CV joint involved, separate the tripod from the housing as follows.

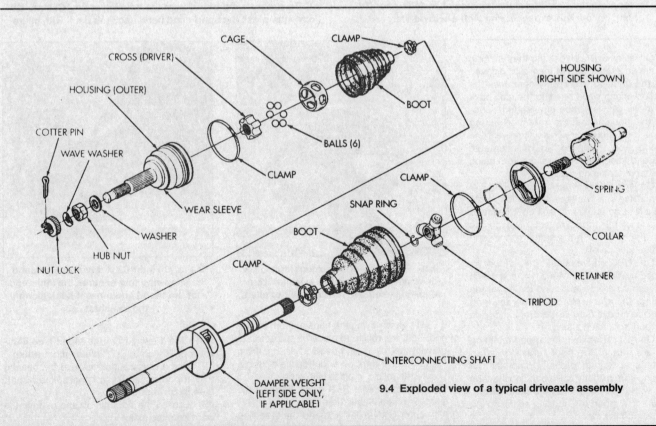

9.4 Exploded view of a typical driveaxle assembly

8

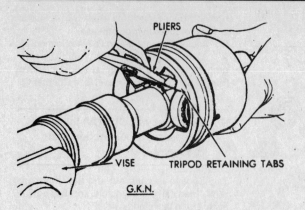

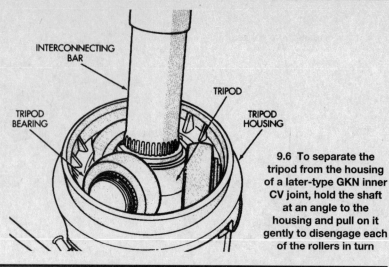

9.5 To separate the tripod from the housing of an early-type GKN inner CV joint, bend up the retaining tabs with a pair of pliers

9.6 To separate the tripod from the housing of a later-type GKN inner CV joint, hold the shaft at an angle to the housing and pull on it gently to disengage each of the rollers in turn

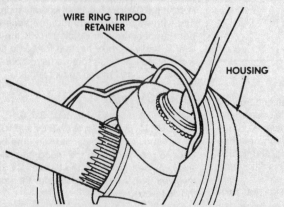

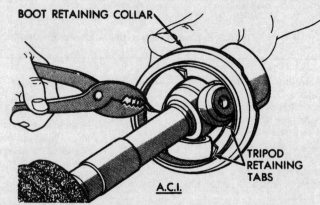

9.7 To separate the tripod from the housing of an SSG inner CV joint, pry out this expander ring with a screwdriver

9.8 To separate the tripod from the housing of an ACI inner CV joint, compress the spring and bend each tab back with pliers

5   On early GKN driveaxles, the retaining tabs are an integral part of the housing cover. Hold the housing and lightly compress the retention spring while bending the tabs back with a pair of pliers **(see illustration)**. Support the housing as the retention spring pushes it off the tripod. This will prevent the housing from reaching an unacceptable angle and keep the tripod rollers from being pulled from the tripod studs.

6   On later GKN driveaxles, secure the CV joint housing in a vise **(see illustration)**. Hold the shaft at an angle and pull on it gently to free one of the tripod rollers. Detach the other tripod rollers in the same manner and take the housing off.

7   On SSG driveaxles, the tripod is retained in the housing with a wire ring which expands into a groove around the top of the housing. Using a screwdriver, pry this ring out of the groove **(see illustration)** and slide the tripod from the housing.

8   On ACI driveaxles, the tripod retaining tabs are part of the boot retaining collar, which is staked in place. Compress the retaining spring lightly while bending the tabs back with a pair of pliers **(see illustration)**. Be sure to support the housing as the spring pushes it off the tripod.

9.10 The tripod on all except later GKN driveaxles is held on the axleshaft by a snap-ring - remove it with a pair of pliers

9   When removing the housing from the tripod, hold the rollers in place on the studs to prevent the rollers and needle bearings from falling. After the tripod is out of the housing, secure the rollers in place with tape.

10   All except later GKN axles: Remove the snap-ring **(see illustration)**.

11   Later GKN axles: Expand the stop ring

9.11a On later GKN driveaxles, expand the snap-ring that secures the inner end of the tripod and move it back along the axleshaft . . .

and slide it away from the tripod **(see illustration)**. Pry off the circlip **(see illustration)**.

12   Use a brass punch to drive the bearing and tripod assembly off the splined shaft **(see illustration)**.

13   Loosen the boot clamp and remove the boot from the axle.

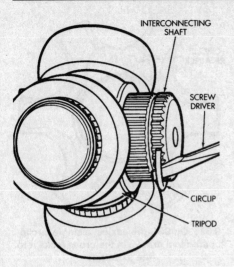

9.11b ... then pry off the circlip with
a screwdriver

9.12 Secure the bearings with tape and
drive the tripod off the shaft with a brass
punch and hammer

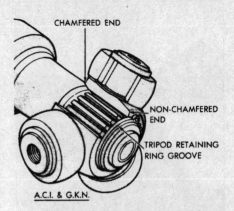

9.18 On ACI and early GKN CV joints, the
non-chamfered end of the tripod must
face out when installed on the
driveaxle splines

14   Clean the grease from the tripod assembly. Check for score marks, wear, corrosion and excessive play. Replace any damaged or worn components.
15   Inspect the inner splined area of the bearing tripod for wear and damage. Replace parts as necessary.
16   Remove all old grease from the housing. Inspect the housing splines, ball races, spring, spring cup and the spherical end of the shaft for wear, damage, nicks and corrosion. Replace parts as necessary.
17   Install the new boot on the axle.
18   On ACI and early GKN driveaxles, slide the tripod onto the shaft with the non-chamfered end facing out (next to the snap-ring groove) (see illustration).
19   On later GKN driveaxles, slide the stop ring into its groove on the driveaxle. Install the tripod with its internally chamfered side toward the stop ring (see illustration), then install the circlip. Try to pull the tripod off the shaft by hand; if it comes off, the circlip isn't properly seated.
20   SSG driveaxles are equipped with tripods that can be installed with either end out (both sides are the same). Be sure to

install the wire ring tripod retainer on the driveaxle shaft before sliding the tripod onto the shaft.
21   If necessary, use a section of pipe or a socket and hammer to carefully tap the tripod onto the shaft until it just clears the snap-ring groove.
22   Install a new snap-ring or circlip and make sure it's seated in the groove.
23   On ACI driveaxles, distribute one of the two supplied packets of grease in the boot and the remaining packet in the housing. On early GKN driveaxles, distribute two of the three or four packets of grease supplied with the kit in the boot and the remaining packet(s) in the housing. On later GKN and all SSG driveaxles, distribute half the supplied grease in the boot and the other half in the housing. Make sure the grease is applied to the bearing grooves in the housing.
24   Position the spring in the housing spring pocket with the cup attached to the exposed end of the spring (see illustration). Apply a small amount of grease to the concave surface of the spring cup.
25   On early GKN driveaxles, slip the tripod into the housing and bend the retaining ring tabs down to their original positions. Make sure the tabs retain the tripod in the housing.

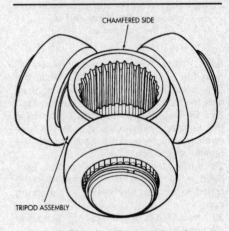

9.19 The chamfer must face in

26   On later GKN driveaxles, secure the shaft in a vise and position the housing over the rollers. Hold the housing at an angle and push it down over each of the tripod rollers in turn so the rollers lock into the housing. Make sure the rollers are locked into the housing.
27   On ACI driveaxles, slip the tripod into the housing but don't bend the retaining tabs (see illustration) back to their original posi-

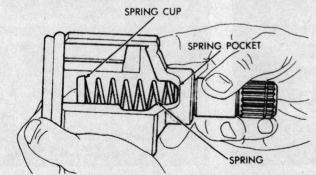

9.24 When assembling the inner CV joint, make sure the spring is
seated securely in the spring pocket and the spring cup is
installed in the outer end

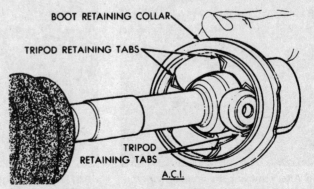

9.27 On ACI driveaxles, press the housing onto the tripod - but
don't try to bend the retaining tabs back to their original positions

8

9.32a On ACI and GKN driveaxles, give the outer CV joint housing a sharp tap with a soft-face hammer to disengage it from the internal circlip installed in a groove on the outer end of the axleshaft . . .

9.32b . . . and remove the outer CV joint from the housing

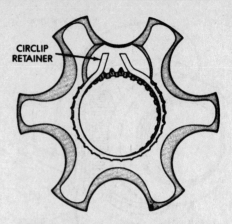

9.32c On SSG driveaxles, a single circlip located in a groove in the cross locks it to the axleshaft

tions. Reattach the boot instead, which will hold the housing on the shaft. When the driveaxle is reinstalled on the vehicle, make sure the tripod is re-engaged in the housing.

28 On SSG driveaxles, install the tripod in the housing and secure it with the wire retainer. Try to pull the housing off; the retainer should hold it on.

29 Make sure the retention spring is centered in the housing spring pocket when the tripod is installed and seated in the spring cup.

30 Install the boot and retaining clamp (see Section 10).

Outer CV joint

Refer to illustrations 9.32a, 9.32b, 9.32c, 9.36, 9.37, 9.38, 9.39, 9.42, 9.46a, 9.46b and 9.50

31 Remove the boot clamps and push the boot back.

32 Wipe the grease out of the joint. Use a soft-face hammer to drive the housing off the axle **(see illustrations)**. Support the CV joint as this is done and rap the housing sharply on the outer edge to dislodge it from the internal circlip installed on the shaft. On SSG driveaxles (axleshaft equipped with a damper weight), a single circlip located in a groove on the cross locks it to the axleshaft **(see illustration)**. To remove this type, mark the position of the damper weight, loosen the damper weight bolts, slide the weight and the boot toward the inner joint, remove the circlip with snap-ring pliers and slide the inner joint off the axle.

33 Slide the boot off the driveaxle. If the CV joint was operating properly and the grease doesn't appear to be contaminated, just replace the boot (see Section 10). Skip the following disassembly procedure. If the CV joint was noisy or the grease was contaminated, proceed with the disassembly procedure to determine if it should be replaced with a new one.

34 Remove the circlip from the driveaxle groove and discard it (the rebuild kit will

include a new circlip). GKN and ACI driveaxles are equipped with a large spacer ring, which must not be removed unless the driveaxle is being replaced with a new one.

35 Clean the axle spline area and check the splines for wear, damage and corrosion.

36 Clean the outer CV joint bearing assembly with a clean cloth to remove excess grease. Mark the relative position of the bearing cage, cross and housing **(see illustration)**.

37 Grip the housing shaft securely in the wood blocks in the vise. Push down one side of the cage and remove the ball bearing from the opposite side. Repeat the procedure in a criss-cross pattern until all of the balls are removed **(see illustration)**. If the joint is tight, tap on the cross (not the cage) with a hammer and brass punch.

38 Remove the bearing cage assembly from the housing by tilting it vertically and aligning two opposing elongated cage windows in the area between the ball grooves **(see illustration)**.

39 Turn the cross 90-degrees to the cage and align one of the spherical lands with an

9.36 After removing the grease, mark the bearing cage, cross and housing to ensure that they're reinstalled in the same relationship to one another

9.37 With the cage and cross lifted like this, remove the ball bearings one at a time

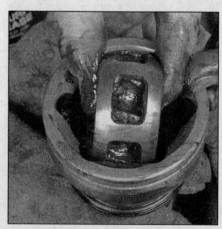

9.38 Tilt the cross and cage 90-degrees, then align the windows in the cage with the lands and rotate the cross up and out of the housing

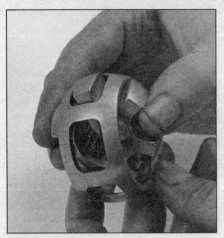

9.39 Turn the cross 90-degrees, align the race lands with the cage windows and rotate the race out of the cage

9.42 If the wear sleeve (on models so equipped) requires replacement, pry it off the housing with a large screwdriver

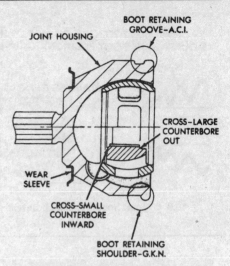

9.46a On GKN and ACI CV joints, make sure the large counterbore faces out when the joint is reassembled

elongated cage window. Raise the land into the window and swivel the cross out of the cage **(see illustration)**.

40   Clean all of the parts with solvent and dry them with compressed air (if available).

41   Inspect the housing, splines, balls and races for damage, corrosion, wear and cracks. Check the cross for wear and scoring in the races. If any of the components are not serviceable, the entire CV joint assembly must be replaced with a new one.

42   Check the outer housing wear sleeve for damage and distortion. If it's damaged or worn, pry the sleeve off the housing **(see illustration)** and replace it with a new one. A special tool is available for installing the new sleeve, but a large section of pipe slightly smaller in diameter than the outer edge of the sleeve will work if care is exercised (don't nick or gouge the seal mating surface).

43   Apply a thin coat of oil to all CV joint components before beginning reassembly.

44   Align the marks and install the cross in the cage so one of the lands fits into the elongated window.

45   Rotate the cross into position in the cage and install the assembly in the CV joint

housing, again using the elongated window for clearance.

46   Rotate the cage into position in the housing. On GKN and ACI driveaxles, the large counterbore of the cross must face out **(see illustration)**. On SSG driveaxles, the internal circlip in the cross will be facing out from the housing **(see illustration)**. On all driveaxles, make sure the marks made during disassembly face out and are aligned.

47   Pack the lubricant from the kit into the ball races and grooves.

48   Install the balls into the elongated holes, one at a time, until they're all in position.

49   Place the driveaxle in the vise and slide the boot over it. On all except SSG driveaxles, install a new circlip in the axle groove, taking care not to twist it. SSG driveaxles have a reusable retainer integral with the driver assembly.

50   Place the CV joint housing in position on the axle, align the splines and rap it sharply with a soft-face hammer **(see illustration)**. Make sure it's seated on the circlip by attempting to pull it off the shaft.

51   Install the boot (see Section 10).

52   Install the driveaxle (see Section 7).

10   Constant velocity (CV) joint boots - replacement

Note: *If the instructions supplied with the replacement boot kit differ from the instructions here, follow the ones with the new boots. A special tool, available at most auto parts stores, is required to install the factory-supplied boot clamps. Do-it-yourself kits which offer greatly simplified installation may be available for your vehicle. Consult an auto parts store or dealer parts department for more information on these kits.*

1   If the boot is cut, torn or leaking, it must be replaced and the CV joint inspected as soon as possible. Even a small amount of dirt in the joint can cause premature wear and failure. Obtain a replacement boot kit before beginning this procedure. There are several different types of boot, each with its own replacement procedure. Compare the boots on your vehicle to the following illustrations to determine which procedure to follow.

8

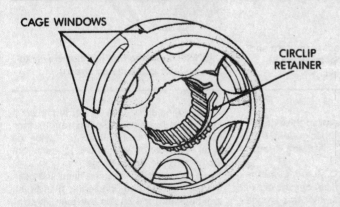

9.46b On SSG driveaxles, make sure the internal circlip in the cross is facing out from the housing

9.50 Strike the end of the housing shaft with a soft-face hammer to engage it with the shaft circlip

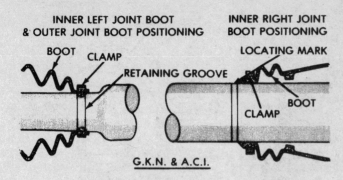

10.8 CV joint boot installation details (GKN and ACI)

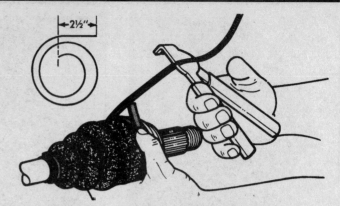

10.10 Wrap the clamp around the boot twice, leaving about 2-1/2 inches of extra material, then cut off the excess

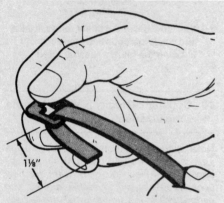

10.11 Pass the strap around the buckle and fold it back about 1-1/8 inch on the inside of the buckle

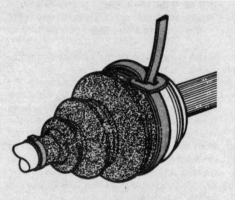

10.13a Install the strap on the boot and bend it back so it can't unwind

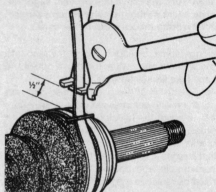

10.13b Attach the tool about 1/2-inch from the buckle . . .

2   Remove the driveaxle (see Section 7).

3   Disassemble the CV joint and remove the boot as described in Section 9.

4   Inspect the CV joint to determine if it's been damaged by contamination or running with too little lubricant. If you have any doubts about the condition of the joint components, perform the inspection procedures described in Section 9.

5   Clean the old grease out of the CV joint and repack it with the grease supplied with the kit.

6   Pack the interior of the new boot with the remaining grease.

7   Install the boot and clamps as follows.

Soft rubber boots (except SSG right inner joint)

Refer to illustrations 10.8, 10.10, 10.11, 10.13a, 10.13b, 10.14, 10.15a and 10.15b

8   Slide the small end of the boot over the shaft and align it with the locating mark or groove **(see illustration)**.

9   Place the large diameter of the boot in the groove **(see illustration 10.8). Note:** *Clamping procedures are identical for attaching the boot to the shaft and the CV joint housing.*

10   Wrap the clamping strap around the boot twice, plus 2-1/2 inches, and cut it off

10.14 . . . then push the tool forward and up to engage the tool hook in the buckle eye

10.15a Close the tool handles slowly to tighten the clamp strap . . .

(see illustration).

11   Pass the end of the strap through the buckle opening and fold it back about 1-1/8 inch on the inside of the buckle **(see illustration)**.

12   Position the clamping strap around the boot, on the clamping surface, with the eye of the buckle facing you. Wrap the strap around the boot once and pass it through the buckle, then wrap it around a second time and pass it through the buckle again.

13   Fold the strap back slightly to prevent it from unwinding itself **(see illustration)**, then open the special tool (C-4653) and place the strap in the narrow slot, about 1/2-inch from the buckle **(see illustration)**.

14   Hold the strap with one hand and push the tool forward and up slightly, then fit the tool hook into the buckle eye **(see illustration)**.

15   Tighten the strap by closing the tool handles **(see illustration)**, then rotate the

10.15b . . . then rotate the tool down while
releasing the pressure on the handles
(allow the handles to open)

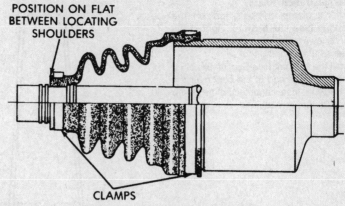

POSITION ON FLAT
BETWEEN LOCATING
SHOULDERS

CLAMPS

10.20 Position the edge of the boot on the flat between the locating shoulders,
then secure it with the clamp

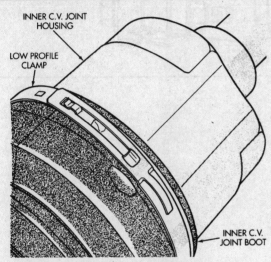

INNER C.V. JOINT
HOUSING

LOW PROFILE
CLAMP

INNER C.V.
JOINT BOOT

10.23a Install the large clamp as shown . . .

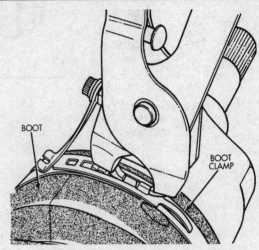

BOOT

BOOT
CLAMP

10.23b . . . then place the prongs of the special tool in the holes in
the clamp and compress the tool until the two ends meet

tool down slowly while releasing the pressure
on the handles (see illustration). Allow the
handles to open progressively, then open the
tool all the way and slide it sideways off the
strap. Caution: *Never fold the strap back or
rotate the tool down while squeezing the handles together (if this is done, the strap will
break).*

16   If the strap isn't tight enough, repeat the
procedure. Always engage the tool about
1/2-inch from the buckle. Make sure the strap
moves smoothly as tightening force is
applied and don't allow the buckle to fold
over as the strap passes through it.

17   When the strap is tight, cut it off 1/8-
inch above the buckle and fold it back neatly.
It must not overlap the edge of the buckle.

18   Repeat the procedure for the remaining
boot clamps.

Soft rubber boots (SSG right inner CV joint only)

*Refer to illustrations 10.20, 10.23a and
10.23b*

19   Slip the clamp for the small end of the
boot onto the driveaxle shaft.

20   Slip the boot onto the shaft and position

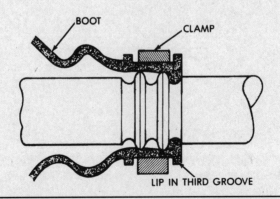

BOOT   CLAMP

10.25 Position the lip of
the boot in the third
groove on the axleshaft

LIP IN THIRD GROOVE

it on the flat between the locating shoulders
(see illustration).

21   Slip the small clamp over the boot and
crimp it with a special tool which is available
at most auto parts stores.

22   Install the CV joint (see Section 9).

23   Install the large end of the boot and
position its clamp. Tighten the clamp with a
special tool for automatic or manual transaxle
models, available at most auto parts stores
(see illustrations).

Hard plastic boots (SSG left inner and both outer CV joints)

Refer to illustrations 10.25 and 10.27

24   Slip the clamp for the small end of the
boot onto the driveaxle shaft.

25   Slip the boot onto the shaft and position
its lip in the third locating groove, nearest the
center of the driveaxle shaft (see illustration).

26   Center the clamp over the end of the

8

boot **(see illustration 10.25).**
27   Install a clamp crimping tool on the clamp bridge **(see illustration)**. Tighten the tool until its jaws touch each other.
28   Release the crimping tool.
29   Install the CV joint (see Section 9).
30   Place the large end of the boot over the CV joint housing. Install and secure the clamp (see Steps 26 through 28).

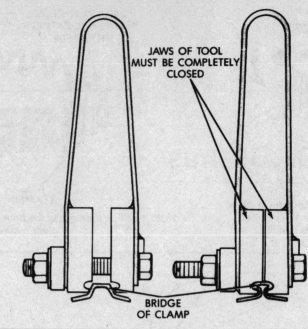

JAWS OF TOOL
MUST BE COMPLETELY
CLOSED

BRIDGE
OF CLAMP

10.27 Because the clamps used with hard plastic boots must generate approximately 100 times the clamping force of those used with rubber boots, this special tool is necessary to crimp the clamps securely

Chapter 9 Brakes

Contents

Specifications

Brake fluid type
See Chapter 1

Disc brakes
Brake pad wear limit	See Chapter 1
Minimum disc thickness	See specs cast into disc
Disc runout (maximum)	0.004 inch
Disc thickness (parallelism) variation limit	0.0005 inch

Drum brakes
Brake shoe wear limit	See Chapter 1
Drum	
Standard diameter	8.66 inches
Maximum diameter	See specs cast into drum
Runout (maximum)	0.006 inch
Out-of-round (maximum)	
In 30-degrees	0.0025 inch
In 360-degrees	0.0035 inch
Parking brake adjustment diameter	6-3/4 inches

Torque specifications
	Ft-lbs (unless otherwise indicated)
Master cylinder mounting nuts	17 to 25
Power brake booster-to-firewall nuts	17 to 25
Caliper guide pin(s)	
1989 through 1991	25 to 35
1992	30
Caliper mounting bracket-to-steering knuckle bolts	
1989 through 1991	130 to 190
1992	160
Brake hose-to-caliper inlet fitting bolt	
1989 through 1991	19 to 29
1992	35
Wheel cylinder-to-brake backing plate bolts	75 in-lbs
Brake backing plate-to-rear axle bolts	
1989 through 1991	45 to 60
1992	80

9

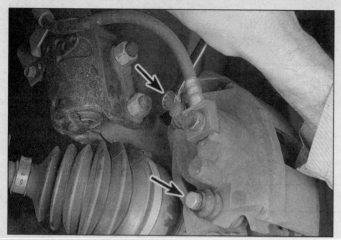

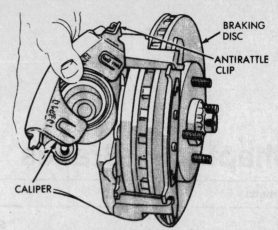

2.2a To get at the pads, remove the guide pins (arrows) (double-pin family caliper shown; some calipers have only a single lower pin) . . .

2.2b . . . and pivot the caliper up off the mounting bracket (pry it loose from the bracket if necessary) – note the anti-rattle clip at the top of the caliper

1　General information

All models are equipped with hydraulically-operated disc front brakes. Rear drum brakes are standard on all models. Rear disc brakes are optional on later models.

The front brakes use a single-piston, floating-caliper design. Three types of caliper, all manufactured by Kelsey-Hayes, are used: single-pin, double-pin family, and double-pin non-family. **Warning:** *The calipers differ in design, so parts are not interchangeable. Using parts from the wrong design could lead to complete brake failure.*

The single-pin caliper, used on early models, floats on a single steel pin that threads into an adapter. The adapter is attached to the steering knuckle. The double-pin family caliper is secured by two steel pins that thread into an adapter, which in turn is attached to the steering knuckle. The double-pin non-family caliper is attached directly to the steering knuckle by two steel pins.

The rear drum brakes are a leading/trailing design with automatic adjustment. The brakes may be manufactured by Kelsey-Hayes or Varga. Service procedures for both designs are nearly identical; differences are pointed out as they occur. The optional rear disc brakes use single-pin floating calipers. **Warning:** *There are two sizes of rear disc brakes. Parts are not interchangeable between the two sizes or between front and rear disc brakes. Use of the wrong parts could cause complete brake failure.*

Front-wheel drive vehicles tend to wear the front brake pads at a faster rate than rear-drive vehicles. Consequently, it's very important to inspect the brake pads frequently to make sure they haven't worn to the point where the disc itself is scored or damaged. Note that the pad thickness limit on these models includes the metal portion of the brake pad, not just the lining material (see Chapter 1).

The hydraulic system consists of two separate circuits. The master cylinder has a separate section in the reservoir for each circuit - in the event of a leak or failure in one hydraulic circuit, the other circuit will remain operative.

Some later models have an Anti-lock Braking system (ABS) that aids vehicle stability during heavy braking or on wet or uneven road surfaces. All non-ABS models have a load sensing dual proportioning valve which modulates the rear brake pressure depending on vehicle load.

All models are equipped with a cable-actuated parking brake, which operates the rear brakes. On vehicles with rear drum brakes, the parking brake expands the brake shoes. On rear disc brake models, the parking brake uses a separate set of drum brakes, mounted inside drums integral with the rear brake discs.

2　Front disc brake pads - replacement

Warning: *Disc brake pads must be replaced on both front wheels at the same time - never replace the pads on only one wheel. Also, the dust created by the brake system may contain asbestos, which is harmful to your health. Never blow it out with compressed air and don't inhale any of it. An approved filtering mask should be worn when working on the brakes. Do not, under any circumstances, use petroleum-based solvents to clean brake parts. Use brake system cleaner or clean brake fluid only!*
Note: *When servicing the disc brakes, use high-quality, nationally-recognized, name-brand parts.*
1　Raise the front of the vehicle and support it securely on jackstands. Block the rear wheels and apply the parking brake, then remove the front wheels. **Note:** *The pad replacement procedure varies, depending on which design you have. Count the caliper mounting pins. If it has one pin, it's a single-*

2.3 Hang the caliper out of the way on a piece of wire – DO NOT let it hang by the brake hose!

pin caliper; if it has two, note whether it's attached directly to the steering knuckle or to an adapter. If the caliper is attached directly to the knuckle, it's a non-family caliper; if attached to an adapter, it's a family caliper.

Single-pin and double-pin family caliper

Refer to illustrations 2.2a, 2.2b, 2.3, 2.4a, 2.4b and 2.6
2　Remove the caliper guide pin(s) **(see illustration)**, swing up the lower end of the caliper and pull it off the caliper mounting bracket **(see illustration)**.
3　Support the caliper out of the way with a wire hanger **(see illustration)**. **Warning:** *Don't allow the caliper to hang by the brake hose!*
4　Detach the outer brake pad from the caliper mounting bracket **(see illustrations)**. If you're replacing the pads on a single-pin or early double-pin caliper, remove the anti-rattle spring from the bottom of the pad and install it on the new outer pad.
5　Remove the brake disc (see Section 4).

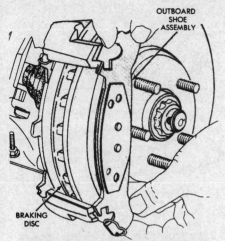

2.4a To remove the outer pad from a single-pin or early double-pin family caliper, simply pull it straight off – then remove the anti-rattle spring at the bottom of the pad and transfer it to the new outer pad

2.4b To remove the outer pad from a later double-pin family caliper, disengage the upper end of the brake backing plate from the anti-rattle spring and remove the pad – after you remove the inner pad, the anti-rattle spring (arrow) will fall out of the caliper mounting bracket, so note how it's installed BEFORE you remove the inner pad

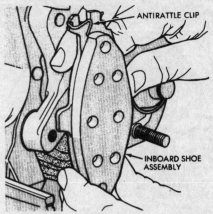

2.6 Slide the inner pad off the mounting bracket – on single-pin and early double-pin family calipers, remove the anti-rattle clip from the top of the pad and transfer it to the new pad

6   Detach the inner brake pad (see illustration). If you're replacing the pads on a single-pin caliper or early double-pin caliper, remove the anti-rattle spring from the top of the inner pad and install it on the new inner pad. If you're replacing the pads on a later double-pin caliper, note how the anti-rattle spring clip is installed on the caliper mounting bracket, in case it falls off before you install the new pads.
7   Inspect the caliper and caliper mounting bracket for wear, damage, rust and evidence of fluid leaks. If the caliper-to-bracket mating surfaces are rusty, clean them thoroughly with a wire brush (the caliper must be able to move freely when the brakes are applied). Also inspect the brake disc (see Section 4).
8   Siphon some brake fluid from the master cylinder reservoir, or place rags or newspapers underneath the reservoir to catch the overflow that will occur when the piston is pushed back to make room for the new pads. Then use a piece of wood to carefully push the piston into the caliper bore far enough to

provide clearance for the new pads.
9   Apply a thin film of Mopar Multipurpose Lubricant or high-temperature brake grease to the adapter-to-brake pad and caliper mating surfaces. Caution: Don't get any grease on the pad lining material, gasket surface or brake disc.
10   Remove the protective paper from the noise suppression gasket on both pads. Install the inner brake pad, making sure the anti-rattle spring is secure.
11   Install the brake disc (see Section 4).
12   Place the outer pad in position in the caliper mounting bracket. Make sure the anti-rattle spring is secure.
13   Slide the caliper into position over the pad and disc assembly. On single-pin or early double-pin types, be sure the anti-rattle clip is engaged correctly.
14   Install the guide pin(s) and tighten it/them to the torque listed in this Chapter's Specifications. Don't cross-thread the guide

pin(s) during installation.
15   Repeat Steps 2 through 14 for the other caliper.
16   Install the wheel, tighten the wheel lug nuts to half the torque listed in the Chapter 1 Specifications and lower the vehicle. Tighten the lug nuts to the torque listed in the Chapter 1 Specifications.
17   Pump the brake pedal several times to bring the pads into contact with the disc. Check the brake fluid level (see Chapter 1). Drive the vehicle in an isolated area and make several stops to wear off any foreign material on the pads and seat them on the disc.

Double-pin non-family caliper

Refer to illustrations 2.18, 2.19, 2.20, 2.21, 2.26a and 2.26b
18   Remove the caliper guide pin bolts (see illustration).
19   Pivot the bottom of the caliper away from the brake disc and lift it off (see illustration), together with the brake pads. Warning: Once the caliper is off, don't let it hang by the brake hose! Support it by hand while remov-

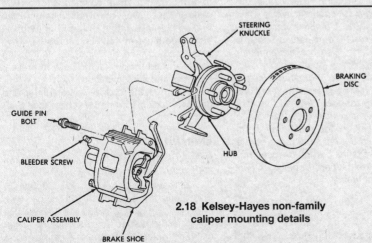

2.18 Kelsey-Hayes non-family caliper mounting details

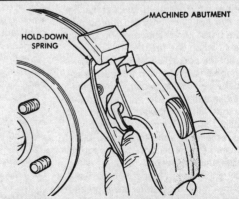

2.19 Work the hold-down spring out from under the machined abutment and remove the caliper together with the pads

9

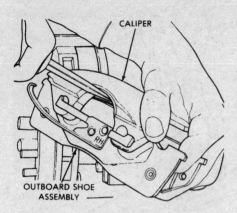

2.20 Pry the outer pad loose from the caliper with a screwdriver

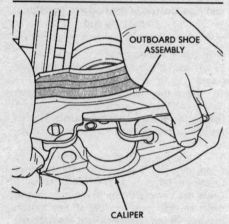

2.26b Work the pad onto the caliper and engage the pad retainer spring with the caliper body

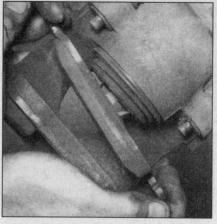

2.21 To disengage the retainer spring (on the back of the inner pad) from the piston, pull the inner pad straight out

25   Install the inner pad by pressing the retainer into the piston recess.
26   Select the correct outer pad for the side of the vehicle you're working on by referring to the identification marks **(see illustration)**. Remove the protective paper from the noise suppression gasket and install the pad on the caliper **(see illustration)**.
27   Install the caliper on the steering knuckle and position the hold-down spring under the steering knuckle abutment **(see illustration 2.19)**. Caution: *Don't damage the steering knuckle bushing seals when you install the caliper.*
28   Repeat Steps 18 through 27 for the other caliper.
29   Perform Steps 16 and 17 to complete the installation.

---

3   Front disc brake caliper - removal, overhaul and installation

---

Warning: *Dust created by the brake system may contain asbestos, which is harmful to your health. Never blow it out with compressed air and don't inhale any of it. An approved filtering mask should be worn when working on the brakes. Do not, under any circumstances, use petroleum-based solvents to clean brake parts. Use brake cleaner or clean brake fluid only!*
Note: *If an overhaul is indicated (usually because of fluid leakage), explore all options before beginning the job. New and factory rebuilt calipers are available on an exchange basis, which makes this job quite easy. If it's decided to rebuild the calipers, make sure a rebuild kit is available before proceeding. Always rebuild the calipers in pairs - never rebuild just one of them.*

Removal

Refer to illustration 3.2
1   Loosen the wheel lug nuts, raise the front of the vehicle and support it securely on

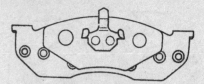

INBOARD SHOE ASSEMBLY (RIGHT AND LEFT COMMON)

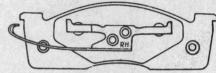

OUTBOARD SHOE ASSEMBLY (RIGHT SIDE SHOWN)

2.26a Inner pads on non-family calipers are interchangeable; outer pads must be installed on the proper side of the vehicle – the pads are marked to indicate the correct side

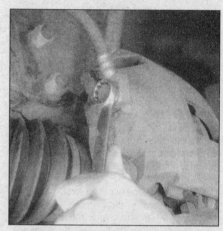

3.2 Place some shop rags or newspapers under the brake hose inlet fitting bore, then plug it to prevent contamination right after you disconnect it

jackstands. Remove the front wheels.
2   **Note:** *Don't remove the brake hose from the caliper if you're only removing the caliper to gain access to other components. If you're removing the caliper for overhaul, remove the brake hose inlet fitting bolt and detach the hose* **(see illustration)**. Have a rag handy to catch spilled fluid and wrap a plastic bag tightly around the end of the hose to prevent fluid loss and contamination.
3   Remove the caliper guide pin(s) and detach the caliper from the vehicle (see Section 2).

Overhaul

Refer to illustrations 3.6, 3.7, 3.8, 3.9a, 3.9b, 3.9c, 3.9d, 3.14 and 3.15
4   Remove the brake pads (see Section 2).
5   Clean the exterior of the caliper with brake cleaner or new brake fluid. Never use gasoline, kerosene or petroleum-based cleaning solvents. Place the caliper on a clean workbench.

---

ing the pads, then hang it from the vehicle with wire **(see illustration 2.3)**.
20   Pry the outer pad away from the caliper **(see illustration)**.
21   Remove the inner pad by pulling it straight away from the piston **(see illustration)**.
22   Inspect the caliper and caliper mounting bracket for wear, damage, rust and evidence of fluid leaks. If the caliper-to-bracket mating surfaces are rusty, clean them thoroughly with a wire brush (the caliper must be able to move freely when the brakes are applied). Also inspect the brake disc (see Section 4).
23   Siphon some brake fluid from the master cylinder reservoir, or place rags or newspapers underneath the reservoir to catch the overflow that will occur when the piston is pushed back to make room for the new pads. Then use a piece of wood to carefully push the piston into the caliper bore far enough to provide clearance for the new pads.
24   Apply a thin film of Mopar Multipurpose Lubricant or high-temperature brake grease to the adapter-to-brake pad and caliper mating surfaces.
Caution: *Don't get any grease on the pad lining material, gasket surface or brake disc.*

3.6 Place a piece of wood between the caliper and piston, then force the piston out of the caliper bore with compressed air – be sure to keep your hands and fingers out of the way during this procedure

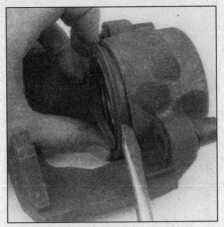

3.7 Use a screwdriver to pry the dust boot out of the cylinder bore

3.8 Remove the piston seal with a wood pencil or a plastic eating utensil so you don't damage the bore and seal groove

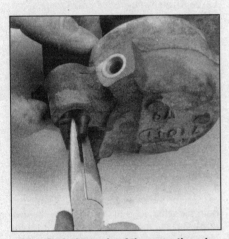

3.9a Grab the ends of the mounting pin bushing with needle-nose pliers and push them through the caliper ears with a twisting motion

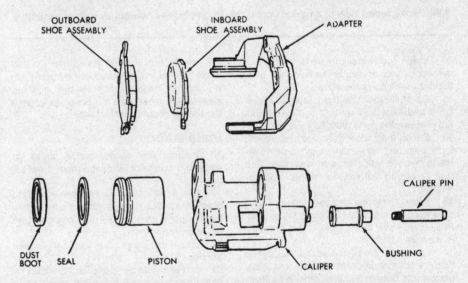

3.9b An exploded view of a typical single-pin Kelsey-Hayes caliper assembly

6 Position a wooden block or several shop rags in the caliper as a cushion, then use compressed air to remove the piston from the caliper **(see illustration)**. Use only enough air pressure to ease the piston out of the bore. If the piston is blown out, even with the cushion in place, it may be damaged. **Warning:** *Never place your fingers in front of the piston in an attempt to catch or protect it when applying compressed air - serious injury could result!*

7 Carefully pry the dust boot out of the caliper bore **(see illustration).**

8 Using a wood or plastic tool, remove the piston seal from the groove in the caliper bore **(see illustration)**. Metal tools may damage the bore.

9 Remove the caliper bleeder screw. On double-pin calipers, remove the bushing sleeves. Remove and discard the caliper (guide) pin bushing(s) from the caliper ears. Discard all rubber parts **(see illustrations).**

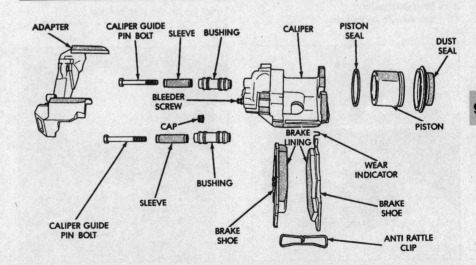

3.9c An exploded view of a typical Kelsey-Hayes double-pin family caliper assembly (late design shown; earlier models use three separate anti-rattle clips)

9

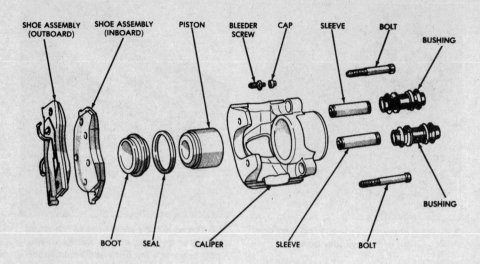

SHOE ASSEMBLY (OUTBOARD)   SHOE ASSEMBLY (INBOARD)   PISTON   BLEEDER SCREW   CAP   SLEEVE   BOLT   BUSHING

BOOT   SEAL   CALIPER   SLEEVE   BOLT   BUSHING

3.9d An exploded view of a typical double-pin Kelsey-Hayes non-family caliper assembly

10   Clean the remaining parts with brake system cleaner or new brake fluid then blow them dry with compressed air.
11   Carefully examine the piston for nicks, burrs and excessive wear. If surface defects are present, the parts must be replaced.
12   Check the caliper bore in a similar way. Light polishing with crocus cloth is permissible to remove light corrosion and stains, but rust or pitting will require caliper replacement.
13   When reassembling the caliper, lubricate the bore and seal with clean brake fluid. Position the seal in the caliper bore groove - make sure it isn't twisted.
14   Lubricate the piston with clean brake fluid, install it squarely in the bore and apply pressure to bottom it in the caliper **(see illustration)**.
15   Stretch the dust boot over the groove in the piston, then carefully seat it in the caliper bore **(see illustration)**.
16   Install the bleeder screw.

17   Install new caliper pin bushings and make sure they're centered in their bores. On double-pin calipers, install the bushing sleeves and make sure the bushings engage the sealing grooves in the sleeves.

Installation

18   Inspect the caliper guide pin(s) for excessive corrosion. Replace them if necessary.
19   Clean the caliper and caliper mounting bracket contact surfaces with a wire brush, then apply a thin film of high-temperature brake grease to them.
20   Install the brake pads and caliper (see Section 2).
21   Install the brake hose and inlet fitting bolt, using new copper washers, then tighten the bolt to the torque listed in this Chapter's Specifications.
22   If the line was disconnected, be sure to bleed the brakes (see Section 9).
23   Install the wheels and lower the vehicle.

Tighten the lug nuts to the torque listed in the Chapter 1 Specifications.
24   After the job has been completed, firmly depress the brake pedal a few times to bring the pads into contact with the disc.
25   Check brake operation before driving the vehicle in traffic.

4   Front brake disc - inspection, removal and installation

1   Loosen the wheel lug nuts, raise the vehicle and support it securely on jackstands. Remove the wheel and reinstall the lug nuts to hold the disc in place.
2   Remove the brake caliper (see Section 2). It's not necessary to disconnect the brake hose. After removing the caliper guide pin(s), suspend the caliper out of the way with a piece of wire. Don't let the caliper hang by the hose and don't stretch or twist the hose. On all except double-pin non-family calipers, remove the outer brake pad.

Inspection

Refer to illustrations 4.4a, 4.4b, 4.5a and 4.5b
3   Visually inspect the disc surface for scoring and other damage. Light scratches and shallow grooves are normal after use and may not affect brake operation, but deep score marks - over 0.015-inch - require disc removal and refinishing by an automotive machine shop. Be sure to check both sides of the disc. If pulsating has been noticed during application of the brakes, suspect disc runout.
4   To check disc runout, mount a dial indicator with the stem resting about 1/2-inch from the outer edge of the disc **(see illustration)**. Set the indicator to zero and turn the disc. The indicator reading should not exceed the maximum allowable runout listed in this Chapter's Specifications. If it does, the disc should be refinished by an automotive machine shop. **Note:** *Professionals recommend resurfacing of brake discs regardless of*

3.14 When you install the piston, make sure it doesn't become cocked as you push it into its bore in the caliper

3.15 If the correct seal driver tool isn't available, use a drift punch to tap around the edge until the dust boot is seated

4.4a make sure the lug nuts are in place and evenly tightened, then measure the disc runout with a dial indicator

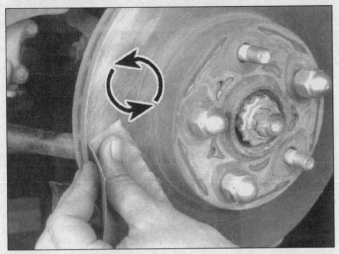

4.4b Using a swirling motion, remove the glaze from the disc surface with sandpaper or emery cloth

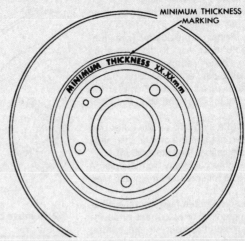

4.5a The disc can be resurfaced by an automotive machine shop, provided the machining operation doesn't result in a disc thickness less than the minimum stamped on it

4.5b Measure the disc thickness with a micrometer at several points around its circumference

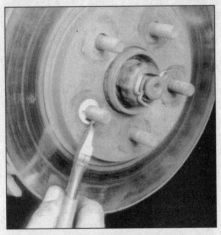

4.6a If the discs on your vehicle use retaining washers like this, pull them off with a pair of needle-nose pliers and discard them

4.6b When you remove the disc, make sure you don't damage the threads on the wheel studs

the dial indicator reading (to produce a smooth, flat surface that will eliminate brake pedal pulsations and other undesirable symptoms related to questionable discs). At the very least, if you elect not to have the discs resurfaced, deglaze them with sandpaper or emery cloth (use a swirling motion to ensure a non-directional finish) **(see illustration)**.

5   The disc must not be machined to a thickness less than the minimum listed in this Chapter's Specifications. The minimum wear (or discard) thickness is also cast into the inside of the disc **(see illustration)**. The disc thickness can be checked with a micrometer **(see illustration)**.

Removal

Refer to illustrations 4.6a and 4.6b

6   Remove the lug nuts you installed to hold the disc in place during inspection. The discs on some models are equipped with retaining washers to prevent them from slipping off while the caliper is removed; if the discs on your vehicle are so equipped, remove the washer with needle-nose pliers **(see illustration)** and discard it. Slide the disc off the threaded studs **(see illustration)**.

Installation

7   Place the disc in position over the threaded studs.

8   Install the caliper and brake pads (see Section 2). Tighten the caliper guide pin(s) to the torque listed in this Chapter's Specifications.

9   Install the wheel and lug nuts, then lower the vehicle to the ground. Tighten the lug nuts to the torque listed in the Chapter 1 Specifications.

10   Depress the brake pedal a few times to bring the brake pads into contact with the disc. Bleeding of the system isn't necessary unless the brake hose was disconnected from the caliper. Check the operation of the brakes carefully before driving the vehicle in traffic.

5   Rear disc brake pads - replacement

Refer to illustrations 5.2, 5.3, 5.4 and 5.5

Warning: *Disc brake pads must be replaced on both rear wheels at the same time - never replace the pads on only one wheel. Also, the dust created by the brake system may contain asbestos, which is harmful to your health. Never blow it out with compressed air and don't inhale any of it. An approved filtering mask should be worn when working on the brakes. Do not, under any circumstances, use petroleum-based solvents to clean brake parts. Use brake system cleaner or clean brake fluid only!*

Note: *When servicing the disc brakes, use high-quality, nationally-recognized, name-brand parts.*

1   Raise the rear of the vehicle and support it securely on jackstands. Block the front wheels so the vehicle can't roll in either direc-

9

tion, then remove the rear wheels.

2   Remove the caliper attaching bolts **(see illustration)**.

3   Lift the caliper off the adapter **(see illustration)**. It's not necessary to disconnect the brake hose. After removing the caliper attaching bolts, suspend the caliper out of the way with a piece of wire. Don't let the caliper hang by the hose and don't stretch or twist the hose.

4   Pry the retaining clip on the outer pad over the raised area on the caliper, then slide the pad off the caliper **(see illustration)**.

5   Pull the inner pad away from the piston to disengage its retainer from the piston **(see illustration)**.

6   Siphon some brake fluid from the master cylinder reservoir, or place rags or newspapers underneath the reservoir to catch the overflow that will occur when the piston is pushed back to make room for the new pads. Then use a piece of wood to carefully push the piston into the caliper bore far enough to provide clearance for the new pads.

7   Apply a thin film of Mopar Multipurpose Lubricant or high-temperature brake grease to the adapter-to-brake pad and caliper mating surfaces. **Caution:** *Don't get any grease on the pad lining material, gasket surface or brake disc.*

8   Push the new inner pad into the piston recess **(see illustration 5.5)**.

9   Slide the new outer pad onto the caliper and make sure the retaining finger locks over the raised area on the caliper **(see illustration 5.4)**.

10   Position the bottom of the caliper on the adapter **(see illustration 5.3)**. Make sure the caliper casting projections and the lower tabs on the pads are beneath the mounting rail, then pivot the caliper and pads over the disc.

11   Install the caliper attaching bolts and tighten them to the torque listed in this Chapter's Specifications.

12   Install the wheel, hand tighten the wheel lug nuts and lower the vehicle. Tighten the

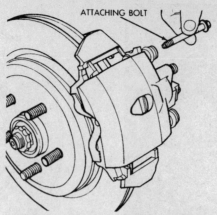

5.2 Remove the caliper attaching bolts . . .

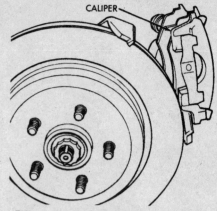

5.3 . . . and lift the caliper away from the disc, together with the pads

lug nuts to the torque listed in the Chapter 1 Specifications.

13   Pump the brake pedal several times to bring the pads into contact with the disc. Check the brake fluid level (see Chapter 1). Drive the vehicle in an isolated area and make several stops to wear off any foreign material on the pads and seat them on the disc.

---

6   Rear disc brake caliper - removal, overhaul and installation

These procedures are the same as for the double-piston non-family front caliper (see Section 3).

---

7   Rear brake disc - removal, inspection and installation

These procedures are the same as for front brake discs (see Section 4).

---

8   Brake shoes - replacement

Refer to illustrations 8.2a, 8.2b, 8.4a, 8.4b, 8.4c, 8.5, 8.6, 8.7, 8.8a, 8.8b, 8.9a, 8.9b, 8.10, 8.11, 8.13, 8.15, 8.16, 8.18, 8.19, 8.20, 8.27, and 8.28

Warning: *Drum brake shoes must be replaced on both wheels at the same time - never replace the shoes on only one wheel. Also, the dust created by the brake system may contain asbestos, which is harmful to your health. Never blow it out with compressed air and don't inhale any of it. An approved filtering mask should be worn when working on the brakes. Do not, under any circumstances, use petroleum-based solvents to clean brake parts. Use brake cleaner or denatured alcohol only!*

Caution: *Whenever the brake shoes are replaced, the retractor and hold-down springs should also be replaced. Due to the continuous heating/cooling cycle that springs are subjected to, they lose their tension over a period of time any may allow the shoes to drag on the drum and wear at a much faster*

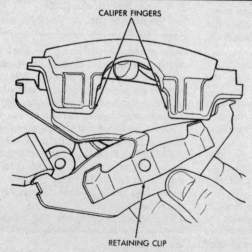

5.4 Lift the tab on the outer pad away from the raised part of the caliper, then slide the pad off

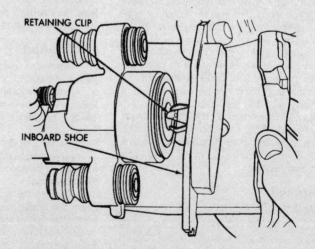

5.5 Pull on the inner pad to disengage its retainer from the piston

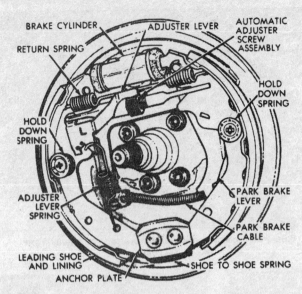

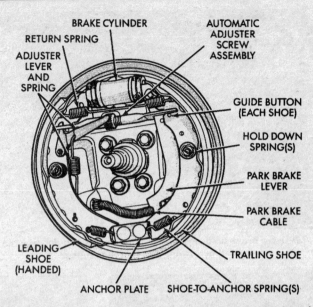

8.2a Typical Kelsey-Hayes rear drum brake assembly (left side shown)

8.2b Typical Varga rear drum brake assembly (left side shown)

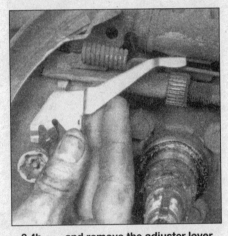

8.4a On Kelsey-Hayes brakes, use pliers to detach the adjuster lever spring . . .

8.4b . . . and remove the adjuster lever

8.4c On Varga brakes, the procedure is the same but the spring location is slightly different

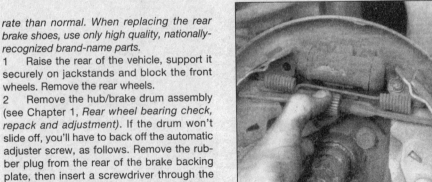

rate than normal. When replacing the rear brake shoes, use only high quality, nationally-recognized brand-name parts.

1   Raise the rear of the vehicle, support it securely on jackstands and block the front wheels. Remove the rear wheels.

2   Remove the hub/brake drum assembly (see Chapter 1, *Rear wheel bearing check, repack and adjustment*). If the drum won't slide off, you'll have to back off the automatic adjuster screw, as follows. Remove the rubber plug from the rear of the brake backing plate, then insert a screwdriver through the hole and use it to push the adjuster lever off the automatic adjuster **(see illustrations)**. Insert another screwdriver or brake adjusting tool and use it to turn the star wheel on the automatic adjuster screw until the drum will pull off.

3   Use brake system cleaner to remove dust and brake fluid from the shoe assembly components.

4   Remove the adjuster lever spring and

8.5 Back off the adjuster star wheel

8.6 Use needle-nose pliers to pull the cable from the parking brake lever

adjuster lever **(see illustrations)**.

5   Back off the adjuster screw star wheel **(see illustration)**.

6   Disconnect the parking brake cable with a pair of pliers **(see illustration)**.

9

8.7 Use a brake hold-down spring tool or pliers to depress the hold-down spring and turn the retainer

8.8a Pull the upper ends of the brake shoes away from the wheel cylinder . . .

8.8b . . . then disengage the lower ends of the shoes from the anchor plate (Kelsey-Hayes brake shown; Varga brakes similar)

8.9a Unhook the lower spring . . .

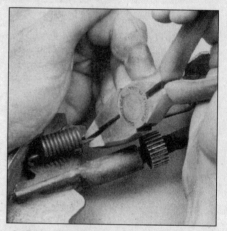

8.9b . . . and use pliers to disengage the upper spring from the shoes

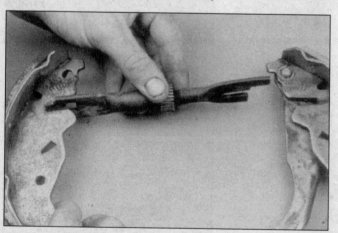

8.10 Detach the adjuster from the shoes

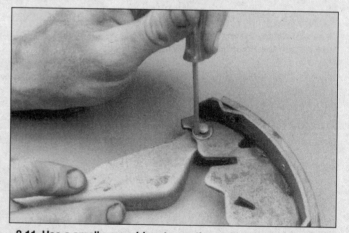

8.11 Use a small screwdriver to pry the parking brake lever clip off the post

7   Remove the hold-down springs by depressing them with a pair of pliers or a special tool and turning the retainer until the slot aligns with the flattened end of the pin, allowing removal **(see illustration)**.

8   Disengage the brake shoe assembly from the wheel cylinder at the top and the anchor plate at the bottom and remove it from the backing plate **(see illustrations)**.

9   Place the assembly on a work surface and remove the springs **(see illustrations)**.

10   Separate the shoes from the adjuster **(see illustration)**.

11   Remove the parking brake lever retainer clip with a small screwdriver and transfer the lever to the new shoe **(see illustration)**.

12   Check the shoe linings to make sure they indicate full contact with the drum.

13   Check the drum for cracks, score marks and signs of overheating. Measure the inside diameter of the drum (most auto parts stores will do this for you) and compare it to the size stamped on the drum **(see illustration)**. Minor imperfections in the drum surface can

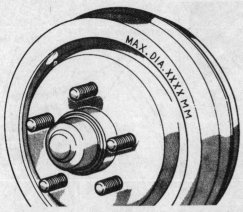

8.13 The maximum allowable inside diameter of the drum is stamped on it

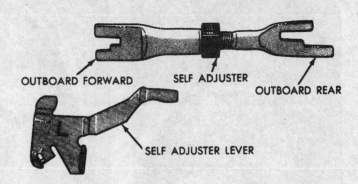

8.15 Adjuster components – exploded view

be removed with fine emery paper. Deeper score marks can be removed by having the drum resurfaced by an automotive machine shop (as long as the maximum diameter is not exceeded). **Note:** *Professionals recommend resurfacing the drums whenever the shoes are replaced.* It's a good idea to replace them as a matter of course.

14   Check the brake springs for signs of discolored paint, indicating overheating, and distorted end coils. It's a good idea to replace them as a matter of course.

15   Check the self-adjuster assembly and threads for bent, corroded and damaged components. Replace the assembly if the screw threads are damaged or rusted. Clean the threads and lubricate them with white lithium-based grease **(see illustration)**.

16   Check the wheel cylinder boots for damage and signs of leakage **(see illustration)**.

17   Rebuild or replace the wheel cylinder if there is any sign of leakage around the boots (see Section 6).

18   Check for rough or rusted shoe contact areas on the backing plate, then lubricate the contact points with high-temperature grease

8.16 Carefully peel back the wheel cylinder boots to check for brake fluid leakage

(see illustration).

19   Assemble the shoes over the adjuster and connect the return springs **(see illustration)**.

20   Place the assembly in position on the backing plate and insert the parking brake

8.18 The area on the backing plate where the brake shoes contact it must be smooth and lubricated with high-temperature grease

cable into the parking brake lever **(see illustration)**.

21   Spread the bottom spring enough to allow the lower ends of the shoes to be seated in the anchor plate.

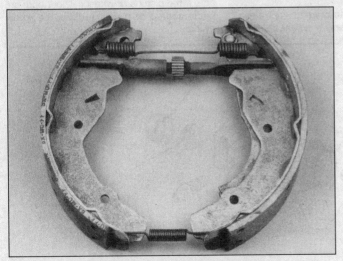

8.19 Assemble the shoes, adjuster and springs prior to installation on the backing plate

8.20 Use pliers to insert the parking brake cable into the lever

9

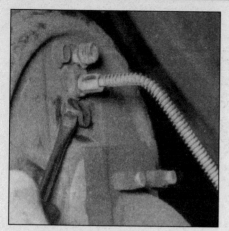

8.27 Pry the rubber plug out of the adjusting hole with a screwdriver

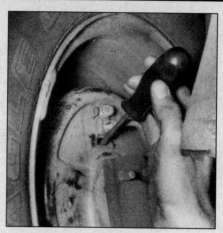

8.28 Insert the screwdriver into the hole and turn the star wheel

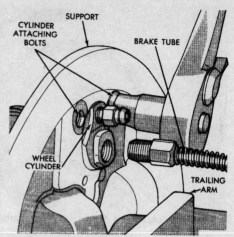

9.4 To detach the wheel cylinder from the brake backing plate, disconnect the brake tube fitting and remove the two attaching bolts

22   Spread the top spring and seat the shoes in the wheel cylinder pistons.
23   Insert the pins through the backing plate from the rear and hold them in place while installing the hold-down springs and retainers.
24   Install the adjuster lever and connect the spring to it.
25   Turn the adjuster until the shoes are retracted enough to allow the drum to be reinstalled.
26   Install the hub/drum assembly and the wheel. Repeat the procedure for the other wheel.
27   Remove the rubber plug from the hole in the backing plate **(see illustration)**.
28   Insert a narrow screwdriver through the hole in the backing plate and turn the star wheel until the brake drags slightly as the tire is turned **(see illustration)**.
29   Back off the star wheel until the tire turns freely.
30   Repeat the adjustment on the opposite wheel.
31   Install the plugs in the backing plate access holes.
32   Adjust the parking brake.
33   Lower the vehicle and check the brake operation very carefully before placing the vehicle into normal service.

9   Wheel cylinder - removal, overhaul and installation

Note: *Before deciding to rebuild a wheel cylinder, make sure parts are available. It's sometimes more practical to simply replace the old wheel cylinder with a new or rebuilt unit instead of rebuilding it.*

Removal

Refer to illustration 9.4
1   Raise the rear of the vehicle and support it securely on jackstands, then block the front wheels. Remove the rear wheels.
2   Remove the rear hub/drum (see Chapter 1) and the brake shoes (see Section 8).
3   Disconnect the brake line (tube) from the back of the wheel cylinder and plug it. Use a flare-nut wrench, if available.
4   Unbolt the wheel cylinder and remove it from the backing plate **(see illustration)**. Clean the backing plate and wheel cylinder mating surfaces.

Overhaul

Refer to illustration 9.5
Note: *You'll need a clean place to work, clean rags, some newspapers, a wheel cylinder*

rebuild kit, a container of brake fluid and some denatured alcohol to perform a wheel cylinder overhaul.
5   Remove the bleeder screw **(see illustration)** and check to make sure it is not obstructed.
6   Carefully pry the boots from the wheel cylinder and remove them.
7   Push in on one piston and force out the opposite piston, cups and spring with the cup expanders from the bore.
8   Clean the wheel cylinder, pistons and spring with clean brake fluid, denatured alcohol or brake system solvent and dry them with compressed air. **Warning:** *Do not, under any circumstances, use petroleum-based solvents or gasoline to clean brake parts.*
9   Check the cylinder bore and pistons for score marks and corrosion (pitting). Slight imperfections in the bore can be removed with fine crocus cloth (use a circular motion). Black stains on the cylinder walls are caused by the cups and will not impair brake operation. If the pistons or wheel cylinder bore are badly scored or pitted, replace the wheel cylinder.

9.5 An exploded view of a typical wheel cylinder assembly

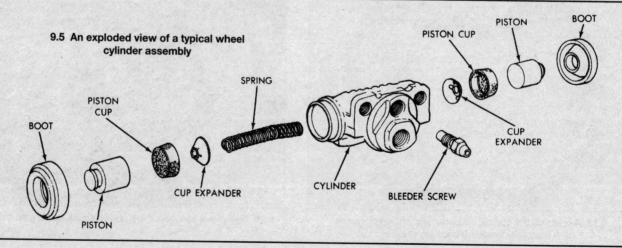

10.2 To remove the master cylinder, disconnect the two brake line fittings (arrows) with a flare nut wrench . . .

10.3a . . . then remove the mounting nuts from the driver's side . . .

10.3b . . . and passenger side of the master cylinder - once the nuts are removed, lift the master cylinder off the booster

10 Lubricate the components with clean brake fluid or brake assembly lubricant prior to installation.

11 With the cylinder bore coated with clean brake fluid or brake assembly lube, install the spring and cup expanders. Install the cups in each end of the cylinder. Make sure the open ends of the cups are facing each other.

12 Engage the boot on the piston and slide the assembly into the bore. Carefully press the boot over the cylinder end until it is seated. Repeat the procedure for the remaining boot and piston.

13 Install the bleeder screw.

Installation

14 Apply RTV-type sealant to the wheel cylinder mating surface of the backing plate.

15 To install the wheel cylinder, hold it in position, install the mounting bolts and tighten them to the specified torque.

16 Unplug the brake line, insert it into the wheel cylinder fitting and carefully thread the flare nut into place. Once the nut is properly started, tighten it securely with a wrench (use a flare nut wrench if available).

17 Install the brake shoes (see Section 8) and the hub/drum (see Chapter 1).

18 Bleed the brakes (see Section 13).

19 Install the wheels and lower the vehicle. Check the brake operation very carefully before placing the vehicle into normal service.

10 Master cylinder - removal and installation

Refer to illustrations 10.2, 10.3a and 10.3b
Note: *The master cylinder installed on these vehicles cannot be rebuilt. If problems are encountered, replace it with a new unit.*

1 Place a container and several layers of newspaper under the master cylinder to catch spilled brake fluid.

2 Unscrew the steel line flare nuts **(see illustration)**, remove the lines and cap them. Use a flare-nut wrench, if available, to

unscrew the nuts. Allow the fluid in the master cylinder to drain into the container.

3 Remove the mounting nuts and detach the master cylinder from the booster **(see illustrations)**. If you are installing a new master cylinder, it may be necessary to transfer the plastic fluid reservoir to the new master cylinder. To do so, first drain the reservoir, then place the aluminum portion of the master cylinder in a vise and use your hand (no tools) to gently pull the reservoir off while gently rocking it back and forth. Replace the two rubber grommets with new ones, put them in place in the master cylinder, lubricate them with clean brake fluid and press the reservoir back into place, using a rocking motion. Make sure the bottom of the reservoir touches the top of each grommet.

4 Every time the master cylinder is removed, the complete hydraulic system must be bled. The time required to bleed the system can be reduced if the master cylinder is filled with fluid and bench bled before the master cylinder is installed on the vehicle.

5 Insert threaded plugs of the correct size into the cylinder outlet holes and fill both reservoirs with brake fluid. The master cylinder should be supported in a level manner so that brake fluid will not spill during the bench bleeding procedure.

6 Loosen one plug at a time and push the piston assembly into the bore to force air from the master cylinder. To prevent air from being drawn back into the cylinder, the plug must be tightened before allowing the piston to return to its original position.

7 Since high pressure is not involved in the bench bleeding procedure, an alternative to the removal and replacement of the plug with each stroke of the piston assembly is available. Before pushing in on the piston assembly, remove the plug, then depress the piston as described above. Before releasing the piston, however, instead of replacing the plug, simply put your finger tightly over the hole to keep air from being drawn back into the master cylinder. Wait several seconds for brake fluid to be drawn from the reservoir into the piston bore, then depress the piston

again, removing your finger as the brake fluid is expelled. Be sure to put your finger back over the hole each time before releasing the piston. When the bleeding procedure is complete for that port, replace the plug and tighten it snugly before going on to the other port to repeat the procedure.

8 Stroke the piston three or four times for each outlet to ensure that all air has been expelled.

9 Refill the master cylinder reservoirs and install the cover assembly. **Note:** *The reservoirs should only be filled to the top of the reservoir divider to prevent overflowing when the cover is installed.*

10 To install the master cylinder, hold it in position, align the pushrod and master cylinder piston and install the mounting nuts. Tighten the nuts to the torque listed in this Chapter's Specifications.

11 Install the lines and carefully start the flare nuts, taking care not to cross-thread them. After they have been started by hand, tighten them securely with a flare-nut wrench.

12 Fill the master cylinder reservoir and bleed the brakes.

11 Brake hoses and lines - inspection and replacement

Refer to illustrations 11.4a and 11.4b

1 About every six months, the flexible hoses which connect the steel brake lines with the rear brakes and the front calipers should be inspected for cracks, chafing of the outer cover, leaks, blisters and other damage.

2 Replacement steel and flexible brake lines are commonly available from dealer parts departments and auto parts stores. Do not, under any circumstances, use anything other than steel lines or approved flexible brake hoses as replacement items.

3 When installing the brake line, leave at least 3/4-inch between the line and any moving or vibrating parts.

9

4   When disconnecting a hose and a line, loosen the fitting with a flare-nut wrench **(see illustration)**. Once the fitting has been loosened, the spring clip can be removed **(see illustration)**.

5   When connecting two hoses, use open-end wrenches on the hose ends. When connecting two hoses, make sure they're not bent, twisted or strained in any way.

6   Steel brake lines are usually retained at several points with clips. Always remove the clips before detaching a steel brake line. Always reinstall the clips (or new ones if the old ones are damaged) when replacing a brake line - they provide support and keep the lines from vibrating, which can eventually break them.

7   After installing a line or hose, bleed the brakes (see Section 13).

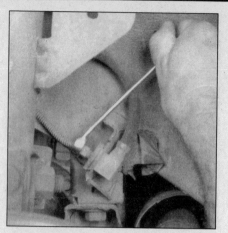

11.4a To detach a metal brake line from the flexible hose, loosen the fitting with a flare-nut wrench . . .

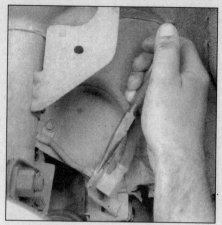

11.4b . . . then pull off the retaining clip with needle-nose pliers

12   Anti-lock Brake System (ABS) - general information

Description

Some 1991 and later models have an Anti-lock Brake System (ABS) designed to maintain vehicle maneuverability, directional stability, and optimum deceleration under severe braking conditions on most road surfaces. It does so by monitoring the rotational speed of the wheels and controlling the brake line pressure to the wheels during braking. This prevents the wheels from locking up prematurely during hard braking.

Components

Pumps

The pumps, one for each hydraulic circuit, are driven by an electric motor. The pumps provide high-pressure brake fluid to the accumulators or hydraulic system when the ABS system is activated.

Modulator assembly

The modulator assembly contains the pump motor and various valves and orifices. It regulates brake pressure during a stop when the ABS system is activated. The modulator is mounted below the battery and protected by an acid shield.

Controller

The controller is mounted on the passenger side frame rail in the engine compartment and is the "brain" for the system. The function of the controller is to accept and process information received from the wheel speed sensors to control the hydraulic line pressure and avoid wheel lock up. It also monitors the system and stores fault codes which indicate specific problems.

Wheel speed sensors

A speed sensor is mounted at each wheel. The speed sensors send voltage signals to the controller indicating wheel rotational speed.

Diagnosis and repair

The ABS system has self-diagnostic capabilities. Each time the vehicle is started, the system runs a self-test. The amber ABS warning light comes on during the test (usually for one to two seconds).
If the amber warning light comes on and stays on during vehicle operation, or if it comes on intermittently, there may be a fault in the ABS system. However, the main brake system will function normally. Faults in the main brake system are indicated by a red warning light.

Although a special electronic tester is necessary to properly diagnose the system, the home mechanic can perform a few preliminary checks before taking the vehicle to a dealer service department which is equipped with this tester.

a) *Make sure the brake calipers are in good condition.*
b) *Check the 60-way electrical connector at the controller.*
c) *Check the fuses.*
d) *Follow the wiring harness to the speed sensors and brake light switch and make sure all connections are secure and the wiring isn't damaged.*

Note: *If the above preliminary checks don't rectify the problem, the vehicle should be diagnosed by a dealer service department.*

13   Brake hydraulic system - bleeding

Refer to illustration 13.8
Warning: *Wear eye protection when bleeding the brake system. If the fluid comes in contact with your eyes, immediately rinse them with water and seek medical attention.*
Note 1: *The main brake system on vehicles equipped with ABS is bled in the same manner as for non-ABS models. The ABS system must also be bled, but this is a separate procedure. Bleeding the ABS system requires*

the same special tester used to diagnose the system and must be done by a dealer service department.
Note 2: *Bleeding the hydraulic system is necessary to remove air that manages to find its way into the system when it's been opened during removal and installation of a hose, line, caliper or master cylinder.*

1   It'll probably be necessary to bleed the system at all four brakes if air has entered the system due to low fluid level, or if the brake lines have been disconnected at the master cylinder.

2   If a brake line was disconnected only at a wheel, then only that caliper or wheel cylinder must be bled.

3   If a brake line was disconnected at a fitting located between the master cylinder and any of the brakes, that part of the system served by the disconnected line must be bled.

4   Remove any residual vacuum from the brake power booster by applying the brake several times with the engine off.

5   Remove the master cylinder reservoir cover and fill the reservoir with brake fluid. Reinstall the cover. **Note:** *Check the fluid level often during the bleeding operation and add fluid as necessary to prevent the fluid level from falling low enough to allow air into the master cylinder.*

6   Have an assistant on hand, as well as a supply of new brake fluid, a clear plastic container partially filled with clean brake fluid, a length of tubing (preferably clear) to fit over the bleeder screw and a wrench to open and close the bleeder screw.

7   Beginning at the right rear wheel, loosen the bleeder screw slightly, then tighten it to a point where it's snug but can still be loosened quickly and easily.

8   Place one end of the tubing over the bleeder screw and submerge the other end in brake fluid in the container **(see illustration)**.

9   Have your assistant pump the brakes slowly a few times to get pressure in the system, then hold the pedal down firmly.

10   While the pedal is held down, open the bleeder screw. Watch for air bubbles to exit

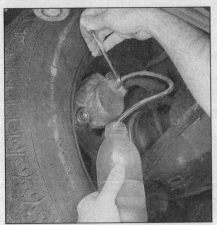

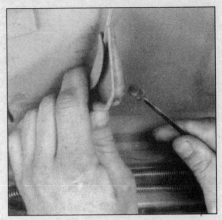

13.8 When bleeding the brakes, push one end of a clear plastic tube onto the bleeder screw at the caliper or wheel cylinder and submerge the other end in a container of brake fluid; build up pressure in the lines with the brake pedal and open the bleeder screw – air expelled from the lines is visible as bubbles; when the bubbles disappear, you've bled the line to that caliper or wheel cylinder

14.4 Turn this nut to adjust the parking brake

15.3 Once you've loosened the equalizer adjusting nut, detach the rear end of the front cable from this connector

the submerged end of the tube. When the fluid flow slows, tighten the screw, then have your assistant release the pedal.

11   Repeat Steps 9 and 10 until no more air is seen leaving the tube, then tighten the bleeder screw and proceed to the left front wheel, the left rear wheel and the right front wheel, in that order, and perform the same procedure. Be sure to check the fluid in the master cylinder reservoir frequently.

12   Never use old brake fluid. It contains moisture which will deteriorate the brake system components and boil when the fluid gets hot.

13   Refill the master cylinder with fluid at the end of the operation.

14   Check the operation of the brakes. The pedal should feel solid when depressed, with no sponginess. If necessary, repeat the entire process. **Warning:** *Don't operate the vehicle if you're in doubt about the condition of the brake system.*

14   Parking brake - adjustment

Refer to illustration 14.4

1   The rear drum brakes must be in proper working order before adjusting the parking brake (see Section 5 or 6).

2   Block the front wheels to prevent vehicle movement, raise the rear of the vehicle and support it securely on jackstands. Release the parking brake.

3   Clean the cable adjuster threads with a wire brush and lubricate them with multi-purpose grease.

4   Loosen the adjusting nut **(see illustration)** until there's slack in the cable.

5   Have an assistant rotate the rear wheels to make sure they turn easily.

6   Tighten the adjusting nut until a slight drag can be felt when the rear wheels are turned. You may have to keep the adjuster rod from turning by holding it with a wrench or pair of pliers.

7   Loosen the nut until the rear wheels turn freely, then back it off an additional two full turns.

8   Apply and release the parking brake several times to make sure it operates properly. It must lock the rear wheels when applied and the wheels must turn easily, without dragging, when it's released.

9   Lower the vehicle.

15   Parking brake cables - removal and installation

1   Raise the rear of the vehicle and support it securely on jackstands.

Front cable

Refer to illustrations 15.3 and 15.8

2   Working under the vehicle, loosen the adjusting nut until there's slack in the cables **(see illustration 14.4)**.

3   Detach the rear end of the front cable from the connector that attaches it to the middle cable **(see illustration)**.

4   From inside the vehicle, remove the driver's side kick panel.

5   Pull up the forward end of the front cable and disconnect it.

6   Pinch the cable retainer with needle-nose pliers and pull it down through the cable retaining bracket.

7   Pull the cable assembly through the grommet in the hole in the floor.

8   Installation is the reverse of removal **(see illustration)**.

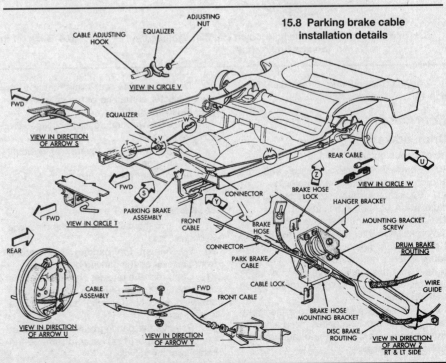

15.8 Parking brake cable installation details

9

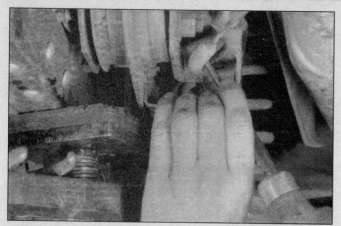

15.14 Using a hammer punch, knock the cable lock loose from the brake cable support bracket on the trailing arm and detach the cable from the bracket

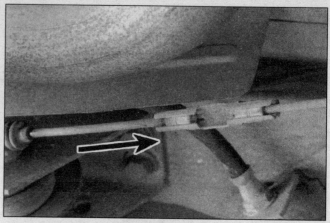

15.15 Pull forward on the rear cable to disconnect it from this connector

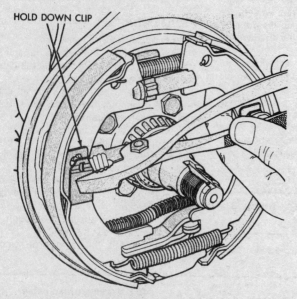

16.3 Use pliers to remove the hold-down clip that secures the forward brake shoe

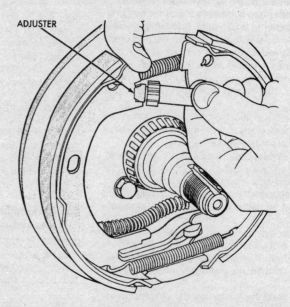

16.4 Back off the adjuster all the way, then remove it from between the shoes

9   Adjust the parking brake (see Section 14).

Rear cable

Drum brakes

Refer to illustrations 15.14 and 15.15

10   Remove the rear wheels and the hub/drum assemblies (see Chapter 1).
11   Back off the equalizer adjusting nut **(see illustration 14.4)** until the cable is slack.
12   Disconnect the rear brake cable from the brake shoe lever **(see illustration 8.6)**.
13   Locate the retainer at the end of the rear cable, where it enters the brake shoe backing plate. Pinch this retainer with pliers (or use a hose clamp) and pull the retainer through the backing plate.
14   Remove the cable lock from the brake cable support bracket on the trailing arm **(see illustration)** and detach the cable from the trailing arm assembly.

15   Disconnect the rear brake cable from the connector at the end of the middle cable **(see illustration)**.
16   The above procedure also applies to the other rear cable.
17   Installation is the reverse of removal **(see illustration 15.8)**.
18   Adjust the parking brake (see Section 14).

Disc brakes

19   Remove the caliper and brake disc (see Sections 5 and 7).
20   Disconnect the parking brake cable from the lever on the parking brake shoe.
21   Compress the retainer on the end of the cable housing with pliers or a hose clamp and feed the cable through the retaining hole in the adapter.
22   Remove the parking brake cable clip at the cable support bracket and remove the cable from the vehicle.

23   The above procedure also applies to the other rear cable.
24   Installation is the reverse of removal.

16   Parking brake shoes (rear disc brake models) - removal and installation

Refer to illustrations 16.3, 16.4, 16.5 and 16.6

1   Remove the brake caliper and disc (See Sections 5, 6 and 7).
2   Remove the hub and bearings (see Chapter 1).
3   Remove the hold-down clip from the forward parking brake shoe **(see illustration)**.
4   Back off the parking brake adjuster all the way, then remove it **(see illustration)**.
5   Remove the upper shoe-to-shoe spring **(see illustration)**.

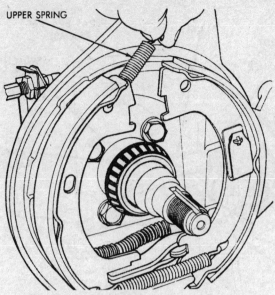

16.5 Remove the upper shoe-to-shoe spring . . .

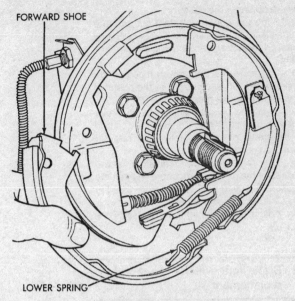

16.6 . . . then pull the forward shoe away from its anchor and disconnect the lower shoe-to-shoe spring from it

6   Pull the forward shoe away from its anchor, then remove the shoe and lower spring (see illustration).
7   Remove the hold-down clip from the rear shoe, then remove the rear shoe.
8   Reverse Steps 3 through 7 to install the shoes. Position the adjuster star wheel toward the front of the vehicle.
9   Turn the star wheel to adjust the parking brake shoes to the diameter listed in this Chapter's Specifications.
10   The remainder of installation is the reverse of the removal steps.
11   Perform Steps 1 through 10 on the other side of the vehicle.

17   Power brake booster - check, removal and installation

Operating check

1   Depress the brake pedal several times with the engine off and make sure there's no change in the pedal reserve distance.
2   Depress the pedal and start the engine. If the pedal goes down slightly, operation is normal.

Airtightness check

3   Start the engine and turn it off after one or two minutes. Slowly depress the brake pedal several times. If the pedal goes down farther the first time but gradually rises after the second or third depression, the booster is airtight.
4   Depress the brake pedal while the engine is running, then stop the engine with the pedal depressed. If there's no change in the pedal reserve travel (distance between the pedal and the floor) after holding the pedal for 30 seconds, the booster is airtight.

Removal and installation

Refer to illustration 17.11

5   Power brake booster units should not be disassembled. They require special tools not normally found in most service stations or shops. They're fairly complex and because of their critical relationship to brake performance it's best to replace a defective booster unit with a new or rebuilt one.
6   To remove the booster, first remove the brake master cylinder (see Section 10).
7   Disconnect the vacuum hose between the engine and the booster. Make sure you don't damage this hose when removing it from the booster fitting. **Caution:** *Disconnect the hose from the check valve on the booster; don't remove the check valve from the booster.*
8   Detach the brackets that secure the

steel heater coolant tube to the dash panel and driver's side frame rail.
9   On vehicles with a manual transaxle, remove the clutch cable mounting bracket. Also push aside the wiring harness on the shock tower. If you need more room, unplug the harness at the multi-connector on the firewall.
10   Working under the dash, position a small screwdriver between the center tang on the retainer clip and the pin in the brake pedal, then rotate the screwdriver enough to allow the retainer clip center tang to pass over the end of the brake pedal pin and pull it from the pin. Disconnect the pushrod from the pedal pin. Discard the retainer clip and use a new one on reassembly.
11   Remove the nuts and washers holding the brake booster to the firewall (see illustration). You may need a light to see them -

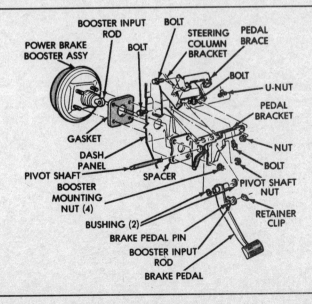

17.11 Power brake booster mounting details

9

they're up under the dash.

12   Slide the booster straight out until the studs clear the holes and lift it (along with any installed gaskets) out of the engine compartment.

13   Lubricate the bearing surfaces of the brake pedal pin and the tip of the pushrod with multi-purpose grease.

14   Install the booster, along with any previously installed gaskets. Connect the pushrod to the pedal pin and install a new retainer clip.

15   The remainder of installation is the reverse of the removal procedure. Tighten the booster mounting nuts to the torque listed in this Chapter's Specifications.

16   Adjust the brake light switch (see Section 18).

18   Brake light switch - check and replacement

Refer to illustration 18.1

1   The brake light switch **(see illustration)** is located under the dash, at the upper end of the brake pedal assembly. A plunger on the switch is in constant contact with a striker at the top of the pedal assembly. When the pedal is depressed, the striker moves forward, releasing the plunger, which closes the circuit to the brake lights.

Check

Note: *Refer to the Wiring Diagrams at the end of Chapter 12.*

2   Use a test light to verify that there's voltage in the wire between the battery and the switch.

a) *If there isn't, find the short or open and fix it (see Chapter 12).*

b) *If there is, proceed to the next Step.*

3   Now use the test light to verify that there's no voltage in the wire between the

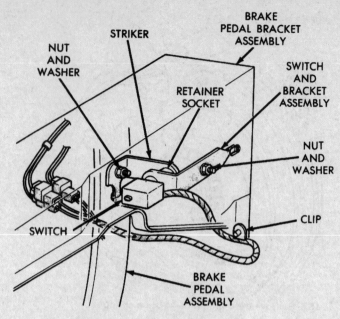

18.1 Brake light switch installation details

switch and the brake lights when the brake pedal is not depressed.

a) *If there is, the switch is shorted - replace it (see below).*

b) *If there isn't, proceed to the next Step.*

4   Now depress the brake pedal and use the test light to verify that there's voltage in the wire between the switch and the brake lights.

a) *If there is, the switch itself is functioning normally - the problem is somewhere between the switch and the brake lights.*

b) *If there isn't, the switch is has an open - replace it (proceed to the next step).*

Replacement

5   Unplug the electrical connector.

6   The retainer socket locks the switch into the mounting bracket, but if you pull on the switch with some force, the retainer socket will come free.

7   To install the new switch, insert the retainer socket through the switch mounting bracket and plug in the electrical connector.

8   Push the switch forward as far as it will go. As you push the retainer socket through the hole in the bracket, it acts like a ratchet - it can be pushed into the bracket but it can't slip back. The brake pedal will move forward slightly.

9   Gently pull back on the brake pedal (very little movement is needed). This brings the plunger toward the switch until the brake pedal can't go any further. The switch then ratchets backward to the correct position. No further adjustment is necessary.

Chapter 10
Suspension and steering systems

Contents

Specifications

Torque specifications

Front suspension

Ft-lbs (unless otherwise indicated)

Balljoint clamp bolt/nut	
1989 and 1990	70
1991 on	105
Driveaxle hub nut	See Chapter 8
Control arm pivot bolt nuts	125
Stabilizer bar bolts (all)	
1989 and 1990	40
1991 on	50
Strut assembly	
Strut-to-steering knuckle nuts	75 plus 1/4 turn
Upper mounting nuts	20
Wheel lug nuts	See Chapter 1

Rear suspension

Trailing arm-to-hanger bracket mounting nuts	
1989 to 1991	40
1992	45
Track bar	
Pivot bolt at axle (lower end)	70
Pivot bolt at frame bracket (upper end)	55
Shock absorber mounting bolts/nuts	45
Spindle/brake assembly mounting bolts (drum and disc brakes)	55

10

Torque specifications

Steering

	Ft-lbs (unless otherwise indicated)
Airbag module-to-steering wheel fasteners	90 to 100 in-lbs
Crossmember mounting bolts	90
Ignition switch/shifter interlock adjustment nut	15 to 25 in-lbs
Inner tie-rod jam nut	
Non-power steering	45 to 65
Power steering	55
Steering gear mounting bolts/nuts	
1989 and 1990	21
1991 on	50
Steering wheel retaining nut	45
Tie-rod end-to-steering knuckle nut	
Non-power steering	25 to 50
Power steering	38

1   General information

Refer to illustrations 1.1 and 1.2

Front suspension is by MacPherson struts. The steering knuckles are located by control arms and both control arms are connected by a stabilizer bar **(see illustration)**.

The rear suspension features a beam-type axle with coil springs, located by trailing arms and a track bar **(see illustration)**. Damping is handled by vertically-mounted shock absorbers located between the axle and the chassis.

The rack-and-pinion steering gear is located behind the engine and actuates the steering arms which are integral with the steering knuckles. Power assist is optional and the steering column is designed to collapse in the event of an accident. **Note:**

These vehicles use a combination of standard and metric fasteners on the various suspension and steering components, so it would be a good idea to have both types of tools available when beginning work.

A shifter-ignition interlock is used on 1992 automatic transaxle models to lock the shifter in Park when the ignition switch is in the Lock or Accessory position.

Frequently, when working on the sus-

1.1 Front suspension and steering components

1	*Strut assembly*	2	*Control arm*	3	*Stabilizer bar*	4	*Steering gear*

1.2 Rear suspension components

1	Shock absorber	2	Coil spring	3	Rear axle assembly	4	Track bar

pension or steering system components, you may come across fasteners which seem impossible to loosen. These fasteners on the underside of the vehicle are continually subjected to water, road grime, mud, etc., and can become rusted or frozen, making them extremely difficult to remove. In order to unscrew these stubborn fasteners without damaging them (or other components), be sure to use lots of penetrating oil and allow it to soak in for a while. Using a wire brush to clean exposed threads will also ease removal of the nut or bolt and prevent damage to the threads. Sometimes a sharp blow with a hammer and punch will break the bond between a nut and bolt threads, but care must be taken to prevent the punch from slipping off the fastener and ruining the threads. Heating the stuck fastener and surrounding area with a torch sometimes helps too, but isn't recommended because of the obvious dangers associated with fire. Long breaker bars and extension, or "cheater", pipes will increase leverage, but never use an extension pipe on a ratchet - the ratcheting mechanism could be damaged. Sometimes tightening the nut or bolt first will help to break it loose. Fasteners that require drastic

measures to remove should always be replaced with new ones.

Since most of the procedures dealt with in this Chapter involve jacking up the vehicle and working underneath it, a good pair of jackstands will be needed. A hydraulic floor jack is the preferred type of jack to lift the

2.3 Mark the position of the camber cam (arrow) in relation to the strut

vehicle, and it can also be used to support certain components during various operations. **Warning:** *Never, under any circumstances, rely on a jack to support the vehicle while working on it. Whenever any of the suspension or steering fasteners are loosened or removed they must be inspected and, if necessary, replaced with new ones of the same part number or of original equipment quality and design. Torque specifications must be followed for proper reassembly and component retention. Never attempt to heat or straighten any suspension or steering components. Instead, replace any bent or damaged part with a new one.*

10

2 Strut assembly - removal and installation

Refer to illustrations 2.3, 2.5, 2.6 and 2.11
1 Loosen the front wheel lug nuts.
2 Raise the vehicle and support it securely on jackstands. Remove the front wheels.
3 Mark the position of the camber cam **(see illustration)**.
4 Remove the strut-to-steering knuckle nuts, bolts, cam and washer plate.

2.5 Remove this bolt (arrow) and detach the brake hose bracket from the strut

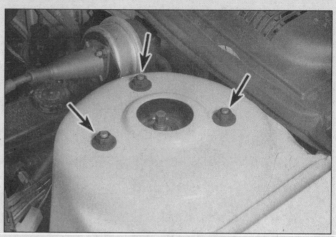

2.6 Remove these three upper mounting nuts (arrows) – DO NOT remove the center nut

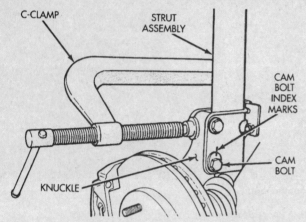

2.11 Install a C-clamp to hold the knuckle and strut together while you align the camber cam, then tighten the knuckle-to-strut bolts and nuts

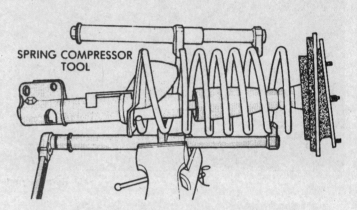

3.4 Install the spring compressor in accordance with the tool manufacturer's instructions and compress the spring until all pressure is removed from the upper spring seat

5   Disconnect the brake hose bracket from the strut **(see illustration)**.

6   Remove the upper mounting nuts **(see illustration)**, disengage the strut from the steering knuckle and detach it from the vehicle.

7   Inspect the strut and coil spring assembly for leaking fluid, dents, damage and corrosion. If the strut is damaged, see Section 3.

8   To install the strut, place it in position with the studs extending up through the shock tower. Install the nuts and tighten them to the torque listed in this Chapter's Specifications.

9   Attach the strut to the steering knuckle, then insert the strut-to-steering knuckle bolts through the cam and washer plate. Install the nuts, but don't tighten them yet.

10   Attach the brake hose bracket to the strut.

11   Install a 4-inch or larger C-clamp on the strut and knuckle **(see illustration)**. Tighten it just enough to remove any looseness between the knuckle and strut. Align the marks you made on the cam and strut. Tighten the steering knuckle-to-strut bolts

and nuts to the torque listed in this Chapter's Specifications.

12   Install the wheels and lower the vehicle.

---

3   Strut - replacement

Refer to illustrations 3.4, 3.5 and 3.6

Note: *You'll need a spring compressor for this procedure. Spring compressors are available on a daily rental basis at most auto parts stores or equipment yards.*

1   If the struts or coil springs exhibit the telltale signs of wear (leaking fluid, loss of damping capability, chipped, sagging or cracked coil springs), explore all options before beginning any work. The strut insert assemblies are not serviceable and must be replaced if a problem develops. However, strut assemblies complete with springs may be available on an exchange basis, which eliminates much time and work. Whichever route you choose to take, check on the cost and availability of parts before disassembling your vehicle. **Warning:** *Disassembling a strut assembly is a potentially dangerous undertak-*

ing and utmost attention must be directed to the job at hand, or serious bodily injury may result. Use only a high-quality spring compressor and carefully follow the manufacturer's instructions furnished with the tool. After removing the coil spring from the strut assembly, set it aside in a safe, isolated area (a steel cabinet is preferred).

2   Remove the strut and spring assembly (see Section 2).

3   Mount the strut assembly in a vise. Line the vise jaws with wood or rags to prevent damage to the unit and don't tighten the vise excessively.

4   Install the spring compressor in accordance with the manufacturer's instructions **(see illustration)**. Compress the spring until you can wiggle the mount assembly and spring seat.

5   To loosen the damper shaft nut, hold the shaft with a box-end wrench while loosening the shaft nut with another box-end wrench **(see illustration)**.

6   Disassemble the strut assembly and lay out the parts in exactly the same order as shown **(see illustration)**. **Warning:** *When*

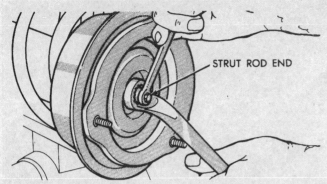

3.5 To remove the damper shaft nut, hold the shaft in place with a box-wrench and loosen the nut with another box-wrench

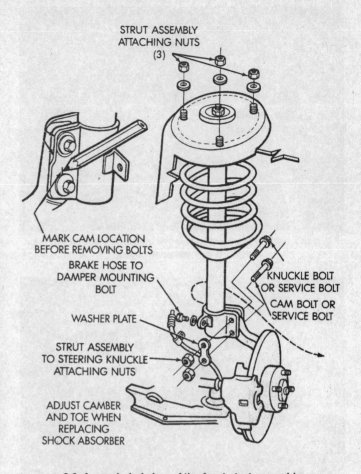

3.6 An exploded view of the front strut assembly

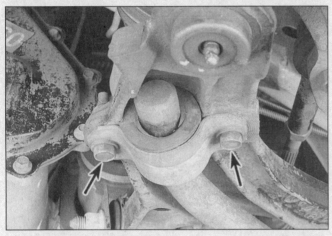

4.2 Put a back-up wrench on each nut (on top of control arm, not visible) and remove these retainer bolts (arrows) and retainers from both control arms

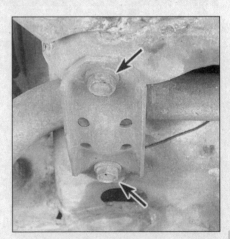

4.3 Remove these clamp bolts (arrows) and both clamps from the crossmember

removing the compressed spring, lift it off very carefully and set it in a safe place, such as a steel cabinet. Keep the ends of the spring away from your body. Note: Mark the spring so it can be reinstalled on the same side of the vehicle from which it was removed.

7   Inspect all rubber parts for damage, cracking and hardness and replace as necessary.

8   Reassembly is the reverse of disassembly. Be careful not to damage the damper shaft or the strut will leak. When installing the spring, be sure the spring ends mesh with the spring anti-rotation stops provided by the spring upper and lower seats.

4   Stabilizer bar - removal and installation

Refer to illustrations 4.2 and 4.3

1   Loosen the front wheel lug nuts, raise the front of the vehicle, support it securely on jackstands and remove the front wheels.

2   Remove the stabilizer bar retainer bolts, nuts and retainers from the control arms **(see illustration)**.

3   Support the stabilizer bar and remove the stabilizer bar clamp bolts and clamps from the crossmember **(see illustration)**. Remove the stabilizer bar from the vehicle.

4   Check the bar for damage, corrosion and signs of twisting.

5   Check the clamps, bushings and retainers for distortion, damage and wear. Replace the inner bushings by prying them open at the split and removing them. Install the new bushings with the curved surface (early models) or external rib (later models) up and the split facing toward the front of the vehicle. The outer bushings can be removed by cutting them off or hammering them from the bar. Force the new bushings onto the end of the bar until 1/2-inch of the bar is protruding. Silicone spray lubricant will ease this process.

6   Attach the bar to the crossmember, then install the clamps, bolts and nuts, but don't tighten them completely yet.

7   Install the bushing retainers and bolts on the control arms, but don't tighten the bolts completely yet.

8   Raise the control arms to normal ride height and tighten the bolts to the torque listed in this Chapter's Specifications.

9   Install the wheels and lower the vehicle.

5   Control arm - removal, inspection and installation

Refer to illustrations 5.3, 5.4, 5.5 and 5.9

1   Raise the front of the vehicle, support it securely on jackstands and remove the front wheels.

2   Disconnect the stabilizer bar from the

10

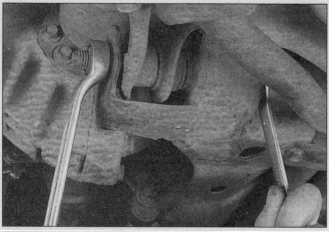

5.3 Use a back-up wrench to remove the pivot bolt and nut from the front of the control arm

5.4 Remove this pivot bolt from the rear of the control arm

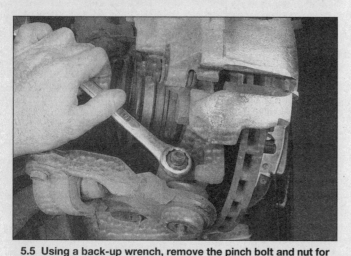

5.5 Using a back-up wrench, remove the pinch bolt and nut for the balljoint stud clamp at the bottom of the steering knuckle, then pull the control arm down to separate the stud from the knuckle

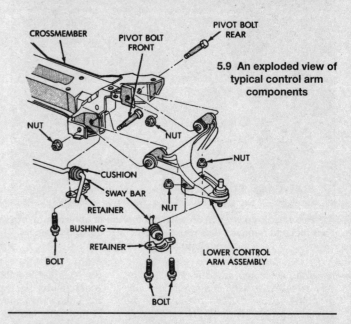

5.9 An exploded view of typical control arm components

control arms (see Section 4) and rotate the bar down, out of the way.

3   Remove the front pivot bolt and nut from the control arm **(see illustration)**.

4   Remove the rear pivot bolt and nut **(see illustration)** from the control arm.

5   Remove the balljoint clamp pinch bolt and nut from the steering knuckle **(see illustration)**.

6   Pull the balljoint stud from the steering knuckle. **Caution:** *Do not move the steering knuckle/strut assembly out or you may separate the inner CV joint.*

7   Remove the control arm by pulling it straight down.

8   Inspect the control arm for distortion and the bushings for wear, damage and deterioration. If the control arm is damaged or bent, replace it. If an inner pivot bushing or a balljoint are worn, have them replaced by a dealer service department or repair shop with the special tools necessary to do the job. **Note:** *Some bushings are not serviceable and the entire control arm must be replaced if the bushings are worn.*

9   Installation is the reverse of removal **(see illustration)**. Don't tighten the pivot bolts until the vehicle is at normal ride height.

10   After you've installed the wheels and lowered the vehicle so that its weight is on the suspension, tighten the pivot bolts to the torque listed in this Chapter's Specifications.

6   Steering knuckle and hub - removal, inspection and installation

Removal

Refer to illustrations 6.1 and 6.15

1   With the vehicle weight resting on the front suspension, remove the hub cap, cotter pin, nut lock and spring washer. Loosen, but do not remove, the front hub (driveaxle) nut and wheel lug nuts **(see illustration)**.

2   Raise the front of the vehicle, support it securely on jackstands and remove the front wheels.

3   Remove the driveaxle hub nut and washer.

4   Push the driveaxle in until it is free of the hub. It may be necessary to tap on the axle end with a brass drift punch and hammer to dislodge the driveaxle from the hub.

5   Remove the cotter pin and nut and use a puller to disconnect the tie-rod end from the steering knuckle (see Section 14).

6   Move the tie-rod out of the way and secure it with a piece of wire.

7   Disconnect the brake hose bracket from the strut by removing the bolt and retainer.

8   Remove the caliper and brake pads (see Chapter 9), then remove the caliper mounting bracket from the steering knuckle. Taking care not to twist the brake hose, hang the caliper out of the way in the wheel well with a piece of wire.

9   Detach the stabilizer bar retainer bolts from the control arms (see Section 4) and pull the stabilizer bar down and out of the way.

10   Remove the retainer washer (if equipped) from the wheel stud and pull off the brake disc.

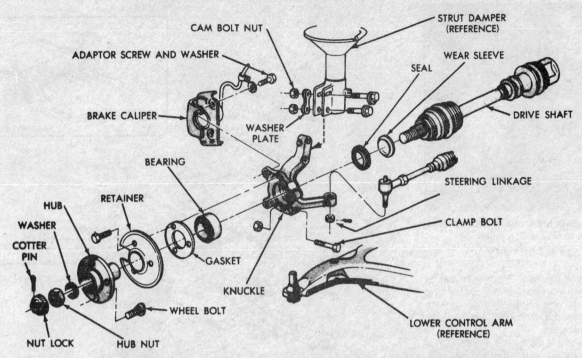

STRUT DAMPER (REFERENCE)
CAM BOLT NUT
ADAPTOR SCREW AND WASHER
WEAR SLEEVE
SEAL
BRAKE CALIPER
WASHER PLATE
DRIVE SHAFT
BEARING
STEERING LINKAGE
HUB
RETAINER
WASHER
CLAMP BOLT
COTTER PIN
GASKET
KNUCKLE
WHEEL BOLT
NUT LOCK   HUB NUT
LOWER CONTROL ARM (REFERENCE)

6.1 An exploded view of a typical steering knuckle assembly and related components (1989 and 1990 model shown; 1991 and later models use a one-piece hub and bearing assembly which is bolted to the hub)

11   Mark the position of the camber cam (see Section 2).
12   Remove the balljoint pinch bolt and nut and disengage the balljoint from the hub (see Section 5).
13   Remove the steering knuckle-to-strut bolts and nuts (see Section 5).
14   With the knuckle and hub assembly in the straight-ahead position, grasp it securely and pull it directly out and off the driveaxle splines. **Caution:** *Be careful not to pull the driveaxle out or you may disengage the inner CV joint.*

Inspection

15   Place the assembly on a clean work surface and wipe it off with a lint-free cloth. Inspect the knuckle for rust, damage and cracks. Check the bearings by rotating them to make sure they move freely, without excessive noise or looseness. The bearings should be packed with an adequate supply of clean grease. If the bearings are bad or in doubtful condition, do the following:

a) *1989 and 1990 models: Further disassembly will have to be left to your dealer service department or a repair shop because of the special tools required.*
b) *1991 and later models: Remove four bolts that secure the hub and bearing assembly to the knuckle, then remove the assembly* **(see illustration)***. Make sure the mounting surfaces are completely clean and free of nicks, then install a new hub and bearing assembly. Tighten the bolts in a criss-cross pattern to the torque listed in this Chapter's Specifications.*

Installation

16   Prior to installation, clean the CV joint seal and the hub grease seal with solvent (don't get any solvent on the CV joint boot). Lubricate the entire circumference of the CV joint wear sleeve and seal contact surface with multi-purpose grease (see Chapter 8).
17   Carefully place the knuckle and hub assembly in position. Align the splines of the axle and the hub and slide the hub into place.
18   Install the knuckle-to-strut bolts, camber cam, washer plate and nuts, followed by the balljoint pinch bolt and nut. Adjust the position of the camber cam (see Section 2) and tighten the nuts to the torque listed in this Chapter's Specifications.
19   Reattach the tie-rod end to the steering knuckle, tighten the nut and install a new cotter pin (see Section 14).
20   Install the brake disc, pads and caliper/adapter assembly (see Chapter 9).
21   Reattach the brake hose bracket to the strut.
22   Attach the ends of the stabilizer bar to the control arms and tighten the retainer fasteners to the torque listed in this Chapter's Specifications.
23   Push the CV joint completely into the hub to make sure it is seated and install the washer and hub nut finger tight.
24   Install the wheels, hand tighten the lug nuts, lower the vehicle and tighten the wheel lug nuts to the torque specified in Chapter 1.
25   With an assistant applying the brakes, tighten the hub nut to the torque specified in Chapter 8. Install the spring washer, nut lock and a new cotter pin.

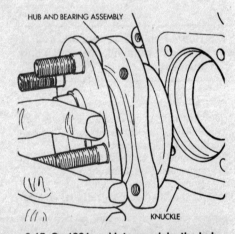

HUB AND BEARING ASSEMBLY

KNUCKLE

6.15 On 1991 and later models, the hub and bearing assembly is unbolted from the knuckle and replaced as a unit

26   With the weight of the vehicle on the suspension, check the steering knuckle and balljoint nuts to make sure they are tightened properly.
27   Have the vehicle front end alignment checked.

7   Balljoints - check and replacement

Refer to illustration 7.2

1   The suspension balljoints are designed to operate without freeplay.

10

7.2 Try to lever the steering knuckle from side to side with a prybar or large screwdriver

2   To check for wear, place a prybar or large screwdriver between the control arm and the underside of the steering knuckle and try to lever the knuckle from side to side **(see illustration)**.
3   If there is any movement, the balljoint is worn and must be replaced with a new one. Remove the control arm (see Section 5) and take it to a dealer service department or automotive machine shop to have the old balljoint pressed out and a new one pressed in.

8   Rear shock absorbers and coil springs - removal, inspection and installation

Removal

Refer to illustrations 8.2a, 8.2b, 8.3a and 8.3b
1   Raise the rear of the vehicle and support it securely on jackstands.
2   Support the axle with a jack and remove the rear wheels **(see illustrations)**.
3   Remove the lower and upper shock mounting bolts **(see illustrations)** and de-

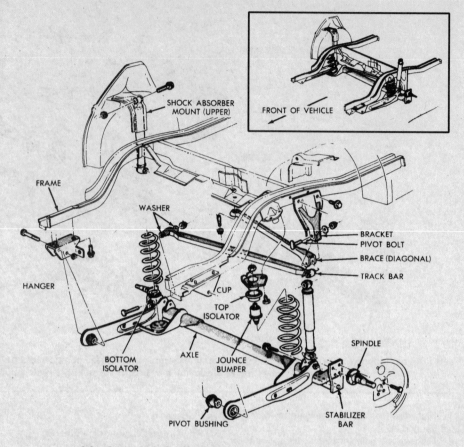

8.2a An exploded view of typical rear suspension components

tach the shock absorber.
4   If you wish to remove the coil springs, carefully lower the jack, supporting the axle until all compression is relieved and remove the coil spring.

Inspection

5   With the shock upright, grasp it at each end and pump it in and out several times. The action should be smooth, with no binding or dead spots.
Check for fluid leakage. Replace the shock with a new one if it is leaking or if the action is rough. Always replace the shocks in pairs.
6   Inspect the jounce bumper at the upper end of the coil spring. If it's cracked or dried out, replace it: remove the two screws that attach the jounce bumper cup to the under-

8.2b Support the rear axle with a jack before removing the shock absorber mounting bolts – if you don't, the coil spring, which is under a great deal of pressure, will snap the axle down violently

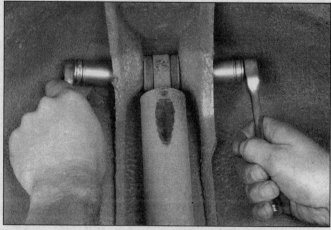

8.3a Use a back-up wrench when removing the upper mounting bolt and nut from the shock absorber

8.3b Use a back-up wrench when removing the lower mounting nut and bolt from the shock absorber (arrow)

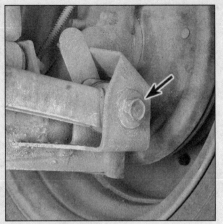

11.3a Remove the track bar-to-axle pivot bolt (arrow) . . .

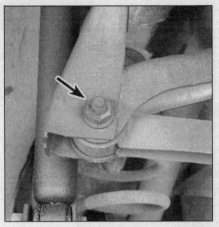

11.3b . . . and the track bar-to-frame pivot bolt (arrow) and remove the track bar

side of the frame rail and remove it. Make sure the new cup fasteners are firmly tightened.

7   Check the springs for breakage, nicks and cracks. Replace the spring if you notice any of these conditions.

Installation

8   To install the coil springs, make sure they're seated properly, then carefully raise the axle back into position with the jack.

9   Hold the shock in position and install the bolts. Tighten the upper bolt to the torque listed in this Chapter's Specifications. Lower the vehicle and tighten the lower bolt to the torque listed in this Chapter's Specifications.

9   Rear hub/drum or disc assembly - removal and installation

This procedure is covered in Chapter 1 as a part of the *Rear wheel bearing check, repack and adjustment* procedure.

10   Rear spindle - inspection, removal and installation

Removal

1   Remove the rear hub/drum or disc (see Section 9).

2   Clean the axle and inspect the bearing contact surfaces for wear and damage.

3   The spindle should be replaced with a new one if it is bent, damaged or worn.

4   Disconnect the parking brake cable from the brake assembly (see Chapter 9).

5   Disconnect and plug the rear brake line at the wheel cylinder (see Chapter 9).

6   Remove the four backing plate mounting bolts and detach the brake assembly and spindle. The bolts may have Torx-type heads, which require a special tool for removal. Be sure to mark the location of any spindle shims.

Installation

7   Place the shim(s) (if equipped), spindle and brake assembly in position, install the bolts and tighten them to the torque listed in this Chapter's Specifications, following a criss-cross pattern.

8   Connect the brake line and parking brake cable.

9   Install the hub/drum or disc (see Section 9), bleed the brakes and adjust the parking brake (see Chapter 9).

11   Track bar assembly - removal and installation

Refer to illustrations 11.3a and 11.3b

1   Loosen the rear wheel lug nuts, raise the vehicle, place it securely on jackstands and remove the rear wheels.

2   Raise the rear axle to normal ride height with a jack.

3   Support the track bar while you remove the track bar-to-axle pivot bolt and the track bar-to-frame pivot bolt **(see illustrations)**.

4   Remove the track bar. Inspect the bushing for cracks and deterioration. A dealer service department or automotive machine shop can install new bushings in the track bar, if necessary.

5   Installation is the reverse of removal.

12   Rear axle assembly - removal and installation

Refer to illustration 12.7

1   Loosen the rear wheel lug nuts, raise the vehicle, place it securely on jackstands and remove the rear wheels.

2   Support the axle at the center with a floor jack.

3   Disconnect the rear parking brake cables from the middle cable at the connectors, detach the retaining brackets and remove the cable retainer clips from the brackets on the trailing arms (see Chapter 9).

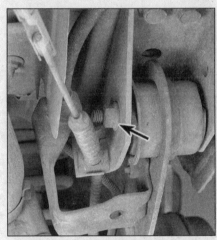

12.7 To remove the pivot bolts for the trailing arms, remove the nuts (arrow) and drive the bolt through the bushing and bracket – it looks as if the bolt will hit the body, but there's a small hole in the body behind the rubber flap on the right

Pull the rear cables through the holes in the trailing arms so they're clear of the axle assembly.

4   Disconnect the brake lines from the hoses at the trailing arm pivot points.

5   Disconnect the lower ends of the shock absorbers (see Section 8) and the track bar (see Section 11). Support the lower end of the track bar with a piece of sturdy wire.

6   Carefully lower the axle assembly until the coil springs are no longer under compression, then remove the coil springs and isolators.

7   Support the forward ends of the trailing arms with stands and remove the pivot bolts **(see illustration)**.

8   Remove the axle assembly.

9   Inspect the pivot bushings. If they're cracked or dried out, replace them.

10   Installation is the reverse of removal. Be sure to bleed the brakes after the job is complete (see Chapter 9).

10

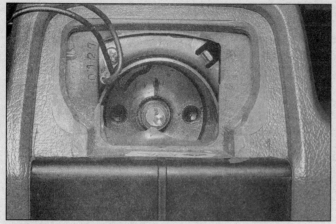

13.3 After you've removed the steering wheel nut, mark the relationship of the steering wheel to the shaft to ensure proper alignment at reassembly

13.4 Use a bolt-type puller like this one to remove the steering wheel

14.2a To disconnect the tie-rod end from the steering knuckle, remove the cotter pin and loosen the castellated nut . . .

14.2b . . . install a puller and separate the tie-rod end from the knuckle; note how the nut is still in place, loosened a few turns – this will prevent the components from separating violently

14.3a Using a back-up wrench on the tie-rod end, loosen the jam nut with another wrench . . .

13   Steering wheel - removal and installation

Refer to illustrations 13.3 and 13.4
Warning: *Some models are equipped with airbags. Always disconnect the negative battery cable and wait at least two minutes before working in the vicinity of the impact sensors, steering column or instrument panel to avoid the possibility of accidental deployment of the airbag, which could cause personal injury (see Chapter 12).*
1   Park the vehicle with the wheels pointing straight ahead. Disconnect the cable from the negative terminal of the battery. On airbag-equipped models, wait at least two minutes before proceeding.
2   On models without an airbag, remove the center pad assembly and disconnect the horn connectors. On models with an airbag, remove the cruise control switch (if equipped) and remove the airbag module retaining fasteners from the backside of the steering wheel. Unplug the horn and airbag electrical connectors and remove the airbag module.
Warning: *Carry the airbag module with the*

trim side facing away from your body, and set it in an isolated area with the trim side facing up.
3   Remove the steering wheel retaining nut and mark the relationship of the steering shaft and hub to simplify installation **(see illustration)**. On automatic transaxle models, remove the damper.
4   Use a bolt-type puller to remove the steering wheel **(see illustration)**. **Caution:** *Do not hammer on the shaft to remove the steering wheel.*
5   To install the wheel, align the mark on the steering wheel hub with the mark made on the shaft during removal and slip the wheel onto the shaft. Install the hub nut (and damper if removed) and tighten it to the torque listed in this Chapter's Specifications.
6   On models without an airbag, connect the horn wires and install the center pad assembly.
7   On models with an airbag, install the airbag module and tighten the fasteners to the torque listed in this Chapter's Specifications.
8   Connect the negative battery cable.

14   Tie-rod ends - removal and installation

Refer to illustrations 14.2a, 14.2b, 14.3a and 14.3b
1   Raise the front of the vehicle, support it securely on jackstands, block the rear wheels and set the parking brake. Remove the front wheels.
2   Remove the tie-rod-to-steering knuckle cotter pin, loosen the nut, then disconnect the tie-rod from the steering knuckle with a puller **(see illustrations)**.
3   Loosen the jam nut **(see illustration)**, mark the position of the tie-rod end on the inner tie-rod **(see illustration)**, unscrew the tie-rod end and remove it.
4   To install the tie-rod end, thread it onto the rod to the marked position and tighten the jam nut securely.
5   Connect the tie-rod end to the steering knuckle, install the nut and tighten it to the torque listed in this Chapter's Specifications. Install a new cotter pin.
6   Have the front end alignment checked by a dealer service department or an alignment shop.

14.3b . . . then paint an alignment mark on the threads of the inner tie-rod to mark the position of the tie-rod end

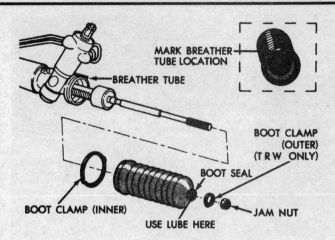

15.4 Steering gear boot replacement details

15 Steering gear boots - replacement

Refer to illustration 15.4

1   Raise the vehicle and support it securely on jackstands.

2   Remove the tie-rod end (see Section 14).

3   Remove the boot clamps.

4   Mark the location of the breather tube, use a small screwdriver to lift the boot out of the groove in the steering gear and remove the boot **(see illustration)**.

5   Prior to installation, lubricate the boot groove in the steering tie-rod with silicone-type grease.

6   Slide the new boot into position on the steering gear until it seats in the groove and install a new inner clamp. Make sure the breather tube fits securely in the boot.

7   Install the clamp(s).

8   Install the tie-rod end.

9   Lower the vehicle.

10   Have the front end alignment checked by a dealer service department or an alignment shop.

16 Steering gear - removal and installation

Warning: *On airbag-equipped models, make sure the steering shaft is not turned while the* steering gear is removed or you could damage the airbag clockspring. To prevent the shaft from turning, place the ignition key in the LOCK position or thread the seat belt through the steering wheel and clip it into place.*

Removal

Refer to illustration 16.3, 16.7, 16.8a and 16.8b

1   Loosen the wheel lug nuts, raise the vehicle, support it securely on jackstands and remove the front wheels.

2   Disconnect the tie-rod ends from the steering knuckles (see Section 14).

3   Support the front crossmember with a jack **(see illustration)**.

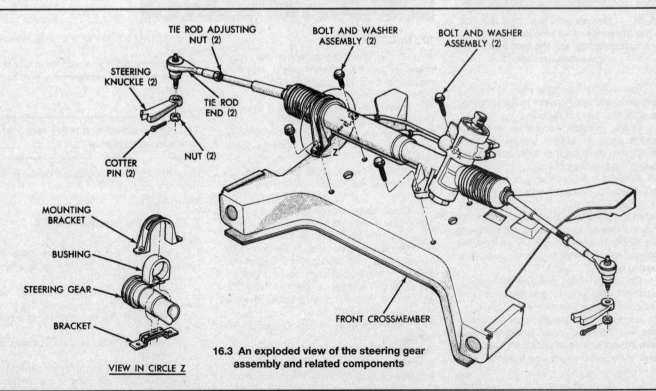

16.3 An exploded view of the steering gear assembly and related components

10

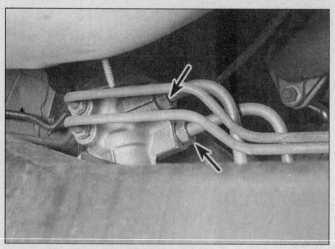

16.7 Disconnect the two fluid line fittings indicated by arrows; leave the others connected

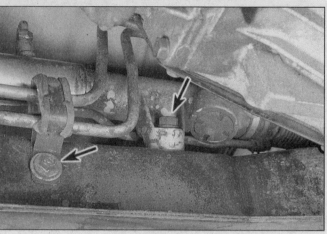

16.8a Remove the fluid line retainer clip bolt and both driver's side mounting bolts (one is behind the gear and not visible in this photo) . . .

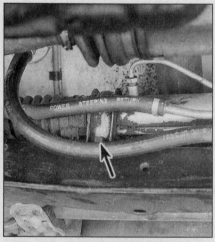

16.8b . . . remove both mounting bolts on the passenger side (one is behind the gear) and detach the gear from the crossmember

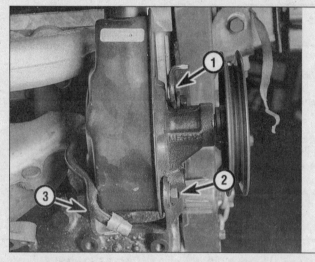

17.2 To detach the power steering pump from its mounting bracket on 2.2L and 2.5L engine models, remove these three fasteners

1) *Drivebelt adjustment bolt*
2) *Lower pivot bolt*
3) *Mounting stud nut*

4   Remove the four bolts (early models) or three bolts and one nut (later models) holding the crossmember to the body.

5   Lower the jack and crossmember far enough to gain access to the U-joint between the steering input shaft and the intermediate shaft of the steering column.

6   Remove the boot that protects the U-joint. Mark the relationship of the U-joint to the intermediate shaft so it can be re-connected the same way. Remove the pinch bolt from the U-joint. Lower the crossmember a little farther to separate the U-joint from the intermediate shaft (the U-joint stays with the steering gear).

7   On power-steering-equipped models, disconnect the lines **(see illustration)** and drain the fluid into a container.

8   Remove the steering gear mounting bolts and fluid line retaining clip bolt **(see illustrations)** and separate it from the crossmember by withdrawing it to the left side of the vehicle.

Installation

9   Position the steering gear on the crossmember, install the steering gear mounting bolts and fluid line retaining clip bolt and tighten them securely.

10   Raise the crossmember and steering gear into position with the jack.

11   On power steering equipped models, reconnect the lines. Use new O-rings on the fittings.

12   Connect the U-joint to the intermediate shaft, aligning the marks made on disassembly.

13   Install the U-joint pinch bolt.

14   Install the U-joint boot.

15   Install the four crossmember bolts (early models) or three bolts and one nut (later models). Start with the right rear bolt or nut, which is the pilot that aligns the crossmember correctly - and tighten them securely.

16   Attach the tie-rod ends to the steering knuckles (see Section 14).

17   Install the front wheels and lower the vehicle.

18   On power steering-equipped models, start the engine and bleed the steering system (see Section 18). While the engine is run-

ning, check for leaks at the hose connections.

19   Have the front end alignment checked by a dealer service department or an alignment shop.

---

17 Power steering pump - removal and installation

Note: *Metric fasteners are used on the power steering pump.*

Removal

2.2L and 2.5L engine models

Refer to illustration 17.2

1   Open the hood and disconnect the two wires from the air conditioner clutch cycling switch (if equipped).

2   Remove the drivebelt adjustment bolt **(see illustration)** from the front of the pump and (if equipped) the nut from the end hose bracket.

3   Raise the vehicle and support it securely on jackstands.

4   Disconnect the pump return hose and drain the fluid from the pump into a container.

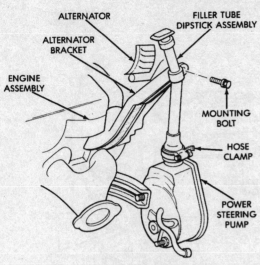

17.10 Power steering filler tube mounting details
(3.0L engine models)

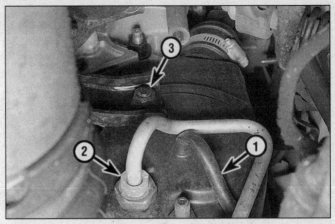

17.13 These components must be disconnected from the rear
side of the pump on 3.0L engine models

1	Fluid return hose (follow the metal fitting to the hose clamp)	2	Fluid pressure line flare nut
		3	Support bracket nut

5   While the pump is draining, remove the right side splash shield that protects the drivebelts.

6   Disconnect both hoses from the pump. Cap all open hose ends to prevent contamination.

7   Loosen the two lower pump mounting fasteners - a bolt and a stud nut, disconnect the drivebelt, then remove the fasteners.

8   To remove the pump, move it rearward to clear the mounting bracket, then remove the bracket. Then rotate the pump clockwise until the pump pulley faces toward the rear of the vehicle and pull the pump up and out.

3.0L engine models

Refer to illustrations 17.10, 17.13 and 17.16

9   Open the hood and remove the serpentine drive belt (see Chapter 1).

10   Unbolt the power steering pump filler tube from the alternator bracket **(see illustration)**. Remove the hose clamp and detach the filler tube from the pump.

11   Raise the vehicle and support it securely on jackstands.

12   Detach the exhaust pipe from the manifold (see Chapter 4). Push the pipe toward the driver's side of the vehicle to provide removal clearance for the pump.

13   Place a drain pan beneath the vehicle to catch dripping fluid. Disconnect the hose from the fluid return fitting **(see illustration)** and let the fluid drain into the pan.

14   While the fluid drains, disconnect the pressure fitting from the pump **(see illustration 17.13)**.

15   Remove the nut that secures the pump to the bracket **(see illustration 17.13)**. Unbolt the bracket from the engine and take it out.

16   Using a deep-drive socket, reach through the holes in the pump pulley and remove the two bolts which secure the front of the pump to the mounting plate **(see illustration)**.

17   Lower the pump away from the engine.

Pass it between the suspension crossmember and the exhaust pipe tunnel in the floorpan, then take it out.

Installation

18   Installation is the reverse of removal. On 2.2L and 2.5L engine models, make sure the tab on the mounting bracket is in the lower left front mounting hole. Be sure to use new O-rings when you attach the hoses to the pump. Don't tighten the fasteners until you've adjusted the belt tension.

19   Adjust the belt to the proper tension (see Chapter l) and tighten the fasteners.

20   Fill the pump with the specified fluid (see Chapter 1).

21   Start the engine, bleed the air from the system (see Section 18) and check the fluid level.

18   Power steering system - bleeding

1   The power steering system must be bled whenever a line is disconnected.

2   Check the fluid level in the reservoir; add the specified fluid to bring it up to the proper level (see Chapter 1 if necessary).

3   Start the engine and slowly turn the steering wheel several times from left to right and back again. Do not turn the wheel fully from lock to lock.

4   Check the fluid level, topping it up as necessary until it remains steady and no more bubbles appear in the reservoir.

19   Ignition switch/shifter interlock - check and adjustment

Check

Refer to illustration 19.1

1   Place the shifter in Park and the shifter

17.16 To detach the front side of the
pump on 3.0L engine models, reach
through the access holes in the pulley
with a deep-drive socket and remove the
two mounting bolts (the lower bolt is
hidden beneath the upper bolt)

knob pushbutton in its fully raised position **(see illustration on the following page)**.

2   Turn the ignition key. The ignition switch should move freely through all of its positions.

3   Place the shifter in the Drive or Overdrive position. It should be impossible to turn the ignition key from the Off or Run position to the Lock position.

4   If the system doesn't perform as described, adjust it (see below).

Adjustment

Refer to illustration 19.8

5   Turn the key to the Accessory position.

6   Remove the retainer screw from the front side of the shift knob, then remove the knob. Leave the release button in the shift lever.

7   Carefully pry the PRNDL plate off the

10

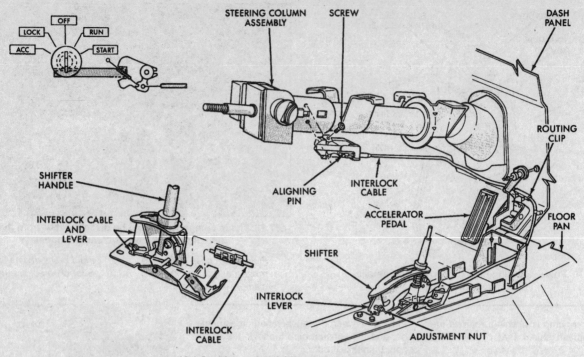

19.1 Ignition switch/shifter interlock system details

console with a screwdriver, taking care not to scratch or gouge it.

8   Place the shift lever in Park. Make sure the green plunger is all the way up and the interlock cable slug is fully seated in the interlock lever **(see illustration)**.

9   With the ignition switch still in the Accessory position, loosen the interlock lever adjustment nut **(see illustration 19.1)**. The spring will automatically position the interlock lever correctly. Once it does, tighten the adjustment nut to the torque listed in this Chapter's Specifications.

10   The remainder of installation is the reverse of the removal steps. Repeat Steps 1 through 3 to check the adjustment. If the system won't adjust properly, take the vehicle to a dealer service department.

20 Wheels and tires - general information

Refer to illustration 20.1

All vehicles covered by this manual are equipped with metric-size fiberglass or steel-belted radial tires **(see illustration)**. The

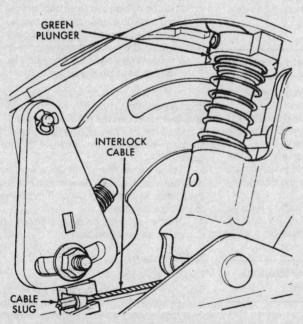

19.8 The green plunger should be all the way up and the cable slug should be fully seated in the interlock lever

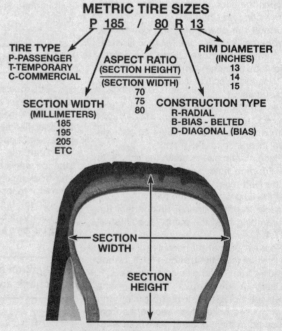

20.1 Metric tire size code

installation of different size or other type tires may affect the ride and handling of the vehicle. Don't mix different types of tires, such as radials and bias belted, on the same vehicle; handling may be seriously affected. Always try to replace tires in pairs on the same axle. However, if only one tire is being replaced, be sure it's the same size, structure and tread design as the other. Because tire pressure has a substantial effect on handling and wear, the pressure in all tires should be checked at least once a month or before any extended trips (see Chapter 1).

Wheels must be replaced if they're bent, dented, leak air, have elongated bolt holes, are heavily rusted, out of vertical symmetry or if the lug nuts won't stay tight. Wheel repairs by welding or peening aren't recommended.

Tire and wheel balance is important to the overall handling, braking and performance of the vehicle. Unbalanced wheels can adversely affect handling and ride characteristics as well as tire life. Whenever a tire is installed on a wheel, the tire and wheel should be balanced by a shop with the proper equipment.

21 Front end alignment - general information

Refer to illustration 21.1

A front end alignment refers to the adjustments made to the front wheels so they're in proper angular relationship to the suspension and the ground. Front wheels that are out of proper alignment not only affect steering control, but also increase tire wear. The front end adjustments normally required are camber and toe-in **(see illustration)**.

Getting the proper front wheel alignment is a very exacting process in which complicated and expensive machines are necessary to perform the job properly. Because of this, you should have a technician with the proper equipment perform these tasks. We will, however, use this space to give you a basic idea of what's involved with front end alignment so you can better understand the process and deal intelligently with the shop that

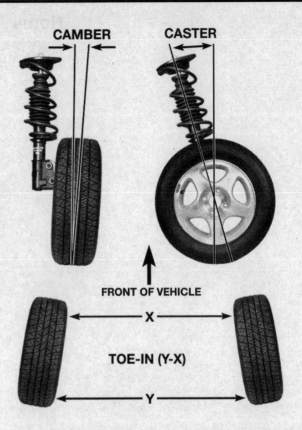

21.1 Caster, camber and toe-in angles

does the work.

Toe-in is the turning in of the front wheels. The purpose of a toe specification is to ensure parallel rolling of the front wheels. In a vehicle with zero toe-in, the distance between the front edges of the wheels will be the same as the distance between the rear edges of the wheels. The actual amount of toe-in is normally only a fraction of an inch. Toe-in adjustment is controlled by the positions of the tie-rod ends on the tie-rods. Incorrect toe-in will cause the tires to wear improperly by making them scrub against the road surface.

Camber is the tilting of the front wheels from vertical when viewed from the front of the vehicle. When the wheels tilt out at the top, the camber is said to be positive (+). When the wheels tilt in at the top the camber is negative (-). The amount of tilt is measured in degrees from vertical - this measurement is called the camber angle. This angle affects the amount of tire tread contacting the road and compensates for changes in the suspension geometry when the vehicle is cornering or traveling over an undulating surface.

Caster is the tilting of the top of the front steering axis from vertical. A tilt toward the rear is positive caster and a tilt toward the front is negative caster. Caster isn't adjustable on these vehicles.

10

Notes

Chapter 11   Body

Contents

1   General information

These models feature a "unibody" layout, using a floor pan with front and rear frame side rails which support the body components, front and rear suspension systems and other mechanical components. Certain components are particularly vulnerable to accident damage and can be unbolted and repaired or replaced. Among these parts are the body moldings, bumpers, the hood and trunk lids and all glass. Only general body maintenance practices and body panel repair procedures within the scope of the do-it-yourselfer are included in this chapter.

2   Body - maintenance

1   The condition of your vehicle's body is very important, because the resale value depends a great deal on it. It's much more difficult to repair a neglected or damaged body than it is to repair mechanical components. The hidden areas of the body, such as the wheel wells, the frame and the engine compartment, are equally important, although they don't require as frequent attention as the rest of the body.
2   Once a year, or every 12,000 miles, it's a good idea to have the underside of the body steam cleaned. All traces of dirt and oil will be removed and the area can then be inspected carefully for rust, damaged brake lines, frayed electrical wires, damaged cables and other problems. The front suspension components should be greased after completion of this job.
3   At the same time, clean the engine and the engine compartment with a steam cleaner or water-soluble degreaser.
4   The wheel wells should be given close attention, since undercoating can peel away and stones and dirt thrown up by the tires can cause the paint to chip and flake, allowing rust to set in. If rust is found, clean down to the bare metal and apply an anti-rust paint.
5   The body should be washed about once a week. Wet the vehicle thoroughly to soften the dirt, then wash it down with a soft sponge and plenty of clean soapy water. If the surplus dirt is not washed off very carefully, it can wear down the paint.
6   Spots of tar or asphalt thrown up from the road should be removed with a cloth soaked in solvent.
7   Once every six months, wax the body and chrome trim. If a chrome cleaner is used to remove rust from any of the vehicle's plated parts, remember that the cleaner also removes part of the chrome, so use it sparingly.

3   Vinyl trim - maintenance

Don't clean vinyl trim with detergents, caustic soap or petroleum-based cleaners. Plain soap and water works just fine, with a soft brush to clean dirt that may be ingrained. Wash the vinyl as frequently as the rest of the vehicle. After cleaning, application of a high-quality rubber and vinyl protectant will help prevent oxidation and cracks. The protectant can also be applied to weatherstripping, vacuum lines and rubber hoses, which often fail as a result of chemical degradation, and to the tires.

11

4   Upholstery and carpets - maintenance

1   Every three months remove the carpets or mats and clean the interior of the vehicle (more frequently if necessary). Vacuum the upholstery and carpets to remove loose dirt and dust.
2   Leather upholstery requires special care. Stains should be removed with warm water and a very mild soap solution. Use a clean, damp cloth to remove the soap, then wipe again with a dry cloth. Never use alcohol, gasoline, nail polish remover or thinner to clean leather upholstery.
3   After cleaning, regularly treat leather upholstery with a leather wax. Never use car wax on leather upholstery.
4   In areas where the interior of the vehicle is subject to bright sunlight, cover leather seats with a sheet if the vehicle is to be left out for any length of time.

5   Body repair - minor damage

Repair of scratches

1   If the scratch is superficial and does not penetrate to the metal of the body, repair is very simple. Lightly rub the scratched area with a fine rubbing compound to remove loose paint and built up wax. Rinse the area with clean water.
2   Apply touch-up paint to the scratch, using a small brush. Continue to apply thin layers of paint until the surface of the paint in the scratch is level with the surrounding paint. Allow the new paint at least two weeks to harden, then blend it into the surrounding paint by rubbing with a very fine rubbing compound. Finally, apply a coat of wax to the scratch area.
3   If the scratch has penetrated the paint and exposed the metal of the body, causing the metal to rust, a different repair technique is required. Remove all loose rust from the bottom of the scratch with a pocket knife, then apply rust inhibiting paint to prevent the formation of rust in the future. Using a rubber or nylon applicator, coat the scratched area with glaze-type filler. If required, the filler can be mixed with thinner to provide a very thin paste, which is ideal for filling narrow scratches. Before the glaze filler in the scratch hardens, wrap a piece of smooth cotton cloth around the tip of a finger. Dip the cloth in thinner and then quickly wipe it along the surface of the scratch. This will ensure that the surface of the filler is slightly hollow. The scratch can now be painted over as described earlier in this section.

Repair of dents

See color photo sequence
4   When repairing dents, the first job is to pull the dent out until the affected area is as close as possible to its original shape. There

is no point in trying to restore the original shape completely as the metal in the damaged area will have stretched on impact and cannot be restored to its original contours. It is better to bring the level of the dent up to a point which is about 1/8-inch below the level of the surrounding metal. In cases where the dent is very shallow, it is not worth trying to pull it out at all.
5   If the back side of the dent is accessible, it can be hammered out gently from behind using a soft-face hammer. While doing this, hold a block of wood firmly against the opposite side of the metal to absorb the hammer blows and prevent the metal from being stretched.
6   If the dent is in a section of the body which has double layers, or some other factor makes it inaccessible from behind, a different technique is required. Drill several small holes through the metal inside the damaged area, particularly in the deeper sections. Screw long, self tapping screws into the holes just enough for them to get a good grip in the metal. Now the dent can be pulled out by pulling on the protruding heads of the screws with locking pliers.
7   The next stage of repair is the removal of paint from the damaged area and from an inch or so of the surrounding metal. This is easily done with a wire brush or sanding disk in a drill motor, although it can be done just as effectively by hand with sandpaper. To complete the preparation for filling, score the surface of the bare metal with a screwdriver or the tang of a file or drill small holes in the affected area. This will provide a good grip for the filler material. To complete the repair, see the section on filling and painting.

Repair of rust holes or gashes

8   Remove all paint from the affected area and from an inch or so of the surrounding metal using a sanding disk or wire brush mounted in a drill motor. If these are not available, a few sheets of sandpaper will do the job just as effectively.
9   With the paint removed, you will be able to determine the severity of the corrosion and decide whether to replace the whole panel, if possible, or repair the affected area. New body panels are not as expensive as most people think and it is often quicker to install a new panel than to repair large areas of rust.
10   Remove all trim pieces from the affected area except those which will act as a guide to the original shape of the damaged body, such as headlight shells, etc. Using metal snips or a hacksaw blade, remove all loose metal and any other metal that is badly affected by rust. Hammer the edges of the hole on the inside to create a slight depression for the filler material.
11   Wire brush the affected area to remove the powdery rust from the surface of the metal. If the back of the rusted area is accessible, treat it with rust inhibiting paint.
12   Before filling is done, block the hole in some way. This can be done with sheet metal riveted or screwed into place, or by stuffing

the hole with wire mesh.
13   Once the hole is blocked off, the affected area can be filled and painted. See the following subsection on filling and painting.

Filling and painting

14   Many types of body fillers are available, but generally speaking, body repair kits which contain filler paste and a tube of resin hardener are best for this type of repair work. A wide, flexible plastic or nylon applicator will be necessary for imparting a smooth and contoured finish to the surface of the filler material. Mix up a small amount of filler on a clean piece of wood or cardboard (use the hardener sparingly). Follow the manufacturer's instructions on the package, otherwise the filler will set incorrectly.
15   Using the applicator, apply the filler paste to the prepared area. Draw the applicator across the surface of the filler to achieve the desired contour and to level the filler surface. As soon as a contour that approximates the original one is achieved, stop working the paste. If you continue, the paste will begin to stick to the applicator. Continue to add thin layers of paste at 20-minute intervals until the level of the filler is just above the surrounding metal.
16   Once the filler has hardened, the excess can be removed with a body file. From then on, progressively finer grades of sandpaper should be used, starting with a 180-grit paper and finishing with 600-grit wet-or-dry paper. Always wrap the sandpaper around a flat rubber or wooden block, otherwise the surface of the filler will not be completely flat. During the sanding of the filler surface, the wet-or-dry paper should be periodically rinsed in water. This will ensure that a very smooth finish is produced in the final stage.
17   At this point, the repair area should be surrounded by a ring of bare metal, which in turn should be encircled by the finely feathered edge of good paint. Rinse the repair area with clean water until all of the dust produced by the sanding operation is gone.
18   Spray the entire area with a light coat of primer. This will reveal any imperfections in the surface of the filler. Repair the imperfections with fresh filler paste or glaze filler and once more smooth the surface with sandpaper. Repeat this spray-and-repair procedure until you are satisfied that the surface of the filler and the feathered edge of the paint are perfect. Rinse the area with clean water and allow it to dry completely.
19   The repair area is now ready for painting. Spray painting must be carried out in a warm, dry, windless and dust free atmosphere. These conditions can be created if you have access to a large indoor work area, but if you are forced to work in the open, you will have to pick the day very carefully. If you are working indoors, dousing the floor in the work area with water will help settle the dust which would otherwise be in the air. If the repair area is confined to one body panel, mask off the surrounding panels. This will

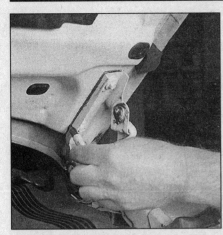

9.2 Use a marking pen to outline the hinge plate and bolt head

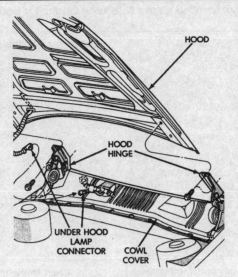

9.4 Hood details

9.10 Adjust the hood vertically by screwing the hood bumpers in or out

help minimize the effects of a slight mismatch in paint color. Trim pieces such as chrome strips, door handles, etc., will also need to be masked off or removed. Use masking tape and several thicknesses of newspaper for the masking operations.

20   Before spraying, shake the paint can thoroughly, then spray a test area until the spray painting technique is mastered. Cover the repair area with a thick coat of primer. The thickness should be built up using several thin layers of primer rather than one thick one. Using 600-grit wet-or-dry sandpaper, rub down the surface of the primer until it is very smooth. While doing this, the work area should be thoroughly rinsed with water and the wet-or-dry sandpaper periodically rinsed as well. Allow the primer to dry before spraying additional coats.

21   Spray on the top coat, again building up the thickness by using several thin layers of paint. Begin spraying in the center of the repair area and then, using a circular motion, work out until the whole repair area and about two inches of the surrounding original paint is covered. Remove all masking material 10 to 15 minutes after spraying on the final coat of paint. Allow the new paint at least two weeks to harden, then use a very fine rubbing compound to blend the edges of the new paint into the existing paint. Finally, apply a coat of wax.

6   Body repair - major damage

1   Major damage must be repaired by an auto body shop specifically equipped to perform unibody repairs. These shops have the specialized equipment required to do the job properly.

2   If the damage is extensive, the body must be checked for proper alignment or the vehicle's handling characteristics may be adversely affected and other components may wear at an accelerated rate.

3   Due to the fact that all of the major body components (hood, fenders, etc.) are separate and replaceable units, any seriously

damaged components should be replaced rather than repaired. Sometimes the components can be found in a wrecking yard that specializes in used vehicle components, often at considerable savings over the cost of new parts.

7   Hinges and locks - maintenance

Once every 3000 miles, or every three months, the hinges and latch assemblies on the doors, hood and trunk should be given a few drops of light oil or lock lubricant. The door latch strikers should also be lubricated with a thin coat of grease to reduce wear and ensure free movement. Lubricate the door and trunk locks with spray-on graphite lubricant.

8   Fixed glass - replacement

Replacement of the windshield and fixed glass requires the use of special fast-setting adhesive/caulk materials and some specialized tools and techniques. These operations should be left to a dealer service department or a shop specializing in glass work.

9   Hood - removal, installation and adjustment

Refer to illustrations 9.2, 9.4 and 9.10
Note: *The hood is heavy and somewhat awkward to remove and install - at least two people should perform this procedure.*

Removal and installation

1   Use blankets or pads to cover the cowl area of the body and the fenders. This will protect the body and paint as the hood is lifted off.

2   Scribe alignment marks around the bolt heads to insure proper alignment during installation (a permanent-type felt-tip marker also will work for this) **(see illustration)**.

3   Disconnect any cables or wire harnesses which will interfere with removal.

4   Have an assistant support the weight of the hood. Remove the hinge-to-hood or bolts **(see illustration)**.

5   Lift off the hood.

6   Installation is the reverse of removal.

Adjustment

7   Fore-and-aft and side-to-side adjustment of the hood is done by moving the hood in relation to the hinge plate after loosening the bolts.

8   Scribe or trace a line around the entire hinge plate so you can judge the amount of movement.

9   Loosen the bolts or nuts and move the hood into correct alignment. Move it only a little at a time. Tighten the hinge bolts or nuts and carefully lower the hood to check the alignment.

10   Adjust the hood bumpers on the radiator support so the hood is flush with the fenders when closed **(see illustration)**.

11   The safety catch assembly on the hood itself can also be adjusted fore-and-aft and side-to-side after loosening the bolts.

12   The hood latch assembly, as well as the hinges, should be periodically lubricated with white lithium-base grease to prevent sticking and wear.

10   Hood latch and cable - removal and installation

Refer to illustrations 10.1 and 10.4
Warning: *On airbag-equipped models, always disconnect the negative battery cable and wait at least two minutes before working in the vicinity of the impact sensors, steering column or center console to avoid the accidental deployment of the airbag, which could cause personal injury.*

11

These photos illustrate a method of repairing simple dents. They are intended to supplement *Body repair - minor damage* in this Chapter and should not be used as the sole instructions for body repair on these vehicles.

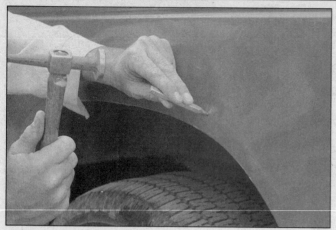

1   If you can't access the backside of the body panel to hammer out the dent, pull it out with a slide-hammer-type dent puller. In the deepest portion of the dent or along the crease line, drill or punch hole(s) at least one inch apart . . .

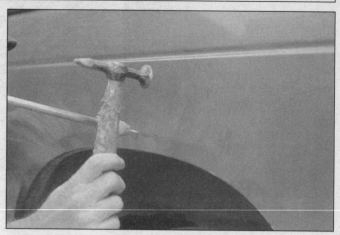

2   . . . then screw the slide-hammer into the hole and operate it. Tap with a hammer near the edge of the dent to help 'pop' the metal back to its original shape. When you're finished, the dent area should be close to its original contour and about 1/8-inch below the surface of the surrounding metal

3   Using coarse-grit sandpaper, remove the paint down to the bare metal. Hand sanding works fine, but the disc sander shown here makes the job faster. Use finer (about 320-grit) sandpaper to feather-edge the paint at least one inch around the dent area

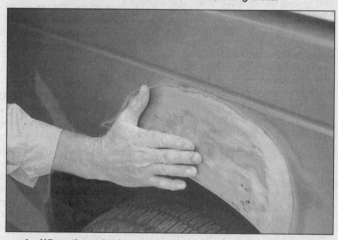

4   When the paint is removed, touch will probably be more helpful than sight for telling if the metal is straight. Hammer down the high spots or raise the low spots as necessary. Clean the repair area with wax/silicone remover

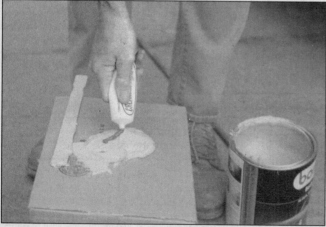

5   Following label instructions, mix up a batch of plastic filler and hardener. The ratio of filler to hardener is critical, and, if you mix it incorrectly, it will either not cure properly or cure too quickly (you won't have time to file and sand it into shape)

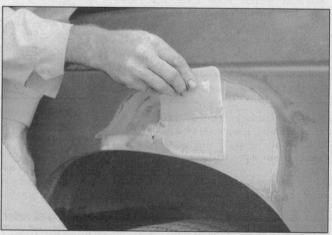

6   Working quickly so the filler doesn't harden, use a plastic applicator to press the body filler firmly into the metal, assuring it bonds completely. Work the filler until it matches the original contour and is slightly above the surrounding metal

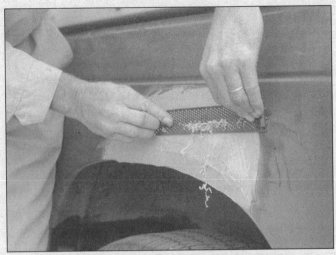

7   Let the filler harden until you can just dent it with your fingernail. Use a body file or Surform tool (shown here) to rough-shape the filler

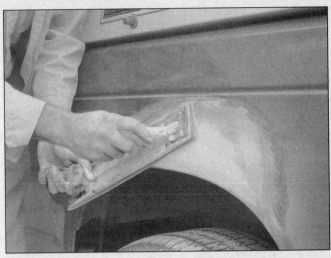

8   Use coarse-grit sandpaper and a sanding board or block to work the filler down until it's smooth and even. Work down to finer grits of sandpaper - always using a board or block - ending up with 360 or 400 grit

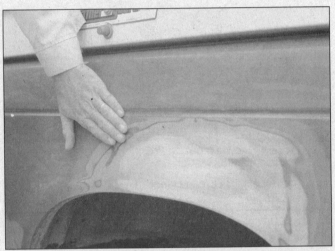

9   You shouldn't be able to feel any ridge at the transition from the filler to the bare metal or from the bare metal to the old paint. As soon as the repair is flat and uniform, remove the dust and mask off the adjacent panels or trim pieces

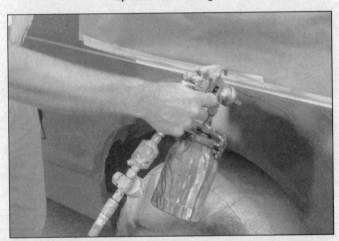

10   Apply several layers of primer to the area. Don't spray the primer on too heavy, so it sags or runs, and make sure each coat is dry before you spray on the next one. A professional-type spray gun is being used here, but aerosol spray primer is available inexpensively from auto parts stores

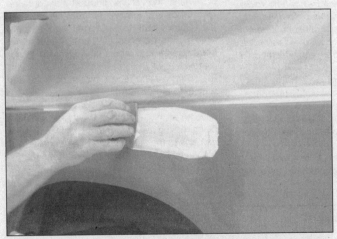

11   The primer will help reveal imperfections or scratches. Fill these with glazing compound. Follow the label instructions and sand it with 360 or 400-grit sandpaper until it's smooth. Repeat the glazing, sanding and respraying until the primer reveals a perfectly smooth surface

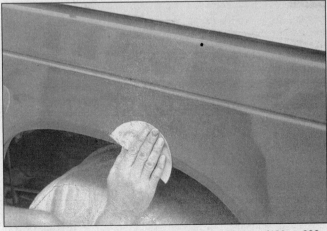

12   Finish sand the primer with very fine sandpaper (400 or 600-grit) to remove the primer overspray. Clean the area with water and allow it to dry. Use a tack rag to remove any dust, then apply the finish coat. Don't attempt to rub out or wax the repair area until the paint has dried completely (at least two weeks)

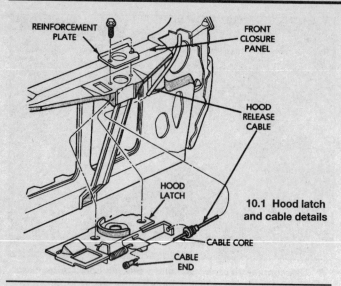

10.1 Hood latch and cable details

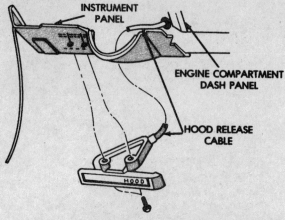

10.4 Hood release cable and handle attachment details

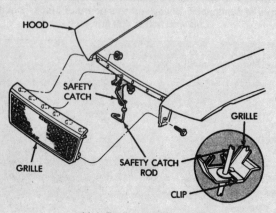

11.1 Radiator grille details

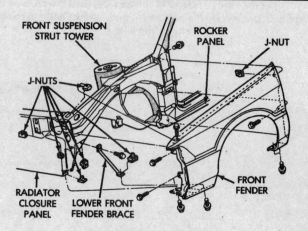

12.3 Front fender details

Latch

1   Remove the bolts, detach the latch assembly, then use a screwdriver to detach the cable end **(see illustration)**.
2   Installation is the reverse of removal.

Cable

3   For access to the cable-latch connection, either remove the latch **(see illustration 10.1)** or use a small screwdriver to pry out the push-in fasteners and detach the black plastic latch cover.
4   In the passenger compartment, remove the screws and detach the hood release cable and handle assembly **(see illustration)**.
5   Under the dash, remove the cable grommet from the firewall.
6   Connect a string or piece of wire to the engine compartment end of the cable, then detach the cable and pull it through the firewall into the passenger compartment.
7   Connect the string or wire to the new cable and pull it through the firewall into the engine compartment.
8   The remainder of installation is the reverse of removal.

11   Radiator grille - removal and installation

Refer to illustration 11.1
Warning: *On airbag-equipped models, always disconnect the negative battery cable and wait at least two minutes before working in the vicinity of the impact sensors, steering column or center console to avoid the accidental deployment of the airbag, which could cause personal injury.*
1   Remove the clip and detach the safety catch rod from the grille assembly **(see illustration)**.
2   Remove the bolts and screws and detach the grille from the hood **(see illustration 11.1)**.
3   To install, place the grille in position, install the bolts and screws, then connect the safety catch rod.

12   Front fender - removal and installation

Refer to illustration 12.3
Warning: *On airbag-equipped models,*

always disconnect the negative battery cable and wait at least two minutes before working in the vicinity of the impact sensors, steering column or center console to avoid the accidental deployment of the airbag, which could cause personal injury.
1   Raise the vehicle, support it securely on jackstands and remove the front wheel.
2   Disconnect the antenna and all light bulb wiring harness connectors and other components that would interfere with fender removal.
3   Remove the fender mounting bolts and nuts **(see illustration)**.
4   Detach the fender. It's a good idea to have an assistant support the fender while it's being moved away from the vehicle to prevent damage to the surrounding body panels.
5   Installation is the reverse of removal.
6   Tighten all nuts, bolts and screws securely.

13   Bumpers - removal and installation

Refer to illustrations 13.4a and 13.4b
Warning: *On airbag-equipped models,*

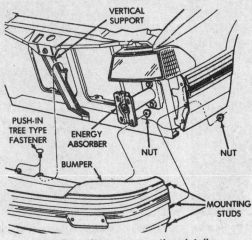

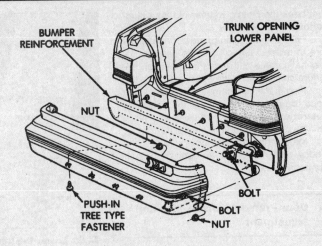

13.4a Front bumper mounting details

13.4b Rear bumper mounting details

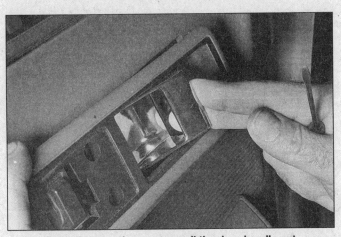

14.2a Remove the screws, pull the door handle out,
lift the bezel off . . .

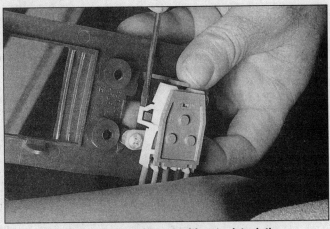

14.2b . . . then use a screwdriver to detach the
electrical connector

*always disconnect the negative battery cable
and wait at least two minutes before working
in the vicinity of the impact sensors, steering
column or center console to avoid the accidental deployment of the airbag, which could
cause personal injury.*

1   Detach the bumper cover.
2   Disconnect any wiring or other components that would interfere with bumper
removal.
3   Support the bumper with a jack or have
an assistant support the bumper as the bolts
are removed.
4   Remove the mounting bolts and detach
the bumper **(see illustrations)**.
5   Installation is the reverse of removal.
6   Tighten the mounting bolts securely.
7   Install the bumper cover and any other
components that were removed.

14   Door trim panel - removal and installation

*Refer to illustrations 14.2a, 14.2b, 14.5, 14.6,
14.8a and 14.8b*

1   Disconnect the negative cable from the
battery.

2   Remove all door trim panel retaining
screws and door pull/armrest assemblies
(see illustrations).
3   On manual window models, remove the
window crank. On power window models,
remove the screw, pry out the control switch
assembly and unplug it.
4   Insert a putty knife between the trim

panel and the door and disengage the retaining clips. Work around the outer edge until
the panel is free.
5   Once all of the clips are disengaged,
detach the trim panel, unplug any wire harness connectors and remove the trim panel
from the vehicle **(see illustrations)**.
6   For access to the inner door, carefully

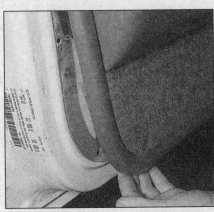

14.5 Pry the clips at the corner free, pull
out sharply on the panel to detach it from
the door, then lift it up and off the door

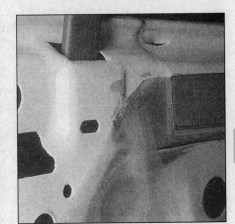

14.6 Pull the watershield off very
carefully, so it won't be torn or distorted

11

peel back the plastic watershield **(see illustration)**.

7   Prior to installation of the door panel, be sure to reinstall any clips in the panel which may have come out during the removal procedure and remain in the door itself.

8   Plug in the wire harness connectors and place the panel in position in the door **(see illustration)**. Press the trim panel into place until the clips are seated **(see illustration)**.

9   Install the armrest/door pulls and the window switch or crank. Re-connect the battery negative cable.

15   Door - removal, installation and adjustment

Refer to illustrations 15.3a and 15.3b

1   Remove the door trim panel. Disconnect any wire harness connectors and push them through the door opening so they won't interfere with door removal.

2   Place a jack under the door or have an assistant on hand to support it when the hinge bolts are removed. **Note:** *If a jack is used, place a rag between it and the door to protect the door's painted surfaces.*

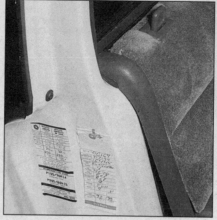

14.8a Lower the top of the trim panel into the door . . .

3   Drive out the pins and carefully lift off the door **(see illustrations)**.

4   Installation is the reverse of removal.

5   Following installation of the door, check the alignment and adjust it if necessary as follows:

a) Up-and-down and forward-and-backward adjustments are made by carefully

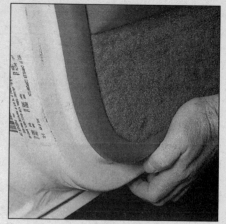

14.8b . . . then use the heel of your hand to seat the clips

bending the hinges slightly, *using a special tool (take the vehicle to a dealer service department or auto body repair shop).*

b) *The door lock striker can also be adjusted both up-and-down and sideways to provide positive engagement with the lock mechanism. This is done by loosening the mounting bolts and moving the striker as necessary.*

16   Door latch, lock cylinder and outside handle - removal and installation

Refer to illustrations 16.2a, 16.2b, 16.3, 16.7, 16.10a and 16.10b

Latch

1   Close the window completely and remove the door trim panel and watershield (see Section 14).

2   Disconnect the link rods from the latch **(see illustrations)**.

3   Remove the three Torx-head mounting

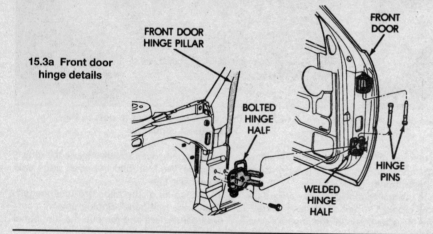

15.3a Front door hinge details

FRONT DOOR HINGE PILLAR

FRONT DOOR

BOLTED HINGE HALF

HINGE PINS

WELDED HINGE HALF

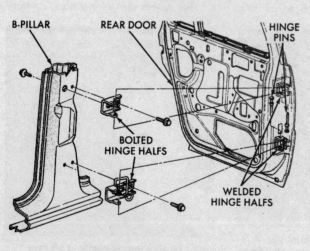

15.3b Rear door hinge details

B-PILLAR

REAR DOOR

HINGE PINS

BOLTED HINGE HALFS

WELDED HINGE HALFS

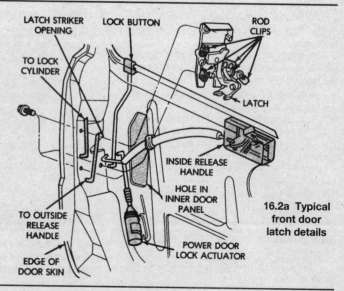

16.2a Typical front door latch details

LATCH STRIKER OPENING

LOCK BUTTON

ROD CLIPS

TO LOCK CYLINDER

LATCH

INSIDE RELEASE HANDLE

HOLE IN INNER DOOR PANEL

TO OUTSIDE RELEASE HANDLE

EDGE OF DOOR SKIN

POWER DOOR LOCK ACTUATOR

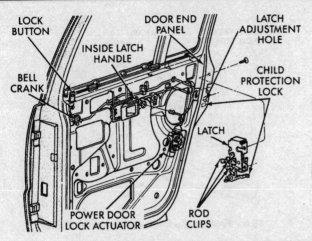

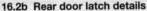

16.2b Rear door latch details

16.3 A Torx-head tool will be required to remove the door latch screws (arrows)

screws **(see illustration)**. It may be necessary to use an impact-type screwdriver to loosen them.

4   Remove the latch from the door.

5   Place the latch in position and install the screws. Tighten the screws securely.

6   Connect the link rods to the latch.

7   Check the door to make sure it closes properly. Readjust the latch (by loosening the screws and moving it) as necessary until the door closes smoothly (with the door handle flush with the door). After installation, loosen the linkage adjusting screw by inserting a 5/32-inch hex-head wrench through the adjustment hole in the end of the door **(see illustration)**. Loosen the adjustment screw and push it up in the slot to remove all slack from the linkage, then tighten it.

Lock cylinder

8   Remove the outside door handle (see below). Disconnect the link, use a screwdriver to push the key lock cylinder retainer off and withdraw the lock cylinder from the door.

9   Installation is the reverse of removal.

Outside handle

10   Disconnect the outside handle (remote control) link from the latch, remove the mounting nuts and detach the handle from the door **(see illustrations)**.

11   Place the handle in position, attach the link and install the nuts. Tighten the nuts securely.

17   Door window glass - removal, installation and adjustment

1   Remove the door trim panel and watershield (see Section 14).

2   Raise the glass to the half-way position in the door opening.

Front door

Refer to illustration 17.3

3   Insert a door glass removal tool (available at your dealer) between the glass slide and the channel retaining lip at a point about

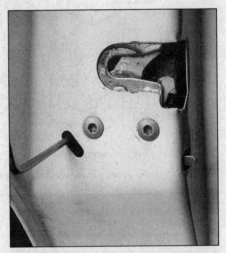

16.7 Insert a hex-head wrench into the adjustment hole, loosen the screw and move it up in the slot to remove the slack from the linkage

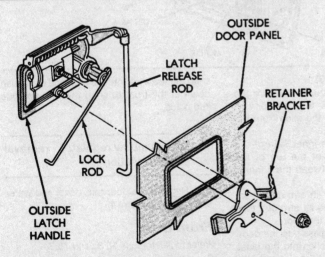

16.10a Front door outside door handle details

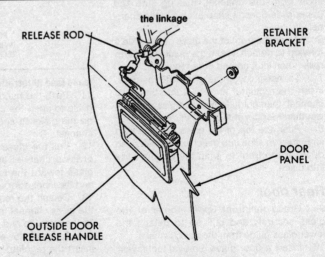

16.10b Rear door handle details

11

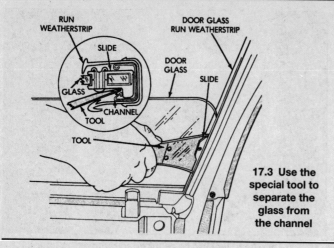

17.3 Use the special tool to separate the glass from the channel

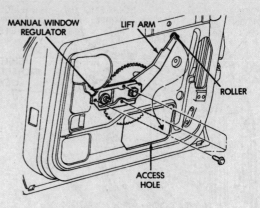

18.3a Front manual window regulator details

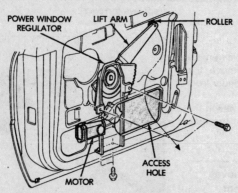

18.3b Front power window regulator details

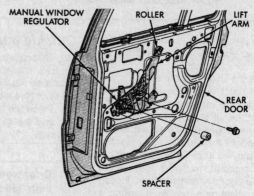

18.6a Rear door manual window details

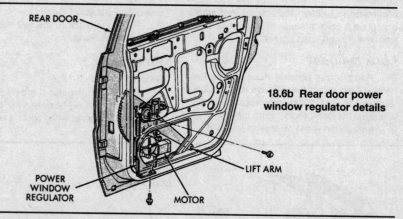

18.6b Rear door power window regulator details

two inches from the top of the glass (see illustration).

4   Push the handle of the tool toward the glass to open the channel, then push it down at the front of the glass to separate the slide from the channel.

5   Insert the tool approximately two inches from the bottom of the glass. Push the tool handle toward the glass to open the channel, then push down at the front to separate the slide from the channel, making sure the upper slide doesn't snap back into the channel.

6   Angle the front of the glass down, slide it forward to detach it from the regulator lift arm roller, then lift it up and out of the door.

7   To install, lower the glass into the door, insert the regulator arm roller into the glass channel, then guide front of the glass into the weatherstripping at the front of the door.

8   Push the top of the glass to the rear to snap the top slide into the channel, then push down at the front to snap the bottom slide into place.

Rear door

9   Grasp the front upper corner of the glass securely and pull up to detach the lower glass guide from the run channel.

10   Insert a door glass removal tool (available at your dealer) between the glass slide and the channel retaining lip at a point about two inches from the top rear corner of the

glass (see illustration 17.3).

11   Push the handle of the tool toward the glass to open the channel, then pull forward on the glass to separate the slide from the channel.

12   Pull the glass to the inner side of the division channel and pivot the top of the glass toward the rear between the channel and the inner door panel.

13   Detach the regulator lift arm roller from the glass channel, hold the lift arm out, then lift the glass up and out of the door.

14   To install, lower the glass into the door, insert the regulator arm roller into the glass channel, then guide front of the glass into the weatherstripping at the front of the door.

15   Push the top of the glass to the rear to

snap the top slide into the channel, then push down at the front to snap the bottom slide into place.

18   Door window regulator - removal and installation

1   Remove the door trim panel and watershield (see Section 14).

Front door

Refer to illustrations 18.3a and 18.3b

2   Raise the glass to the within in one inch of the top of the door opening, then tape it in place. On power window models, disconnect

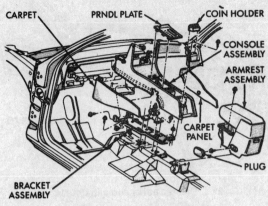

19.3 Floor console details

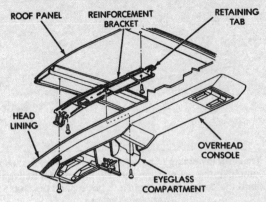

19.13 Overhead console details

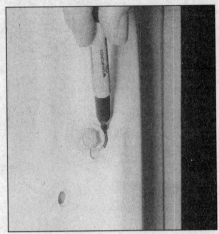

20.3 Draw around the bolt heads with a
marking pen so the trunk lid can be
installed in the same position

the negative battery cable.
3   Remove the regulator bolts and detach
the lift arm roller from the glass. Rotate the
regulator and lift it out through the opening in
the door (see illustrations).
4   Installation is the reverse of removal.

Rear door

Refer to illustrations 18.6a and 18.6b
5   Raise the window glass up six inches
into the window opening, then grasp the
glass securely and pull the front edge up
sharply to detach the glass from the lower
glass guide from the division run channel.
6   Remove the window regulator-to-door
bolts (see illustrations).
7   Slide the lift arm roller out of the window
lift channel.
8   Raise the glass to within six inches of
the top of the door opening and tape it in
place.
10   Rotate the regulator and lift it out
through the opening in the door.
11   Installation is the reverse of removal.

19   Center console - removal and installation

Refer to illustrations 19.3 and 19.13
Warning: *On airbag-equipped models,
always disconnect the negative battery cable
and wait at least two minutes before working
in the vicinity of the impact sensors, steering
column or center console to avoid the accidental deployment of the airbag, which could
cause personal injury.*

Floor console

1   Disconnect the negative battery cable.
2   Move the seats all the way forward.
3   Use a small screwdriver to pry out the
screw access plugs in the sides of the console (see illustration).
4   Lift out the coin holder and remove the
arm rest riser screws.
5   Move the seats to the rear.
6   Use a small screwdriver to pry around
the center bezel and detach the clips, then

pull the bezel off.
7   Remove the shift knob. On manual shift
models the knob is held in place by a set
screw while on automatic models the shift
knob can be removed by grasping it securely
and pulling straight it up and off.
8   Remove the gearshift boot.
9   On automatic models, pry the shift position (PRNDL) plate off.
10   Remove the mounting screws/bolts,
detach the console and lift it up.
11   Unplug any electrical connectors and
remove the console from the vehicle.
12   Installation is the reverse of removal.

Overhead console

13   Remove the console-to-reinforcement
bracket screws (see illustration).
14   Slide the console to rear, detach it from
the bracket and lower it sufficiently to unplug
the electrical connectors, then remove it from
the vehicle.
15   Installation is the reverse of removal.

20   Trunk lid - removal, installation and adjustment

Refer to illustration 20.3
1   Open the trunk lid and cover the edges
of the trunk compartment with pads or cloths
to protect the painted surfaces when the lid is
removed.
2   Disconnect any cables or electrical connectors attached to the trunk lid that would
interfere with removal.
3   Use a marking pen to make alignment
marks around the hinge bolt mounting
flanges (see illustration).
4   While an assistant supports it's weight,
remove the hinge bolts from both sides and
lift the trunk lid off.
5   Installation is the reverse of removal.
Note: *When reinstalling the trunk lid, align the
hinge bolt flanges with the marks made during removal.*
6   After installation, close the lid and see if
it's in proper alignment with the surrounding
panels. Fore-and-aft and side-to-side adjust-

ments of the lid are controlled by the position
of the hinge bolts in the slots. To adjust it,
loosen the hinge bolts, reposition the lid and
retighten the bolts.
7   The height of the lid in relation to the
surrounding body panels when closed can be
adjusted by loosening the lock striker bolts,
repositioning the striker and retightening the
bolts.

21   Instrument cluster bezel - removal and installation

Refer to illustrations 21.3 and 21.4
Warning: *On airbag-equipped models,
always disconnect the negative battery cable
and wait at least two minutes before working
in the vicinity of the impact sensors, steering
column or center console to avoid the accidental deployment of the airbag, which could
cause personal injury.*
1   On column shift models, place the shift
lever in Neutral.
2   On tilt steering models, lower the steering wheel to it's lowest position.
3   The bezel is held in place by clips. A
special tool (available at auto parts stores)

11

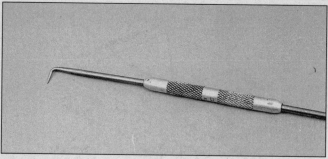

21.3 This tool (available at most auto parts stores) makes the job of detaching the bezel clip easy – simply insert it between the bezel and the dashboard, rotate it to get a good purchase on the bezel and pull out

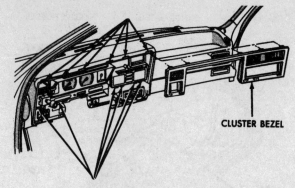

21.4 Cluster bezel and clip details

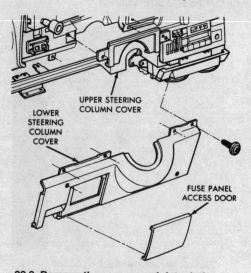

22.3 Remove the screws and detach the lower steering column cover

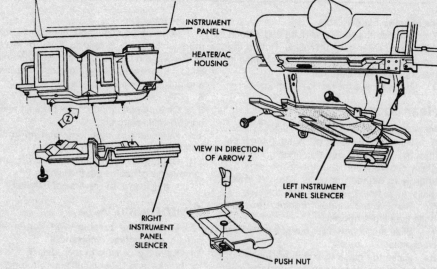

22.7 Instrument panel silencer details

makes the job of detaching the clips easier **(see illustration)**. Insert the tool into the gap between the bezel and surrounding dashboard panel, rotate the end of the tool behind the bezel until you have a good purchase and pull out sharply to detach the clips.

4   Work around the outer circumference until all of the clips are detached, then lift the bezel off **(see illustration)**.

5   Place the bezel in position and push it into place until the clips are seated.

22 Dashboard panels - removal and installation

Warning: *On airbag-equipped models, always disconnect the negative battery cable and wait at least two minutes before working in the vicinity of the impact sensors, steering column or center console to avoid the accidental deployment of the airbag, which could cause personal injury.*

Lower steering column cover

Refer to illustration 22.3

1   Detach the parking brake release rod.

2   Pry off the fuse panel access door.

3   Remove the screws and detach the cover from the dashboard **(see illustration)**.

4   Installation is the reverse of removal.

Instrument panel silencers

Refer to illustration 22.7

5   On floor shift models, remove the floor console (Section 19).

6   On column shift models, remove the center brace bracket.

7   Remove the screws and push nuts, then detach the silencer panels **(see illustration)**.

8   Installation is the reverse of removal.

Glove box

Refer to illustration 22.11

9   Open the glove box and detach the check strap.

10   Reach up behind the glove box light, pull it back, unplug the connectors, then remove it.

11   Remove the glove box retaining screws (there are 11 of them - four on the top, five on the bottom and one in each lower corner); detach the glove box and remove it from the dashboard **(see illustration)**.

12   Installation is the reverse of removal.

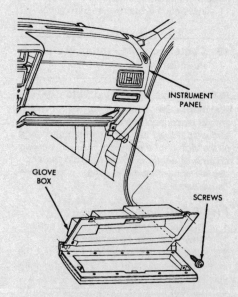

22.11 There are 11 glove box mounting screws (four on the top, five on the bottom and one in each lower corner)

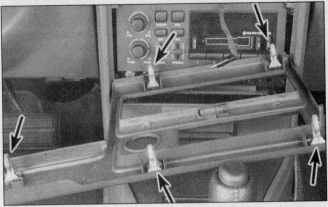

22.13a To remove the center bezel, simply grasp it as shown and carefully pull it off the dash . . .

22.13b . . . where the five retaining clips (arrows) are located – unplug the electrical connector for the courtesy light and remove the bezel

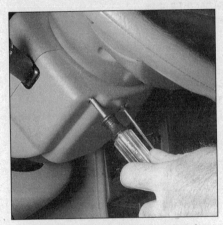

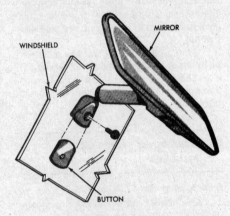

23.2 Two different size Torx-head screwdrivers are need to remove the column cover screws with the larger (#20) on the left and the #15 on the right

23.3 Unscrew the tilt lever to allow the upper column cover half to be lifted off

24.1 The interior mirror fits over the button on the glass and is held in position by the screw

Center bezel

Refer to illustrations 22.13a and 22.13b

13   Grasp the center bezel with your hand as shown **(see illustration)** and carefully pull it off the dashboard. There are five retaining clips **(see illustration)** on the backside of the bezel. Unplug the electrical connector for the courtesy light and remove the center bezel.

14   To install the bezel, plug in the courtesy light, place the bezel in position and push the retaining clips back into their respective clips.

23   Steering column cover - removal and installation

Refer to illustrations 23.2 and 23.3

Warning: *On airbag-equipped models, always disconnect the negative battery cable and wait at least two minutes before working in the vicinity of the impact sensors, steering column or center console to avoid the accidental deployment of the airbag, which could cause personal injury.*

1   Disconnect the negative battery cable.
2   Remove the screws and detach the

lower half of the column cover **(see illustration).**

3   Unscrew the steering column tilt lever and remove the upper half of the cover **(see illustration).**

24   Mirrors - removal and installation

Refer to illustrations 24.1 and 24.4

Interior

1   Use a Phillips head screwdriver to remove the set screw, then slide the mirror up off the button on the windshield **(see illustration).**

2   Installation is the reverse of removal.

Exterior

3   Remove the door trim panel (see Section 14).

4   Remove the screws and detach the mirror knob and bezel **(see illustration).** On power mirrors, unplug the electrical connector.

5   Remove the nuts and detach the mirror from the door.

6   Installation is the reverse of removal.

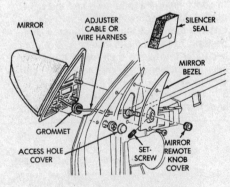

24.4 Exterior mirror details

25   Engine drivebelt and wheelhouse splash shields - removal and installation

Refer to illustrations 25.2a and 25.2b

1   Loosen the wheel lug nuts, raise the front of the vehicle and support it securely on jackstands. Remove the wheel(s).

2   The wheelhouse splash shield is retained by screws and plastic (tree-type) fasteners, which generally aren't reusable

11

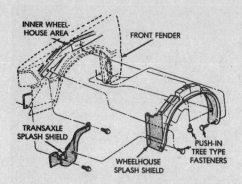

25.2a Wheelhouse and transaxle splash
shield details

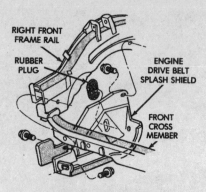

25.2b Engine drivebelt splash
shield details

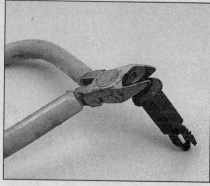

26.2 Use wire cutters as shown here to
gently remove the black plastic screw out
of the expanding fastener (don't cut the
head off!), then remove the fastener

after removal. Carefully pry the fasteners out
with pliers or wire cutters (see illustration).
The transaxle and engine drivebelt splash
shields are held in place by bolts (see illustration).

3   After all the screws and fasteners have
been removed, detach the splash shield.

4   To install a splash shield, hold it in position and install the screws and new plastic
fasteners.

26   Cowl cover - removal and installation

Refer to illustrations 26.2 and 26.3

1   Disconnect the windshield washer
hoses and remove the wiper arms.

2   Remove the plastic expanding fasteners. While these look like plastic Phillips head
screws, they are actually press in fasteners.
Use wire cutters
to gently pry out and remove first the screw
portion, then the expanding portion of the
fastener (don't cut the head off!) (see illustration). To install these fasteners, press the
expander into place then insert the screw
fully by pushing it in with a Phillips head
screwdriver.

3   After removing the fasteners, lift up the
back of the cowl cover and separate it from

26.3 Cowl cover
components

the rubber seal (see illustration). Remove
the cover toward the windshield.

4   Installation is the reverse of removal.

27   Seats - removal and installation

Refer to illustrations 27.2 and 27.5

Front

1   Move the seat forward.

2   Remove the seat-to-track nuts, then
move the seat rearward and remove the bolts
at the front (see illustration). Unplug any

electrical connectors attached to the seat.

3   Lift the seat from the vehicle.

4   Installation is the reverse of removal.

Rear

5   Remove the seat cushion-to-floor bolts,
push the seat belts through the cushion
openings, then detach the cushion and lift it
out (see illustration).

6   Fold the back of the seat forward and
detach the push-in fasteners holding the carpet to the seat back. Remove the seat back-
to-hinge arm bolts and lift the seat back out
of the vehicle.

7   Installation is the reverse of removal.

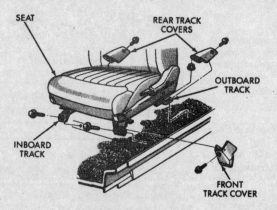

27.2 Front seat details

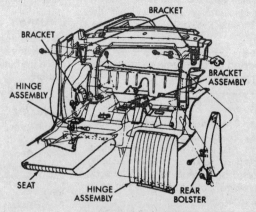

27.5 Rear seat details

Chapter 12
Chassis electrical system

Contents

Specifications

Light bulb types

Front

Headlight	9004
Park/turn signal light	194NA
Side marker light	168

Interior

Speedometer and instrument cluster light	194
Dome light	211-2

Rear

License plate light	168
Back-up light	3157
Brake/tail light	3157
High-mounted brake light	921
Turn signal light	3157
Side marker light	916

1 General information

The electrical system is a 12-volt, negative ground type. Power for the lights and all electrical accessories is supplied by a lead/acid-type battery which is charged by the alternator.

This Chapter covers repair and service procedures for the various electrical components not associated with the engine. Information on the battery, alternator, distributor and starter motor can be found in Chapter 5.

Warning: *When working on the electrical system, disconnect the negative battery cable from the battery to prevent electrical shorts and/or fires.*

2 Electrical troubleshooting - general information

A typical electrical circuit consists of an electrical component, any switches, relays, motors, fuses, fusible links or circuit breakers related to the component and the wiring and connectors that link the component to both the battery and the chassis. To help pinpoint an electrical circuit problem, wiring diagrams are included at the end of this Chapter.

Before tackling any troublesome electrical circuit, first study the appropriate wiring diagrams to get a complete understanding of what makes up that individual circuit. Trouble spots, for instance, can often be narrowed down by noting if other components related to the circuit are operating properly. If several components or circuits fail at one time, chances are the problem is in a fuse or ground connection, because several circuits are often routed through the same fuse and ground connections.

Electrical problems usually stem from simple causes, such as loose or corroded connections, a blown fuse, a melted fusible link or a bad relay. Visually inspect the condition of all fuses, wires and connections in a problem circuit before troubleshooting it.

If testing instruments are going to be utilized, use the diagrams to plan ahead of time where to make the necessary connections to accurately pinpoint the trouble spot.

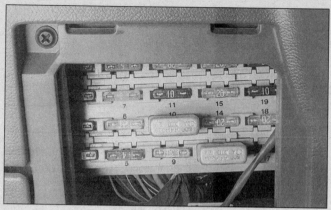

3.1 The fuse block is located under the left side of the instrument panel

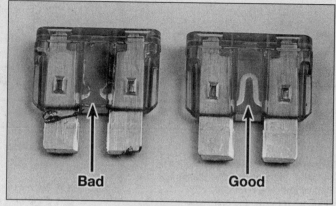

3.3 When a fuse blows, the element between the terminals melts - the fuse on the left is blown, the fuse on the right is good

The basic tools needed for electrical troubleshooting include a circuit tester or voltmeter (a 12-volt bulb with a set of test leads can also be used), a continuity tester (which includes a bulb, battery and set of test leads) and a jumper wire, preferably with a circuit breaker incorporated, which can be used to bypass electrical components. Before attempting to locate a problem with test instruments, use the wiring diagram(s) to decide where to make the connections.

Voltage checks

Voltage checks should be performed if a circuit isn't functioning properly. Connect one lead of a circuit tester to either the negative battery terminal or a known good ground. Connect the other lead to a connector in the circuit being tested, preferably nearest to the battery or fuse. If the bulb of the tester lights, voltage is present, which means the part of the circuit between the connector and the battery is problem free. Continue checking the rest of the circuit in the same fashion. When you reach a point where no voltage is present, the problem lies between that point and the last test point with voltage. Most of the time the problem can be traced to a loose connection. **Note:** *Keep in mind that some circuits receive voltage only when the ignition key is in the Accessory or Run position.*

Finding a short

One method of finding a short in a circuit is to remove the fuse and connect a test light or voltmeter in its place to the fuse terminals. There should be no voltage present in the circuit. Move the wiring harness from side-to-side while watching the test light. If the bulb lights, there's a short to ground somewhere in that area, probably where the insulation has rubbed through. The same test can be performed on each component in the circuit, even a switch.

Ground check

Perform a ground test to check whether a component is properly grounded. Disconnect the battery and connect one lead of a self-powered test light, known as a continuity

tester, to a known good ground. Connect the other lead to the wire or ground connection being tested. If the bulb lights, the ground is good. If the bulb doesn't light, the ground is no good.

Continuity check

A continuity check is done to determine if there are breaks in a circuit - if it's capable of passing electricity properly. With the circuit off (no power in the circuit), a self-powered continuity tester can be used to check it. Connect the test leads to both ends of the circuit (or to the "power" end and a good ground) - if the test light comes on the circuit is passing current properly. If the light does-n't come on, there's a break (open) some-where in the circuit. The same procedure can be used to test a switch by connecting the continuity tester to the switch terminals. With the switch on, the test light should come on.

Finding an open circuit

When diagnosing for possible open cir-cuits, it's often difficult to locate them by sight because oxidation or terminal misalign-ment are hidden by the connectors. Merely wiggling a connector on a sensor or in the wiring harness may correct the open circuit condition. Remember this when an open is indicated when troubleshooting a circuit. Intermittent problems may also be caused by oxidized or loose connections. Electrical troubleshooting is simple if you keep in mind that all electrical circuits are basically elec-tricity running from the battery, through the wires, switches, relays, fuses and fusible links to each electrical component (light bulb, motor, etc.) and to ground, where it's passed back to the battery. Any electrical problem is an interruption in the flow of electricity to and from the battery.

3   Fuses - general information

Refer to illustrations 3.1 and 3.3

The electrical circuits of the vehicle are protected by a combination of fuses, circuit

breakers and fusible links. The fuse block is located under the instrument panel on the left side of the dashboard **(see illustration)**.

Each of the fuses is designed to protect a specific circuit, and the various circuits are identified on the fuse panel itself.

Miniaturized fuses are employed in the fuse block. These compact fuses, with blade terminal design, allow fingertip removal and replacement. If an electrical component fails, always check the fuse first. The best way to check the fuses is with a test light. Check for power at the exposed terminal tips of each fuse. If power is present at one side of the fuse but not the other, the fuse is blown. A blown fuse can also be identified by visually inspecting it **(see illustration)**.

Be sure to replace blown fuses with the correct type. Fuses of different ratings are physically interchangeable, but only fuses of the proper rating should be used. Replacing a fuse with one of a higher or lower value than specified is not recommended. Each electri-cal circuit needs a specific amount of protec-tion. The amperage value of each fuse is molded into the fuse body.

If the replacement fuse immediately fails, don't replace it again until the cause of the problem is isolated and corrected. In most cases, the cause will be a short circuit in the wiring caused by a broken or deterio-rated wire.

4   Fusible links - general information

Refer to illustrations 4.2a and 4.2b

Some circuits are protected by fusible links. The links are used in circuits which are not ordinarily fused, such as the ignition cir-cuit.

Although the fusible links appear to be a heavier gauge than the wires they're protect-ing, the appearance is due to the thick insula-tion **(see illustration)**. All fusible links are four wire gauges smaller than the wire they're designed to protect. fusible links can't be repaired, but a new link of the same size wire can be installed. The procedure is as follows:

4.2a The fusible links (arrow) are located in the engine compartment adjacent to the battery

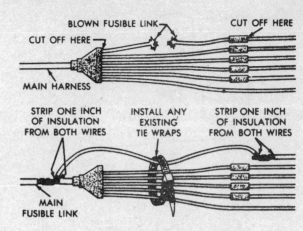

4.2b Fusible link repair details

a) *Disconnect the negative cable from the battery.*
b) *Disconnect the fusible link from the wiring harness.*
c) *Cut the damaged fusible link out of the wire just behind the connector.*
d) *Strip the insulation back approximately 1-inch (see illustration).*
e) *Position the connector on the new fusible link and crimp it into place.*
f) *Use rosin core solder at each end of the new link to obtain a good connection.*
g) *Use plenty of electrical tape around the soldered joint. No wires should be exposed.*
h) *Connect the negative battery cable. Test the circuit for proper operation.*

5 Circuit breakers - general information

Circuit breakers protect components such as power windows, power door locks and headlights. Some circuit breakers are located in the fuse box. On some models the circuit breaker resets itself automatically, so an electrical overload in the circuit will cause it to fail momentarily, then come back on. If the circuit doesn't come back on, check it immediately. Once the condition is corrected, the circuit breaker will resume its normal function. Some circuit breakers have a button on top and must be reset manually.

6 Relays - general information

Refer to illustration 6.1

Several electrical accessories in the vehicle utilize relays to transmit current to the component (see illustration). If the relay is defective, the component won't operate properly.

If a faulty relay is suspected, it can be removed and tested by a dealer service department or a repair shop. Defective relays must be replaced as a unit.

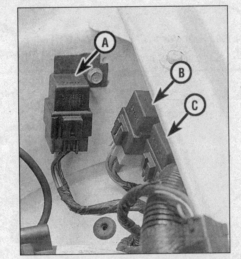

6.1 Several relays are located in the engine compartment, near the battery

  A   *Starter relay*
  B   *Radiator fan relay*
  C   *Air conditioning cutout relay*

7 Turn signal and hazard flashers - check and replacement

Warning: *On airbag-equipped models, always disconnect the negative battery cable and wait at least two minutes before working in the vicinity of the impact sensors, steering column or center console to avoid the accidental deployment of the airbag, which could cause personal injury.*

Turn signal flasher

Refer to illustration 7.1

1   The turn signal flasher, a small canister-shaped unit located on a bracket under the driver's side air conditioning duct, flashes the turn signals (see illustration).
2   When the flasher unit is functioning properly, an audible click can be heard during its operation. If the turn signals fail on one

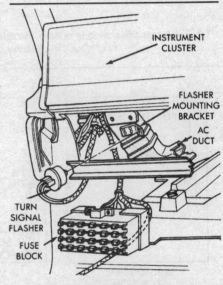

7.1 The turn signal flasher is mounted on a bracket under the dash

side or the other and the flasher unit doesn't make its characteristic clicking sound, a faulty turn signal bulb is indicated.
3   If both turn signals fail to blink, the problem may be due to a blown fuse, a faulty flasher unit, a broken switch or a loose or open connection. If a quick check of the fuse box indicates the turn signal fuse has blown, check the wiring for a short before installing a new fuse.
4   To replace the flasher, simply detach it from its electrical connector and plug in the new one.
5   Make sure the replacement is identical to the original. Compare the old one to the new one before installing it.
6   Installation is the reverse of removal.

Hazard flasher

Refer to illustration 7.7

7   The hazard flasher, a small canister-shaped unit located in the relay module

12

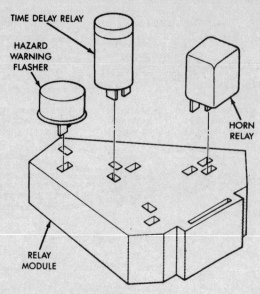

7.7 The hazard flasher is located in the relay module under the dash above the fuse block

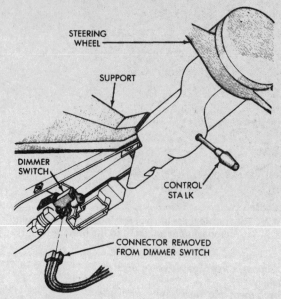

8.2 Unplug the electrical connector from the dimmer switch

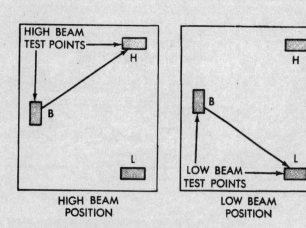

8.3 Terminal continuity guide for a typical electrical connector of headlight dimmer switch (non-airbag models)

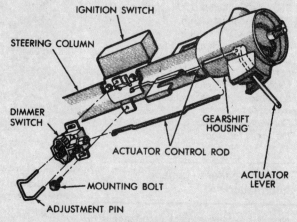

8.6 An exploded view of a typical dimmer switch assembly – you can fabricate your own adjustment pin using a piece of coat hanger or paper clip, or use proper size drill bits

under the left side of the dash, flashes all four turn signals simultaneously when activated **(see illustration)**.

8   The hazard flasher is checked just like the turn signal flasher (see Steps 2 and 3).

9   To replace the hazard flasher, pull it out of the back of relay module.

10   Make sure the replacement is identical to the original. Compare the old one to the new one before installing it.

11   Installation is the reverse of removal.

---

8   Headlight dimmer switch (non-airbag equipped models) - check and replacement

Refer to illustrations 8.2, 8.3 and 8.6
Warning: *On airbag-equipped models, always disconnect the negative battery cable*

and wait at least two minutes before working in the vicinity of the impact sensors, steering column or center console to avoid the accidental deployment of the airbag, which could cause personal injury.

Check

1   Remove the steering column cover.
2   Unplug the electrical connector from the switch **(see illustration)**.
3   Use an ohmmeter to check the continuity between the switch terminals. There should be continuity between the B and H terminals with the switch in the high beam position and the B and L terminals in the low beam position **(see illustration)**. If there isn't, replace the switch.

Replacement

4   Remove the two bolts and lower the

switch from the steering column.
5   Place the new switch in position and install the mounting bolts finger tight.
6   Insert an adjustment pin fabricated from a piece of wire. Push the switch to the rear to take up the slack in the actuator control rod, then tighten the bolts securely **(see illustration)**.
7   Remove the pin, plug in the connector and install the steering column cover.

---

9   Turn signal/hazard warning switch (non-airbag equipped models) - check and replacement

Refer to illustrations 9.4, 9.5 and 9.11
Warning: *On airbag-equipped models, always disconnect the negative battery cable and wait at least two minutes before working*

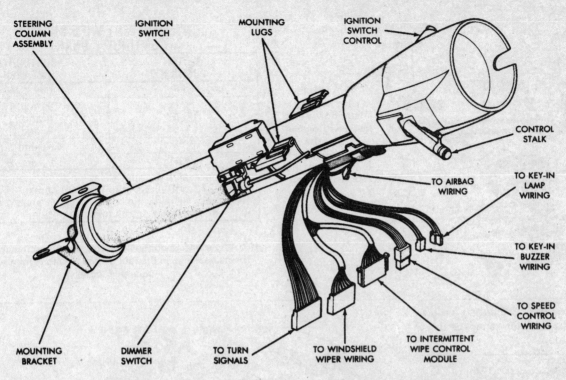

9.4 Details of the steering column electrical connectors (typical non-airbag models)

SWITCH CONTINUITY CHART

Turn Signal Switch			
Switch Position:	Left	Neutral	Right
Continuity Between:	7 and 4	10 and 9	7 and 5
Continuity Between:	7 and 8	10 and 8	7 and 9
Continuity Between:*	21 and 23	—	22 and 21
Continuity Between:	10 and 9	—	10 and 8
Hazard Warning Switch			
Switch Position:	Off		On
Continuity Between:	10 and 9		6 and 4
Continuity Between:	10 and 8		6 and 5
Continuity Between:	—		6 and 8
Continuity Between:	—		6 and 9
*Cornering Lamps Only			

9.5 Typical turn signal and hazard switch continuity check details

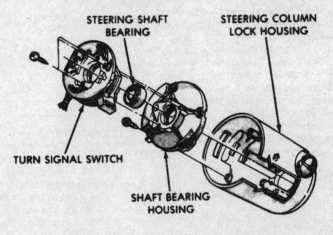

9.11 Typical turn signal switch mounting details

in the vicinity of the impact sensors, steering column or center console to avoid the accidental deployment of the airbag, which could cause personal injury.

1 The turn signal switch is located at the top end of the steering column and is operated by the multi-function control stalk. The hazard warning switch is mounted under the turn signal switch, next to the ignition key light.

Check

2 Disconnect the negative cable from the battery.

3 Remove the steering column lower cover.

4 Unplug the turn signal switch electrical connector (see illustration).

5 Use an ohmmeter or self-powered test light to check for continuity between the indicated switch connector terminals (see illustration).

6 Replace the turn signal or hazard switch if the continuity is not as specified.

Replacement

7 Disconnect the negative battery cable, then remove the steering wheel (see Chapter 10).

8 Detach the wiring harness trough from the steering column.

9 Unplug the electrical connector (see illustration 9.4).

10 Remove the wiper/washer switch pivot screw, leaving the control stalk in place.

11 Remove the three screws and detach the turn signal switch (see illustration). Carefully pull the wiring harness out through the top of the steering column.

12 Installation is the reverse of removal, remembering to lubricate the steering shaft contact surfaces with multi-purpose grease and to make sure the dimmer switch rod is located securely in the pocket of the control stalk.

12

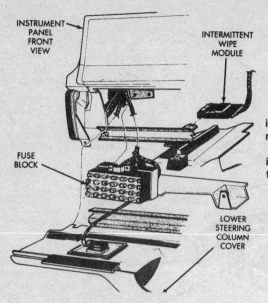

10.1 On all models, the intermittent wiper module is located under the instrument panel, to the right of the steering column

INTERMITTENT WIPE SWITCH CONTINUITY CHART

SWITCH POSITION	CONTINUITY BETWEEN
OFF	L and P_2
DELAY	P_1 and I_1 R and I_1* I_2 and G
LOW	P_1 and L
HIGH	P_1 and H

*Resistance at maximum delay position should be between 270,000 ohms and 330,000 ohms.
*Resistance at minimum delay position should be zero with ohmmeter set on the high ohm scale.

10.5 Wiper switch continuity check chart – continuity should be as specified in the four switch positions (non-airbag equipped models)

10   Wiper/washer switch (non-airbag equipped models) - check and replacement

Refer to illustrations 10.1 and 10.5
Warning: *On airbag-equipped models, always disconnect the negative battery cable and wait at least two minutes before working in the vicinity of the impact sensors, steering column or center console to avoid the accidental deployment of the airbag, which could cause personal injury.*

1   These models are equipped with a multi-function lever located on the left side of the steering column which controls the wiper/washer, turn signal and dimmer switches mounted on the steering column. On all models, the wipers are two-speed with an intermittent feature, operated by a module located under the instrument panel to the right of the steering column **(see illustration)**.

Check

2   Disconnect the negative cable from the battery.
3   Remove the steering column lower cover.
4   Unplug the electrical connector **(see illustration 9.4)**.
5   Use an ohmmeter or self-powered test light to check for continuity between the switch terminals at the electrical connector **(see illustrations)**.
6   Replace the wiper/washer switch if the continuity is not as specified.

Replacement

7   Perform the procedures in Steps 2 and 3, then remove the steering wheel (see Chapter 10).
8   Detach the wiring harness trough from the steering column.
9   Unplug the electrical connector **(see illustration 9.4)**.
10   Remove the lock housing cover screws

and pull the cover off.
11   Pull the switch hider out for access.
12   Remove the two screws and detach the switch from the stalk, then remove the wiper knob from the end of the stalk.
13   Rotate the control stalk fully clockwise, align the slot and pin, then pull the stalk out.
14   Installation is the reverse of removal.

11   Ignition switch - check and replacement

Warning: *On airbag-equipped models, always disconnect the negative battery cable and wait at least two minutes before working in the vicinity of the impact sensors, steering column or center console to avoid the accidental deployment of the airbag, which could cause personal injury.*

Non-tilt column
Check

Refer to illustrations 11.1 and 11.3
1   The ignition switch is located on the

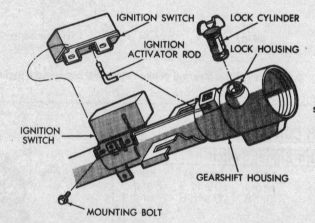

11.1 On non-tilt columns, the ignition switch is located on the top right side of the steering column

steering column and is actuated by a rod attached to the key lock cylinder **(see illustration)**.
2   Remove the switch (Steps 5 through 8).
3   Use an ohmmeter or self-powered test light and the accompanying diagram to check for continuity between the switch terminals **(see illustration)**.
4   If the switch does not have correct continuity, replace it.

Replacement

5   Disconnect the negative cable from the battery.
6   Insert the key into the lock cylinder and turn it to the ACC position.
7   Remove the steering column cover (see Chapter 11). On some models it may be necessary to remove the bolts or nuts and lower the steering column for access to the switch.
8   Unplug the electrical connector, remove the bolts, then detach the switch from the actuator rod and lower it from the steering column.
9   Installation is the reverse of removal. With the switch in the Lock position engage it to the actuator rod, then push up on the

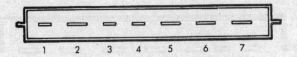

IGNITION SWITCH CONNECTOR LOOKING INTO SWITCH

WIRE CAVITY	WIRE COLOR	APPLICATION
1	YELLOW	STARTER RELAY
2	DARK BLUE	IGNITION RUN/START
3	GRAY/BLACK	BRAKE WARNING LAMP
4	PINK/BLACK	IGNITION SWITCH BATTERY FEED
	PINK OR PINK/WHITE	
5	BLACK/ORANGE OR BLACK/TAN	RUN ACCESSORY
6	BLACK OR BLACK/WHITE	ACCESSORY
7	RED	IGNITION SWITCH BATTERY FEED

11.3 Ignition switch continuity chart

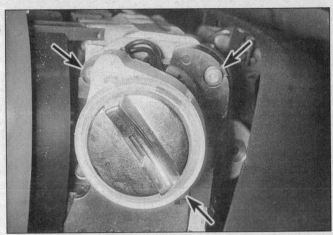

11.16 The tilt column ignition switch is held in place by three Torx-head tamper proof screws (the lower screw is located under the cover)

switch to remove any slack from the rod before fully tightening the bolts.

Tilt column models

Check

Refer to illustrations 11.16, 11.17, 11.18 and 11.19

10   The ignition switch is located on right side of the steering column and is held in place by three Torx T-20 tamper proof screws which require a special tool for removal (available at auto parts stores).

11   Remove the switch (see Steps 14 through 16).

12   Use an ohmmeter or self-powered test light and check for continuity between the switch terminals (see illustration 11.3).

13   If the switch does not have correct continuity, replace it.

Replacement

14   Disconnect the negative cable from the battery.

15   Remove the steering column cover (see Chapter 11).

16   Remove the tamper proof screws, detach the switch from column, then unplug the electrical connector and remove switch from the steering column (see illustration).

17   If it is necessary to remove the lock cylinder, insert the key and turn it to the Lock position. Press the retaining pin in with a small screwdriver until it is flush with the surface (see illustration).

18   Turn the key clockwise to the Off position, which will unseat the lock cylinder, but don't try to remove it yet (see illustration). With the cylinder unseated, rotate the key counterclockwise to the Lock position, remove the key, then remove the lock cylinder from the ignition switch.

19   Installation is the reverse of removal, making sure that on column shift models the shifter is in Park. As the switch is engaged to

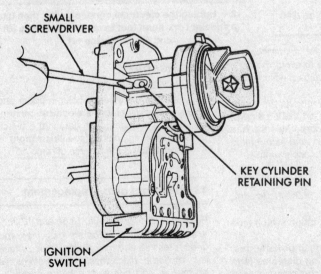

11.17 Push the retaining pin in to unseat the lock cylinder

11.18 The lock cylinder will protrude about 1/8-inch from the switch once it's unseated – don't try to remove it until you rotate it to the Lock position and remove the key

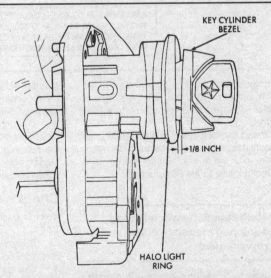

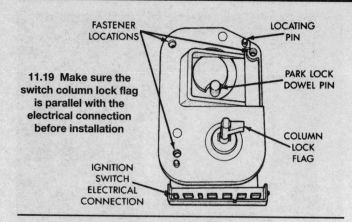

11.19 Make sure the switch column lock flag is parallel with the electrical connection before installation

FASTENER LOCATIONS
LOCATING PIN
PARK LOCK DOWEL PIN
COLUMN LOCK FLAG
IGNITION SWITCH ELECTRICAL CONNECTION

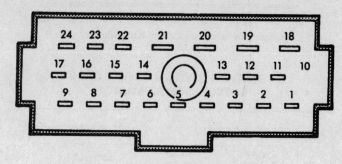

12.3a The multi-function switch terminal details

SWITCH POSITIONS		
TURN SIGNAL	**HAZARD WARNING**	**CONTINUITY BETWEEN**
NEUTRAL	OFF	12 AND 14 AND 15
LEFT	OFF	15 AND 16 AND 17
LEFT	OFF	12 AND 14
LEFT	OFF	22 AND 23 WITH OPTIONAL CORNER LAMPS
RIGHT	OFF	11 AND 12 AND 17
RIGHT	OFF	14 AND 15
RIGHT	OFF	23 AND 24 WITH OPTIONAL CORNER LAMPS
NEUTRAL	ON	11 AND 12 AND 13 AND 15 AND 16

12.3b Turn signal and hazard flasher continuity details – the switch must be in the indicated position for each check

SWITCH POSITION	CONTINUITY BETWEEN
LOW BEAM	18 AND 19
HIGH BEAM	19 AND 20
OPTICAL HORN	20 AND 21

12.3c Headlight dimmer switch continuity details

12.3d Make the continuity checks for the windshield wiper/intermittent wiper with the multi-function switch in the indicated positions

INTERMITTENT WIPE SWITCH CONTINUITY CHART	
SWITCH POSITION	**CONTINUITY BETWEEN**
OFF	PIN 6 & PIN 7
DELAY	PIN 8 & PIN 9 PIN 2 & PIN 4 PIN 1 & PIN 2
LOW	PIN 4 & PIN 6
HIGH	PIN 4 & PIN 5

*RESISTANCE AT MAXIMUM DELAY POSITION SHOULD BE BETWEEN 270,000 OHMS AND 300,000 OHMS.
*RESISTANCE AT MINIMUM DELAY POSITION SHOULD BE ZERO WITH OHMMETER SET ON HIGH OHM SCALE.

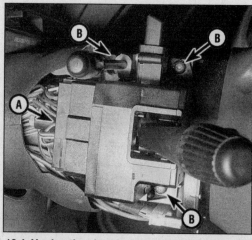

12.4 Unplug the electrical connector (A), then use a special Torx-head tool to remove the bolts (B) and lift the switch off

the column shift park slider linkage, make sure the column lock flag on the switch is parallel with the electrical connectors **(see illustration)**.
20 Insert the lock cylinder in the Lock position until it bottoms in the switch. While pushing the lock cylinder in, insert the key and turn it clockwise to the Run position.

12 Multi-function switch (airbag equipped models) - check and replacement

Warning: *On airbag-equipped models, always disconnect the negative battery cable and wait at least two minutes before working in the vicinity of the impact sensors, steering*

column or center console to avoid the accidental deployment of the airbag, which could cause personal injury.
1   On airbag equipped models the multi-function switch is located on the left side of the steering column. It incorporates the turn signal, headlight dimmer and windshield wiper/washer functions into one switch.

Check

Refer to illustrations 12.3a, 12.3b, 12.3c and 12.3d
2   Remove the multi-function switch (see Steps 5 through 8).
3   Use an ohmmeter or self-powered test light and the accompanying diagrams **(see illustrations)** to check for continuity between the switch terminals with the switch in each position.

Replacement

Refer to illustration 12.4
4   Remove the steering column upper and lower covers. Unplug the electrical connector, remove the bolts, then detach the switch from the steering column **(see illustration)**.
5   Installation is the reverse of removal.

13 Headlight bulb - replacement

Refer to illustrations 13.3a, 13.3b and 13.3c
Warning: *Halogen bulbs are gas-filled and under pressure and may shatter if the surface is scratched or the bulb is dropped. Wear eye protection and handle the bulbs carefully, grasping only the base whenever possible. Don't touch the surface of the bulb with your*

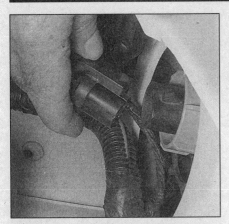

13.3a Depress the retainer and unplug the connector

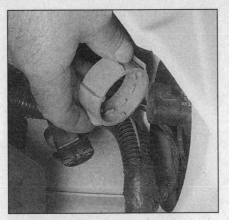

13.3b Unscrew the plastic collar . . .

13.3c . . . then grasp the bulb holder and pull it out of the housing

14.1a The Torx-head screw (arrow) at the top of the housing adjusts the headlight up-and-down movement

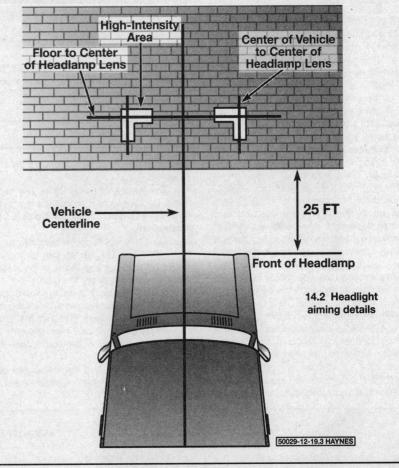

14.2 Headlight aiming details

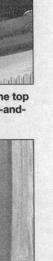

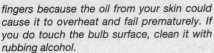

14.1b Left-and-right headlight adjustments is made with this screw (arrow)

fingers because the oil from your skin could cause it to overheat and fail prematurely. If you do touch the bulb surface, clean it with rubbing alcohol.

1   Disconnect the negative cable from the battery.
2   Open the hood.
3   Reach behind the headlight assembly, unplug the electrical connector, unscrew the bulb retaining ring and pull the holder assembly out for access to the bulb **(see illustrations)**.

4   Grasp the bulb base and unplug it from the holder.
5   Insert the new bulb into the holder.
6   Install the bulb holder in the headlight assembly.

14   Headlights - adjustment

Refer to illustrations 14.1a, 14.1b and 14.2
Warning: *The headlights must be aimed correctly. If adjusted incorrectly, they could temporarily blind the driver of an oncoming vehicle and cause an accident or seriously reduce*

your ability to see the road. The headlights should be checked for proper aim every 12 months and any time a new headlight is installed or front end body work is performed. The following procedure is only an interim step to provide temporary adjustment until the headlights can be adjusted by a properly equipped shop.

1   Headlights have two spring loaded adjusting screws, one on the top controlling up-and-down movement and one on the side controlling left and right movement **(see illustrations)**.
2   This procedure requires a blank wall 25

12

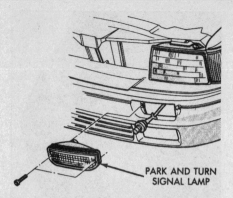

15.1 The park and turn signal light bulbs can be replaced after removing the lens housings

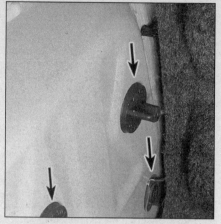

15.3a Unscrew the plastic holders (arrows) and remove the tail light housing covers for access to the bulbs

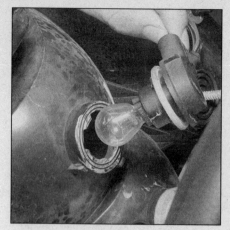

15.3b Pull the bulb holder out . . .

feet in front of the vehicle and a level floor **(see illustration)**.

3   Position masking tape vertically on the wall in reference to the vehicle centerline and the centerlines of both headlights.

4   Position a horizontal tape line in reference to the centerline of all the headlights. **Note:** *It may be easier to position the tape on the wall with the vehicle parked only a few inches away.*

5   Adjustment should be made with the vehicle sitting level, the gas tank half-full and no unusually heavy load in the vehicle.

6   Starting with the low beam adjustment, position the high intensity zone so it's two inches below the horizontal line and two inches to the right of the headlight vertical line. Adjustment is made by turning the top adjusting screw clockwise to raise the beam and counterclockwise to lower the beam. The adjusting screw on the side should be used in the same manner to move the beam left or right.

7   With the high beams on, the high intensity zone should be vertically centered with the exact center just below the horizontal line. **Note:** *It may not be possible to position the headlight aim exactly for both high and low beams. If a compromise must be made, keep in mind that the low beams are the most*

used and have the greatest effect on driver safety.

8   Have the headlights adjusted by a dealer service department or service station at the earliest opportunity.

15   Bulb replacement

Refer to illustrations 15.1, 15.3a, 15.3b and 15.3c

1   The lenses of many lights are held in place by screws, which makes it a simple procedure to gain access to the bulbs **(see illustration)**.

2   On some lights the lenses are held in place by clips. The lenses can be removed either by unsnapping them or by using a small screwdriver to pry them off.

3   Several types of bulbs are used. Some are removed by pushing in and turning them counterclockwise **(see illustration)**. Others can simply be unclipped from the terminals or pulled straight out of the socket **(see illustrations)**.

4   To gain access to the instrument panel lights, the instrument cluster must be removed first.

16   Headlight switch - removal and installation

Refer to illustration 16.3

Warning: *On airbag-equipped models, always disconnect the negative battery cable and wait at least two minutes before working in the vicinity of the impact sensors, steering column or center console to avoid the accidental deployment of the airbag, which could cause personal injury.*

1   Disconnect the negative battery cable.

2   Remove the instrument cluster bezel (Chapter 11).

3   Remove the mounting plate screws **(see illustration)**.

4   Pull the switch assembly out of the dash and unplug the electrical connector.

5   Press the release button on the side of the switch and withdraw the switch knob and shaft.

6   Remove the screws, detach the switch from the mounting plate and remove the switch.

7   Snap the escutcheon out of the dash, then remove the nut holding the switch on the mounting plate.

8   Installation is the reverse of removal.

15.3c . . . then pull the bulb out of the holder

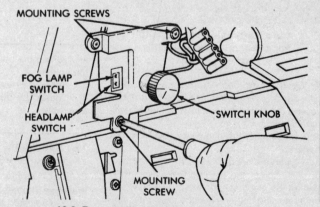

16.3 Remove the mounting plate screws

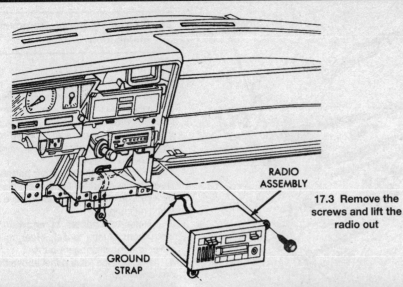

17.3 Remove the screws and lift the radio out

17.6a The speakers are held in place by Phillips head screws (arrow) around the outer edge of the housing

17.6b Once the speaker is removed from the opening, the connector can be unplugged

18.3a Unscrew the antenna mast with a small wrench

18.3b Use needle-nose pliers to unscrew the cap nut – be careful, the pliers can easily slip and scratch the fender

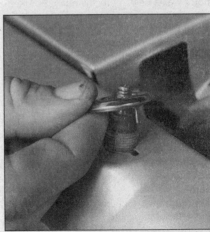

18.3c Lift the adapter off the fender

17   Radio and speakers - removal and installation

Warning: *On airbag-equipped models, always disconnect the negative battery cable and wait at least two minutes before working in the vicinity of the impact sensors, steering column or center console to avoid the accidental deployment of the airbag, which could cause personal injury.*

Radio

Refer to illustration 17.3

1   Disconnect the negative battery cable.
2   Remove the center bezel (Chapter 11).
3   Remove the mounting screws, pull the radio out of the instrument panel, disconnect the electrical connectors and antenna lead, then remove it from the vehicle (see illustration).
4   Installation is the reverse of removal.

Speakers

Refer to illustrations 17.6a and 17.6b

5   Remove the door trim panels (Chapter 11).

6   Remove the screws and detach the speaker (see illustration). Pull the speaker out of the door, unplug the electrical connector and remove the speaker from the vehicle (see illustration).
7   Installation is the reverse of removal.

18   Antenna - removal and installation

Refer to illustrations 18.3a, 18.3b and 18.3c
Warning: *On airbag-equipped models, always disconnect the negative battery cable and wait at least two minutes before working in the vicinity of the impact sensors, steering column or center console to avoid the accidental deployment of the airbag, which could cause personal injury.*

1   Disconnect the negative battery cable.
2   Working under the dash, unplug the antenna cable.
3   Use a small open-end wrench to unscrew the antenna mast, then remove the cap nut and lift off the upper adapter and gasket (see illustrations).
4   Working under the vehicle, remove the three plastic rivets from the rear edge of the inner fender splash shield and pull the shield away for access to the antenna.
5   Detach the antenna from the fender and remove it from the vehicle.
6   Installation is the reverse of removal.

12

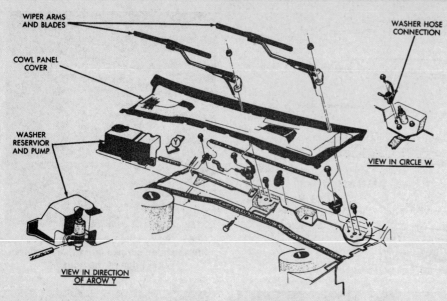

19.10 Windshield wiper motor details

19 Windshield wiper motor - check and replacement

Refer to illustration 19.10

Check

1 If the wiper motor does not run at all, first check the fuse block for a blown fuse (see Section 3).
2 Check the wiper switch (see Section 10 or 12).
3 Turn the ignition switch and wiper switch on.
4 Connect a jumper wire between the wiper motor and ground, then retest. If the motor works now, repair the ground connection.
5 If the wipers still don't work, turn on the wipers and check for voltage at the motor connector. If there's voltage, remove the motor and check it off the vehicle with fused jumper wires from the battery. If the motor now works, check for binding linkage. If the motor still doesn't work, replace it.
6 If there's no voltage at the motor, the problem is in the switch or wiring.

Replacement

7 Disconnect the negative cable from the battery.
8 Mark their locations, remove the nuts and detach the wiper arms.
9 Remove the cowl cover (see Chapter 11).
10 Unplug the wiper motor electrical connector and remove the mounting bolts **(see illustration)**.
11 Hold the motor drive crank with a wrench, remove the crank nut and detach the crank, then lift the motor out.
12 Installation is the reverse of removal.

20 Instrument cluster - removal and installation

Warning: *On airbag-equipped models, always disconnect the negative battery cable and wait at least two minutes before working in the vicinity of the impact sensors, steering column or center console to avoid the accidental deployment of the airbag, which could cause personal injury.*
1 Disconnect the negative cable from the battery.
2 Remove the cluster bezel (see Chapter 11).
3 Remove the cluster mounting screws. Pull the assembly out and disconnect the electrical connectors.
4 Installation is the reverse of removal.

21 Instrument panel - removal and installation

Refer to illustration 21.11
Warning: *On airbag-equipped models, always disconnect the negative battery cable and wait at least two minutes before working in the vicinity of the impact sensors, steering column or center console to avoid the accidental deployment of the airbag, which could cause personal injury.*
1 Disconnect the negative battery cable. Have the air conditioning system discharged by a service station or an automotive air conditioning shop.
2 Refer to Chapter 11 and remove the instrument cluster bezel, steering column cover and the dashboard panels.
3 Remove the relay panel above the glove box opening.
4 Remove the left and right side cowl and scuff plate panels.
5 Remove the hood release handle.
6 Remove the center floor console (Chapter 11).
7 Remove the radio and heater/air conditioner controls.
8 Unplug the instrument panel bulkhead electrical connector.
9 Disconnect the heater/air conditioner electrical and vacuum lines.
10 Remove the instrument panel top cover.
11 Loosen the left and right hand instrument panel pivot bolts **(see illustration)**.
12 Remove the screws attaching the instrument panel to the cowl.
13 Roll the instrument panel back for access and unplug any remaining electrical connectors.
14 With an assistant supporting the weight, remove the pivot bolts, then remove the instrument panel from the vehicle.
15 Installation is the reverse of removal.

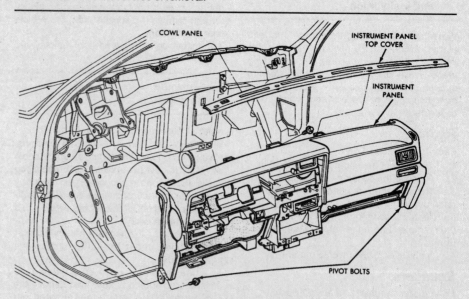

21.11 Instrument panel and top cover details

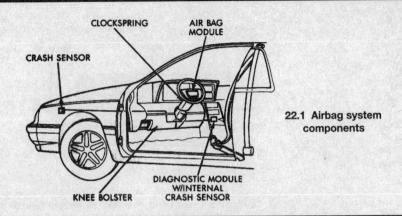

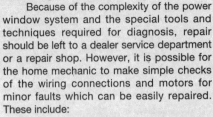

22.1 Airbag system components

22 Airbag system - general information

Refer to illustration 22.1

Later models are equipped with a Supplemental Restraint System (SRS), more commonly called an airbag system. This system is designed to protect the driver from serious injury in the event of head-on or frontal collision. It consists of an airbag module in the center of the steering wheel, a passenger's side airbag mounted in the right side of the dash (some models), two crash sensors mounted at the front of the vehicle and a diagnostic module which also contains a crash sensor located inside the passenger compartment **(see illustration)**.

Airbag module

The airbag module contains a housing incorporating the cushion (airbag) and inflator unit. The inflator assembly is mounted on the back of the housing over a hole through which gas is expelled, inflating the bag almost instantaneously when an electrical signal is sent from the system. On the driver's side, a specially wound wire, called a clockspring, carries this signal to the module **(see illustration 22.1)**. The clockspring is a flat, ribbon-like electrically conductive tape which is wound with 20 turns so it can transmit an electrical signal regardless of steering wheel position.

Sensors

The system has three sensors: two crash sensors at the front of the vehicle behind the bumper and a safing sensor in the Airbag System Diagnostic Module (ASDM) located under the instrument panel, just in front of the center console.

The front crash sensors are basically pressure sensitive switches that complete an electrical circuit during an impact of sufficient G force. The electrical signal from the crash sensors is sent to the safing sensor in the ASDM, which then completes the circuit and inflates the airbag.

Airbag System Diagnostic Module (ASDM)

The ASDM contains the safing sensor

and an on-board microprocessor which monitors the operation of the system. It checks this system every time the vehicle is started, causing the AIRBAG light to go on, then off, if the system is operating properly. If there is a fault in the system, the light will go on and stay on and the ASDM will store fault codes indicating the nature of the fault. If the AIRBAG light does go on and stay on, the vehicle should be taken to your dealer immediately for service.

23 Power door lock system - description and check

The power door lock system operates the door lock actuators mounted in each door. The system consists of the switches, actuators and associated wiring. Since special tools and techniques are required to diagnose the system, it should be left to a dealer service department or a repair shop. However, it is possible for the home mechanic to make simple checks of the wiring connections and actuators for minor faults which can be easily repaired. These include:

a) *Check the system fuse and/or circuit breaker.*

b) *Check the switch wires for damage and loose connections. Check the switches for continuity.*

c) *Remove the door panel(s) and check the actuator wiring connections to see if they're loose or damaged. Inspect the actuator rods (if equipped) to make sure they aren't bent or damaged. Inspect the actuator wiring for damaged or loose connections. The actuator can be checked by applying battery power momentarily. A discernible click indicates that the solenoid is operating properly.*

24 Power window system - description and check

The power window system operates the electric motors mounted in the doors which lower and raise the windows. The system consists of the control switches, the motors

(regulators), glass mechanisms and associated wiring.

Because of the complexity of the power window system and the special tools and techniques required for diagnosis, repair should be left to a dealer service department or a repair shop. However, it is possible for the home mechanic to make simple checks of the wiring connections and motors for minor faults which can be easily repaired. These include:

a) *Inspect the power window actuating switches for broken wires and loose connections.*

b) *Check the power window fuse/and or circuit breaker.*

c) *Remove the door panel(s) and check the power window motor wires to see if they're loose or damaged. Inspect the glass mechanisms for damage which could cause binding.*

25 Cruise control system - description and check

The cruise control system maintains vehicle speed with a vacuum actuated servo motor located in the engine compartment, which is connected to the throttle linkage by a cable. The system consists of the servo motor, clutch switch, brake switch, control switches, a relay and associated vacuum hoses.

Because of the complexity of the cruise control system and the special tools and techniques required for diagnosis, repair should be left to a dealer service department or a repair shop. However, it is possible for the home mechanic to make simple checks of the wiring and vacuum connections for minor faults which can be easily repaired. These include:

a) *Inspect the cruise control actuating switches for broken wires and loose connections.*

b) *Check the cruise control fuse.*

c) *The cruise control system is operated by vacuum so it's critical that all vacuum switches, hoses and connections are secure. Check the hoses in the engine compartment for tight connections, cracks and obvious vacuum leaks.*

26 Rear window defogger - check and repair

Refer to illustrations 26.4 and 26.13

1   The rear window defogger consists of a number of horizontal elements baked onto the glass surface.

2   Small breaks in the element can be repaired without removing the rear window.

Check

3   Turn the ignition switch and defogger system switches On.

12

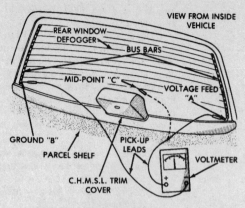

26.4 Rear window defogger test points

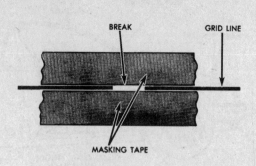

26.13 To repair a broken grid, first apply a strip of tape to either side of the grid to mask off the area

4   Ground the negative lead of a voltmeter to terminal B and the positive lead to terminal A **(see illustration)**.

5   The voltmeter between 10 and 15 volts. If the reading is lower, there is a poor ground connection.

6   Contact the negative lead to a good body ground. The reading should stay the same.

7   Connect the negative lead to terminal B, then touch each grid line at the mid-point with the positive lead.

8   The reading should be approximately six volts. If the reading is 0, there is a break between mid-point "C" and terminal "A".

9   A 10 to 14 volt reading is an indication of a break between mid-point "C". Move the lead toward the break; the voltage will change when the break is crossed.

Repair

10   Repair the break in the line using repair kit recommended specifically for this purpose. Included in this kit is plastic conductive epoxy.

11   Prior to repairing a break, turn off the system and allow it to de-energize for a few minutes.

12   Lightly buff the element area with fine steel wool, then clean it thoroughly with rubbing alcohol.

13   Use masking tape to mask off the area of repair **(see illustration)**.

14   Mix the epoxy thoroughly, according to the instructions on the package.

15   Apply the epoxy material to the slit in the masking tape, overlapping the undamaged

WIRE COLOR CODE CHART					
COLOR CODE	COLOR	STANDARD TRACER COLOR	COLOR CODE	COLOR	STANDARD TRACER CODE
BK	BLACK	WT	PK	PINK	BK OR WH
BR	BROWN	WT	RD	RED	WT
DB	DARK BLUE	WT	TN	TAN	WT
DG	DARK GREEN	WT	VT	VIOLET	WT
GY	GRAY	BK	WT	WHITE	BK
LB	LIGHT BLUE	BK	YL	YELLOW	BK
LG	LIGHT GREEN	BK	*	WITH TRACER	
OR	ORANGE	BK			

27.4a Wire color code chart

area about 3/4-inch on either end.

16   Allow the repair to cure for 24 hours before removing the tape and using system.

27   Wiring diagrams - general information

Refer to illustrations 27.4a and 27.46

Since it isn't possible to include all wiring diagrams for every year covered by this manual, the following diagrams are those that are typical and most commonly needed.

Prior to troubleshooting any circuits, check the fuse and circuit breakers (if equipped) to make sure they're in good condition. Make sure the battery is properly charged and check the cable connections (see Chapter 1).

When checking a circuit, make sure that all connectors are clean, with no broken or loose terminals. When unplugging a connector, do not pull on the wires. Pull only on the connector housings themselves.

Refer to the accompanying table and legend for the wire color codes applicable to your vehicle **(see illustrations)**.

LEGEND OF SYMBOLS USED ON WIRING DIAGRAMS			
+	POSITIVE		CONNECTOR
−	NEGATIVE		MALE CONNECTOR
	GROUND		FEMALE CONNECTOR
	FUSE		DENOTES WIRE CONTINUES ELSEWHERE
	GANG FUSES WITH BUSS BAR		DENOTES WIRE GOES TO ONE OF TWO CIRCUITS
	CIRCUIT BREAKER		SPLICE
	CAPACITOR	J2 2	SPLICE IDENTIFICATION
Ω	OHMS		THERMAL ELEMENT
	RESISTOR	TIMER	TIMER
	VARIABLE RESISTOR		MULTIPLE CONNECTOR
	SERIES RESISTOR		OPTIONAL WIRING WITH / WIRING WITHOUT
	COIL		"Y" WINDINGS
	STEP UP COIL	88:88	DIGITAL READOUT
	OPEN CONTACT		SINGLE FILAMENT LAMP
	CLOSED CONTACT		DUAL FILAMENT LAMP
	CLOSED SWITCH		L.E.D. — LIGHT EMITTING DIODE
	OPEN SWITCH		THERMISTOR
	CLOSED GANGED SWITCH		GAUGE
	OPEN GANGED SWITCH		SENSOR
	TWO POLE SINGLE THROW SWITCH		FUEL INJECTOR
	PRESSURE SWITCH	#36	DENOTES WIRE GOES THROUGH BULKHEAD DISCONNECT
	SOLENOID SWITCH	#19 STRG COLUMN	DENOTES WIRE GOES THROUGH STEERING COLUMN CONNECTOR
	MERCURY SWITCH	INST PANEL #14	DENOTES WIRE GOES THROUGH INSTRUMENT PANEL CONNECTOR
	DIODE OR RECTIFIER	ENG #7	DENOTES WIRE GOES THROUGH GROMMET TO ENGINE COMPARTMENT
	BY-DIRECTIONAL ZENER DIODE		DENOTES WIRE GOES THROUGH GROMMET
	MOTOR		HEATED GRID ELEMENTS
	ARMATURE AND BRUSHES		

27.4b Wiring diagram symbol legend

12

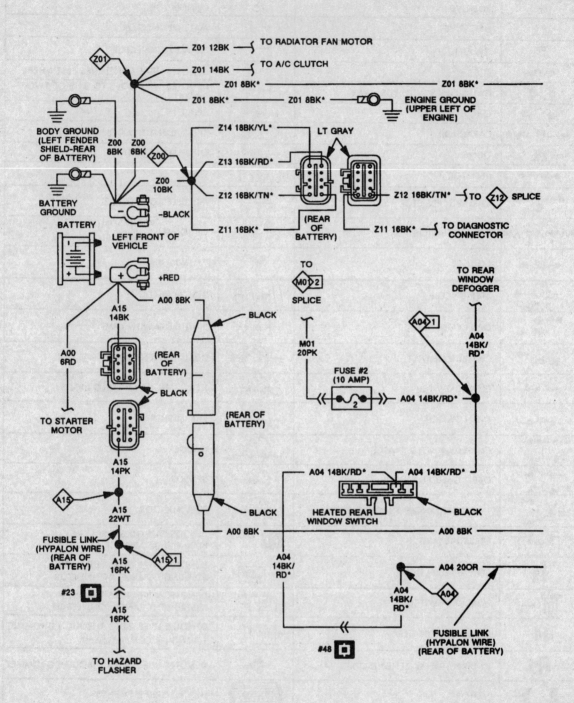

Typical four-cylinder engine charging system wiring diagram (1 of 2)

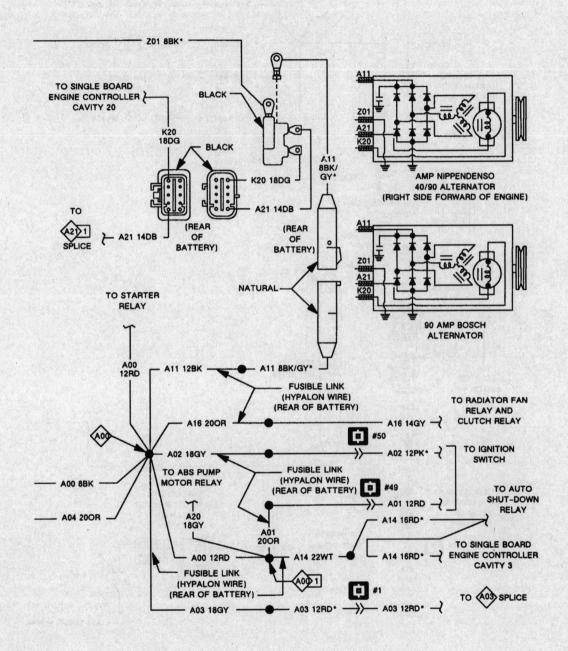

Typical four-cylinder engine charging system wiring diagram (2 of 2)

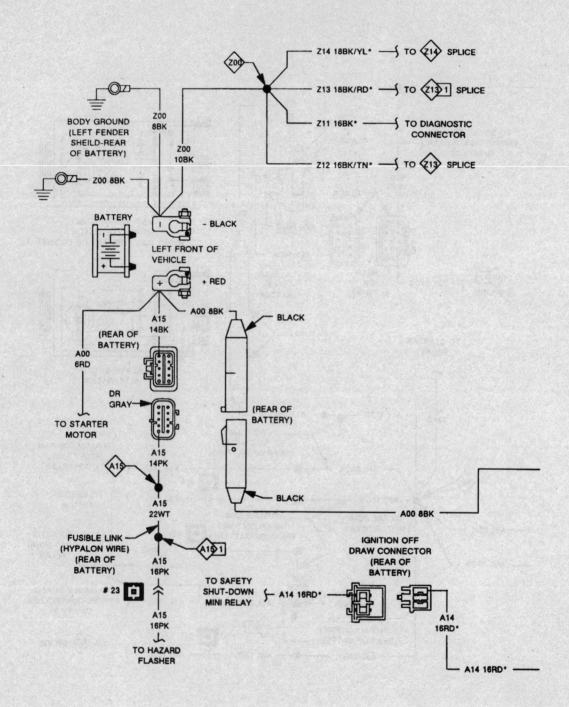

Typical V6 engine charging system wiring diagram (1 of 2)

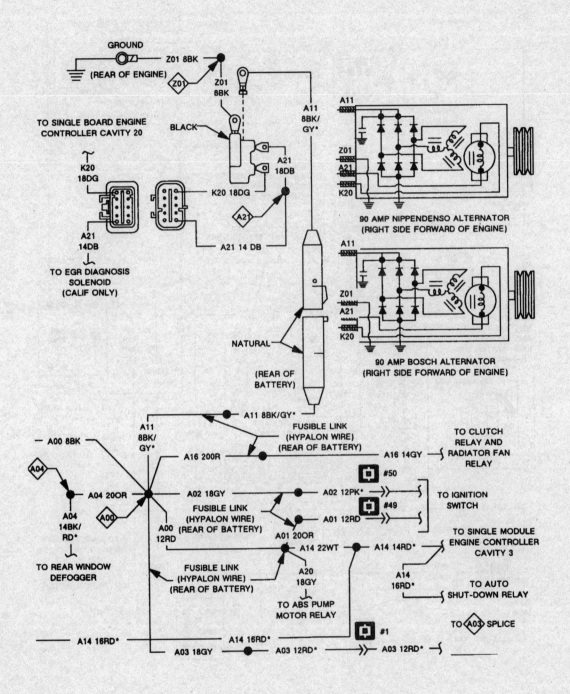

Typical V6 engine charging system wiring diagram (2 of 2)

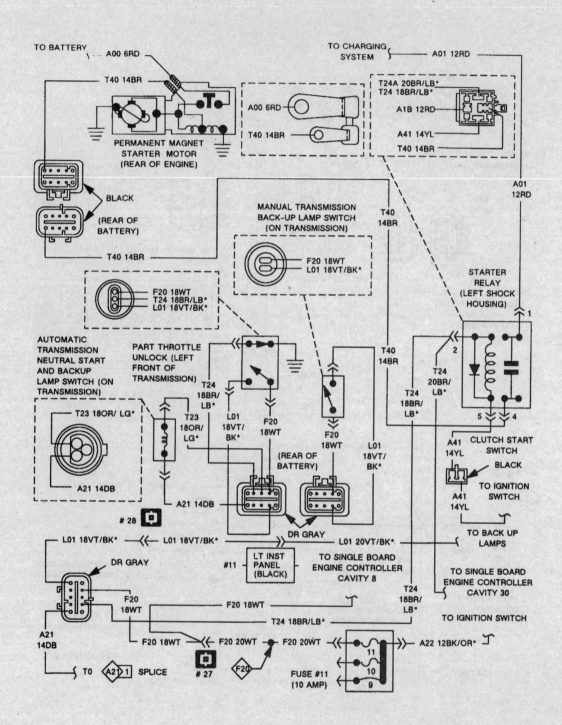

Typical four-cylinder engine starting system wiring diagram

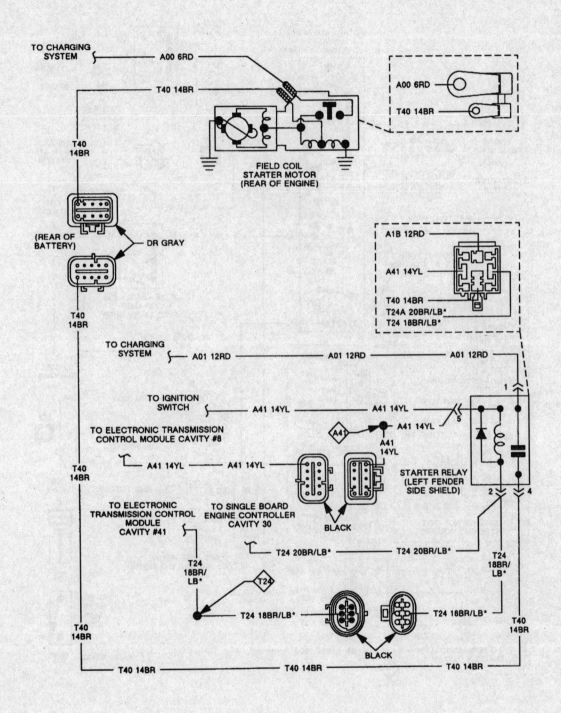

Typical V6 engine starting system wiring diagram

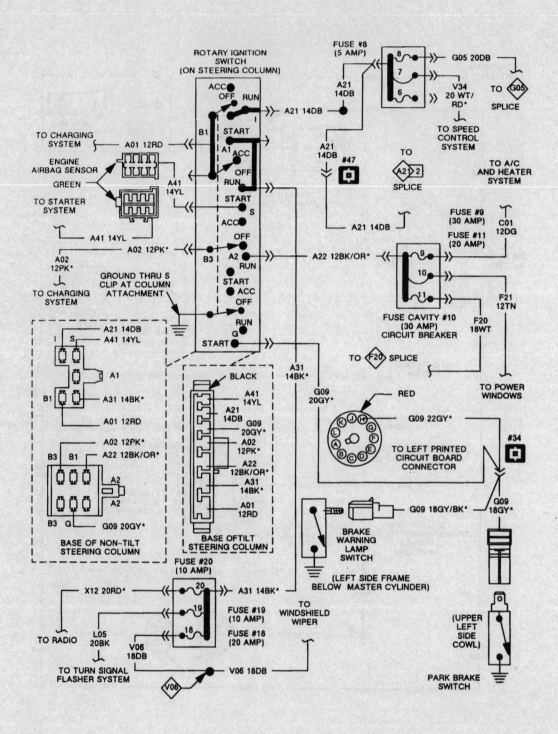

Typical ignition switch wiring diagram

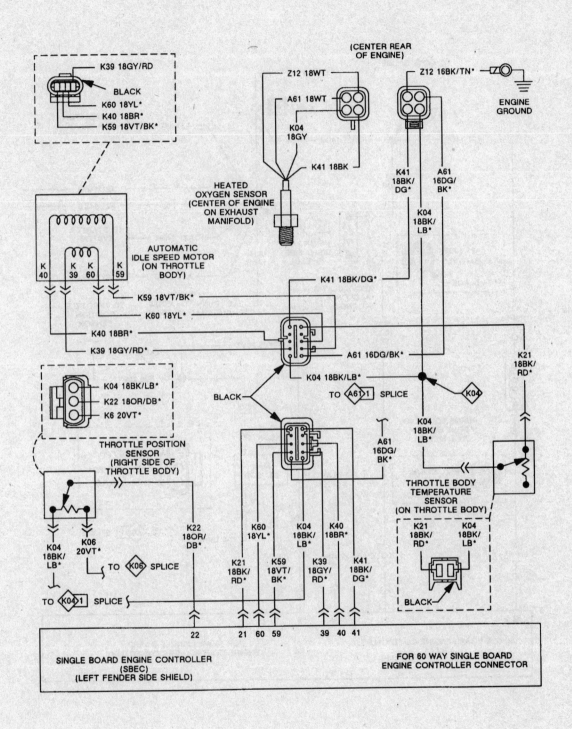

Typical engine management system wiring diagram (1 of 3)

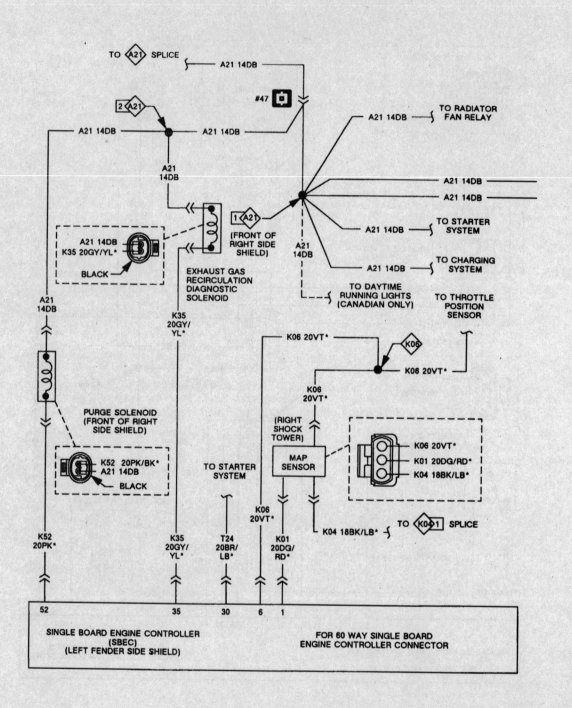

Typical engine management system wiring diagram (2 of 3)

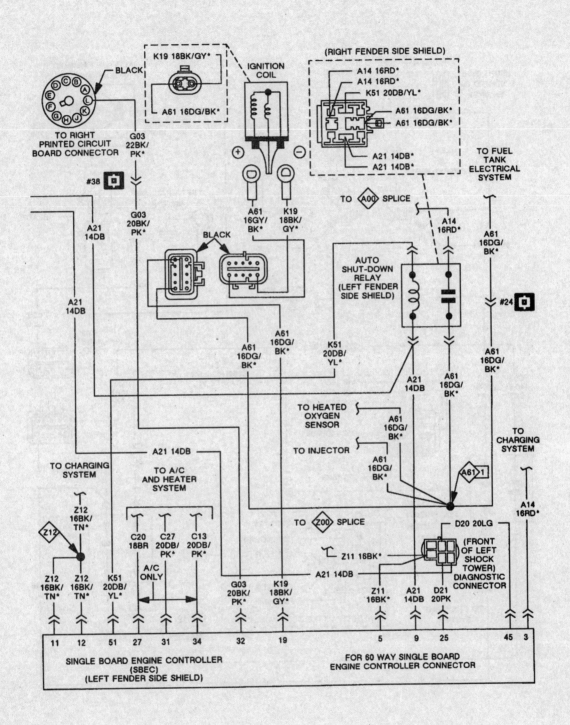

Typical engine management system wiring diagram (3 of 3)

12

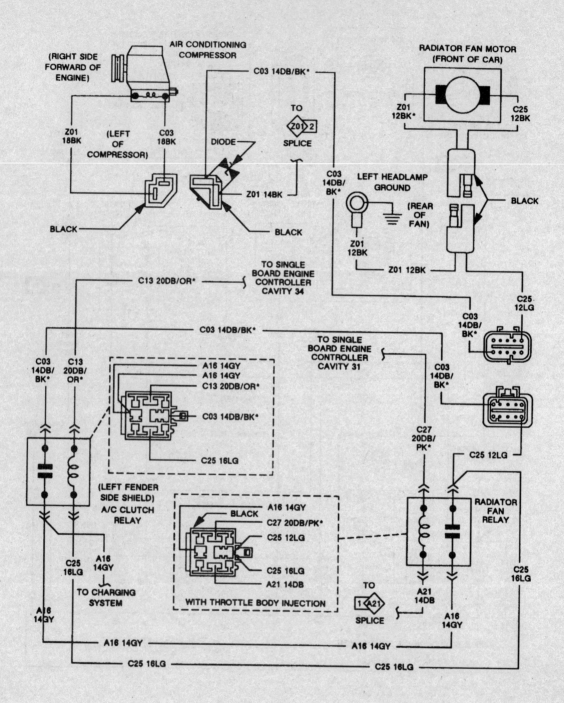

Typical four-cylinder engine radiator fan system wiring diagram

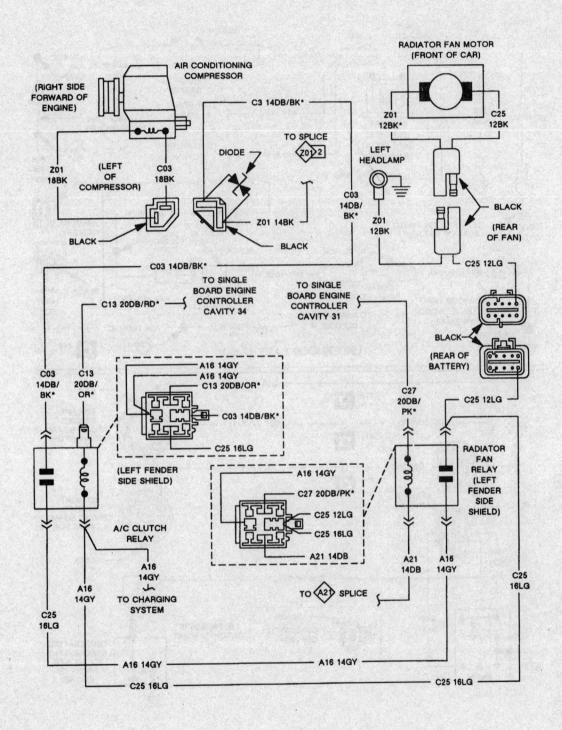

Typical V6 engine radiator fan system wiring diagram

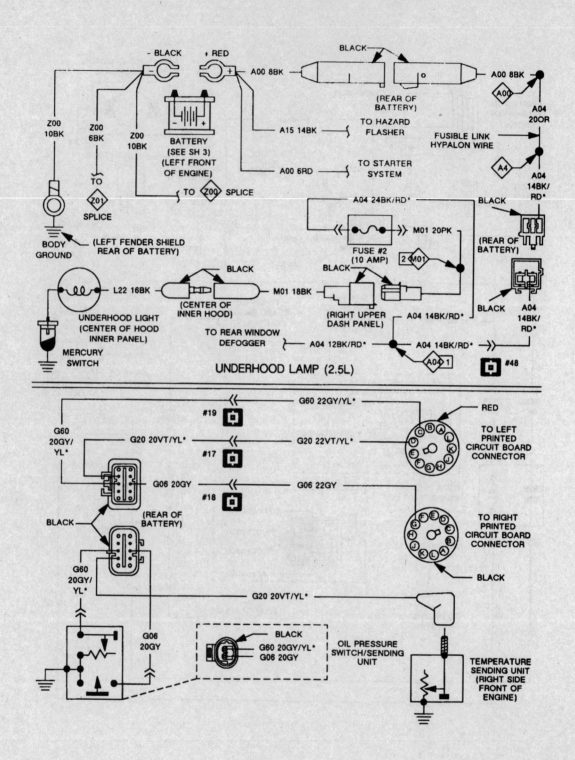

Typical four-cylinder engine underhood lamp and oil pressure/temperature warning system wiring diagram

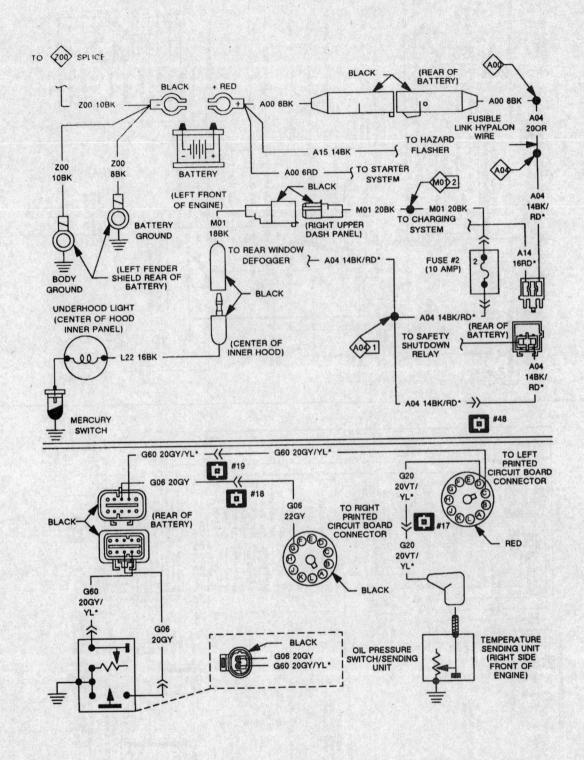

Typical V6 engine underhood lamp and oil pressure/temperature warning system wiring diagram

12

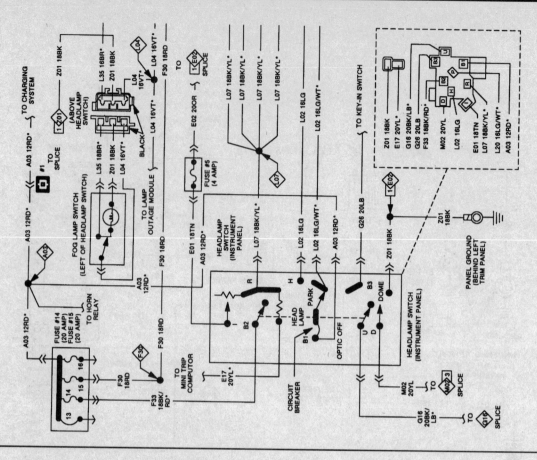

Typical headlight and fog lamp switch wiring diagram (1 of 2)

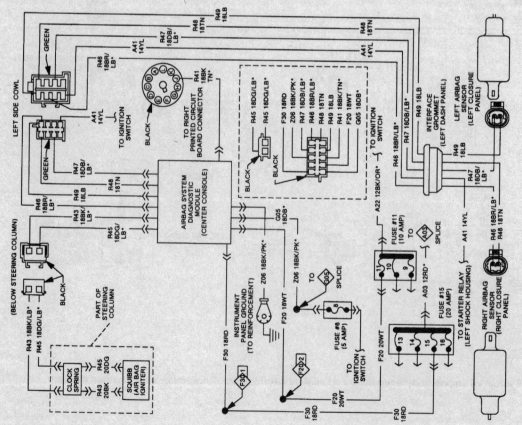

Typical airbag system wiring diagram

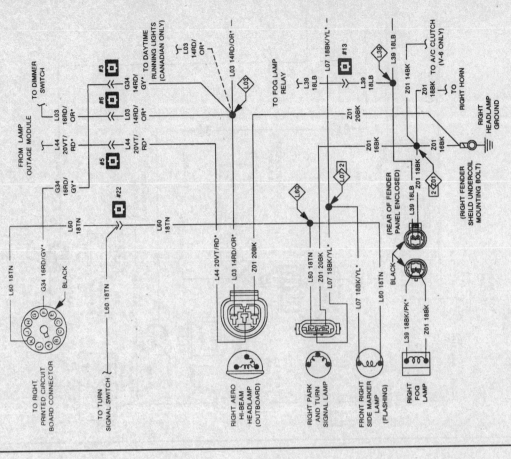

Typical front end lighting wiring diagram (1 of 2)

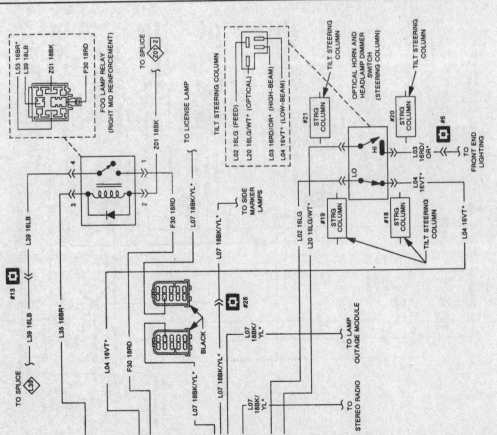

Typical headlight and fog lamp switch wiring diagram (2 of 2)

12

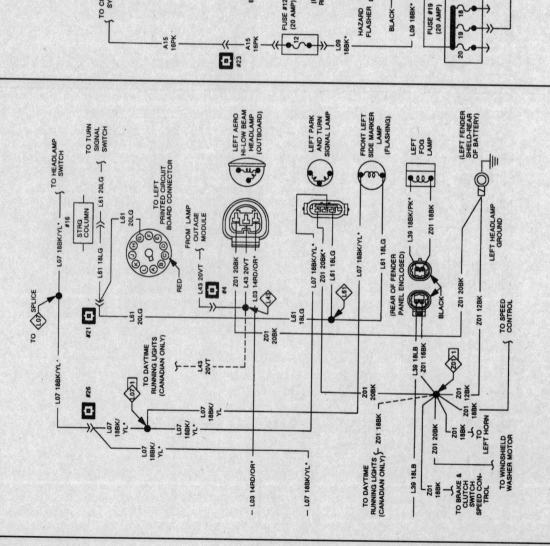

Typical turn signal/hazard flasher wiring diagram (1 of 2)

Typical front end lighting wiring diagram (2 of 2)

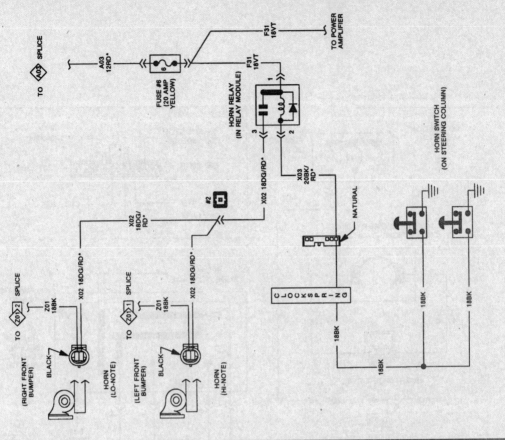

Typical horn system wiring diagram

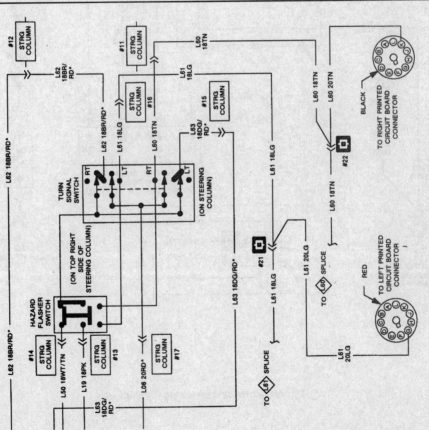

Typical turn signal/hazard flasher wiring diagram (2 of 2)

12

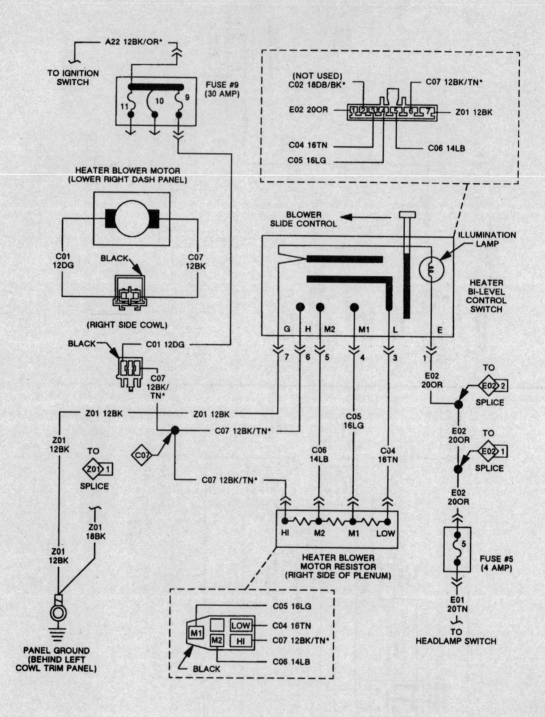

Typical heater system wiring diagram

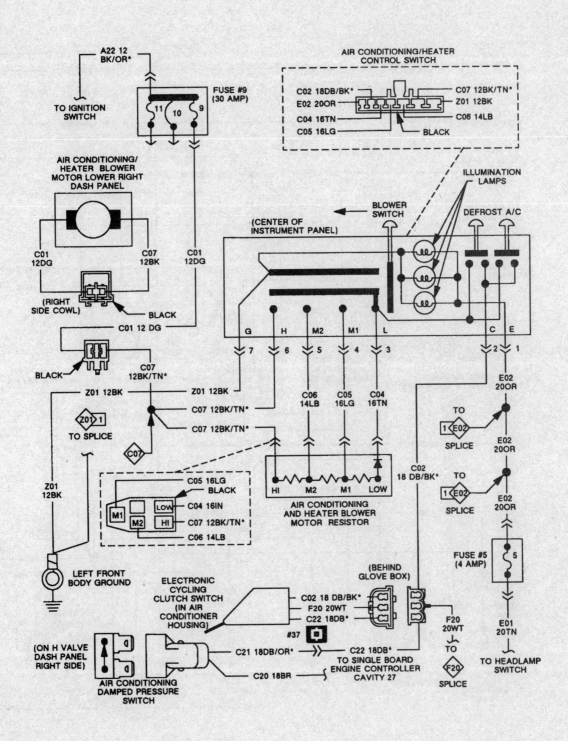

Typical four-cylinder air conditioning system wiring diagram

12

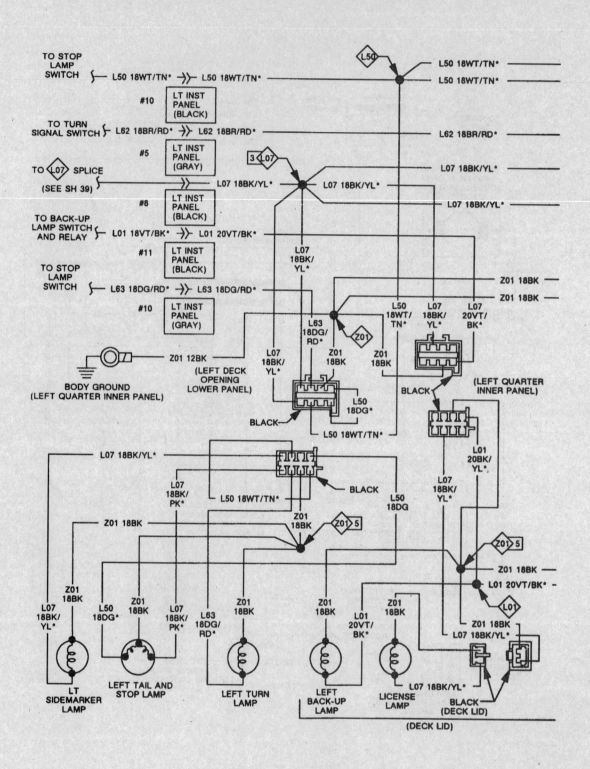

Typical rear end lighting system wiring diagram (1 of 2)

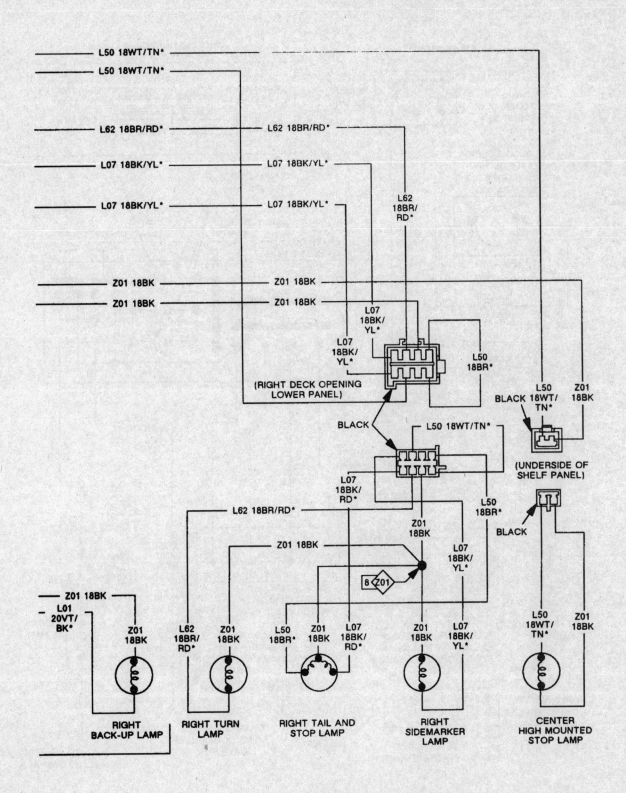

Typical rear end lighting system wiring diagram (2 of 2)

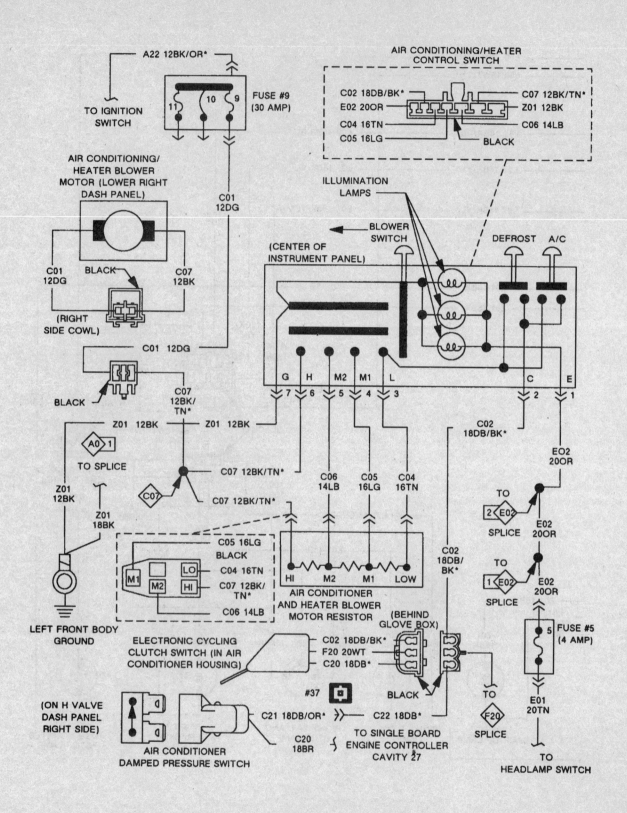

Typical V6 air conditioning system wiring diagram

Index

Haynes Automotive Manuals

NOTE: New manuals are added to this list on a periodic basis. If you do not see a listing for your vehicle, consult your local Haynes dealer for the latest product information.

ACURA
12020 Integra '86 thru '89 & Legend '86 thru '90
12021 Integra '90 thru '93 & Legend '91 thru '95

AMC
Jeep CJ - see JEEP (50020)
14020 Concord/Hornet/Gremlin/Spirit '70 thru '83
14025 (Renault) Alliance & Encore '83 thru '87

AUDI
15020 4000 all models '80 thru '87
15025 5000 all models '77 thru '83
15026 5000 all models '84 thru '88

AUSTIN
Healey Sprite - see MG Midget (66015)

BMW
*18020 3/5 Series '82 thru '92
18021 3 Series including Z3 models '92 thru '98
18025 320i all 4 cyl models '75 thru '83
18050 1500 thru 2002 except Turbo '59 thru '77

BUICK
*19010 Buick Century '97 thru '02
Century (FWD) - see GM (38005)
*19020 Buick, Oldsmobile & Pontiac Full-size (Front wheel drive) '85 thru '02
19025 Buick Oldsmobile & Pontiac Full-size (Rear wheel drive) '70 thru '90
19030 Mid-size Regal & Century '74 thru '87
Regal - see GENERAL MOTORS (38010)
Skyhawk - see GM (38030)
Skylark - see GM (38020, 38025)
Somerset - see GENERAL MOTORS (38025)

CADILLAC
21030 Cadillac Rear Wheel Drive '70 thru '93
Cimarron, Eldorado & Seville - see GM (38015, 38030, 38031)

CHEVROLET
10305 Chevrolet Engine Overhaul Manual
*24010 Astro & GMC Safari Mini-vans '85 thru '03
24015 Camaro V8 all models '70 thru '81
24016 Camaro all models '82 thru '92
Cavalier - see GM (38015)
Celebrity - see GM (38005)
24017 Camaro & Firebird '93 thru '02
24020 Chevelle, Malibu, El Camino '69 thru '87
24024 Chevette & Pontiac T1000 '76 thru '87
Citation - see GENERAL MOTORS (38020)
24032 Corsica/Beretta all models '87 thru '96
24040 Corvette all V8 models '68 thru '82
24041 Corvette all models '84 thru '96
24045 Full-size Sedans Caprice, Impala, Biscayne, Bel Air & Wagons '69 thru '90
24046 Impala SS & Caprice and Buick Roadmaster '91 thru '96
Lumina '90 thru '94 - see GM (38010)
*24048 Lumina & Monte Carlo '95 thru '03
Lumina APV - see GM (38035)
24050 Luv Pick-up all 2WD & 4WD '72 thru '82
Malibu - see GM (38026)
24055 Monte Carlo all models '70 thru '88
Monte Carlo '95 thru '01 - see LUMINA
24059 Nova all V8 models '69 thru '79
24060 Nova/Geo Prizm '85 thru '92
24064 Pick-ups '67 thru '87 - Chevrolet & GMC, all V8 & in-line 6 cyl, 2WD & 4WD '67 thru '87; Suburbans, Blazers & Jimmys '67 thru '91
24065 Pick-ups '88 thru '98 - Chevrolet & GMC, all full-size models '88 thru '98; C/K Classic '99 & '00; Blazer & Jimmy '92 thru '94; Suburban '92 thru '99; Tahoe & Yukon '95 thru '99
*24066 Pick-ups '99 thru '02 - Chevrolet Silverado & GMC Sierra '99 thru '02; Suburban/Tahoe/Yukon/Yukon XL '00 thru '02
24070 S-10 & GMC S-15 Pick-ups '82 thru '93
*24071 S-10, Gmc S-15 & Jimmy '94 thru '01
*24072 Chevrolet TrailBlazer & TrailBlazer EXT, GMC Envoy & Envoy XL, Oldsmobile Bravada '02 and '03
24075 Sprint '85 thru '88, Geo Metro '89 thru '01
24080 Vans - Chevrolet & GMC '68 thru '96

CHRYSLER
10310 Chrysler Engine Overhaul Manual
25015 Chrysler Cirrus, Dodge Stratus, Plymouth Breeze, '95 thru '98
25020 Full-size Front-Wheel Drive '88 thru '93
K-Cars - see DODGE (30008)
Laser - see DODGE Daytona (30030)
25025 Chrysler LHS, Concorde & New Yorker, Dodge Intrepid, Eagle Vision, '93 thru '97
*25026 Chrysler LHS, Concorde, 300M, Dodge Intrepid '98 thru '03
25030 Chrysler/Plym. Mid-size '82 thru '95
Rear-wheel Drive - see DODGE (30050)
*25035 PT Cruiser all models '01 thru '03
*25040 Chrysler Sebring/Dodge Avenger '95 thru '02

DATSUN
28005 200SX all models '80 thru '83
28007 B-210 all models '73 thru '78
28009 210 all models '78 thru '82
28012 240Z, 260Z & 280Z Coupe '70 thru '78
28014 280ZX Coupe & 2+2 '79 thru '83
300ZX - see NISSAN (72010)
28016 310 all models '78 thru '82
28018 510 & PL521 Pick-up '68 thru '73
28020 510 all models '78 thru '81
28022 620 Series Pick-up all models '73 thru '79
720 Series Pick-up - see NISSAN (72030)
28025 810/Maxima all gas models, '77 thru '84

DODGE
400 & 600 - see CHRYSLER (25030)
30008 Aries & Plymouth Reliant '81 thru '89
30010 Caravan & Ply. Voyager '84 thru '95
*30011 Caravan & Ply. Voyager '96 thru '02
30012 Challenger/Plymouth Saporro '78 thru '83
Challenger '67-'76 - see DART (30025)
30016 Colt/Plymouth Champ '78 thru '87
30020 Dakota Pick-ups all models '87 thru '96
*30021 Durango '98 & '99, Dakota '97 thru '99
30025 Dart, Challenger/Plymouth Barracuda & Valiant 6 cyl models '67 thru '76
30030 Daytona & Chrysler Laser '84 thru '89
Intrepid - see Chrysler (25025, 25026)
*30034 Dodge & Plymouth Neon '95 thru '99
*30035 Omni & Plymouth Horizon '78 thru '90
30040 Pick-ups all full-size models '74 thru '93
*30041 Pick-ups all full-size models '94 thru '01
*30045 Ram 50/D50 Pick-ups & Raider and Plymouth Arrow Pick-ups '79 thru '93
30050 Dodge/Ply./Chrysler RWD '71 thru '89
30055 Shadow/Plymouth Sundance '87 thru '94
30060 Spirit & Plymouth Acclaim '89 thru '95
*30065 Vans - Dodge & Plymouth '71 thru '03

EAGLE
Talon - see MITSUBISHI (68030, 68031)
Vision - see CHRYSLER (25025)

FIAT
34010 124 Sport Coupe & Spider '68 thru '78
34025 X1/9 all models '74 thru '80

FORD
10355 Ford Automatic Transmission Overhaul
10320 Ford Engine Overhaul Manual
36004 Aerostar Mini-vans '86 thru '97
Aspire - see FORD Festiva (36030)
36006 Contour/Mercury Mystique '95 thru '00
36008 Courier Pick-up all models '72 thru '82
*36012 Crown Victoria & Mercury Grand Marquis '88 thru '00
36016 Escort/Mercury Lynx '81 thru '90
36020 Escort/Mercury Tracer '91 thru '00
36022 Expedition - see FORD Pick-up (36059)
*36024 Ford Escape & Mazda Tribute '01 thru '03
36025 Ford Explorer & Mercury Mountaineer '02 and '03
36028 Fairmont & Mercury Zephyr '78 thru '83
36030 Festiva & Aspire '88 thru '97
36032 Fiesta all models '77 thru '80
*36034 Focus all models '00 thru '05
36036 Ford & Mercury Full-size '75 thru '87
36044 Ford & Mercury Mid-size '75 thru '86
36048 Mustang V8 all models '64-1/2 thru '73
36049 Mustang II 4 cyl, V6 & V8 '74 thru '78
36050 Mustang & Mercury Capri '79 thru '86
*36051 Mustang all models '94 thru '03
36054 Pick-ups and Bronco '73 thru '79
36058 Pick-ups and Bronco '80 thru '96
*36059 Pick-ups, Expedition & Lincoln Navigator '97 thru '02
*36060 Super Duty Pick-ups, Excursion '97 thru '02
36062 Pinto & Mercury Bobcat '75 thru '80
36066 Probe all models '89 thru '92
36070 Ranger/Bronco II gas models '83 thru '92
*36071 Ford Ranger '93 thru '00 & Mazda Pick-ups '94 thru '00
36074 Taurus & Mercury Sable '86 thru '95
*36075 Taurus & Mercury Sable '96 thru '01
36078 Tempo & Mercury Topaz '84 thru '94
36082 Thunderbird/Mercury Cougar '83 thru '88
36086 Thunderbird/Mercury Cougar '89 thru '97
36090 Vans all V8 Econoline models '69 thru '91
*36094 Vans full size '92 thru '01
*36097 Windstar Mini-van '95 thru '03

GENERAL MOTORS
10360 GM Automatic Transmission Overhaul
38005 Buick Century, Chevrolet Celebrity, Olds Cutlass Ciera & Pontiac 6000 '82 thru '96
*38010 Buick Regal, Chevrolet Lumina, Oldsmobile Cutlass Supreme & Pontiac Grand Prix front wheel drive '88 thru '02
38015 Buick Skyhawk, Cadillac Cimarron, Chevrolet Cavalier, Oldsmobile Firenza Pontiac J-2000 & Sunbird '82 thru '94
*38016 Chevrolet Cavalier/Pontiac Sunfire '95 thru '04
38020 Buick Skylark, Chevrolet Citation, Olds Omega, Pontiac Phoenix '80 thru '85
38025 Buick Skylark & Somerset, Olds Achieva, Calais & Pontiac Grand Am '85 thru '98
*38026 Chevrolet Malibu, Olds Alero & Cutlass, Pontiac Grand Am '97 thru '00
38030 Cadillac Eldorado & Oldsmobile Toronado '71 thru '85, Seville '80 thru '85, Buick Riviera '79 thru '85
*38031 Cadillac Eldorado & Seville '86 thru '91, DeVille & Buick Riviera '86 thru '93, Fleetwood & Olds Toronado '86 thru '92
38032 DeVille '94 thru '02, Seville '92 thru '02
38035 Chevrolet Lumina APV, Oldsmobile Silhouette & Pontiac Trans Sport '90 thru '96
*38036 Chevrolet Venture, Olds Silhouette, Pontiac Trans Sport & Montana '97 thru '01
General Motors Full-size Rear-wheel Drive - see BUICK (19025)

GEO
Metro - see CHEVROLET Sprint (24075)
Prizm - see CHEVROLET (24060) or TOYOTA (92036)
40030 Storm all models '90 thru '93
Tracker - see SUZUKI Samurai (90010)

GMC
Vans & Pick-ups - see CHEVROLET

HONDA
42010 Accord CVCC all models '76 thru '83
42011 Accord all models '84 thru '89
42012 Accord all models '90 thru '93
42013 Accord all models '94 thru '97
*42014 Accord all models '98 thru '02
42020 Civic 1200 all models '73 thru '79
42021 Civic 1300 & 1500 CVCC '80 thru '83
42022 Civic 1500 CVCC all models '75 thru '79
42023 Civic all models '84 thru '91
42024 Civic & del Sol '92 thru '95
*42025 Civic '96 thru '00, CR-V '97 thru '00, Acura Integra '94 thru '00
Passport - see ISUZU Rodeo (47017)
42026 Civic '01 thru '04, CR-V '02 thru '04
*42040 Prelude CVCC all models '79 thru '89

HYUNDAI
*43010 Elantra all models '96 thru '01
43015 Excel & Accent all models '86 thru '98

ISUZU
Hombre - see CHEVROLET S-10 (24071)
*47017 Rodeo '91 thru '02, Amigo '89 thru '02, Honda Passport '95 thru '02
47020 Trooper '84 thru '91, Pick-up '81 thru '93

JAGUAR
49010 XJ6 all 6 cyl models '68 thru '86
49011 XJ6 all models '88 thru '94
49015 XJ12 & XJS all 12 cyl models '72 thru '85

JEEP
50010 Cherokee, Comanche & Wagoneer Limited all models '84 thru '01
50020 CJ all models '49 thru '86
*50025 Grand Cherokee all models '93 thru '04
50029 Grand Wagoneer & Pick-up '72 thru '91
*50030 Wrangler all models '87 thru '00
50035 Liberty '02 thru '04

LEXUS
ES 300 - see TOYOTA Camry (92007)

LINCOLN
Navigator - see FORD Pick-up (36059)
*59010 Rear Wheel Drive all models '70 thru '01

MAZDA
61010 GLC (rear wheel drive) '77 thru '83
61011 GLC (front wheel drive) '81 thru '85
61015 323 & Protegé '90 thru '00
*61016 MX-5 Miata '90 thru '97
61020 MPV all models '89 thru '94
Navajo - see FORD Explorer (36024)
61030 Pick-ups '72 thru '93
Pick-ups '94 on - see Ford (36071)
61035 RX-7 all models '79 thru '85
61036 RX-7 all models '86 thru '91
61040 626 (rear wheel drive) '79 thru '82
61041 626 & MX-6 (front wheel drive) '83 thru '91
61042 626 '93 thru '01, MX-6/Ford Probe '93 thru '97

MERCEDES-BENZ
63012 123 Series Diesel '76 thru '85
63015 190 Series 4-cyl gas models, '84 thru '88
63020 230, 250 & 280 6 cyl sohc '68 thru '72
63025 280 123 Series gas models '77 thru '81
63030 350 & 450 all models '71 thru '80

MERCURY
64200 Villager & Nissan Quest '93 thru '01
All other titles, see FORD listing.

MG
66010 MGB Roadster & GT Coupe '62 thru '80
66015 MG Midget & Austin Healey Sprite Roadster '58 thru '80

MITSUBISHI
68020 Cordia, Tredia, Galant, Precis & Mirage '83 thru '93
68030 Eclipse, Eagle Talon & Plymouth Laser '90 thru '94
*68031 Eclipse '95 thru '01, Eagle Talon '95 thru '98
68035 Mitsubishi Galant '94 thru '03
68040 Pick-up '83 thru '96, Montero '83 thru '93

NISSAN
72010 300ZX all models incl. Turbo '84 thru '89
72015 Altima all models '93 thru '04
72020 Maxima all models '85 thru '92
*72021 Maxima all models '93 thru '01
72030 Pick-ups '80 thru '97, Pathfinder '87 thru '95
*72031 Frontier Pick-up '98 thru '01, Xterra '00 & '01, Pathfinder '96 thru '01
72040 Pulsar all models '83 thru '86
72050 Sentra all models '82 thru '94
72051 Sentra & 200SX all models '95 thru '99
72060 Stanza all models '82 thru '90

OLDSMOBILE
*73015 Cutlass '74 thru '88
For other OLDSMOBILE titles, see BUICK, CHEVROLET or GM listings.

PLYMOUTH
For PLYMOUTH titles, see DODGE.

PONTIAC
79008 Fiero all models '84 thru '88
79018 Firebird V8 models except Turbo '70 thru '81
79019 Firebird all models '82 thru '92
79040 Mid-size Rear-wheel Drive '70 thru '87
For other PONTIAC titles, see BUICK, CHEVROLET or GM listings.

PORSCHE
80020 911 Coupe & Targa models '65 thru '89
80025 914 all 4 cyl models '69 thru '76
80030 924 all models incl. Turbo '76 thru '82
80035 944 all models incl. Turbo '83 thru '89

RENAULT
Alliance, Encore - see AMC (14020)

SAAB
*84010 900 including Turbo '79 thru '88

SATURN
*87010 Saturn all models '91 thru '02
87020 Saturn all L-series models '00 thru '04

SUBARU
89002 1100, 1300, 1400 & 1600 '71 thru '79
89003 1600 & 1800 2WD & 4WD '80 thru '94

SUZUKI
90010 Samurai/Sidekick/Geo Tracker '86 thru '01

TOYOTA
92005 Camry all models '83 thru '91
92006 Camry all models '92 thru '96
*92007 Camry/Avalon/Solara/Lexus ES 300 '97 thru '01
92015 Celica Rear Wheel Drive '71 thru '85
92020 Celica Front Wheel Drive '86 thru '99
92025 Celica Supra all models '79 thru '92
92030 Corolla all models '75 thru '79
92032 Corolla rear wheel drive models '80 thru '87
92035 Corolla front wheel drive models '84 thru '92
92036 Corolla & Geo Prizm '93 thru '02
92040 Corolla Tercel all models '80 thru '82
92045 Corona all models '74 thru '82
92050 Cressida all models '78 thru '82
92055 Land Cruiser FJ40/43/45/55 '68 thru '82
92056 Land Cruiser FJ60/62/80/FZJ80 '80 thru '96
92065 MR2 all models '85 thru '87
92070 Pick-up all models '69 thru '78
92075 Pick-up all models '79 thru '95
*92076 Tacoma '95 thru '00, 4Runner '96 thru '00, T100 '93 thru '98
*92078 Tundra '00 thru '02, Sequoia '01 thru '02
92080 Previa all models '91 thru '95
*92082 RAV4 all models '96 thru '02
92085 Tercel all models '87 thru '94

TRIUMPH
94007 Spitfire all models '62 thru '81
94010 TR7 all models '75 thru '81

VW
96008 Beetle & Karmann Ghia '54 thru '79
*96009 New Beetle '98 thru '00
96016 Rabbit, Jetta, Scirocco, & Pick-up gas models '74 thru '91 & Convertible '80 thru '92
96017 Golf, GTI & Jetta '93 thru '98, Cabrio '95 thru '98
*96018 Golf, GTI, Jetta & Cabrio '99 thru '02
96020 Rabbit, Jetta, Pick-up diesel '77 thru '84
96023 Passat '98 thru '01, Audi A4 '96 thru '01
96030 Transporter 1600 all models '68 thru '79
96035 Transporter 1700, 1800, 2000 '72 thru '79
96040 Type 3 1500 & 1600 '63 thru '73
96045 Vanagon air-cooled models '80 thru '83

VOLVO
97010 120, 130 Series & 1800 Sports '61 thru '73
97015 140 Series all models '66 thru '74
97020 240 Series all models '76 thru '93
97025 260 Series all models '75 thru '82
97040 740 & 760 Series all models '82 thru '88

TECHBOOK MANUALS
10205 Automotive Computer Codes
10210 Automotive Emissions Control Manual
10215 Fuel Injection Manual, 1978 thru 1985
10220 Fuel Injection Manual, 1986 thru 1999
10225 Holley Carburetor Manual
10230 Rochester Carburetor Manual
10240 Weber/Zenith/Stromberg/SU Carburetor
10305 Chevrolet Engine Overhaul Manual
10310 Chrysler Engine Overhaul Manual
10320 Ford Engine Overhaul Manual
10330 GM and Ford Diesel Engine Repair
10340 Small Engine Repair Manual
10345 Suspension, Steering & Driveline
10355 Ford Automatic Transmission Overhaul
10360 GM Automatic Transmission Overhaul
10405 Automotive Body Repair & Painting
10410 Automotive Brake Manual
10415 Automotive Detailing Manual
10420 Automotive Eelectrical Manual
10425 Automotive Heating & Air Conditioning
10430 Automotive Reference Dictionary
10435 Automotive Tools Manual
10440 Used Car Buying Guide
10445 Welding Manual
10450 ATV Basics

SPANISH MANUALS
98903 Reparación de Carrocería & Pintura
98905 Códigos Automotrices de la Computadora
98915 Frenos Automotriz
98915 Inyección de Combustible 1986 al 1999
99040 Chevrolet & GMC Camionetas '67 al '87
99041 Chevrolet & GMC Camionetas '88 al '98
99042 Chevrolet Camionetas Cerradas '68 al '95
99055 Dodge Caravan/Ply. Voyager '84 al '95
99075 Ford Camionetas y Bronco '80 al '94
99077 Ford Camionetas Cerradas '69 al '91
99088 Ford Modelos de Tamaño Mediano '75 al '86
99091 Ford Taurus & Mercury Sable '86 al '95
99095 GM Modelos de Tamaño Grande '70 al '90
99100 GM Modelos de Tamaño Mediano '70 al '88
99110 Nissan Camionetas '80 al '96, Pathfinder '87 al '95
99118 Nissan Sentra '82 al '94
99125 Toyota Camionetas y 4-Runner '79 al '95

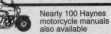

Nearly 100 Haynes motorcycle manuals also available

2-05

Listings shown with an asterisk (*) indicate model coverage as of this printing. These titles will be periodically updated to include later model years - consult your Haynes dealer for more information.

Haynes North America, Inc., 861 Lawrence Drive, Newbury Park, CA 91320 • (805) 498-6703